FROM SLAVERY TO 9/11

READINGS IN THE SOCIOLOGY AND SOCIAL PSYCHOLOGY OF EXTREME SITUATIONS

Sidney Langer

Kean University

Boston   Columbus   Indianapolis   New York   San Francisco   Upper Saddle River
Amsterdam   Cape Town   Dubai   London   Madrid   Milan   Munich   Paris   Montréal   Toronto
Delhi   Mexico City   São Paulo   Sydney   Hong Kong   Seoul   Singapore   Taipei   Tokyo

Editorial Director: Craig Campanella
Editor in Chief: Dickson Musslewhite
Publisher: Karen Hanson
Executive Marketing Manager: Kelly May
Marketing Assistant: Janeli Bitor
Production Manager: Fran Russello
Cover Design Manager: Jayne Conte
Cover Designer: Bruce Kenselaar
Cover Image Credit: Fotolia: © GIS
Editorial Production and Composition Service: Sneha Pant/PreMediaGlobal
Printer/Binder: Courier Companies, Inc.

Credits and acknowledgments borrowed from other sources and reproduced, with permission, in this textbook appear on appropriate page within text.

Library of Congress Cataloging-in-Publication Data

Langer, Sidney.
  From slavery to 9/11 : readings in the sociology and social psychology of extreme situations / Sidney Langer.
      p. cm.
  Includes bibliographical references.
  ISBN-13: 978-0-205-73134-3
  ISBN-10: 0-205-73134-1
  1. Totalitarianism—Psychological aspects.   2. Extreme environments.   I.
  Title.
  JC480.L357 2013
  302.5—dc23

                                                                    2011039123

10 9 8 7 6 5 4 3 2 1—CRW—16 15 13 12 11

ISBN-10: 0-205-73134-1
ISBN-13: 978-0-205-73134-3

Dedicated to … those who did not survive

CONTENTS

PREFACE

My interest in total institutions and extreme situations was heightened many years ago when I was asked to teach a course titled the "Sociology of Extreme Situations," at Kean University. This unique subject matter had originally been proposed and designed by a former faculty member of the university. As I began to develop and teach the course over the years, I focused in the first half of the curriculum on the sociological and social psychological dynamics of the concentration camp experience of World War II. The second half examined prisons, asylums and other total institutions.

In the Fall of 1982, the Holocaust Resource Center opened at Kean University, and I became the first director of its Oral History Project, the videotaped interviewing of Holocaust survivors. During the interviews, the survivors spoke of their experiences before, during and after the Holocaust. I began to show some of those interviews to my students in the extreme situations course and they were asked to write short reaction papers. Although students were familiar in general terms with the nature of the concentration camp, the taped narratives of survivors provided a human dimension to their understanding. Viewing these tapes in the classroom proved a particularly informative, dynamic and poignant experience.

A central theme in the study of extreme situations and total institutions is the analysis of the survival techniques and coping mechanisms employed by those who have been touched by them. Unfortunately, many of the defining events of the 19th and 20th centuries and the early 21st century have been man-made and natural disasters which have propelled individuals and societies into a complex web of total institutions and extreme situations. This has challenged man's ability to persevere and survive in the face of powerful adversity. If the reader's knowledge of these historical and contemporary events is increased, and if there are lessons to be learned from these experiences that will enhance the reader's appreciation of man's resilience and the urgent need for mutual tolerance and respect, then this volume will have succeeded in its purpose.

ACKNOWLEDGMENTS

It is a pleasure to acknowledge so many individuals who have had some role to play in the publication of this anthology. I would surmise that some might be surprised to find their name here but they should know that in some way they had a meaningful impact on me during the preparation of this manuscript.

At my host institution, Kean University, I would like to thank President Dawood Farahi and my colleagues James Conyers, Frank Esposito, Henry Kaplowitz, Dennis Klein, Celene Krauss, Mary Lou Mayo, Frank Naughton and Barbara Wheeler.

In addition, several academic colleagues provided guidance and encouragement: Norman Adler, Karen Bacon, Ruth Bevan-Dunner, Andrea Rosso Efthymiou, Ethel Orlian and Roberta Farber.

Over the course of this project, I have benefited from conversations with and the support of numerous friends and individuals: Rebecca Balsam, Edith Bayme, Diana Benmergui, Isaac Chavel, Aniruddha Das, John Gorman, Harvey Greenberg, Amy Katz, Tova Katz, Talia Langer, Hindishe Lee, Ezra Levin, Jason Mirvis, Bernadette McCarthy, Judy Putterman and Marc Wilson.

Several students have been helpful to me in bringing this project to fruition: Tami Adelson, Chana Czarka, Alana Ebin, Nicole Grubner, Sara Hyman, Gila Yarmush and Meira Zack.

Special thanks to the Schneidman Scholarship Program, Yeshiva University, which provided funds for student research assistance and to Arlene Schulman, who was instrumental in securing this grant.

Thanks to a friend and legal scholar of international renown, Joseph Weiler, for helping me to crystallize the thematic structure and presentation of the book.

No individual was more helpful to me in the development and enhancement of this book than my good friend of many decades, Steven Bayme. Steve's insights, suggestions and critical comments were invaluable in the preparation of this manuscript. I thank Steve for always making himself available to me in a most gracious manner.

At Pearson, I owe a special debt of gratitude to Jeff Lasser, who recognized the significance of this project and signed the book. The book moved from Jeff's desk to Karen Hanson, Publisher, and I thank her for her sage advice and support. Special thanks to Frances Russello, Production Manager, and Sneha Pant, Project Manager, for their patience and professionalism.

Finally, no project of this kind is possible without the support and patience of one's family. I respectfully acknowledge my mother, Zmira, and late father of blessed memory, Moshe Yitzchak. A special note of thanks and appreciation to my wife, Yonina, my children, Nomi, Akiva and Tali, and my grandchildren, Ami, Eliora and Tamara.

Introduction

On September 11, 2001, at approximately 8:40 a.m., I exited from Grand Central Station on 42nd Street and Park Avenue, New York City. Scheduled to give a lecture at 9:00 a.m. at a venue located several blocks south of Grand Central, I thoroughly enjoyed the short walk on what could only be described as a magnificently brilliant and exhilarating fall morning. In greeting my audience of approximately thirty individuals, not one of us was aware that the World Trade Center (a short subway ride away) had already been struck. At 8:46 a.m., a hijacked American Airlines passenger aircraft had slammed into the North Tower of the financial center.

At approximately 9:20 a.m., a young woman who had once been a student of mine, knocked on the glass window of our door and motioned to get my attention. Visibly shaken and distraught, she recounted that she was working in the Empire State Building located nearby, looked out the window, and had seen what she believed was a plane fly into the World Trade Center. My immediate thought and comforting response to her was rational, logical and predictable. It must have been one of those popular sightseeing propeller planes that encircle the city. Within minutes, however, as additional pieces of information trickled in, we had our worst fears confirmed and the normative feelings of security and predictability in our lives shattered.

The mainland of the United States of America was under attack by terrorists who had hijacked four passenger airliners and were using them as deadly weapons of destruction. I knew at that moment that the world had changed forever. If you were a passenger on any of those airplanes, if you were in the World Trade Center, the Pentagon or anywhere in proximity of those sites, you were the target, the enemy. Your age, sex, race, religion, ethnicity, occupation, social relationships, value system or life history was irrelevant to your status as target. Nearly 3,000 people perished on that day.

In their discussion of thermonuclear war as an extreme situation, sociologists Rosenberg, Gerver and Howton (1964) make the following point that may illuminate also the events and ramifications of September 11:

> The individual is an object of interest to wartime functionaries not for what he does but for *what he is* [emphasis mine]: part of a social category designated "the enemy." Moreover he is "the enemy" in a new and dehumanized form. In the functionaries' decision to kill him or not to kill him, and how, is entirely an expression of functional rationality. Against those who have the power and may find it necessary (that is, rational) to annihilate him and his social type, he has no moral or legal claim (p. 167).

It is against this backdrop that so many of us were thrust into the confusion, fears, insecurities and trauma of that fatal September day that began in brilliant sunshine but quickly turned into ashen darkness. Our minds were bombarded with uncertainty about our families, friends, neighbors and acquaintances, whom we were unable to reach. I spent that day, as did so many others, glued to a television screen projecting images of the destruction and of people jumping out of the windows of the World Trade Center as our world was literally and figuratively crumbling before our eyes. Like so many others, I was devastated by the events of that day. At the same time, September 11 catalyzed my ongoing interest in and reflections on human behavior in extreme situations.

This volume of readings is a sociological and social psychological analysis of extreme situations, total institutions and survival. The concept of "extreme situation" was coined by the psychologist Bruno Bettelheim to describe the Nazi concentration camp experience of World War II. His analysis is based on his own experience in a camp and his observations of its social structure and impact on his fellow inmates. According to Bettelheim (1952/1980),

> [w]e find ourselves in an extreme situation when we are suddenly catapulted into a set of conditions where our old adaptive mechanisms and values do not apply any more and when some of them may even endanger the life they were meant to protect. Then we are, so to say, stripped of our whole defensive system and thrown back to rock bottom—whence we must carve out a new set of attitudes, values, and way of living as required by the new situation (p. 11).

Psychologist Paul Marcus (1999) describes Bettelheim's concept of an extreme situation:

> [W]hen an individual is faced with an extremely confusing, rapidly changing, contingent reality, when his routine and valued modes of thought and acting (i.e., beliefs and values) are in the process of being destroyed, he feels himself to be in what Bettelheim calls an "extreme situation"—a social context in which the inmate is suddenly, massively and decisively threatened with the destruction of his world, fostering intense death anxiety (p. 80).

The theoretical underpinning of the "extreme situation" in its relationship to the events of 9/11 is striking and deserves further attention. This discussion will follow in a further chapter in this volume.

Bettelheim's description of the concentration camp as an extreme situation would seem to fit neatly into the category of what has been called "total institution." The concept of "total institution" was first developed by the sociologist Erving Goffman and generally refers to such institutions as prisons, mental asylums, military establishments, monasteries etc. According to Goffman (1961),

> a total institution may be defined as a place of residence and work where a large number of like-situated individuals, cut off from the wider society for an appreciable period of time together lead an enclosed formally administered round of life (p. xiii).

While total institutions clearly vary in the extent to which control is manifest, it is apparent that the intersection of the concepts of extreme situation and total institution can be found when the totality of the total institution is introduced into our analysis (Rosenberg et al., 1964, p. 160). Sociologist Samuel Wallace (1971) noted in his book on total institutions that

> [t]otal institutions are not a separate class of social establishments, but rather specific institutions which exhibit to an intense degree certain characteristics found in all institutions. The issue is not which institutions are total and which are not, but rather, how much totality does each display? (p. 2).

In other words, can we identify and place various institutions on a continuum of ever increasing control and mortification of self? Does the extreme situation (concentration camp) represent the most total of all total institutions? Are extreme situations the product of total institutions or are they to be seen as unique constructs within the analysis of control and "inmate functionary relationships"? (Rosenberg et al., 1964, pp. 157–168).

The concentration camp, and specifically the extermination camps, and genocidal atrocities are man-made disasters conceived to control and destroy life in the most efficient and functional manner. So too was the bombing of the World Trade Center on September 11, 2001, when more civilians were killed in the United States than in any previous man-made disaster. How do people in total institutions, survivors of man-made disasters, and victims of natural disasters, such as Hurricane Katrina (2005), the Haiti earthquake (2010), the floods in Pakistan (2010), and the recent earthquake and tsunami in Japan (2011), negotiate their respective experiences?

This anthology is meant to explore these issues by describing the social structure of these institutions and events and the coping mechanisms used by those whose lives have been touched by them. The total institutions/extreme situations included in this book represent many of the defining events of the 19th and 20th centuries and the beginning of the 21st century: institutionalized slavery; genocidal atrocities and the Holocaust; September 11, 2001; and Hurricane Katrina. On first glance one might question the connectedness between these events/institutions. After all, what might be the relationship between Goffman's discussion of mental asylums and the institution of slavery in the United States? How might one compare a nursing home or hospital, whose goal is caring and healing, with a prison or concentration camp, whose purpose is to punish or exterminate? Is it possible that the organizational response to a natural disaster like Katrina has any commonality with the designation of Darfur as genocide? Can we identify common survival mechanisms or adaptive techniques employed in different extreme situations? Are there gender-specific differences in the coping mechanisms of men and women in extreme situations? These are some of the questions that we will explore as we familiarize ourselves with some of these watershed events of our recent history.

The first chapter of the book includes seminal readings that are illustrative of our discussion of extreme situations and total institutions. The vocabulary of the book is defined in an examination of the dynamics and social structure of extreme situations, total institutions and their interrelationships. Each subsequent chapter focuses on the sociological and social psychological dimension (social structure and dynamic) of a *specific* total institution and/or extreme situation. I have included articles that are scientific in their presentation and context as well as personal accounts and biographies of survival that should be understood within the framework of established sociological and social psychological theory.

The second chapter of the book focuses on slavery in the United States as a total institution/extreme situation. The readings include a discussion of the techniques employed by the slave masters in their attempt to mold the "ideal" slave and a critical analysis of the typology of adaptive responses and self-identities that the slaves assumed. The chapter concludes with the searing personal narratives of Frederick Douglass and Harriet Jacobs, two of the most prolific writers on the slave experience.

Chapter three begins with a discussion of the goals underlying the creation of the first concentration camp and the identification and distinguishing features of the various types of camps. This is followed by a series of readings that include several of the standard and most frequently cited accounts of survival in the camps. The concluding article is a compelling narrative of the unique experiences of female camp inmates.

The fourth chapter of the book is an examination of the "birth" of the prison as an institution of control in modern society and the "pains of imprisonment" experienced by its inmates. In addition to traditional readings of survival and adaptation, I have included an article that details rich anecdotal accounts of women in prison. Another reading explores the utility of analyzing contemporary first-person oral histories of prison life within the framework of standard prison texts. The concluding article applies Goffman's discussion of the mortification process in a total institution in its analysis of Jonestown, a community in Guyana, where more than 900 people committed mass suicide in 1978.

Chapter five begins with an ethnographic analysis of how the unique social and professional background of "first responders" impacted their reaction to the devastation of September 11, 2001. Also included in this chapter are the personal and professional psychological insights of a well-known radio host and author. The concluding article presents a sociological analysis of manifestations of communal "ritual solidarity" in response to the attacks of September 11, 2001.

Several readings in chapter six explore the controversy surrounding our understanding of Hurricane Katrina as a purely natural disaster or an event "triggered" by natural causes, but significantly redefined by racial, socioeconomic and political variables. One article examines the intersection of racial and social factors in individual and organizational responses to Katrina, while another reading evaluates the impact of the media's biased presentation of the behavior of the citizens of New Orleans. The last article is an emotive oral history of a survivor's experience during the hurricane and concluding reflections on the human costs of the disaster.

The final chapter of the book is a comparative analysis of the Holocaust and other genocidal atrocities. This chapter is not intended to be a presentation of "competitive suffering," but rather to familiarize the reader with the events, and to highlight some of the critical issues that frame the discussion surrounding genocide. Readings include one that situates the Holocaust as unique in genocidal destruction, while another article posits that the Holocaust and the Armenian genocide are "prototypically" different in their relationships to other mass disasters. Another selection chronicles the "events and circumstances" that resulted in the Armenian genocide, and is followed by a reading that explores the centrality of violence against women in the Armenian genocide. Also included in this chapter is an analysis of the differences between "genocide" and "politicide" as they relate to the mass murders in Rwanda, Ethiopia and Cambodia. The next article briefly describes the dynamics of the relationship between the Hutus and Tutsis as a precursor to the Rwandan genocide, and then explores the victimization of a young Tutsi woman. The concluding reading presents an analysis of the evolutionary forces that influenced the formal organizational response to the "crisis" of violence in Darfur and the role that the "memory" of Rwanda ultimately played in positioning Darfur in the "framework" of the genocidal debate.

It has been almost five decades since the publication of *Mass Society in Crisis* (1964) by sociologists Bernard Rosenberg, Israel Gerver and F. William Howton. I owe a special debt of gratitude to them for providing me with the intellectual and theoretical context within which to present many of the readings in this volume. Their sociological paradigm of viewing extreme situations as the product of total institutions has given me the conceptual framework to link what might appear to be distinct and unrelated manifestations of man-made and natural disasters, extreme situations and total institutions. In fact, this volume is intended to illustrate the commonalities inherent in these events and institutions and to document the individual's ability to survive and persevere in the face of crushing adversity.

The organization of this book is structured in the following tripartite paradigm. In order to familiarize the reader with the dynamics of a specific total institution/extreme situation, the significant background information regarding a particular event or institution is described. This descriptive presentation is culled from both standard source material and contemporary readings. Second, I have included classic readings from the sociological and psychological literature that illustrate adaptive techniques in total institutions/extreme situations. A primary goal of this anthology has been to include selections from volumes that are often not easily accessible to the reader. These articles have been excerpted in order to enhance their readability. Finally, first-person narratives of coping and survival are presented within the framework of our sociological and psychological paradigm of total institutions and extreme situations. Several of these oral histories are gender specific and highlight the unique experiences of women in extreme situations. It is my hope that the scope of the reader's knowledge and contextual understanding of many of the defining events of our recent history will be enhanced by this volume.

CHAPTER 1

Total Institutions
and Extreme Situations

In his groundbreaking essay, "The Ultimate Limit," Bruno Bettelheim (1952/1980) introduces us to the concept of extreme situation as it relates to death anxiety. He suggests that as long as things go "reasonably well" in our lives we generally tend to avoid grappling with the philosophical dilemmas associated with such complex issues as life's purpose or meaning. This changes, however, when we are suddenly challenged by an unpredictable or particularly overwhelming or threatening problem or event which shakes our psychological calm and equilibrium, and forces us to confront the ultimate purpose of life. According to Bettelheim man can be thrust into the deepest of all anxieties, death anxiety, unless the individual can anchor his life in a belief or value system which allows him to be guided by his appreciation and understanding of the ultimate meaning of life (pp. 3–4).

Bettelheim notes that historically man was thrown into the abyss of death anxiety by *natural* catastrophic events such as earthquakes, floods and plagues. These disasters attacked those very belief systems that gave meaning to life (p. 7). They were somewhat neutralized when we entered the 20th century and scientific discovery and progress provided us with the tools to anticipate and control these natural catastrophes more effectively. However, these scientific achievements, which gave new meaning to our lives and acted as a buffer to protect us from death anxiety, were soon to betray us and become the very tools of mass destruction and death that would destroy man in violent spasms of technological efficiency. According to Bettelheim the development of the atomic bomb and the Nazi death camps "became the indicators of the ineffectiveness of our civilization's defenses against the reality of death. Progress not only failed to preserve life but it deprived millions of their lives more effectively than had been possible ever before" (p. 8). Bettelheim (1952/1980) used the term "extreme situation" to describe the

> combined and sudden breakdown of all these defenses against death anxiety [wherein] . . . we are suddenly catapulted into a set of conditions where our old adaptive mechanisms and values do not apply any more and when some of them may even endanger the life they were meant to protect (p. 11).

Erving Goffman's classic work, *Asylums* (1961), published almost five decades ago, remains one of the most significant contributions to the sociological enterprise and to our understanding of the dynamics of institutional life. According to Goffman, "The handling of many human needs by the bureaucratic organization of whole blocks of people . . . is the key fact of total institutions" (p. 6). In his description, the "central feature of total institutions can be described as a breakdown of the barriers" (Goffman, 1961, p. 6) that usually separate the basic spheres of a person's life, that is, sleeping, playing, and working. He then goes on to delineate five different categories of total institutions, which include such varied types as homes for the aged, mental hospitals, prisons, boarding schools and monasteries. Goffman is not suggesting that one can compare a concentration camp or prison to a nursing home or army barracks. Rather he suggests that these institutions share in different degrees certain "common characteristics" that are part of "a family of attributes" of total institutions (p. 5).

Similarly, the process of degradation, depersonalization and humiliation that is experienced as one enters the world of the total institution will vary considerably in its intensity and transformative power as determined by the specific nature of that total institution. This mortification process is intended to strip the individual of his unique sense of self and transform him into an object which is more easily controlled and fits neatly into the bureaucratic machinery of the total institution. Goffman carefully describes the objectification of the individual as it is accomplished through such dynamics as "role dispossession," "property dispossession," "obedience tests" and "contaminative exposure," which can be both physical and experiential (pp. 14–35). As presented later in this volume, Terrence Des Pres's (1976) discussion of excremental assault, the relationship between bodily function and human behavior in the concentration camp, is a powerful portrayal of this contaminative exposure.

In *Mass Society in Crisis*, Rosenberg et al. (1964) construct a sociological paradigm of extreme situations wherein extreme situations are to be seen as the *products* of total institutions. The sociological perspective is concerned with how social conditions impact the lives of individuals and focuses on *similarities* in behavior that result from these forces, while the focal point of study in psychology is the mind and individual *differences*. Rosenberg et al. thus suggest that Bettelheim's concept of extreme situations is uniquely psychological in that it focuses on the dynamics of individual *differences* rather than *similarities* that are employed by persons in response to their environmental stimuli. In their sociological *"reformulation"* of the concept, they focus on the social structural condition itself and how the nature of those structural forces are the crucial variables in producing observable responses that are both similar and characteristic of that social group. Indeed, Rosenberg et al. suggest that Erving Goffman's concept of the "total institution" intersects with Bettelheim's extreme situation which, in fact, is the product of the total institution; " . . . our leading proposition is this: *Total institutions produce extreme situations*. Moreover, the totalness of institutions in modern society is a product of universal and pervasive bureaucratization" (p. 161). They suggest that total institutions can be organized on a continuum wherein the level of bureaucratization as measured by the nature of the "functionary–inmate relationship" is the crucial factor in determining the degree of totality of the total institution. They further assert that "[t]he more total the institution, the more specifically and completely bureaucratic is this relationship" (p. 160). "Extreme situations . . . are those in which the interaction between functionary and inmate is carried on without effective governance by societal norms" (p. 161).

They further suggest that the extreme situation is "de-moralized (humanitarian sentiment is ruled out) and de-legalized (law, in the form of guarantees of civil rights, is ruled out). The process viewed comprehensively may be called denormatization" (p. 161). In other words, there is a complete breakdown or suspension of the norms which are the regulatory and guiding standards or rules of behavior that govern social relationships.

In their empirical typology of extreme situations, Rosenberg et al. include mental hospitalization, concentration camps, the ineffective state, the totalitarian state, genocide and thermonuclear war. This expansive listing of extreme situations must be understood as examples of situations which are characterized by varying degrees of demoralization, de-legalization and functional rationalization. The analysis is not grounded in presenting equivalency of extreme situations but rather in employing the relative process of denormatization as the critical factor in the understanding of extreme situations. As indicated by Rosenberg et al.,

> the situation of the hospital inmate is certainly less extreme than that of his counterpart in a concentration camp . . . the Negro in the American rural South at first place has little in common with the inmate of a mental hospital or concentration camp . . . [however] the situation of Negroes in the American South is significantly demoralized and de-legalized and functional rationality rather than simple corruption (which is functionally irrational) is the spirit of its structure (pp. 162–164).

The relative nature of this denormatization process in the extreme situation is further amplified in their discussion of genocide:

> Hilberg appropriately speaks of the destruction of the European Jews. Terms like "killing" or "murder" do not convey the meaning of genocide, because they have moral and legal overtones . . . we have here, finally the very essence of the extreme situation: the individual has neither a moral nor a legal claim on society. He is bereft and victimized or simply destroyed (p. 166).

In *Autonomy in the Extreme Situation*, Marcus (1999) explores the linkage between Bettelheim's analysis of survival in the concentration camp and the challenge of maintaining individuality in a mass society. He suggests that the salient point in Bettelheim's observation is that "the inmates' struggle in a concentration camp is the extreme example of the modern dilemma of maintaining autonomy in a mass state" (p. 2).

Marcus's discussion of Bettelheim's essay on mass society is particularly poignant in that it explores the themes that have also captured the attention of such important theorists as Weber, Foucault, Fromm, Giddens and Goffman. The thread that binds them together is their commentary on the inherent incompatibility between mass society/bureaucracy and individuality. Indeed, the appeal of mass society and its promise of economic rewards and security cannot be achieved without the consequent mortification of one's self and the "intense psychological anxiety and fear rooted in the sense of losing individual identity" (Marcus, 1999, p. 43). Weber, Foucault and Giddens have examined the feelings of powerlessness, depersonalization, and regulatory control that are the by products of bureaucratization. Foucault and Giddens have both paid special attention to the power of both institutional and societal surveillance as the unique instruments of social control in modern/mass society (Marcus, 1999, pp. 40–41).

In Foucault's discussion of the modern "disciplinary society," he emphasizes the profound impact of surveillance as a mechanism of regulatory and disciplinary control. O'Farrell (2005) notes that whether these individuals are inmates, workers or school children, they would come to believe and behave "as though they were being watched all the time" (p. 104). Foucault (1977) asserts that

> there is no need for weapons, physical violence, material constraints. Just a gaze. An inspecting gaze, a gaze which each person feeling its weight will end up by interiorising to the point of observing himself; thus each person will exercise this surveillance over and against himself (as cited in O'Farrell, 2005, p. 104).

Similarly, Giddens (1991) sees surveillance as

> the basis of the massive increase in organizational power associated with the emergence of modern social life. Surveillance refers to the supervisory control of subject populations, whether this control takes the form of "visible" supervision in Foucault's sense, or the use of information to coordinate social activities (p. 15).

As discussed later in this volume (chapter four), British social philosopher Jeremy Bentham's (1791) architectural/spatial design of the prison as Panopticon is the foundational underpinning of the principle of Panopticism or surveillance as the tool of control in modern society. The Panopticon was designed to allow the prison guards to observe the inmates at all times while the inmates were unable to see them. However, it has been suggested, in symbolic terms, that "the Panopticon is not a prison. It is a general principle of construction, the polyvalent apparatus of surveillance, the universal optical machine of human groupings" (Miller & Miller, 1987, p. 3).

It should be noted at this time that Bettelheim does not lack for severe and passionate critics. More specifically, he has been accused of "blurring" the differences between extermination camps and labor camps, inappropriately applying psychoanalytic theory to behavior in the camps and even of defaming survivors of the experience (e.g. Des Pres, 1977; Langer, 1982; Krell, 1997; discussion and references as cited in Marcus, 1999, p. 2). (Also see T. Pytell, 2007.)

To be sure, Goffman too has been subject to criticism regarding interpretive confusion and reformulations of the concept of total institution. Some have questioned the "utility and meaning" of the concept as they point to its emphasis on similarities in institutional dynamics rather than the extensive variations that exist in its organizational structure. These variations may be related to levels of bureaucratization and the relationship of an institution to its "external environment" and cultural milieu (McEwen, 1980; Davies, 1989).

Notwithstanding these criticisms, I do employ the core concepts of extreme situations and total institutions as the constructs upon which this volume is grounded. As first adumbrated by Rosenberg et al. (1964), the paradigm of seeing extreme situations as the products of total institutions provides an excellent lens by which to view the commonalities linking diverse illustrations of man's inhumanity to man and the capacity of victims to persevere. Indeed, "the fact that extreme situations can be demonstrated to occur *outside* (emphasis mine) the confines of total institutions is evidence that their spirit and structure tend to pervade modern society" (p. 167). One need not agree necessarily with the specific findings of Bettelheim's research in order to appreciate the validity and endurance of the concept of extreme situation. As Volpato and Contarello (1999) have observed,

> in the literature of clinical psychology and that of psychoanalytic orientation in particular, the term "extreme situation" was taken up again by various authors who used it in a broader sense to indicate traumatic situations in which the defensive barrier of the Ego is defeated (p. 241).

Its presentation in this volume has been significantly expanded and enhanced in its descriptive meaning, scope and application. Bettelheim has compelled us to confront the realities of human behavior in extreme situations and has posed powerful questions about the impact of mass society and its effect on the pursuit of individuality.

Similarly, limitations and modifications to the nature of Goffman's total institution do not detract from its significance as the foundation for studying a particularistic organizational structure. An extensive body of analysis is grounded in Goffman's detailed understanding of the mortification of the individual in the total institution. The presentation of extreme situations as the products of total institutions is necessarily grounded in an expanded and dynamic interpretation of Goffman's original construct. Goffman's detailed description of the mortification process in the total institution has provided us with the interpretive underpinning for enhancing our understanding of the degradation and humiliation associated with the loss of adult self-determination in the institutional world of regulation and social control.

As suggested previously, one of the goals of this anthology is to expand the reader's informational familiarity with several of the most significant and tragic events of our recent human experience. The selected readings represent an analysis of these events/institutions as recorded both by the most informed, critical and prolific observers of our history and by the personal narratives of men and women who were fortunate enough to survive their ordeals. The paradigm of total institutions and extreme situations provides an excellent contextual setting for our discussion.

THE ULTIMATE LIMIT

Bruno Bettelheim

Unless philosophically inclined, people are content to take life as it comes when things go reasonably well, preferring to evade the troublesome question of life's purpose or meaning. While we are quite ready to accept intellectually that man in general is but the chance product of a long and complex evolutionary process, and that we in particular came into being as the consequence of our parents' procreative instinct and—so we hope—also their desire to have *us* for a child, I doubt that this rational explanation is ever truly convincing to our emotions. From time to time we cannot help wondering what life's purpose for human beings might be, if any. But it is not a problem that oppresses us greatly in the normal course of events.

In times of trouble, however, the problem of life's purpose, or meaning, forces itself on our awareness. The greater the hardship we experience, the more pressing the question becomes for us. It makes good sense psychologically that we begin to worry about life's meaning when we already suffer from serious trials and tribulations, because then our search for answers has a purpose. It seems that if we could just grasp life's deeper significance, then we would also comprehend the true meaning of our agony—and incidentally that of others—and this would answer the burning question of why we have to bear it, why it was inflicted on us. If in the light of our understanding of life's design our suffering is needed to achieve its purpose, or is at least an essential part of it, then as an integral element of life's great design our affliction becomes meaningful, and thus more bearable.

Great as one's pain may be, it becomes more tolerable when one is certain that one will survive the sickness that caused it and eventually be cured. The worst calamity becomes bearable if one believes its end is in sight. The worst agony is mitigated as soon as one believes the state of distress is reversible and will be reversed. Only death is absolute, irreversible, final; first and foremost our own, but equally that of others. That is why death anxiety, when not relieved by a firm belief in an afterlife, surpasses all other anxieties in depth. Death, life's ultimate denial, poses most acutely the problem of life's meaning.

So intricately, so inextricably interwoven are death and life's meaning that when life seems to have lost all meaning, suicide seems the inescapable consequence. Suicidal attempts further elucidate this connection. Very few suicides are due to the wish to end insufferable pain which prevents any further enjoyment of life, when the condition causing the pain is definitely irreversible. More frequently suicides are the consequence of an unalterable conviction that the person's life has completely and irremediably lost all meaning. From my experience with persons who tried to commit suicide, I believe that the majority of suicides are accidents in attempts which are expected to be aborted, but unfortunately are not.

The vast majority of suicide attempts are desperate cries for help to become able to continue living. Such suicide attempts are serious, because if the help is not forthcoming, then the person may indeed end his life. What the suicidal person needs to be able to continue living, and the response which he tries to evoke, is the restoration of meaning to his existence.

A suicide attempt is thus most often an utterly desperate demand directed at some real or imaginary, but always emotionally significant person. This very special person's response to the suicidal action should demonstrate clearly, tellingly, beyond any possible doubt, that—contrary to the suicidal person's fear—there is meaning to his life. The more or less specific demand inherent in the suicide attempt is usually that this other person, through his action, should show that he is willing to go to extreme lengths—not to prevent suicide, as is all too often the inadequate response—but to give meaning to the afflicted person's life by convincingly showing that his existence is of singular importance to the intended rescuer. The suicidal person believes that only through his being important on the deepest level to this uniquely significant person can meaning be restored to his life. By virtue of being so meaningful to this all-important person, the suicidal individual's life becomes also meaningful to himself, and death is no longer an acceptable alternative to life.

To have found meaning in life is thus the only certain antidote to the deliberate seeking of death. But at the same time, in a strange dialectical way, it is death that endows life with its deepest, most unique meaning.

We cannot really imagine what life would be like, had it no end; how it would feel, how we would live it, what would give it importance. Those cultures which believe in successive reincarnations desire most that their chain should end; not only is the final goal of all reincarnations their cessation, but each separate existence also has its definite conclusion. If there have been civilizations which believed in the desirability of an unending life, it seems they could imagine it only as the eternal repetition of the same well-known daily events, or as an existence without any problems, challenges, change.

Even the poets have found it difficult to visualize a paradisal existence with any other content besides eternal bliss. Whatever the experience of life may have been for those who believed it to be without end, and whatever their ideas about the continuation of life after death, to us an existence in which nothing ever changes seems devoid of interest. Thus it is the finiteness of life—much as we may dislike contemplating it and dread life's end—which gives life its unique quality and makes us wish to savor every one of its moments to the fullest.

It is man's struggle to find the significance of life, and of its finiteness, and through his search master his fear of death, which defines not only his religion, but also much of what he considers best in his culture and the personal style of his life. Essentially man has dealt with the inescapability of death in three ways: through acceptance or resignation, making all of life a mere preparation for death and what supposedly comes after it; through denial; and through efforts at temporary mastery.

During the centuries when Christianity shaped life for Western man, he tried to both accept death and deny it. It was largely the denial that made the acceptance possible, because only the belief in a life eternal in the hereafter enabled man to face the knowledge that on this earth even "in the midst of life we are in death."

Later, when a rational-scientific view of the world began to emerge, belief in the hereafter crumbled. Acceptance and resignation became less possible, because from the start these had been based on denial. In the mood of this new age of reason, with its commitment to this world here and now rather than to the next, a good life on earth was thought to be assured through social, economic, and scientific progress.

With this, the widely held faith in life's definite goal of gaining salvation and, with it, life eternal, underwent a radical change: it became the struggle to achieve progress—which was thought to be limitless—which was to give life its ultimate meaning. This is the Faustian solution to the enigma of life's significance, and it found its most beautiful and concise expression at the end of Goethe's poem, when Faust had overcome his dread of death through his efforts to reshape the world for the better. Because of the improvements he had worked, Faust, the archetypical modern Western man, felt sure that

The imprints of my earthly days.
In aeons shall not disappear.

But the monumental improvement which Faust believed he bequeathed to the world, and which he trusted would guarantee the permanent continuation, if not of himself as a person, then of his life's achievement, is but a mirage.

By putting his trust in what progress could achieve, man sought to free himself ever more from the terror of death. Science would conquer disease, extend the span of life, make it ever safer, less painful, more satisfying. Because of decline in faith, the denial of death through the religious promise of life eternal wore thin, and came to be replaced by a concentration on postponing death. Man cannot worry about too many things at once; one anxiety easily replaces another. By concentrating his attention, as well as his anxieties, for example, on cancer and on cancer-causing agents, pollution, etc., man manages to push death anxiety so much into the background of his mind that for all practical purposes it is denied.

Since it is reasonable to assume that a solution to the cancer problem will be found, belief in progress seems to have proven its capacity to combat death anxiety, since with all the emphasis on fighting cancer the question is hardly considered of what will then cause the death of those who now die of cancer. Innumerable health fads serve the same purpose of trying to repress death anxiety by devoting one's mental—and often also one's physical—energies to prolonging life, so that thoughts about its end will not permit death anxiety to come to awareness.

For the rest, Western man has relied on hiding stark death anxiety behind soothingly scientific and less threatening euphemisms. Since anxiety is a psychological phenomenon, death anxiety came to be viewed as but a special form of "separation anxiety" or "fear of abandonment." Such terms, born of trust in unlimited progress, suggest that remedies for the fear of abandonment will eventually be forthcoming. And they can indeed be found for temporary desertion—although not, of course, for the ultimate one. Still, by using the same concept—anxiety—to refer to reversible and to irreversible events, to the feelings which both a temporary and the ultimate, eternal abandonment evoke, the irreversible event is made to seem similar to the reversible one.

But whatever man's psychological defenses against death anxiety, they have always broken down whenever catastrophe struck and vast numbers of people were suddenly and unexpectedly killed in a very short time. Probably the first such disaster for which we have ample records was the Black Death in the fourteenth century. This event resulted in an image of life as being nothing but a dance with death, a visual and poetic expression of the death anxiety then sweeping the Western world.

The earthquake which destroyed Lisbon in 1755 and caused great loss of life was widely experienced as a cataclysmic event which called the wisdom and benevolence of God seriously into question. With this doubt, men were deprived of the belief which until then had served them well to ward off death anxiety and had given meaning to their temporary existence on earth. This was also true for the boy Goethe, as he described in his autobiography a lifetime later;[1] it may very well have been this shattering experience at the beginning of his conscious existence which led Goethe to embrace the Faustian solution quoted above.

In the past it was mainly natural catastrophes: plagues, earthquakes, floods, devastating conflagrations—all of which came to be known as holocausts—which shook man's trust in those of his beliefs which gave deeper meaning to his life and at the same time served as his defense against death anxiety. When a war wiped out cities and countries, it was regarded as the scourge of God, as were natural disasters. As such, they led in religious times to renewed efforts to do God's will, to pacify His wrath through greater devotion.

All this changed with this century. In the twentieth century, man's mastery over natural catastrophes became more effective than ever. But at the same time it seemed he became the hapless victim of manmade cataclysms even more devastating than the natural disasters which had thrown him into panic death anxiety in the preceding centuries. Worse, progress in the sciences and in the rational organization of society, into which man had put his faith as the best defense against death anxiety and as that which would give meaning to his life, turned out to provide the tools for a much more radical destruction of life than man had imagined possible.

The modern defense against death anxiety—belief in the unlimited blessings of progress—was severely undermined by World War I and its aftermath. That war led Freud to recognize that death is as powerful a force in our mind and in shaping our actions as is our love of life. Unfortunately he cast this important insight into theories that paralleled his earlier concept of the libido (the sex instinct, or the life drives) and proposed a theoretical death drive. Actually it is not the battle between the life and the death drives that governs man's life, but a struggle of the life drives against being overwhelmed by death anxiety. In short, there is an omnipresent fear of extinction which threatens to run destructively rampant when not successfully kept under safe control by our conviction of the positive value of life.

The full impact of this recognition came much less from World War II (which was essentially a continuation of the First World War) than from the concentration camps with their gas chambers and from the first atomic bomb. These confronted us with the stark reality of overwhelming death, not so much one's own—this each of us has to face sooner or later and however uneasily most of us manage not to be overpowered by our fear of it—but the unnecessary and untimely death of millions. Senseless mass murder in the gas chambers, genocide, the leveling of an entire city by the dropping of one single bomb—these became the indicators of the ineffectiveness of our civilization's defenses against the reality of death. Progress not only failed to preserve life, but it deprived millions of their lives more effectively than had been possible ever before.

Years ago Freud wrote of the three great blows dealt to our narcissism by the discoveries of science. The first was the Copernican revolution, which revealed that man's home the earth was not the center of the universe. The second was the Darwinian, since it removed man from his unique position and placed him squarely in the animal world.

---

[1]*Dichtung und Wahrheit*, part one, book one.

Finally, the Freudian revolution showed that man is not even fully aware of his motives, so that often they drive him to act in ways he does not understand.[2]

It seems that in addition to these basic blows to man's self-oriented world, he has sustained three additional shattering blows in this century alone. The first crisis was World War I, which destroyed the belief that in and of itself progress would solve our problems, provide meaning to our life, and help us master our existential anxiety—the human fear of death. It forced us to realize that despite great scientific, technological, and intellectual progress man is still prey to irrational forces which push him to engage in violence and wreak destruction.

In World War II Auschwitz and Hiroshima showed that progress through technology has escalated man's destructive impulses into more precise and incredibly more devastating form. It was progress toward an all-powerful social organization that made Auschwitz—which epitomizes man's organized cruelty to man—possible. The atomic bomb demonstrated the destructive potentials of science and called the very benefits of scientific progress into question.

When the holocausts of past times were viewed as God's will, they had to be accepted as such. Inscrutable as His decisions were, men believed a catastrophe was a warning from Him to mend their ways while there was still time, so that they would not end in Hell, but gain eternal salvation. Thus while what happened was terrible, it neither undermined belief in the purpose and meaning of life nor disintegrated the individual man's personal system of beliefs, and with it his personality. Although the event was horrible, it was in harmony with the existing image of things. To accept without flinching the suffering God inflicted on man was a demonstration of the strength of man's faith, and with it of the solidity of his integration. It changed neither life's goal: salvation; nor its purpose: to do God's will; nor the way to achieve both: religious piety. Far from leading man to doubt his defenses against death anxiety, it strengthened them through religious fervor. With this, it also increased the resilience of an integration which was based on a system of religious beliefs.

Exactly the opposite holds true for the impact of modern holocausts. Far from fitting into our world picture, or the image of man which we would like to hold on to, they are utterly destructive to both. Since we realize that these mass murders are man-made, we can no longer ascribe some deeper meaning to them which potentially could benefit the survivor.

To our dismay we have been forced to realize that what rational man felt confident was life-enhancing stood revealed to be also life-destroying. Despite all the advantages which scientific and technological progress has brought us, it has also led to atomic fission and the holocaust of Hiroshima. Social organization which we believed would bring about ever greater security and well-being was used in Auschwitz to murder millions more efficiently. The reorganization of Russian society for the purpose of achieving a more beneficial social system resulted in the death of untold millions of citizens.

It is most destructive to a person—and when it happens to many at the same time and in the same way, to an entire culture—when the beliefs which gave direction to life are revealed as unreliable, and when the psychological defenses which were depended upon to secure physical and psychological well-being and protect against death

---

[2] "A Difficulty in the Path of Psychoanalysis," *The Standard Edition of the Complete Psychological Works of Sigmund Freud*, vol. 17 (London: The Hogarth Press, 1955).

anxiety—psychological structures which in their entirety form our personality—turn out to be untrustworthy. That experience is sufficient to disintegrate a personality built up on the basis of these beliefs.

It can become completely shattering to a person's integration when the system of beliefs on which he relied for his integration, and for offering protection against death anxiety, not only lets him down, but worse, is about to destroy him psychologically and physically. Then nothing seems left that can offer protection. Furthermore, we now no longer can feel confident that we will be able ever again to know reliably what to trust, and what to defend against.

Thus modern man's Faustian defense against death anxiety, and the system of beliefs which gave meaning to his life—striving to work for progress, although with no specific goal—have become shaky even under normal circumstances. The sheer prospect of death is not all that haunts us; there is also the anxiety we feel when the social structures we created to protect us from abandonment collapse, or when the personality structure we built up for the same purpose disintegrates.

While either source of protection, the personal or social, can easily crumble in moments of great stress, if normal life continues around us, it permits us to soon reestablish our protective stances, unless insanity or senility occurs. Matters are different when not only does the trust we put in man and society suddenly turn out to have been an illusion, but also our personality structure no longer protects us from a fear of abandonment. The only worse situation occurs when we really are abandoned and immediate death is possible and likely, although we feel our time is not yet ripe. Then the effects are catastrophic. The combined and sudden breakdown of all these defenses against death anxiety projects us into what I called some thirty-five years ago, for want of available terms, an *extreme situation.*

Extreme Situations

We find ourselves in an extreme situation when we are suddenly catapulted into a set of conditions where our old adaptive mechanisms and values do not apply any more and when some of them may even endanger the life they were meant to protect. Then we are so to say, stripped of our whole defensive system and thrown back to rock bottom whence we must carve out a new set of attitudes, values, and way of living as required by the new situation.

This is what happened to me, as it did to thousands of others, when in the spring of 1938, immediately after the annexation of Austria, I was first arrested in my home and deprived of my passport, making orderly emigration impossible, and a few weeks later imprisoned for a few days and then transported into the concentration camp at Dachau. It happened to tens of thousands in November of the same year as part of the huge pogrom in the wake of the murder of vom Rath,[3] and in an even more horrible form to the millions who were shipped into the extermination camps during the war.

In some ways I was better prepared for the immediate shock of this "extreme experience" than many of my fellow prisoners, because out of political interest I had

---

[3]On November 7, 1938, Herschel Grynszpan, a young Polish Jew, deeply upset by the Nazi persecution of Jews, went to the German embassy in Paris and there shot Ernst vom Rath, the third secretary, who died two days later. This served as the excuse for a terrible pogrom in Germany in which thousands of Jews were murdered and tens of thousands put into concentration camps.

become familiar with the few reports which had trickled out of the Third Reich, telling what life in these camps was like. In addition, through the teachings of psychoanalysis I had become cognizant of the dark sides of man—his hatreds and destructive potentials, the power of those forces which Freud had named the death drive.

In a way, I also was lucky. During the transport I had been hurt badly enough to be looked at by an SS physician on the morning following my arrival at Dachau. He permitted me three days of complete rest, to be followed by a week of preferred treatment (*Schonung*).[4] This gave me a chance to recuperate to some measure. What may have been more beneficial in the long run, it was also an opportunity to attempt taking stock of my experience, to sort out first impressions of what being in this horrible predicament was doing to my comrades and to me, and of how those prisoners who had been in the camps for some years seemed to cope.

This demonstrated the validity of what I had learned during my psychoanalysis: how psychologically reconstructive it is to try to comprehend one's mental responses to an experience, and how helpful it is to fathom what goes on in the minds of others who are subjected to the same experience. This effort to gain at least some limited awareness probably convinced me that something of my old system of mastery might be salvaged, that some aspects of the belief in the value of rational examination—such as in what could be learned from psychoanalysis—might be of some use, even under these radically changed conditions of living. Had I been projected immediately into the dreadfully destructive grind of deadly mistreatments and utterly exhausting labor, as were my comrades, I do not know whether I would have succeeded equally well in reestablishing some parts of my psychological protective system.

Of course, at the time nothing was further from my mind than salvaging something of my old defensive system. All my thoughts, all my energies went into the desperate struggle to survive the day, to fight off depressive moods, to keep up the will to resist, to gain some small advantages that might make seemingly impossibly difficult efforts to survive just a bit more likely to succeed, and to frustrate as much as possible the SS's unrelenting efforts to break the spirit of the prisoners. When I was not too exhausted or downhearted to do so, I tried to understand what went on in me and in others because this was of interest to me, and it was one of the rare satisfactions that the SS could not deprive me of.

---

[4]On the train ride from Vienna to Dachau, which had lasted a night and the better part of a day, all the prisoners were severely mistreated. Of the approximately 700 to 800 prisoners who were part of this particular transport, at least twenty were killed during the night. Hardly anybody escaped unharmed, and many were wounded severely. Compared to them I was relatively lucky to suffer no permanent damage, although I received a few severe blows on the head and some other-minor wounds. The horn-rimmed glasses I happened to be wearing when I was imprisoned marked me as an intellectual in the eyes of the SS, and this particularly aroused their antagonism, which may explain the blows on the head, the first of which smashed my glasses.

On my arrival at Dachau, my state was sufficiently bad—mainly due to loss of blood—that on the next morning the prisoner in command of the barrack (the so-called *Blockältester*) included me among the few whom he took to the camp clinic. There the SS orderly chose me as one of those to be looked at by the SS physician, who granted me a few days of rest. Since my glasses had been broken, and since without them I am near-blind, the physician also permitted me to write home for a replacement. Having learned my lesson, I requested—and a while later received—glasses of the simplest and cheapest kind. Even so, I found it best to hide my glasses and do without them whenever the SS went on a rampage; I was much safer this way. This was but one of the many precautions a prisoner had to learn to take if he wanted to increase his chances for survival.

Only with the passing of months did I very slowly come to realize that without any conscious planning, by doing only what came naturally, I had unconsciously hit on what would "protect this individual against a disintegration of his personality." Stating it so confidently was possible only in hindsight; while still a prisoner in the camps, it was whistling in the dark on my part to view it so positively. I did view it thus, however, to fight off the lurking anxiety that the SS might succeed in their efforts to disintegrate my personality further, as they tried to do to all prisoners.

Source: From *Surviving and Other Essays* by Bruno Bettelheim, copyright © 1979 by Bruno Bettelheim and Trude Bettelheim as Trustees. Used by permission of Alfred A. Knopf, a division of Random House, Inc.

CHARACTERISTICS OF TOTAL INSTITUTIONS

Erving Goffman

Every institution captures something of the time and interest of its members and provides something of a world for them; in brief, every institution has encompassing tendencies. When we review the different institutions in our Western society, we find some that are encompassing to a degree discontinuously greater than the ones next in line. Their encompassing or total character is symbolized by the barrier to social intercourse with the outside and to departure that is often built right into the physical plant, such as locked doors, high walls, barbed wire, cliffs, water, forests, or moors. These establishments I am calling *total institutions,* and it is their general characteristics I want to explore.[1]

The total institutions of our society can be listed in five rough groupings. First, there are institutions established to care for persons felt to be both incapable and harmless; these are the homes for the blind, the aged, the orphaned, and the indigent. Second, there are places established to care for persons felt to be both incapable of looking after themselves and a threat to the community, albeit an unintended one: TB sanitaria, mental hospitals, and leprosaria. A third type of total institution is organized to protect the community against what are felt to be intentional dangers to it, with the welfare of the persons thus sequestered not the immediate issue: jails, penitentiaries, P.O.W. camps, and concentration camps. Fourth, there are institutions purportedly established the better to pursue some worklike task and justifying themselves only on these instrumental grounds: army barracks, ships, boarding schools, work camps, colonial compounds, and large mansions from the point of view of those who live in the servants' quarters. Finally, there are those establishments designed as retreats from the world even while often serving also as training stations for the religious; examples are abbeys, monasteries, convents, and other cloisters. This classification of total institutions is not neat, exhaustive, nor of immediate analytical use, but it does provide a purely denotative definition of the category as a concrete starting point. By anchoring the initial definition of total institutions in this way, I hope to be able to discuss the general characteristics of the type without becoming tautological.

Before I attempt to extract a general profile from this list of establishments, I would like to mention one conceptual problem: none of the elements I will describe seems peculiar to total institutions, and none seems to be shared by every one of them; what is distinctive about total institutions is that each exhibits to an intense degree many items in this family of attributes. In speaking of "common characteristics," I will be using this phrase in a way that is restricted but I think logically defensible. At the same time this

---

[1]The category of total institutions has been pointed out from time to time in the sociological literature under a variety of names, and some of the characteristics of the class have been suggested, most notably perhaps in Howard Rowland's neglected paper, "Segregated Communities and Mental Health," in *Mental Health Publication of the American Association for the Advancement of Science,* No. 9, edited by F. R. Moulton, 1939. A preliminary statement of the present paper is reported in *Group Processes,* Transactions of the Third (1956) Conference, edited by Bertram Schaffner (New York: Josiah Macy, Jr. Foundation, 1957). The term "total" has also been used in its present context in Amitai Etzioni, "The Organizational Structure of 'Closed' Educational Institutions in Israel," *Harvard Educational Review,* XXVII (1957), p. 115.

permits using the method of ideal types, establishing common features with the hope of highlighting significant differences later.

A basic social arrangement in modern society is that the individual tends to sleep, play, and work in different places, with different co-participants, under different authorities, and without an over-all rational plan. The central feature of total institutions can be described as a breakdown of the barriers ordinarily separating these three spheres of life. First, all aspects of life are conducted in the same place and under the same single authority. Second, each phase of the member's daily activity is carried on in the immediate company of a large batch of others, all of whom are treated alike and required to do the same thing together. Third, all phases of the day's activities are tightly scheduled, with one activity leading at a prearranged time into the next, the whole sequence of activities being imposed from above by a system of explicit formal rulings and a body of officials. Finally, the various enforced activities are brought together into a single rational plan purportedly designed to fulfill the official aims of the institution.

Individually, these features are found in places other than total institutions. For example, our large commercial, industrial, and educational establishments are increasingly providing cafeterias and free-time recreation for their members; use of these extended facilities remains voluntary in many particulars, however, and special care is taken to see that the ordinary line of authority does not extend to them. Similarly, housewives or farm families may have all their major spheres of life within the same fenced-in area, but these persons are not collectively regimented and do not march through the day's activities in the immediate company of a batch of similar others.

The handling of many human needs by the bureaucratic organization of whole blocks of people—whether or not this is a necessary or effective means of social organization in the circumstances—is the key fact of total institutions. From this follow certain important implications.

When persons are moved in blocks, they can be supervised by personnel whose chief activity is not guidance or periodic inspection (as in many employer-employee relations) but rather surveillance—a seeing to it that everyone does what he has been clearly told is required of him, under conditions where one person's infraction is likely to stand out in relief against the visible, constantly examined compliance of the others. Which comes first, the large blocks of managed people, or the small supervisory staff, is not here at issue; the point is that each is made for the other.

In total institutions there is a basic split between a large managed group, conveniently called inmates, and a small supervisory staff. Inmates typically live in the institution and have restricted contact with the world outside the walls; staff often operate on an eight-hour day and are socially integrated into the outside world.[2] Each grouping tends to conceive of the other in terms of narrow hostile stereotypes, staff

---

[2]The binary character of total institutions was pointed out to me by Gregory Bateson, and has been noted in the literature. See, for example, Lloyd E. Ohlin, *Sociology and the Field of Corrections* (New York: Russell Sage Foundation, 1956), pp. 14, 20. In those situations where staff are also required to live in, we may expect staff to feel they are suffering special hardships and to have brought home to them a status dependency on life on the inside which they did not expect. See Jane Cassels Record, "The Marine Radioman's Struggle for Status," *American Journal of Sociology,* LXII (1957), p. 359.

often seeing inmates as bitter, secretive, and untrustworthy, while inmates often see staff as condescending, highhanded, and mean. Staff tends to feel superior and righteous; inmates tend, in some ways at least, to feel inferior, weak, blameworthy, and guilty.[3]

Social mobility between the two strata is grossly restricted; social distance is typically great and often formally prescribed. Even talk across the boundaries may be conducted in a special tone of voice, as illustrated in a fictionalized record of an actual sojourn in a mental hospital:

> "I tell you what," said Miss Hart when they were crossing the dayroom. "You do everything Miss Davis says. Don't think about it, just do it. You'll get along all right."
>
> As soon as she heard the name Virginia knew what was terrible about Ward One. Miss Davis. "Is she the head nurse?"
>
> "And how," muttered Miss Hart. And then she raised her voice. The nurses had a way of acting as if the patients were unable to hear anything that was not shouted. Frequently they said things in normal voices that the ladies were not supposed to hear; if they had not been nurses you would have said they frequently talked to themselves. "A most competent and efficient person, Miss Davis," announced Miss Hart.[4]

Although some communication between inmates and the staff guarding them is necessary, one of the guard's functions is the control of communication from inmates to higher staff levels. A student of mental hospitals provides an illustration:

> Since many of the patients are anxious to see the doctor on his rounds, the attendants must act as mediators between the patients and the physician if the latter is not to be swamped. On Ward 30, it seemed to be generally true that patients without physical symptoms who fell into the two lower privilege groups were almost never permitted to talk to the physician unless Dr. Baker himself asked for them. The persevering, nagging delusional group—who were termed "worry warts," "nuisances," "bird dogs," in the attendants' slang—often tried to break through the attendant-mediator but were always quite summarily dealt with when they tried.[5]

Just as talk across the boundary is restricted, so, too, is the passage of information, especially information about the staff's plans for inmates. Characteristically, the inmate is excluded from knowledge of the decisions taken regarding his fate. Whether the official grounds are military, as in concealing travel destination from enlisted men, or medical, as in concealing diagnosis, plan of treatment, and approximate length of stay from

---

[3]For the prison version, see S. Kirson Weinberg, "Aspects of the Prison's Social Structure," *American Journal of Sociology*, XLVII (1942), pp. 717–26.

[4]Mary Jane Ward, *The Snake Pit* (New York: New American Library, 1955), p. 72.

[5]Ivan Belknap, *Human Problems of a State Mental Hospital* (New York: McGraw-Hill, 1956), p. 177.

tuberculosis patients,[6] such exclusion gives staff a special basis of distance from and control over inmates.

All these restrictions of contact presumably help to maintain the antagonistic stereotypes.[7] Two different social and cultural worlds develop, jogging alongside each other with points of official contact but little mutual penetration. Significantly, the institutional plant and name come to be identified by both staff and inmates as somehow belonging to staff, so that when either grouping refers to the views or interests of "the institution," by implication they are referring (as I shall also) to the views and concerns of the staff.

The staff-inmate split is one major implication of the bureaucratic management of large blocks of persons; a second pertains to work.

In the ordinary arrangements of living in our society, the authority of the work place stops with the worker's receipt of a money payment; the spending of this in a domestic and recreational setting is the worker's private affair and constitutes a mechanism through which the authority of the work place is kept within strict bounds. But to say that inmates of total institutions have their full day scheduled for them is to say that all their essential needs will have to be planned for. Whatever the incentive given for work, then, this incentive will not have the structural significance it has on the outside. There will have to be different motives for work and different attitudes toward it. This is a basic adjustment required of the inmates and of those who must induce them to work.

Sometimes so little work is required that inmates, often untrained in leisurely pursuits, suffer extremes of boredom. Work that is required may be carried on at a very slow pace and may be geared into a system of minor, often ceremonial, payments, such as the weekly tobacco ration and the Christmas presents that lead some mental patients to stay on their jobs. In other cases, of course, more than a full day's hard labor is required, induced not by reward but by threat of physical punishment. In some total institutions, such as logging camps and merchant ships, the practice of forced saving postpones the usual relation to the world that money can buy; all needs are organized by the institution and payment is given only when a work season is over and the men leave the premises. In some institutions there is a kind of slavery, with the inmate's full time placed at the convenience of staff; here the inmate's sense of self and sense of possession can become alienated from his work capacity. T. E. Lawrence gives an illustration in his record of service in an R.A.F. training depot:

> The six-weeks men we meet on fatigues shock our moral sense by their easy-going. "You're silly—, you rookies, to sweat yourselves" they say. Is it our new keenness, or a relic of civility in us? For by the R.A.F. we shall be paid all the twenty-four hours a day, at three halfpence an hour; paid to work, paid to eat, paid to sleep: always those halfpence are adding up. Impossible, therefore, to dignify a job by doing it well. It must take as much time as it can for afterwards there is not a fireside waiting, but another job.[8]

---

[6]A very full case report on this matter is provided in a chapter titled "Information and the Control of Treatment," in Julius A. Roth's forthcoming monograph on the tuberculosis hospital. His work promises to be a model study of a total institution. Preliminary statements may be found in his articles, "What is an Activity?" Etc., XIV (Autumn 1956), pp. 54–56, and "Ritual and Magic in the Control of Contagion," *American Sociological Review*, XXII (1957), pp. 310–14.

[7]Suggested in Ohlin, *op. cit.*, p. 20.

[8]T. E. Lawrence, *The Mint* (London: Jonathan Cape, 1955), p. 40.

Whether there is too much work or too little, the individual who was work-oriented on the outside tends to become demoralized by the work system of the total institution. An example of such demoralization is the practice in state mental hospitals of "bumming" or "working someone for" a nickel or dime to spend in the canteen. Persons do this—often with some defiance—who on the outside would consider such actions beneath their self-respect. (Staff members, interpreting this begging pattern in terms of their own civilian orientation to earning, tend to see it as a symptom of mental illness and one further bit of evidence that inmates really are unwell.)

There is an incompatibility, then, between total institutions and the basic work-payment structure of our society. Total institutions are also incompatible with another crucial element of our society, the family. Family life is sometimes contrasted with solitary living, but in fact the more pertinent contrast is with batch living, for those who eat and sleep at work, with a group of fellow workers, can hardly sustain a meaningful domestic existence.[9] Conversely, maintaining families off the grounds often permits staff members to remain integrated with the outside community and to escape the encompassing tendency of the total institution.

Whether a particular total institution acts as a good or bad force in civil society, force it will have, and this will in part depend on the suppression of a whole circle of actual or potential households. Conversely, the formation of households provides a structural guarantee that total institutions will not be without resistance. The incompatibility of these two forms of social organization should tell us something about the wider social functions of them both.

The total institution is a social hybrid, part residential community, part formal organization; therein lies its special sociological interest. There are other reasons for being interested in these establishments, too. In our society, they are the forcing houses for changing persons; each is a natural experiment on what can be done to the self.

Some of the key features of total institutions have been suggested. I want now to consider these establishments from two perspectives: first, the inmate world; then the staff world. Finally, I want to say something about contacts between the two.

The Inmate World

It is characteristic of inmates that they come to the institution with a "presenting culture" (to modify a psychiatric phrase) derived from a "home world"—a way of life and a round of activities taken for granted until the point of admission to the institution. (There is reason, then, to exclude orphanages and foundling homes from the list of total institutions, except in so far as the orphan comes to be socialized into the outside world by some process of cultural osmosis even while this world is being systematically denied him.) Whatever the stability of the recruit's personal organization, it was part of a wider framework lodged in his civil environment—a round of experience that confirmed a tolerable conception of self and allowed for a set of defensive maneuvers, exercised at his own discretion, for coping with conflicts, discreditings, and failures.

Now it appears that total institutions do not substitute their own unique culture for something already formed; we deal with something more restricted than acculturation

---

[9]An interesting marginal case here is the Israeli *kibbutz*. See Melford E. Spiro, *Kibbutz, Venture in Utopia* (Cambridge: Harvard University Press, 1956), and Etzioni, *op. cit.*

or assimilation. If cultural change does occur, it has to do, perhaps, with the removal of certain behavior opportunities and with failure to keep pace with recent social changes on the outside. Thus, if the inmate's stay is long, what has been called "disculturation"[10] may occur—that is, an "untraining" which renders him temporarily incapable of managing certain features of daily life on the outside, if and when he gets back to it.

The full meaning for the inmate of being "in" or "on the inside" does not exist apart from the special meaning to him of "getting out" or "getting on the outside." In this sense, total institutions do not really look for cultural victory. They create and sustain a particular kind of tension between the home world and the institutional world and use this persistent tension as strategic leverage in the management of men.

The recruit comes into the establishment with a conception of himself made possible by certain stable social arrangements in his home world. Upon entrance, he is immediately stripped of the support provided by these arrangements. In the accurate language of some of our oldest total institutions, he begins a series of abasements, degradations, humiliations, and profanations of self. His self is systematically, if often unintentionally, mortified. He begins some radical shifts in his *moral career*, a career composed of the progressive changes that occur in the beliefs that he has concerning himself and significant others.

The processes by which a person's self is mortified are fairly standard in total institutions;[11] analysis of these processes can help us to see the arrangements that ordinary establishments must guarantee if members are to preserve their civilian selves.

Although there are solidarizing tendencies such as fraternalization and clique formation, they are limited. Constraints which place inmates in a position to sympathize and communicate with each other do not necessarily lead to high group morale and solidarity. In some concentration camps and prisoner-of-war installations the inmate cannot rely on his fellows, who may steal from him, assault him, and squeal on him, leading to what some students have referred to as anomie.[12] In mental hospitals, dyads and triads may keep secrets from the authorities, but anything known to a whole ward of patients is likely to get to the ear of the attendant. (In prisons, of course, inmate organization has sometimes been strong enough to run strikes and short-lived insurrections; in prisoner-of-war camps, it has sometimes been possible to organize sections of the prisoners to operate escape channels;[13] in concentration camps there have been periods of thoroughgoing underground organization;[14] and on ships there have been mutinies; but these concerted actions seem to be the exception, not the rule.) But though there is usually little group loyalty in total institutions, the expectation that group loyalty should prevail forms part of the inmate culture and underlies the hostility accorded those who break inmate solidarity.

---

[10]A term employed by Robert Sommer, "Patients who grow old in a mental hospital," *Gerlatrics*, XIV (1959), pp. 586–87. The term "desocialization," sometimes used in this context would seem to be too strong, implying loss of fundamental capacities to communicate and co-operate.

[11]An example of the description of these processes may be found in Gresham M. Sykes, *The Society of Captives* (Princeton: Princeton University Press, 1958), ch. iv, "The Pains of Imprisonment," pp. 63–83.

[12]A full statement of this theme may be found in D. Cressey and W. Krassowski, "Inmate Organization and Anomie in American Prisons and Soviet Labor Camps," *Social Problems*, V (Winter 1957–58), pp. 217–30.

[13]See, for example, P. R. Reid, *Escape from Colditz* (New York: Berkley Publishing Corp., 1956).

[14]See Paul Foreman, "Buchenwald and Modern Prisoner-of-War Detention Policy," *Social Forces*, XXXVII (1959), pp. 289–98.

The privilege system and the mortifying processes that have been discussed represent the conditions to which the inmate must adapt. These conditions allow for different individualistic ways of meeting them, apart from any effort at collective subversive action. The same inmate will employ different personal lines of adaptation at different phases in his moral career and may even alternate among different tacks at the same time.

First, there is the tack of "situational withdrawal." The inmate withdraws apparent attention from everything except events immediately around his body and sees these in a perspective not employed by others present. This drastic curtailment of involvement in interactional events is best known, of course, in mental hospitals, under the title of "regression." Aspects of "prison psychosis" or going "stir simple" represent the same adjustment,[15] as do some forms of "acute depersonalization" described in concentration camps and "tankeritis" apparently found among confirmed merchant mariners.[16] I do not think it is known whether this line of adaptation forms a single continuum of varying degrees of withdrawal or whether there are standard plateaus of disinvolvement. Given the pressures apparently required to dislodge an inmate from this status, as well as the currently limited facilities for doing so, this line of adaptation is often effectively irreversible.

Secondly, there is the "intransigent line": the inmate intentionally challenges the institution by flagrantly refusing to co-operate with staff.[17] The result is a constantly communicated intransigency and sometimes high individual morale. Many large mental hospitals, for example, have wards where this spirit prevails. Sustained rejection of a total institution often requires sustained orientation to its formal organization, and hence, paradoxically, a deep kind of involvement in the establishment. Similarly, when staff take the line that the intransigent inmate must be broken (as they sometimes do in the case of hospital psychiatrists prescribing electroshock[18] or military tribunals prescribing the stockade), then the institution shows as much special devotion to the rebel as he has shown to it. Finally, although some prisoners of war have been known to take a staunchly intransigent stance throughout their incarceration, intransigence is typically a temporary and initial phase of reaction, with the inmate shifting to situational withdrawal or some other line of adaptation.

A third standard alignment in the institutional world is "colonization": the sampling of the outside world provided by the establishment is taken by the inmate as the whole, and a stable, relatively contented existence is built up out of the maximum satisfactions procurable within the institution.[19] Experience of the outside world is used as a point of reference to demonstrate the desirability of life on the inside, and the usual tension between the two worlds is markedly reduced, thwarting the motivational scheme based upon this felt discrepancy which I described as peculiar to total institutions. Characteristically, the individual who too obviously takes this line may be

---

[15]For an early treatment, see P. Nitsche and K. Wilmanns, *The History of Prison Psychosis,* Nervous and Mental Disease Monograph Series No. 13 (1912).

[16]Richardson, *op. cit.,* p. 42.

[17]See, for example, the discussion of "The Resisters," in Schein, *op. cit.,* pp. 166–67.

[18]Belknap, *op. cit.,* p. 192.

[19]In the case of mental hospitals, those who take this line are sometimes called "institutional cures" or are said to suffer from "hospitalitis."

accused by his fellow inmates of "having found a home" or of "never having had it so good." The staff itself may become vaguely embarrassed by this use that is being made of the institution, sensing that the benign possibilities in the situation are somehow being misused. Colonizers may feel obliged to deny their satisfaction with the institution, if only to sustain the counter-mores supporting inmate solidarity. They may find it necessary to mess up just prior to their slated discharge to provide themselves with an apparently involuntary basis for continued incarceration. Significantly, the staff who try to make life in total institutions more bearable must face the possibility that doing so may increase the attractiveness and likelihood of colonization.

A fourth mode of adaptation to the setting of a total institution is that of "conversion": the inmate appears to take over the official or staff view of himself and tries to act out the role of the perfect inmate. While the colonized inmate builds as much of a free community for himself as possible by using the limited facilities available, the convert takes a more disciplined, moralistic, monochromatic line, presenting himself as someone whose institutional enthusiasm is always at the disposal of the staff. In Chinese P.O.W. camps, we find Americans who became "Pros" and fully espoused the Communist view of the world.[20] In army barracks there are enlisted men who give the impression that they are always "sucking around" and always "bucking for promotion." In prisons there are "square johns." In German concentration camps, a long-time prisoner sometimes came to adapt the vocabulary, recreation, posture, expressions of aggression, and clothing style of the Gestapo, executing the role of straw boss with military strictness.[21] Some mental hospitals have the distinction of providing two quite different conversion possibilities—one for the new admission, who can see the light after an appropriate inner struggle and adopt the psychiatric view of himself, and another for the chronic patient, who adopts the manner and dress of attendants while helping them to manage the other patients, employing a stringency sometimes excelling that of the attendants themselves. And of course in officer training camps we find trainees who quickly become "G.I.," espousing a torment of themselves that they will soon be able to inflict on others.[22]

Here is a significant way in which total institutions differ: many, like progressive mental hospitals, merchant ships, TB sanitaria, and brainwashing camps, offer the inmate an opportunity to live up to a model of conduct that is at once ideal and staff-sponsored—a model felt by its advocates to be in the best interests of the very persons to whom it is applied; other total institutions, like some concentration camps and some prisons, do not officially sponsor an ideal that the inmate is expected to incorporate.

The alignments that have been mentioned represent coherent courses to pursue, but few inmates seem to pursue any one of them very far. In most total institutions, most inmates take the tack of what some of them call "playing it cool." This involves a somewhat opportunistic combination of secondary adjustments, conversion, colonization,

[20]Schein, *op. cit.,* pp. 167–69.

[21]See Bruno Bettelheim, "Individual and Mass Behavior in Extreme Situations," *Journal of Abnormal and Social Psychology,* XXXVIII (1943), pp. 447–51. It should be added that in concentration camps, colonization and conversion often seemed to go together. See Cohen, *op. cit.,* pp. 200–03, where the role of the "Kapo" is discussed.

[22]Brewster Smith (Stouffer, *op. cit.*), p. 390.

and loyalty to the inmate group, so that the inmate will have a maximum chance, in the particular circumstances, of eventually getting out physically and psychologically un-damaged.[23] Typically, the inmate when with fellow inmates will support the counter-mores and conceal from them how tractably he acts when alone with the staff.[24] Inmates who play it cool subordinate contacts with their fellows to the higher claim of "keeping out of trouble"; they tend to volunteer for nothing; and they may learn to cut their ties to the outside world just enough to give cultural reality to the world inside but not enough to lead to colonization.

I have suggested some of the lines of adaptation that inmates can take to the pressures present in total institutions. Each tack represents a way of managing the tension between the home world and the institutional world. Sometimes, however, the home world of the inmate has been, in fact, such as to immunize him against the bleak world on the inside, and for these persons no particular scheme of adaptation need be carried very far. Some lower-class mental-hospital patients who have lived all their previous lives in orphanages, reformatories, and jails tend to see the hospital as just another total institution, to which they can apply the adaptive techniques learned and perfected in similar institutions. For these persons, playing it cool does not rep-resent a shift in their moral career but an alignment that is already second nature. Similarly, Shetland youths recruited into the British merchant service are apparently not much threatened by the cramped, arduous life on board, because island life is even more stunted; they make uncomplaining sailors because from their point of view they have little to complain about.

Something similar in effect to immunization is achieved by inmates who have spe-cial compensations inside the institution or special means of being impervious to its as-saults. In the early period of German concentration camps, criminals apparently derived compensative satisfaction from living with middle-class political prisoners.[25] Similarly, the middle-class vocabulary of group psychotherapy and the classless ideology of "psy-chodynamics" give to some socially ambitious and socially frustrated lower-class mental patients the closest contact with the polite world that they have ever had. Strong religious and political convictions have served to insulate the true believer against the assaults of a total institution. Failure to speak the staff's language may make the staff give up its efforts at reformation, freeing the non-speaker from certain pressures.[26]

---

[23]See the discussion in Schein, *op. cit.,* pp. 165–66, of the "Get-Alongers," and Robert J. Lifton, "Home by Ship: Reaction Patterns of American Prisoners of War Repatriated from North Korea," *American Journal of Psychiatry,* CX (1954), p. 734.

[24]This two-facedness is very commonly found in total institutions. In the state mental hospital studied by the writer, even the few elite patients selected for individual psychotherapy, and hence in the best position to espouse the psychiatric approach to self, tended to present their favorable view of psychotherapy only to the members of their intimate cliques. For a report on the way in which army prisoners concealed from fellow offenders their interest in "restoration" to the Army, see the comments by Richard Cloward in Session Four of *New Perspectives for Research on Juvenile Delinquency,* eds. Helen L. Witmer and Ruth Kotinsky, U.S. Dept. of Health, Education, and Welfare, Children's Bureau Publication No. 356 (1956), especially p. 90.

[25]Bettelheim, *op. cit.,* p. 425.

[26]Thus, Schein, *op. cit.,* p. 165 fn., suggests that the Chinese gave up on Puerto Ricans and other non-English-speaking prisoners of war and allowed them to work out a viable routine of menial chores.

Source: From *Asylums: Essays on the Social Situation of Mental Patients & Other Inmates* by Erving Goffman, copyright © 1961 by Erving Goffman. Used by permission of Doubleday, a division of Random House, Inc.

EXTREME SITUATIONS

Bernard Rosenberg, Israel Gerver and F. William Howton

The term *extreme situations* was introduced into the social science literature by Bruno Bettelheim, a psychologist who was interested in explaining why some individuals confined in Nazi concentration camps were better able to survive than others. Drawing from his own experience as a former inmate, he noted that the extreme harshness of camp life killed off a high proportion of new prisoners within months. He concluded that those who survived either were capable of great self-discipline (such as Bettelheim himself), or else were able to accept being remade morally in the image of the SS guards and commanders.

The Bettelheim thesis has been criticized by other camp survivors and social scientists. Luchterhand interviewed fifty-two individuals in depth. He concluded, contrary to Bettelheim, that the individuals most likely to survive extreme situations are those who have established a strong personal bond with another individual. This sometimes makes it possible for him to enter a wider network of sustaining and nurturing social relationships.

What makes the situation of the concentration camp inmate extreme is that typically he is deprived of practically everything he needs to live and to make him want to go on living: food, rest, warmth, health care, and the social and psychological amenities that make life worthwhile. He is continuously in danger of deteriorating, mentally and morally as well as physically. What he wanted in the German camps, above all else, was to come out alive and *unchanged*. The special agony he had to endure was that often he had to choose between survival and self-alteration.

Extreme situations take on a new dimension of sociological interest when they are considered in relation to what Erving Goffman calls total institutions: jails, prisons, mental hospitals, military barracks, ships at sea, convents, monasteries, boarding schools—and, of course, concentration camps.

The mental patient's situation is less extreme than the camp inmate's, but the two are similar enough in character to be of the same species. Goffman describes the patient's "moral career" in a way that strikingly recalls the concentration camp literature. The "unmanageable" patient is punished repeatedly until he learns to accept the role laid out for him. He goes through "degradation ceremonies"—and witnesses others as part of a process whose end result is sociological reincarnation: a *patient* is born. The same thing happens in some degree in all total institutions, even boarding schools. A staff of functionaries oversees in intimate, totalitarian detail the daily lives of a body of inmates, with the objective of changing them.

The distinguishing feature of the functionary-inmate relationship is that, in logic, the inmate is not a person but a thing: a horse to be trained, "broken" to saddle or harness, or a block of wood to be carved into a useful implement. Any legal or moral restraint on the functionary's freedom to reshape the inmate is an obstacle to be worked around: Civil rights are a nuisance, administratively speaking, and moral scruples against treating a human being as a thing are a deplorable source of inefficiency. Rationality in operations—functional rationality—can be realized only to the extent that the functionary's freedom to act in a way that manifests the logic of his situation is unhindered.

The term *institution* is fruitfully ambiguous in sociology. An institution such as a school, a hospital, or a military installation is an organization of people—staff and inmates, or clients—that has a certain character and makes use of certain facilities. Monogamous marriage, slavery, and the American two-party system in politics are examples of institutions in a different sense: they are established ways of doing things in a given society at a given moment in its history. The common quality is that each is an established way of acting, in accord with the values a society upholds and the material conditions of its existence. An institution, whether as organizational instrument or social pattern, exists because it has been found workable and morally acceptable. As it changes it reflects new features of both technology and the moral order. New ways of doing things become available, and demands arise for doing old things differently and for trying new things previously thought out of reach. Evidently the conception of extreme situations can be broadened to cover a wider range of human experience than Bettelheim had in mind. *Total institutions breed extreme situations.* The whole institutional character of modern society tends to be totalitarian. Extreme situations are not confined within total institutions like jails but are found everywhere—their quality of extremeness varying as a function of the totalness of the environing institutional structure. The point requires some development.

The special quality of the functionary-inmate relationship in a (relatively) total institution makes for the (relatively) extreme situation in which the individual inmate finds himself. However, an inmate is only a special kind of client (a client in general is one who has something done *to* him in the course of having something done *for* him). What happens when the citizen becomes a client, as in a totalitarian state like Nazi Germany or Maoist China or in the Stalinist period of the Soviet Union? He loses his political existence as a subject and becomes an acted-for or acted-upon object; he loses his civil rights and liberties. The people he formerly related to as elected officials and civil servants are now caretakers ("leaders") and state functionaries, and he has undergone a metamorphosis from constituent to client.

Hannah Arendt makes it clear that the existence of a totalitarian secret police puts everyone within its reach, at least latently, into an extreme situation. The Nazi doctrine that Jews are "objectively criminalistic" had its echo in the Communist doctrine, in the USSR under Stalin and in China under Mao that to be of the bourgeoisie is to be categorically an "enemy of the state." In the United States the genocidal doctrine of the nineteenth century that "the only good Indian is a dead Indian" and the institutionalized police vigilantism in the South and parts of the North (with its rationale that "you've got to keep the nigger in his place") remind us that the United States has not been backward in producing its share of the extreme situation breeding structural totalitarianism.

Finally, extreme situations are found in a third mode: that generated by the existence of the weapons and techniques of thermonuclear war.

Wars of extermination against whole populations are as old as history. But never before has it been possible, as it is now, to strike one massive blow and be certain that it will effectively achieve that end. Instant genocide is forestalled only by the "balance of terror": our thousands of hydrogen-bomb-tipped ballistic missiles hold the Soviet Union's cities in hostage, just as the Soviet Union's retaliatory force threatens our cities. Neither the United States nor the Soviet Union can strike the other without being struck back with catastrophic force.

The functionary-inmate or the broader functionary-client model does not at first seem to fit very well into a scheme that postulates that total weapons as well as total institutions produce extreme situations. But then we reflect that an actual relationship between persons is not essential. What makes a situation extreme is the fact that the individual is encompassed in the (collective) object of a collective someone who may want to kill him (it) and can, and is not bound by legal or moral considerations in deciding whether or not he should.

Functional rationality is concerned with means, not ends, with "how," not "what." The way the system is supposed to operate is that functionary types man it, but the signal to "go" is the exclusive prerogative of a level of command above and apart from operations. Statesmen decide whether and when, after making a rational calculation of self-interest. But in practice the advance of technology tends to shrink the statesman's sphere and extend effective responsibility for deciding to act to the functionary. (The case of the Sentinel or Safeguard anti-ballistic missile [ABM] system is illustrative. If it is to work, reaction time will have to be so short that the decision to fire an interceptor missile will be shifted down to an operational-level functionary—ultimately a machine, the computer.)

The logic and the ethic of functional rationality erodes even self-interest as a factor inhibiting action. The ultimate horror is not so much that the thermonuclear holocaust may be triggered by a strategic mistake as that it may be triggered by a "computer malfunction," if we bear in mind that the logic of computer operation and the logic of functionary operation are substantially the same.

The worldwide proliferation of thermonuclear weapons and the corresponding advance in technology of their control and delivery systems must result in placing everyone on the globe in an extreme situation: man is a hostage to a functionary who takes him into account not as a human being with existence and rights and a claim to compassion but as a cipher in a projection of probable megadeaths.

Source: Rosenberg, B., Gerver, I., and Howton, F. W. (1971). *Mass Society in Crisis: Social Problems and Social Pathology.* (2nd ed.). Reproduced by permission of Pearson Education, Inc.

BETTELHEIM'S ANALYSIS OF THE MASS SOCIETY

Paul Marcus

In this chapter I will elaborate on Bettelheim's analysis of how the mass society under-mines the individual's autonomy and integration, including what I think is his novel conceptualization of there being a dangerous continuity between the mass society, the total mass state of Nazi Germany and the concentration camps. I will further suggest that the insights that Bettelheim offered in his analysis of the mass society have rel-evance to understanding some of the compelling problems that our society faces today. As we shall see, many of the themes that Bettelheim was concerned with are those that a number of contemporary social theorists, frequently from very different theoretical perspectives, have suggested are crucial to understanding the individual's struggle to maintain his autonomy and integration in late modernity.

Mass society, according to Bettelheim, has a seductive lure: Its positive elements such as modern technology and mass production promise material wealth and security to many. However, says Bettelheim, with this comes its negative aspects; "the imper-sonal bureaucracy, impersonal taste makers, and impersonal sources of information."[1] In organized industrial society the immutable impersonal principles of organization [allot] to each member a circumscribed, routinized task; his uniqueness has no place in the system. The speed with which mass society appeared on the cultural scene has given the individual little time to adapt. Furthermore, says Bettelheim, the mass so-ciety's ability to exert powerful control over the individual through mass media and intrusive surveillance capabilities also lead the individual to feel ineffective, weak and powerless to look for satisfactions suited to his own particular personality and circum-stances. He thus relies on others for guidance. Likewise, the vastness of the political system and its bureaucracy, and the bigness of most modern technological enterprises foster a loss of autonomy because just at the point where man begins to feel he is los-ing control of his destiny and may be motivated to do something about it, he is offered a convenient excuse for evading responsibility. Bettelheim mentions, for instance, that many Germans, when confronted with the horrors they supposedly consented to, in-stead of admitting that they were not able to maintain their independence in the face of outside pressure, claimed "I was only a little man, what could I do."[2] Mass society, according to Bettelheim, is so complex that man can justify his saying helplessly that he does not understand his role in the political or productive processes. Says Bettelheim, "The trouble is that the justification does not help; it just lowers his own confidence in himself. His distance from the managers adds the often valid excuse that he is power-less to reach them, let alone influence anyone directly."[3] The individual thus relinquish-es much of his autonomy amidst an endless maze of obstacles to self-assertion.

Bettelheim focused on the dangers of impersonal bureaucracy, the trend-setting mass media and intrusive surveillance in undermining the individual's autonomy and integration, which are issues that have been and continue to be of great concern to a

---

[1]Bruno Bettelheim, *The Informed Heart: Autonomy in a Mass Age* (Glencoe, Ill.: Free Press, 1960), p. 99.
[2]Ibid., pp. 84–85.
[3]Ibid., p. 84.

number of contemporary social theorists. To some extent, Bettelheim's formulations are compatible with some of the current theorizing and they also provide useful insights into social processes. For example, Bettelheim's observations about the depersonalizing impact of bureaucracy calls to mind Foucault's discussion of the disciplinary power and Max Weber's analysis of modern bureaucracy. As Giddens points out, in both Foucault and Weber (and I think to some extent in Bettelheim), "there is a stress upon the emergence of a novel type of administrative power, generated by the concentrated organization of human activities through their precise specification and coordination."[4] In other words, says Giddens, in modern times disciplinary power is characterized by "new modes of regularizing activities in time-space."[5] He mentions, following Foucault, the farming of space such as in a classroom with its lines, columns and measured walled intervals and the division of time such as in the way a day is a temporally regulated in a precise and ordered fashion.[6] The timing and spacing of human activity is thus a prime means of regulating social life. Bettelheim, like Foucault and Giddens, recognized that "the vastness of the political system and its bureaucracy, and the bigness of most modern technological enterprises, now add still another factor—distance"[7] to its list of elements, which fosters, in Bettelheim's language, personality disintegration. By distance Bettelheim means, in part, the pervasive feeling of helplessness, of being "only a little man," an object of manipulation in an incredibly complex and impersonal society where one is "distant" from those who make the decisions determining one's fate.[8] For instance, says Bettelheim, "physical distance from the managers [in a workplace] keeps a man from testing against reality his belief in their good will, a process that might prove disastrous to his sense of economic and social security."[9] Elsewhere says Bettelheim, "distance in time is used by the boss in our society who lets an inferior wait before seeing him," which is meant to impress "the person with the boss' power and his own inferiority."[10] The result, says Bettelheim, is that the individual becomes demoralized as his sense of agency is diminished. He tends to relinquish his autonomy to those in power, to the "system," and to the "expert," thus fostering compliance and conformity, becoming a docile body.

Bettelheim, like Foucault and Giddens, had concern about the invasive surveillance in contemporary society. In his essay "Some Comments on Privacy," for example, Bettelheim is troubled by the "ever more frequent, pervasive, and intrusive invasion of privacy by governmental agencies, private organizations, and the mass media aggravated by requests from researchers for all kinds of detailed information on one's activities, opinions, and preferences."[11] What Bettelheim is insinuating, Giddens has argued succinctly: that the processes of surveillance within modern society constitute

---

[4]Anthony Giddens, *The Constitution of Society* (Berkeley: University of California Press, 1984), p. 151.

[5]Anthony Giddens, *The Nation-State and Violence* (Cambridge, U.K.: Polity Press, 1985), p. 183.

[6]Ibid., p. 147.

[7]Bettelheim, *The Informed Heart*, p. 84.

[8]Ibid., p. 85.

[9]Ibid., p. 86.

[10]Ibid., p. 87.

[11]Bettelheim, "Some Comments on Privacy," in *Surviving and Other Essays* (New York: Knopf, 1979), p. 399.

one of its major institutional dimensions.[12] It should be made clear that by surveillance I am not simply referring to its manifestation solely in terms of the police or security apparatus, but rather, I am describing the fact that "organizations of many kinds know us only as coded sequences of numbers and letters . . . [by computers]. Precise details of our personal lives are collected, stored, retrieved and processed every day within huge computer databases belonging to big corporations and government departments. This is the 'surveillance society.'"[13] As David Lyon has suggested, it is this widespread adoption of information technologies that has amplified and accelerated certain tendencies and processes in contemporary society.[14]

Bettelheim recognized that in the mass society, social control, both in terms of social reproduction and self-identity, were correlated with the development of administrative power brought about by the accelerating processes of surveillance. Says Bettelheim, "the paramount task of those who wish to safeguard individual freedom is to find ways to protect it despite the power of modern mass control and mass persuasion."[15] As Giddens has pointed out, the expansion of surveillance capabilities is the main medium of the control of social activity by social means.[16] He suggests that surveillance is fundamental to all the kinds of organizations associated with modernity. It is visible, for example, in capitalist workplace supervision, government administration and the monopoly by the nation-state of the means of violence. Foucault, perhaps more than any other social theorist, has shown how surveillance acts as a medium of social control. Through the relentless reporting and documentation of the behavior of individuals throughout the entire social body, and through the normalizing judgment that emanates from the hierarchy of continuous and functional surveillance, the individual's autonomy and integration is weakened. Says Foucault, "He who is subjected to a field of visibility, and who knows it, assumes responsibility for the constraints of power; he makes them play spontaneously upon himself; he inscribes in himself the power relation in which he simultaneously plays both roles; he becomes the principle of his own subjection."[17] It is precisely this point that Bettelheim was suggesting in his study of the mass society. With the enormous expansion in the administrative, bureaucratic "reach" of the state, with the ever-increasing coding of information of the individual—the transparency of behavior can become an instrument for undermining the individual's autonomy and fostering conformity to deadening social norms. As Foucault notes in his discussion of Bentham's Panopticon, Bentham made "visibility a trap," the transformation of the field of visibility into the domain of power. In its extreme form, intimates Bettelheim, such processes involving surveillance technology and bureaucracy can contribute to subtly undermining and destroying democratic institutions and processes, a point that Giddens has emphasized when he wrote that "Totalitarianism is, first of all, an extreme focusing of surveillance."[18]

---

[12]Anthony Giddens, *The Consequences of Modernity* (Cambridge, U.K.: Polity Press, 1990).

[13]David Lyon, *The Electronic Eye* (Minneapolis: University of Minnesota Press, 1993), p. 3.

[14]Ibid., pp. 226–27.

[15]Bettelheim, *The Informed Heart,* p. 103.

[16]Anthony Giddens, *Modernity and Self-identity* (Stanford, Calif.: Stanford University Press, 1990), p. 149.

[17]Michel Foucault, "The Subject and Power." An afterword by Foucault in H.L. Dreyfus and P. Rabinow, *Michel Foucault: Beyond Structuralism and Hermeneutics* (Chicago: University of Chicago Press, 1983), pp. 221–22.

[18]Giddens, *The Nation-State and Violence,* p. 303.

Bettelheim emphasizes that a major negative consequence for the individual in the mass society is the development of intense psychological anxiety and fear rooted in the sense of loosing individual identity. This makes the individual more prone to look to the external for direction. The acquiescence in looking to society to provide the individual's personal agenda further reinforces the sense of depletion and loss of personal identity. For example, while the mass society robs the individual of his self-confidence in his decision-making ability, he tends to look to the "expert" for direction and leadership. The mass man begins to feel that the expert knows what is best for him; it is the expert, often via the mass media, from which the individual derives his preferences and fashions his values. Gone is his attempt to gratify his particular propensities according to his own personality needs and circumstances, for the man in mass society no longer can determine what he really wants, but rather his needs and tastes are defined by the expert. In this situation the individual has surrendered much of his autonomy to the state and his personality integration suffers because of it: "while the process of uncritical acceptance usually starts with externals, it does not often stop there because external and internal life are too closely interwoven. So once a person begins to rely on others for decision making in externals it can soon extend to inner conflicts as well."[19] Thus, according to Bettelheim, where other regimes only aimed at getting their citizens to comply and conform to their edicts in terms of external behavior, the mass society also tries to dominate the internal experience of the person; it aims at controlling his thoughts and affective life by undermining his autonomy. Bettelheim is here describing the corrosive psychological impact of living in a disciplinary society, and in particular, he is suggesting in the language of Foucault, how power—understood as a strategy, a "multiplicity of force relations," that invests individuals, is transmitted by and through them—helps foster a subjectivity characterized by dependence on external authority and passivity. John Dewey, like Bettelheim, was well aware that such a reliance on authority is extremely dangerous to democratic society. Says Dewey, "The serious threat to our democracy is not the existence of foreign totalitarian states. It is the existence without our own personal attitudes and within our own institutions of conditions which have given a victory to external authority, discipline, uniformity and dependence on The Leader in foreign countries. The battlefield is also accordingly here—within ourselves and our institutions."[20]

It was Erich Fromm, perhaps more than any other social theorist, who was concerned with many of the same themes as Bettelheim; in particular, elaborating in what ways individuals relinquish personal freedom in contemporary capitalist society. Like Bettelheim, Fromm says that the difficulty with contemporary society is that the requirements it levels for "normalcy" often conflict with the individual's own needs for growth and happiness. Two courses of action are open to him as he tries to overcome his painful state of helplessness and aloneness, the existential coordinates that Fromm thinks characterize twentieth-century capitalist man. Says Fromm, "By one course he can progress to 'positive freedom'; he can relate himself spontaneously to the world in love and work, in the genuine expression of his emotional, sensuous, and intellectual capacities; he can thus become one again with man, nature, and himself, without giving

[19]Bettelheim, *The Informed Heart*, p. 80.

[20]John Dewey, *Freedom and Culture* (New York: G.P. Putnam's Sons, 1939). Quoted in Erich Fromm, *Escape from Freedom* (New York: Avon Books, 1969), pp. 19–20 (no page number from Dewey given).

up the independence and integrity of his individual self."[21] This solution to the conflict between freedom and helplessness he regards as basically a healthy one. The second course of action open to the individual, according to Fromm, involves the unhealthy strategy of relinquishing personal freedom completely. Individuals, he says, seek to merge themselves, or surrender their identity to, the conglomerate we call society. The person, in other words, strives to "escape from freedom." In Bettelheim's language, this means giving up one's autonomy and integration and identifying with the conformist values of the mass society.

Fromm describes a number of methods that individuals use to obliterate their consciousness of freedom and the integrity of the self such as "authoritarianism," and "destructiveness." However, it is his notion of "automaton conformity" that best correlates with Bettelheim's description of the "mass man" with his extreme dependence on social norms and reliance on external authority for direction. Automaton conformity, says Fromm, involves a strategy of escape from freedom by default: "To put it briefly, the individual ceases to be himself; he adopts entirely the kind of personality offered to him by cultural patterns; and he therefore becomes exactly as all others are and as they expect him to be."[22] Like the protective coloring of some animals, the individual who is a conforming automaton takes on the coloring, shading, and emotional texture of his surroundings. Because he mimics millions of other people, the automaton no longer feels alone. But, for this reduction in his feelings of aloneness, he pays the price of what Fromm describes as a loss of selfhood. According to Fromm, in his surrender of his "true" self to the facade of sameness with others, the individual does not achieve the security for which he hoped. Instead, he finds himself adopting a pseudo-self to compensate for the loss of his spontaneity. Similar to Bettelheim, Fromm believed that whether it is automaton conformity, authoritarian submission or domination, or destructiveness, these attempts to numb the feelings of aloneness that inevitably accompany the responsibilities of freedom are partial, temporary and inadequate. Moreover, both Bettelheim and Fromm believed that without a "genuine self," one can be alienated. Without genuine selfhood, one becomes an unfeeling, robot-like mass man.

Losing a World

According to Bettelheim the Nazis aimed at completely destroying the inmate's world, rubbing out his entire "social existence by depriving one of all previous support systems such as family, friends, position in life, while at the same time subjecting one to utter terrorization and degradation through the severest mistreatment and the omnipresent, inescapable, immediate threat to one's very life."[23] Says Bettelheim, "To be incarcerated in a camp meant to be cut off from all aspects of one's previous life. The SS and the Nazi state made it amply clear that the life the person had been living was ended; they denied one's former life all validity, now and forever."[24] Other scholars and survivors have made similar observations. Des Pres writes that "In the camps prisoners lost their possessions, their social identity, the whole of the cultural matrix which

---

[21]Erich Fromm, *Escape from Freedom* (New York: Avon, 1969), p. 161.

[22]Ibid., pp. 208–09.

[23]Bettelheim, "Trauma and Reintegration," in *Surviving and Other Essays*, p. 25.

[24]Ibid., p. 31.

had previously sustained them. They lost, in other words, the delicate web of symbolic identifications available to men and women in normal times" and which provides perhaps, most of what we think we are.[25] Elie Cohen notes that "every feature of human beings in normal life . . . [was] to be obliterated."[26] And Viktor Frankl says that inmates had to "strike out . . . [their] whole former life."[27] In a word, Bettelheim and others are describing the impact of an "extreme situation" on one's world. As Bettelheim has written, in an extreme situation one finds oneself totally overpowered:

> Characterizing this situation were its shattering impact on the individual, for which he was totally unprepared; its inescapability; the expectation that the situation would last for an undetermined period, potentially a lifetime; the fact that, throughout its entirety, one's very life would be in jeopardy at every moment; and the fact that one was powerless to protect oneself.[28]

In the language of Giddens, such an extreme situation, or "critical situation" as he calls it, fundamentally involves "circumstances of radical disjuncture of an unpredictable kind which affect substantial numbers of individuals, situations that threaten or destroy the certitudes of institutionalized routines."[29] With such a sustained assault on the inmate's agency and pre-incarceration routines that underpinned his ontological security, the inmate was inundated with disorganizing affects and intense death anxiety. This condition made it nearly impossible to maintain his autonomy and integration or any kind of coherent narrative of self-identity. Trapped in a maze of grotesque happenings, the inmate's options were greatly limited and he was often without hope.

As Bettelheim points out, the Nazi assault on the world of the prospective inmate usually began with his arrest late at night so as to intensify its shock, terror and Kafkaesque nature. After a few days in jail, which was in itself an extremely stressful ordeal for people with no experience in the prison system, the prisoners then faced the next major shock, that of being transported to the camp.[30] As is well-known, prisoners were often transported in cattle cars instead of passenger cars; they were overcrowded and sealed in without adequate toileting facilities, air, food and water, in conditions that Stanley Elkins has compared to the infamous Middle Passage of the American Black slave trade.[31] As Bettelheim has written, the inmates' "'initiation' to the concentration camp, which took place on transport, was often the first torture prisoners had ever experienced and was, for most of them, the worst torture they would be exposed to either physically or psychologically."[32] Goffman has remarked that this fact was not by

---

[25]Des Pres, *The Survivor*, p. 214.

[26]Elie A. Cohen, *Human Behavior in the Concentration Camp* (London: Free Association Books, 1988), p. 147.

[27]Viktor E. Frankl, *Man's Search for Meaning* (New York: Pocket Books, 1963), p. 21.

[28]Bettelheim, "Schizophrenia as a Reaction to Extreme Situations," in *Surviving and Other Essays*, p. 115.

[29]Anthony Giddens, *The Constitution of Society* (Berkeley: University of California Press, 1984), p. 60.

[30]It should be remembered that many Eastern European Jews had a period of forced ghettoization before being deported to camps. Bettelheim is describing the experiences of many German Jews living in Nazi Germany during about 1938–1939, the period he was incarcerated in Dachau and Buchenwald.

[31]Stanley Elkins, *Slavery* (Chicago: University of Chicago Press, 1976), p. 106.

[32]Bettelheim, *The Informed Heart*, p. 119.

chance. In such total institutions as the Nazi concentration camp the "theory of human nature" that was applied to inmates was one that emphasized that if the initial demands put upon the inmate were severe and brutal enough, the inmates' "resistance" or "spirit" would be broken.[33] Elkins also indicates that the "initiation" phase involved a planned series of brutalities inflicted by guards making repeated rounds through the train over a twelve-to thirty-six-hour period during which the inmate was prevented from resting.[34] Thus, being suddenly taken away from family, friends and community, being brutalized and tortured during transportation to the camps was almost completely physically and emotionally overwhelming for many inmates and tended to foster an expectation of personal collapse.

As Goffman's work suggests, this initial torture, sometimes called the prisoner's "welcome" to the concentration camp by the Gestapo, can be conceptualized as a mortification process, a series of abasements, degradations, humiliations and profanations of the self.[35] It was this process that generated in the inmate the feeling that he had indeed lost much of his former world and was trapped in a chaotic and violent nightmare. The curtailment of the inmate's contact with the outside world, the disinfecting, haircutting, assigning numbers rather than using names, searching, undressing, issuing institutional clothing, the control of his activities in the camp, the lack of privacy, the besmearing and defiling of the body such as having to empty one's own excrement, instructing as to rules, assigning quarters and the verbal and physical abuse; these indignities are all examples of how the Nazis implemented this mortification process.[36] These abasements, as well as the continual hunger; the fact that inmates were almost always in a state of chronic anxiety about being punished if they did not follow the rules; the omnipresent threat of suddenly being killed; and the fact that the imprisonment did not have an obvious endpoint created an entirely different social context that emphasized to the inmates that the "normality" associated with their former world (e.g., the habitual,

---

[33]Goffman, *Asylums*, p. 89.

[34]Elkins, *Slavery*, p. 106.

[35]Goffman, *Asylums*, p. 14.

[36]Ibid., pp. 14–42. According to one biographer of Bettelheim, Richard Pollak, in Dachau when Bettelheim was imprisoned there, there was a library that inmates could use after working; the SS allowed soccer and other sports and arranged concerts and other cultural events usually exploiting the talent among the inmates. Pollak also claims that Bettelheim testified that in Dachau the food was adequate and could be supplemented with food from the canteen if one could buy it (*The Creation of Dr. B.* New York: Simon and Schuster, 1997, pp. 65–66). While I think that Pollak to some extent reports all of this to somehow undermine the basis of Bettelheim's narrative on the camps, insinuating that "he did not have it so tough" (my words) in Dachau and that his experience can not reasonably be generalized to other camps, it should be remembered that the above-described features of Dachau existed within the context of extreme violence, terror, death, humiliation, brutal forced labor, totalitarian controls and deprivation of freedom. Moreover, according to Nina Sutton, Bettelheim's other biographer, in Dachau the prisoner's daily ration when Bettelheim was there was "around a half a pound of bread" and "dinner was a bowl of soup, which on good days might contain a scrap of sausage or whale meat." Given the forced labor that inmates were doing, this amount of food was, in general, hardly adequate despite what Bettelheim may have said. Incidentally, it should be stressed that while he was not in a death camp, Bettelheim's incarceration involved significant suffering. For example, says Sutton, "Bettelheim had weighed 150 pounds when he arrived at Dachau [on June 3, 1938; he was transferred to Buchenwald in September 1938 and released in April 1939]; by April 1939 he weighed a mere 86. He had lost most of his hair . . . and his teeth were in a terrible state. He was also suffering from a stomach ulcer" (Nina Sutton, *Bettelheim: A Life and a Legacy*. New York: Basic Books, 1996, pp. 141–42, 162). Moreover, as far as I can tell from reading both of his biographers, and from what Bettelheim has insinuated in his writings, he, like so many of his fellow survivors, was something of a psychological "mess" after he was liberated.

taken-for-granted character of the vast bulk of the activities of day-to-day social life[37]) was more or less inoperable, and a new notion of "normality" took its place (e.g., new styles and forms of conduct).[38]

Goffman makes it clear that the mortification process in the concentration camp was designed to force the inmate to give up his old "self" in part by "breaking" his sense of self-efficacy and executive competency (i.e., agency). Loss of self-determination, for example, was ceremonialized; inmates had to roll in the mud, stand on their heads in the snow, work at ludicrously useless tasks, swear at themselves, or, in the case of Jewish prisoners, sing anti-Semitic songs.[39] Says Goffman, "Whatever the form or the source of these various indignities, the inmate has to engage in activity whose symbolic implications are incompatible with his [prior] conception of self."[40] The main purpose of this mortification process was thus to destroy the inmate's self-concept made possible by certain stable social arrangements and routines in his home world.[41] In such circumstances, says Goffman, the individual cannot feel himself to be a person "with 'adult' self-determination, autonomy, and freedom of action."[42] As I have already noted, following Richard Rorty, when the story that a person has been telling himself about his life, when the narrative which constituted his self-identity is grossly defiled, the individual feels humiliated; his self and world have been rendered almost completely meaningless, cutting deeply into his motivation to carry on.[43] In Bettelheim's language, the person's autonomy and integration has been subverted if not destroyed.

For example, according to Bettelheim, it was the non-political, non-religious middle-class prisoners that had the greatest difficulty responding to the initial period of internment, because these prisoners had lost the world that their self-respect and self-esteem were based on. Their self-esteem had heavily relied on a status and respect that came with their positions, depended on their jobs, on being head of a family, or similar external factors. Without these external structures to prop them up they collapsed into despair soon after their arrival into the camp.[44] Says Bettelheim,

> It can become completely shattering to a person's integration when the system of beliefs on which he relied for his integration . . . not only lets him down, but worse, is about to destroy him psychologically and physically. Then nothing seems left that can offer protection. Furthermore, we now no longer can feel confident that we will be able ever again to know reliably what to trust, and what to defend against.[45]

In other words, such inmates, without their familiar world of meaning—their social position, prestige and power to command—without a sense of their world as orderly, stable,

---

[37]Giddens, *The Constitution of Society*, p. 376.

[38]Elkins, *Slavery*, pp. 107–08.

[39]Goffman, *Asylums*, p. 44.

[40]Ibid., p. 23.

[41]Ibid., p. 14.

[42]Ibid., p. 43.

[43]Richard Rorty, *Contingency, Irony, and Solidarity* (Cambridge, U.K.: Cambridge University Press, 1989), p. 179.

[44]Bettelheim, *The Informed Heart*, pp. 120–22.

[45]Bettelheim, "The Ultimate Limit," in *Surviving and Other Essays*, p. 10.

continuous and comprehensible, were unable to maintain their prior narrative of self-identity. The security of their being was threatened, and their sense of self was shattered.[46] Moreover, as Erich Fromm has pointed out, without the props on which their self-esteem and sense of identity rested, these non-political, non-religious middle-class inmates collapsed "morally like a deflatable balloon."[47] They were, in Rorty's language humiliated. In contrast, the religious and politically committed prisoners, the "believers," had deeply internalized, consistent values and strong beliefs that could better sustain their autonomy and integration. Bettelheim succinctly distinguishes these two groups on this point:

> [H]ow soon and completely [the inmate] lost all of his autonomy, and how far the disintegration of his personality went were mainly conditioned by two factors: the severity of the traumatization he was subjected to, as objectively evaluated; and how shattering it was experienced subjectively by him. The latter depended to a very large degree on how securely a person's autonomy had become established in his pre-camp existence; that is, how well his personality had been integrated and his self-respect developed. . . . Most important . . . was whether and to what degree his self-respect and security had been anchored in his innermost life—that is in who he was [the "believers"]—or to what degree he had relied for security and self-image on the externals of existence—that is on what he only seemed to be [the non-religious, non-political middle-class inmates].[48]

Returning to the initiation phase of the inmates ordeal, perhaps the reason why Bettelheim thought the initiation phase was the worst torture that inmates had to endure was best summed up by Auschwitz survivor Jean Améry, who himself was tortured when he was captured as part of the French Resistance. Wrote Améry,

> At the first blow . . . trust [ontological security] in the world breaks down . . . the certainty that by reason of written or unwritten social contracts the other person will spare me . . . that he will respect my physical, and with it also my metaphysical, being. . . . Whoever has succumbed to torture can no longer feel at home in the world. Trust in the world, . . . under torture, fully, will not be regained.[49]

It is this loss of trust in the world, of ontological security that signifies the beginning of the corrosive and shattering process of the inmate losing his pre-incarceration world. Without trust in the world, the inmate is not able to maintain either his autonomy or a coherent narrative of self-identity.

Bettelheim has further suggested why during the initiation process into the camp world the "vast majority of the thousands of prisoners who died at Buchenwald each

---

[46]Fred Weinstein, *The Dynamics of Nazism* (New York: Academic Press, 1980), pp. 8, 18.

[47]Erich Fromm, *The Anatomy of Human Destructiveness* (Greenwich, Conn.: Fawcett Crest Books, 1973), p. 86. See also my paper, "The Religious Believer, the Psychoanalytic Intellectual, and the Challenge of Sustaining the Self in the Concentration Camps" (*Journal for the Psychoanalysis of Culture and Society*, Volume 3, Number 1, 1998, pp. 61–75), for an analysis of why the psychoanalytic "intellectual" compared to the religious or political "believer" in general faired psychologically worse in the camps.

[48]Bettelheim, "Owners of Their Faces," in *Surviving and Other Essays*, p. 108.

[49]Jean Améry, *At the Mind's Limits: Contemplations by a Survivor on Auschwitz and Its Realities*, translated by Sidney and Stella P. Rosenfeld (Bloomington: Indiana University Press, 1980), pp. 28, 40.

year died soon."[50] He says that the main reason is that they "died of exhaustion, both physical and psychological, due to a loss of desire to live."[51] As Des Pres has pointed out, loss of desire to live, not striving for life with every fiber of one's being, is a symptom of the period of initial collapse but not a cause. He says that inmates "died soon" from a complex of conditions and forces which nothing in their lives had prepared them to face or even imagine; "from prolonged terror and shock; from radical loss, both of identity and of faith in the capacity of goodness to prevail against evil surrounding them. They died simply for lack of information, because they did not know what to do or how to act. Very often, too, they died of mourning, of grief for the deaths of their family and friends."[52] However, Des Pres emphasizes the important point that the deepest cause of early death was the "horror and irreparable hurt felt by the prisoner when he or she first encounters the spectacle of atrocity. Moral disgust, if it arises too abruptly or becomes too intense, expresses itself in the desire to die, to have done with such a world. . . . No feeling remains except absolute refusal to go on existing when existence itself seems vile beyond redemption."[53] Some religious inmates, for example, who firmly believed in a loving, compassionate, omnipotent and providential God, were not able to sustain themselves amidst an environment that so radically violated their core conviction that they lived in an ethically caring universe. These inmates usually gave up the struggle to survive and died. Similar to Rorty, Des Pres is emphasizing that when one feels humiliated, in this case by the awareness that one is enmeshed in the defiling world of atrocity, one cannot easily maintain the rudiments of a coherent, trusting and dignified narrative of self-identity. Most often, one "loses the desire to live" and dies.

Thus, it was amidst this extreme situation, with its brutalizing mortification process and new "normality," that the concentration camp inmate was faced with the fact that much of his "old" self, his routines, roles and values and beliefs, were no longer functional and had, to a great extent, to be changed and adapted to his new circumstances.[54] As Des Pres has written, "The first encounter with extremity immersed prisoners in a world of pure terror, a world in which nothing made sense or promised hope. The impact was so sudden and overwhelming that the self floundered and began to disintegrate. In shock and disbelief, prisoners went about as if asleep, as if locked in a horrid dream, not responding intelligently, not looking out for themselves."[55] Des Pres concludes, "The otherness of the camps, their horror and apparent chaos, was not real by past standards; unable to root itself in familiar ground, the old self fell apart."[56] In my view, it is within the extreme or critical situation, when the established modes of the inmate's accustomed daily life were drastically undermined or shattered, that we can best understand how it came to be that many inmates gradually adopted a "survival at any price" orientation to their ordeal.

---

[50]Bettelheim, *The Informed Heart*, p. 146.

[51]Ibid.

[52]Des Pres, *The Survivor*, pp. 88–89.

[53]Ibid., p. 89.

[54]As I have stressed earlier, in light of my dialectical conceptualization of the inmate's experience, at the same time as the inmate was falling apart, he was trying to fend off the destructive impact of the mortification process, to "hold on" to fragments of his pre-incarceration world. As Giddens has remarked, "human agents never passively accept external conditions of action, but more or less continuously reflect upon them and reconstitute them in light of their particular circumstances" (*Modernity and Self-Identity*. Stanford, Calif.: Stanford University Press, 1991, p. 175).

[55]Des Pres, *The Survivor*, p. 85.

[56]Ibid., p. 86.

As a consequence of the Nazi attempt to brutalize the inmates into a powerless, help-less, dependent, deindividualized condition, most inmates (including the "new" prisoners but excluding those inmates with a consistent set of values and strong beliefs) were in general unable to avoid a range of childlike attitudes, such as a very marked diminution in time sense, the capacity to "think ahead," and volatile mood swings in response to entirely trivial happenings. Says Bettelheim, "The prisoners lived, like children only in the imme-diate present; they lost feeling for the sequence of time; they became unable to plan for the future or to give up immediate pleasure satisfactions to gain greater ones in the near future. They were unable to establish durable object relationships. Friendships developed as quickly as they broke up."[57] Bettelheim further describes inmates as being filled with impotent rage, a situation frequent in childhood, but extremely undermining for the adult personality. Therefore, the inmate's aggressions had to be dealt with somehow, and one of the safest ways was to turn it against the self, contributing to "increased masochistic, passive-dependent, and childlike attitudes which were 'safe' because they kept the pris-oner out of conflict with the SS."[58] In other words, the inmate without a consistent set of values and strong beliefs had lost his adult conception of himself because he had lost the freedom to behave like an adult, including performing the crucial ordinary daily routines that sustained his sense of autonomy and integration in his pre-incarceration world.

In summary, for Bettelheim the Nazis facilitated this regressive mode of being in many inmates by the disruption and sustained attack upon the ordinary routines of the inmate's pre-incarceration adult world. By destroying the inmate's sense of himself as being in control of the security and management of his body and having a predict-able framework of social life, the inmate's ontological security was subverted, fostering intense fear and death anxiety.[59] This in turn had a kind of corrosive effect upon his cus-tomary behavior; he no longer felt himself to be a competent, purposeful adult with re-sources to effectively influence his situation or protect himself from mortification of the self. His regressive self-experience and behavior thus reflected the dependent, helpless, powerless state that he was actually in by virtue of the Nazi assault. In my framework, the inmate could be described as having lost his pre-incarceration world; he was unable to maintain the rudiments of an enduring, integral, motivating coherent narrative of self-identity. As Bettelheim indicates, in such a context "our old adaptive mechanisms and values do not apply any more and . . . some of them may even endanger the life they were meant to protect. . . . We are, so to say, stripped of our whole defensive system and thrown back to rock bottom—whence we must carve out a new set of attitudes, values, and way of living as required by the new situation."[60] Most importantly, in such circum-stances where one's world has been undermined or destroyed, the individual tends to display a heightened suggestibility, or vulnerability to the promptings of others.[61]

---

[57]Bettelheim, "Individual and Mass Behavior in Extreme Situations," in *Surviving and Other Essays*, p. 76.

[58]Bettelheim, *The Informed Heart*, p. 131.

[59]Giddens, *The Constitution of Society*, p. 63.

[60]Bettelheim, "The Ultimate Limit," in *Surviving and Other Essays*, p. 11.

[61]Anthony Giddens, *Central Problems in Social Theory* (Berkeley: University of California Press, 1979), p. 126.

Source: From *Autonomy in the Extreme Situation: Bruno Bettelheim, the Nazi Concentration Camps and the Mass Society* by Paul Marcus. Copyright © 1999. Reproduced with permission of ABC-CLIO Inc. in the format Textbook via Copyright Clearance Center.

CHAPTER 2

Institutionalized Slavery in the United States

In Kenneth Stampp's (1963) classic study of slavery in the ante-bellum South, *The Peculiar Institution*, he notes that "to understand the South is to feel the pathos in its history. . . . Their tragedy did not begin with the ordeal of Reconstruction, or with the agony of civil war, but with the growth of a 'peculiar institution' (as they called it) in ante-bellum days" (p. 3). It is commonly held that the first group of African slaves arrived in Virginia in 1619. However, " . . . [t]he African slave trade was already over a hundred years old when the Dutch ship landed twenty Africans at the Jamestown colony in 1619" (Lester, 1968, p. 16). It was eighteen years later that an American slave ship, the *Desire*, sailed to Africa to bring back black slaves to North America (Lester, 1968, p. 18).

It was not until 1798, however, "when Georgia finally took action, [that] all the Atlantic seaboard states had prohibited the importation of slaves from Africa or the Caribbean. . . . By January 1, 1808 . . . the federal government finally outlawed the African slave trade" (Davis, 2006, p. 156). In 1863, the Emancipation Proclamation ended slavery in the Confederate states and in 1865, the Thirteenth Amendment to the U.S. Constitution abolished slavery in the United States.

In an article published in the *American Journal of Sociology*, H. G. Adler (1958), the novelist and poet, offers the following comments toward a definition of slavery:

> In the short pregnant definition of my late friend, the social anthropologist of Oxford, Franz Baerman Steiner, slavery is *exploitation of men without contract*. Wherever slavery is found in unmitigated form, we must recognize in the slave a man deprived of all the rights society attributes to other men. In slavery one man has power over another without standing to him in any relation the law would consider as creating mutual rights (p. 515).

As discussed previously, this relationship of the slave to society is the essence of the process of "denormatization," the suspension of morality and the rule of law.

The first reading in this chapter by Stampp (1963) suggests that the institution of slavery in the South was an evolutionary process pursued in the quest for cheap labor and greater economic return, and was not the product of some "inherent depravity" of the Southern population. He proposes that the complexities of individual personalities (masters and slaves) and the dynamics of human interaction were clearly evident in the diverse relationships that existed between master and slave. It was precisely this understanding of the anomalous nature of the "peculiar institution" that necessitated the masters' adherence to a prescribed sequence of steps in the molding of the "perfect slave."

There has been much discussion and controversy in the literature regarding the slave experience and personality type[s] of the slaves and their respective adjustments to institutionalized slavery. John Blassingame (1972) suggests that "[i]n order to understand the resources and choices theoretically open to Southern slaves it is necessary to examine 'total' institutions" (p. 189). He cites psychological studies of the concentration camp and other total institutions indicating that the inmates' adaptive mode (e.g. docile and/or infantile versus independent and/or rebellious) was directly related to their treatment by the "superordinate." "When the plantation is viewed as a total institution, it is obvious that the slave's personality was intimately bound up with the use of coercive power by his master" (Blassingame, 1972, p. 190). This "coercive power" could be measured by the frequency and nature of punishment experienced by slaves at the hand of their "masters" and in situations of extreme cruelty a slave could become "docile, submissive and Sambo-like" (Blassingame, 1972, p. 193).

The reading in this chapter by Stanley Elkins (1963), "Slavery and Personality," critically evaluates the controversy surrounding the identification of the "Sambo" type of plantation slave. He postulates that in fact the characteristics associated with the Sambo type (e.g. docility and infantilism) are not racially based, but rather may be adaptive mechanisms to the situational character of the plantation system, which in many ways are analogous to the experience of concentration camp inmates. He traces the cumulative force of "shock and detachment" that began with the slaves' capture and culminated in his confinement in the "closed plantation system." Kolchin (1993) suggests that the controversy surrounding the Sambo thesis

> played a major role in redirecting historical scholarship on slavery. As historians sought to rebut Elkins's assertion of slave docility, they found it necessary to focus far more than they previously had on the slaves as subjects in their own right rather than as objects of white treatment (p. 136).

Michael Tadman's (1996) introduction to his book *Speculators and Slaves* is noteworthy for its excellent review and critique of the most significant portrayals of the conflicting interpretations that describe the relationship that existed between master and slave. These theories range from Philip's "conservative, racist and accommodationist theory" to the "rejectionist theory" of Aptheker, and to other representations that "support some sort of accommodation thesis" (p. xxiv). Tadman points out the importance of one's source material (e.g. primary sources vs. "black oral tradition") used in framing one's analysis and that "[e]vidence in the present study supports Gutman's views on the resilience of the slaves' family culture and on the racist indifference of white owners to black families" (p. xxv). He suggests that the special relationship between "key slaves" or the "most privileged slaves" (e.g. the master's driver) and their masters is often the narrative of "white manuscript records" and is not reflective or representative of the majority of slave/master relationships. He concludes that "[t]he idea of an 'integrated' antebellum past (based on close accommodation under slavery) seems to be largely inaccurate, as, unfortunately is an integrated present" (p. xxxvii).

The narratives of Frederick Douglass (1845) and Harriet Jacobs (1861) are wrenching testimonies of the slave experience and should be read within the context of the research presented in the previous readings. What can we learn from Jacob's comments about the corruptive nature of slavery for both whites and blacks and the gender-specific experiences described in what she refers to as the "cage of obscene birds?" (as cited in Andrews and Gates, 2000, p. 798).

Frederick Douglass "was one of the most eminent human rights leaders of the 19th century. His oratorical and literary brilliance thrust him into the forefront of the U.S. abolition movement, and he became the first black citizen to hold high rank in the U.S. government" (Encyclopaedia Britannica Online, 2011). His graphic descriptions of the brutal murders of both male and female slaves by their "superordinates" and his comment that, "killing a slave, or any colored person . . . is not treated as a crime either by the courts or the community" (as cited in Andrews and Gates, 2000, p. 297) is searing testimony to the extent of denormatization previously discussed. Oral histories project images onto a screen that can be viewed by the reader in a manner not often seen in traditional research findings.

THE SETTING

Kenneth M. Stampp

To understand the South is to feel the pathos in its history. This aura of pathos is more than a delusion of historians, more than the vague sensation one gets when looking down an avenue of somber, moss-draped live oaks leading to stately ruins or to nothing at all. For Southerners live in the shadow of a real tragedy; they know, better than most other Americans, that little ironies fill the history of mankind and that large disasters from time to time unexpectedly help to shape its course.

Their tragedy did not begin with the ordeal of Reconstruction, or with the agony of civil war, but with the growth of a "peculiar institution" (as they called it) in antebellum days. It began, in short, with chattel slavery whose spiritual stresses and unremitting social tensions became an inescapable part of life in the Old South.

What caused the growth of this institutional affliction which had so severe an impact upon the lives of so many Southerners? Some historians have traced the origin of southern slavery to a morbific quality in the southern climate. Though admitting great climatic variations within the South and the normal mildness of the winter season, they have emphasized the weather's fiercer moods—the torrential rains, the searing droughts, above all, the humid heat of subtropical summers. Since Southerners were unable to control the weather, they had to come to terms with it. So it was the climate that determined the nature of their institutions and the structure of their society. "Let us begin by discussing the weather," wrote one historian who saw here "the chief agency in making the South distinctive."[1] To such climatic determinists the social significance of "ninety degrees in the shade" was too real to be ignored.

If climate alone could not explain everything, then perhaps certain additional factors, such as soil, topography, and watercourses, contributed to a broader geographical determinism. Combine the hot summers and long growing seasons with the rich southern soils—the alluvial river bottoms, the sandy loams of the coastal plains, the silt loams of the Black Belt, and the red clays of the piedmont—and an agricultural economy was the logical result. Add the many navigable rivers which facilitated the movement of bulky staples from considerable distances inland to coastal ports, and all the requirements for a commercial form of agriculture were at hand. Commercial agriculture induced a trend toward large landholdings which in turn created a demand for labor. Thus some have argued that Southerners, in permitting slavery to grow, had merely submitted to compelling natural forces.

Human institutions, however, have not been formed by forces as rigidly deterministic as this. To be sure, men must inevitably make certain adjustments to fixed environmental conditions. But, within limits, these adjustments may take a variety of forms. At different times and in different places roughly similar environmental conditions have produced vastly different human responses. Some human adaptations have been far more successful than others. For this reason one must examine the forms of southern institutions as closely as the facts of the southern environment.

---

[1]Ulrich B. Phillips, *Life and Labor in the Old South* (Boston, 1929), p. 1.

It may be that unfree labor alone made possible the early rise of the plantation system, but this proves neither the necessity nor the inevitability of slavery. Actually, the southern plantation was older than slavery and survived its abolition. More important, there was nothing inevitable about the plantation. Without a continuing supply of bondsmen, southern agriculture, in its early development at least, would probably have depended more upon small-farm units and given less emphasis to the production of staple crops. Under these circumstances the South might have developed more slowly, but it would not have remained a wilderness. There was no crop cultivated by slaves that could not have been cultivated by other forms of labor, no area fit for human habitation that would have been passed by for want of a slave force. The slave-plantation system answered no "specific need" that could not have been answered in some other way.[2]

Slavery, then, cannot be attributed to some deadly atmospheric miasma or some irresistible force in the South's economic evolution. The use of slaves in southern agriculture was a deliberate choice (among several alternatives) made by men who sought greater returns than they could obtain from their own labor alone, and who found other types of labor more expensive. "For what purpose does the master hold the servant?" asked an ante-bellum Southerner. "Is it not that by his labor he, the master, may accumulate wealth?"[3] The rise of slavery in the South was inevitable only in the sense that every event in history seems inevitable after it has occurred.

Southerners who chose to develop and to preserve slavery could no more escape responsibility for their action than they could escape its consequences. But to judge them without compassion is to lack both the insight and the sensitivity needed to understand the nature of their tragedy. For the South began with good human material; its tragedy did not spring from the inherent depravity of its people. Southerners did not create the slave system all at once in 1619; rather, they built it little by little, step by step, choice by choice, over a period of many years; and all the while most of them were more or less blind to the ultimate consequences of the choices they were making. Somehow, at crucial times, their vision failed them; somehow it was their misfortune to have built a social structure wanting in flexibility. Ultimately Southerners became the victims of their own peculiar institution; they were unwilling to adjust it, or themselves, to the ideological and cultural realities of the nineteenth century.

Not that slavery failed as a practical labor system. In that narrow sense it was a success, and it was still flourishing as late as 1860. In terms of its broad social consequences for the South as a whole, however, slavery must be adjudged a failure. Few slaves ever really adapted successfully to their servitude, and few whites could defend the system without betraying the emotional stresses to which slavery subjected them. Eventually the omnipresent slave became the symbol of the South and the cornerstone of its culture. When that happened, disaster was close at hand—in fact, that in itself was a disaster.

To Make Them Stand in Fear

It is a pity," a North Carolina planter wrote sadly, "that agreeable to the nature of things Slavery and Tyranny must go together and that there is no such thing as having an obedient and useful Slave, without the painful exercise of undue and tyrannical authority."

---

[2]For such a defense of the system see Ulrich B. Phillips (ed.), *Plantation and Frontier: 1649–1863* (Cleveland, 1910), I, p. 71.

[3]*Farmer's Journal*, II (1853), p. 52.

The legislatures and courts of the ante-bellum South recognized this fact and regulated the relationship of master and slave accordingly. "The power of the master must be absolute, to render the submission of the slave perfect," a southern judge once affirmed.[4] Short of deliberately killing or maliciously maiming them, the owner did have almost absolute power over his chattels.

If a bondsman ran away, if he stole the goods, injured the property, or disobeyed the commands of the master, he was guilty of a private and not a public offense; and the state left the prevention and punishment of such offenses to the owner.[5] In governing his bondsmen, therefore, the master made the law, tried offenders, and administered penalties. Whether he exercised his despotic authority benevolently or malevolently depended upon his nature.

Masters were not all alike. Some governed their slaves with great skill and induced them to submit with a minimum of force. Others, lacking the personal qualities needed to accomplish this, governed inefficiently. For example, an Alabama woman with an undisciplined temper found it nearly impossible to control her domestics. Two of them, Alex and Hampton, obeyed her commands only when they found it agreeable to do so; the rest of the time they treated her orders with "the utmost contempt." Hampton "has often laughed in my face and told me that I was the only mistress he ever failed to please, on my saying he should try another soon, he said he could not be worsted, and was willing to go." During a dinner with a friend this mistress was astonished to see how smoothly his household ran. His servants were perfectly trained: "you hear no noise, see no confusion, . . . and their master has no need to point them to their duty. By what secret does he manage all this? The contrast with me is mortifying, truly."[6]

Slaves were not all alike either. They reacted to a particular master or overseer in different ways, some acquiescing in his authority and others rebelling against it. Some, because of their temperaments, found it impossible to get along with even a humane master. Ephraim, the property of a kind and pious small Virginia slaveholder, was in trouble so frequently that his master labeled him a "bad negro." After running away Ephraim was sold to a New Orleans slave trader; according to his owner, it was "his wish . . . to be sold."[7] Sometimes a restless slave became passive when transferred to another owner.

A master valued each slave not only on the basis of his physical condition and proficiency as a worker but also in terms of mutual compatibility. For this reason southern courts repeatedly ruled that it was impossible to give any slave an objective valuation. "One man will give or take fifty or one hundred dollars more or less in the purchase of one [bondsman] than another man will," declared a judge. Two prospective purchasers might come to opposite conclusions about the character of a slave: "A habit that would render him useless to one man, would scarcely be considered a blot upon his character in the hands of another." Indeed, the value of slaves depended "upon a thousand things"; it was in the "wretched market of the mere slave trader" that they were rated only "by pound avoirdupois."[8]

---

[4]Charles Pettigrew to Ebenezer Pettigrew May 19, 1802, Pettigrew Family Papers; Catterall (ed.), *Judicial Cases*, II, p. 57.

[5]Catterall (ed.), *Judicial Cases*, I, p. 382; V, p. 249.

[6]Sarah A. Gayle Ms. Journal, entries for March 24, September 15, November 10, 1833.

[7]Walker Diary, entry for October 5, 1846.

[8]Catterall (ed.), *Judicial Cases*, II, pp. 97, 318, 530.

The successful master was often a keen student of human psychology. Those who discussed the problem of managing slaves advised owners to study carefully the character of each chattel. "As . . . some negroes are greater offenders than others, so does it require different management for differently disposed negroes. You should *not* 'treat them all alike.'" "Too many masters did not understand this. Some bondsmen, warned a Virginian, required "spurring up, some coaxing, some flattery, and others nothing but good words." Many a valuable slave had been "broken down by injudicious management."[9]

It was within this framework of human relationships that the peculiar institution had to operate. To achieve the "perfect" submission of his slaves, to utilize their labor profitably, each master devised a set of rules by which he governed. These were the laws of his private domain—and the techniques which enabled him to minimize the bondsmen's resistance to servitude. The techniques of control were many and varied, some subtle, some ingenious, some brutal. Slaveholders generally relied upon more than one.

A wise master did not take seriously the belief that Negroes were natural-born slaves. He knew better. He knew that Negroes freshly imported from Africa had to be broken in to bondage; that each succeeding generation had to be carefully trained. This was no easy task, for the bondsman rarely submitted willingly. Moreover, he rarely submitted completely. In most cases there was no end to the need for control—at least not until old age reduced the slave to a condition of helplessness.

Masters revealed the qualities they sought to develop in slaves when they singled out certain ones for special commendation. A small Mississippi planter mourned the death of his "faithful and dearly beloved servant" Jack: "Since I have owned him he has been true to me in all respects. He was an obedient trusty servant. . . . I never knew him to steal nor lie and he ever set a moral and industrious example to those around him. . . . I shall ever cherish his memory." A Louisiana sugar planter lost a "very valuable Boy" through an accident: "His life was a very great one. I have always found him willing and obedient and never knew him to fail to do anything he was put to do."[10] These were "ideal" slaves, the models slaveholders had in mind as they trained and governed their workers.

How might this ideal be approached? The first step, advised those who wrote discourses on the management of slaves, was to establish and maintain strict discipline. An Arkansas master suggested the adoption of the "Army Regulations as to the discipline in Forts." "They must obey at all times, and under all circumstances, cheerfully and with alacrity," affirmed a Virginia slaveholder. "It greatly impairs the happiness of a negro, to be allowed to cultivate an insubordinate temper. Unconditional submission is the only footing upon which slavery should be placed. It is precisely similar to the attitude of a minor to his parent, or a soldier to his general." A South Carolinian limned a perfect relationship between a slave and his master: "that the slave should know that his master is to govern absolutely, and he is to obey implicitly. That he is never for a moment to exercise either his will or judgment in opposition to a positive order."[11]

---

[9]*Southern Cultivator*, XVIII (1860), p. 287; *Farmers' Register*, I (1834), pp. 564–65; IV (1836), p. 115.

[10]Baker Diary, entry for July 1, 1854; Alexander Franklin Pugh Ms. Plantation Diary, entry for June 21, 1860.

[11]*Southern Cultivator*, IV (1846), pp. 43–44; XVIII (1860), pp. 304–05; *Farmers' Register*, V (1837), p. 32.

The second step was to implant in the bondsmen themselves a consciousness of personal inferiority. They had "to know and keep their places," to "feel the difference between master and slave," to understand that bondage was their natural status. They had to feel that African ancestry tainted them, that their color was a badge of degradation. In the country they were to show respect for even their master's nonslaveholding neighbors; in the towns they were to give way on the streets to the most wretched white man. The line between the races must never be crossed, for familiarity caused slaves to forget their lowly station and to become "impudent."[12]

Frederick Douglass explained that a slave might commit the offense of impudence in various ways: "in the tone of an answer; in answering at all; in not answering; in the expression of countenance; in the motion of the head; in the gait, manner and bearing of the slave." Any of these acts, in some subtle way, might indicate the absence of proper subordination. "In a well regulated community," wrote a Texan, "a negro takes off his hat in addressing a white man. . . . Where this is not enforced, we may always look for impudent and rebellious negroes."[13]

The third step in the training of slaves was to awe them with a sense of their master's enormous power. The only principle upon which slavery could be maintained, reported a group of Charlestonians, was the "principle of fear." In his defense of slavery James H. Hammond admitted that this, unfortunately, was true but put the responsibility upon the abolitionists. Antislavery agitation had forced masters to strengthen their authority: "We have to rely more and more on the power of fear. . . . We are determined to continue masters, and to do so we have to draw the reign tighter and tighter day by day to be assured that we hold them in complete check." A North Carolina mistress, after subduing a troublesome domestic, realized that it was essential "to make them stand in fear"![14]

In this the slaveholders had considerable success. Frederick Douglass believed that most slaves stood "in awe" of white men; few could free themselves altogether from the notion that their masters were "invested with a sort of sacredness." Olmsted saw a small white girl stop a slave on the road and boldly order him to return to his plantation. The slave fearfully obeyed her command. A visitor in Mississippi claimed that a master, armed only with a whip or cane, could throw himself among a score of bondsmen and cause them to "flee with terror." He accomplished this by the "peculiar tone of authority" with which he spoke. "Fear, awe, and obedience . . . are interwoven into the very nature of the slave."[15]

The fourth step was to persuade the bondsmen to take an interest in the master's enterprise and to accept his standards of good conduct. A South Carolina planter explained: "The master should make it his business to show his slaves, that the advancement of his individual interest, is at the same time an advancement of theirs. Once they feel this, it will require but little compulsion to make them act as it becomes them."[16]

---

[12]*Southern Planter*, XII (1852), pp. 376–79; *Southern Cultivator*, VIII (1850), p. 163; *Farmer's Register*, I (1834), pp. 564–65.

[13]Douglass, *My Bondage*, p. 92; Austin *Texas State Gazette*, October 10, 1857.

[14]Phillips (ed.), *Plantation and Frontier*, II, pp. 108–11; *De Bow's Review*, VII (1849), p. 498; Mary W. Bryan to Ebenezer Pettigrew, October 20, 1835, Pettigrew Family Papers.

[15]Douglass, *My Bondage*, pp. 250–51; Olmsted, *Back Country*, pp. 444–45; [Ingraham], *South-West*, II, pp. 260–61.

[16]*Farmer's Register*, IV (1837), p. 574.

Though slaveholders induced only a few chattels to respond to this appeal, these few were useful examples for others.

The final step was to impress Negroes with their helplessness, to create in them "a habit of perfect dependence" upon their masters.[17] Many believed it dangerous to train slaves to be skilled artisans in the towns, because they tended to become self-reliant. Some thought it equally dangerous to hire them to factory owners. In the Richmond tobacco factories they were alarmingly independent and "insolent." A Virginian was dismayed to find that his bondsmen, while working at an iron furnace, "got a habit of roaming about and *taking care of themselves*." Permitting them to hire their own time produced even worse results. "No higher evidence can be furnished of its baneful effects," wrote a Charlestonian, "than the unwillingness it produces in the slave, to return to the regular life and domestic control of the master."[18]

A spirit of independence was less likely to develop among slaves kept on the land, where most of them became accustomed to having their master provide their basic needs, and where they might be taught that they were unfit to look out for themselves. Slaves then directed their energies to the attainment of mere "temporary ease and enjoyment." "Their masters," Olmsted believed, "calculated on it in them—do not wish to cure it—and by constant practice encourage it."[19]

Here, then, was the way to produce the perfect slave: accustom him to rigid discipline, demand from him unconditional submission, impress upon him his innate inferiority, develop in him a paralyzing fear of white men, train him to adopt the master's code of good behavior, and instill in him a sense of complete dependence. This, at least, was the goal.

But the goal was seldom reached. Every master knew that the average slave was only an imperfect copy of the model. He knew that some bondsmen yielded only to superior power—and yielded reluctantly. This complicated his problem of control.

---

[17]*Southern Cultivator*, IV (1846), p. 44.

[18]*Southern Planter*, XII (1852), pp. 376–79; Olmsted, *Seaboard*, pp. 58–59; Charleston *Courier*, September 12, 1850.

[19]Olmsted, *Seaboard*, pp. 128–29.

SLAVERY AND PERSONALITY

Stanley M. Elkins

Personality Types and Stereotypes

An examination of American slavery, checked at certain critical points against a very different slave system, that of Latin America, reveals that a major key to many of the contrasts between them was an institutional key: The presence or absence of other powerful institutions in society made an immense difference in the character of slavery itself. In Latin America, the very tension and balance among three kinds of organizational concerns—church, crown, and plantation agriculture—prevented slavery from being carried by the planting class to its ultimate logic. For the slave, in terms of the space thus allowed for the development of men and women as moral beings, the result was an "open system": a system of contacts with free society through which ultimate absorption into that society could and did occur with great frequency. The rights of personality implicit in the ancient traditions of slavery and in the church's most venerable assumptions on the nature of the human soul were thus in a vital sense conserved, whereas to a staggering extent the very opposite was true in North American slavery. The latter system had developed virtually unchecked by institutions having anything like the power of their Latin counterparts; the legal structure which supported it, shaped only by the demands of a staple-raising capitalism, had defined with such nicety the slave's character as chattel that his character as a moral individual was left in the vaguest of legal obscurity. In this sense American slavery operated as a "closed" system—one in which, for the generality of slaves in their nature as men and women, *sub specie aeternitatis*, contacts with free society could occur only on the most narrowly circumscribed of terms. The next question is whether living within such a "closed system" might not have produced noticeable effects upon the slave's very personality.

The name "Sambo" has come to be synonymous with "race stereotype." Here is an automatic danger signal, warning that the analytical difficulties of asking questions about slave personality may not be nearly so great as the moral difficulties. The one inhibits the other; the morality of the matter has had a clogging effect on its theoretical development that may not be to the best interests of either. And yet theory on group personality is still in a stage rudimentary enough that this particular body of material—potentially illuminating—ought not to remain morally impounded any longer.

Is it possible to deal with "Sambo" as a type? The characteristics that have been claimed for the type come principally from Southern lore. Sambo, the typical plantation slave, was docile but irresponsible, loyal but lazy, humble but chronically given to lying and stealing; his behavior was full of infantile silliness and his talk inflated with childish exaggeration. His relationship with his master was one of utter dependence and childlike attachment: it was indeed this childlike quality that was the very key to his being. Although the merest hint of Sambo's "manhood" might fill the Southern breast with scorn, the child, "in his place" could be both exasperating and lovable.

Was he real or unreal? What order of existence, what rank of legitimacy, should be accorded him? Is there a "scientific" way to talk about this problem? For most Southerners in 1860 it went without saying not only that Sambo was real—that he was a dominant plantation type—but also that his characteristics were the clear product of racial inheritance. That was one way to deal with Sambo, a way that persisted a good many years after 1860. But in recent times, the discrediting, as unscientific, of racial explanations for any feature of plantation slavery has tended in the case of Sambo to discredit not simply the explanation itself but also the thing it was supposed to explain. Sambo is a mere stereotype—"stereotype" is itself a bad word, insinuating racial inferiority and invidious discrimination.[1] This modern approach to Sambo had a strong counterpart in the way Northern reformers thought about slavery in ante-bellum times: they thought that nothing could actually be said about the Negro's "true" nature because that nature was veiled by the institution of slavery. It could only be revealed by tearing away the veil.[2] In short, no order of reality could be given to assertions about slave character, because those assertions were illegitimately grounded on race, whereas their only basis was a corrupt and "unreal" institution. "To be sure," a recent writer concedes, "there were plenty of opportunists among the Negroes who played the role assigned to them, acted the clown, and curried the favor of their masters in order to win the maximum rewards within the system. . . . "[3] To impeach Sambo's legitimacy in this way is the next thing to talking him out of existence.

There ought, however, to be still a third way of dealing with the Sambo picture, some formula for taking it seriously. The picture has far too many circumstantial details, its hues have been stroked in by too many different brushes, for it to be denounced as counterfeit. Too much folk-knowledge, too much plantation literature, too much of the Negro's own lore, have gone into its making to entitle one in good conscience to condemn it as "conspiracy." One searches in vain through the literature of the Latin-American slave systems for the "Sambo" of our tradition—the perpetual child

---

[1]The historian Samuel Eliot Morison was taken to task a few years ago by students of Queens College, Long Island, for his use of the name "Sambo" (in Volume I of his and H. S. Commager's text, *The Growth of the American Republic*) and for referring to the pre-Civil War Negroes as "a race with exasperating habits" and to the typical slave as "childlike, improvident, humorous, prevaricating, and superstitious." As a result, the use of the text at Queens was discontinued. See *Time*, February 26, 1951, pp. 48–49.

The following is from the "Concluding Summary" of one of the series of studies begun in the late 1930's under the inspiration of Gunnar Myrdal: "The description of the stereotypes held concerning the American Negro indicates the widespread tendency to look upon the Negro as inferior, and to ascribe to him qualities of intellect and personality which mark him off with some definiteness from the surrounding white American population . . . [;] not all these alleged characteristics of the Negro are uncomplimentary, but even those which may be regarded as favorable have the flavor of inferiority about them. When the Negro is praised, he is praised for his childlike qualities of happiness and good nature or for his artistic and musical gifts. . . . Negro writers do express much more frequently, as one would expect, the belief that whites and Negroes have essentially equal potentialities, and that it is only the accidents of training and economic opportunity which have produced temporary differences; even among Negro writers, however, some have accepted the prevailing stereotype." Otto Klineberg (ed.), *Characteristics of the American Negro* (New York: Harper, 1944). Instead of proposing an actual program of inquiry, the intentions of this line of thought appear to be primarily moral and its objectives to be of a normative sort: desistance from the use of stereotypes.

[2]See below, Part IV, pp. 190–91.

[3]Kenneth Stampp, "The Historian and Southern Negro Slavery," *American Historical Review*, LVII (April, 1952), 617.

incapable of maturity. How is this to be explained?[4] If Sambo is not a product of race (that "explanation" can be consigned to oblivion) and not simply a product of "slavery" in the abstract (other societies have had slavery),[5] then he must be related to our peculiar variety of it. And if Sambo is uniquely an American product, then his existence, and the reasons for his character, must be recognized in order to appreciate the very scope of our slave problem and its aftermath. The absoluteness with which such a personality ("real" or "unreal") had been stamped upon the plantation slave does much to make plausible the ante-bellum Southerner's difficulty in imagining that blacks anywhere could be anything but a degraded race—and it goes far to explain his failure to see any sense at all in abolitionism. It even casts light on the peculiar quality of abolitionism itself; it was so all-enveloping a problem in human personality that our abolitionists could literally not afford to recognize it. Virtually without exception, they met this dilemma either by sidetracking it altogether (they explicitly refused to advance plans for solving it, arguing that this would rob their message of its moral force) or by countering it with theories of infinite human perfectibility. The question of personality, therefore, becomes a crucial phase of the entire problem of slavery in the United States, having conceivably something to do with the difference—already alluded to—between an "open" and a "closed" system of slavery.

If it were taken for granted that a special type existed in significant numbers on American plantations, closer connections might be made with a growing literature on personality and character types, the investigation of which has become a widespread,

---

[4]There is such a word as "Zambo" in Latin America, but its meaning has no relation to our "Sambo." "A Zambo or Sambo (Spanish, *Zambo*, 'bandy-legged') is a cross between a Negro and an Amerindian (sometimes this name is given to the cross between a pure Negro and a mulatto, which the French called 'griffe')." Sir Harry Johnston, *The Negro in the New World* (London: Methuen, 1910), p. 3. I am not implying that racial stigma of some kind did not exist in South America (see above, pp. 77–78, n. 113); indeed, anthropological research has shown that the Latin-Americans were, and are, a good deal more conscious of "race" than such writers as Gilberto Freyre have been willing to admit. Even in Brazil, derogatory Negro stereotypes are common, and are apparently of long standing. On this point see Charles Wagley, *Race and Class in Rural Brazil* (Paris: UNESCO, 1952). On the other hand, it would be very difficult to find evidence in the literature of Brazil, or anywhere else in Latin America, of responsible men seriously maintaining that the Negro slave was constitutionally incapable of freedom. The views of a man like James H. Hammond, or for that matter the views of any average Southerner during the ante-bellum period, would have had little meaning in nineteenth-century Latin America. One is even inclined to think that these Latin-American stereotypes would compare more closely with the stereotypes of eastern and southern European immigrants that were held by certain classes in this country early in the twentieth century. See, e.g., Madison *Grant's Passing of the Great Race* (New York: Scribner, 1916). There are stereotypes and stereotypes: it would be quite safe to say that our "Sambo" far exceeds in tenacity and pervasiveness anything comparable in Latin America.

[5]It is, however, one thing to say that no longer are there any responsible men of science to be found advancing the racial argument, and quite another to assert the argument is closed. In an odd sense we still find any number of statements indicating that the *other* side of the controversy is still being carried on, long after the bones of the enemy lie bleaching on the sands. For example, in the preface to a recent study on the American Negro by two distinguished psychologists, the authors define their "scientific position" by announcing that their book was "conceived and written on the premise that group characteristics are adaptive in nature and therefore not inborn, but acquired" and that "anyone who wishes to quote from [its] conclusions . . . to uphold any other thesis risks doing injustice to the material in the book, to the intentions of the authors, and to the Negro people." They then quote a kind of manifesto, signed by a group of prominent psychologists and social scientists, attesting that "as social scientists we know of no evidence that any ethnic group is inherently inferior." This is followed by a portion of the 1950 UNESCO "Statement on Race" which declares that "biological studies lend support to the ethic of universal brotherhood." From Abram Kardiner and Lionel Ovesey, *The Marl of Oppression: A Psychosocial Study of the American Negro* (New York: Norton, 1951), pp. v–vi. While these are sentiments which may (and must) be pronounced on any number of occasions among men of good will (the President regularly conceives it his duty to do this), their *scientific* content (which is the level at which they are here being offered) has long since ceased to be a matter of controversy.

respectable, and productive enterprise among our psychologists and social scientists.[6] Realizing that, it might then seem not quite so dangerous to add that the type corresponded in its major outlines to "Sambo."

Let the above, then, be a preface to the argument of the present essay. It will be assumed that there were elements in the very structure of the plantation system—its "closed" character—that could sustain infantilism as a normal feature of behavior. These elements, having less to do with "cruelty" per se than simply with the sanctions of authority, were effective and pervasive enough to require that such infantilism be characterized as something much more basic than mere "accommodation." It will be assumed that the sanctions of the system were in themselves sufficient to produce a recognizable personality type.[7]

It should be understood that to identify a social type in this sense is still to generalize on a fairly crude level—and to insist for a limited purpose on the legitimacy of such generalizing is by no means to deny that, on more refined levels, a great profusion of individual types might have been observed in slave society. Nor need it be claimed that the "Sambo" type, even in the relatively crude sense employed here, was a universal type. It was, however, a plantation type, and a plantation existence embraced well over half the slave population.[8] Two kinds of material will be used in the effort to picture the mechanisms whereby this adjustment to absolute power—an adjustment whose end product included infantile features of behavior—may have been effected. One is drawn from the theoretical knowledge presently available in social psychology, and the other, in the form of an analogy, is derived from some of the data that have come out of the German concentration camps. It is recognized in most theory that social behavior is regulated in some general way by adjustment to symbols of authority—however diversely "authority" may be defined either in theory or in culture itself—and that such adjustment is closely related to the very formation of personality. A corollary would be, of course, that the more diverse those symbols of authority may be, the greater is the permissible variety of adjustment to them—and the wider the margin of individuality, consequently, in the development of the self.

---

[6]Among such studies are Robert K. Merton, "Bureaucratic Structure and Personality," *Social Forces*, XVIII (May, 1940), 560–68; Erich Fromm, *Man for Himself* (New York: Rinehart, 1947); David Riesman, *The Lonely Crowd* (New Haven: Yale University Press, 1950); and Theodore Adorno and Others, *The Authoritarian Personality* (New York: Harper, 1950)—a work which is itself subjected to examination in Richard Christie and Marie Jahoda (eds.), *Studies in the Scope and Method of "The Authoritarian Personality"* (Glencoe, Ill.: Free Press, 1954); and H. H. Gerth and C. Wright Mills, *Character and Social Structure: The Psychology of Social Institutions* (New York: Harcourt, Brace, 1953). For a consideration of this field in the broadest terms, see Alex Inkeles and Daniel J. Levinson, "National Character: The Study of Modal Personality and Sociocultural Systems," *Handbook of Social Psychology*, ed. Gardner Lindzey (Cambridge, Mass.: Addison-Wesley, 1954), II, 977–1020.

[7]The line between "accommodation" (as conscious hypocrisy) and behavior inextricable from basic personality, though the line certainly exists, is anything but a clear and simple matter of choice. There is reason to think that the one grades into the other, and vice versa, with considerable subtlety. In this connection, the most satisfactory theoretical mediating term between deliberate role-playing and "natural" role-playing might be found in role-psychology. See below, pp. 131–33.

[8]Although the majority of Southern slaveholders were not planters, the majority of slaves were owned by a planter minority. "Considerably more than half of them lived on plantation units of more than twenty slaves, and one-fourth lived on units of more than fifty. That the majority of slaves belonged to members of the planter class, and not to those who operated small farms with a single slave family, is a fact of crucial importance concerning the nature of bondage in the ante-bellum South." Stampp, *Peculiar Institution*, p. 31.

The question here has to do with the wideness or narrowness of that margin on the ante-bellum plantation.

The other body of material, involving an experience undergone by several million men and women in the concentration camps of our own time, contains certain items of relevance to the problem here being considered. The experience was analogous to that of slavery and was one in which wide-scale instances of infantilization were observed. The material is sufficiently detailed, and sufficiently documented by men who not only took part in the experience itself but who were versed in the use of psychological theory for analyzing it, that the advantages of drawing upon such data for purposes of analogy seem to outweigh the possible risks.

The introduction of this second body of material must to a certain extent govern the theoretical strategy itself. It has been recognized both implicitly and explicitly that the psychic impact and effects of the concentration-camp experience were not anticipated in existing theory and that consequently such theory would require some major supplementation. It might be added, parenthetically, that almost any published discussion of this modern Inferno, no matter how learned, demonstrates how "theory," operating at such a level of shared human experience, tends to shed much of its technical trappings and to take on an almost literary quality. The experience showed, in any event, that infantile personality features could be induced in a relatively short time among large numbers of adult human beings coming from very diverse backgrounds. The particular strain which was thus placed upon prior theory consisted in the need to make room not only for the cultural and environmental sanctions that sustain personality (which in a sense Freudian theory already had) but also for a virtually unanticipated problem: actual change in the personality of masses of adults. It forced a reappraisal and new appreciation of how completely and effectively prior cultural sanctions for behavior and personality could be detached to make way for new and different sanctions, and of how adjustments could be made by individuals to a species of authority vastly different from any previously known. The revelation for theory was the process of detachment.

These cues, accordingly, will guide the argument on Negro slavery. Several million people were detached with a peculiar effectiveness from a great variety of cultural backgrounds in Africa—a detachment operating with infinitely more effectiveness upon those brought to North America than upon those who came to Latin America. It was achieved partly by the shock experience inherent in the very mode of procurement but more specifically by the type of authority-system to which they were introduced and to which they had to adjust for physical and psychic survival. The new adjustment, to absolute power in a closed system, involved infantilization, and the detachment was so complete that little trace of prior (and thus alternative) cultural sanctions for behavior and personality remained for the descendants of the first generation. For them, adjustment to clear and omnipresent authority could be more or less automatic—as much so, or as little, as it is for anyone whose adjustment to a social system begins at birth and to whom that system represents normality. We do not know how generally a full adjustment was made by the first generation of fresh slaves from Africa. But we do know—from a modern experience—that such an adjustment is possible, not only within the same generation but within two or three years. This proved possible for people in a full state of complex civilization, for men and women who were not black and not savages.

Shock and Detachment

We may suppose that every African who became a slave underwent an experience whose crude psychic impact must have been staggering and whose consequences superseded anything that had ever previously happened to him. Some effort should therefore be made to picture the series of shocks which must have accompanied the principal events of that enslavement.

The majority of slaves appear to have been taken in native wars,[9] which meant that no one—neither persons of high rank nor warriors of prowess—was guaranteed against capture and enslavement.[10] Great numbers were caught in surprise attacks upon their villages, and since the tribes acting as middlemen for the trade had come to depend on regular supplies of captives in order to maintain that function, the distinction between wars and raiding expeditions tended to be very dim.[11] The first shock, in an experience destined to endure many months and to leave its survivors irrevocably changed, was thus the shock of capture. It is an effort to remember that while enslavement occurred in Africa every day, to the individual it occurred just once.[12]

The second shock—the long march to the sea—drew out the nightmare for many weeks. Under the glaring sun, through the steaming jungle, they were driven along like beasts tied together by their necks; day after day, eight or more hours at a time, they would stagger barefoot over thorny underbrush, dried reeds, and stones. Hardship, thirst, brutalities, and near starvation penetrated the experience of each exhausted man and woman who reached the coast.[13] One traveler tells of seeing hundreds of bleaching

---

[9]There were other pretexts, such as crime or debt, but war was probably the most frequent mode of procurement. Snelgrave, *New Account*, p. 158; "John Barbot's Description," in Donnan, *Documents*, I, pp. 284, 289, 294, 298; "Observations on the Slave Trade, 1789" [C. B. Wadström] in *ibid.*, II, p. 599; Matthews, *Voyage to Sierra-Leone*, pp. 145–46, 163. See also below, n. 34.

[10]As to "character types," one might be tempted to suppose that as a rule it would be only the weaker and more submissive who allowed themselves to be taken into slavery. Yet it appears that a heavy proportion of the slaves were in fact drawn from among the most warlike. "In a country divided into a thousand petty states, mostly independent and jealous of each other; where every freeman is accustomed to arms, and fond of military achievements; where the youth who has practised the bow and spear from his infancy, longs for nothing so much as an opportunity to display his valour; it is natural to imagine that wars frequently originate from very frivolous provocation." Park, *Travels*, p. 328. "The most potent negroe," wrote William Bosman, "can't pretend to be insured from slavery; for if he ever ventures himself in the wars it may easily become his lot." *New and Accurate Description*, p. 183. It has often been pointed out that slavery already existed among the tribes themselves and that a considerable proportion of Africans were used to it and had in fact been born into it. It may be doubted, however, if substantial numbers of these slaves came to America, for apparently the native chiefs tended to sell only their war captives to the Europeans and to keep their hereditary and customary slaves—together with their most docile captives—for themselves. Park, *Travels*, p. 332. It has even been asserted that in many places the tribal laws themselves forbade the selling of domestic slaves, except for crimes, though apparently it was simple enough to trump up an accusation if one wanted to get rid of a slave. Matthews,*Voyage to Sierra-Leone*, p. 153; Edwards, History, II, p. 312.

[11]"The Wars which the inhabitants of the interior parts of the country, beyond Senegal, Gambia, and Sierra Leona, carry on with each other, are chiefly of a predatory nature, and owe their origin to the yearly number of slaves, which the Mandingoes, or the inland traders suppose will be wanted by the vessels that will arrive on the coast." "Observations" [Wadström], in Donnan; *Documents*, II, p. 599.

[12]A number of excerpts describing these raids are cited in Thomas Fowell Buxton, *Letter on the Slave Trade to the Lord Viscount Melbourne* (London, 1838), pp. 34–38.

[13]Descriptions of the march may be found in Park, *Travels*, pp. 371 ff.; Buxton, *Letter*, pp. 41–44; Rinchon, *La traite et l'esclavage*, pp. 174–75; L. Degrandpré, *Voyage à la côte occidentale d'Afrique, fait dans les années 1786 et 1787* (Paris, 1801), II, pp. 48–50.

skeletons strewn along one of the slave caravan routes.[14] But then the man who must interest us is the man who survived—he who underwent the entire experience, of which this was only the beginning.

The next shock, aside from the fresh physical torments which accompanied it, was the sale to the European slavers. After being crowded into pens near the trading stations and kept there overnight, sometimes for days, the slaves were brought out for examination. Those rejected would be abandoned to starvation; the remaining ones—those who had been bought—were branded, given numbers inscribed on leaden tags, and herded on shipboard.[15]

The episode that followed—almost too protracted and stupefying to be called a mere "shock"—was the dread Middle Passage, brutalizing to any man, black or white, ever to be involved with it. The holds, packed with squirming and suffocating humanity, became stinking infernos of filth and pestilence. Stories of disease, death, and cruelty on the terrible two-month voyage abound in the testimony which did much toward ending the British slave trade forever.[16]

The final shock in the process of enslavement came with the Negro's introduction to the West Indies. Bryan Edwards, describing the arrival of a slave ship, writes of how in times of labor scarcity crowds of people would come scrambling aboard, manhandling the slaves and throwing them into panic. The Jamaica legislature eventually "corrected the enormity" by enacting that the sales be held on shore. Edwards felt a certain mortification at seeing the Negroes exposed naked in public, similar to that felt by the trader Degrandpré at seeing them examined back at the African factories.[17] Yet here they did not seem to care. "They display . . . very few signs of lamentation for their past or of apprehension for their future condition; but . . . commonly express great eagerness to be sold."[18] The "seasoning" process which followed completed the series of steps whereby the African Negro became a slave.

The mortality had been very high. One-third of the numbers first taken, out of a total of perhaps fifteen million, had died on the march and at the trading stations;

---

[14]Buxton, *Letter*, p. 43.

[15]"When these slaves come to fida, they are put in prison all together, and when we treat concerning buying them, they are all brought out together in a large plain; where, by our Chirurgeons, whose province it is, they are thoroughly examined, even to the smallest member, and that naked too both men and women, without the least distinction and modesty. Those which are approved as good are set on one side; and the lame or faulty are set by as *invalides*, which are here called *mackrons*. These are such as are above five and thirty years old, or are maimed in the arms, legs, hands or feet, have lost a tooth, are grey-haired, or have films over their eyes; as well as all those which are affected by any venereal distemper, or with several other diseases." Bosman, *New and Accurate Description*, p. 364. See also Degrandpré, *Voyage*, II, pp. 53–56; Buxton, *Letter*, pp. 47–49; Rinchon, *La traite et l'esclavage*, pp. 188–89; "John Barbot's Description," in Donnan, *Documents*, I, pp. 289, 295; Park, *Travels*, p. 360.

[16]Descriptions of the Middle Passage may be found in *An Abstract of the Evidence Delivered before a Select Committee of the Home of Commons in the Years 1790, and 1791; on the Part of the Petitioners for the Abolition of the Slave Trade* (London, 1791); Alexander Falconbridge, *An Account of the Slave Trade on the Coast of Africa* (London: T. Phillips, 1788); Rinchon, *La traite et l'esclavage*, pp. 196–209; Edwards, *History*, II; Brantz Mayer, *Captain Canot* (New York: D. Appleton, 1854); Averil Mackenzie-Grieve, *The Last Years of the English Slave Trade, Liverpool 1750–1807* (London: Putnam, 1941).

[17]Degrandpré, *Voyage*, II, pp. 55–56.

[18]Edwards, *History*, II, 340. See also *Abstract of Evidence*, pp. 46–47, and Falconbridge, *Account*, pp. 33–36.

another third died during the Middle Passage and the seasoning.[19] Since a majority of the African-born slaves who came to the North American plantations did not come directly but were imported through the British West Indies, one may assume that the typical slave underwent an experience something like that just outlined. This was the man—one in three—who had come through it all and lived and was about to enter our "closed system." What would he be like if he survived and adjusted to that?

Actually, a great deal had happened to him already. Much of his past had been annihilated; nearly every prior connection had been severed. Not that he had really "forgotten" all these things—his family and kinship arrangements, his language, the tribal religion, the taboos, the name he had once borne, and so on—but none of it any longer carried much meaning. The old values, the sanctions, the standards, already unreal, could no longer furnish him guides for conduct, for adjusting to the expectations of a complete new life. Where then was he to look for new standards, new cues—who would furnish them now? He could now look to none but his master, the one man to whom the system had committed his entire being: the man upon whose will depended his food, his shelter, his sexual connections, whatever moral instruction he might be offered, whatever "success" was possible within the system, his very security—in short, everything.

The thoroughness with which African Negroes coming to America were detached from prior cultural sanctions should thus be partly explainable by the very shock sequence inherent in the technique of procurement. But it took something more than this to produce "Sambo," and it is possible to overrate—or at least to overgeneralize—this shock sequence in the effort to explain what followed.[20] A comparable experience was also undergone by slaves coming to Latin America, where very little that resembled our "Sambo" tradition would ever develop. We should also remember that, in either case, it was only the first generation that actually experienced these shocks. It could even be argued that the shock sequence is not an absolute necessity for explaining "Sambo" at all.

So whereas the Middle Passage and all that went with it must have been psychologically numbing, and should probably be regarded as a long thrust, at least, toward the end product, it has little meaning considered apart from what came later. It may be assumed that the process of detachment was completed—and, as it were, guaranteed—by the kind of "closed" authority-system into which the slave was introduced and to which he would have to adjust.[21] At any rate, a test of this detachment and its thoroughness is virtually ready-made. Everyone who has looked into the problem of African cultural features surviving among New World Negroes agrees that the contrast between North America and Latin America is immense. In Brazil, survivals from African religion are not only to be encountered everywhere, but such carry-overs are

---

[19]Tannenbaum, *Slave and Citizen*, p. 28. As for the total exports of slaves from Africa throughout the entire period of the trade, estimates run as high as twenty million. "Even a conservative estimate," notes Mr. Tannenbaum, "would hardly cut this figure in half." *ibid.*, p. 32.

[20]Its rigors, at least prior to the sea passage, were clearly not experienced with uniform intensity by all. For example, Onwuka Dike claims that among the tribes east of the Niger, nearly as many, and perhaps even more, of the slaves sold to Europeans were procured by non-violent means, through the judgment of the Oracle, as were taken in wars. See Dike, *Trade and Politics*, pp. 40–41. It might also be added that the "long march" was probably not a universal experience either, since there was in West Africa a network of navigable rivers down which cargoes of slaves could be transported in canoes. On this point see *ibid.*, pp. 19–20.

[21]See above, pp. 37–63.

so distinct that they may even be identified with particular tribal groups. "The Negro religions and cults," Arthur Ramos adds, "were not the only form of cultural expression which survived in Brazil. The number of folklore survivals is extremely large, the prolongation of social institutions, habits, practices and events from Africa."[22] Fernando Ortiz, writing of Cuba in 1905, saw the African witchcraft cults flourishing on the island as a formidable social problem.[23] One of our own anthropologists, on the other hand, despite much dedicated field work, has been put to great effort to prove that in North American Negro society any African cultural vestiges have survived at all.[24]

---

[22]Arthur Ramos, *The Negro in Brazil* (Washington: Associated Publishers, 1939), p. 94. Ramos devotes two full chapters to "The Cultural Heritage of the Brazilian Negro." Donald Pierson, in his *Negroes in Brazil* (Chicago: University of Chicago Press, 1942), likewise devotes two chapters to African influences in the customs of the Negroes of Bahia.

[23]Fernando Ortiz, *Los Negros Brujos* (Madrid: Libería de F. Fé, 1906). This entire book is devoted to occult African practices in Cuba, including a chapter called "The Future of Witchcraft."

[24]Herskovits, *Myth of the Negro Past*. The real aim of this study seems more often than not to be that of "promoting" African culture in the United States by insisting on its values instead of describing its actual survivals—which the author himself admits are decidedly on the scanty side compared with those to be found in Latin America. Such "Africanisms" do not seem to go much beyond esoteric vestiges of a suspiciously circumstantial nature, in speech rhythms, certain symbols in folk-tales, habits of "temporary mating," etc. Professor Herskovits reveals, perhaps unwittingly, that efforts to convince American Negro audiences that they do, in fact, have an African cultural heritage, have met with hostility and tension.

Source: From *Slavery: A Problem in American Institutional and Intellectual Life* by Stanley Elkins. Copyright © 1959. Reprinted by permission of University of Chicago Press and the author.

KEY SLAVES AND THE POVERTY OF PATERNALISM

Michael Tadman

For those interested in the nature of American slavery, crucial questions have always been how far masters were benign or cruel, and how far slaves were rebellious, docile, or resilient. Since the racist legacies of slavery still stretch across America today, these questions are significant, not just for academic historians, but for society at large. It is important to know upon what traditions—invented and real—modern black-white relations have been founded. The task of exploring master-slave relations is complex, however—and is so, in part, precisely because slavery, for its very survival, called for the making of myths and false traditions. Slavery required a racist ideology that would seem to legitimize its existence, and which would rationalize the treatment of blacks as slaves. Such myth making built much that was treacherous into the primary documentation of slavery. The first purpose of this introduction is to comment on available primary sources (especially slaveholders' records), and to discuss, rather more substantially than I do elsewhere in the book, some of the most significant investigations of antebellum slavery. Second, building upon my framework of evidence on the slave trade, I want to develop an overall interpretation of relations between masters and slaves in the American South. This interpretation differs substantially from the theses of close accommodation which Robert Fogel and Stanley Engerman, and Eugene Genovese, have proposed. It emphasizes the resilience of slaves, and their fundamental resistance to the values and culture of masters. It argues, further, that the relationship with "key slaves" (defined below) allowed masters to maintain a self-image of benevolent patriarchs, while in practice treating nearly all slaves with racist indifference.

Sources, Theories, and Key Slaves

If we start in very general terms, we might talk of two main historical interpretations of slaveowners—owners as being straightforwardly exploitative of slaves, and owners as being in some sort of paternal relationship with their slaves (where masters had certain "responsibilities" and where slaves had certain "privileges"). So far as the slaves are concerned, historians have employed three basic schemes of analysis—slave submission to the system of bondage, rejection of the system, and accommodation within slavery. We shall, in fact, have to make important distinctions between different accommodation theories—because such theories range from ideas of a very close set of understandings between masters and slaves to notions of strictly limited accommodation and of minimal cultural interpenetration between masters and slaves.

Disagreement among historians [has] arisen for many reasons, but [has] tended to be perpetuated by certain features of the primary documentation on slavery. First, although there are vitally important slave sources, historians have always been restricted by the limited extent of surviving evidence from slaves. Second, so far as white records are concerned, they have faced a mix—of apparently unquantifiable proportions—of, on the one hand, cases of brutality and indifference toward blacks, with, on the other hand, cases of apparent white benevolence and of black-white affection. Thus, if the historian is content simply to compile illustrative quotations, rather than including systematic sampling, parallel histories of benevolence and can readily be developed. The goal of the good historian has always been to find sources, techniques, or frameworks that reveal the relative importance of different patterns.

We could talk of other difficulties with sources, but a problem which has hitherto been largely ignored deserves special emphasis. This is the problem that white manuscript records tend very much to be skewed toward "key slaves." By key slaves, I mean especially drivers (assistants to white overseers or planters), drivers' wives, and certain senior domestics. One expects, in slaveholder sources, strong racist biases, but in addition one faces the problem that, in slaveholders' diaries and letters, rank-and-file slaves are almost invisible. Instead, two or three key slaves, referred to by name, will appear time and again. Significantly, key slaves were the most privileged slaves, and were exactly those for whom masters were most likely to make claims of affection (and, indeed, claims of mutual affection between slaves and masters). As well as racist biases in slaveholders' records, then, one has a skew toward comment on the more advantaged slaves. It becomes particularly difficult, therefore, to write a history of slaves, rather than of key slaves. In a slaveholder's manuscripts, the temperaments, skills, "limitations," and activities of key slaves might be commented on at length; and the death of a key slave might be much lamented. Rank-and-file slaves, however, rarely appear as individuals referred to by name. We might find a brief note that a rank-and-file slave was ill, or that "Jim, a valuable Negro" had died. But we find, from such white records, next to nothing about the personalities and lives of rank-and-file slaves—about the great majority, that is. We shall return to the problem of key slaves after reviewing some of the main historical analyses of slavery.

In subsequent chapters of this study I have tried to overcome the biases of typical slaveholder sources by attempting to establish a reliable basic framework for the study of master-slave relationships. This frame of reference has been what slaveowners did to slaves, rather than what they said they did. Instead of focusing initially on rationalization and on the slaveholders' world view, I have started by trying to establish the *behavior* of slaveholders in critically important areas of master-slave relationships— these areas being slave sales and family separations. One might argue that the slave trade was the worst aspect of slavery, and that to focus on it introduces biases. But when the trade turns out to have been so pervasive, it becomes necessary to make it a central reference point. Evidence on the scale and nature of the trade clearly shows a profound gulf between the masters' world view and their actual treatment of slaves. And this practical framework of analysis seems to cut much of the ground away from any theory of close accommodation between masters and slaves. Even so, the world view of masters, with all of its biases, rationalization, and self-deception, does, indirectly, have a great deal to reveal. Later in this introduction, by turning to the world view of the slaveholders—and in particular by exploring the role of key slaves—I shall undertake to develop a theory of master-slave relations which will be supported by the evidence of the following chapters.

Slavery and the Historians: Rejection, Submission, or Accommodation?

The first half of this century was dominated by a thesis of close accommodation between masters and slaves—the conservative, racist thesis of Ulrich B. Phillips. According to Phillips,

> The problem of accommodation [between slave and master], which was the central problem of life, was on the whole happily resolved. . . . The adjustments and readjustments were continually made, for although the masters had by far the major power of control, the slaves themselves were by no means devoid of influence. . . . The general regime was in fact shaped by mutual requirements, concessions, and understandings, producing reciprocal codes of conventional morality. . . . In short, their [the masters'] despotism, so far as it might properly be so called, was benevolent in intent and on the whole benevolent in effect.

The great mass of masters, according to Phillips, promoted Christianity and marriage, and gave occasional rewards and indulgences. And, he continued, "they refrained from selling slaves, except under the stress of circumstances . . . , and endeavored to inspire effort through affection rather than through fear. "This classic accommodation thesis was based on a skillful reworking of the proslavery literature, together with an effortless prose style and a great knowledge of plantation manuscripts. More fundamentally, however, it was based on racist assumptions about black character. Blacks were assumed to be inherently lazy and irresponsible. They could not, Phillips claimed, be made to work beyond certain modest limits. This "idleness," he maintained, forced slaveowners to tolerate "a slackness in every concern not vital to routine." From this, Phillips asserted, there was born a southern tradition which was leisurely, gentlemanly, tolerant of modest returns, and which was rich in its human values.[1]

Such a thesis was consciously created in order to make a white supremacist society confident about itself and at ease with its past. In this romantic view of the Old South, masters gave leadership and protection, and in return slaves gave loyalty, affection, and moderate labor. Racist premises, however, clearly made this formulation of the accommodation thesis untenable. And after that, there were the further problems of bias and of narrowness of perspective in the slaveowner sources on which the study so heavily relied.

A significant challenge to Phillips came with Frederic Bancroft's *Slave Trading in the Old South* (1931), where Bancroft argued that typical masters did not protect slave families. Indeed, he argued that the interregional slave trade assumed massive proportions. Bancroft's study grew steadily in influence, but, on its own, failed to shake Phillips's dominance. Important in limiting Bancroft's impact was the continued dominance of racist assumptions in society at large. Furthermore, Bancroft's evidence was mainly on slave trading at urban centers, and this left open the possibility that the great mass of the rural South might not have been deeply influenced by slave selling and by its attendant destruction of families. Beyond that, there was the fact that Bancroft offered no general thesis on slavery. He rejected Phillips's idea of blacks' innate inferiority

---

[1]Ulrich B. Phillips, *American Negro Slavery: A Survey of the Supply, Employment and Control of Negro Labor as Determined by the Plantation Regime* (New York, 1918; Boston Rouge, 1966), pp. 328, 287.

to whites; and his emphasis on the cruelty of slavery ran counter to Phillips's thesis of close accommodation. But Bancroft's assumption that slaves had not been allowed to move far beyond what he saw as "African barbarity" meant that he failed to develop an explicit thesis of slave culture and of master-slave interaction.[2]

In a series of studies, but most notably in his *American Negro Slave Revolts* (New York, 1943), the Marxist historian Herbert Aptheker advanced a "rejection" thesis—which directly attacked Phillips's accommodation theory. Aptheker argued that, far from accommodating to slavery, American slaves comprehensively rejected it—and showed this rejection in a vigorous tradition of revolt. This work, though it demonstrated the existence of considerable white fear of revolt, failed, however, to establish that open rebellion was widespread.

The two landmark studies of the 1950s—by Kenneth Stampp and Stanley Elkins—both gave considerable weight to slave trading and to family separations, and (like Aptheker's work) both rejected the accommodation thesis. Stampp's *Peculiar Institution* (1956) had elements of a rejection thesis, but saw slaves as "caught between two cultures" (white and African). "In slavery," he wrote, "the Negro existed in a kind of cultural void. He lived in a twilight world between two ways of life and was unable to obtain from either many of the attributes which distinguished man from beast."[3] Stampp's study, although it provided a much-needed counterweight to the racism of Phillips, was limited in that (like Phillips's work, and like that of many other historians) it was built upon illustrative quotations from primary sources, rather than upon the inclusion of explicit sampling of documentation on critical issues. Stanley Elkins's *Slavery* (1959) adopted a "slave submission" thesis, arguing that North American slavery was so extreme in its brutality that it turned blacks (through no fault of their own) into infantilized "Samboes." Elkins's work, however, was very much theory-driven (using psychological theories, and drawing analogies with the Nazi concentration camps of the Second World War). It drew very little from primary sources. In major studies of slave culture, other historians (especially Lawrence Levine and Herbert Gutman) would, by the imaginative use of primary sources, compile impressive evidence of a resilient—rather than infantilized—slave society.

The work of Lawrence Levine and Herbert Gutman supports some sort of accommodation thesis, but—as my own research finds—it is a thesis of strictly limited adjustment to the sheer power of masters.[4] Both Levine and Gutman—although they acknowledged that much of what slaves did was determined by masters—emphasized, too, what slaves concealed from masters, what masters did not understand, and what was special to slaves. Levine broke out of the problems of more commonly used primary sources by exploring black oral tradition, folk tales, and songs. The themes of the folk tales—the moral worth of the underdog and the outwitting of the powerful master—did not suggest the cultural dominance of whites in the slave cabin. Nor did the themes

---

[2]For detailed comments on Bancroft's ideas, see Tadman, Introduction to new edition of Frederic Bancroft, *Slave Trading in the Old South* (University of South Carolina Press, Columbia, 1996).

[3]Kenneth B. Stampp, *The Peculiar Institution: Slavery in the Antebellum South* (New York, 1956), p. 364; Stanley M. Elkins, *Slavery: A Problem in American Institutional and Intellectual Life* (Chicago, 1959).

[4]See Lawrence W. Levine, *Black Culture and Black Consciousness: Afro-American Folk Thought from Slavery to Freedom* (New York, 1977); Herbert G. Gutman, *The Black Family in Slavery and Freedom, 1750–1925* (New York and Oxford, 1976).

of religious songs, which emphasized that the slaves were God's chosen people. The dominance of such themes—of resilience, resistance, and worthiness—suggests that, whatever compromises they made with masters, the slaves had an alternative set of values to those of their oppressors.

Herbert Gutman's work on the slave family made major breakthroughs by using white sources in new ways. He found, from the way that first names were passed on from father to son (but not from mother to daughter), and passed on from grandparents and from aunts and uncles, that slaves knew who their kin, and their extended kin, were—and that they valued ties of kin. He found, too, great enthusiasm for marriage among slaves—and this despite his strong evidence that masters (when their own convenience and financial interests were at stake) showed indifference to slave unions. When masters did not forcibly break a slave marriage, that union would only very rarely be broken by the actions of the slaves. With the coming of freedom, he found that slaves were keen to be reunited with lost relatives; and he found that from the Civil War to the end of the nineteenth century blacks, overwhelmingly, lived in two-parent families, and were equally as keen as whites to have new marriages officially sanctioned. Such a pattern, with a massive predominance of attachment to two-parent families, could not have suddenly and successfully been implanted in 1865, and must have had its roots in slave attitudes to family. Significantly, Gutman argued, the tradition of family resilience came *despite* masters. Rather than supporting the culture of a strong slave family, masters, in practice, were overwhelmingly its enemies. But family identities gave slaves a strong sense of collective resistance. Evidence in the present study supports Gutman's views on the resilience of the slaves' family culture and on the racist indifference of white owners to black families.

Theories of Close Accommodation: Capitalist and Anticapitalist Masters

Recent thinking on antebellum slavery has been very strongly influenced by the overlapping, but essentially different, accommodation theories of Robert Fogel and Stanley Engerman, and of Eugene Genovese.[5] Fogel and Engerman's thesis was built on the economics of slavery; it saw slavery as an efficient capitalistic system, whose work ethic the slaves shared with their enterprising masters. For Genovese, antebellum slavery was precapitalist and antibourgeois. Master-slave relations were based on a paternalist accommodation, with slaves expecting, and usually receiving, at least certain minimum standards of treatment from their masters. The theories just mentioned, though different from each other, both saw strong slaveholder influence on the cultural values of the slaves.

Fogel and Engerman's work has sought to break out of the problem of narrative primary sources by developing a striking econometric model (combining economic theory with quantitative methods). Impressive evidence was developed on the profitability of slavery and on the strength of the profit motive among masters. Slave work rates and morale, Fogel and Engerman argued, were high—and, supposedly, this to a great extent was because masters gave their slaves positive incentives, especially the

---

[5]Robert W. Fogel and Stanley L. Engerman, *Time on the Cross: The Economics of American Negro Slavery* (Boston, 1974), and Fogel, *Without Consent on Contract: The Rise and Fall of American Slavery* (New York, 1989); and Eugene D. Genovese, *Roll, Jordan, Roll: The World the Slaves Made* (New York, 1974), and other studies by Genovese, including very recent work which is discussed below.

protection of families. While their conclusions on the levels of profit were convincing, their arguments on the means by which profits were achieved were much less persuasive. For their theory of high morale and protected families to work, the internal slave trade had to be of minor numerical significance and family separations had to be quite rare. Their samples on the trade and on separations were, however, demonstrably atypical. Fogel and Engerman's thesis of willing workers, within a system of capitalist accommodation, was not consistent with the evidence of the slave trade. The record of family separations suggests a very different slave culture from that in Fogel and Engerman's model—and suggests a culture where slaves distrusted masters and held much of their feelings back from masters.

Eugene Genovese has been in part concerned with economic analysis, but has been much more interested in the class and social relationships produced by antebellum slavery. He has taken these systems very seriously—seeing class formations in the "precapitalist" or "anticapitalist" slave South as the great exception to the dominant capitalist pattern of the United States. Because he has developed an explicit theory about social relationships within slavery, his work is of especial importance for the present study, and his analysis is therefore commented upon at some length. Genovese's accommodation thesis was founded on his view that the slaveowning class—though in some senses hybrid, and though producing staples for the capitalist world—was precapitalist and antibourgeois in its values. According to Genovese, precisely because they owned their labor force (the slaves), American slaveholders stood in a very different relationship to their laborers compared with capitalist employers, who simply hired and fired free labor as they required it. Southern slavery, Genovese tells us, was based essentially upon "relationships of class power in racial form."[6] Out of this "class power," he argues, a system of paternalism developed.

While white violence was always available to secure power, relationships, we are told, came to be based on negotiations over minimum standards of treatment *within the system* of slavery. Masters saw themselves as giving slaves privileges (like protection of family, moderate rather than excessive physical discipline, certain breaks from work, reasonable food), while slaves reinterpreted these "privileges" as "rights." Because they felt that they had rights, and because of their Christian faith, the slaves, we are told, knew that they had human worth. They were involved in a class struggle with their masters, but hegemony and cultural dominance had been achieved by the slaveowners. This was because conflicts with masters were essentially over rights or privileges which were to be preserved within the system. The property base of the slaveholder was not threatened. The slaves, we are told, while seeing slavery as illegitimate, accepted paternalism and worked within the rules of paternalism.[7]

Genovese goes on to insist, in *Roll, Jordan, Roll* (1974), in *The Slaveholders' Dilemma* (1992), and elsewhere, that the slaveholders were confident in their position as owners of slaves and were confident in their world view. And, he argues, in order to feel this confidence and to justify their position, they needed to feel that they were benevolent paternalists. Their intellectuals argued that slavery was necessary for the preservation of morality and for the gradual advancement of liberty in society. Slavery, the proslavery intellectuals argued, gave a reliable support to the lowest stratum in society. Without

---

[6]Genovese, *Roll, Jordan, Roll,* p. 4.

[7]On the arguments just summarized, see especially Genovese, *Roll, Jordan, Roll,* pp. 25–26, 148, 597–98.

slavery, they maintained, a proletariat would grow, conflict between capital and labor would develop, and chaos, violence, and the collapse of morality would be unstoppable. We are told, then, that slaveholders were a highly self-conscious class, confident in the legitimacy of their position and convinced that they acted benevolently.[8]

Essential for Genovese's thesis was the idea of the patriarchal household—which included not just the slaveholder's white family but his "family, white and black." Everywhere, Genovese found, masters talked of their "family, white and black." The concept, he argued, was found so widely that, although there was a measure of "rationalization and self-serving cant" in this slaveholder usage, it must, he claimed, also have contained something of genuine substance.[9] Similarly, he maintained, planters' ideal lists of rules for the governing of slaves should not be dismissed as mere hypocrisy. Furthermore, he found substance in the claim of antebellum proslavery writers that the slaveholding community often intervened against unduly harsh slaveowners within its ranks.[10] And, Genovese claimed, in order to sustain their self-image slaveholders expected from their slaves not only duty and respect, but love.[11] The thesis, then, saw bonds of affection between master and slave as being possible, and, one has to assume, common. With force always available in the background, the master's hegemony, we are told, operated on a day-to-day basis through the owner's "command of culture."[12]

It is sometimes difficult to be sure how deeply, and in what ways, Genovese sees slave mentalities as being dominated by white "control of culture." At some points in his work "culture" and "cultural dominance" seem to be so narrowly defined (as bargaining power) that differences between Genovese and historians such as Gutman are substantially reduced.[13] He has also characteristically combined, within a single paragraph, contrasting elements, as when he wrote:

> This special sense of [a "white and black"] family shaped southern culture. In its positive aspect, it brought white and black together and welded them into one people with genuine elements of affection and intimacy. . . . But in its overwhelming negative aspect—its arrogant doctrine of domination and its inherent cruelty towards disobedient "children"—it pitted blacks against whites in bitter antagonism and simultaneously poisoned the life of the dominant white community itself.[14]

But "control of culture" is of great importance for Genovese. He has insisted that many historians (Herbert Gutman being a particular target) have ignored the

---

[8]Eugene D. Genovese, *The Slaveholders, Dilemma: Freedom and Progress in Southern Conservative Thought, 1820–1860* (Columbia, S.C., 1992).

[9]See Genovese, *Roll, Jordan, Roll*, pp. 70–75; and, for an important development of this, see Eugene D. Genovese, "'Our Family, White and Black:' Family and Household in the Southern Slaveholders' World View," pp. 69–87 in Carol Bleser (ed.) *In Joy and in Sorrow: Women, Family, and Marriage in the Victorian South, 1830–1900.* (New York, 1991). See also Elizabeth Fox-Genovese, *Within the Plantation Household: Black and White Women of the Old South* (Chapel Hill, N.C., 1988).

[10]Genovese, *Roll, Jordan, Roll*, pp. 70–71, 41–43.

[11]Genovese, *Roll, Jordan, Roll*, p. 97.

[12]Genovese, *Roll, Jordan, Roll*, p. 658.

[13]For an apparent de-emphasis of cultural interpenetration, see for example Eugene D. Genovese, "Master-slave Relations," pp. 449–54 in Randall M. Miller and John David Smith (eds.), *Dictionary of Afro-American Slavery* (New York, 1988).

[14]Genovese, *Roll, Jordan, Roll*, p. 74.

"cultural interpenetration" between masters and slaves, and he has argued that the work of Gutman and others was "one-sided" in that, supposedly, it neglected the master's dominance of slave culture.[15] Indeed, the idea of strong "cultural penetration" of slaves by masters must be seen as central to Genovese, or his work loses a major part of its distinctiveness. Briefly stated, then, Genovese's, thesis seems to be that antebellum slavery was non-capitalist and antibourgeois, that it emphasized personal relationships (rather than the impersonal market), that slaves accepted "paternalism" (and therefore accepted some of the premises of slavery), that many (probably most) slaves saw themselves as being part of the master's family or "household," and that there were significant bonds of affection between household members.

In building his interpretation of master-slave relations, Genovese had first put in place (in a series of studies) his ideas on the slaveholders' world view.[16] He considered that masters could not have sustained their world view (of benevolent paternalism, based on the plantation "household" and "family") unless it was reflected to a significant extent in their behavior toward slaves. His class-based analysis of the slaveholders' world view, therefore, drove him to conclude that benevolent paternalism was significant in practice. From this base, it seemed to follow, furthermore, that slave mentalities and culture must have been formed to an important extent by that paternalism. Genovese's work has great ingenuity and sophistication, and reveals much about slaveholders that is of great significance. Nevertheless, there are very important problems when a world-view model is used not just to explain the dominant group's self-image and rationalization process, but to reveal the *behavior* of the dominant group (the slaveholders) and the attitudes of the subordinate group (the slaves).

The real behavior of slaveholders in connection with slave selling and family separations is not hinted at in the slaveholders' world view—but it was probably the most important aspect of the master's behavior, and it had a controlling influence on how slaves thought about masters. Genovese wrote that paternalism was a "fragile bridge" between black and white, and he added that

> Perceived cruelty seems to have been intolerable to society as a whole primarily because it threatened a delicate fabric of implicit duties, the acceptance of which by both masters and slaves alone could keep the regime intact.

On the family specifically, he wrote:

> A master who used the whip too often or with too much vigor risked their [the slaves'] hatred. Masters who failed to respect family sensibilities or who separated husbands from wives would be sure of it. The slaves grieved over the sale of their children but accepted it as a fact of life; however much they suffered, they did not necessarily hate their individual masters for it. But a husband and wife who cared for each other could never accept being parted.

---

[15]Elizabeth Fox-Genovese and Eugene D. Genovese, *Fruits of Merchant Capital: Slavery and Bourgeois Property in the Rise and Expansion of Capitalism* (Oxford, 1983), pp. 136–71.

[16]For early studies, see Eugene D. Genovese, *The Political Economy of Slavery: Studies in the Economy and Society of the Slave South* (New York, 1965); Genovese, *The World the Slaveholders Made: Two Essays in Interpretation* (New York, 1969). See also, for strong emphasis on the masters' world view, Fox-Genovese and Genovese, *Fruits of Merchant Capital*, and Genovese, *The Slaveholders' Dilemma*.

Evidence in the present study suggests that Genovese greatly underestimated the emotional significance of parent-child separations, and this study also demonstrates that he very seriously underestimated the scale of family separations generally. Indeed, the pervasiveness of slave sales and of family separations suggests that the theory of a "delicate web of paternalism" is inappropriate. The "hatred" which Genovese associated with marriage separations must have been very widespread indeed. For a people who (as I try to show later in this study) deeply valued family, separations and the threat of separation must have confined paternalism to something that, although important for the master's self-image, meant very little to the typical slave. Masters in the exporting states routinely cashed in on the natural increase of their "people" by selling slaves to traders who would remove them to the regions where demand was greatest; and in those buying regions masters routinely bought "good young women with first child" and other obviously broken families. Slaveholders and traders respected market prices far more than slave families. A paternal social system based on "delicate compromises" could not have been dominant in a white South which paid so little heed to the black family.[17]

There seems to be no reason to doubt that slaveholders were a confident class, secure in their belief that slavery was legitimate and safe in their conviction that the "peculiar institution" was beneficial to blacks and to civilization. The fact that the slaveholders' attitude to the market in slaves approached quite closely the capitalist hiring and firing process in a crude free-labor market is, however, one reason to wonder whether owners were not, after all, capitalists rather than precapitalists. It seems, too, that racism played a much bigger part in the proslavery literature and in the slaveholders' world view than Genovese suggested. As George Fredrickson found in his work on southern white intellectuals, Negrophobia and racist contempt for blacks were all-pervasive.[18] Indeed, it seems likely that racism—even more than a self-image based on class—was the fundamental basis of slaveholder confidence. Racism meant that whites could act as they wished toward blacks and still feel superior. Furthermore, awareness of the whites' racist contempt, and knowledge that white society saw them and their families in market terms, must have meant that the great majority of slaves had little respect for white values and culture.

Key Slaves and Others

It is true that an important paradox exists between the slaveholders' very widespread use of the term "my family, white and black" and the pervasiveness of slave trading and forcible family separations. The puzzle seems, however, to be resolved when we consider the role of key slaves (defined earlier as a small minority of favored slaves, including especially the driver and his wife, and certain domestics). The notion of key slaves was critically important in the construction and durability of the slaveholders' world view.[19]

---

[17]The Genovese quotations are from *Roll, Jordan, Roll*, pp. 5, 73, 124–25.

[18]See George M. Fredrickson, *Black Image in the White Mind: The Debate on Afro-American Character and Destiny, 1817–1914* (New York, 1971); and Fredrickson's essays, "Masters and Mudsills: The Role of Race in the Planter Ideology of South Carolina," and "The Challenge of Marxism: The Genoveses on Slavery and Merchant Capital," pp. 15–27 and 125–33, in his *The Arrogance of Race: Historical Perspectives on Slavery, Racism, and Social Inequality* (Middletown, Conn., 1988).

[19]The brief comments on key slaves in this section will be developed at length (and with more systematic sampling of probate records and other sources) in my book, provisionally titled *The Worlds of Masters and Slaves* (forthcoming, The University of Wisconsin Press).

In terms of discipline and plantation organization, it made sense to give certain protections to a small number of elite slaves. To preserve their special character, these slaves might, up to a point, be spared the humiliation of whipping and of open criticism by the owner and the white overseer. And for the smooth running of the plantation and of the big house, it made sense to try to keep the families of key slaves together. As we noted earlier, such slaves overwhelmingly predominated among those blacks who, in owners' letters and diaries, were mentioned in any detail. Masters and mistresses, then, needed key slaves for the practical business of being effective slaveholders. There was, however, another even more important level on which they needed key slaves—the level of their self-image. The favoring of key slaves had the critically important role of allowing a slaveholder to tell himself or herself that he or she treated slaves well. The all-important thing was that, by considering that they treated "worthy" and "more sensible" slaves (key slaves) well, they could treat the rest with racist indifference—and could still maintain a self-image of benevolence.

Slaveholder references to "my people" and to "my family, white and black" were part of the language of self-image and rationalization. Sometimes mutual affection might indeed develop between slaveholder and key slave. For his self-image, how-ever, what really mattered was that the patriarch could see himself presiding over a household where all were considered to be part of the "family, white and black"—even though the black family was made up of key slaves, and then of others who were as-sumed to merit much less consideration. The slaveowner might be as interested as any Yankee in profit and enterprise, and he could take the slave trade comfortably in his stride—but, still, he was the patriarch. Still he could be confident that slavery was right, and that he treated his "people" with benevolence.

Slaveholder reminiscences give one indication of the ideological and psychologi-cal role of key slaves for the slaveowner. After the Civil War, "attachment" to key slaves allowed slavery to be fitted comfortably into the southern white heritage—just as in the antebellum period it allowed the slaveholders to sustain a benevolent self-image. Over the half century or so following the ending of slavery, many volumes of romantic white reminiscences of the days of slavery were written, and J. G. Clinkscales's *On the Old Plantation* (1916) is a classic of this type. In such reminiscences, a few key slaves would typically be used to make the case for the benevolent master. "I can say of a truth," Clinkscales wrote, "and for that truth I am profoundly grateful, my father's slaves not only respected and obeyed him but loved him." Of the 110 slaves on this South Carolina plantation, those on whom the story focused were two key slaves—the crippled domestic servant Dick ("a pet on the plantation" who "looked with a kind of contempt upon the ordinary 'field hand'") and the driver, Essex (Unc' Essick). These, we are told, were the slaves with whom Clinkscales, as a boy, had spent much time, and for whom he felt particular affection. The "helpless cripple" Dick had asked to be taught to read, and, even though it was illegal to teach slaves such things, Clinkscales's sisters had consented, because "somehow not a member of the family regarded Dick as a slave." When, as a young lad, Clinkscales had been frightened by talk of fighting and war, he had run to Unc' Essick. Essex soon made him feel safe, and as Clinkscales wrote:

> The faithful guardian pressed me trembling to his great, throbbing heart, and, brushing the tears from my cheeks with his big rough hand, said with

peculiar tenderness: "Nuver min', honey, nuver min'; don' you know if dat big gun bodder dis chile, Unc' Essick chaw it up an' spit it out on de groun'?

Essick, he thought, was a "nobleman in black" and was proof to the world of the loyal "ole-time slav'ry nigger." Clinkscales wrote of his sadness when, after the Civil War, Essex died:

> Need I blush to confess I brushed the tears from my cheek when I heard of the tragic death of Unc' Essick? No reader; if you knew slavery at its best—if you knew the close relationship and tender feeling existing between master and slave on some plantations—then I need not blush.[20]

Diaries of slaveholders were less romantic in their depiction of key slaves, but again and again they point to their special role. The diary of a South Carolina planter, David Gavin, provides an example. His diary, started in 1855 (and running beyond the Civil War), recorded his day-to-day life as a slaveowner (of thirty-five slaves by 1864). Again, in this less self-conscious piece (not apparently written for publication) we find little about individual slaves—with the exceptions of comments on Friday (a trusted octogenarian) and a note on Gavin's waiting-man Little Jim (as well as references to Team, a persistent runaway). We hear about Gavin buying several slaves, and selling several (including two sold to the traders Fly & Witherspoon). We hear about his appraising of estates and of his dividing the slaves into lots and about his chasing runaways with dogs. But, as was usually the case in slaveholders' diaries, we find very little emphasis on affection for slaves. Only on old Friday's death, and when Gavin's waiting-man Little Jim ("a smart, good boy") fell ill do we find hints of anything like close bonds with slaves. On Friday's death, Gavin wrote:

> Old man Friday . . . [had] served my Grandfather and grandmother Gavin. . . . He seemed like a link between me and grandfather and grandmother Gavin for he could talk to and tell me of the actings and doings of them and of others of the olden days.

Friday had been confined to light tasks with the livestock, but had possibly been a driver in earlier years. By 1859, we find that Gavin had, over the years, "buried eleven Negroes," but only Friday's death was given special mention in his diary.[21]

Slaveholders' wills again point to the special position of key slaves and to the protection that they (and sometimes their families) were given. In the late 1850s, the executors of the estate of Dr. E. T. Heriot of South Carolina divided Heriot's slaves among his heirs. At first sight, Heriot appeared to have provided well for his slaves. The executors noted:

> Tom the Driver and Molly his wife are appraised & assigned to this list (No. 1) in order that they may go with their children. They are never to be sold out of the family except it be with their consent first obtained. Under the will they are to be provided for as long as they live.

---

[20]J. G. Clinkscales, On the Old Plantation: Reminiscences of his Childhood (Spartanburg, S.C., 1916), pp. 13, 39–41, 45–50, 1–2, 35.

[21]David Gavin Diary (SHC), especially entries for 13 Sept. 1856, 30 Aug. 1857, 15 Nov. 1859.

Another note indicated that a third slave (Jacob) was also to get special protection, and again Tom and Molly were mentioned. The executors' note stated

> 5th—That Tom, Molly & Jacob, three slaves specially named in the will of the Testator, and commended to the care and kindness of the family shall be appraised . . . separately from the Gang, . . . and shall be permitted to select their individual owners from the heirs, without bias or hindrance.

The full significance of Heriot's will only emerges, however, when one finds that he had owned almost four hundred slaves, spread among several plantations. In other words, he made special provision for less than 1 percent of his slaves. The rest were divided among heirs in lots based on value, except for at least eighty-one, who were sold. These latter, moreover, were nearly all sold to long-distance slave traders—including the speculators Benjamin Mordecai, Ziba Oakes, J. S. Riggs, G. V. Anker, Delap & Co., G. W. Wylly, and A. J. Salinas. By favoring the three key slaves in his will, Heriot no doubt felt that he had done well by his "black family," but the slaves would have known differently.[22]

Only a small minority of slaveholders' wills indicate special protective provisions for any of their slaves. This itself suggests something of the priorities of the head of household between his "white family" (and their pecuniary interests) and his "black family" (and its well-being). But small slaveholders, like major planters of Heriot's rank, sometimes made such provisions. Whatever the size of the slaveholding in such cases, however, one is quite likely to find either that the white family and inheritors ignored any provisions involving substantial financial disadvantage or that the testator himself (or herself) added a proviso that the slaves' interests should be considered only so long as the pecuniary "sacrifice" by the white family would not be too great. The will of Emanuel A. Wingard of South Carolina provides an example. He was a small slaveholder, with just five slaves, and his will provided that two of these slaves should be able to choose their owners at his death. The will recorded that

> I desire and empower my said Executor to sell at private sale for what sums they may decree just and reasonable prices my negro boy (yellow) Alfred or Al as he is generally called, and my negro woman Frances to such person or persons as may be chosen by the above named negroes for their owners or to such other person or persons as they are willing to live with.

The will continued, however:

> I desire and direct that if my said Executors cannot effect a private sale of the above named negroes after a reasonable time given *without too great a sacrifice* [emphasis added] then and in that case my said Executors do have the said Negroes appraised and then sold at public auction to the highest bidder for the same.

[22]Manuscript bound volume 1853–1859 ("Records of Dirleton Plantation by Jas. R. Sparkman"), esp. pp. 44–51; "Articles Agreed by Executors," 24 May 1858; and sale papers of P. J. Porcher & Baya, auctioneers. All of these records are from James Ritchie Sparkman Papers (SCL).

Wingard's other slaves were not to be given any special consideration, and were to be sold to the highest bidder—so that his heirs (the white family, comprising his wife and daughter) would gain immediate advantage. Again, with this sort of case, whites could congratulate themselves that they had looked after their "black family," while the slaves (even the key slaves) would have had reason to see white "affection" and "protective care" differently.[23]

As we have seen then, even for key slaves (who were so important for the slaveholder's self-image), protection was far from being total. Key slaves—drivers and special domestic slaves—were in an awkward position. They were given certain latitude by owners, and might be distrusted by other hands. But they did not necessarily internalize the roles that the owner saw for them; and deep frustration could develop on the part of both owner and key slave. The planter-politician James H. Hammond was aware of these dangers, and tried to avoid them. In his "Plantation Manual," he set out guidelines for running his plantation, and wrote of the driver:

> The head driver is the most important negro on the plantation. . . . He is to be treated with more respect than any other negro by both master & overseer. He is on no occasion to be treated with any indignity calculated to lose the respect of the other negroes without breaking him. He is required to maintain proper discipline at all times, to see that no negro idles or does bad work in the field & to punish it with discretion on the spot.

And Hammond added, significantly, that

> The driver is permitted to visit the master at any time without being required to get a card. . . . He is a confidential agent & may be a guard against any excesses or omissions on the part of the overseer.[24]

If Hammond's driver was ever humiliated before the other slaves, he had, then, to be "broken" (demoted) for the sake of future plantation discipline. The driver needed to be given special privileges, was not to be humiliated, but had to have links with the other slaves (as well as with the master). The driver's situation, thus, was very likely to involve "delicate compromises"; but his position was very different from that of rank-and-file slaves.

All masters who reflected at all about the ethics of slavery needed key slaves—and not just for reasons of practicality (as when drivers supervised and disciplined field hands). They needed them, too, so that their world view as benevolent slaveholders could be kept intact. Although by no means all key slaves completely satisfied their masters' definitions of ideal slaves, their presence as a notional type was vital in satisfying the owners' psychological and ideological needs.[25]

---

[23]"Inventory and Appraisal of all Goods, Chattels, and Personal Estate of Emanuel A. Wingard," and will of Wingard, in Muller Family Papers (SCL).

[24]James H. Hammond, "Plantation Manual [1844]," p. xv, James H. Hammond Papers (SCL).

[25]For numerous examples of rebellious drivers, see William L. Van Deburg, *The Slave Drivers: Black Agricultural Labor Supervisors in the Antebellum South* (Westport, Conn., 1979), esp. pp. 93–112.

    The complex position of key slaves seems to explain some of the most important features of antebellum slavery. The notion of key slaves allowed masters, even if they casually broke up slave families, to maintain positive, benevolent self-images. Through their notion of treating "worthy" (mainly) key slaves with "consideration" and "benevolence" (while treating the "less worthy" rank-and-file with indifference), they could preserve their positive, confident self-images. This meant that slaveowners were not necessarily consciously misleading and hypocritical when they referred to mutual bonds of affection between master and slave. A benevolent self-image was, then, in practice the logical partner to a racist contempt or indifference toward the great mass of slaves. There could be cases of genuine affection between owners and slaves, but the framework established by evidence on the slave trade shows that such cases must have been unusual. Instead, the dominant patterns must have been deep distrust of owners by the great mass of slaves, and a very strictly limited accommodation between masters and slaves. The idea of an "integrated" antebellum past (based on close accommodation under slavery) seems to be largely inaccurate, as, unfortunately, is an integrated present. Sadly, America today is at best desegregated, rather than integrated. Perhaps a necessary step toward a fairer and more integrated future is a recognition of the scale and the long-run nature of nonintegration and of black exclusion.

Source: From Tadman, Michael, *Speculators and Slaves,* © 1996 by the Regents of the University of Wisconsin System. Reprinted by permission of The University of Wisconsin Press.

NARRATIVE OF THE LIFE OF FREDERICK DOUGLASS

Frederick Douglas

I was born in Tuckahoe, near Hillsborough, and about twelve miles from Easton, in Talbot county, Maryland. I have no accurate knowledge of my age, never having seen any authentic record containing it. By far the larger part of the slaves know as little of their ages as horses know of theirs, and it is the wish of most masters within my knowl-edge to keep their slaves thus ignorant. I do not remember to have ever met a slave who could tell of his birthday. They seldom come nearer to it than planting-time, harvest-time, cherry-time, spring-time, or fall-time. A want of information concerning my own was a source of unhappiness to me even during childhood. The white children could tell their ages. I could not tell why I ought to be deprived of the same privilege. I was not allowed to make any inquiries of my master concerning it. He deemed all such in-quiries on the part of a slave improper and impertinent, and evidence of a restless spirit. The nearest estimate I can give makes me now between twenty-seven and twenty-eight years of age. I come to this, from hearing my master say, some time during 1835, I was about seventeen years old.

My mother was named Harriet Bailey. She was the daughter of Isaac and Betsey Bailey, both colored, and quite dark. My mother was of a darker complexion than either my grandmother or grandfather.

My father was a white man. He was admitted to be such by all I ever heard speak of my parentage. The opinion was also whispered that my master was my father; but of the correctness of this opinion, I know nothing; the means of knowing was withheld from me. My mother and I were separated when I was but an infant—before I knew her as my mother. It is a common custom, in the part of Maryland from which I ran away, to part children from their mothers at a very early age. Frequently, before the child has reached its twelfth month, its mother is taken from it, and hired out on some farm a considerable distance off, and the child is placed under the care of an old woman, too old for field labor. For what this separation is done, I do not know, unless it be to hinder the development of the child's affection toward its mother, and to blunt and destroy the natural affection of the mother for the child. This is the inevitable result.

I never saw my mother, to know her as such, more than four or five times in my life; and each of these times was very short in duration, and at night. She was hired by a Mr. Stewart, who lived about twelve miles from my home. She made her journeys to see me in the night, travelling the whole distance on foot, after the performance of her day's work. She was a field hand, and a whipping is the penalty of not being in the field at sunrise, unless a slave has special permission from his or her master to the contrary—a permission which they seldom get, and one that gives to him that gives it the proud name of being a kind master. I do not recollect of ever seeing my mother by the light of day. She was with me in the night. She would lie down with me, and get me to sleep, but long before I waked she was gone. Very little communication ever took place between us. Death soon ended what little we could have while she lived, and with it her hardships and suffering. She died when I was about seven years old, on one of my master's farms, near Lee's Mill. I was not allowed to be present during her illness, at her death, or burial. She was gone long before I knew any thing about it. Never having enjoyed, to any considerable extent, her soothing presence, her tender and watchful care, I received the tidings of her death with much the same emotions I should have probably felt at the death of a stranger.

Called thus suddenly away, she left me without the slightest intimation of who my father was. The whisper that my master was my father, may or may not be true; and, true or false, it is of but little consequence to my purpose whilst the fact remains, in all its glaring odiousness, that slaveholders have ordained, and by law established, that the children of slave women shall in all cases follow the condition of their mothers; and this is done too obviously to administer to their own lusts, and make a gratification of their wicked desires profitable as well as pleasurable; for by this cunning arrangement, the slaveholder, in cases not a few, sustains to his slaves the double relation of master and father.

I know of such cases; and it is worthy of remark that such slaves invariably suffer greater hardships, and have more to contend with, than others. They are, in the first place, a constant offence to their mistress. She is ever disposed to find fault with them; they can seldom do any thing to please her; she is never better pleased than when she sees them under the lash, especially when she suspects her husband of showing to his mulatto children favors which he withholds from his black slaves. The master is frequently compelled to sell this class of his slaves, out of deference to the feelings of his white wife; and, cruel as the deed may strike any one to be, for a man to sell his own children to human flesh-mongers, it is often the dictate of humanity for him to do so; for, unless he does this, he must not only whip them himself, but must stand by and see one white son tie up his brother, of but few shades darker complexion than himself, and ply the gory lash to his naked back; and if he lisp one word of disapproval, it is set down to his parental partiality, and only makes a bad matter worse, both for himself and the slave whom he would protect and defend.

Every year brings with it multitudes of this class of slaves. It was doubtless in consequence of a knowledge of this fact, that one great statesman of the south predicted the downfall of slavery by the inevitable laws of population. Whether this prophecy is ever fulfilled or not, it is nevertheless plain that a very different-looking class of people are springing up at the south, and are now held in slavery, from those originally brought to this country from Africa; and if their increase will do no other good, it will do away the force of the argument, that God cursed Ham, and therefore American slavery is right. If the lineal descendants of Ham are alone to be scripturally enslaved, it is certain that slavery at the south must soon become unscriptural; for thousands are ushered into the world, annually, who, like myself, owe their existence to white fathers, and those fathers most frequently their own masters.

I have had two masters. My first master's name was Anthony. I do not remember his first name. He was generally called Captain Anthony—a title which, I presume, he acquired by sailing a craft on the Chesapeake Bay. He was not considered a rich slaveholder. He owned two or three farms, and about thirty slaves. His farms and slaves were under the care of an overseer. The overseer's name was Plummer. Mr. Plummer was a miserable drunkard, a profane swearer, and a savage monster. He always went armed with a cowskin and a heavy cudgel. I have known him to cut and slash the women's heads so horribly, that even master would be enraged at his cruelty, and would threaten to whip him if he did not mind himself. Master, however, was not a humane slaveholder. It required extraordinary barbarity on the part of an overseer to affect him. He was a cruel man, hardened by a long life of slaveholding. He would at times seem to take great pleasure in whipping a slave. I have often been awakened at the dawn of day by the most heart-rending shrieks of an own aunt of mine, whom he used to tie up to a joist, and whip upon her naked back till she was literally covered with blood. No words, no tears, no prayers, from his gory victim, seemed to move his iron heart from its bloody purpose. The louder she screamed, the harder he whipped; and where the blood ran fastest, there he whipped longest. He would whip her to make her scream, and whip her to make her hush; and not until overcome by fatigue, would he cease to swing the blood-clotted cowskin. I remember the first time I ever witnessed this horrible exhibition. I was quite a child, but I well remember it. I never shall forget it whilst I remember any thing. It was the first of a long series of such outrages, of which I was doomed to be a witness and a participant. It struck me with awful force. It was the blood-stained gate, the entrance to the hell of slavery, through which I was about to pass. It was a most terrible spectacle. I wish I could commit to paper the feelings with which I beheld it.

This occurrence took place very soon after I went to live with my old master, and under the following circumstances. Aunt Hester went out one night,—where or for what I do not know,—and happened to be absent when my master desired her presence. He had ordered her not to go out evenings, and warned her that she must never let him catch her in company with a young man, who was paying attention to her, belonging to Colonel Lloyd. The young man's name was Ned Roberts, generally called Lloyd's Ned. Why master was so careful of her, may be safely left to conjecture. She was a woman of noble form and of graceful proportions, having very few equals, and fewer superiors, in personal appearance, among the colored or white women of our neighborhood.

Aunt Hester had not only disobeyed his orders in going out, but had been found in company with Lloyd's Ned; which circumstance, I found, from what he said while whipping her, was the chief offence. Had he been a man of pure morals himself, he might have been thought interested in protecting the innocence of my aunt; but those who knew him will not suspect him of any such virtue. Before he commenced whipping Aunt Hester, he took her into the kitchen, and stripped her from neck to waist, leaving her neck, shoulders, and back, entirely naked. He then told her to cross her hands, calling her at the same time a d——d b——h. After crossing her hands, he tied them with a strong rope, and led her to a stool under a large hook in the joist, put in for the purpose. He made her get upon the stool, and tied her hands to the hook. She now stood fair for his infernal purpose. Her arms were stretched up at their full length, so that she stood upon the ends of her toes. He then said to her, "Now, you d——d b——h, I'll learn you how to disobey my orders!" and after rolling up his sleeves, he commenced to lay on the heavy cowskin, and soon the warm, red blood (amid heart-rending shrieks from her, and horrid oaths from him) came dripping to the floor. I was so terrified and horror-stricken at the sight, that I hid myself in a closet, and dared not venture out till long after the bloody transaction was over. I expected it would be my turn next. It was all new to me. I had never seen any thing like it before. I had always lived with my grandmother on the outskirts of the plantation, where she was put to raise the children of the younger women. I had therefore been, until now, out of the way of the bloody scenes that often occurred on the plantation.

My master's family consisted of two sons, Andrew and Richard; one daughter, Lucretia, and her husband, Captain Thomas Auld. They lived in one house, upon the home plantation of Colonel Edward Lloyd. My master was Colonel Lloyd's clerk and superintendent. He was what might be called the overseer of the overseers. I spent two years of childhood on this plantation in my old master's family. It was here that I witnessed the bloody transaction recorded in the first chapter; and as I received my first impressions of slavery on this plantation, I will give some description of it, and of slavery as it there existed. The plantation is about twelve miles north of Easton, in Talbot county, and is situated on the border of Miles River. The principal products raised upon it were tobacco, corn, and wheat. These were raised in great abundance; so that, with the products of this and the other farms belonging to him, he was able to keep in almost constant employment a large sloop, in carrying them to market at Baltimore. This sloop was named Sally Lloyd, in honor of one of the colonel's daughters. My master's son-in-law, Captain Auld, was master of the vessel; she was otherwise manned by the colonel's own slaves. Their names were Peter, Isaac, Rich, and Jake. These were esteemed very highly by the other slaves, and looked upon as the privileged ones of the plantation; for it was no small affair, in the eyes of the slaves, to be allowed to see Baltimore.

Colonel Lloyd kept from three to four hundred slaves on his home plantation, and owned a large number more on the neighboring farms belonging to him. The names of the farms nearest to the home plantation were Wye Town and New Design. "Wye Town" was under the overseership of a man named Noah Willis. New Design was under the overseership of a Mr. Townsend. The overseers of these, and all the rest of the farms, numbering over twenty, received advice and direction from the managers of the home plantation. This was the great business place. It was the seat of government for the whole twenty farms. All disputes among the overseers were settled here. If a slave was convicted of any high misdemeanor, became unmanageable, or evinced a determination to run away, he was brought immediately here, severely whipped, put on board the sloop, carried to Baltimore, and sold to Austin Woolfolk, or some other slave-trader, as a warning to the slaves remaining.

Here, too, the slaves of all the other farms received their monthly allowance of food, and their yearly clothing. The men and women slaves received, as their monthly allowance of food, eight pounds of pork, or its equivalent in fish, and one bushel of corn meal. Their yearly clothing consisted of two coarse linen shirts, one pair of linen trousers, like the shirts, one jacket, one pair of trousers for winter, made of coarse negro cloth, one pair of stockings, and one pair of shoes; the whole of which could not have cost more than seven dollars. The allowance of the slave children was given to their mothers, or the old women having the care of them. The children unable to work in the field had neither shoes, stockings, jackets, nor trousers, given to them; their clothing consisted of two coarse linen shirts per year. When these failed them, they went naked until the next allowance-day. Children from seven to ten years old, of both sexes, almost naked, might be seen at all seasons of the year.

There were no beds given the slaves, unless one coarse blanket be considered such, and none but the men and women had these. This, however, is not considered a very great privation. They find less difficulty from the want of beds, than from the want of time to sleep; for when their day's work in the field is done, the most of them having their washing, mending, and cooking to do, and having few or none of the ordinary facilities for doing either of these, very many of their sleeping hours are consumed in preparing for the field the coming day; and when this is done, old and young, male and female, married and single, drop down side by side, on one common bed,—the cold, damp floor,—each covering himself or herself with their miserable blankets; and here they sleep till they are summoned to the field by the driver's horn. At the sound of this, all must rise, and be off to the field. There must be no halting; every one must be at his or her post; and woe betides them who hear not this morning summons to the field; for if they are not awakened by the sense of hearing, they are by the sense of feeling: no age nor sex finds any favor. Mr. Severe, the overseer, used to stand by the door of the quarter, armed with a large hickory stick and heavy cowskin, ready to whip any one who was so unfortunate as not to hear, or, from any other cause, was prevented from being ready to start for the field at the sound of the horn.

Mr. Severe was rightly named: he was a cruel man. I have seen him whip a woman, causing the blood to run half an hour at the time; and this, too, in the midst of her crying children, pleading for their mother's release. He seemed to take pleasure in manifesting his fiendish barbarity. Added to his cruelty, he was a profane swearer. It was enough to chill the blood and stiffen the hair of an ordinary man to hear him talk. Scarce a sentence escaped him but that was commenced or concluded by some horrid oath. The field was the place to witness his cruelty and profanity. His presence made it both the field of blood and of blasphemy. From the rising till the going down of the sun, he was cursing, raving, cutting, and slashing among the slaves of the field, in the most frightful manner. His career was short. He died very soon after I went to Colonel Lloyd's; and he died as he lived, uttering, with his dying groans, bitter curses and horrid oaths. His death was regarded by the slaves as the result of a merciful providence.

Mr. Gore was proud, ambitious, and persevering. He was artful, cruel, and obdurate. He was just the man for such a place, and it was just the place for such a man. It afforded scope for the full exercise of all his powers, and he seemed to be perfectly at home in it. He was one of those who could torture the slightest look, word, or gesture, on the part of the slave, into impudence, and would treat it accordingly. There must be no answering back to him; no explanation was allowed a slave, showing himself to have been wrongfully accused. Mr. Gore acted fully up to the maxim laid down by slaveholders,—"It is better that a dozen slaves suffer under, the lash, than that the overseer should be convicted, in the presence of the slaves, of having been at fault." No matter how innocent a slave might be—it availed him nothing, when accused by Mr. Gore of any misdemeanor. To be accused was to be convicted, and to be convicted was to be punished; the one always following the other with immutable certainty. To escape punishment was to escape accusation; and few slaves had the fortune to do either, under the overseership of Mr. Gore. He was just proud enough to demand the most debasing homage of the slave, and quite servile enough to crouch, himself, at the feet of the master. He was ambitious enough to be contented with nothing short of the highest rank of overseers, and persevering enough to reach the height of his ambition. He was cruel enough to inflict the severest punishment, artful enough to descend to the lowest trickery, and obdurate enough to be insensible to the voice of a reproving conscience. He was, of all the overseers, the most dreaded by the slaves. His presence was painful, his eye flashed confusion; and seldom was his sharp, shrill voice heard, without producing horror and trembling in their ranks.

Mr. Gore was a grave man, and, though a young man, he indulged in no jokes, said no funny words, seldom smiled. His words were in perfect keeping with his looks, and his looks were in perfect keeping with his words. Overseers will sometimes indulge in a witty word, even with the slaves; not so with Mr. Gore. He spoke but to command,

and commanded but to be obeyed; he dealt sparingly with his words, and bountifully with his whip, never using the former where the latter would answer as well. When he whipped, he seemed to do so from a sense of duty, and feared no consequences. He did nothing reluctantly, no matter how disagreeable; always at his post, never inconsistent. He never promised but to fulfil. He was, in a word, a man of the most inflexible firmness and stone-like coolness.

His savage barbarity was equalled only by the consummate coolness with which he committed the grossest and most savage deeds upon the slaves under his charge. Mr. Gore once undertook to whip one of Colonel Lloyd's slaves, by the name of Demby. He had given Demby but few stripes, when, to get rid of the scourging, he ran and plunged himself into a creek, and stood there at the depth of his shoulders, refusing to come out. Mr. Gore told him that he would give him three calls, and that, if he did not come out at the third call, he would shoot him. The first call was given. Demby made no response, but stood his ground. The second and third calls were given with the same result. Mr. Gore then, without consultation or deliberation with any one, not even giving Demby an additional call, raised his musket to his face, taking deadly aim at his standing victim, and in an instant poor Demby was no more. His mangled body sank out of sight, and blood and brains marked the water where he had stood.

A thrill of horror flashed through every soul upon the plantation, excepting Mr. Gore. He alone seemed cool and collected. He was asked by Colonel Lloyd and my old master, why he resorted to this extraordinary expedient. His reply was (as well as I can remember) that Demby had become unmanageable. He was setting a dangerous example to the other slaves,—one which, if suffered to pass without some such demonstration on his part, would finally lead to the total subversion of all rule and order upon the plantation. He argued that if one slave refused to be corrected, and escaped with his life, the other slaves would soon copy the example; the result of which would be, the freedom of the slaves, and the enslavement of the whites. Mr. Gore's defence was satisfactory. He was continued in his station as overseer upon the home plantation. His fame as an overseer went abroad. His horrid crime was not even submitted to judicial investigation. It was committed in the presence of slaves, and they of course could neither institute a suit, nor testify against him; and thus the guilty perpetrator of one of the bloodiest and most foul murders goes unwhipped of justice, and uncensured by the community in which he lives. Mr. Gore lived in St. Michael's, Talbot county, Maryland, when I left there; and if he is still alive, he very probably lives there now; and if so, he is now, as he was then, as highly esteemed and as much respected as though his guilty soul had not been stained with his brother's blood.

I speak advisedly when I say this,—that killing a slave, or any colored person, in Talbot county, Maryland, is not treated as a crime, either by the courts or the community. Mr. Thomas Lanman, of St. Michael's, killed two slaves, one of whom he killed with a hatchet, by knocking his brains out. He used to boast of the commission of the awful and bloody deed. I have heard him do so laughingly, saying, among other things, that he was the only benefactor of his country in the company, and that when others would do as much as he had done, we should be relieved of "the d—d niggers."

The wife of Mr. Giles Hick, living but a short distance from where I used to live, murdered my wife's cousin, a young girl between fifteen and sixteen years of age, mangling her person in the most horrible manner, breaking her nose and breastbone with a stick, so that the poor girl expired in a few hours afterward. She was immediately buried, but had not been in her untimely grave but a few hours before she was taken up and examined by the coroner, who decided that she had come to her death by severe beating. The offence for which this girl was thus murdered was this:—She had been set that night to mind Mrs. Hick's baby, and during the night she fell asleep, and the baby cried. She, having lost her rest for several nights previous, did not hear the crying. They were both in the room with Mrs. Hicks. Mrs. Hicks, finding the girl slow to move, jumped from her bed, seized an oak stick of wood by the fireplace, and with it broke the girl's nose and breastbone, and thus ended her life. I will not say that this most horrid murder produced no sensation in the community. It did produce sensation, but not enough to bring the murderess to punishment. There was a warrant issued for her arrest, but it was never served. Thus she escaped not only punishment, but even the pain of being arraigned before a court for her horrid crime.

Whilst I am detailing bloody deeds which took place during my stay on Colonel Lloyd's plantation, I will briefly narrate another, which occurred about the same time as the murder of Demby by Mr. Gore.

Colonel Lloyd's slaves were in the habit of spending a part of their nights and Sundays in fishing for oysters, and in this way made up the deficiency of their scanty allowance. An old man belonging to Colonel Lloyd, while thus engaged, happened to get beyond the limits of Colonel Lloyd's, and on the premises of Mr. Beal Bondly. At this trespass, Mr. Bondly took offence, and with his musket came down to the shore, and blew its deadly contents into the poor old man.

Mr. Bondly came over to see Colonel Lloyd the next day, whether to pay him for his property, or to justify himself in what he had done, I know not. At any rate, this whole fiendish transaction was soon hushed up. There was very little said about it at all, and nothing done. It was a common saying, even among little white boys, that it was worth a half-cent to kill a "nigger," and a half-cent to bury one.

Source: Andrews, William L., Henry Gates Jr. (2000). *Slave Narratives.* Library of America. pp. 281–288, 295–298.

INCIDENTS IN THE LIFE OF A SLAVE GIRL

Harriet A. Jacobs

There was a planter in the country, not far from us, whom I will call Mr. Litch. He was an ill-bred, uneducated man, but very wealthy. He had six hundred slaves, many of whom he did not know by sight. His extensive plantation was managed by well-paid overseers. There was a jail and a whipping post on his grounds; and whatever cruelties were perpetrated there, they passed without comment. He was so effectually screened by his great wealth that he was called to no account for his crimes, not even for murder.

Various were the punishments resorted to. A favorite one was to tie a rope round a man's body, and suspend him from the ground. A fire was kindled over him, from which was suspended a piece of fat pork. As this cooked, the scalding drops of fat continually fell on the bare flesh. On his own plantation, he required very strict obedience to the eighth commandment. But depredations on the neighbors were allowable, provided the culprit managed to evade detection or suspicion. If a neighbor brought a charge of theft against any of his slaves, he was browbeaten by the master, who assured him that his slaves had enough of every thing at home, and had no inducement to steal. No sooner was the neighbor's back turned, than the accused was sought out, and whipped for his lack of discretion. If a slave stole from him even a pound of meat or a peck of corn, if detection followed, he was put in chains and imprisoned, and so kept till his form was attenuated by hunger and suffering.

A freshet once bore his wine cellar and meat house miles away from the plantation. Some slaves followed, and secured bits of meat and bottles of wine. Two were detected; a ham and some liquor being found in their huts. They were summoned by their master. No words were used, but a club felled them to the ground. A rough box was their coffin, and their interment was a dog's burial. Nothing was said.

Murder was so common on his plantation that he feared to be alone after nightfall. He might have believed in ghosts.

His brother, if not equal in wealth, was at least equal in cruelty. His bloodhounds were well trained. Their pen was spacious, and a terror to the slaves. They were let loose on a runaway, and, if they tracked him, they literally tore the flesh from his bones. When this slaveholder died, his shrieks and groans were so frightful that they appalled his own friends. His last words were, "I am going to hell; bury my money with me."

After death his eyes remained open. To press the lids down, silver dollars were laid on them. These were buried with him. From this circumstance, a rumor went abroad that his coffin was filled with money. Three times his grave was opened, and his coffin taken out. The last time, his body was found on the ground, and a flock of buzzards were pecking at it. He was again interred, and a sentinel set over his grave. The perpetrators were never discovered.

Cruelty is contagious in uncivilized communities. Mr. Conant, a neighbor of Mr. Litch, returned from town one evening in a partial state of intoxication. His body servant gave him some offence. He was divested of his clothes, except his shirt, whipped, and tied to a large tree in front of the house. It was a stormy night in winter. The wind blew bitterly cold, and the boughs of the old tree crackled under falling sleet. A member of the family, fearing he would freeze to death, begged that he might be taken down; but the master would not relent. He remained there three hours; and, when he was cut down, he was more dead than alive. Another slave, who stole a pig from this master, to appease his hunger, was terribly flogged. In desperation, he tried to run away. But at the end of two miles, he was so faint with loss of blood, he thought he was dying. He had a wife, and he longed to see her once more. Too sick to walk, he crept back that long distance on his hands and knees. When he reached his master's, it was night. He had not strength to rise and open the gate. He moaned, and tried to call for help. I had a friend living in the same family. At last his cry reached her. She went out and found the prostrate man at the gate. She ran back to the house for assistance, and two men returned with her. They carried him in, and laid him on the floor. The back of his shirt was one clot of blood. By means of lard, my friend loosened it from the raw flesh. She bandaged him, gave him cool drink, and left him to rest. The master said he deserved a hundred more lashes. When his own labor was stolen from him, he had stolen food to appease his hunger. This was his crime.

Another neighbor was a Mrs. Wade. At no hour of the day was there cessation of the lash on her premises. Her labors began with the dawn, and did not cease till long after night-fall. The barn was her particular place of torture. There she lashed the slaves with the might of a man. An old slave of hers once said to me, "It is hell in missis's house. 'Pears I can never get out. Day and night I prays to die:"

The mistress died before the old woman, and, when dying, entreated her husband not to permit any one of her slaves to look on her after death. A slave who had nursed her children, and had still a child in her care, watched her chance, and stole with it in her arms to the room where lay her dead mistress. She gazed a while on her, then raised her hand and dealt two blows on her face, saying, as she did so, "The devil is got you *now*!" She forgot that the child was looking on. She had just begun to talk; and she said to her father, "I did see ma, and mammy did strike ma, so," striking her own face with her little hand. The master was startled. He could not imagine how the nurse could obtain access to the room where the corpse lay; for he kept the door locked. He questioned her. She confessed that what the child had said was true, and told how she had procured the key. She was sold to Georgia.

In my childhood I knew a valuable slave, named Charity, and loved her, as all children did. Her young mistress married, and took her to Louisiana. Her little boy, James, was sold to a good sort of master. He became involved in debt, and James was sold again to a wealthy slaveholder, noted for his cruelty. With this man he grew up to manhood, receiving the treatment of a dog. After a severe whipping, to save himself from further infliction of the lash, with which he was threatened, he took to the woods. He was in a most miserable condition—cut by the cowskin, half naked, half starved, and without the means of procuring a crust of bread.

Some weeks after his escape, he was captured, tied, and carried back to his master's plantation. This man considered punishment in his jail, on bread and water, after receiving hundreds of lashes, too mild for the poor slave's offence. Therefore he decided, after the overseer should have whipped him to his satisfaction, to have him placed between the screws of the cotton gin, to stay as long as he had been in the woods. This wretched creature was cut with the whip from his head to his feet, then washed with strong brine, to prevent the flesh from mortifying, and make it heal sooner than it other wise would. He was then put into the cotton gin, which was screwed down, only allowing him room to turn on his side when he could not lie on his back. Every morning a slave was sent with a piece of bread and bowl of water, which were placed within reach of the poor fellow. The slave was charged, under penalty of severe punishment, not to speak to him.

Four days passed, and the slave continued to carry the bread and water. On the second morning, he found the bread gone, but the water untouched. When he had been in the press four days and five nights, the slave informed his master that the water had not been used for four mornings, and that a horrible stench came from the gin house. The overseer was sent to examine into it. When the press was unscrewed, the dead body was found partly eaten by rats and vermin. Perhaps the rats that devoured his bread had gnawed him before life was extinct. Poor Charity! Grandmother and I often asked each other how her affectionate heart would bear the news, if she should ever hear of the murder of her son. We had known her husband, and knew that James was like him in manliness and intelligence. These were the qualities that made it so hard for him to be a plantation slave. They put him into a rough box, and buried him with less feeling than would have been manifested for an old house dog. Nobody asked any questions. He was a slave; and the feeling was that the master had a right to do what he pleased with his own property. And what did *he* care for the value of a slave? He had hundreds of them. When they had finished their daily toil, they must hurry to eat their little morsels, and be ready to extinguish their pine knots before nine o'clock, when the overseer went his patrol rounds. He entered every cabin, to see that men and their wives had gone to bed together, lest the men, from over-fatigue, should fall asleep in the chimney corner, and remain there till the morning horn called them to their daily task. Women are considered of no value, unless they continually increase their owner's stock. They are put on a par with animals. This same master shot a woman through the head, who had run away and been brought back to him. No one called him to account for it. If a slave resisted being whipped, the bloodhounds were unpacked, and set upon him, to tear his flesh from his bones. The master who did these things was highly educated, and styled a perfect gentleman. He also boasted the name and standing of a Christian, though Satan never had a truer follower.

I could tell of more slaveholders as cruel as those I have described. They are not exceptions to the general rule. I do not say there are no humane slaveholders. Such characters do exist, notwithstanding the hardening influences around them. But they are "like angels' visits—few and far between."

I knew a young lady who was one of these rare specimens. She was an orphan, and inherited as slaves a woman and her six children. Their father was a free man. They had a comfortable home of their own, parents and children living together. The mother and eldest daughter served their mistress during the day, and at night returned to their dwelling, which was on the premises. The young lady was very pious, and there was some reality in her religion. She taught her slaves to lead pure lives, and wished them to enjoy the fruit of their own industry. *Her* religion was not a garb put on for Sunday, and laid aside till Sunday returned again. The eldest daughter of the slave mother was promised in marriage to a free man; and the day before the wedding this good mistress emancipated her, in order that her marriage might have the sanction of *law*.

Report said that this young lady cherished an unrequited affection for a man who had resolved to marry for wealth. In the course of time a rich uncle of hers died. He left six thousand dollars to his two sons by a colored woman, and the remainder of his property to this orphan niece. The metal soon attracted the magnet. The lady and her weighty purse became his. She offered to manumit her slaves—telling them that her marriage might make unexpected changes in their destiny, and she wished to insure their happiness. They refused to take their freedom, saying that she had always been their best friend, and they could not be so happy any where as with her. I was not surprised. I had often seen them in their comfortable home, and thought that the whole town did not contain a happier family. They had never felt slavery; and, when it was too late, they were convinced of its reality.

When the new master claimed this family as his property, the father became furious, and went to his mistress for protection. "I can do nothing for you now, Harry," said she. "I no longer have the power I had a week ago. I have succeeded in obtaining the freedom of your wife; but I cannot obtain it for your children." The unhappy father swore that nobody should take his children from him. He concealed them in the woods for some days; but they were discovered and taken. The father was put in jail, and the two oldest boys sold to Georgia. One little girl, too young to be of service to her master, was left with the wretched mother. The other three were carried to their master's plantation. The eldest soon became a mother; and, when the slaveholder's wife looked at the babe, she wept bitterly. She knew that her own husband had violated the purity she had so carefully inculcated. She had a second child by her master, and then he sold her and his offspring to his brother. She bore two children to the brother, and was sold again. The next sister went crazy. The life she was compelled to lead drove her mad. The third one became the mother of five daughters. Before the birth of the fourth the pious mistress died. To the last, she rendered every kindness to the slaves that her unfortunate circumstances permitted. She passed away peacefully, glad to close her eyes on a life which had been made so wretched by the man she loved.

This man squandered the fortune he had received, and sought to retrieve his affairs by a second marriage; but, having retired after a night of drunken debauch, he was found dead in the morning. He was called a good master; for he fed and clothed his slaves better than most masters, and the lash was not heard on his plantation so frequently as on many others. Had it not been for slavery, he would have been a better man, and his wife a happier woman.

No pen can give an adequate description of the all-pervading corruption produced by slavery. The slave girl is reared in an atmosphere of licentiousness and fear. The lash and the foul talk of her master and his sons are her teachers. When she is fourteen or fifteen, her owner, or his sons, or the overseer, or perhaps all of them, begin to bribe her with presents. If these fail to accomplish their purpose, she is whipped or starved into submission to their will. She may have had religious principles inculcated by some pious mother or grandmother, or some good mistress; she may have a lover, whose good opinion and peace of mind are dear to her heart; or the profligate men who have power over her may be exceedingly odious to her. But resistance is hopeless.

"The poor worm
Shall prove her contest vain. Life's little day
Shall pass, and she is gone!"

The slaveholder's sons are, of course, vitiated, even while boys, by the unclean influences every where around them. Nor do the master's daughters always escape. Severe retributions sometimes come upon him for the wrongs he does to the daughters of the slaves. The white daughters early hear their parents quarrelling about some female slave. Their curiosity is excited, and they soon learn the cause. They are attended by the young slave girls whom their father has corrupted; and they hear such talk as should never meet youthful ears, or any other ears. They know that the women slaves are subject to their father's authority in all things; and in some cases they exercise the same authority over the men slaves. I have myself seen the master of such a household whose head was bowed down in shame; for it was known in the neighborhood that his daughter had selected one of the meanest slaves on his plantation to be the father of his first grandchild. She did not make her advances to her equals, nor even to her father's more intelligent servants. She selected the most brutalized, over whom her authority could be exercised with less fear of exposure. Her father, half frantic with rage, sought to revenge himself on the offending black man; but his daughter, foreseeing the storm that would arise, had given him free papers, and sent him out of the state.

In such cases the infant is smothered, or sent where it is never seen by any who know its history. But if the white parent is the *father*, instead of the mother, the off-spring are unblushingly reared for the market. If they are girls, I have indicated plainly enough what will be their inevitable destiny.

You may believe what I say; for I write only that whereof I know. I was twenty one years in that cage of obscene birds. I can testify, from my own experience and ob-servation, that slavery is a curse to the whites as well as to the blacks. It makes the white fathers cruel and sensual; the sons violent and licentious; it contaminates the daughters, and makes the wives wretched. And as for the colored race, it needs an abler pen than mine to describe the extremity of their sufferings, the depth of their degradation.

Yet few slaveholders seem to be aware of the widespread moral ruin occasioned by this wicked system. Their talk is of blighted cotton crops—nor of the blight on their children's souls.

If you want to be fully convinced of the abominations of slavery, go on a southern plantation, and call yourself a negro trader. Then there will be no concealment; and you will see and hear things that will seem to you impossible among human beings with immortal souls.

Source: Jacobs, Harriet A. (1861). *Incidents in the Life of a Slave Girl*, Written by Herself. Edited by L. Maria Child. Andrews, William L., Henry Gates Jr. (2000). *Slave Narratives*. Library of America. pp. 791–798.

CHAPTER 3

Concentration Camps

The term "concentration camp" is generally used as the generic descriptor for all institutionalized camps constructed and maintained by the Nazi regime. Historically this term has referred to a collection or concentration of people in a restricted area "who are detained or confined, usually under harsh conditions and without regard to legal norms of arrest and imprisonment that are acceptable in a constitutional democracy" (United States Holocaust Memorial Museum, n.d.). In fact, the types of camps used by the Nazi regime were varied and included prisoner of war camps, labor camps, transit camps and extermination or death camps. It should be noted that the Nazi propaganda machine disseminated information on the use of concentration camps by the British in the Boer War (1899–1902). This was a component of their anti-Western posturing and their attempt to justify their construction of the camps as centers of preventive detention. As such, there was no need for the Nazis to conceal the existence of the concentration camp as compared to their attempts to conceal the *extermination* camps. The construction and use of the numerous Nazi concentration camps can be delineated into the following three time periods: 1933 to 1936, 1936 to 1942 and 1942 to 1944–1945 (Yad Vashem, n.d., pp. 1–3).

The first concentration camp in National Socialist Germany was set up in March 1933 in Dachau, an area close to the city of Munich. By that time, the many local prisons could no longer accommodate the thousands of individuals detained by the Nazis who had been "arrested in 'preventive' measures to eliminate 'threats from subversive elements.' . . . By the summer of 1933 there were ten or more camps and detention centers . . . with over 25,000 inmates—Social Democrats, Communists, members of other opposition parties, journalists and writers (especially Jews), and various other 'unpopular' categories" (Dawidowicz, 1976, p. 100).

The Enabling Act of March 1933 had given Hitler the "legal authority for dictatorship . . . [and] the government the power for four years to promulgate legislation even if it deviated from the Constitution" (Dawidowicz, 1976, p. 68).

As noted in the first chapter reading by Bettelheim, during this first period those imprisoned included not only political enemies but also the "work shy," Jehovah's

Witnesses and other "asocial elements" (e.g. Gypsies and homosexuals) in the German population. The primary goal during this first phase of incarceration was preventive detention in an effort to crush all opposition to the Nazi regime.

During the second period in this chronology (1936–1942), most of the camps used during the first period were closed, with the exception of Dachau. In his detailed sociological analysis of the concentration camp, Wolfgang Sofsky (1997) notes that Dachau was the first camp that was regulated and controlled exclusively by the German secret police known as the SS. He further comments that Dachau "served as the paragon for the reorganization of the entire system of concentration camps" (p. 32), in that it became the "paradigm for the everyday practice of terror, which the camp personnel was able to carry out according to its own experience, habits, and whim" (p. 32). Both Sofsky and Bettelheim discuss some of the differences between the various concentration camps and the extermination or death camps which were built to implement the "Final Solution," the annihilation of the Jewish community. As suggested previously, the Nazis made every effort to hide the death camps. While the existence of the concentration camp was well known, its operational activities were shrouded in "secrecy, mystery and innuendos" in an effort to terrorize the population and increase its deterrent effect on those who might oppose the government. Bettelheim (1952/1980) cautions that "because this method of control through terror and secrecy was so effective in Nazi Germany, there is danger that it may be used again" (p. 41).

Sofsky (1997) posits that the "distinctive feature of the concentration camp [is] absolute power that has broken free, fundamentally and totally, from the familiar forms of social power." He notes that "the concentration camp demolished the central concepts of civilization, the ideals of reason, progress, freedom, and understanding" (p. 10). While clearly recognizing the numerous historical instances of mass murders and killings perpetrated in the name of politics, wars etc., he sees the concentration camp as the "locus of organized terror and extermination . . . an invention of the twentieth century. What remains historically unique and unparalleled is the state-initiated and industrially organized mass annihilation of Jews and Gypsies by the Germans" (pp. 11–12). In his analysis of the creation of the extermination/death camps, he states that

> the setting up of death factories, to which an entire people, from infants to the aged, was transported over thousands of kilometers to be obliterated without a trace and "exploited as raw material" was not just a new mode of murder; it represented a climactic high point in the negative history of social power and modern organization (p. 12).

In Dachau and in many other camps, including Buchenwald, Auschwitz and Majdanek, Jews were forced to engage in hard labor, often for private companies, under the harshest of conditions. The Auschwitz complex was the largest of its kind and included three camps, all of which had forced labor. In addition, it was "[c]hosen as the central location for the annihilation of the Jewish people" (Yad Vashem, n.d.). Later, the camp inmates were used primarily for activities relating to the German war effort. The Jewish prisoners "were beaten relentlessly by supervisors and were subjected to reduced and pilfered food rations by staff at all levels. Deprived of medicines and exposed to ceaseless brutality, more than half a million Jews died in the labor camps" (Yad Vashem, n.d.).

In November of 1938, a sixteen-year-old Polish Jew, Herschel Grynszpan, assassinated a staff member of the German embassy in Paris. His parents were part of a group of approximately 17,000 Polish Jews who had been deported from Germany and were left to languish in a no-mans-land on the German–Polish border. His attempted act of revenge, in turn, provided the rationale for a government-inspired pogrom against the Jews known as Kristallnacht or Night of Broken Glass. In fact, it is evident that plans for such a pogrom had been developed well in advance. On that evening in numerous German towns and cities, Jewish synagogues, institutions, businesses and homes were burned to the ground. Many Jews were killed and approximately thirty thousand Jewish men were sent to Buchenwald, Dachau and Sachsenhausen (Dawidowicz, 1976, p. 136). Jews were now to be sent to concentration camps simply because they were Jews. Additionally, after the German invasion of the Soviet Union in June 1941, "tens of thousands of Soviet prisoners of war were imprisoned in Nazi concentration camps, and subsequently murdered" (Yad Vashem, n.d.).

In pursuit of the *Final Solution*, the Nazis built the first extermination camp, Chelmno, in Poland in December 1941 and began to liquidate Jews in gas vans. In March 1942, three additional death camps with permanent gas chambers—Belzec, Sobibor and Treblinka—were built adjacent to railroad tracks to accelerate the extermination. Approximately 1,700,000 Polish Jewish men, women and children were killed in these three camps (Yad Vashem, n.d.). An additional camp, Majdanek, was established in late 1941, for Soviet prisoners of war and as a concentration camp for Poles. The gas chambers and crematoria were built in 1942. In the spring of that year, thousands of Jews, Slovaks, Czechs, Germans and Poles were murdered in Majdanek. Approximately 78,000 people were murdered in Majdanek.

Extermination continued until late 1944 in Chelmno, Majdanek and Auschwitz. "The gas chambers in the Auschwitz complex constituted the largest and most efficient extermination method employed by the Nazis . . . approximately one million Jews had been murdered there" (Yad Vashem, n.d.). In addition, several hundred thousand Poles, Sinti and Roma and people of various nationalities were murdered there. Approximately 6 million Jews or two-thirds of European Jewry were killed during the Holocaust (Yad Vashem, n.d.).

The chapter continues with a series of readings that include several of the standard, most powerful and frequently cited accounts of survival in the camps. The concluding article is a compelling narrative of the unique experiences of female camp inmates.

In Bettelheim's (1943) discussion of behavior in extreme situations, he posits that as long as the concentration camp experiences fell within the "normal frame of reference of a prisoner's life experience, [they] were dealt with by means of normal psychological mechanisms" (p. 433). If, however, one's experience, "transcended this frame of reference, . . . new psychological mechanisms were needed" (p. 433). Bettelheim suggests that the extreme nature of an experience produced in the individual a "split" between the subjective "me" who actually experienced the event and the objective "me" who had stepped outside of the experience to become "an interested but detached observer" (p. 434). This "split" allowed the prisoner to detach his emotions from the extreme situation and free himself, if only temporarily, from the horror of the experience.

Bettelheim asserts that the prisoners' debasing experiences caused them to "regress" into infantile and childlike behavior such that they were consumed by the need for immediate gratification and not able to project into the future. Bettelheim cautions that his observations are "preliminary" and suggests that the impact of the concentration camp on both the prisoners and its Gestapo keepers has implications for the individual in mass society. Concerted action is needed to break the shackles of totalitarian control whose goal is to objectify and transform its citizens into a state of "childlike dependency" on its leaders. He suggests that only through the resistance and strength of productive and democratic group solidarity can the person prevent the "disintegration" of one's individuality.

Terrence Des Pres's (1976) description of excremental assault, the deliberate attack on the relationship between bodily function and human behavior in the concentration camp is one of the most powerful portrayals of the degradation, humiliation and mortification imposed by the Nazis on its victims. The horrific contaminative exposure and destruction of adult self-determination in regards to excretory functions was compounded by the pervasive suffering of dysentery and "while prisoners in the Nazi camps were virtually drowning in their own waste . . . death by excrement was common" (p. 58).

Des Pres takes exception with the analysis put forth by Bettelheim and others that the extreme nature of the camp experience produced a regression to "childlike" or "infantile" behaviors, and a "fixation on pre-oedipal stages" (p. 56) (e.g. obsession with excretory activity). Des Pres contends that while in fact "the prisoners were forced to wet and soil themselves" (p. 57), this was a function of the aberrant situational forces and context of the camp such that their "action was not the index of infantile wishes but of response to hideous necessity" (p. 57). In other words, their behavior was not a "regression," but rather an adaptive behavioral response to a milieu of "sub-human" proportion. Des Pres further posits that the deliberate objectification, dehumanization and destruction of self-esteem of the prisoners allowed the SS to become desensitized to the prisoners' "humanity," thus neutralizing any guilt or other feelings that might inhibit one's murderous behavior. In the face of these debasements, the prisoners knew that in order to survive, they had to attend to what might otherwise be the most mundane detail of physical appearance in an effort to restore their human dignity.

Finally, Des Pres reemphasizes his criticism of the assumptions made by Stanley Elkins, Bettelheim and others regarding "infantile regression," "survival egotism" and the dissolution of all "prior standards" of behavior. Des Pres concludes that in fact "social bonding" between prisoners was clearly evident, acts of great courage to save others were numerous and adaptations to the camp experience were a product of informed, practical and considered choices (pp. 151–155).

In his standard text *Man's Search for Meaning* (1959/1985), Viktor Frankl posits the following distinction between his "therapeutic doctrine," *logotherapy*, and the more traditional Freudian psychoanalysis: ". . . logotherapy, in comparison with psychoanalysis, is a method less *retrospective* and less *introspective*. Logotherapy focuses rather on the future, that is to say, on the meaning to be fulfilled by the patient in his future. . . . [I]n logotherapy the patient is actually confronted with and reoriented toward the meaning of his life" (p. 120).

In his analysis of the concentration camp experience, Frankl identifies three distinct "phases of the inmate's mental reaction to camp life . . . the period following his admission; the period when he is well entrenched in camp routine; and the period following his release and liberation" (p. 26). While Frankl describes the "shock" experienced during the first stage, he also talks of the inmates' feelings of "cold curiosity" which allow for an experiential detachment from their surroundings. This defensive maneuver is similar to Bettelheim's discussion of the "split" between the subjective "me" and the objective "me" who has stepped outside of the experience. Frankl observes that in the second stage of the inmate's mental reaction he experiences, "[a]pathy, the blunting of the emotions and the feeling that one could not care anymore . . . [by] means of this insensibility the prisoner soon surrounded himself with a very necessary protective shell . . ." (p. 42). "Reality dimmed, and all efforts and all emotions were centered on one task: preserving one's own life and that of the other fellow" (p. 47).

Notwithstanding the fact that the inmates were propelled into a world of primitive thoughts and desires with only their dreams providing some ephemeral refuge and relief, Frankl suggests that "it was possible for spiritual life to deepen . . . [where] they were able to retreat from their terrible surrounding to a life of inner riches and spiritual freedom" (p. 55). According to Frankl, man has the capacity to move beyond even the most debasing and debilitating sociological, psychological and physical pain, and capture a deep "spiritual freedom" which will ultimately give purpose and meaning to one's life. Frankl expresses great optimism in man's ability to locate freedom in the private domain of one's mind that is accessible only to the individual and to no one else. While human beings can be forced to do certain things, they cannot be forced to adopt another's attitude toward what they are doing. Frankl emphasizes the importance of identifying a future goal that could lift the person out of his degrading paralysis, find deeper meaning in his suffering and strengthen his "spiritual hold." "The prisoner who had lost faith in the future—his future—was doomed. With his loss of belief in the future he also lost his spiritual hold; he let himself decline and became subject to mental and physical decay" (p. 95). Frankl concludes this reading with an affirmation of man's individuality in the identification and pursuit of his unique goals, meaning and purpose in life.

In the preface to his classic work, *Survival in Auschwitz* (1958/1996), Primo Levi comments on the urgent and cathartic need for the survivor to write of his experience:

> The need to tell our story to "the rest," to make "the rest" participate in it, had taken on for us, before our liberation and after, the character of an immediate and violent impulse, to the point of competing with our elementary needs. The book has been written to satisfy this need: first and foremost, therefore, as an interior liberation (p. 9).

Referring to the concentration camp by its German name, *Lager*, Levi speaks of the "drowned and the saved," those who have fallen into a perpetual state of decay and those who could find salvation and be saved. Levi describes the breakdown of the moral order in the camp, the extreme isolation and aloneness of its captives and their consequent adaptive techniques

> to he that has, will be given; from he that has not, will be taken away. In the *Lager*, where man is alone and where the struggle for life is reduced to its primordial mechanism, this unjust law is openly in force, is recognized by all (pp. 88–89).

Levi describes the drowned, the *muselmann*, as pitiful creatures destined to be consumed and forgotten in the fires of the crematoria. The German word *muselmann*

> refer[s] to prisoners who are near death due to exhaustion, starvation or hopelessness . . . many victims, totally lacking the wherewithal to adapt, reached this stage soon after arrival in a camp . . . ; they were lethargic, indifferent to their surroundings, and could not stand up for more than a short period of time (Yad Vashem, n.d.).

It has been suggested by some that the term "muselmann" "originated from the similarity between the near-death prone state of a concentration camp *Muselmann* and the image of a Muslim prostrating himself on the ground in prayer" (Yad Vashem, n.d.).

Levi then comments on the tenacity, inner strength and resourcefulness of those who were able to survive. Generally, this was made possible only by the suspension of one's conscience and morality. "Survival without renunciation of any part of one's own moral world . . . was conceded only to very few superior individuals, made of the stuff of martyrs and saints" (p. 92). Levi's brilliant and prosaic anecdotal accounts of the survival mechanisms of several individuals illuminate their varied and often atavistic paths to salvation in the perverse world of Auschwitz.

Myrna Goldenberg's (1996) reading on women's holocaust narratives suggests that while female survivors did share similar experiences with their male counterparts, their stories of survival reveal their unique "double" victimization as both female and Jewish. She asserts that the backdrop for this double marginality was grounded in a Nazi ideology that was misogynistic, patriarchal and racist. Goldenberg provides searing narratives of sexual violence, sadism and degradation that are central themes of women's oral histories. In addition, she notes the horrific choices and events confronting women that resulted from pregnancy and childbirth. At the same time, however, the oral histories describe the vital role that friendship networks, mutual bonding and resourcefulness played in creating "surrogate families" which sustained an "alternative social structure of women's values" that contributed to their survival. Finally, Goldenberg states that while some Holocaust scholars and survivors are not supportive of a gender-specific analysis, she emphasizes the importance of feminist values as a foundation for understanding and improving individual and communal development.

GERMAN CONCENTRATION CAMPS

Bruno Bettelheim

It is difficult to remember today, when thinking of the German concentration camps, that there were a variety of camps, with quite different purposes. The unfathomable horror of the death camps, with their gas chambers in which millions were asphyxiated, overshadows the memory of the other camps and the innumerable murders committed in them as well. According to the best estimates, between 5.5 and 6 million Jews were killed by the Germans, most of them in the gas chambers of the death camps, in addition to vast numbers of Poles, Gypsies, and others considered undesirable by the Nazis.[1] When the death camps were organized in December of 1941, the gas chambers had not yet been used, but there had been precursors—mobile vans in which people were killed by the exhaust from the engines. The concentration camps as an institution by this time already had quite an abominable history of their own.

The first concentration camps were established immediately after the Nazis came to power in 1933; these were not yet for the purpose of killing those whom the Nazis considered undesirables—although quite a few of them were murdered in somewhat haphazard fashion all along—but mainly to terrorize those who might try to oppose the Nazis, and also to spread terror of retribution for opposition among the rest of the German population. The Nazis hoped to force all Germans to turn themselves into willing and obedient subjects of the Nazi Reich. So they maintained all along to some degree the fiction that the purpose of these camps was to reeducate opponents of the regime, and to destroy those who resisted such reeducation. A third, large group of camps came into being during the war, for the purpose of providing German industry with extremely cheap, readily expendable, and practically unpaid foreign slave labor.[2]

Possibly because my own concentration camp experience antedates the inception of the "Final Solution of the Jewish Problem," with its carefully planned and systematically executed murder of all persons of Jewish descent, I have been concerned in my writings mainly with the meaning of the concentration camp phenomenon and its consequences rather than with the incredibly greater abomination of the death camps. But something else also contributed to this choice.

---

[1] There is considerable literature on this. Two books may be mentioned which state the facts concerning the extermination of European Jewry: Raul Hilberg, *The Destruction of the European Jews* (Chicago: Quadrangle Books, 1961), and Lucy S. Dawidowicz, *The War Against the Jews, 1933–1945* (New York: Holt, Rinehart and Winston, 1975).

[2] From the ample literature on the concentration camps for so-called political prisoners again two books may be cited: Eugen Kogon, *The Theory and Practice of Hell: The Concentration Camps and the System Behind Them* (New York: Farrar, Straus, 1950), whose original German title, *The SS State*, indicates more accurately its scope, and my *The Informed Heart* (New York: The Free Press, 1960). The most complete accounts of all concentration camps, including the death and slave labor camps, are contained in International Military Tribunal, *Trial of the Major War Criminals Before the International Military Tribunal: Official Text*, 42 vols. (Nuremberg, 1947–49). Further, see Office of the United States Chief of Counsel for the Prosecution of Axis Criminality, *Nazi Conspiracy and Aggression*, 11 vols. (Washington, D.C., 1946–48). (Both publications include incidentally my depositions as a witness.)

Of the three types of camps, the slave labor camps—terrible as they were—present the least interesting problems. They were not all that different from the worst of other slave labor situations known throughout history. Given the totalitarian nature of the Nazi state, and the ruthless and near-absolute power of the SS, conditions in the slave labor camps were much worse than those prevalent in even very bad prison labor camps, because the inmates did not enjoy even those small human considerations and the significant protections of the law which are the prerogatives of common criminals. But dreadful as life in the slave labor camps was, these camps did not present new or unique theoretical or psychological problems. Quite the opposite is true for the Nazi death camps, and for the concentration camps.

The death camps were established for the one purpose of perpetrating the "Final Solution of the Jewish Problem," that is, killing all Jews within reach in the most efficient manner possible. The destruction of the Jews, of the Gypsies—of whom about 100,000 were murdered—and of some other groups also considered racially inferior and thus dangerous to the superiority and purity of the German race, was the consequence of paranoic delusions peculiar to Hitler with which he infected his followers—although this could not so easily have led to the destruction of millions had it not drawn support from centuries old prejudices, discrimination, and hatred, and had not masses of Hitler's followers made this delusion their own, as expressed, among many other ways, in the often-chanted slogan "Awake, Germany! Exterminate the Jews!" (*Deutschland erwache! Juda verrecke!*) In any event, terrible as it was that those given to fantasies about a pure Aryan race had the absolute power to act them out by destroying millions of hapless victims over much of Europe, I am optimistic enough to believe that there is little likelihood of a similar concatenation of circumstances ever again conspiring so that a parallel delusion will lead to an analogous destruction of millions.

I am not equally sanguine in regard to the possible use of the concentration camps as a means to establish total control in a mass society because of the fact that very similar concentration camp systems were spontaneously created for the same purpose by the two otherwise radically different totalitarian mass societies: Leninist and Stalinist Russia, and Hitler's Germany. In both countries these institutions were administered along very similar lines by a secret police.

Although the concentration camps were sometimes located in the same places as the death camps, and although they incidentally provided slave labor (including Jews) for the SS, their purpose was to terrorize, and through the anxiety thus created, permit the state to control all that its subjects did and thought. The specific method used to make the concentration camp an instrument for controlling the entire population was this terror shrouded in secrecy, which vastly increases its power to create incapacitating anxiety. Thus, the existence of concentration camps as the places where opponents of the regime were severely punished was widely and frequently advertised, but what went on in the camps was only suggested through fear-creating innuendos. (Quite the opposite was true for the death camps; more serious—albeit mostly ineffective—efforts were made to keep secret and covert their existence and purpose.)

When before the war sizable numbers of Jews were imprisoned in the concentration camps, this was done to terrorize all Jews so that they would emigrate immediately and leave all their possessions behind—which nearly all did who were psychologically able to contemplate leaving everything behind and starting life anew in a foreign land, and who had the strength to arrange for their move, or to induce others to help them do so—even though in many cases the only places which would accept them were those they would not have chosen, had they had a choice.[3] The large number of Jews who did leave Germany after they, their relatives, or their friends had been imprisoned in the camps illustrates once more the effectiveness of the concentration camp as an instrument of total control not only over the prisoners, but also over the rest of the population. The terror of the concentration camps as a means of altering behavior, and with it attitudes and even personality, is an inherent potential of a technologically oriented totalitarian mass society when its anti-humanistic tendencies are no longer tempered by moral or religious scruples.

Self-interest demands that each person try to reduce his anxiety as much as possible; the best way to do so in a mass state is to become a willing and obedient subject of the state, which means doing the state's bidding all on one's own. Just because this method of control through terror and secrecy was so effective in Nazi, Germany, there is danger that it may be used again.

Some Facts about German Concentration Camps[*]

Until 1933, concentration camps had never been deliberately employed by a government to intimidate its own subjects except by Stalinist Russia. The German National Socialist government was therefore the first Western regime to use them as a major instrument for establishing control and ensuring its continuation in power. Because the camps were new inventions of the regime, no rules or regulations inherited from the German republic interfered with their organization. Moreover, the camps were entirely under the control of the secret state police, removed from any interference by any other governmental institutions such as the courts, which might have exercised a mitigating influence.

The history of the camps, as central institutions of the government, followed closely that of the National Socialist state, and changes reflected developments in the dictatorship itself. Whenever the regime felt threatened, the tools safeguarding it were used more viciously and extensively. As the regime expanded and encompassed all of Germany's life, the concentration camps increased also in size and purpose. The camps then became used for goals not contemplated when they were first established. As time passed, the old types of concentration camps could no longer fulfill the various purposes assigned to them, and new types were developed. During the regime's decline, the camps reflected the disintegration and chaos of a government which was no longer able to control even its central institutions of power.

---

[3] During various periods it was quite possible to enter some Central American countries, at least for a limited time; and up to the beginning of the war it was fairly easy to go to Shanghai, although for penniless newcomers it was very difficult to earn a living there.

[*]What follows are selected and updated parts of an article, "Concentration Camps, German," which appeared in *10 Eventful Years,* Vol. 2 (Chicago: Encyclopaedia Britannica, Inc., 1947), pp. 1–12.

At least three factors combined in influencing the history of the concentration camp: the history of the regime itself and the various needs it tried to meet by means of the concentration camps; the independent development of the concentration camps as institutions; and, finally, the counter-actions of the prisoners in the camps.

Legally, the creation of the concentration camps was indirectly based on the German constitution, which in its article 48, paragraph 2, gave the president far-reaching emergency powers. These were used by Paul von Hindenburg in 1933 to promulgate a law permitting protective custody (*Schutzhaft*) to protect the state's security. An edict from the Ministry of the Interior of April 12, 1934, introduced into the rules governing protective custody legal grounds for establishment of the camps. It also decreed that persons sent to a concentration camp came under the jurisdiction of the gestapo and that their release was at its discretion. Later, courts ruled that such prisoners could have no access to the courts.

The administration of the law for protecting people and state was entrusted to the secret state police, *Geheime Staats Polizei*, whose name was shortened to the use of the first letters of each word so that it became known as the gestapo. The gestapo never gave any public account of its activities, did not tell why anybody had been imprisoned, never told for how long; and did not even inform prisoners' relations as to whether their kin were still alive—all to increase terrorization through secrecy and uncertainty. It was staffed by the most trusted and fanatic followers of Hitler, the SS troops. Later, when the SS expanded, elite formations were created whose officers administered and ruled the concentration camps while the soldiers served as guards. These specially selected and trained soldiers of the secret state police (*Schutz Staffeln*, hence SS) wore as a distinctive insignia a skull (death's-head) and from this were known as the death's-head (*Totenkopf*) units. The insignia signified both their inhumanity and their commitment to kill and die unhesitatingly for the Reich.

At first only the regime's political enemies were brought into the camps, and from among them, only those who could not be prosecuted successfully in the courts of law. But soon others were included, when it seemed undesirable for the government to make public their imprisonment or any specific grounds for it.

As soon as the Nazi party was securely entrenched in power the situation changed, because then former left-wing opponents were no longer the most dangerous foes of the government. In 1934, the radical element within the party, including followers of Ernst Roehm, became the first party members to enter the concentration camps which some of them had helped create.

The next group considered troublesome included those who opposed what was then the party's main task—preparation for war. Therefore, pacifists, conscientious objectors, and so-called "work-shy" persons were sent to the concentration camps.

The ideology of the Germans as *the* superior race, which became a central concept of the party, was soon reflected in the constituency of the camps. Persons of so-called non-Aryan race who had sexual relations with members of the German "race" were either prosecuted in the courts or sent to the concentration camps. Later, when the party decided to prosecute them, homosexual prisoners were added since these persons had all committed so-called racial crimes, and were considered race polluters.

Defection and disobedience among the SS and within the party were even more dangerous to the regime than opposition outside it. Therefore, the concentration camps came into more use against restive party members themselves.

At the beginning of 1938, there were less than 30,000 prisoners in the German concentration camps. At that time the two main camps were at Dachau, near Munich, with about 6,000 prisoners, and at Sachsenhausen, near Berlin, with about 8,000 inmates. To them had been recently added the camp at Buchenwald, near Weimar, which at that time had about 2,000 inmates. There were also a few quite small camps, one of them at Ravensbrück for women. There were also a probably equally large number of political prisoners in the regular jails, where they were treated much better, pretty much as prisoners are treated in jails in the rest of the world.

Up to 1938 most prisoners in the concentration camps were political opponents of the Nazis. The rest consisted of several hundred persons charged with being "work-shy"; a few hundred conscientious objectors, most of them Jehovah's Witnesses; less than 500 Jewish prisoners, many of them "race polluters"; a few so-called incorrigible criminals; and a miscellaneous group of less than 100 which included such persons as former members of the French Foreign Legion who had returned to Germany and were considered traitors because they had accepted service under a foreign power.

Within months of the annexation of Austria, in the spring of 1938, the population of the camp at Dachau, for example, increased from not quite 6,000 to well over 9,000. All in all, during 1938 some 60,000 prisoners were added to the camp population. From 1939 on, the number of concentration camp prisoners grew steadily at an ever-increasing rate. More and more Jews were brought into the camps to force all of them to get out of Germany. In an obvious preparation for war, the gestapo tried to incarcerate or intimidate all those inhabitants of Germany who might oppose or impede the war effort. From then on, the character of the camps' populations changed; the number of Jewish, asocial, and criminal prisoners increased much faster than that of political prisoners.

The racial and eugenic notions of National Socialist ideology exercised their influence on the camps as early as 1937. At that time, a few prisoners, mostly so-called sex offenders (homosexuals, rapists, Jews who had had sexual relations with gentile women without being married to them), were sterilized. Later, beginning in 1940, prisoners who were deemed incurably sick, or insane, were killed. Thereafter, the policy intended to improve the race was implemented in the camps by exterminating persons who were considered to carry undesirable genes. While all exterminations were the result of racial dogmas, the use of the extermination camps on a large scale was probably not envisaged when such doctrines were first developed.

The first racial "problem" attacked on a large scale was that of the Jews, culminating in the huge pogroms in the fall of 1938 and the transportation of tens of thousands of Jews into the then-existing concentration camps. During the war, both the desire to execute the racial policy and the fear of having Jews living in German cities spread. So the Jews were first forced to live in ghettos, and later sent to the camps, mainly to the extermination camps built in what had been Poland.

From the beginning of the war in September of 1939, a policy of decimation was inaugurated, mainly for the Jews as "the enemies of the German people," for the

Gypsies as carriers of particularly undesirable genes, and for the Polish and Russian elite who might possibly threaten Germany's hegemony on conquered lands. The tools used in the camps were inadequate food and shelter, exhaustingly hard labor, absence of medical care, and so on; but during the first years of the war actual murder, although frequent, was partly selective and partly unsystematic.

The last step was inaugurated with the establishment of the extermination camps. Experiments with the gas chamber had started at the Oswiecim (Auschwitz) camp near Cracow. Extermination was in full swing in July 1942; it was finally stopped in September 1944, on orders from Berlin in the hope of thus gaining more favorable peace terms. Nobody knows how many had died by then in the camps. The estimates vary from 11,000,000 (which official East German sources consider the lowest reasonable estimate) to well over 18,000,000; according to the most reliable estimates, between 5.5 and 6 million of these were Jews. Aside from the extermination camps, in which practically everybody died, the best guess is that from 1933 until 1945 1,600,000 were sent to the non-extermination concentration camps, of whom at least 1,180,000 died. At best 530,000 survived the various camps, and many of these died after liberation from the after-effects of what had happened to them while in the camps.[4]

Each of the concentration camps had its separate history, with better and worse periods, with emphasis on one rather than another of the manifold purposes for which the camps were created and used by the gestapo. Thus, for instance, conditions in Dachau in 1938 were typical for the then-existing concentration camps. Buchenwald, from its founding late in 1937 until 1939, was the worst of all the camps. But from 1942 until its total disintegration during 1944/45 (due to Allied bombings), Buchenwald was one of the best, and so was Dachau from about 1943 on. In general, the concentration camps located in Germany proper and in Czechoslovakia (at Theresienstadt, for example) fared better during the later war years, while conditions were worst in those camps located in occupied Polish territory.

---

[4] Since the extermination camps and most of the concentration camps were located either in Poland or in what is now East Germany, and since many of the surviving archives are located there, East German sources seem most reliable. As mentioned above, according to them the lowest reasonable estimate of the number of prisoners murdered in the concentration and extermination camps is 11,000,000. (*Meyers Neues Lexikon* [Leipzig: Bibliographisches Institut, 1974].)

According to West German sources, while there were 60,000 prisoners in the concentration camps at the end of 1938 and 100,000 in 1942, their number had swollen to 715,000 in 1945, at which time 40,000 SS were assigned to rule the various camps. In 1945 there were about 20 concentration camps, and, either connected with them or separate from them, some 165 slave labor camps. Auschwitz was all three: an extermination, a concentration, and a slave labor camp. So it might be of interest that according to the commander of this camp, from its inception until December 1, 1943 (that is, long before it was abandoned) 2,500,000 were murdered there—mainly in the gas chambers—while an additional 500,000 died of starvation, exhaustion, or sickness. (*Meyers Enzyklopädisches Lexikon*, 1975.) The German estimates are close to the French, since according to the *Encyclopedia Universalis* (Paris, 1968) at least 12,000,000 died in the concentration and extermination camps.

According to the *Encyclopaedia Britannica* (15th ed., 1974), "It is estimated that in all the camps of Germany and its occupied territories, 18,000,000 to 26,000,000 persons—prisoners of war, political prisoners, and nationals of occupied and invaded countries—were put to death through hunger, cold, pestilence, torture, medical experimentation, and other means of extermination such as gas chambers."

INDIVIDUAL AND MASS BEHAVIOR IN EXTREME SITUATIONS

Bruno Bettelheim

The Adaptation to the Camp Situation

Differences in the Response to Extreme and to Suffering Experiences

It seems that camp experiences which remained within the normal frame of reference of a prisoner's life experience were dealt with by means of the normal psychological mechanisms. Once the experience transcended this frame of reference, the normal mechanisms seemed no longer able to deal adequately with it and new psychological mechanisms were needed. The experience during the transportation was one of those transcending the normal frame of reference and the reaction to it may be described as "unforgettable, but unreal."

The prisoners' dreams were an indication that the extreme experiences were not dealt with by the usual mechanisms. Many dreams expressed aggression against Gestapo members, usually combined with wish fulfillment in such a way that the prisoner was taking his revenge on them. Interestingly enough, the reason he took revenge on them—if a particular reason could be ascertained—was always for some comparatively small mistreatment, never an extreme experience. The author had had some previous experience concerning his reaction to shocks in dreams. He expected that his dreams after the transportation would follow the pattern of repetition of the shock in dreams, the shock becoming less vivid and the dream finally disappearing. He was astonished to find that in his dreams the most shocking events did not appear. He asked many prisoners whether they dreamed about the transportation and he was unable to find a single one who could remember having dreamed about it.

Attitudes similar to those developed toward the transportation could be observed in other extreme situations. On a terribly cold winter night when a snow storm was blowing, all prisoners were punished by being forced to stand at attention without overcoats—they never wore any—for hours.[1] This, after having worked for more than 12 hours in the open, and having received hardly any food. They were threatened with having to stand all through the night. After about 20 prisoners had died from exposure the discipline broke down. The threats of the guards became ineffective. To be exposed to the weather was a terrible torture; to see one's friends die without being able to help, and to stand a good chance of dying, created a situation similar to the transportation, except that the prisoners had by now more experience with the Gestapo. Open resistance was impossible, as impossible as it was to do anything definite to safeguard oneself. A feeling of utter indifference swept the prisoners. They did not care whether the guards shot them; they were indifferent to acts of torture committed by the guards. The guards had no longer any authority, the spell of fear and death was broken. It was again as if what happened did not "really" happen to oneself. There was again the split

---

[1] The reason for this punishment was that two prisoners had tried to escape. On such occasions all prisoners were always punished very severely, so that in the future they would give away secrets they had learned, because otherwise they would have to suffer. The idea was that every prisoner ought to feel responsible for any act committed by any other prisoner. This was in line with the principle of the Gestapo to force the prisoners to feel and act as a group, and not as individuals.

between the "me" to whom it happened and the "me" who really did not care and was just an interested but detached observer. Unfortunate as the situation was, they felt free from fear and therefore were actually happier than at most other times during their camp experiences.

Whereas the extremeness of the situation probably produced the split mentioned above, a number of circumstances concurred to create the feeling of happiness in the prisoners. Obviously it was easier to withstand unpleasant experiences when all found themselves in "the same boat." Moreover, since everybody was convinced that his chances to survive were slim, each felt more heroic and willing to help others than he would feel at other moments when helping others might endanger him. This helping and being helped raised the spirits. Another factor was that they were not only free of the fear of the Gestapo, but the Gestapo had actually lost its power, since the guards seemed reluctant to shoot all prisoners.[2] After more than 80 prisoners had died, and several hundred had their extremities so badly frozen that they had later to be amputated, the prisoners were permitted to return to the barracks. They were completely exhausted, but did not experience that feeling of happiness which some of them had expected. They felt relieved that the torture was over, but felt at the same time that they no longer were free from fear and no longer could strongly rely on mutual help. Each prisoner as an individual was now comparatively safer, but he had lost the safety originating in being a member of a unified group. This event was again freely discussed, in a detached way, and again the discussion was restricted to facts; the prisoners' emotions and thoughts during this night were hardly ever mentioned. The event itself and its details were not forgotten, but no particular emotions were attached to them; nor did they appear in dreams.

The psychological reactions to events which were somewhat more within the sphere of the normally comprehensible were decidedly different from those to extreme events. It seems that prisoners dealt with less extreme events in the same way as if they had happened outside of the camp. For example, if a prisoner's punishment was not of an unusual kind, he seemed ashamed of it, he tried not to speak about it. A slap in one's face was embarrassing, and not to be discussed. One hated individual guards who had kicked one, or slapped one, or verbally abused one much more than the guard who really had wounded one seriously. In the latter case one eventually hated the Gestapo as such, but not so much the individual inflicting the punishment. Obviously this differentiation was unreasonable, but it seemed to be inescapable. One felt deeper and more violent aggressions against particular Gestapo members who had committed minor vile acts than one felt against those who had acted in a much more terrible fashion.

The following tentative interpretation of this strange phenomenon should be accepted with caution. It seems that all experiences which might have happened during the prisoner's "normal" life history provoked a "normal" reaction. Prisoners seemed, for instance, particularly sensitive to punishments similar to those which a parent might inflict on his child. To punish a child was within their "normal" frame of reference, but that they should become the object of the punishment destroyed their adult frame of reference. So they reacted to it not in an adult, but in a childish way—with

---

[2] This was one of the occasions in which the antisocial attitudes of certain middle-class prisoners became apparent. Some of them did not participate in the spirit of mutual help, some even tried to take advantage of others for their own benefit.

embarrassment and shame, with violent, impotent, and unmanageable emotions directed, not against the system, but against the person inflicting the punishment. A contributing factor might have been that the greater the punishment, the more could one expect to receive friendly support which exerted a soothing influence. Moreover, if the suffering was great, one felt more or less like a martyr, suffering for a cause, and the martyr is supposed not to resent his martyrdom.

This, incidentally, raises the question as to which psychological phenomena make it possible to submit to martyrdom and which are those leading others to accept it as such. This problem transcends the frame of this presentation, but some observations pertinent to it may be mentioned. Prisoners who died under tortures *qua* prisoners, although martyrs to their political conviction, were not considered martyrs. Those who suffered due to efforts to protect others were accepted as martyrs. The Gestapo was usually successful in preventing the creation of martyrs, due either to insight into the psychological mechanisms involved or to its anti-individualistic ideology. If a prisoner tried to protect a group, he might have been killed by a guard, but if his action came to the knowledge of the camp administration then the whole group was always more severely punished than it would have been in the first place. In this way the group came to resent the actions of its protector because it suffered under them. *The protector was thus prevented from becoming a leader, or a martyr, around whom group resistance might have been formed.*

Let us return to the initial question of why prisoners resented minor vile acts on the part of the guards more than extreme experiences. It seems that if a prisoner was cursed, slapped, pushed around "like a child" and if he was, like a child, unable to defend himself, this revived in him behavior patterns and psychological mechanisms which he had developed when a child. Like a child he was unable to see his treatment in the general context of the behavior of the Gestapo and hated the individual Gestapo member. He swore that he was going "to get even" with him, well knowing that this was impossible. He could develop neither a detached attitude nor an objective evaluation which would have led him to consider his suffering as minor when compared with other experiences. The prisoners as a group developed the same attitude to minor sufferings; not only did they not offer any help, on the contrary they blamed the prisoner who suffered for having brought about his suffering by his stupidity of not making the right reply, of letting himself get caught, of not being careful enough, in short accused him of having behaved like a child. So the degradation of the prisoner by means of being treated like a child took place not only in his mind, but in the minds of his fellow prisoners, too. This attitude extended to small details. So, for instance, a prisoner did not resent being cursed by the guards when it occurred during an extreme experience, but he hated the guards for similar cursing, and was ashamed of suffering from it, when it occurred during some minor mistreatment. It should be emphasized that as time went on the difference in the reaction to minor and major sufferings slowly seemed to disappear. This change in reaction was only one of many differences between old and new prisoners. A few others ought to be mentioned.

Hopes about Life after Liberation

Closely connected with the prisoners' beliefs about, and attitudes toward, their families were their beliefs and hopes concerning their life after release from camp. Here the prisoners embarked a great deal on individual and group daydreams. To indulge in them was one of the favorite pastimes if the general emotional climate in the camp was not too depressed. There was a marked difference between the daydreams of the new and the old prisoners. *The longer the time a prisoner had spent in camp, the less true to reality were his daydreams*; so much so that the hopes and expectations of the old prisoners often took the form of eschatological or messianic hopes; this was in line with their expectation that only such an event as the end of the world would liberate them. They would daydream of the coming world war and world revolution. They were convinced that out of this great upheaval they would emerge as the future leaders of Germany at least, if not of the world. This was the least to which their sufferings entitled them. These grandiose expectations were coexistent with great vagueness as to their future private lives. In their daydreams they were certain to emerge as the future secretaries of state, but they were less certain whether they would continue to live with their wives and children. Part of these daydreams may be explained by the fact that they seemed to feel that only a high public position could help them to regain their standing within their families.

The hopes and expectations of the new prisoners about their future lives were much more true to reality. Despite their open ambivalence about their families, they never doubted that they were going to continue to live with them just where they had left off. They hoped to continue their public and professional lives in the same way as they used to live them.

Most of the adaptations to the camp situation mentioned so far were more or less individual behaviors, according to our definition. The changes discussed in the next section, namely, the regression to infantile behavior, was according to our definition a mass phenomenon. The writer is of the opinion—partly based on introspection, and partly on discussions with the few other prisoners who realized what was happening—that this regression would not have taken place if it had not happened in all prisoners. Moreover, whereas the prisoners did not interfere with another's daydreams or with his attitudes to his family, they asserted their power as a group over those prisoners who objected to deviations from normal adult behavior. They accused those who would not develop a childlike dependency on the guards as threatening the security of the group, an accusation which was not without foundation, since the Gestapo always punished the group for the misbehavior of individual members. This regression into childlike behavior was, therefore, even more inescapable than other types of behavior imposed on the individual by the impact of the conditions in the camp.

Regression into Infantile Behavior

The prisoners developed types of behavior which are characteristic of infancy or early youth. Some of these behaviors developed slowly, others were immediately imposed on the prisoners and developed only in intensity as time went on. Some of these more or less infantile behaviors have already been discussed, such as ambivalence to one's family, despondency, finding satisfaction in daydreaming rather than in action.

Whether some of these behavior patterns were deliberately produced by the Gestapo is hard to ascertain. Others were definitely produced by it, but again we do not know whether it was consciously done. It has been mentioned that even during the transportation the prisoners were tortured in a way in which a cruel and domineering father might torture a helpless child; here it should be added that the prisoners were also debased by techniques which went much further into childhood situations. They were forced to soil themselves. In the camp the defecation was strictly regulated; it was one of the most important daily events, discussed in great detail. During the day the prisoners who wanted to defecate had to obtain the permission of the guard. It seemed as if the education to cleanliness would be once more repeated. It seemed to give pleasure to the guards to hold the power of granting or withholding the permission to visit the latrines. (Toilets were mostly not available.) This pleasure of the guards found its counterpart in the pleasure the prisoners derived from visiting the latrines, because there they usually could rest for a moment, secure from the whips of the overseers and guards. They were not always so secure, because sometimes enterprising young guards enjoyed interfering with the prisoners even at these moments.

The prisoners were forced to say "thou" to one another, which in Germany is indiscriminately used only among small children. They were not permitted to address one another with the many titles to which middle- and upper-class Germans are accustomed. On the other hand, they had to address the guards in the most deferential manner, giving them all their titles.

The prisoners lived, like children, only in the immediate present; they lost the feeling for the sequence of time, they became unable to plan for the future or to give up immediate pleasure satisfactions to gain greater ones in the near future. They were unable to establish durable object-relations. Friendships developed as quickly as they broke up. Prisoners would, like early adolescents, fight one another tooth and nail, declare that they would never even look at one another or speak to one another, only to become close friends within a few minutes. They were boastful, telling tales about what they had accomplished in their former lives, or how they succeeded in cheating foremen or guards, and how they sabotaged the work. Like children they felt not at all set back or ashamed when it became known that they had lied about their prowess.

Another factor contributing to the regression into childhood behavior was the work the prisoners were forced to perform. New prisoners particularly were forced to perform nonsensical tasks, such as carrying heavy rocks from one place to another, and after a while back to the place where they had picked them up. On other days they were forced to dig holes in the ground with their bare hands, although tools were available. They resented such nonsensical work, although it ought to have been immaterial to them whether their work was useful. They felt debased when forced to perform "childish" and stupid labor, and preferred even harder work when it produced something that might be considered useful. There seems to be no doubt that the tasks they performed, as well as the mistreatment by the Gestapo which they had to endure, contributed to their disintegration as adult persons.

The author had a chance to interview several prisoners who before being brought into the camp had spent a few years in prison, some of them in solitary confinement. Although their number was too small to permit valid generalizations, it seems that to spend time in prison does not produce the character changes described in this paper. As far as the regression into childhood behaviors is concerned, the only feature prison and camp seem to have in common is that in both the prisoners are prevented from satisfying their sexual desires in a normal way, which eventually leads them to the fear of losing their virility. In the camp this fear added strength to the other factors detrimental to adult types of behavior and promoted childlike types of behavior.

Summary. Significant differences could be observed when comparing old and new prisoners. They seemed to originate in personality changes which were brought about by the impact of the camp experiences on the prisoners. One of the differences was a changed frame of reference, indicated by the difference in evaluating extreme experiences as "real" or unreal. Old prisoners had more or less lost contact with their families and the world outside the camp. Their evaluation of their own importance had become fantastic, as could be seen from their hopes about their lives after liberation. These exaggerated hopes were partly due to the feeling that they were atoning for others and were, therefore, entitled to reward. All changes produced by living in the camp seemed to force the prisoners back into childhood attitudes and behaviors and they became in this way more or less willing tools of the Gestapo.

In conclusion it should be emphasized again that this essay is a preliminary report and does not pretend to be exhaustive. The author feels that the concentration camp has an importance reaching far beyond its being a place where the Gestapo takes revenge on its enemies. It is the main training ground for young Gestapo soldiers who are planning to rule and police Germany and all conquered nations; it is the Gestapo's laboratory where it develops methods for changing free and upright citizens not only into grumbling slaves, but into serfs who in many respects accept their masters' values. They still think that they are following their own life goals and values, whereas in reality they have accepted the Nazis' values as their own.

It seems that what happens in an extreme fashion to the prisoners who spend several years in the concentration camp happens in less exaggerated form to the inhabitants of the big concentration camp called greater Germany. It might happen to the inhabitants of occupied countries if they are not able to form organized groups of resistance. The system seems too strong for an individual to break its hold over his emotional life, particularly if he finds himself within a group which has more or less accepted the Nazi system. It seems easier to resist the pressure of the Gestapo and the Nazis if one functions as an individual; the Gestapo seems to know that and therefore insists on forcing all individuals into groups which they supervise. Some of the methods used for this purpose are the hostage system and the punishment of the whole group for whatever a member of it does; not permitting anybody to deviate in his behavior from the group norm, whatever this norm may be; discouraging solitary activities of any kind, etc. The main goal of the efforts seems to be to produce in the subjects' childlike attitudes and childlike dependency on the will of the leaders. The most effective way to break this influence seems to be the formation of democratic groups of [resistance] of independent, mature, and self-reliant persons, in which every member backs up, in all other members, the ability to resist. If such groups are not formed it seems very difficult not to become subject to the slow process of personality disintegration produced by the unrelenting pressure of the Gestapo and the Nazi system.

Inasmuch as the concentration camp is the laboratory of the Gestapo for subjecting not only free men, but even the most ardent foes of the Nazi system, to the process of disintegration from their position as autonomous individuals, it ought to be studied by all persons interested in understanding what happens to a population subject to the methods of the Nazi system. It is hoped that by understanding what happens to the unhappy persons under Nazi domination it will be possible to devise methods by means of which they will be helped to resurrect within a short time as autonomous and self-reliant persons.

Source: Bettelheim, Bruno. (1943). "Individual and Mass Behavior in Extreme Situations," *Journal of Abnormal and Social Psychology*, Volume 38, Pages 433–437, 443–447, 451–452.

THE SURVIVOR: AN ANATOMY OF LIFE IN THE DEATH CAMPS

Terrence Des Pres

It began in the trains, in the locked boxcars—eighty to a hundred people per car—crossing Europe to the camps in Poland:

> The temperature started to rise, as the freight car was enclosed and body heat had no outlet. . . . The only place to urinate was through a slot in the skylight, though whoever tried this usually missed, spilling urine on the floor. . . . When dawn finally rose . . . we were all quite ill and shattered, crushed not only by the weight of fatigue but by the stifling, moist atmosphere and the foul odor of excrement. . . . There was no latrine, no provision. . . . On top of everything else, a lot of people had vomited on the floor. We were to live for days on end breathing these foul smells, and soon we lived in the foulness itself (Kessel, 50–51).

Transport by boat, in the case of many Soviet prisoners, was even worse: "most people were seasick and they just had to vomit on those down below. That was the only way to perform their natural functions too" (Knapp, 59). From the beginning, that is, subjection to filth was an aspect of the survivor's ordeal. In Nazi camps especially, dirt and excrement were permanent conditions of existence. In the barracks at night, for example, "buckets of excrement stood in a little passage by the exit. There were not enough. By dawn, the whole floor was awash with urine and feces. We carried the filth about the hut on our feet, the stench made people faint" (Birenbaum, 226). Sickness made things worse:

> Everybody in the block had typhus . . . it came to Belsen Bergen in its most violent, most painful, deadliest form. The diarrhea caused by it became uncontrollable. It flooded the bottom of the cages, dripping through the cracks into the faces of the women lying in the cages below, and mixed with blood, pus and urine, formed a slimy, fetid mud on the floor of the barracks (Perl, 171).

The latrines were a spectacle unto themselves:

> There was one latrine for thirty to thirty-two thousand women and we were permitted to use it only at certain hours of the day. We stood in line to get into this tiny building, knee-deep in human excrement. As we all suffered from dysentery, we could rarely wait until our turn came, and soiled our ragged clothes, which never came off our bodies, thus adding to the horror of our existence by the terrible smell which surrounded us like a cloud. The latrine consisted of a deep ditch with planks thrown across it at certain intervals. We squatted on these planks like birds perched on a telegraph wire, so close together that we could not help soiling one another (Perl, 33).

Prisoners lucky enough to work in one of the camp hospitals, and therefore able to enjoy some measure of privacy, were not thereby exempt from the latrine's special horror: "I had to step into human excreta, into urine soaked with blood, into stools of patients suffering from highly contagious diseases. Only then could one reach the hole, surrounded by the most inexpressible dirt" (Weiss, 69). The new prisoner's initiation into camp life was complete when he "realized that there was no toilet paper"—

> that there was no paper in the whole of Auschwitz, and that I would have to "find another way out." I tore off a piece of my scarf and washed it after use. I retained this little piece throughout my days in Auschwitz; others did likewise (Unsdorfer, 102).

Problems of this kind were intensified by the fact that, at one time or another, *everyone* suffered from diarrhea or dysentery. And for prisoners already starved and exhausted, it was fatal more often than not: "Those with dysentery melted down like candles, relieving themselves in their clothes, and swiftly turned into stinking repulsive skeletons who died in their own excrement" (Donat, 269). Sometimes whole camp populations sickened in this way, and then the horror was overwhelming. Men and women soiled themselves and each other. Those too weak to move relieved themselves where they lay. Those who did not recover were slowly enveloped in their own decomposition: "Some of the patients died before they ever reached the gas chambers. Many of them were covered all over with excrement, for there were no sanitary facilities, and they could not keep themselves clean" (Newman, 39).

Diarrhea was a deadly disease and a source of constant befoulment, but it was also dangerous for another reason—it forced prisoners to break rules:

> Many women with diarrhea relieved themselves in soup bowls or the pans for "coffee"; then they hid the utensils under the mattress to avoid the punishment threatening them for doing so: twenty-five strokes on the bare buttocks, or kneeling all night long on sharp gravel, holding up bricks. These punishments often ended in the death of the "guilty" (Birenbaum, 134).

In another case a group of men were locked day after day in a room without ventilation or toilet facilities of any kind. Next to a window by which guards passed they discovered a hole in the floor. But to use it a man had to risk his life, since those caught were beaten to death. "The spectacle of these unfortunates, shaking with fear as they crawled on hands and knees to the hole and relieved themselves lying down, is one of my most terrible memories of Sachsenhausen" (Szalet, 51).

The anguish of existence in the camps was thus intensified by the mineral movement of life itself. Death was planted in a need which could not, like other needs, be repressed or delayed or passively endured. The demands of the bowels are absolute, and under such circumstances men and women had to oppose, yet somehow accommodate, their own most intimate necessities:

> Imagine what it would be like to be forbidden to go to the toilet; imagine also that you were suffering from increasingly severe dysentery, caused and aggravated by a diet of cabbage soup as well as by the constant cold. Naturally, you would try to go anyway. Sometimes you might succeed. But your absences would be noticed and you would be beaten, knocked down and trampled on. By now, you would know what the risks were, but urgency would

> oblige you to repeat the attempt, cost what it might. . . . I soon learned to deal
> with the dysentery by tying strings around the lower end of my drawers
> (Maurel, 38–39).

With only one exception, so far as I know, psychoanalytic studies of the camp experience maintain that it was characterized by regression to "childlike" or "infantile" levels of behavior. This conclusion is based primarily on the fact that men and women in the concentration camps were "abnormally" preoccupied with food and excretory functions. Infants show similar preoccupations, and the comparison suggests that men and women react to extremity by "regression to, and fixation on, pre-oedipal stages" (Hoppe, 77). Here, as in general from the psychoanalytic point of view, context is not considered. The fact that the survivor's situation was itself abnormal is simply ignored. That the preoccupation with food was caused by literal starvation does not count; and the fact that camp inmates were *forced* to live in filth is likewise overlooked.

The case for "infantilism" has been put most forcefully by Bruno Bettelheim. A major thesis of his book *The Informed Heart* is that in extreme situations men are reduced to children; and in a section entitled "Childlike Behavior" he simply equates the prisoners' objective predicament with behavior inherently regressive. Bettelheim observes, for example—and of course this was true—that camp regulations were designed to transform excretory functions into moments of crisis. Prisoners had to ask permission in order to relieve themselves, thereby becoming exposed to the murderous whim of the SS guard to whom they spoke. During the twelve-hour workday, furthermore, prisoners were often not allowed to answer natural needs, or they were forced to do so *while* they worked and on the actual spot *where* they worked. As one survivor says: "If anyone of us, tormented by her stomach, would try to go to a nearby ditch, the guards would release their dogs. Humiliated, goaded, the women did not leave their places— they waded in their own excrement" (Zywulska, 67). Worst of all were the days of the death marches, when prisoners who stopped for any reason were instantly shot. To live they simply had to keep going:

> Urine and excreta poured down the prisoners' legs, and by nightfall the excrement, which had frozen to our limbs, gave off its stench. We were really no longer human beings in the accepted sense. Not even animals, but putrefying corpses moving on two legs (Weiss, 211).

Under such conditions, excretion does indeed become, as Bettelheim says, "an important daily event"; but the conclusion does not follow, as he goes on to say, that prisoners were therefore reduced "to the level they were at before toilet training was achieved" (132). Outwardly, yes; men and women were very much concerned with excretory functions, just as infants are, and prisoners were "forced to wet and soil themselves" just as infants do—except that infants are not forced. Bettelheim concludes that for camp inmates the ordeal of excremental crisis "made it impossible to see themselves as fully adult persons any more" (134). He does not distinguish between behavior in extremity and civilized behavior; for of course, if in civilized circumstances an adult worries about the state of his bowels, or sees the trip to the toilet as some sort of ordeal, then neurosis is evident. But in the concentration camps behavior was governed by immediate death threat; action was not the index of infantile wishes but of response to hideous necessity.

The fact is that prisoners were *systematically* subjected to filth. They were the deliberate target of excremental assault. Defilement was a constant threat, a condition of life from day to day, and at any moment it was liable to take abruptly vicious and sometimes fatal forms. The favorite pastime of one *Kapo* was to stop prisoners just before they reached the latrine. He would force an inmate to stand at attention for questioning; then make him "squat in deep knee-bends until the poor man could no longer control his sphincter and 'exploded'"; then beat him; and only then, "covered with his own excrement, the victim would be allowed to drag himself to the latrine" (Donat, 178). In another instance prisoners were forced to lie in rows on the ground, and each man, when he was finally allowed to get up, "had to urinate across the heads of the others"; and there was "one night when they refined their treatment by making each man urinate into another's mouth" (Wells, 91). In Birkenau, soup bowls were periodically taken from the prisoners and thrown into the latrine, from which they had to be retrieved: "When you put it to your lips for the first time, you smell nothing suspicious. Other pairs of hands trembling with impatience wait for it, they seize it the moment you have finished drinking. Only later, much later, does a repelling odor hit your nostrils" (Szmaglewska, 154). And as we have seen, prisoners with dysentery commonly got around camp rules and kept from befouling themselves by using their own eating utensils:

> The first days our stomachs rose up at the thought of using what were actually chamber pots at night. But hunger drives, and we were so starved that we were ready to eat any food. That it had to be handled in such bowls could not be helped. During the night, many of us availed ourselves of the bowls secretly. We were allowed to go to the latrines only twice each day. How could we help it? No matter how great our need, if we went out in the middle of the night we risked being caught by the SS, who had orders to shoot first and ask questions later (Lengyel, 26).

There was no end to this kind of degradation. The stench of excrement mingled with the smoke of the crematoria and the rancid decay of flesh. Prisoners in the Nazi camps were virtually drowning in their own waste, and in fact death by excrement was common. In Buchenwald, for instance, latrines consisted of open pits twenty-five feet long, twelve feet deep and twelve feet wide. There were railings along the edge to squat on, and "one of the favorite games of the SS, engaged in for many years," was to catch men in the act of relieving themselves and throw them into the pit: "In Buchenwald ten prisoners suffocated in excrement in this fashion in October 1937 alone" (Kogon, 56). These same pits, which were always overflowing, were emptied at night by prisoners working with nothing but small pails:

> The location was slippery and unlighted. Of the thirty men on this assignment, an average of ten fell into the pit in the course of each night's work. The others were not allowed to pull the victims out. When work was done and the pit empty, then and then only were they permitted to remove the corpses (Weinstock, 157–158).

Again, conditions like these were not accidental; they were determined by a deliberate policy which aimed at complete humiliation and debasement of prisoners. Why this was necessary is not at first apparent, since none of the goals of the camp system—to spread terror, to provide slaves, to exterminate populations—required the kind of thoroughness with which conditions of defilement were enforced. But here too, for all its madness, there was method and reason. This special kind of evil is a natural outcome of power when it becomes absolute, and in the totalitarian world of the camps it very nearly was. The SS could kill anyone they happened to run into. Criminal *Kapos* would walk about in groups of two and three, making bets among themselves on who could kill a prisoner with a single blow. The pathological rage of such men, their uncontrollable fury when rules were broken, is evidence of a boundless desire to annihilate, to destroy, to smash everything not mobilized within the movement of their own authority. And inevitably, the mere act of killing is not enough; for if a man dies without surrender, if something within him remains unbroken to the end, then the power which destroyed him has not, after all, crushed everything. Something has escaped its reach, and it is precisely this something—let us call it "dignity"—that must die if those in power are to reach the orgasmic peak of their potential domination.

As power grows, it grows more and more hostile to everything outside itself. Its logic is inherently negative, which is why it ends by destroying itself (a consolation which no longer means much, since the perimeter of atomic destruction is infinite). The exercise of totalitarian power, in any case, does not stop with the demand for outward compliance. It seeks, further, to crush the spirit, to obliterate that active inward principle whose strength depends on its freedom from entire determination by external forces. And thus the compulsion, felt by men with great power, to seek out and destroy all resistance, all spiritual autonomy, all sign of dignity in those held captive. It was not enough just to shoot the Old Bolsheviks; Stalin had to have the show trials. He had to demonstrate publicly that these men of enormous energy and spirit were so utterly broken as to openly repudiate themselves and all they had fought for. And so it was in the camps. Spiritual destruction became an end in itself, quite apart from the requirements of mass murder. The death of the soul was aimed at. It was to be accomplished by terror and privation, but first of all by a relentless assault on the survivor's sense of purity and worth. Excremental attack, the physical inducement of disgust and self-loathing, was a principal weapon.

But defilement had its lesser logic as well. "In Buchenwald," says one survivor, "it was a principle to depress the morale of prisoners to the lowest possible level, thereby preventing the development of fellow-feeling or co-operation among the victims" (Weinstock, 92). How much self-esteem can one maintain, how readily can one respond with respect to the needs of another, if both stink, if both are caked with mud and feces? We tend to forget how camp prisoners looked and smelled, especially those who had given up the will to live, and in consequence the enormous revulsion and disgust which naturally arose among prisoners. Here was an effective mechanism for intensifying the already heightened irritability of prisoners towards each other, and thus for stifling in common loathing the impulse toward solidarity. Within the camp world all visible signs of human beauty, of bodily pride and spiritual radiance, were thereby to be eliminated from the ranks of the inmates. The prisoner was made to feel subhuman, to see his self-image only in the dirt and stink of his neighbor. The SS, on the contrary, appeared superior not only by virtue of their guns and assurance, but by their elegant apartness from the filth of the prisoner's world. In Auschwitz prisoners were forced to march in the mud, whereas the clean roadway was reserved for the SS.

And here is a final, vastly significant reason why in the camps the prisoners were so degraded. This made it easier for the SS to do their job. It made mass murder less terrible to the murderers, because the victims appeared less than human. They *looked* inferior. In Gitta Sereny's series of interviews with Franz Stangl, commandant of Treblinka, there are moments of fearful insight. Here is one of the most telling:

> "*Why*," I asked Stangl, "*if they were going to kill them anyway, what was the point of all the humiliation, why the cruelty?*"
>
> "To condition those who actually had to carry out the policies," he said. "To make it possible for them to do what they did" (101).

In a lecture at the New School (New York, 1974), Hannah Arendt remarked that it is easier to kill a dog than a man, easier yet to kill a rat or frog, and no problem at all to kill insects—"It is in the glance, in the eyes." She means that the perception of subjective being in the victim sparks some degree of identification in the assailant, and makes his act difficult in proportion to the capacity for suffering and resistance he perceives. Inhibited by pity and guilt, the act of murder becomes harder to perform and results in greater psychic damage to the killer himself. If, on the other hand, the victim exhibits self-disgust; if he cannot lift his eyes for humiliation, or if lifted they show only emptiness—then his death may be administered with ease or even with the conviction that so much rotten tissue has been removed from life's body. And it is a fact that in camp the procedure of "selection"—to the left, life; to the right, death—was based on physical appearance and on a certain sense of inward collapse or resilience in the prospective victim. As a survivor of Auschwitz puts it:

> Yes, here one rotted alive, there was no doubt about it, just like the SS in Bitterfield had predicted. Yet it was vitally important to keep the body clear. . . . Everyone [at a "selection"] had to strip and one by one, parade before them naked. Mengele in his immaculate white gloves stood pointing his thumb sometimes to the right, sometimes to the left. Anyone with spots on the body, or a thin *Muselmann*, was directed to the right. That side spelt death, the other meant one was allowed to rot a little longer (Hart, 65).

With water in permanent shortage; with latrines submerged in their own filth; with diarrhea rife and mud everywhere, strict cleanliness was just not possible. Simply to *try* to stay clean took extraordinary effort. As one survivor says: "To pick oneself up, to wash and clean oneself—all that is the simplest thing in the world, isn't it? And yet it was not so. Everything in Auschwitz was so organized as to make these things impossible. There was nothing to lean on; there was no place for washing oneself. Nor was there time" (Lewinska, 43). That conditions *were* "so organized" was a dreadful discovery:

> At the outset the living places, the ditches, the mud, the piles of excrement behind the blocks, had appalled me with their horrible filth. . . . And then I saw the light! I saw that it was not a question of disorder or lack of organization but that, on the contrary, a very thoroughly considered conscious idea was in the back of the camp's existence. They had condemned us to die in our own filth, to drown in mud, in our own excrement. They wished to abase us, to destroy our human dignity, to efface every vestige of humanity,

to return us to the level of wild animals, to fill us with horror and contempt toward ourselves and our fellows (Lewinska, 41–42).

With this recognition the prisoner either gave up or decided to resist. For many survivors this moment marked the birth of their will to fight back:

> But from the instant when I grasped the motivating principle . . . it was as if I had been awakened from a dream. . . . I felt under orders to live. . . . And if I did die in Auschwitz, it would be as a human being, I would hold on to my dignity. I was not going to become the contemptible, disgusting brute my enemy wished me to be. . . . And a terrible struggle began which went on day and night (Lewinska, 50).

Or as another survivor says:

> There and then I determined that if I did not become the target of a bullet, or if I were not hanged, I would make every effort to endure. No longer would I succumb to apathy. My first impulse was to concentrate on making myself more presentable. Under the circumstances this may sound ludicrous; what real relation was there between my new-found spiritual resistance and the unsightly rags on my body? But in a subtle sense there *was* a relationship, and from that moment onwards, throughout my life in the camps, I knew this for a fact. I began to look around me and saw the beginning of the end for any woman who might have had the opportunity to wash and had not done so, or any woman who felt that the tying of a shoe-lace was wasted energy (Weiss, 84).

Washing, if only in a ritual sense—and quite apart from reasons of health—was something prisoners needed to do. They found it necessary to survival, odd as that may seem, and those who stopped soon died:

> At 4:30, "coffee"—a light mint infusion without nourishment and with a repulsive taste—was distributed. We often took a few swallows and used the rest for washing, but not all of us were able to do without this poor substitute for coffee and consequently many inmates ceased to wash. This was the first step to the grave. It was an almost iron law: those who failed to wash every day soon died. Whether this was the cause or the effect of inner breakdown, I don't know; but it was an infallible symptom (Donat, 173).

Another survivor describes the initial disappearance of concern for his appearance, and the gradual realization that without such care he would not survive:

> Why should I wash? Would I be better off than I am? Would I please someone more? Would I live a day, an hour longer? I would probably live a shorter time, because to wash is an effort, a waste of energy and warmth. . . . But later I understood. . . . In this place it is practically pointless to wash every day in the turbid water of the filthy wash-basins for purposes of cleanliness and health; but it is most important as a symptom of remaining vitality, and necessary as an instrument of moral survival (Levi, 35).

By passing through the degradation of the camps, survivors discovered that in extremity a sense of dignity is something which men and women cannot afford to lose. Great damage has to be borne, much humiliation suffered. But at some point a steady resistance to their obliteration as human beings must be made. They learned, furthermore, that when conditions of filth are enforced, befoulment of the body is experienced as befoulment of the soul. And they came to recognize, finally, that when this particular feeling—of something inwardly untouchable—is ruined beyond repair, the will to live dies. To care for one's appearance thus becomes an act of resistance and a necessary moment in the larger structure of survival. Life itself depends on keeping dignity intact, and this, in turn, depends on the daily, never finished battle to remain *visibly* human:

> So we must certainly wash our faces without soap in dirty water and dry ourselves on our jackets. We must polish our shoes, not because the regulation states it, but for dignity and propriety. We must walk erect, without dragging our feet, not in homage to Prussian discipline but to remain alive, not to begin to die (Levi, 36).

In many of the Nazi camps, women who gave birth were automatically sent with their children to the ovens. To save at least *some* of these lives required the following decision by members of the hospital staff in Auschwitz: "One day we decided we had been weak long enough. We must at least save the mothers. To carry out our plan, we would have to make the infants pass for stillborn" (Lengyel, 99). The pain of such decisions was the price which members of the resistance had to pay, just to salvage something rather than nothing in a world where, without this kind of hard choice, all would have died:

> And so, the Germans succeeded in making murderers of even us. To this day the picture of those murdered babies haunts me. . . . The only meager consolation is that by these murders we saved the mothers. Without our intervention they would have endured worse sufferings, for they would have been thrown into the crematory ovens while still alive (Lengyel, 100).

Death was thereby cheated, made less than absolute, which is as much as survivors can hope for. They never win, in a conventional sense, but only lose less than all. And even to accomplish victories so small, so apparently insignificant against defeats so appalling, they must make choices painful often past bearing. Many could not bear it. They chose to die, rather than survive on such terms. The hardness of the survivor's choice, in other words, requires a toughness equal in its way to the forces he or she resists; life goes on by using the methods of the enemy.

Thus when lists were made up of prisoners to be gassed or sent on especially dangerous work details, as many places as possible were filled with criminals, informers, or men lost in any case. The underground was forced to make its own "selection" in strategic mimicry of the Nazi procedure, and as one survivor says, "it was the crudest task that any Underground has ever faced. . . . The Nazi system was so thorough that anti-Nazis, too, had to use death as a tool" (Weinstock, 118). Here is another example: a young man breaks down when told of the death of his family. He decides that in the morning he will commit suicide by attacking an SS officer. Because of the Nazi practice of mass reprisal, his act will cost the lives of all four hundred men in his barracks (remember that the population of Lidice was wiped out because Heydrich, one of the SS high command, was assassinated by a man from that village). All night, therefore, the crazed man's comrades try to talk him back to sanity, but his grief is stronger than their appeals. So two members of the underground must decide:

> "Do you think he'd do it?"
> "I don't know. Maybe not. Maybe he'll calm down."

Maybe. Before roll-call next morning the camp hospital sent for the man, who was not seen again (Weinstock, 150). On the same principle, an informer who "did not shrink from denouncing anyone with whom he had ever had the most trivial dispute" got sick and was "unwise enough to report to the hospital" (Kogon, 229). He too disappeared.

Life was preserved because men and women did not hesitate when moments of hard choice arose. If, as happened at Auschwitz, some members of the resistance got caught, the rest of the organization had to be protected:

> If those men cracked under torture, it would mean more than their deaths, more than fierce reprisals against the rest of us. It would mean that the underground movement . . . would be liquidated. . . . The leaders of the underground were fully aware of the danger and took swift evasive action. They smuggled poison into Block Eleven and within a few hours the men in Block Eleven were dead. Rather than risk revealing the names of their comrades, they had committed suicide (Vrba, 168–169).

As in any war, those who fight cannot afford sentiment. If one's comrade falls, that is that. The battle goes on, as did the smuggling of explosives in Auschwitz:

> A young boy who only a day before had accepted a package from me swung on the gallows. One of my comrades, numb with fright, whispered to me, "Tell me, isn't that the same boy who was in the infirmary yesterday?"
> "No," I replied. "I have never seen him before."
> That was the rule. Whoever fell was forgotten (Lengyel, 156).

Compassion was seldom possible, self-pity never. Emotion not only blurred judgment and undermined decisiveness, it jeopardized the life of everyone in the underground. To oppose their fate in the death camps, survivors had to choose life at the cost of moral injury; they had to sustain spiritual damage and still keep going without losing sight of the difference between strategic compromise and demoralization. Hard choices had to be made and not everyone was equal to the task, no one less than the kind of person whose goodness was most evident, most admired, but least available for action:

> It was the pure in heart who suffered the least damage . . . and . . . their lives shed radiance and beneficence on the rest of us. But on no account could they be placed in situations where they had to take part in making decisions vital to the very existence of the camp. . . . And the more tender one's conscience, the more difficult it was to make such decisions. Since they had to be made, and made swiftly, it was perhaps better that they should have fallen to the more robust spirits, lest all of us became martyrs instead of surviving witnesses (Kogon, 278).

In 1959 Stanley M. Elkins put forward his slave-as-sambo thesis in *Slavery*, arguing that the personality of the American slave had been fundamentally regressive and infantile. Elkins does not examine direct evidence; he uses a "comparative" method, and his main comparison is with inmates of the German concentration camps. To identify the Southern plantation with Auschwitz is senseless, of course; but the comparison is still significant, not for what it tells us of either slaves or survivors, but for the assumptions that are made about behavior in extremity. Elkins takes it for granted that in the camps men and women lost their capacity to act as morally responsible adults, and the point of his comparison is to demonstrate that this also happened to American slaves. Specifically, he states that "old prisoners," by which he means the survivors, suffered "deep disintegrative effects" (107); that the "most immediate aspect of the old inmates' behavior . . . was its *childlike* quality" (111); and finally that "all" survivors were "reduced to complete and childish dependence upon their masters" (113). Elkins goes on to say that regression began with the abandonment of previous ethical standards, and to make his point he quotes as representative a brief statement by a survivor of Auschwitz. In Elkins' context, here is her remark:

> One part of the prisoner's being was thus, under sharp stress, brought to the crude realization that he must thenceforth be governed by an entire new set of standards in order to live. Mrs. Lingens-Reiner puts it bluntly: "Will you survive or shall I? As soon as one sensed that this was at stake everyone turned egotist" (109–10).

In extremity, in other words, everyone fights alone, and the "entire new set of standards" comes from the camp system itself. But is there not a contradiction here? Childlike behavior is not the same as rapacious battle in one's best self-interest. The former entails passivity and preference for illusion; the latter demands intelligent calculation and a capacity for quick, objective judgment. All the same, that survivors suffered regression to infantile stages, *and* that they were amoral monsters, are very widespread notions. They constitute nothing less than the prevailing view of survival behavior. Not surprisingly, in *Death in Life* Robert Lifton has used the same quotation—"Will you survive, or shall I?"—as a representative expression of the "competition for survival" which, in his view, lies at the root of the "guilt" survivors are supposed to feel (490). What, then, are we to make of the Lingens-Reiner statement? Is it a fair summation of her own view?

In *Prisoners of Fear* she aims to tell the very worst; and the most striking thing about her testimony is the double vision we have already noted in reports by survivors. The viciousness and horror are certainly there, but also examples of morally intelligent behavior, and many references to resistance and solidarity among camp inmates. There is the moment when the narrator exposes herself by taking action to get another prisoner's name off a death list. She does this, all the time calling herself a fool for taking the risk, because she sees an opportunity: there was a *way* to save someone and that decided her. The incident takes four pages to describe (79–82) and is not an example of "survival egotism" or of "infantile regression." It is one instance among many of men and women acting with courage and intelligence to help others. The following are typical:

> There were girls among them who lived through a typhus attack without staying in bed. Two of their friends would take the sick comrade between them, when she had a temperature of 103° F and saw everything as a blur,

and drag her along with their labour gang; out in the fields they would lay her down under a shrub, and in the evening they would march her back to camp—all to avoid her being sent to the hospital hut and so being exposed to the danger of a selection (122).

The camp doctor would line up all the Jewish patients. . . . All those who were too ill to get out of bed were lost from the outset. . . . The rest of the prisoners did everything in their power to obstruct the doctor and to save one or other of the victims; I do not think that a single one among us withheld her help. We would hide women somewhere in the hut. . . . We would smuggle them into "Aryan" huts. . . . We would put their names on the list of patients due for release (76-7).

Under the pressure of a concentration camp you grew more closely attached to people than you would have done otherwise in such a short time (162).

The pursuit of self-interest was certainly a determinant of behavior in the camps, but it was everywhere countered by an unsuppressible urge toward decency and care, a multitude of small deeds against the grain of one's "best" interest. Prisoners looked out for themselves first of all, but also for one another when and however they could. In the whole body of testimony by survivors there is no better description of this contradiction than in the book by Lingens-Reiner:

Ena Weiss, our Chief Doctor—one of the most intelligent, gifted and eminent Jewish women in the camp—once defined her attitude thus, in sarcastic rejection of fulsome flattery and at the same time with brutal frankness: "How did I keep alive in Auschwitz? My principle is: myself first, second and third. Then nothing. Then myself again—and then all the others." This formula expressed the only principle which was possible for Jews who intended—almost insanely intended—to survive Auschwitz. Yet, because this woman had the icy wisdom and strength to accept the principle, she kept for herself a position in which she could do something for the Jews. Hardly anybody else in the camp did as much for them and saved so many lives as she did (118).

At least in this instance, Elkins' thesis is not borne out by the evidence from which he quotes, and if for a time his "sambo" theory of slave behavior was accepted, that was not because he had offered solid evidence but because by comparing slavery to the camp experience he was able to mobilize the deeply disturbing and largely uncontrolled range of reaction which attends our idea of the concentration camps. Here is how he sums it up:

Daily life in the camp, with its fear and tensions, taught over and over the lesson of absolute power. It prepared the personality for a drastic shift in standards. It crushed whatever anxieties might have been drawn from prior standards; such standards had become meaningless. It focused the prisoner's attention constantly on the moods, attitudes, and standards of the only man who mattered [the SS guard]. A truly childlike situation was thus created: utter and abject dependency. . . . It is thus no wonder that the prisoners should become "as children." It is no wonder that their obedience became unquestioning, that they did not revolt, that they could not "hate" their masters (122).

Elkins is simply reiterating accepted ideas. But power is never absolute, especially over time, and it is not true that the SS guard was the "one significant other" on whom the prisoners' needs depended. Social bonding among prisoners themselves was a universal phenomenon in the camps. And of course it is not true that survivors were morally crushed, that they lost all sense of prior standards, that moral sanity was meaningless. Certainly it is not true that they did not revolt; to live was to resist, every day, all the time, and in addition to dramatic events like the burning of Treblinka and Sobibor there were many small revolts in which all perished. Prisoners who were capable, furthermore, of organizing an underground and of systematically subverting SS intentions were not behaving "as children." And it is not true, finally, that hatred was absent. Survivors seethed with it, they speak of it often, they describe terrible acts of revenge. In *Prisoners of Fear* the author praises one of her comrades for "the ice-cold self-control by which she hid her abysmal hatred of the German rulers" (123) in order to exploit them. Ella Lingens-Reiner's own rage rings through her prose on every page.

   No, most of this was not true, not for many survivors in many camps. Hence these disturbing questions: Why do we insist that prisoners died "like sheep"? Why is it easy to believe, despite the contradiction, that survivors were infantile *and* that they were cunning manipulators using every kind of betrayal and base trick to stay alive? Why, in short, do we insist that survivors did not really survive: that they suffered "death in life" and that if they are alive in body their spirit was destroyed beyond salvaging? Here is how one psychoanalytic commentator summed up the opinions of his colleagues in a symposium on the camp experience: "To one degree or another, they all stifled their true feelings, they all denied the dictates of conscience and social feeling in hope of survival, and they were all warped and distorted as a result" (Hoppe, 83). That word "all"—its assurance, its contempt—must be accounted for.

Source: From *The Survivor: An Anatomy of Life in Death Camps* by Terrence Des Pres (1976) pp. 53–65, 151–155, © 1976 by Oxford University Press, Inc. By permission of Oxford University Press, Inc., and by permission of Georges Borchardt, Inc., on behalf of the Estate of Terrence Des Pres.

EXPERIENCES IN A CONCENTRATION CAMP

Viktor Frankl

In attempting this psychological presentation and a psychopathological explanation of the typical characteristics of a concentration camp inmate, I may give the impression that the human being is completely and unavoidably influenced by his surroundings. (In this case the surroundings being the unique structure of camp life, which forced the prisoner to conform his conduct to a certain set pattern.) But what about human liberty? Is there no spiritual freedom in regard to behavior and reaction to any given surroundings? Is that theory true which would have us believe that man is no more than a product of many conditional and environmental factors—be they of a biological, psychological or sociological nature? Is man but an accidental product of these? Most important, do the prisoners' reactions to the singular world of the concentration camp prove that man cannot escape the influences of his surroundings? Does man have no choice of action in the face of such circumstances?

We can answer these questions from experience as well as on principle. The experiences of camp life show that man does have a choice of action. There were enough examples, often of a heroic nature, which proved that apathy could be overcome, irritability suppressed. Man *can* preserve a vestige of spiritual freedom, of independence of mind, even in such terrible conditions of psychic and physical stress.

We who lived in concentration camps can remember the men who walked through the huts comforting others, giving away their last piece of bread. They may have been few in number, but they offer sufficient proof that everything can be taken from a man but one thing: the last of the human freedoms—to choose one's attitude in any given set of circumstances, to choose one's own way.

And there were always choices to make. Every day, every hour, offered the opportunity to make a decision, a decision which determined whether you would or would not submit to those powers which threatened to rob you of your very self, your inner freedom; which determined whether or not you would become the plaything of circumstance, renouncing freedom and dignity to become molded into the form of the typical inmate.

Seen from this point of view, the mental reactions of the inmates of a concentration camp must seem more to us than the mere expression of certain physical and sociological conditions. Even though conditions such as lack of sleep, insufficient food and various mental stresses may suggest that the inmates were bound to react in certain ways, in the final analysis it becomes clear that the sort of person the prisoner became was the result of an inner decision, and not the result of camp influences alone. Fundamentally, therefore, any man can, even under such circumstances, decide what shall become of him—mentally and spiritually. He may retain his human dignity even in a concentration camp. Dostoevski said once, "There is only one thing that I dread: not to be worthy of my sufferings." These words frequently came to my mind after I became acquainted with those martyrs whose behavior in camp, whose suffering and death, bore witness to the fact that the last inner freedom cannot be lost. It can be said that they were worthy of their sufferings; the way they bore their suffering was a genuine inner achievement. It is this spiritual freedom—which cannot be taken away—that makes life meaningful and purposeful.

An active life serves the purpose of giving man the opportunity to realize values in creative work, while a passive life of enjoyment affords him the opportunity to obtain fulfillment in experiencing beauty, art, or nature. But there is also purpose in that life which is almost barren of both creation and enjoyment and which admits of but one possibility of high moral behavior: namely, in man's attitude to his existence, an existence restricted by external forces. A creative life and a life of enjoyment are banned to him. But not only creativeness and enjoyment are meaningful. If there is a meaning in life at all, then there must be a meaning in suffering. Suffering is an ineradicable part of life, even as fate and death. Without suffering and death human life cannot be complete.

The way in which a man accepts his fate and all the suffering it entails, the way in which he takes up his cross, gives him ample opportunity—even under the most difficult circumstances—to add a deeper meaning to his life. It may remain brave, dignified and unselfish. Or in the bitter fight for self-preservation he may forget his human dignity and become no more than an animal. Here lies the chance for a man either to make use of or to forgo the opportunities of attaining the moral values that a difficult situation may afford him. And this decides whether he is worthy of his sufferings or not.

Do not think that these considerations are unworldly and too far removed from real life. It is true that only a few people are capable of reaching such high moral standards. Of the prisoners only a few kept their full inner liberty and obtained those values which their suffering afforded, but even one such example is sufficient proof that man's inner strength may raise him above his outward fate. Such men are not only in concentration camps. Everywhere man is confronted with fate, with the chance of achieving something through his own suffering.

Take the fate of the sick—especially those who are incurable. I once read a letter written by a young invalid, in which he told a friend that he had just found out he would not live for long, that even an operation would be of no help. He wrote further that he remembered a film he had seen in which a man was portrayed who waited for death in a courageous and dignified way. The boy had thought it a great accomplishment to meet death so well. Now—he wrote—fate was offering him a similar chance.

One of the prisoners, who on his arrival marched with a long column of new inmates from the station to the camp, told me later that he had felt as though he were marching at his own funeral. His life had seemed to him absolutely without future. He regarded it as over and done, as if he had already died. This feeling of lifelessness was intensified by other causes: in time, it was the limitlessness of the term of imprisonment which was most acutely felt; in space, the narrow limits of the prison. Anything outside the barbed wire became remote—out of reach and, in a way, unreal. The events and the people outside, all the normal life there, had a ghostly aspect for the prisoner. The outside life, that is, as much as he could see of it, appeared to him almost as it might have to a dead man who looked at it from another world.

A man who let himself decline because he could not see any future goal found himself occupied with retrospective thoughts. In a different connection, we have already spoken of the tendency there was to look into the past, to help make the present, with all its horrors, less real. But in robbing the present of its reality there lay a certain danger. It became easy to overlook the opportunities to make something positive of camp life, opportunities which really did exist. Regarding our "provisional existence" as unreal was in itself an important factor in causing the prisoners to lose their hold on life; everything in a way became pointless. Such people forgot that often it is just such an exceptionally difficult external situation which gives man the opportunity to grow spiritually beyond himself. Instead of taking the camp's difficulties as a test of their inner strength, they did not take their life seriously and despised it as something of no consequence. They preferred to close their eyes and to live in the past. Life for such people became meaningless.

Naturally only a few people were capable of reaching great spiritual heights. But a few were given the chance to attain human greatness even through their apparent worldly failure and death, an accomplishment which in ordinary circumstances they would never have achieved. To the others of us, the mediocre and the half-hearted, the words of Bismarck could be applied: "Life is like being at the dentist. You always think that the worst is still to come, and yet it is over already." Varying this, we could say that most men in a concentration camp believed that the real opportunities of life had passed. Yet, in reality, there was an opportunity and a challenge. One could make a victory of those experiences, turning life into an inner triumph, or one could ignore the challenge and simply vegetate, as did a majority of the prisoners.

Any attempt at fighting the camp's psychopathological influence on the prisoner by psychotherapeutic or psychopathological methods had to aim at giving him inner strength by pointing out to him a future goal to which he could look forward. Instinctively some of the prisoners attempted to find one on their own. It is a peculiarity of man that he can only live by looking to the future—*sub specie aeternitatis*. And this is his salvation in the most difficult moments of his existence, although he sometimes has to force his mind to the task.

I remember a personal experience. Almost in tears from pain (I had terrible sores on my feet from wearing torn shoes), I limped a few kilometers with our long column of men from the camp to our work site. Very cold, bitter winds struck us. I kept thinking of the endless little problems of our miserable life. What would there be to eat tonight? If a piece of sausage came as extra ration, should I exchange it for a piece of bread? Should I trade my last cigarette, which was left from a bonus I received a fortnight ago, for a bowl of soup? How could I get a piece of wire to replace the fragment which served as one of my shoelaces? Would I get to our work site in time to join my usual working party or would I have to join another, which might have a brutal foreman? What could I do to get on good terms with the Capo, who could help me to obtain work in camp instead of undertaking this horribly long daily march?

I became disgusted with the state of affairs which compelled me, daily and hourly, to think of only such trivial things. I forced my thoughts to turn to another subject. Suddenly I saw myself standing on the platform of a well-lit, warm and pleasant lecture room. In front of me sat an attentive audience on comfortable upholstered seats. I was giving a lecture on the psychology of the concentration camp! All that oppressed me at that moment became objective, seen and described from the remote viewpoint of science. By this method I succeeded somehow in rising above the situation, above the sufferings of the moment, and I observed them as if they were already of the past. Both I and my troubles became the object of an interesting psychoscientific study undertaken by myself. What does Spinoza say in his *Ethics?*—"*Affectus, qui passio est, desinit esse passio simulatque eius claram et distinctam formamus ideam.*" Emotion, which is suffering, ceases to be suffering as soon as we form a clear and precise picture of it.

The prisoner who had lost faith in the future—his future—was doomed. With his loss of belief in the future, he also lost his spiritual hold; he let himself decline and became subject to mental and physical decay. Usually this happened quite suddenly, in the form of a crisis, the symptoms of which were familiar to the experienced camp inmate. We all feared this moment—not for ourselves, which would have been pointless, but for our friends. Usually it began with the prisoner refusing one morning to get dressed and wash or to go out on the parade grounds. No entreaties, no moving. If this crisis was brought about by an illness, he refused to be taken to the sick-bay or to do anything to help himself. He simply gave up. There he remained, lying in his own excreta, and nothing bothered him any more.

I once had a dramatic demonstration of the close link between the loss of faith in the future and this dangerous giving up. F——, my senior block warden, a fairly well-known composer and librettist, confided in me one day: "I would like to tell you something, Doctor. I have had a strange dream. A voice told me that I could wish for something that I should only say what I wanted to know, and all my questions would be answered. What do you think I asked? That I would like to know when the war would be over for me. You know what I mean, Doctor—for me! I wanted to know when we, when our camp, would be liberated and our sufferings come to an end."

"And when did you have this dream?" I asked.
"In February 1945," he answered. It was then the beginning of March.
"What did your dream voice answer?"
Furtively he whispered to me, "March thirtieth."

When F—— told me about his dream, he was still full of hope and convinced that the voice of his dream would be right. But as the promised day drew nearer, the war news which reached our camp made it appear very unlikely that we would be free on the promised date. On March twenty-ninth, F—— suddenly became ill and ran a high temperature. On March thirtieth, the day his prophecy had told him that the war and suffering would be over for him, he became delirious and lost consciousness. On March thirty-first, he was dead. To all outward appearances, he had died of typhus.

Those who know how close the connection is between the state of mind of a man—his courage and hope, or lack of them—and the state of immunity of his body will understand that the sudden loss of hope and courage can have a deadly effect. The ultimate cause of my friend's death was that the expected liberation did not come and he was severely disappointed. This suddenly lowered his body's resistance against the latent typhus infection. His faith in the future and his will to live had become paralyzed and his body fell victim to illness—and thus the voice of his dream was right after all.

The observations of this one case and the conclusion drawn from them are in accordance with something that was drawn to my attention by the chief doctor of our concentration camp. The death rate in the week between Christmas, 1944, and New Year's, 1945, increased in camp beyond all previous experience. In his opinion, the explanation for this increase did not lie in the harder working conditions or the deterioration of our food supplies or a change of weather or new epidemics. It was simply that the majority of the prisoners had lived in the naïve hope that they would be home again by Christmas. As the time drew near and there was no encouraging news, the prisoners lost courage and disappointment overcame them. This had a dangerous influence on their powers of resistance and a great number of them died.

As we said before, any attempt to restore a man's inner strength in the camp had first to succeed in showing him some future goal. Nietzsche's words, "He who has a *why* to live for can bear with almost any *how*," could be the guiding motto for all psychotherapeutic and psychohygienic efforts regarding prisoners. Whenever there was an opportunity for it, one had to give them a why—an aim—for their lives, in order to strengthen them to bear the terrible *how* of their existence. Woe to him who saw no more sense in his life, no aim, no purpose, and therefore no point in carrying on. He was soon lost. The typical reply with which such a man rejected all encouraging arguments was, "I have nothing to expect from life any more." What sort of answer can one give to that?

What was really needed was a fundamental change in our attitude toward life. We had to learn ourselves and, furthermore, we had to teach the despairing men, that *it did not really matter what we expected from life, but rather what life expected from us.* We needed to stop asking about the meaning of life, and instead to think of ourselves as those who were being questioned by life—daily and hourly. Our answer must consist, not in talk and meditation, but in right action and in right conduct. Life ultimately means taking the responsibility to find the right answer to its problems and to fulfill the tasks which it constantly sets for each individual.

These tasks, and therefore the meaning of life, differ from man to man, and from moment to moment. Thus it is impossible to define the meaning of life in a general way. Questions about the meaning of life can never be answered by sweeping statements. "Life" does not mean something vague, but something very real and concrete, just as life's tasks are also very real and concrete. They form man's destiny, which is different and unique for each individual. No man and no destiny can be compared with any other man or any other destiny. No situation repeats itself, and each situation calls for a different response. Sometimes the situation in which a man finds himself may require him to shape his own fate by action. At other times it is more advantageous for him to make use of an opportunity for contemplation and to realize assets in this way. Sometimes man may be required simply to accept fate, to bear his cross.

Every situation is distinguished by its uniqueness, and there is always only one right answer to the problem posed by the situation at hand.

When a man finds that it is his destiny to suffer, he will have to accept his suffering as his task: his single and unique task. He will have to acknowledge the fact that even in suffering he is unique and alone in the universe. No one can relieve him of his suffering or suffer in his place. His unique opportunity lies in the way in which he bears his burden.

For us, as prisoners, these thoughts were not speculations far removed from reality. They were the only thoughts that could be of help to us. They kept us from despair, even when there seemed to be no chance of coming out of it alive. Long ago we had passed the stage of asking what was the meaning of life, a naïve query which understands life as the attaining of some aim through the active creation of something of value. For us, the meaning of life embraced the wider cycles of life and death, of suffering and of dying.

Once the meaning of suffering had been revealed to us, we refused to minimize or alleviate the camp's tortures by ignoring them or harboring false illusions and entertaining artificial optimism. Suffering had become a task on which we did not want to turn our backs. We had realized its hidden opportunities for achievement, the opportunities which caused the poet Rilke to write,"*Wie viel ist aufzuleiden!*" (How much suffering there is to get through!) Rilke spoke of "getting through suffering" as others would talk of "getting through work." There was plenty of suffering for us to get through. Therefore, it was necessary to face up to the full amount of suffering, trying to keep moments of weakness and furtive tears to a minimum. But there was no need to be ashamed of tears, for tears bore witness that a man had the greatest of courage, the courage to suffer. Only very few realized that. Shamefacedly some confessed occasionally that they had wept, like the comrade who answered my question of how he had gotten over his edema, by confessing, "I have wept it out of my system."

The tender beginnings of a psychotherapy or psychohygiene were, when they were possible at all in the camp, either individual or collective in nature. The individual psychotherapeutic attempts were often a kind of "life-saving procedure." These efforts were usually concerned with the prevention of suicides. A very strict camp ruling forbade any efforts to save a man who attempted suicide. It was forbidden, for example, to cut down a man who was trying to hang himself. Therefore, it was all important to prevent these attempts from occurring.

I remember two cases of would-be suicide, which bore a striking similarity to each other. Both men had talked of their intentions to commit suicide. Both used the typical argument—they had nothing more to expect from life. In both cases it was a question of getting them to realize that life was still expecting something from them; something in the future was expected of them. We found, in fact, that for the one it was his child whom he adored and who was waiting for him in a foreign country. For the other it was a thing, not a person. This man was a scientist and had written a series of books which still needed to be finished. His work could not be done by anyone else, any more than another person could ever take the place of the father in his child's affections.

This uniqueness and singleness which distinguishes each individual and gives a meaning to his existence has a bearing on creative work as much as it does on human love. When the impossibility of replacing a person is realized, it allows the responsibility which a man has for his existence and its continuance to appear in all its magnitude. A man who becomes conscious of the responsibility he bears toward a human being who affectionately waits for him, or to an unfinished work, will never be able to throw away his life. He knows the "why" for his existence, and will be able to bear almost any "how."

THE DROWNED AND THE SAVED

Primo Levi

What we have so far said and will say concerns the ambiguous life of the Lager. In our days many men have lived in this cruel manner, crushed against the bottom, but each for a relatively short period; so that we can perhaps ask ourselves if it is necessary or good to retain any memory of this exceptional human state.

To this question we feel that we have to reply in the affirmative. We are in fact convinced that no human experience is without meaning or unworthy of analysis, and that fundamental values, even if they are not positive, can be deduced from this particular world which we are describing. We would also like to consider that the Lager was pre-eminently a gigantic biological and social experiment.

Thousands of individuals, differing in age, condition, origin, language, culture and customs, are enclosed within barbed wire: there they live a regular, controlled life which is identical for all and inadequate to all needs, and which is more rigorous than any experimenter could have set up to establish what is essential and what adventitious to the conduct of the human animal in the struggle for life.

We do not believe in the most obvious and facile deduction: that man is fundamentally brutal, egoistic and stupid in his conduct once every civilized institution is taken away, and that the Häftling is consequently nothing but a man without inhibitions. We believe, rather, that the only conclusion to be drawn is that in the face of driving necessity and physical disabilities many social habits and instincts are reduced to silence.

But another fact seems to us worthy of attention: there comes to light the existence of two particularly well differentiated categories among men—the saved and the drowned. Other pairs of opposites (the good and the bad, the wise and the foolish, the cowards and the courageous, the unlucky and the fortunate) are considerably less distinct, they seem less essential, and above all they allow for more numerous and complex intermediary gradations.

This division is much less evident in ordinary life; for there it rarely happens that a man loses himself. A man is normally not alone, and in his rise or fall is tied to the destinies of his neighbours; so that it is exceptional for anyone to acquire unlimited power, or to fall by a succession of defeats into utter ruin. Moreover, everyone is normally in possession of such spiritual, physical and even financial resources that the probabilities of a shipwreck, of total inadequacy in the face of life, are relatively small. And one must take into account a definite cushioning effect exercised both by the law, and by the moral sense which constitutes a self-imposed law; for a country is considered the more civilized the more the wisdom and efficiency of its laws hinder a weak man from becoming too weak or a powerful one too powerful.

But in the Lager things are different: here the struggle to survive is without respite, because everyone is desperately and ferociously alone. If some Null Achtzehn vacillates, he will find no one to extend a helping hand; on the contrary, someone will knock him aside, because it is in no one's interest that there will be one more 'musselman'* dragging himself to work every day; and if someone, by a miracle of savage patience and cunning, finds a new method of avoiding the hardest work, a new art which yields him an ounce

---

*This word *'Muselmann'*, I do not know why, was used by the old ones of the camp to describe the weak, the inept, those doomed to selection.

of bread, he will try to keep his method secret, and he will be esteemed and respected for this, and will derive from it an exclusive, personal benefit; he will become stronger and so will be feared, and who is feared is, ipso facto, a candidate for survival.

In history and in life one sometimes seems to glimpse a ferocious law which states: 'to he that has, will be given; from he that has not, will be taken away.' In the Lager, where man is alone and where the struggle for life is reduced to its primordial mechanism, this unjust law is openly in force, is recognized by all. With the adaptable, the strong and astute individuals, even the leaders willingly keep contact, sometimes even friendly contact, because they hope later to perhaps derive some benefit. But with the musselmans, the men in decay, it is not even worth speaking, because one knows already that they will complain and will speak about what they used to eat at home. Even less worthwhile is it to make friends with them, because they have no distinguished acquaintances in camp, they do not gain any extra rations, they do not work in profitable Kommandos and they know no secret method of organizing. And in any case, one knows that they are only here on a visit, that in a few weeks nothing will remain of them but a handful of ashes in some near-by field and a crossed-out number on a register. Although engulfed and swept along without rest by the innumerable crowd of those similar to them, they suffer and drag themselves along in an opaque intimate solitude, and in solitude they die or disappear, without leaving a trace in anyone's memory.

The result of this pitiless process of natural selection could be read in the statistics of Lager population movements. At Auschwitz, in 1944, of the old Jewish prisoners (we will not speak of the others here, as their condition was different), 'kleine Nummer', low numbers less than 150,000, only a few hundred had survived; not one was an ordinary Häftling, vegetating in the ordinary Kommandos, and subsisting on the normal ration. There remained only the doctors, tailors, shoemakers, musicians, cooks, young attractive homosexuals, friends or compatriots of some authority in the camp; or they were particularly pitiless, vigorous and inhuman individuals, installed (following an investiture by the SS command, which showed itself in such choices to possess satanic knowledge of human beings) in the posts of Kapos, Blockältester, etc.; or finally, those who, without fulfilling particular functions, had always succeeded through their astuteness and energy in successfully organizing, gaining in this way, besides material advantages and reputation, the indulgence and esteem of the powerful people in the camp. Whosoever does not know how to become an 'Organisator,' 'Kombinator,' 'Prominent' (the savage eloquence of these words!) soon becomes a 'musselman.' In life, a third way exists, and is in fact the rule; it does not exist in the concentration camp.

To sink is the easiest of matters; it is enough to carry out all the orders one receives, to eat only the ration, to observe the discipline of the work and the camp. Experience showed that only exceptionally could one survive more than three months in this way. All the musselmans who finished in the gas chambers have the same story, or more exactly, have no story; they followed the slope down to the bottom, like streams that run down to the sea. On their entry into the camp, through basic incapacity, or by misfortune, or through some banal incident, they are overcome before they can adapt themselves; they are beaten by time, they do not begin to learn German, to disentangle the infernal knot of laws and prohibitions until their body is already in decay, and nothing can save them from selections or from death by exhaustion. Their life is short, but their number is endless: they, the Muselmänner, the drowned, form the backbone of the camp, an anonymous mass, continually renewed and always identical, of non-men who march and labour in silence, the divine spark dead within them, already too empty to really suffer. One hesitates to call them living: one hesitates to call their death death, in the face of which they have no fear, as they are too tired to understand.

They crowd my memory with their faceless presences, and if I could enclose all the evil of our time in one image, I would choose this image which is familiar to me: an emaciated man, with head dropped and shoulders curved, on whose face and in whose eyes not a trace of a thought is to be seen.

If the drowned have no story, and single and broad is the path to perdition, the paths to salvation are many, difficult and improbable.

The most travelled road, as we have stated, is the '*Prominenz.*' '*Prominenten*' is the name for the camp officials, from the Häftling-director (*Lagerältester*) to the Kapos, the cooks, the nurses, the night-guards, even to the hut-sweepers and to the *Scheissminister* and *Bademeister* (superintendents of the latrines and showers). We are more particularly interested in the Jewish prominents, because while the others are automatically invested with offices as they enter the camp in virtue of their natural supremacy, the Jews have to plot and struggle hard to gain them.

The Jewish prominents form a sad and notable human phenomenon. In them converge present, past and atavistic sufferings, and the tradition of hostility towards the stranger makes of them monsters of asociality and insensitivity.

They are the typical product of the structure of the German Lager: if one offers a position of privilege to a few individuals in a state of slavery, exacting in exchange the betrayal of a natural solidarity with their comrades, there will certainly be someone who will accept. He will be withdrawn from the common law and will become untouchable; the more power that he is given, the more he will be consequently hateful and hated. When he is given the command of a group of unfortunates, with the right of life or death over them, he will be cruel and tyrannical, because he will understand that if he is not sufficiently so, someone else, judged more suitable, will take over his post. Moreover, his capacity for hatred, unfulfilled in the direction of the oppressors, will double back, beyond all reason, on the oppressed; and he will only be satisfied when he has unloaded on to his underlings the injury received from above.

We are aware that this is very distant from the picture that is usually given of the oppressed who unite, if not in resistance, at least in suffering. We do not deny that this may be possible when oppression does not pass a certain limit, or perhaps when the oppressor, through inexperience or magnanimity, tolerates or favours it. But we state that in our days, in all countries in which a foreign people have set foot as invaders, an analogous position of rivalry and hatred among the subjected has been brought about; and this, like many other human characteristics, could be experienced in the Lager in the light of particularly cruel evidence.

About the non-Jewish prominents there is less to say, although they were far and away the most numerous (no 'Aryan' Häftling was without a post, however modest). That they were stolid and bestial is natural when one thinks that the majority were ordinary criminals, chosen from the German prisons for the very purpose of their employment as superintendents of the camps for Jews; and we maintain that it was a very apt choice, because we refuse to believe that the squalid human specimens whom we saw at work were an average example, not of Germans in general, but even of German prisoners in particular. It is difficult to explain how in Auschwitz the political German, Polish and Russian prominents rivalled the ordinary convicts in brutality. But it is known that in Germany the qualification of political crime also applied to such acts as clandestine trade, illicit relations with Jewish women, theft from Party officials. The "real" politicals lived and died in other camps, with names now sadly famous, in notoriously hard conditions, which, however, in many aspects differed from those described here.

But besides the officials in the strict sense of the word, there is a vast category of prisoners, not initially favoured by fate, who fight merely with their own strength to survive. One has to fight against the current; to battle every day and every hour against exhaustion, hunger, cold and the resulting inertia; to resist enemies and have no pity for rivals; to sharpen one's wits, build up one's patience, strengthen one's will-power. Or else, to throttle all dignity and kill all conscience, to climb down into the arena as a beast against other beasts, to let oneself be guided by those unsuspected subterranean forces which sustain families and individuals in cruel times. Many were the ways devised and put into effect by us in order not to die: as many as there are different human characters. All implied a weakening struggle of one against all, and a by no means small sum of aberrations and compromises. Survival without renunciation of any part of one's own moral world – apart from powerful and direct interventions by fortune – was conceded only to very few superior individuals, made of the stuff of martyrs and saints.

We will try to show in how many ways it was possible to reach salvation with the stories of Schepschel, Alfred L., Elias and Henri.

Schepschel has been living in the Lager for four years. He has seen the death of tens of thousands of those like him, beginning with the pogrom which had driven him from his village in Galicia. He had a wife and five children and a prosperous business as a saddler, but for a long time now he has grown accustomed to thinking of himself only as a sack which needs periodic refilling. Schepschel is not very robust, nor very courageous, nor very wicked; he is not even particularly astute, nor has he ever found a method which allows him a little respite, but he is reduced to small and occasional expedients, 'kombinacje' as they are called here.

Every now and again he steals a broom in Buna and sells it to the *Blockältester*; when he manages to set aside a little bread-capital, he hires the tools of the cobbler in the Block, his compatriot, and works on his own account for a few hours; he knows how to make braces with interlaced electric wires. Sigi told me that he has seen him during the midday interval singing and dancing in front of the hut of the Slovak workers, who sometimes reward him with the remainders of their soup.

This said, one would be inclined to think of Schepschel with indulgent sympathy, as of a poor wretch who retains only a humble and elementary desire to live, and who bravely carries on his small struggle not to give way. But Schepschel was no exception, and when the opportunity showed itself, he did not hesitate to have Moischl, his accomplice in a theft from the kitchen, condemned to a flogging, in the mistaken hope of gaining favour in the eyes of the *Blockältester* and furthering his candidature for the position of *Kesselwäscher*, 'vat-washer.'

The story of engineer Alfred L. shows among other things how vain is the myth of original equality among men.

In his own country L. was the director of an extremely important factory of chemical products, and his name was (and is) well-known in industrial circles throughout Europe. He was a robust man of about fifty; I do not know how he had been arrested, but he entered the camp like all others: naked, alone and unknown. When I knew him he was very wasted away, but still showed on his face the signs of a disciplined and methodical energy; at that time, his privileges were limited to the daily cleaning of the Polish workers' pots; this work, which he had gained in some manner as his exclusive monopoly, yielded him half a ladleful of soup per day. Certainly it was not enough to satisfy his hunger; nevertheless, no one had ever heard him complain. In fact, the few words that he let slip implied imposing secret resources, a solid and fruitful 'organization.'

This was confirmed by his appearance. L. had a 'line': with his hands and face always perfectly clean, he had the rare self-denial to wash his shirt every fortnight, without waiting for the bi-monthly change (we would like to point out here that to wash a shirt meant finding soap, time and space in the over-crowded washroom; adapting oneself to carefully keep watch on the wet shirt without losing attention for a moment, and to put it on, naturally still wet, in the silence-hour when the lights are turned out); he owned a pair of wooden shoes to go to the shower, and even his striped suit was singularly adapted to his appearance, clean and new. L. had acquired in practice the whole appearance of a prominent considerably before becoming one; only a long time after did I find out that L. was able to earn all this show of prosperity with incredible tenacity, paying for his individual acquisitions and services with bread from his own ration, so imposing upon himself a regime of supplementary privations.

His plan was a long-term one, which is all the more notable as conceived in an environment dominated by a mentality of the provisional; and L. carried it out with rigid inner discipline, without pity for himself or – with greater reason – for comrades who crossed his path. L. knew that the step was short from being judged powerful to effectively becoming so, and that everywhere, and especially in the midst of the general levelling of the Lager, a respectable appearance is the best guarantee of being respected. He took every care not to be confused with the mass; he worked with stubborn duty, even occasionally admonishing his lazy comrades in a persuasive and deprecatory tone of voice; he avoided the daily struggle for the best place in the queue for the ration, and prepared to take the first ration, notoriously the most liquid, every day, so as to be noticed by his *Blockältester* for his discipline. To complete the separation, he always behaved in his relations with his comrades with the maximum courtesy compatible with his egotism, which was absolute.

When the Chemical Kommando was formed, as will be described, L. knew that his hour had struck: he needed no more than his spruce suit and his emaciated and shaved face in the midst of the flock of his sordid and slovenly colleagues to at once convince both Kapo and *Arbeitsdienst* that he was one of the genuinely saved, a potential prominent; so that (to he who has, shall be given) he was without hesitation appointed 'specialist,' nominated technical head of the Kommando, and taken on by the Direction of the Buna as analyst in the laboratory of the styrene department. He was subsequently appointed to examine all the new intake to the Chemical Kommando, to judge their professional ability; which he always did with extreme severity, especially when faced with those in whom he smelled possible future rivals.

I do not know how his story continued; but I feel it is quite probable that he managed to escape death, and today is still living his cold life of the determined and joyless dominator.

Elias Lindzin, 141565, one day rained into the Chemical Kommando. He was a dwarf, not more than five feet high, but I have never seen muscles like his. When he is naked you can see every muscle taut under his skin, like a poised animal; his body, enlarged without alteration of proportions, would serve as a good model for a Hercules: but you must not look at his head.

Under his scalp, the skull sutures stand out immoderately. The cranium is massive and gives the impression of being made of metal or stone; the limit of his shaven hair shows up barely a finger's width above his eyebrows. The nose, the chin, the forehead, the cheekbones are hard and compact, the whole face looks like a battering ram, an instrument made for butting. A sense of bestial vigour emanates from his body.

To see Elias work is a disconcerting spectacle; the Polish *Meister*, even the Germans sometimes stop to admire Elias at work. Nothing seems impossible to him. While we barely carry one sack of cement, Elias carries two, then three, then four, keeping them balanced no one knows how, and while he hurries along on his short, squat legs, he makes faces under the load, he laughs, curses, shouts and sings without pause, as if he had lungs made of bronze. Despite his wooden shoes Elias climbs like a monkey on to the scaffolding and runs safely on cross-beams poised over nothing; he carries six bricks at a time balanced on his head; he knows how to make a spoon from a piece of tin, and a knife from a scrap of steel; he finds dry paper, wood and coal everywhere and knows how to start a fire in a few moments even in the rain. He is a tailor, a carpenter, a cobbler, a barber; he can spit incredible distances; he sings, in a not unpleasant bass voice, Polish and Yiddish songs never heard before; he can ingest ten, fifteen, twenty pints of soup without vomiting and without having diarrhea, and begin work again immediately after. He knows how to make a big hump come out between his shoulders, and goes around the hut, bow-legged and mimicking, shouting and declaiming incomprehensibly, to the joy of the Prominents of the camp. I saw him fight a Pole a whole head taller than him and knock him down with a blow of his cranium into the stomach, as powerful and accurate as a catapult. I never saw him rest, I never saw him quiet or still, I never saw him injured or ill.

Of his life as a free man, no one knows anything; and in any case, to imagine Elias as a free man requires a great effort of fantasy and induction; he only speaks Polish, and the surly and deformed Yiddish of Warsaw; besides it is impossible to keep him to a coherent conversation. He might be twenty or forty years old; he usually says that he is thirty-three, and that he has begot seventeen children – which is not unlikely. He talks continuously on the most varied of subjects; always in a resounding voice, in an oratorical manner, with the violent mimicry of the deranged; as if he was always talking to a dense crowd – and as is natural, he never lacks a public. Those who understand his language drink up his declamations, shaking with laughter; they pat him enthusiastically on the back – a back as hard as iron—inciting him to continue; while he, fierce and frowning, whirls around like a wild animal in the circle of his audience, apostrophizing now one, now another of them; he suddenly grabs hold of one by the chest with his small hooked paw, irresistibly drags him to himself, vomits into his face an incomprehensible invective, then throws him back like a piece of wood, and amidst the applause and laughter, with his arms reaching up to the heavens like some little prophetic monster, continues his raging and crazy speech.

His fame as an exceptional worker spread quite soon, and by the absurd law of the Lager, from then on he practically ceased to work. His help was requested directly by the *Meister* only for such work as required skill and special vigour. Apart from these services he insolently and violently supervised our daily, flat exhaustion, frequently disappearing on mysterious visits and adventures in who knows what recesses of the yard, from which he returned with large bulges in his pockets and often with his stomach visibly full.

Elias is naturally and innocently a thief: in this he shows the instinctive astuteness of wild animals. He is never caught in the act because he only steals when there is a good chance; but when this chance comes Elias steals as fatally and foreseeably as a stone drops. Apart from the fact that it is difficult to surprise him, it is obvious that it would be of no use punishing him for his thefts: to him they imply a vital act like breathing or sleeping.

We can now ask who is this man Elias. If he is a madman, incomprehensible and para-human, who ended in the Lager by chance. If he is an atavism, different from our modern world, and better adapted to the primordial conditions of camp life. Or if he is perhaps a product of the camp itself, what we will all become if we do not die in the camp, and if the camp itself does not end first.

There is some truth in all three suppositions. Elias has survived the destruction from outside, because he is physically indestructible; he has resisted the annihilation from within because he is insane. So, in the first place, he is a survivor: he is the most adaptable, the human type most suited to this way of living.

If Elias regains his liberty he will be confined to the fringes of human society, in a prison or a lunatic asylum. But here in the Lager there are no criminals nor madmen; no criminals because there is no moral law to contravene, no madmen because we are wholly devoid of free will, as our every action is, in time and place, the only conceivable one.

In the Lager Elias prospers and is triumphant. He is a good worker and a good organizer, and for this double reason, he is safe from selections and respected by both leaders and comrades. For those who have no sound inner resources, for those who do not know how to draw from their own consciences sufficient force to cling to life, the only road to salvation leads to Elias: to insanity and to deceitful bestiality. All the other roads are dead-ends.

This said, one might perhaps be tempted to draw conclusions, and perhaps even rules for our daily life. Are there not all around us some Eliases, more or less in embryo? Do we not see individuals living without purpose, lacking all forms of self-control and conscience, who live not *in spite of* these defects, but like Elias precisely because of them?

The question is serious, but will not be further discussed as we want these to be stories of the Lager, while much has already been written on man outside the Lager. But one thing we would like to add: Elias, as far as we could judge from outside, and as far as the phrase can have meaning, was probably a happy person.

Henri, on the other hand, is eminently civilized and sane, and possesses a complete and organic theory on the ways to survive in Lager. He is only twenty-two, he is extremely intelligent, speaks French, German, English and Russian, has an excellent scientific and classical culture.

His brother died in Buna last winter, and since then Henri has cut off every tie of affection; he has closed himself up, as if in armour, and fights to live without distraction with all the resources that he can derive from his quick intellect and his refined education. According to Henri's theory, there are three methods open to man to escape extermination which still allow him to retain the name of man: organization, pity and theft.

He himself practises all three. There is no better strategist than Henri in seducing ('cultivating' he says) the English PoWs. In his hands they become real geese with golden eggs—if you remember that in exchange for a single English cigarette you can make enough in the Lager not to starve for a day. Henri was once seen in the act of eating a real hard-boiled egg.

The traffic in products of English origin is Henri's monopoly, and this is all a matter of organization; but his instrument of penetration, with the English and with others, is pity. Henri has the delicate and subtly perverse body and face of Sodoma's San Sebastian: his eyes are deep and profound, he has no beard yet, he moves with a natural languid elegance (although when necessary he knows how to run and jump like a cat, while the capacity of his stomach is little inferior to that of Elias). Henri is perfectly aware of his natural gifts and exploits them with the cold competence of a physicist using a scientific instrument: the results are surprising. Basically it is a question of a discovery: Henri has discovered that pity, being a primary and instinctive sentiment, grows quite well if ably cultivated, particularly in the primitive minds of the brutes who command us, those very brutes who have no scruples about beating us up without a reason, or treading our faces into the ground; nor has the great practical importance of the discovery escaped him, and upon it he has built up his personal trade.

As the ichneumon paralyses the great hairy caterpillar, wounding it in its only vulnerable ganglion, so Henri at a glance sizes up the subject, *'son type'*; he speaks to him briefly, to each with the appropriate language, and the *'type'* is conquered: he listens with increasing sympathy, he is moved by the fate of this unfortunate young man, and not much time is needed before he begins to yield returns.

There is no heart so hardened that Henri cannot breach it if he sets himself to it seriously. In the Lager, and in Buna as well, his protectors are very numerous: English soldiers, French, Ukrainian, Polish civilian workers: German 'politicals'; at least four *Blockältester*, a cook, even an SS man. But his favourite field is Ka-Be: Henri has free entry into Ka-Be; Doctor Citron and Doctor Weiss are more than his protectors, they are his friends and take him in whenever he wants and with the diagnosis he wants. This takes place especially immediately before selections, and in the periods of the most laborious work: 'hibernation,' as he says.

Possessing such conspicuous friendships, it is natural that Henri is rarely reduced to the third method, theft; on the other hand, he naturally does not talk much about this subject.

It is very pleasant to talk to Henri in moments of rest. It is also useful: there is nothing in the camp that he does not know and about which he has not reasoned in his close and coherent manner. Of his conquests, he speaks with educated modesty, as of prey of little worth, but he digresses willingly into an explanation of the calculation which led him to approach Hans asking him about his son at the front, and Otto instead showing him the scars on his shins.

To speak with Henri is useful and pleasant: one sometimes also feels him warm and near; communication, even affection seems possible. One seems to glimpse, behind his uncommon personality, a human soul, sorrowful and aware of itself. But the next moment his sad smile freezes into a cold grimace which seems studied at the mirror; Henri politely excuses himself ('. . .j'ai quelque chose à faire.' '. . .j'ai quelqu'un à voir') and here he is again, intent on his hunt and his struggle; hard and distant, enclosed in armour, the enemy of all, inhumanly cunning and incomprehensible like the Serpent in Genesis.

From all my talks with Henri, even the most cordial, I have always left with a slight taste of defeat; of also having been, somehow inadvertently, not a man to him, but an instrument in his hands.

I know that Henri is living today. I would give much to know his life as a free man, but I do not want to see him again.

LESSONS LEARNED FROM GENTLE HEROISM: WOMEN'S HOLOCAUST NARRATIVES

Myrna Goldenberg

Memoirs written by women survivors of the Holocaust share certain characteristics with those written by men, such as a narrative structure that begins with belonging and then moves to humiliation, isolation, deprivation, and finally annihilation. Men and women survivors both describe gratuitous and deliberate violence by Kapos and SS. However, women's memoirs also share strikingly similar characteristics with each other that differ from men's memoirs and that stem from their experiences as women and as Jews—thus as double victims—in a misogynistic, racist totalitarian society. Women's memoirs yield anecdotes that demonstrate women's resourcefulness in the hells of the ghettos and camps. Thus women's narratives are rich sources of the characteristics of an alternative social structure based on traditional feminine values. The experience of women during the Holocaust shows that traditionally feminist values of cooperating and caring are important conditions for the perpetuation of civilization, irrespective of religious, ethnic, or nationalist identification.

"If you are sisterless, you do not have the pressure, the absolute responsibility to end the day alive."[1] Written by Auschwitz survivor Isabella Leitner, who was a prisoner in Auschwitz, these words provoke an examination of women's experiences during the Holocaust. Her memoir, together with hundreds of other descriptions of concentration camp experiences from the perspective of a woman, provides a new dimension to Holocaust studies. Although an enormous amount of material has already been generated about the Holocaust, most of it has focused on the historical events, whether from German, American, or Russian sources, and most of it has assumed a male-centered perspective. That is, the experiences of Jewish men have been documented and generalized as if they were as true for women as they were for men.[2] Although Nazis carefully defined the Jew in Germany, they distinguished between Jews by sex, officially renaming them either Israel or Sara. This measure was an attempt to disconnect them from the custom that linked them to their ancestors, the specific persons for whom they were named, and thus their Jewish heritage.[3] Hence all German Jews, regardless of class or other variables, were categorized only as either Jewish men or Jewish women.[4]

The examination of the literature of women Holocaust survivors suggests that we are confronted with a unique genre, one that is driven by the twin circumstances of racism and gender. Analysis of the differences and similarities in the experiences of Jewish men and women is controversial. A few scholars and survivors have suggested that

---

[1] Isabella Leitner, *Fragments of Isabella* (New York: Dell, 1978), p. 44.

[2] Marion Kaplan, *The Making of the Jewish Middle Class: Women, Family, and Identity in Imperial Germany* (New York: Oxford University Press, 1991), pp. vii–xi. Kaplan explains that "there has been an unfortunate tendency among historians to view a history of Jewish men as Jewish history but a history of Jewish women as women's history, thereby marginalizing women's lives and history." See also Kaplan, *The Jewish Feminist Movement in Germany: The Campaigns of the JFB, 1904–1938* (Westport, CT: Greenwood Press, 1979).

[3] It is the custom among European Jews to name their children after an admired deceased relative.

[4] For an excellent discussion of German Jewish women during the Nazi era, see Sybil Milton, "Women and the Holocaust: The Case of German and German-Jewish Women," *Monthly Review Press*, pp. 297–333 (1984).

such comparisons are inappropriate, divisive, or politically motivated. On the other hand, as Raul Hilberg points out, "The road to annihilation was marked by events that specifically affected men as men and women as women."[5] Thus women's memoirs reveal "different horrors" of the "same Hell."[6] Generally, the discussions of the experiences of women that were unique to women document the particular cruelties women endured, but few scholars have discussed the implications of women's experiences.[7] It can hardly be overemphasized that the literature about and by Jewish women who lived under Nazi control reflects a double vulnerability as both Jews and women. Their writings reflect their experiences from three perspectives, all three of which are a function of a double vulnerability as Jewish women: (1) biological differences from men; (2) gender-specific socialization patterns; and (3) as implied by Leitner's admonition, the ethic of caring that both reflected and was generated from their experiences as women.

That women were regarded differently from men stems from deep-seated Nazi ideology that was rooted in patriarchy and racism. Hitler's frequently repeated statement, "The Nazi Revolution will be an entirely male event,"[8] forewarned us of the political goal of male Aryan supremacy and of a social structure that denied all Jews both essence and existence. Although Hitler praised the prolific Aryan mother as the equal of the Aryan soldier, National Socialism rendered German women invisible except as child bearers and child rearers. The ideal Nazi wife was the wholesome, athletic, peasant type—a domestic mother and helper to her husband: "Her whole world is her husband, her family, her children, her house."[9] This unrealistic vision of women as mothers of the Aryan race delayed Hitler's approval of their conscription in the war effort.[10]

His vision of Jewish women, however, was far more costly. When, in 1934, Hitler equated Jewish intellectualism with the emancipated "new woman," he essentially informed the world that his social plans would reflect his political aims. To Hitler, activist Jewish women, such as Rosa Luxemburg, symbolized the evils of Jewishness and, in particular, Jewish women: "She and other women activists, Jewish and non-Jewish

---

[5] Raul Hilberg, *Perpetrators, Victims, and Bystanders* (New York: Harper Collins, 1992), p. 126.

[6] Myrna Goldenberg, "Different Horrors, Same Hell: Women Remembering the Holocaust," in *Thinking the Unthinkable: Meanings of the Holocaust*, ed. Roger Gottlieb (Mahwah, NJ: Paulist Press, 1990), pp. 150–66.

[7] Carol Rittner and John Roth, eds., *Different Voices: Women and the Holocaust* (New York: Paragon House, 1993), the first anthology in English devoted to women's experiences in the Holocaust. See also Sybil Milton, "Women and the Holocaust: The Case of German and German-Jewish Women," in *When Biology Became Destiny*, ed. Renate Bridenthal, Atina Grossman, and Marion Kaplan (New York: Monthly Review Press, 1984), pp. 297–333; Marlene Heinemann, *Gender and Destiny: Women Writers of the Holocaust* (New York: Greenwood Press, 1986); Joan Ringelheim, "Thoughts About Women and the Holocaust," in *Thinking the Unthinkable*, ed. Gottlieb, pp. 141–9; Goldenberg, "Different Horrors, Same Hell"; idem, "Testimony, Narrative, and Nightmare: The Experiences of Jewish Women in the Holocaust," in *Women and Jewish Culture*, ed. Maurie Sacks (Champaign: University of Illinois Press, 1995), pp. 94–106.

[8] Claudia Koonz, *Mothers in the Fatherland: Women, the Family, and Nazi Politics* (New York: St Martin's Press, 1987), p. 56.

[9] Adolf Hitler, from *Volkischer Beobachter*, 9 Sept. 1934, in *Inside Hitler's Germany: A Documentary History of Life in the Third Reich*, ed. Benjamin C. Sax and Dieter Kunz (Lexington, MA: D.C. Heath, 1992).

[10] Jill Stephenson, "The Wary Response of Women," in *The Nazi Revolution*, ed. Allan Mitchell (New York: D.C. Heath, 1990), pp. 167–75; idem, *Women in Nazi Society* (New York: Harper & Row, 1976), esp. pp. 185–99. See also Elaine Martin, *Gender, Patriarchy, and Fascism in the Third Reich: The Response of Women Writers* (Detroit, MI: Wayne State University Press, 1993), for a superb collection of essays on the interconnections of patriarchy and fascism in twentieth-century Germany.

alike, were remembered with fear and loathing as examples of what National Socialism was pledged to prevent."[11] One woman survivor, the daughter of a Jewish father and Christian mother, noted sardonically that "the Nazis were so male-oriented that they considered children of Jewish fathers more Jewish than children of Jewish mothers, the opposite of [what holds true in] traditional Jewish law."[12]

The treatment of men and women differed during the course of the Third Reich according to the needs of the Reich at any given time and to the needs and whims of leaders and individual soldiers of the Reich. Joan Ringelheim argues forcefully that the Nazis deported more Jewish women than Jewish men and, for a variety of reasons, killed more women than men.[13] Raul Hilberg cites similar demographics but, drawing from ghetto statistics and Einsatzgruppen records, states categorically that men were killed earlier in the war years than women. He attributes this difference in death rate to the fact that many more men than women were given hard labor assignments in the ghettos and were killed in the first mass murders in the USSR and Serbia. Furthermore, explains Hilberg, because of the need to develop a huge slave labor supply for the concentration and work camps, far more women than men were gassed immediately upon their arrival at Auschwitz and other camps.[14] Presumably, in the first few years of Nazi expansion, men were more valued as laborers than were women. It is also probable that more women than men were gassed because their small children clung to them when SS doctors separated men and women as they disembarked from the trains that brought them to the death camps.

Survival figures, though, are unreliable because of the loss of written records in the chaos of war and liberation.[15] The German sources themselves are suspect because Nazi statistics were prepared with an eye toward documenting the success of a 1000 year Third Reich. More troubling perhaps is the fact that we are forced to acknowledge that, in a society that perverted both morality and truth, statistics take on an impossible burden of proof. We are required, therefore, to supplement German sources by relying on inferences drawn from the confluences of many sources, written and oral, about the same events as well as from primary materials that are strongly corroborated by other primary materials.

Violence and Sexuality as a Theme in Memoirs by Women Survivors

Among the documents about the Holocaust are hundreds of memoirs by survivors. Many, such as those by Aharon Appelfeld, Primo Levi, Ida Fink, Elie Wiesel, and

---

[11] Yaffa Eliach, "Women and the Holocaust: Historical Background," *Women of Valor: Partisans and Resistance Fighters*, 6(4):8 (Spring 1990).

[12] Alison Owings, *Frauen: German Women Recall the Third Reich* (New Brunswick, NJ: Rutgers University Press, 1993), p. 453. Eliach also says that "while the status of the Aryan woman in Nazi Germany was distinctly second class, Jewish women were not just inferior to men, but to the entire Aryan race." Ibid., p. 8.

[13] Ringelheim, "Thoughts About Women and the Holocaust," p. 147.

[14] Hilberg, *Perpetrators, Victims, and Bystanders*, pp. 126–30.

[15] Yet it must be remembered that the Holocaust was and still is unique and that "in Auschwitz, more persons were killed than anywhere ever before at one place on this planet," according to Lore Shelley, ed., *Auschwitz: The Nazi Civilization: Twenty-Three Women Prisoners' Accounts* (Lanham, MD: University Press of America, 1992), p. 1. One of Shelley's narrators, who worked in the Political Section as secretary to Pery Broad, explained that when the Russians approached Auschwitz, the "SS tried to destroy as much incriminating evidence as possible. For many weeks we had to burn documents." Ibid., p. 10.

Charlotte Delbo, are, paradoxically, beautifully written literary works about atrocity. Others, also gripping accounts of unspeakable horror (though less artistically narrated), are no less substantial as primary source material. Memoirs written by women survivors share certain characteristics with those written by men, such as a narrative structure that begins with belonging (to the Jewish family or community) and then moves to humiliation, isolation, deprivation, and finally annihilation.[16] Men and women survivors both describe gratuitous and deliberate violence by *Kapos* and SS, but the differences in responses by Jewish men and women to Nazi deprivation and cruelty are illuminating although, up to very recently, ignored or neglected. Jewish women "belonged," as Marion Kaplan explains, "to a sex-segregated religion and a sex-segregated society."[17] The complexities of religious activity, class, and gender had, by the time of the Holocaust, already diminished women's social and political status. The growing number of survivor narratives by women and the testimony taken in preparation for war crimes trials testify to these differences.[18]

Women's narratives echo several themes that are unique to women's biology, such as amenorrhea and its psychological effects, vulnerability to rape and other sexual offenses, pregnancy, and childbirth. Gerda Klein feared that she would never again menstruate and thus, even if she did survive, would eventually give Hitler a victory. Desperately wanting to have a baby, the possibility of forced sterilization and the reality of amenorrhea terrified her. She "would endure anything willingly so long as that hope was not extinguished."[19] Isabella Leitner opens her memoir with a chilling understatement that she had not "menstruated for a long time," introducing the idea of the Final Solution as planned sterility.[20] Ironically, these women, and indeed most women in the Western world during this era, accepted their biological destiny unquestioningly. Few women, however, measured themselves as completely in biological terms as Hitler proposed.

Fear of rape permeates 16-year-old Judith Isaacson's memoir. Hyena, the name she and her bunkmates gave to the sadistic *Kapo* of her work *Kommando*, understood Isaacson's tensions and taunted her:

> I can read your face. But dreaming is all that's left for you, bitch. After the war, you'll be transported to a desert island. No males—not even natives. Much use'll be your fancy looks, with snakes for company. Do you suppose the Americans will win the war? That would be your death sentence. We'll shoot you Jewish bitches before the Americans come—it's the Fuhrer's decree. Your fate is sealed either way: No men. No sex. No seed of Sarah.[21]

Many years later, when Isaacson and her daughter returned to Hungary, her daughter asked about the fate of her mother's friends. Isaacson explained that most

---

[16] Goldenberg, "Testimony, Narrative, and Nightmare."

[17] Kaplan, *Making of the Jewish Middle Class*, p. ix.

[18] Goldenberg, "Different Horrors," pp. 150–66; idem, "Testimony, Narrative, and Nightmare."

[19] Gerda Klein, *All But My Life* (New York: Hill & Wong, 1957), pp. 155–6.

[20] Leitner, *Fragments of Isabella*, p. 14.

[21] Judith Isaacaon, *Seed of Sarah: Memoirs of a Survivor* (Urbana: University of Illinois Press, 1990), p. 108.

had been raped and killed, by Russians if not by Nazis. When her daughter sighed that "thousands of women were raped during the war, but no one hears about them," Isaacson answered, "The Anne Franks who survived rape don't write their stories."[22]

Prior to being murdered in Einsatzgruppen actions, single girls and young women were often raped,[23] despite the fact that the 1935 Law for the Protection of German Blood and German Honor prohibited intercourse between Aryans and Jews.[24] Although some autobiographical Holocaust fiction deals with rape and the bartering of sex for temporary rescue,[25] very few memoirs or other historical sources discuss actual rapes, and, owing to the age of the survivors and to the seriousness of the crime of *Rassenschande* ("race defilement"), there is virtually no likelihood that extensive Nazi documentation will be found.[26]

In rape situations, women were victims of their biology and their social and political status. In sexual bartering, women controlled the use of their bodies as if their sexuality were a commodity. The difference is subtle but significant. Though seldom written about, forced sexual activities were common in ghettos and in partisan camps and were not infrequent in concentration camps. In ghettos and concentration camps, "women prepared to sell their bodies for food" for their children.[27] In Terezin, and presumably other places, *Kapos* seduced women and gave them food in return; neither was prostitution unknown. Male prisoners who had jobs to do in the women's sections of the camps sold food for sex, but some survivors also note that starvation caused a striking absence of the sex drive. Others confide that there was "everlasting talk about sex and smut [which] may be considered as compensatory satisfaction."[28]

After her parents both died from starvation, 17-year-old Lucille Eichengreen was left to take care of herself and Karin, her 12-year-old sister. Trying to find her a place in one of the Lodz ghetto factories that fronted for schools, she encountered a manager who offered Karin a place but demanded something in return. When Lucille "explained that [she] had neither money nor valuables, he laughed and said that that was not what he had in mind." Lucille, in her näiveté was "stunned. The realization was sudden and painful: there were favors to be bought, but they had to be paid for by one way or another—even among our own."[29] But later in a labor camp, she could not resist stealing a "dirty piece of cloth in splashy shades of rust red and olive green" from the rubble she was supposed to clear. She wanted the "threadbare cloth" to cover her bald head. She hid it between her thighs. When her SS guard ordered her to a secluded place where

---

[22] Ibid., pp. 144–5.

[23] Eliach, "Women and the Holocaust: Historical Background," p. 8.

[24] Rittner and Roth, *Different Voices*, p. 23.

[25] See, for example, Ida Fink, "Aryan Papers," *A Scrap of Time* (New York: Schocken Books, 1987); Arnost Lustig, *The Unloved* (New York: Arbor House, 1985); idem. *Indecent Dreams* (Evanston: Northwestern Illinois Press, 1988).

[26] An interesting and ironic side note is the eyewitness accounts of Nazi use of blood from Jewish prisoners of Auschwitz for donations to the German army. See Gisela Perl, *I Was a Doctor in Auschwitz* (1948; Salem, NH: Ayer, 1984), pp. 74–5.

[27] Elie A. Cohen, *Human Behavior in the Concentration Camp* (1954; London: Association Books, 1988), p. 135.

[28] Ibid., p. 141.

[29] Lucille Eichengreen, *From Ashes to Life: My Memories of the Holocaust* (San Francisco: Mercury House, 1994), pp. 48–9.

he could rape her unseen, he found the scarf and disgustedly flung her aside with the words, "You filthy, useless bitch! Pfui! Menstruating!"[30]

Felicia Berland Hyatt, raised in strict Orthodoxy in Chelm, was cautioned by her mother to "do anything anybody asks you to do, just so you save your life." Hyatt and her mother parted, convinced that separation increased their chances to survive. She was grateful for her mother's parting words, which stunned her at the time: "The instructions she gave me when we parted were truly a revelation and they became even more meaningful, when months later I was faced with a situation in which I had to make a snap decision about bestowing a sexual favor in exchange for a temporary rescue from the German authorities."[31] Ironically, the same sexual vulnerability that victimized women also provided them with a small but significant measure of control.

In the concentration camps, the Nazis perfected a process of sexual humiliation that disoriented girls and women at the very same time that they were separated from their families. Girls and women who, on their arrival at a camp, were not chosen for immediate death underwent a gamut of humiliations, including exposure, crude body searches for hidden jewelry, painful body shaves, and sexual ridicule. Even at the moments before death, SS men tried to demoralize Jewish women. As a member of the *Sonderkommando*, Leib Langfuss wrote his observations of such activity and hid his manuscript for posterity. One SS officer, he wrote, "had the custom of standing at the doorway . . . and feeling the private parts of the young women entering the gas bunker. There were also instances of SS men of all ranks pushing their fingers into the sexual organs of pretty young women."[32] An SS officer explained that "mothers with small children are on principle unfit for work. [After they were gassed, they] were also searched to see if they had not hidden jewelry in the intimate parts of their bodies, and their hair was cut off and methodically placed in sacks for industrial purposes."[33] Not only were they violated in life, but they were violated in death as well.

Many women describe their horror at being required to undress in front of leering SS men and at being shaved by male prisoners. Rose Meth, one of the women who smuggled gunpowder to the *Sonderkommando* in Auschwitz, said, "They made us undress completely naked in front of the Nazi soldiers. We wanted to die. They shaved our heads. They shaved all our hair, everywhere."[34] Sarah Nomberg-Przytyk, an Auschwitz prisoner, explained that they were treated like cattle and hit and kicked as they were processed: "in silence with tears streaming down our cheeks," they were made to spread their legs and "the body hair was shorn too."[35] Fifteen-year-old Livia

[30] Ibid., pp. 105–7.

[31] Felicia Berland Hyatt, *Close Calls: The Autobiography of a Survivor* (New York: Holocaust Library, 1991), pp. 76–77.

[32] Leib Langfuss, "The Horrors of Murder," in *The Scrolls of Auschwitz*, ed. Ber Mark (Tel Aviv: Am Oved, 1985), p. 209.

[33] J. Noakes and G. Pridham, eds., *Nazism 1919–1945: A History in Documents and Eyewitness Accounts* (New York: Schocken Books, 1983), 2:1178–80.

[34] Oral history from interview by Bonnie Gurewitsch, 28 Oct. 1985, in *Women of Valor: Partisans and Resistance Fighters*, 6(4):38–41 (Spring 1990).

[35] Sarah Nomberg-Przytyk, *True Tales from a Grotesque Land* (Chapel Hill: University of North Carolina Press, 1985), p. 14.

Bitton Jackson was too embarrassed to expose her breasts, "two growing buds, taut and sensitive," until the sound of a rifle shot jolted her and she removed her bra quickly.[36]

The ordeal of deliberate humiliation began in the ghetto for Cecilie Klein, just before being loaded onto cattle cars:

> We were marched off in groups to a brick factory near the station for a degrading body search. First we were ordered to strip naked, men and women together. Then the women and the girls were lined up on one side and were ordered to lie on our sides on a wooden table. While an SS officer gawked and jeered, a woman with a stick poked around our private parts. My burning cheeks betrayed my sense of shame and humiliation. I sobbed for my mother, subjected to this bestial invasion.

Klein was to endure more degradation upon her arrival at Auschwitz, where she and other naked women were required to stand on stools: "Five male prisoners appear alongside the stools, scissors in hand. . . . In seconds, the men cut off their [the women's] hair, shave their heads, then their intimate parts. The cut hair around the stools was collected by three male prisoners."[37]

Although Klein's narrative focuses on the violence endured by the women, it is quite reasonable that the Jewish men, from the same culture as the women, felt humiliation at having to inflict degradation on the women at the cost of their own survival. SS men, on the other hand, extended sadism to the slave labor sites. A non-Jewish political prisoner recalls overhearing the lewd boasting of an SS officer to his fellow officers about the Jewish women, stripped to their underpants, who "stood barefoot, knee-deep in muddy contaminated water, sore all over the body, exposed to the burning sun and stinging mosquitoes" and who drowned or sank as he speeded up the rate at which they were to mow the reed in the water.[38] Although malaria claimed the lives of 50 percent of the *Kommando*, 100 percent of the victims experienced sadism. In another account, a survivor reported the chilling story she heard from a "mother who told [her] that she was forced to undress her daughter and to look on while the girl was violated by dogs whom the Nazis had specially trained for this sport." That particular brutality was not an isolated event, but rather a "favorite form of amusement" of the SS guards in Auschwitz.[39]

Childbirth as Sadistic Irony

Childbirth was a particularly difficult experience for Jewish women in concentration camps. It was an acutely complex and ironic experience, turning "mothers into murderers, forcing them to kill their newborns in order to prevent reprisals to the women in their barracks."[40] Gisela Perl witnessed SS guards' acts of sadism to pregnant Jewish women that changed her into a peculiar type of activist. She saw "SS men and women"

---

[36] Livia E. Bitton Jackson, *Elli: Coming of Age in the Holocaust* (New York: Times Books, 1980), pp 59–61.

[37] Cecilie Klein, *Sentenced to Live* (New York: Holocaust Library, 1988), pp. 73, 77.

[38] Shelley, ed., *Auschwitz*, pp. 50, 66.

[39] Olga Lengyel, *Five Chimneys* (1947; New York: Granada, 1972), p. 193.

[40] Goldenberg, "Different Horrors," p. 161.

amuse themselves by beating pregnant women "with clubs and whips, [being] torn by dogs, dragged around by the hair and kicked in the stomach with heavy German boots. Then, when [the pregnant Jewish women] collapsed, they were thrown into the crematory—alive."[41] Sometimes, pregnant women were spared until they delivered, after which the Nazis killed both baby and mother. To save the lives of these women, Perl and other Jewish women doctors "pinched and closed" the newborn's "nostrils and when it opened its mouth to breathe . . . gave it a dose of a lethal product"[42] or drowned it in a pail of whatever liquid was available, rather than watch it starve to death, according to Mengele's orders.[43] Several memoirs by survivors and incarcerated female physician survivors document the horrors of delivering babies in such circumstances. One non-Jewish female plumber in Ravensbrück described a macabre event. She was asked to help "solve a monumental plumbing problem" that plagued the camp for over three days during which no water flowed at all. "After days of pumping," trying to unclog the pipes, something came loose. "'It's a pig down there, a little pig,' because it was light-colored. What do they pull out? A boy. A newborn baby boy."[44]

Many survivor memoirs describe a childbirth in the concentration or death camp. In March 1945, on her first day at Bergen-Belsen, her third camp, Eichengreen witnessed a birth of a stillborn that weighed less than two pounds. Eight months earlier, before she knew she was pregnant, the new mother had been deported to Auschwitz and had eventually been sent to Belsen. She did not even know that she was pregnant until her labor pains began.[45] Perhaps the baby was spared by being born dead; certainly, the mother was spared further agony and suffering. But live babies were born and, in very rare circumstances, hidden. The birth of a live full-term baby under such conditions was a result of women's active collaboration, if not resistance.

The Role of Friendship among Women in the Camps

Although all respected Holocaust sources by survivors and scholars emphasize the fact that survival, first and foremost, was random, virtually all memoirs by women implicitly or explicitly credit survival to some manner of women's friendships and collaboration. Clearly, there were no strategies that could save a prisoner from sadistic *Kapos* or SS men and women or from inhuman and unspeakable medical experiments. Thus, given that survival was the responsibility of a prisoner in a very limited way only and that prisoners were faced with choiceless choices, any strategy for coping merits scrutiny. Women had been socialized to use their domestic skills to improve their living conditions, and, writes one woman, even in the concentration camp, "men had to learn behaviors that women already knew."[46] Most women describe situations in which they confronted their new reality and devised strategies that actively engaged them in fighting for their survival. Essentially, as women cleaned their surroundings, sewed pockets into their ragged clothes, created menus to mitigate their hunger, nursed and nurtured

[41] Perl, *I Was a Doctor in Auschwitz*, p. 80.

[42] Lengyel, *Five Chimneys*, p. 111.

[43] Perl, *I Was a Doctor in Auschwitz*, pp. 80–6.

[44] Owings, *Frauen*, p. 169.

[45] Eichengreen, *From Ashes to Life*, p. 121.

[46] Koonz, *Mothers in the Fatherland*, p. 382.

one another, they created the illusion of taking some measure of both control and re-sponsibility for their well-being. In these efforts, they worked collaboratively and, in doing so, imparted a sense of being needed by others. Indeed, they created the illusion of actively improving their chances for survival while most men conveyed a sense of passivity and defeat. Seldom does a woman's memoir describe *Musselmen;*[47] in contrast, men's memoirs are replete with examples and discussions of *Musselmen.*

Since women's memoirs yield anecdotes that demonstrate women's resourceful-ness in the hells of the ghettos and camps, these narratives are rich sources about the characteristics of an alternative social structure based on traditional women's values. Memoirs describe the bonding that was the natural extension of women's caretaking roles in pre-Hitler days. Women survivors recall that they created surrogate families when their own families were separated. Survivor participants in a conference on the Holocaust, wary of generalizing, nevertheless concluded that women, whether by na-ture or socialization, developed friendships that contributed palpably to their survival:

> Men were demoralized and women went right on nurturing. . . . I found that every woman talks about bonding in relation to somebody else: whether it is a mother or a father or a substitute mother or daughter or sister. The men are likely to talk about only me in relation to myself. . . . There was no men to men relationship other than [survival]. . . . It is somewhat mysterious to me as to why [men] can't do some version of that role in protecting a younger person, allowing oneself to be protected by an older man? Why can women convert nurturance into nurturing other women in the camps? Why can't the men convert their roles as protectors?[48]

Friendships, bonding, nurturance, and other permutations of caring can hardly be said to be genetic and exclusive characteristics of women. Yet, in regard to the Holocaust, we read women's narrative after women's narrative that focuses on such bonding. For ex-ample, after her sister was deported in an action in the Lodz ghetto, Lucille Eichengreen was left completely alone. Three sisters whose parents were also deported asked Lucille to move in with them, thus offering her a surrogate family, which meant companion-ship and thus some level of protection.[49]

While the capacity for and the experience of nurturing gave women a mental or emo-tional advantage, other routine women's skills also contributed to their survival. Women, it has been found, kept themselves cleaner longer than men did, thus warding off disease for longer periods. In Auschwitz I, where conditions were much better than in Auschwitz II (Birkenau), water was often unavailable during the day, and inmates report that they "got up in the middle of the night" to wash.[50] Jewish survivors from Birkenau testify to the absence of water except for the mud and slime that characterized the grounds. After marveling about the excessive mud and wretchedness of conditions, Pelagia Lewinska

---

[47] *"Musselmen"* is a term of unknown and debatable origin but widely used to denote "emaciated walking corpses." Milton, "Women and the Holocaust," pp. 297–333. *Musselmen* were those prisoners who were phys-ically and psychologically worn out, those who surrendered their will to live.

[48] Esther Katz and Joan Miriam Ringelheim, *Women Surviving the Holocaust: Proceedings of the Conference* (New York: Institute for Research in History, 1983), pp. 172–6.

[49] Eichengreen, *From Ashes to Life,* p. 53.

[50] Shelley, *Auschwitz,* p. 63.

came to the insight that filth and excrement were part of the Nazi plan to "abase us, to destroy our human dignity, to efface every vestige of humanity, to return us to the level of wild animals, to fill us with horror and contempt toward ourselves and our fellows." She rejected the Nazi plan for her and devised an alternative designed to retain human dignity and human community. Therefore she and her friends made a pact "never to leave each other dying in the mud." Although to help someone rise from the mud meant to risk staying with her in the mud, they pledged to help one another and to keep clean:

> I felt under orders to live. It was my duty toward those who were gone, to those who remained and those who awaited us in the free world. . . . I got a new grip on myself to sustain the heritage from my beloved friends and teachers. I had to keep living. . . . And if I did die at Auschwitz, it would be as a human being. I would hold on to my dignity. I was not going to become the contemptible, disgusting brute my enemy wished me to be.[51]

The Impact of Hunger on Male and Female Prisoners

Starving male and female prisoners dealt with their hunger from different perspectives. Deprived of food, "men . . . fantasized about splendid meals" of the past, but women survivors reported that they exchanged recipes and menus and discussed ways they "stretched" food to make ends meet.[52] Neither men nor women satisfied their hunger, but the approach that women took was creative, allowing them to use their previous experience and imagination and to prepare for the future. Women survivors confess that "the main topic of conversation was food, the most beautiful recipes that anybody could think of, and also a hot bath as soon as the war was over." Ironically, another stated, "The funny thing was that many of us were at the age where we had never been to cooking school, but we had the wildest imagination about what we would cook. I don't think I ever became as good a cook as I was with my mouth."[53] One woman survivor vividly recalls her conversations: "We'd rub our stomachs while imaginary feasts rose before us . . . and we'd laugh at our cleverness . . . gastronomic masturbation."[54] Socialization as cooks or food planners for their families was their vehicle for building community, and building community was an important strategy for coping with their unbearable hunger. In contrast, very few men had enough experience in the kitchen to form a community of men who could transcend their wretched condition by sharing past experiences. Most women also knew enough sewing skills to make pockets if they were given large-sized clothes, pockets that could hide potato peels or similar garbage.

One prisoner considered herself privileged because, as a clerk in the Auschwitz Administration Office who worked directly under the supervision of SS officers, she bathed regularly, ate more and better food than the regular Jewish prisoners, was housed in a barracks with flush toilets, and wore appropriate prison clothing rather than rags. Nevertheless, to survive, she asserted, one needed friends: "You needed others who

---

[51] Pelagia Lewinska, "Twenty Months at Auschwitz," in *Different Voices*, ed. Rittner and Roth, pp. 84–93.

[52] Goldenberg, "Testimony, Narrative, and Nightmare."

[53] Katz and Ringelheim, *Women Surviving the Holocaust*, p. 153.

[54] Gerda Haas, *These I Do Remember: Fragments from the Holocaust* (Freeport, ME: Cumberland Press, 1982), pp. 43–4.

helped you with food or clothing or just advice or sympathy to surmount all the hardship you encountered during all those many months and years in incarceration."[55] In their memoirs and testimony, many other women assume that they derived their courage and strength from the surrogate families they formed: "Four of us girls befriended each other from the beginning. We tried to stay together because no matter how bad it was, it made the pain more tolerable to suffer with friends. In addition, we were all separated from our families and we all had a need to belong to someone."[56] Acknowledging and then satisfying that need provided spiritual sustenance in the absence of material sustenance.

The Practical and Political Effects of Solidarity

Most important, women's narratives reflect an ethic of caring that redefines traditional definitions of courage and heroism. How are we to evaluate the courage of mothers of young children who chose to accompany their children to the gas chambers so that they would not have to suffer death alone? Auschwitz Commandant Rudolf Höss noted that time and time again he witnessed "mothers with laughing or crying children [who] went into the gas chambers" together.[57] One of the manuscripts written by a member of the *Sonderkommando* and hidden in the ashes of Auschwitz tells of a children's transport in winter 1943. The children were undressing in the anteroom to the gas chamber, and the head of the *Sonderkommando* sent some of his men to speed the process. One eight-year-old girl resisted such assistance and cried: "Go away, you Jewish murderer! Don't put your hand covered in Jewish blood on my sweet brother. I am his good mother now, and he will die in my arms."[58] The eight-year-old girl redefined the word "courage" in her protection of her brother! The incident may also reflect early socialization of older sisters as caregivers, a common assignment for girls in European families.

Sisterhood or solidarity often forms the organizational principle of women's narratives. The memoirs are short tales of near death, thwarted both by luck and by women helping women. In August 1942, before Birkenau became widely known as a killing factory, Czech Lotte Frankl Weiss had been in Auschwitz about five months. Barely recovered from meningitis, she dragged herself back to the barracks from the Auschwitz hospital to join her two sisters but within a month found herself alone because her sisters caught typhus and died. Her former *Kapo* had heard of her loss and subsequent desperation and hopelessness, sought her out, and brought her to her own barracks where she fed and nurtured her. She found Lotte an indoor job sorting clothing of Jewish victims and later a job in the SS administrative offices.[59] In essence, the *Kapo* saved Lotte's life. In another SS administrative office, a prisoner-worker described a different kind of solidarity: "We also practiced solidarity. One night, when it was dark and almost everybody was asleep, we administered a sound beating to Boezsi Reich. We threw a blanket over her so that she would not see anything and gave her a good thrashing because she had betrayed Alice Balla who had smoked and had been punished with bunker arrest."[60]

---

[55] Shelley, *Auschwitz*, p. 36.

[56] Ibid., p. 76.

[57] Quoted in *Inside Hitler's Germany*, ed. Sax and Kuntz, p. 445.

[58] Mark, ed., *Scrolls of Auschwitz*, p. 208.

[59] Shelley, *Auschwitz*, p. 94.

[60] Ibid., p. 121.

In another instance, a group of Belgian women prisoners at Auschwitz formed an ad hoc insurrectionist organization founded on the principle of "mutual solidarity." Through "connections," this group became attached to the Schuh-Kommando, sorting the shoes of prisoners, a job that allowed them to "organize" shoes for themselves and their friends. A second group of Belgian women was incarcerated and attached to the Pilz-Kommando, sorting jewelry and other valuables from victims' belongings. A third group of women who were assigned to the Union factory joined the first two groups, forming an organization devoted to resistance and survival. They made contact with the "general insurrectionist organization in the camp," but kept their cohesion through "cultural, educational, and political activities." They organized meetings and lectures, which "played an important role in encouraging the women inmates, for, by momentarily detaching them from the reality of Auschwitz, they gave them additional hope and strength." Although their participation in preparation for armed revolt gave them purpose, their day-to-day existence was made bearable by their "sisterhood":

> Despite the suffering, the cold, the hunger, the punishments of being forced to stand for long hours with arms raised, despite the roll calls which went on for many hours, and the beatings—life in the Schuh-Kommando was still easier, thanks to the mutual solidarity. One woman would give her slice of bread to her starving friend or another would do her sick friend's work for her. . . . While I had typhus, I was in a state of nervous excitement bordering on madness; I was delirious from fever and unaware of what I was saying. Out of the twilight of high fever, I once asked for an apple. My friends went and exchanged their bread rations for an apple. Thus, solidarity saved my life—and the lives of other women comrades.[61]

These informal surrogate families played an incredible role in sustenance: "Everyone knew everyone else, expressed concern for their fellow inmates and encouraged each other not to become depressed and to maintain personal hygiene, a matter of supreme importance." Their concern for one another eliminated "systematic thieving" within a relatively large group of women, prompted them to distribute through the group victims' goods that were housed in storerooms, motivated them to contact similar groups of women, and enabled the women to persevere in the face of random brutality. These surrogate families, bound by shared origins or ideology, "showed the most stability and perseverance in their activities and from these groups developed the camp underground . . . in that hell called Auschwitz."[62] Obviously, the bonding between women was an important factor in their day-to-day and ultimate survival.

While it may be reasonable to assume that such bonding was not exclusive to women, it is difficult to find consistent evidence of men caring about one another to the extent that women did. Besides, caring should not be confused with comradeship. Elie Cohen points out the "necessity" of comradeship, the fact that while survival could not be guaranteed by comradeship, "lone wolf" behavior could almost guarantee death. In the men's camps, Cohen quotes a very early source, "everybody demanded

---

[61] Mark, ed., *Scrolls of Auschwitz*, pp. 75–7.

[62] Ibid., p. 79. For more descriptions of male and female groups organized to rebel against Nazi control, see ibid., pp. 94–6.

comradeship from the other man and only very few were prepared to extend it." In fact, Cohen found that comradeship was "occasional," even rare, and that the "absence of comradeship was most conspicuous": "I found that, if everybody's life is at stake, very little comradeship is evident."[63] Bonding between men was more a factor of political proclivities than of the ethic of caring. This is a stark contrast with women's analyses, which uniformly describe sisterhood and caring.

We are faced with recalculating our definitions of courage in light of Helena Rotstein's quiet challenge to uncritical thinking: "Families were broken up, crying children were taken away from their mothers and the mothers chosen for work. But the mothers didn't abandon their children and went with them to the gas chambers."[64] For years, Janusz Korczak has been lionized for his refusal to abandon his orphans as they were deported and marched to their death. The Nazis recognized Korczak's prominence and offered him the opportunity to live on the condition that he abandon his orphans to the gas chambers. It is time to extend, not displace, the image of protection and dedication to so-called ordinary mothers who, unlike Korczak, were young and healthy and therefore selected to live as forced laborers but chose instead to protect their children in the greatest need. In the perverted context of the concentration camps, where giving comfort was criminal and caring was an act of courage, spiritual courage is heroic.

There are also examples of women's physical courage that appear to be motivated by a profound sense of community and pride in their Jewishness. Women were active resistance fighters, partisans, and, in the concentration camps, insurrectionists. The women in the gunpowder unit of the Union factory supplied the *Sonderkommandos* with the powder that blew up Crematorium IV in the revolt of 7 October 1944 at Auschwitz.[65] They never revealed the names of their contacts in the men's camp. Mala Zimetbaum, famous for her heroic escape from Auschwitz with her lover Edek Galinski and her defiance to her executioners after she was caught, is also well known by camp inmates for her "cheerful optimism" to her Auschwitz "sisters." Using her status as a runner to arrange for lighter camp assignments for weak inmates and to "organize" help in getting medicines to the sick, "she became the living spirit of rescue in the camp and rapidly acquired a reputation among the inmates—especially the Belgian Jewish women . . . [as] the embodiment of all the spiritual and physical courage of the Jewish girls and women in Auschwitz."[66] Zimetbaum was mother and sister to other women prisoners and courageous hero to all prisoners. These acts of heroism and martyrdom were not limited to either men or women, but the less familiar acts of courage—and women's acts of courage have until recently been largely overlooked—have much to teach us. Thus the recovery and consideration of women's words are enormously important.

Rethinking Traditional Responses

Jewish behavior during the Holocaust poses more issues. How, for example, do we categorize the effects of isolation that Jews experienced? Given what we know about women's bonding and socialization as nurturers and caregivers, can we assume this isolation affected women and men differently? If so, in what ways? One recent study suggests that Jewish women were victimized early through isolation by German women. In

---

[63] Cohen, *Human Behavior in the Concentration Camp*, pp. 182–3.

[64] Shelley, *Auschwitz*, p. 14

[65] Mark, ed., *Scrolls of Auschwitz*, pp. 147–54.

[66] Ibid., pp. 116–23.

Frauen, Allison Owings studied 29 representative German women who lived through the war. Almost universally, the German women described the extraordinary fear that gripped the nation—fear of dissent at any level. Repeatedly, they defended their passivity by invoking a ubiquitous fear of the Gestapo. For one German woman about to take a vacation with her husband and child, "letting a Jewish woman water [her] plants would have been enough" to arouse the Gestapo's suspicion.[67] Yet ambiguity persists: some of the women were embarrassed by their fear of being suspected of helping Jews, but they also unashamedly defended Hitler: "What he gave us young girls back then somehow must still be there, that one cannot condemn it all. . . . We did love our Fuehrer, really! It was true. And when that's inside you as a young person, it doesn't leave so quickly."[68]

Perhaps even more relevant is the fact that German women were far more involved with church-related and secular charities than men. Nazi racism, "the linchpin of National Socialist and domestic policy," shaped so-called social welfare programs throughout Germany.[69] Awareness of legalized discrimination, if not genocide, was unavoidable, yet women—even those who attended church regularly—managed to ignore it, focusing instead on rewriting their role in the new Germany to compensate for their diminished status.[70] Church-related women deceived themselves into concentrating on strengthening their churches rather than on acting devoutly. That most Protestant women saw Hitler as their savior led one historian to claim that women were more ideologically influenced by racism than were men.[71] Nazi emphasis on motherhood appealed to Catholic women.[72] In either case, organized religion in Germany—which involved far more women than men—served Nazi purposes: "Indeed, one could invoke religion in defense of one's anti-Semitism."[73] Thus, from the perspective of the victim or the bystander, women experienced the war differently from the way men did. And the usual vehicles for establishing and perpetuating the ethic of caring and community and principle of spiritual courage worked in the service of an amoral government.

The Nazi machine was fueled by an official unrestrained racist policy and a profound and long-standing attitude of patriarchy and misogyny. Although the ultimate lessons of the Holocaust do not focus on gender specifics, traditionally feminist values of cooperating and caring are important conditions for the perpetuation of civilization, irrespective of religious, ethnic, or nationalist identification. Women's experiences, particularly in response to societies mired in violence and struggles for power, teach us to reexamine the values and characteristics that have been associated with the literature and lives of women with an eye toward internalizing them in our development as reasoning individuals and as members of a responsible community.

---

[67] Owings, *Frauen*, p. 76.

[68] Ibid., pp. 181–3.

[69] Michael Phayer, *Protestant and Catholic Women in Nazi Germany* (Detroit, MI: Wayne State University Press, 1990), p. 100.

[70] Ibid., p. 71.

[71] Ibid., p. 49.

[72] Ibid., pp. 62–4.

[73] Ibid., p. 83.

Source: Goldenberg, Myrna. (1996). "Lessons Learned from Gentle Heroism: Women's Holocaust Narratives," *Annals of the American Academy of Political and Social Science*, Volume 548, pp. 78–93. Copyright © 1996. Reprinted by permission of Annals of the American Academy of Political & Social Science.

CHAPTER **4**

Prison

Fyodor Dostoyevsky (1862), the renowned Russian novelist, famously observed that the "degree of civilization in a society can be judged by entering its prisons" (as cited in Shapiro, 2006, p. 210). Others have similarly commented that a society can be judged by how it treats its weakest members, a reference to the poor, the infirm and the prisoners.

Historically, persons accused of a crime were often punished in the public square by the most brutal of physical tortures, which included stoning, flogging and hanging. It is interesting to note that the empirical sociologist Emile Durkheim (1938) commented extensively on the functional role of the deviant in society. He observed that punishment of the offender would serve to reinforce the importance of conformity to the norms in society by crystallizing the boundaries of acceptable and unacceptable behavior. Punishment of the accused in the town square allowed the community to observe this spectacle of retribution, which served to help shape the "normative contours of society . . . morality and immorality meet at the public scaffold, and it is during this meeting that the community declares where the line between them should be drawn" (Erikson, 1962, p. 310). The feeling of uniqueness and cohesiveness of the community is solidified in their response to the deviant. While most modern societies no longer punish the offender in their respective "Times Square," the message of punishment is transmitted to the community by the mass media and, most recently, the global explosion of the Internet. One should note the recent case of an Iranian woman, Sakineh Mohammadi Ashtiani, convicted of adultery:

> After a spirited international campaign joined by Western politicians and celebrities, the Iranian government apparently will not stone a woman accused of adultery . . . Ashtiani would not be stoned to death, a gruesome process in which a person is buried up to their chest or neck and then pelted with medium-sized rocks until they die (Daragahi and Katz, 2010).

It should be mentioned that in August 2010 in northern Kunduz Province, Afghanistan, hundreds of villagers participated in a public stoning, ordered by the Taliban, of a young couple who had eloped (Nordland, 2010).

The incarceration of prisoners in correctional institutions is generally viewed as having its origins in the late 18th and early 19th centuries. The prison was a product of liberal reform and was to be seen as a "humane alternative" to the cruelties of physical punishment and death. The most notable institutions erected at that time were the Walnut Street Jail (1790) in Philadelphia, the Auburn Prison, New York (1816), and the Western (1818) and Eastern (1820) penitentiaries in Pennsylvania (Siegel, 2009, pp. 526–528). While variations in prison design and penal philosophies existed, relative degrees of solitary confinement and prohibitions in communication between prisoners were the order of the day. While the Auburn (congregate) system was more liberal than the Pennsylvania (separate) system, goals of the prisons included punishment of the offender, opportunity for penance, resocialization and insulation of the inmates from the corrupting influences of their peers.

As indicated earlier, the social philosopher Jeremy Bentham (1791) revealed his schematic for the construction of the prison or Panopticon based on an "optical mechanical technique" wherein the inmate could be seen at all times by the guards in a central tower while the inmates could not see the guards. As described by Foucault (1979) in this chapter, the significance of the Panopticon is the creation of a configuration of power and control wherein the prisoner never knows when he is actually being watched. It is precisely this fact, the inmates' awareness of the omnipotence of surveillance, that defines the Panopticon as the ultimate "laboratory of power" (p. 204): "that the eye may observe, without being seen—that is the most cunning thing about the Panopticon . . . [i]f the eye is hidden, it looks at me even when it is not actually observing me" (Miller and Miller, 1987, p. 4).

It is ironic that East Jersey State Prison (formerly Rahway State Prison), which resembles the Panopticon in its circular design, later became the home of the high profile, *inmate* run "Scared Straight" juvenile awareness program (1976). While the portrayal of the inmates in the Panopticon is one of passivity, powerlessness and objectification, the inmates at Rahway Prison initiated, designed and sustained a program that received international recognition and was the subject of an Oscar winning documentary. That program involved bringing youthful offenders to the prison in an attempt to "scare them straight" and deter them from continued involvement in delinquent activity. After the inmates led the juveniles on a tour of the prison, the group moved to a room where an intense and dramatic "encounter session" between the inmates and juveniles ensued. During that session, individual inmates verbally assaulted and intimidated the youths in the harshest of terms on such themes as the futility of a life of crime and the degradations of prison life.

While the program was highly controversial and empirical evaluations of its effectiveness revealed conflicting findings, my own research concluded that the program had a positive effect on a select sample of juvenile offenders. The study revealed that at the conclusion of the analysis (an average of 22 months after their participation in the program) there was a significant difference between the experimental and control groups; the extent of delinquent activity for the program participants was significantly lower than for the nonparticipants. Interestingly enough, there was an increase in delinquent activity for both groups. However, the increase in delinquent activity for the program participants was slight and not statistically significant while the increase for the control group was sharp and significant. This "long term finding" was in contrast to the "short term finding" (ten months after participation in the program) when both the experimental and control groups had significant increases in their delinquent activity (Langer, 1980).

In his landmark study of prison life, *Society of Captives*, Gresham Sykes (1958) moves from a discussion of power as seen from the perspective of the "custodians" to a description of the inmates' "pains of imprisonment" (p. 63). Sykes's analysis of the inmates' condition in prison is strikingly compatible with Goffman's (1961) analysis of the mortification process in the total institution. Sykes notes that while the situational deprivation of liberty in prison "is a double one—first, by confinement to the institution and second, by confinement within the institution" (p. 65) it is the experiential "moral rejection" of the inmate by the community which is most painful. Sykes suggests that while the deprivation of heterosexual relationships might be less severe for those in "concentration camps or similar extreme situations where starvation, torture, and physical exhaustion have reduced life to a simple struggle for survival" (p. 70), that is not the case for the inmate in prison who generally retains his sexual interest. The prisoner's sexual frustration is certainly physical but also psychological and generates within the inmates serious concerns about their masculinity and restrictions in their ability to define their selves in a world devoid of women.

This heightened concern with issues of latent homosexuality and masculinity is a central theme of Hans Toch's (1977) reading on inmate victimization in prison. Toch suggests that while the act of homosexual rape is not pervasive in prison, the innuendos, stress and symbolism of rape as ultimate power and control of one inmate over another define the essence of victimization. The rich anecdotal comments of the inmates expose their concerns regarding being able to negotiate their presentation of self such that they will not fail the test of these emasculating sexual overtones. Failure to affirm their masculinity would serve to reveal weakness and enhance their victimization.

Lori Girshick's (1997) article on women "doing time" in prison is particularly interesting in that she highlights several differences in how men and women adjust their lives to the prison experience. She references homosexuality in prison and its relationship to "prisonization," which is the process of assimilation into prison culture. She also describes the stages of adjustment or the "moral career" (Goffman, 1961) of the inmate in the institutional setting. Finally, the comments of the female inmates regarding their "distrust" of the other prisoners are revealing in that separation from others in prison becomes an important tactic for dealing with being thrown into the situation of "forced interaction" in the total institution. In his book *Asylums*, Goffman (1961) comments on the fact that inmates in prisons and mental institutions feel "contaminated" when forced into contact with others who might be considered undesirable.

John Riley's (2002) article in this chapter speaks to the compelling "symbiotic relationship" that can be achieved when analyzing contemporary personal accounts of prison life within the conceptual framework of classical theory. While Riley makes it clear that additional research subsequent to Sykes's analysis of the "pains of imprisonment" and Goffman's "total institutions" has criticized and challenged many of their original formulations, he maintains that they still retain their importance and endurance as core concepts in understanding institutional life. Using Sykes's "pains of imprisonment" as an example, Riley analyzes the first-person accounts of two prisoners and one correctional officer to illustrate that these narratives can be both supportive of and at times diverge from Sykes's original paradigm. While the phenomenon of institutional structures and the relationship of their charges to their milieu are dynamic, much can be learned from using the classic text as a reference point for enhancing our understanding of contemporary experiences.

The last reading in this chapter is an examination of a communal organization or social movement known as the Peoples Temple, or Jonestown, which was located in Guyana, South America. On November 18, 1978, more than 900 people committed mass suicide at the behest of its founder and leader Jim Jones. Gardner et al. (2008) apply the concepts of "destructive group" and Goffman's analysis of the mortification process in the total institution in an attempt to explore the dynamics of this group that led its members to obedient commitment and their eventual death. While Jonestown was not a prison in the traditional sense, and its members were not sentenced to its confines by a court of law, it is certainly "prison like" in its institutional characteristics, and its analysis complements the other readings in this chapter.

PANOPTICISM

Michel Foucault

Bentham's *Panopticon* is the architectural figure of this composition. We know the principle on which it was based: at the periphery, an annular building; at the centre, a tower; this tower is pierced with wide windows that open onto the inner side of the ring; the peripheric building is divided into cells, each of which extends the whole width of the building; they have two windows, one on the inside, corresponding to the windows of the tower; the other, on the outside, allows the light to cross the cell from one end to the other. All that is needed, then, is to place a supervisor in a central tower and to shut up in each cell a madman, a patient, a condemned man, a worker or a schoolboy. By the effect of backlighting, one can observe from the tower, standing out precisely against the light, the small captive shadows in the cells of the periphery. They are like so many cages, so many small theatres, in which each actor is alone, perfectly individualized and constantly visible. The panoptic mechanism arranges spatial unities that make it possible to see constantly and to recognize immediately. In short, it reverses the principle of the dungeon; or rather of its three functions – to enclose, to deprive of light and to hide – it preserves only the first and eliminates the other two. Full lighting and the eye of a supervisor capture better than darkness, which ultimately protected. Visibility is a trap.

To begin with, this made it possible – as a negative effect – to avoid those compact, swarming, howling masses that were to be found in places of confinement, those painted by Goya or described by Howard. Each individual, in his place, is securely confined to a cell from which he is seen from the front by the supervisor; but the side walls prevent him from coming into contact with his companions. He is seen, but he does not see; he is the object of information, never a subject in communication. The arrangement of his room, opposite the central tower, imposes on him an axial visibility; but the divisions of the ring, those separated cells, imply a lateral invisibility. And this invisibility is a guarantee of order. If the inmates are convicts, there is no danger of a plot, an attempt at collective escape, the planning of new crimes for the future, bad reciprocal influences; if they are patients, there is no danger of contagion; if they are madmen there is no risk of their committing violence upon one another; if they are schoolchildren, there is no copying, no noise, no chatter, no waste of time; if they are workers, there are no disorders, no theft, no coalitions, none of those distractions that slow down the rate of work, make it less perfect or cause accidents. The crowd, a compact mass, a locus of multiple exchanges, individualities merging together, a collective effect, is abolished and replaced by a collection of separated individualities. From the point of view of the guardian, it is replaced by a multiplicity that can be numbered and supervised; from the point of view of the inmates, by a sequestered and observed solitude (Bentham, 1843, 60–64).

Hence the major effect of the Panopticon: to induce in the inmate a state of conscious and permanent visibility that assures the automatic functioning of power. So to arrange things that the surveillance is permanent in its effects, even if it is discontinuous in its action; that the perfection of power should tend to render its actual exercise unnecessary; that this architectural apparatus should be a machine for creating and sustaining a power relation independent of the person who exercises it; in short, that the inmates should be caught up in a power situation of which they are themselves the bearers. To achieve this, it is at once too much and too little that the prisoner should be constantly observed by an inspector: too little, for what matters is that he knows himself to be observed; too much, because he has no need in fact of being so. In view of this, Bentham laid down the principle that power should be visible and unverifiable. Visible: the inmate will constantly have before his eyes the tall outline of the central tower from which he is spied upon. Unverifiable: the inmate must never know whether he is being looked at at any one moment; but he must be sure that he may always be so. In order to make the presence or absence of the inspector unverifiable, so that the prisoners, in their cells, cannot even see a shadow, Bentham envisaged not only venetian blinds on the windows of the central observation hall, but, on the inside, partitions that intersected the hall at right angles and, in order to pass from one quarter to the other, not doors but zig-zag openings; for the slightest noise, a gleam of light, a brightness in a half-opened door would betray the presence of the guardian.[1] The Panopticon is a machine for dissociating the see/being seen dyad: in the peripheric ring, one is totally seen, without ever seeing; in the central tower, one sees everything without ever being seen.[2]

It is an important mechanism, for it automatizes and disindividualizes power. Power has its principle not so much in a person as in a certain concerted distribution of bodies, surfaces, lights, gazes; in an arrangement whose internal mechanisms produce the relation in which individuals are caught up. The ceremonies, the rituals, the marks by which the sovereign's surplus power was manifested are useless. There is a machinery that assures dissymmetry, disequilibrium, difference. Consequently, it does not matter who exercises power. Any individual, taken almost at random, can operate the machine: in the absence of the director, his family, his friends, his visitors, even his servants (Bentham, 45). Similarly, it does not matter what motive animates him: the curiosity of the indiscreet, the malice of a child, the thirst for knowledge of a philosopher who wishes to visit this museum of human nature, or the perversity of those who take pleasure in spying and punishing. The more numerous those anonymous and temporary observers are, the greater the risk for the inmate of being surprised and the greater his anxious awareness of being observed. The Panopticon is a marvellous machine which, whatever use one may wish to put it to, produces homogeneous effects of power.

A real subjection is born mechanically from a fictitious relation. So it is not necessary to use force to constrain the convict to good behaviour, the madman to calm, the worker to work, the schoolboy to application, the patient to the observation of the regulations. Bentham was surprised that panoptic institutions could be so light: there were no more bars, no more chains, no more heavy locks; all that was needed was that the separations should be clear and the openings well arranged. The heaviness of the old 'houses of security', with their fortress-like architecture, could be replaced by the simple, economic geometry of a 'house of certainty'. The efficiency of power, its constraining force have, in a sense, passed over to the other side – to the side of its surface of application. He who is subjected to a field of visibility, and who knows it, assumes

---

[1]In the *Postscript to the Panopticon*, 1791, Bentham adds dark inspection galleries painted in black around the inspector's lodge, each making it possible to observe two storeys of cells.

[2]In his first version of the *Panopticon*, Bentham had also imagined an acoustic surveillance, operated by means of pipes leading from the cells to the central tower. In the *Postscript* he abandoned the idea, perhaps because he could not introduce into it the principle of dissymmetry and prevent the prisoners from hearing the inspector as well as the inspector hearing them.

responsibility for the constraints of power; he makes them play spontaneously upon himself; he inscribes in himself the power relation in which he simultaneously plays both roles; he becomes the principle of his own subjection. By this very fact, the external power may throw off its physical weight; it tends to the non-corporal; and, the more it approaches this limit, the more constant, profound and permanent are its effects: it is a perpetual victory that avoids any physical confrontation and which is always decided in advance.

Bentham does not say whether he was inspired, in his project, by Le Vaux's menagerie at Versailles: the first menagerie in which the different elements are not, as they traditionally were, distributed in a park (Loisel, 104–7). At the centre was an octagonal pavilion which, on the first floor, consisted of only a single room, the king's *salon*; on every side large windows looked out onto seven cages (the eighth side was reserved for the entrance), containing different species of animals. By Bentham's time, this menagerie had disappeared. But one finds in the programme of the Panopticon a similar concern with individualizing observation, with characterization and classification, with the analytical arrangement of space. The Panopticon is a royal menagerie; the animal is replaced by man, individual distribution by specific grouping and the king by the machinery of a furtive power. With this exception, the Panopticon also does the work of a naturalist. It makes it possible to draw up differences: among patients, to observe the symptoms of each individual, without the proximity of beds, the circulation of miasmas, the effects of contagion confusing the clinical tables; among school children, it makes it possible to observe performances (without there being any imitation or copying), to map aptitudes, to assess characters, to draw up rigorous classifications and, in relation to normal development, to distinguish 'laziness and stubbornness' from 'incurable imbecility'; among workers, it makes it possible to note the aptitudes of each worker, compare the time he takes to perform a task, and if they are paid by the day, to calculate their wages (Bentham, 60–64).

So much for the question of observation. But the Panopticon was also a laboratory; it could be used as a machine to carry out experiments, to alter behaviour, to train or correct individuals. To experiment with medicines and monitor their effects. To try out different punishments on prisoners, according to their crimes and character, and to seek the most effective ones. To teach different techniques simultaneously to the workers, to decide which is the best. To try out pedagogical experiments – and in particular to take up once again the well-debated problem of secluded education, by using orphans. One would see what would happen when, in their sixteenth or eighteenth year, they were presented with other boys or girls; one could verify whether, as Helvetius thought, anyone could learn anything; one would follow 'the genealogy of every observable idea'; one could bring up different children according to different systems of thought, making certain children believe that two and two do not make four or that the moon is a cheese, then put them together when they are twenty or twenty-five years old; one would then have discussions that would be worth a great deal more than the sermons or lectures on which so much money is spent; one would have at least an opportunity of making discoveries in the domain of metaphysics. The Panopticon is a privileged place for experiments on men, and for analysing with complete certainty the transformations that may be obtained from them. The Panopticon may even provide an apparatus for supervising its own mechanisms. In this central tower, the director may spy on all the employees that he has under his orders: nurses, doctors, foremen, teachers, warders; he will be able to judge them continuously, alter their behaviour, impose upon them the methods he thinks best; and it will even be possible to observe the director himself. An inspector arriving unexpectedly at the centre of the Panopticon will be able to judge at a glance, without anything being concealed from him, how the entire establishment is functioning. And, in any case, enclosed as he is in the middle of this architectural mechanism, is not the director's own fate entirely bound up with it? The incompetent physician who has allowed contagion to spread, the incompetent prison governor or workshop manager will be the first victims of an epidemic or a revolt. '"By every tie I could devise", said the master of the Panopticon, "my own fate had been bound up by me with theirs" ' (Bentham, 177). The Panopticon functions as a kind of laboratory of power. Thanks to its mechanisms of observation, it gains in efficiency and in the ability to penetrate into men's behaviour; knowledge follows the advances of power, discovering new objects of knowledge over all the surfaces on which power is exercised.

The plague-stricken town, the panoptic establishment – the differences are important. They mark, at a distance of a century and a half, the transformations of the disciplinary programme. In the first case, there is an exceptional situation: against an extraordinary evil, power is mobilized; it makes itself everywhere present and visible; it invents new mechanisms; it separates, it immobilizes, it partitions; it constructs for a time what is both a counter-city and the perfect society; it imposes an ideal functioning, but one that is reduced, in the final analysis, like the evil that it combats, to a simple dualism of life and death: that which moves brings death, and one kills that which moves. The Panopticon, on the other hand, must be understood as a generalizable model of functioning; a way of defining power relations in terms of the everyday life of men. No doubt Bentham presents it as a particular institution, closed in upon itself. Utopias, perfectly closed in upon themselves, are common enough. As opposed to the ruined prisons, littered with mechanisms of torture, to be seen in Piranese's engravings, the Panopticon presents a cruel, ingenious cage. The fact that it should have given rise, even in our own time, to so many variations, projected or realized, is evidence of the imaginary intensity that it has possessed for almost two hundred years. But the Panopticon must not be understood as a dream building: it is the diagram of a mechanism of power reduced to its ideal form; its functioning, abstracted from any obstacle, resistance or friction, must be represented as a pure architectural and optical system: it is in fact a figure of political technology that may and must be detached from any specific use.

It is polyvalent in its applications; it serves to reform prisoners, but also to treat patients, to instruct schoolchildren, to confine the insane, to supervise workers, to put beggars and idlers to work. It is a type of location of bodies in space, of distribution of individuals in relation to one another, of hierarchical organization, of disposition of centres and channels of power, of definition of the instruments and modes of intervention of power, which can be implemented in hospitals, workshops, schools, prisons. Whenever one is dealing with a multiplicity of individuals on whom a task or a particular form of behaviour must be imposed, the panoptic schema may be used.

Source: From *Discipline and Punish* by Michel Foucault. English translation, copyright © 1977 by Alan Sheridan (New York: Pantheon). Originally published in French as *Surveiller et Punir*. Copyright © 1975 by Editions Gallimard. Reprinted by permission of Georges Borchardt, Inc., for Editions Gallimard.

THE PAINS OF IMPRISONMENT

Gresham Sykes

In our discussion of the New Jersey State Prison, the bulk of our remarks has been directed to the custodians—their objectives, their procedures, and their limitations. We have been looking at the prison's system of power from the position of the rulers rather than that of the ruled, and only in passing have we noted the meaning of imprisonment for the prisoners. Now, however, we must examine this society of captives from the viewpoint of the inmates more systematically and in more detail.

It might be argued, of course, that there are certain dangers in speaking of the inmates' perspective of captivity, since it is apt to carry the implication that all prisoners perceive their captivity in precisely the same way. It might be argued that in reality there are as many prisons as there are prisoners—that each man brings to the custodial institution his own needs and his own background and each man takes away from the prison his own interpretation of life within the walls. We do not intend to deny that different men see the conditions of custody somewhat differently and accord these conditions a different emphasis in their personal accounting. Yet when we examine the way the inmates of the New Jersey State Prison perceive the social environment created by the custodians, the dominant fact is the hard core of consensus expressed by the members of the captive population with regard to the nature of their confinement. The inmates are agreed that life in the maximum security prison is depriving or frustrating in the extreme.

In part, the deprivations or frustrations of prison life today might be viewed as punishments which the free community deliberately inflicts on the offender for violating the law; in part, they might be seen as the unplanned (or, as some would argue, the unavoidable) concomitants of confining large groups of criminals for prolonged periods. In either case, the modern pains of imprisonment are often defined by society as a humane alternative to the physical brutality and the neglect which constituted the major meaning of imprisonment in the past. But in examining the pains of imprisonment as they exist today, it is imperative that we go beyond the fact that severe bodily suffering has long since disappeared as a significant aspect of the custodians' regime, leaving behind a residue of apparently less acute hurts such as the loss of liberty, the deprivation of goods and services, the frustration of sexual desire, and so on. These deprivations or frustrations of the modern prison may indeed be the acceptable or unavoidable implications of imprisonment, but we must recognize the fact that they can be just as painful as the physical maltreatment which they have replaced. As Maslow has indicated, there are some frustrating situations which appear as a serious attack on the personality, as a "threat to the life goals of the individual, to his defensive system, to his self-esteem, or to his feelings of security."[1] Such attacks on the psychological level are less easily seen than a sadistic beating, a pair of shackles in the floor, or the caged man on a treadmill, but the destruction of the psyche is no less fearful than bodily affliction and it must play a large role in our discussion. Whatever may be the pains of imprisonment, then,

---

[1]Cf. A. H. Maslow, "Deprivation, Threat, and Frustration," in *Readings in Social Psychology,* edited by T. M. Newcomb and F. L. Hartley, New York: Henry Holt and Company, 1947.

in the custodial institution of today, we must explore the way in which the deprivations and frustrations pose profound threats to the inmate's personality or sense of personal worth.

The Deprivation of Liberty

Of all the painful conditions imposed on the inmates of the New Jersey State Prison, none is more immediately obvious than the loss of liberty. The prisoner must live in a world shrunk to thirteen and a half acres and within this restricted area his freedom of movement is further confined by a strict system of passes, the military formations in moving from one point within the institution to another, and the demand that he remain in his cell until given permission to do otherwise. In short, the prisoner's loss of liberty is a double one—first, by confinement to the institution and second, by confinement within the institution.

The mere fact that the individual's movements are restricted, however, is far less serious than the fact that imprisonment means that the inmate is cut off from family, relatives, and friends, not in the self-isolation of the hermit or the misanthrope, but in the involuntary seclusion of the outlaw. It is true that visiting and mailing privileges partially relieve the prisoner's isolation—if he can find someone to visit him or write to him and who will be approved as a visitor or correspondent by the prison officials. Many inmates, however, have found their links with persons in the free community weakening as the months and years pass by. This may explain in part the fact that an examination of the visiting records of a random sample of the inmate population, covering approximately a one-year period, indicated that 41 percent of the prisoners in the New Jersey State Prison had received no visits from the outside world.

It is not difficult to see this isolation as painfully depriving or frustrating in terms of lost emotional relationships, of loneliness and boredom. But what makes this pain of imprisonment bite most deeply is the fact that the confinement of the criminal represents a deliberate, moral rejection of the criminal by the free community. Indeed, as Reckless has pointed out, it is the moral condemnation of the criminal—however it may be symbolized—that converts hurt into punishment, i.e. the just consequence of committing an offense, and it is this condemnation that confronts the inmate by the fact of his seclusion.

Now it is sometimes claimed that many criminals are so alienated from conforming society and so identified with a criminal subculture that the moral condemnation, rejection, or disapproval of legitimate society does not touch them; they are, it is said, indifferent to the penal sanctions of the free community, at least as far as the moral stigma of being defined as a criminal is concerned. Possibly this is true for a small number of offenders such as the professional thief described by Sutherland[2] or the psychopathic personality delineated by William and Joan McCord.[3] For the great majority of criminals in prison, however, the evidence suggests that neither alienation from the ranks of the law-abiding nor involvement in a system of criminal value is sufficient to eliminate the threat to the prisoner's ego posed by society's rejection.[4] The signs pointing to the

---

[2]Cf. Edwin H. Sutherland, *The Professional Thief*, Chicago: The University of Chicago Press, 1937.

[3]Cf. William and Joan McCord, *Psychopathy and Delinquency*, New York: Grune and Stratton, 1956.

[4]For an excellent discussion of the symbolic overtones of imprisonment, see Walter C. Reckless, *The Crime Problem*, New York: Appleton-Century-Crofts, Inc., 1955, pp. 428–429.

prisoner's degradation are many—the anonymity of a uniform and a number rather than a name, the shaven head,[5] the insistence on gestures of respect and subordination when addressing officials, and so on. The prisoner is never allowed to forget that, by committing a crime, he has foregone his claim to the status of a full-fledged, *trusted* member of society. The status lost by the prisoner is, in fact, similar to what Marshall has called the status of citizenship—that basic acceptance of the individual as a functioning member of the society in which he lives.[6] It is true that in the past the imprisoned criminal literally suffered civil death and that although the doctrines of attainder and corruption of blood were largely abandoned in the 18th and 19th Centuries, the inmate is still stripped of many of his civil rights such as the right to vote, to hold office, to sue in court, and so on.[7] But as important as the loss of these civil rights may be, the loss of that more diffuse status which defines the individual as someone to be trusted or as morally acceptable is the loss which hurts most.

In short, the wall which seals off the criminal, the contaminated man, is a constant threat to the prisoner's self-conception and the threat is continually repeated in the many daily reminders that he must be kept apart from "decent" men. Somehow this rejection or degradation by the free community must be warded off, turned aside, rendered harmless. Somehow the imprisoned criminal must find a device for rejecting his rejectors, if he is to endure psychologically.[8]

The Deprivation of Goods and Services

There are admittedly many problems in attempting to compare the standard of living existing in the free community and the standard of living which is supposed to be the lot of the inmate in prison. How, for example, do we interpret the fact that a covering for the floor of a cell usually consists of a scrap from a discarded blanket and that even this possession is forbidden by the prison authorities? What meaning do we attach to the fact that no inmate owns a common piece of furniture, such as a chair, but only a homemade stool? What is the value of a suit of clothing which is also a convict's uniform with a stripe and a stencilled number? The answers are far from simple although there are a number of prison officials who will argue that some inmates are better off in prison, in strictly material terms, than they could ever hope to be in the rough-and-tumble economic life of the free community. Possibly this is so, but at least it has never been claimed by the inmates that the goods and services provided the prisoner are equal to or better than the goods and services which the prisoner could obtain if he were left to his own devices outside the walls. The average inmate finds himself in a harshly Spartan environment which he defines as painfully depriving.

---

[5]Western culture has long placed a peculiar emphasis on shaving the head as a symbol of degradation, ranging from the enraged treatment of collaborators in occupied Europe to the more measured barbering of recruits in the Armed Forces. In the latter case, as in the prison, the nominal purpose has been cleanliness and neatness, but for the person who is shaved the meaning is somewhat different. In the New Jersey State Prison, the prisoner is clipped to the skull on arrival but not thereafter.

[6]See T. H. Marshall, *Citizenship and Social Class*, Cambridge, England: The Cambridge University Press, 1950.

[7]Paul W. Tappan, "The Legal Rights of Prisoners," *The Annals of the American Academy of Political and Social Science*, Vol. 293, May 1954, pp. 99–111.

[8]See Lloyd W. McCorkle and Richard R. Korn, "Resocialization Within Walls." *Ibid.*, pp. 88–98.

Now it is true that the prisoner's basic material needs are met—in the sense that he does not go hungry, cold, or wet. He receives adequate medical care and he has the opportunity for exercise. But a standard of living constructed in terms of so many calories per day, so many hours of recreation, so many cubic yards of space per individual, and so on, misses the central point when we are discussing the individual's feeling of deprivation, however useful it may be in setting minimum levels of consumption for the maintenance of health. A standard of living can be hopelessly inadequate, from the individual's viewpoint, because it bores him to death or fails to provide those subtle symbolic overtones which we invest in the world of possessions. And this is the core of the prisoner's problem in the area of goods and services. He wants—or needs, if you will—not just the so-called necessities of life but also the amenities: cigarettes and liquor as well as calories, interesting foods as well as sheer bulk, individual clothing as well as adequate clothing, individual furnishings for his living quarters as well as shelter, privacy as well as space. The "rightfulness" of the prisoner's feeling of deprivation can be questioned. And the objective reality of the prisoner's deprivation—in the sense that he has actually suffered a fall from his economic position in the free community—can be viewed with skepticism, as we have indicated above. But these criticisms are irrelevant to the significant issue, namely that legitimately or illegitimately, rationally or irrationally, the inmate population defines its present material impoverishment as a painful loss.

Now in modern Western culture, material possessions are so large a part of the individual's conception of himself that to be stripped of them is to be attacked at the deepest layers of personality. This is particularly true when poverty cannot be excused as a blind stroke of fate or a universal calamity. Poverty due to one's own mistakes or misdeeds represents an indictment against one's basic value or personal worth and there are few men who can philosophically bear the want caused by their own actions. It is true some prisoners in the New Jersey State Prison attempt to interpret their low position in the scale of goods and services as an effort by the State to exploit them economically. Thus, in the eyes of some inmates, the prisoner is poor not because of an offense which he has committed in the past but because the State is a tyrant which uses its captive criminals as slave labor under the hypocritical guise of reformation. Penology, it is said, is a racket. Their poverty, then, is not punishment as we have used the word before, i.e. the just consequence of criminal behavior; rather, it is an unjust hurt or pain inflicted without legitimate cause. This attitude, however, does not appear to be particularly widespread in the inmate population and the great majority of prisoners must face their privation without the aid of the wronged man's sense of injustice. Furthermore, most prisoners are unable to fortify themselves in their low level of material existence by seeing it as a means to some high or worthy end. They are unable to attach any significant meaning to their need to make it more bearable, such as present pleasures foregone for pleasures in the future, self-sacrifice in the interests of the community, or material asceticism for the purpose of spiritual salvation.

The inmate, then, sees himself as having been made poor by reason of his own acts and without the rationale of compensating benefits. The failure is *his* failure in a world where control and possession of the material environment are commonly taken as sure indicators of a man's worth. It is true that our society, as materialistic as it may be, does not rely exclusively on goods and services as a criterion of an individual's value; and, as we shall see shortly, the inmate population defends itself by stressing alternative or supplementary measures of merit. But impoverishment remains as one of the most bitter attacks on the individual's self-image that our society has to offer and the prisoner cannot ignore the implications of his straitened circumstances.[9] Whatever the discomforts and irritations of the prisoner's Spartan existence may be, he must carry the additional burden of social definitions which equate his material deprivation with personal inadequacy.

The Deprivation of Heterosexual Relationships

Unlike the prisoner in many Latin-American countries, the inmate of the maximum security prison in New Jersey does not enjoy the privilege of so-called conjugal visits. And in those brief times when the prisoner is allowed to see his wife, mistress, or "female friend," the woman must sit on one side of a plate glass window and the prisoner on the other, communicating by means of a phone under the scrutiny of a guard. If the inmate, then, is rejected and impoverished by the facts of his imprisonment, he is also figuratively castrated by his involuntary celibacy.

Now a number of writers have suggested that men in prison undergo a reduction of the sexual drive and that the sexual frustrations of prisoners are therefore less than they might appear to be at first glance. The reports of reduced sexual interest have, however, been largely confined to accounts of men imprisoned in concentration camps or similar extreme situations where starvation, torture, and physical exhaustion have reduced life to a simple struggle for survival or left the captive sunk in apathy. But in the American prison these factors are not at work to any significant extent and Linder has noted that the prisoner's access to mass media, pornography circulated among inmates, and similar stimuli serve to keep alive the prisoner's sexual impulses.[10] The same thought is expressed more crudely by the inmates of the New Jersey State Prison in a variety of obscene expressions and it is clear that the lack of heterosexual intercourse is a frustrating experience for the imprisoned criminal and that it is a frustration which weighs heavily and painfully on his mind during his prolonged confinement. There are, of course, some "habitual" homosexuals in the prison—men who were homosexuals before their arrival and who continue their particular form of deviant behavior within the all-male society of the custodial institution. For these inmates, perhaps, the deprivation of heterosexual intercourse cannot be counted as one of the pains of imprisonment. They are few in number, however, and are only too apt to be victimized or raped by aggressive prisoners who have turned to homosexuality as a temporary means of relieving their frustration.

Yet as important as frustration in the sexual sphere may be in physiological terms, the psychological problems created by the lack of heterosexual relationships can be even more serious. A society composed exclusively of men tends to generate anxieties in its members concerning their masculinity regardless of whether or not they are

---

[9]Komarovsky's discussion of the psychological implications of unemployment is particularly apposite here, despite the markedly different context, for she notes that economic failure provokes acute anxiety as humiliation cuts away at the individual's conception of his manhood. He feels useless, undeserving of respect, disorganized, adrift in a society where economic status is a major anchoring point. Cf. Mirra Komarovsky, *The Unemployed Man and His Family*, New York: The Dryden Press, 1940, pp. 74–77.

[10]See Robert M. Lindner, "Sex in Prison," *Complex*, Vol. 6, Fall 1951, pp. 5–20.

coerced, bribed, or seduced into an overt homosexual liaison. Latent homosexual tendencies may be activated in the individual without being translated into open behavior and yet still arouse strong guilt feelings at either the conscious or unconscious level. In the tense atmosphere of the prison with its known perversions, its importunities of admitted homosexuals, and its constant references to the problems of sexual frustration by guards and inmates alike, there are few prisoners who can escape the fact that an essential component of a man's self conception—his status of male—is called into question. And if an inmate has in fact engaged in homosexual behavior within the walls, not as a continuation of a habitual pattern but as a rare act of sexual deviance under the intolerable pressure of mounting physical desire, the psychological onslaughts on his ego image will be particularly acute.[11]

In addition to these problems stemming from sexual frustration per se, the deprivation of heterosexual relationships carries with it another threat to the prisoner's image of himself—more diffuse, perhaps, and more difficult to state precisely and yet no less disturbing. The inmate is shut off from the world of women which by its very polarity gives the male world much of its meaning. Like most men, the inmate must search for his identity not simply within himself but also in the picture of himself which he finds reflected in the eyes of others; and since a significant half of his audience is denied him, the inmate's self image is in danger of becoming half complete, fractured, a monochrome without the hues of reality. The prisoner's looking-glass self, in short—to use Cooley's fine phrase—is only that portion of the prisoner's personality which is recognized or appreciated by men and this partial identity is made hazy by the lack of contrast.

The Deprivation of Autonomy

We have noted before that the inmate suffers from what we have called a loss of autonomy in that he is subjected to a vast body of rules and commands which are designed to control his behavior in minute detail. To the casual observer, however, it might seem that the many areas of life in which self-determination is withheld, such as the language used in a letter, the hours of sleeping and eating, or the route to work, are relatively unimportant. Perhaps it might be argued, as in the case of material deprivation, that the inmate in prison is not much worse off than the individual in the free community who is regulated in a great many aspects of his life by the iron fist of custom. It could even be argued, as some writers have done, that for a number of imprisoned criminals the

---

[11]Estimates of the proportion of inmates who engage in homosexuality during their confinement in the prison are apt to vary. In the New Jersey State Prison, however, Wing Guards and Shop Guards examined a random sample of inmates who were well known to them from prolonged observation and identified 35 percent of the men as individuals believed to have engaged in homosexual acts. The judgments of these officials were substantially in agreement with the judgments of a prisoner who possessed an apparently well-founded reputation as an aggressive homosexual deeply involved in patterns of sexual deviance within the institution and who had been convicted of sodomy. But the validity of these judgments remains largely unknown and we present the following conclusions, based on a variety of sources, as provisional at best: First, a fairly large proportion of prisoners engage in homosexual behavior during their period of confinement. Second, for many of those prisoners who do engage in homosexual behavior, their sexual deviance is rare or sporadic rather than chronic. And third, as we have indicated before, much of the homosexuality which does occur in prison is not part of a life pattern existing before and after confinement; rather, it is a response to the peculiar rigors of imprisonment. A further discussion of the meaning and range of sexual behavior in the New Jersey State Prison will be presented in the next chapter.

extensive control of the custodians provides a welcome escape from freedom and that the prison officials thus supply an external Super-Ego which serves to reduce the anxieties arising from an awareness of deviant impulses. But from the viewpoint of the inmate population, it is precisely the triviality of much of the officials' control which often proves to be most galling. Regulation by a bureaucratic staff is felt far differently than regulation by custom. And even though a few prisoners do welcome the strict regime of the custodians as a means of checking their own aberrant behavior which they would like to curb but cannot, most prisoners look on the matter in a different light. Most prisoners, in fact, express an intense hostility against their far-reaching dependence on the decisions of their captors and the restricted ability to make choices must be included among the pains of imprisonment along with restrictions of physical liberty, the possession of goods and services, and heterosexual relationships.

Source: From *The Society of Captives* by Gresham M. Sykes. Copyright © 1958 by Princeton University Press. Reprinted by permission of Princeton University Press.

INMATE VICTIMIZATION

Hans Toch

The inmates we shall portray in this account are under stress from other inmates. They are "victimized" in the sense of the term as used by Fisher and applied by Bartollas, Miller, and Dinitz. "Victimization" is a process that is defined by Fisher as "a predatory practice whereby inmates of superior strength and knowledge of inmate lore prey on weaker and less knowledgeable inmates" (p. 89). Issues of "weakness" or "strength," "superiority" or "knowledge," must be seen as *relative to victimization, and to no other transactions*. We don't know how "strong" or "weak" the victims or aggressors are in other settings, such as at work, in school, or at home. We know that aggressors select the arena of the victimization contest ("prison lore"), initiate the stressful encounter, and pick the indices of evaluation. The victim walks into situations where his presence lends itself to a game in which the aggressor arranges things deliberately so he can make the victim look as helpless, "weak," and inferior as possible.

The extreme form of inmate victimization is homosexual rape, which is extremely rare in prisons but has been prevalent in some institutions, including the Philadelphia–detention facility publicized by Davis. Though rape literally is not at issue in most victimization of inmates, it is figuratively always involved. It lurks (as does execution over the criminal justice system) as the ultimate penalty, the most extreme form of power that may be held over the victim. Moreover, the motives of victimizers and of rapists overlap heavily. Prison rapists and victimizers derive from similar backgrounds, and they select victims who are culturally similar to each other. Moreover, rape is almost always threatened by prison aggressors and is always feared by the victims.

The aim of victimization is complex, and we can describe and illustrate it later. The apparent or superficial object of victimization is sexual exploitation, and it is sex that the aggressor most often demands of the victim. But we noted that rape is an infrequent event. Though it is possible that the aggressor's hope springs eternal, irrespective of his past experience, this interpretation is unlikely. It is more likely that the nature of the aggressor's threat is incidental to his real purpose, which is to be threatening. The latter assumption suggests that the medium in inmate victimization is in fact its message, that the aim of the activity is to provoke stress and to make stress visible. The gain of such interactions would be that implied by Fisher's definition: to "demonstrate" the aggressor's "superior strength and knowledge" and to pinpoint the victim as "weaker and less knowledgeable." The aim succeeds best where victims are unfamiliar with the arena of testing, which includes violence and its threatened deployment.

Culture Shock

In the first act of *The Pajama Game*, the new superintendent of the Sleep-Tite Pajama Factory complains that

> A new town is a blue town
> A "who do you know" and "show me what you can do" town.

> There's no red carpet at your feet
> If you're not tough they'll try to beat you down.*

When any of us enters a new setting, we usually work on the assumption that our past experience will prove helpful to us. We assume that situations we have resolved in the past will help us to understand new situations, and we assume that the skills we have used to solve past problems will work with new problems. We look for familiar opportunities and familiar challenges that can be dealt with in familiar ways.

Almost everyone scans a new setting when he arrives in it. Such scanning is not idle curiosity but a means of orienting oneself to environmental presses to see where they fall in relation to one's needs. The process is similar to that of driving into a new town and locating key features on a map so that one knows how to get places without getting lost.

A stress-free transition presupposes (1) that the information one needs to deal with new settings can be readily obtained, (2) that one encounters no major problems before he has acquired sufficient familiarity to respond to them, (3) that one sees himself as still able to reach his currently important life goals.

Transition stress can be reduced if the new setting provides a moratorium to environmental adjustment, if it supplies data about itself or offers bridging experiences from other environments. The average arrival has the best chance of avoiding stress if he can be helped to see new configurations as comprising familiar features. A cliff one must climb is less forbidding if it contains handholds and crevices such as one has negotiated elsewhere.

At the most stressful end of the spectrum the new arrival is confronted—preferably without warning—with a strange world that firmly challenges his most basic assumptions. Such experiences are sufficiently disequilibrating to be "used" by some settings (such as concentration camps) to make people dazed, helpless, and malleable (Bettelheim, 1960). An unscheduled transition trauma of this kind faces some young male inmates entering jails or prisons in which other young inmates are housed. This trauma can start at the earliest point of entry into the setting with the discovery that one has become target for what appears to be homosexual attention:

Cox R 6: We were standing in the line and they yelled it down, "Three niggers and one homo," like that. . . . And then I heard the guys talking about me, and then the accidental ass-grabbing started.

• • •

Att R2 10: Any new person, they hollered obscenities at them and all sorts of names, and throwing things down from the gallery and everything. They told me to walk down the middle of this line like I was on exhibition, and everybody started to throw things and everything, and I was shaking in my boots. . . . They were screaming things like, "That is for me" and "This one won't take long—he will be easy." And, "Look at his eyes" and "her eyes" or whatever, and making all kinds of remarks.

---

*From "A New Town Is a Blue Town" by Richard Adler & Jerry Ross. © 1954. 1955 Frank Music Corp., 1350 Avenue of the Americas, N.Y., N.Y., 10019. International Copyright Secured. All Rights Reserved. Used by permission.

The experience of being targeted challenges a number of basic premises of the average young male. One such assumption is that of his own sex role, which he has taken for granted himself, and has assumed that other people will stipulate:

Cox R 27: When you get in your cell sometimes, you get in there and you look at yourself and you say, "Why is this guy saying these things?" I had never thought of that myself. I always thought I was a good looking man and I never thought about myself being a girl. . . . I've sat around a guy a lot of times, I've had my arm around a guy, somebody. We really got wrecked with each other, and then we went out the door and we had a good feeling, a friendship thing, and here I could never put my arm next to somebody. The person would think that I was either trying to make advances or he would turn around and say, "This is a freaky thing, baby." . . . Out there you wouldn't even think about it. You would pick up this *Midnight* magazine or some crazy thing like that, some crazy newspaper or something like that. And you read about a man being sodomized or something. And in here it's something that happens every day, and you have to watch out. . . . When they first start saying things to me like, "Hey baby," I would expect to see a secretary walking by or something. I just could not believe that a male would be saying those kinds of things to me. And I thought that the guy must be goofing on me or something, playing jokes. And I knew then after a while that, if the guy had a chance, he would want to kiss me and have sex with me. That is something you say to yourself, "This can't be true." And it's a freaky thing in the head, man. It's really hard to tell you the feeling that you get. It's like threatening your life, only instead he is threatening your manhood.

The experience also raises the question of one's status as an autonomous human being. As a person one usually deals reciprocally with other persons. One's fate always hinges partly, or largely, on one's own actions. One is not prepared to encounter junctures where one is matter-of-factly regarded as an object available for the asking. Yet in prison the way one is defined and verbally addressed may make it clear that one is seen by other men as impotent, that others feel free to question one's capacity to keep oneself from being used or exploited:

PC 3: From one minute to the next you don't know what an inmate is going to say. You don't. You could be discussing a fishing trip for a few minutes and the next thing you know the guy next to him is yelling that he is going to get into your buns or he thinks you're cute or how about a blow job or something like this. But the few minutes that you were talking about this fishing trip your mind was relaxed and you were settled down and then right away somebody has to start. And it's always that way. Somebody has to start. No matter what the conversation is, it always comes into it. . . . He'll say, "How's your buns today?" Just to keep his image up. And then you have to start, because if you don't start on the defensive then they're going to say that so-and-so doesn't defend himself, so we'll ride him a little more.

• • •

Cox R 27: Sometimes there is twenty or thirty people in the showers, and they're always making remarks to you, and you don't feel free. I'm used to on the streets, where you don't have any paranoia. Taking a shower is a beautiful thing. Here it's a paranoia thing, where they have you back against the wall. And if you turn around and wash your legs and you're bent over, besides getting remarks you might really get hurt. . . . And you take your shower in thirty seconds, and you feel really stupid, and you just pull your pants down, and there is all these guys waiting for you to pull your pants down. It's a sick thing. Even though the physical pressure is there for a short time, the mental pressure is there permanently. And if you're on the toilet and everybody is just walking by, then it's really an intense thing. I've been to the bathroom in front of people on the streets, and it's just nothing at all like it is in here. You just want to say, "Jesus, leave me alone." But you can't close the door, and it's a cell, and people are looking at you. . . . Sometimes I have some heavy thoughts in my cell, thinking about why all this happened. Is this pressure going to build up to the point where I say I'm actually going to be a fag? I really wonder where and why all this is happening. What I was into. I never dreamed that I was going to be in this condition and in this kind of place and around these kind of people and around this kind of environment, where I would want to leave and couldn't.

The physical environment adds to the impression produced by the interpersonal setting. Confinement adds to the impact of social pressure, because it seems to cut off physical retreat (at least initially) and produces an unfamiliar "back to the wall" feeling—a panic state and sense of resourcelessness.

One discovers not only one's sense of fear but one's lack of preparedness for dealing with fear. Part of the problem rests with the Alice in Wonderland flavor of the new experience, where sharper contrasts seem to be generated for oneself than for others. On the simplest level, one sees the cultural discrepancies that make one a favored target. But one also knows oneself to be mystified, lost, and visibly helpless:

Cox R 29:   I can see it from anybody else that comes in from where I live—they just don't fit in with the rest of this population. The population is almost 50 percent, 75 percent, 80 percent from the city—we just don't fit in. . . . They don't act the same and they don't even think the same. It's what I do that is normal. Every one of them that comes through down up north to here has been called a "pussy," and they really have more put on them than guys that come from the city or Rochester or somewhere else. They have had more pressure put on them.

• • •

PC 15:   The farmers like me were being approached or lured into something like that. . . . I was scared, and I didn't know how to react to certain predicaments, and I didn't actually know who to turn to, as far as I didn't know anybody. And I didn't know if I should go to the officers, the other inmates, or the homies, people from your home town. I didn't know what the difference was between all these persons. I didn't know one from the other.

Tests of Resourcefulness

If the inmate does not succumb to panic, he learns over time that the threats to which he is subjected are incidental to his dilemma. He is not a serious target of rape but an object of maneuvers designed to test his "manliness" or coping competence. Aggressors and spectators seem concerned with his reactions or nonreactions to aggressive overtures. The man is on trial, and he is fatefully examined. The penalty for failure is accelerated victimization. If a man acquits himself fully, he ensures his immunity to attack.

The issue is Manliness. The criterion is courage. Courage is evidenced by willingness to fight and by the capacity for doing so:

Cox R 27:   We just recently got this guy on the division that is from Schenectady, and he's in here. Like, he's sort of a gangster, and they don't say boo to him. They sit back and watch him. They don't say boo to him. They don't pop any shit on him, because he kicks their ass.

• • •

Cox C–2 23:   Now, each and every inmate goes through a trial period where someone is going to say, "I want your ass." But if he straightens it out himself, and he gets into a fight or something with the guy, it will show everyone that he is not going to take that kind of shit, you know?—he will be all right.

• • •

P 1: If you don't react to that one word in the right way, you lose something, and then they will test you a little further. . . . Everybody is trying to prove that they're not going to be an underdog. They're not going to be pushed around. And sometimes in so doing they also have to prove that they're going to be more aggressive than you are and they have to show that. And that is the only way that they can prove it.

Doing Time – No Safe Haven: Stories of Women in Prison

Lori B. Girshick

"Doing time" has many meanings for those in prison. To do "hard time" is to dwell on events in the outside world; to do "easy time" is to learn to become emotionally uninvolved in outside events. In the latter, the inmate's thoughts and energies are focused on her daily life and goings-on within prison, protecting her from things over which she has no control (Giallombardo 1966b). Part of hard time is "going through changes," involving mood swings, worry, and adjustment to being incarcerated (Mahan 1984).

Women and men serve their sentences differently. Men concentrate on "doing their own time," keeping others at bay and showing invulnerability. Women generally try to remain involved in the lives of their children and families (Lord 1995). Charles Turnbo (1993, 13) has found that, compared to men, women talk more to staff members, are more openly emotional, have more suicidal thoughts, and are more vocal about issues involving their family and children.

When considering the experiences covered in this chapter, inmates frequently spoke in relative terms—comparing Black Mountain to the North Carolina Correctional Institution for Women in Raleigh (referred to hereinafter as Raleigh). Every woman incarcerated in North Carolina enters the system there. She may stay as briefly as one night, or she may stay for years.

Inmates can be transferred to several different minimum security facilities during their incarceration, but the major point of comparison is the state's main prison. Housing over one thousand women, Raleigh is characterized by long lines, high noise levels, waits to see one's case manager, running out of food at meals, inadequate medical care, and the general problems of overcrowding. It is a self-contained "city" within the state's capital, and inmates never have to leave the prison grounds except for certain circumstances, such as giving birth at Wake County Hospital. It is also dangerous compared to Black Mountain.

> I hated that place. I felt that was the pits of hell for me. . . . The officers there, they don't have the means or the control of that place. It's so overcrowded that someone could get hurt there very easily. It's happened. I was on reception there and a girl got attacked with a straight razor, and by the time, the place is so large, they could get any help to that girl, she was cut all to pieces. And I remember laying on my bed crying, thinking, "Dear God, I can't live like this." It was hell.

Doing time at Black Mountain, therefore, is easier in many respects, and most women do not want to be sent back to Raleigh, where the only privilege is visiting. There are no opportunities for work or study release or community-volunteer passes, all ways to normalize life.

The average time already served when I interviewed the Black Mountain prisoners was two years, five months; the shortest stay was four months, and the longest was sixteen years. One woman gave this advice: "I got a saying, 'Do the time, don't let it do you.' You have to work with the system instead of working against it." "Time" has different meanings in the prison system. For example, every woman referred to "good time," which is time off for good behavior, for programming, or for working extra tasks; it is officially labeled good time, GAIN time, or merit time. "Doing my own time" refers to keeping to oneself, avoiding write-ups or conflict. "Straight time," or flat time, refers to a sentence without the benefit of good time or parole time. And, of course, the number indicating sentence length is another indicator of time, as is a parole date (Mahan 1984).

The Moral Career

Erving Goffman (1961) describes the life of inmates in total institutions, facilities that limit and control their movements, activities, surroundings, and ability for self-definition. Such institutions are characterized by rules and regulations, a strict barrier between those who are in power and those who are not, uniforms, their own lingo, and degradation of personal status. Catharine MacKinnon (1987, 170) observes, "To be a prisoner means to be defined as a member of a group for whom rules of what can be done to you, or what is seen as abuse of you, are reduced as part of the definition of your status." She goes on to say, "To be a woman is that kind of definition and has that kind of meaning." Social control of female prisoners, according to Meda Chesney-Lind and Jocelyn Pollock (1995, 166), compared to control of male inmates, parallels that of women in society—it includes all types of behavior and is more relationship based.

Thomas Arcaro (1984, 75–86) outlines seven stages in the moral career of the female inmate. A moral career is the progression of changes that occurs in sense of self and in relationship to others (Goffman 1961) as an inmate adjusts to the setting of a total institution. The process begins with a literal stripping of the self through strip searching, followed by accepting state-issued clothing and losing personal belongings. Impression management is threatened, since newcomers have few of the "props" needed to manipulate an individualized personality. Thus begins the process of status degradation, characterized not only by lack of distinct individuality but by loss of freedom and heightened external control (see also Moyer 1984).

The second stage involves distancing from the role of prisoner, wherein a new arrival will keep to herself and avoid identifying as an insider. This is a process of denial, which changes as contact with the outside is superseded by contact with life on the inside. In stage three, learning the ropes, the woman comes to understand the social structure of the prison, including hard lessons about trust, gossip, and how to monitor one's own behavior. Culture shock is common.

Learning how to do time marks the fourth stage. This involves figuring out how to cope with boredom, arbitrary enforcement of rules, lack of privacy, and unvarying schedules, as well as developing various coping strategies, such as establishing substitute family relations or involving oneself romantically with another inmate. This stage varies with the length of sentence, and can last from months to years.

Stage five, dealing with fear of denial around parole dates, essentially involves the experience of dashed hopes. An inmate longs for release, but she is denied time after time (and sees this happen to others as well). She comes to view the system as capricious, without fairness, and she needs to develop psychological defenses against this emotional roller coaster. Stage six, getting papers, takes place in this context. As a woman has her home plan accepted and gets a release date, mental strain can become unbearable. Fear that another inmate may undermine her impending release may verge on paranoia.

Finally, stage seven, getting out and shedding the inmate role, is necessarily a lengthy process. Upon release, the former prisoner has many adjustments to make, including rebuilding her sense of self and reestablishing social roles; she also, most likely, faces parole stipulations. Arcaro (1984, 86) observes, "This final stage in the moral career is marked by the ex-inmate becoming aware that she has been permanently affected by her life at [prison], and that she will continually have to deal with the social stigma of being an ex-con."

Powerlessness and Dependency

An environment as controlled as prison—in which women are told when to eat, get up, or go to bed, in which they are transported wherever they go, in which their contact with the outside is strictly regulated—fosters dependency and powerlessness (Clark 1995, Faith 1993). A "no touch" rule fractures any natural connection and spontaneity the women might feel and exhibit with each other that would provide nurturance and support under stressful conditions. Since adult roles and responsibilities are now limited (and in many cases eliminated), women not only have to accept authority but are given the message that they are not to be trusted with responsibility (Clark 1995, 312). The prison becomes the punitive parent, regulating the child through rules and sanctions (Clark 1995, 315). Keeping female prisoners in the status of dependent children makes them easier to control (Carlen 1983, Moyer 1984), and the women themselves feel infantilized. As one inmate told me, "This place here, they're not really hard on you. It's really, speaking for myself, it's feeling low self-esteem, feeling like you got a parent telling you what to do, and that's hard to accept, but you have to. . . . You start feeling like a kid." Another woman said:

> Honestly, [the officers] make me sick. They have an ego thing going. If you treat a person with respect, then you'll get respect. Sometimes there's one bad apple. But the majority of the ladies here, they just want to be treated like somebody. We know we are incarcerated. We're already tried and sentenced. No need to do it over again. They tell you you should act like adults and then talk to you like you're two. I will never understand that, talking down to me.

Female prisoners receive a double message: to take responsibility for themselves, yet to not become too independent (Clark 1995). There is tight regulation over activities such as loaning personal items like toiletries, helping each other out with duties, and sharing possessions like clothing—normal activities that are prohibited within a prison (Fletcher et al. 1993). Such actions, now viewed as "trafficking" or "trading," are generally not even an issue in men's prisons (Belknap 1996), but in women's prisons they are met with write-ups, loss of privileges, or extra work duty. Many write-ups result from misunderstandings that are not negotiable, regardless of fault. One inmate shared this example with me:

> I went home on my home pass and I was told to have my daughter to have me back, and I don't even know what time, a certain time, right. But on the card that they give you the time is on there. She [the guard] told one time and on the card was another time. It messed me up, we went by what the card said. . . . And then another one was I gave my daughter twenty dollars to get her

hair fixed, and my daughter wrote on a piece of paper the statement of why I gave her twenty dollars. But they said I was supposed to give her a money order, and I never gave money orders before. So I wasn't right then. They wrote me up for both of them, gave me forty hours' extra duty, twenty for each one, and, what else—took my home passes for a month.

Many women felt the rules and regulations were more strict at Black Mountain, a minimum security facility, than at Raleigh. The inmates wanted to avoid confrontations and not get sent back to the main prison, yet matters seemed out of their control.

The rules will change from day to day, like one officer will say do it this way and another officer will say, "No, you can't do that," and write you up, and so-and-so said you could but that don't matter. You gonna take a write-up. We just go through a lot of mental anguish every day. We don't know what kind of mood the officer may be in or sergeant or even another inmate. You might just say something in joking and they might take it serious and it creates a problem there.

Another woman remarked,

To me, this prison right here, it seems like a private prison 'cause it seems like they got their own rules. There's nothing here I see that says "DOC." Some of the rules here you wouldn't believe. . . . It's just petty. I mean, you can't sit down, you can't comb a lady's hair outside; one person in the bathroom at a time [after 10 P.M.]

And more than one inmate told me that officers claimed they had to fulfill a write-up quota.

Well, their policy was that if they don't get an inmate, to write them up, there's so many times, they're not doing their job. That was told me by an officer. . . . She said, "Hell, it puts another extra paycheck in our pocket because we get a bonus." I'm like, "What?" "Yeah," she said, "We can get raises by as many write-ups we get."

What seems to be arbitrary control over actions is made worse by the lack of privacy in most prisons. There are no places to be alone, since prisoners must be accounted for at all times (Mahan 1984). Still, one of the benefits of the honor grade included, as one woman said, "doors on the bathroom stalls, shower curtains," and "when you're changing your clothes in your room you can shut your door."

Boredom is another consequence of control and loss of freedoms. According to Karlene Faith (1993, 167), boredom can be the "most miserable feature of the prison experience," given the regimentation of daily life and the herdlike atmosphere. Deprived of agency over their lives, many inmates gain weight, chain-smoke, sleep too much or not enough, become irritable over waits in line, and in general resent mail censorship, strip searches, and orders to "Move, *now*, ladies." Many prisoners I interviewed cited boredom as a prominent feature of daily life, although others felt they could be no busier than they already were with work, passes, and in some cases school.

For example, this inmate said, "It's boring, but that's about it. They don't have no kind of activity here. None whatsoever. Nothing but volleyball and badminton. It's nothing." Another woman remarked.

> I have more freedom [than at Raleigh], and I don't even take advantage of the freedom that I do have. I go out every day to work. I don't do nothing on my job, I don't jeopardize my job in any kind of way. I work around some good people and I don't have nobody to try to bring me this or bring me that in. 'Cause I can go home and get the personal things that I need for myself or I can go out on CV passes to get it.

Adjustment

Being in prison is stressful and can create physical as well as psychological problems. Stress results from loss of freedom, loss of control of one's environment, loss of contact with family and friends, rupture of social roles, fear of losing bonds with one's children, and insults to self-esteem and self-concept (Fogel 1993, Giallombardo 1966a). Regina Arnold (1994, 182) reminds us that these women, structurally dislocated from the primary institutions of society, adopted strategies of survival that were criminalized, and now need to be resocialized within a criminal network and relocated structurally within the prison. Their ties to the prison world will increase as their ties to the conventional world decrease.

All inmates go through a similar adaptation, or prisonization process, though not all of them will experience every aspect of it. For example, Rose Giallombardo (1966b) and David Ward and Gene Kassebaum (1964) argue in two early studies of homosexuality among female inmates that such behaviour was the major mode of adaptation to the prison environment. Other investigators focus on pseudo-families (Mahan 1984, Propper 1982). Zelma Henriques (1996, 83–84) suggests that homosexuality among incarcerated mothers may be one means of dealing with the depression caused by separation from their children, whereas participating in a surrogate family allows for the continuation of mothering roles. Other researchers cite the importance of programming that includes support groups and information, education, drug rehabilitation, and job training (Sultan et al. 1984). Inmates themselves mention focusing on accepting the fact of incarceration, admitting responsibility for their crimes, and learning the difference between associates and friends.

James Larson and Joey Nelson (1984) and Doris MacKenzie et al. (1989) found that length of sentence and time already served had an impact on adaptation to prison. Persons who had served more time seemed better adjusted to prison life, a point with which the Black Mountain inmates agree. "You can tell a person who's been locked down two, three, four years because they more or less know what it's like. They've settled down, their wild streak is not there. They're getting serious with whatever it is that's going on." Another woman, in talking about who she can trust, says. "There's some ladies here you can trust. A lot of them is women that's been locked up for a while, that's kind of settled into it. In for two years or more, there's a big difference."

The types of adaptation that Larson and Nelson (1984) identify include isolation (withdrawing from outside bonds and constructing a life inside prison), solidarity (developing primary relationships with others in prison, especially through family or homosexual ties), and efficacy (transforming a sense of powerlessness to one of limited control through friendship). Although friendship and affiliation are major components of the female gender role, the finding that friendship and trust were important responses to powerlessness seems at odds with what I heard over and over again in the interviews regarding lack of trust. The prisoners at Black Mountain spoke of adaptation based on acceptance, isolation, state families, religious dedication, and resignation. Following are some comments about adjusting to prison life.

> I do know this, that when you do get put in prison you need to just set your mind to the fact that you are in prison, make the best of it, and to learn, immediately, that you have some people over you and that you have to do as they say. This makes it much easier. If you will just go along with the authority that's over you. Also to work as much as possible. This passes the time really nice. To make yourself tired out physically so that mentally you'll be all right.

And,

> Prison can be either good or bad. For some people, for most women it's bad because they don't accept the time they've got, and they always blame it on everybody else. Once you accept the crime and say, "I did it," whether you took it for someone else or whatever you had to make that decision to do it. You have to live with your decision. Once you say, "Ok, I did this, this and this, and this is what I got," and you start looking at it as time, and start living your life the best way DOC allows you, then you can't complain about it.

For some women, incarceration brought about a greater caution in interactions with others. For example, as this prisoner says.

> [I]t's hard in here, it's hard to live with women day in and day out. And sometimes I've found myself putting up shields and guards towards people. I don't want that to carry over with me. I was never like that. In some ways prison has affected me in a negative way because I'm not that trusting, free-spirited, free-hearted person I used to be. I'm very cautious. I feel like in prison, not speaking of on the streets, I feel like in here that you really have to watch what you say and do, and there's always an ulterior motive behind someone's actions.

For others, interaction was welcome within the spiritual context fostered by Bible study.

> Before I would go around preaching to someone, I want to make sure that I'm where I should be. I want God's light to shine through me. I don't want to cuss somebody out and then turn around and say but you should read this in the Bible or you should read that in the Bible because that turns people off. That's not God's love coming through you. . . . But I love to sing, and I love to hear God's word, but I don't go around preaching to everybody. If we're having Bible study and they'd like to join us, I welcome them, they're more than welcome to come in and join us.

Relationships with Other Inmates

Once a woman is incarcerated, however long she takes to observe her fellow prisoners and the routine and rhythm of her new life, she will begin to interact with those around her, making her own impression and aligning with or avoiding other inmates. She learns to make herself scarce when certain guards are around, and she establishes relationships with other prisoners she feels comfortable with. Basically, she "learns the ropes."

When asked about free time, virtually all the women mentioned staying in their rooms. There they slept or read, where it was "safer and quieter." Half the inmates spent free time outside, sitting at the picnic tables, talking in small groups, and smoking. Less than a quarter of the women mentioned the day room as a place to spend time. Generally the television is on, and at the time of the study visiting took place there. The "smoke room" was cited by less than 20 percent of the women as a place to spend time. Since the time of my interviews, smoking has been banned inside prison buildings.

As Sue Mahan (1984, 359) says, "incarceration means forced interaction." There are people, perhaps sharing her room, with whom the new prisoner ordinarily would never associate. Some inmates are uncomfortable with those of another race, some despise prostitutes, some feel other women are not clean enough or look down on their personal habits (Giallombardo 1966a). As one inmate said, "I don't like it. I'm not used to this type of people. It's a new experience for me 'cause I've never had to be around people that lived on the streets, had to sell themselves for what they wanted." And another prisoner, although she was a drug addict, felt she was not like the other women. This belief helped her do her time.

> What influenced me the most was knowing I had nothing in common with these people, and I don't want to say that I'm better than anybody else, 'cause I hate when people say that, it's just that I'm from, I have my values and morals instilled in me and a lot of people don't in here.

Given the limitations on prison activities, "prisoners establish their relationships through talk." Mahan (1984, 359) found that friends shared stories and gossip, whereas those who were not friends ignored each other. Perhaps the most frequent comment I heard about interaction with other inmates was that there are no friends in prison, only associates, so the term "friend" is always used loosely. There may be one or two people to talk to, but one never really trusts them. The element of distrust is *always* present.

> Well, I don't believe I would say [I] trust anybody in prison 'cause you don't really know 'em. Don't matter if you done ten years with them, you'll never know them because everybody will stick you in the back to get what they wanna get. You just don't know who will and who won't, so to just be on the safe side . . . you don't want to tell nobody nothing in here.

These two women echo her pessimism:

> The inmates, you have your certain little groups of friends. Those friends are supportive of you. As far as widespread support from the inmates, there is

none. They'd rather tell on you and get you in trouble than they had to help you. I've found that out since I've been in here that women just will not help other women.

And,

> Trust is not something you have within these walls. . . . Women are evil. I want to believe people are basically good, but every time I believe it, I get knocked down. . . . As much as this is my word, this awful place, there's no trust, there's no dignity, there's no loyalty, there's no honor. I still believe there's good people in the world; this happens to be the place that draws the trash.

Indeed, Giallombardo (1966b, 100) found that inmates commonly held these views of women's nature: you can't trust another woman; every woman is a sneaking, lying bitch; and, with women, "you never really know."

Learning to distrust those around you in prison is based on experience. Gossip and the inaccurate retelling of stories create problems. Women can try to avoid gossip by keeping to themselves or displaying "false fronts" (Arcaro 1984). Says one prisoner:

> Here you don't have friends, you have associates. You really don't have anybody you could call a friend in prison, period. . . . You may say something and it goes and it may be turned three or four ways once it gets back. It's best to keep to yourself.

Or, as another woman remarked, "It doesn't pay to be honest. The one thing you learn from coming to prison is you learn how to lie, and if you didn't know when you got here, you better learn quick. You can't be honest, you just can't do it."

There seems to be no defense against an inmate who chooses to turn someone in with a lie, which sometimes lands a woman on a bus back to Raleigh. It is usually the accuser who is believed, not the person who must defend herself. One woman explained,

> See, what happened, I had a CV sponsor and a girl here who I know, she's gone now, well, she got really jealous of this lady's relationship, come back to the unit and told them that we were gay. And they stripped me of my CV passes to her. I can no longer go out with her. She cannot become a sponsor until the year I make parole. Because they believed it.

Here is another inmate's story:

> I got railroaded just because somebody wrote a statement on me and told a lie. It was a, I got charged with a 23 [a write-up for a sexual act], but what it was was that the girl said that I hemmed her up and exposed myself to her. Now anybody that knows me knows that that's not true. I mean, that's so out of my character. [But, I got sent back to Raleigh.]

The most trusted prisoners seem to be those from one's home town (the home girls, or "homeys") and those who have done long stretches of time together. As one woman said, "I have a girl that's here who's a real good friend of mine from home and I got another girl that she and I are pretty good friends. We've done this whole sentence together just about. But other than that, if they speak, I speak. I don't talk a lot." Homeys "talk about the old days" and are not as likely to twist stories:

> I don't communicate with half of the women here. I stay, if I'm not into a book, I start crocheting. It's very few of the women that I really talk to. Now, my homeys, from my hometown, I communicate with them. Other than that, I don't 'cause I come here to do my time and sometimes there's a mistake when you talk to other people, they stretch and take it elsewhere. . . . Women are trouble.

Source: From Chapter 5 (pp. 75–85) in *No Safe Haven: Stories of Women in Prison* by Lori Girshick, copyright © 1997 by University Press of New England, Lebanon, NH. Reprinted with permission.

THE PAINS OF IMPRISONMENT: EXPLORING A CLASSIC TEXT WITH CONTEMPORARY AUTHORS

John Riley

Firsthand accounts of prison experience have long been a staple of Western literature. While such works are rarely written by authors whose backgrounds prepare them to honor the conventions of scholarship or social science, they can be gripping, well written, and well informed. They offer a portrait of prison life that is largely consistent with academic research findings, while providing color and detail that would otherwise be unavailable. The best firsthand accounts of prison life move the reader to focus on the modern tragedy of mass incarceration in a way that few standard academic offerings ever do. In the classroom, they can stimulate curiosity and support exploration of the academic literature. In short, they can make the sometimes less accessible findings of scholarship and social science come alive.

Serious scholarship on correctional issues eventually requires students to obtain some firsthand familiarity with major works in the field. This essay argues that contemporary, firsthand accounts of prison life can play an important role in classes that introduce students to classic texts on corrections. The goal of this essay is to show how contemporary firsthand accounts of prison may extend and update the analysis found in classic texts and provide students with a foundation for critical reflection on major theoretical issues. This essay focuses on some of the ways in which recent accounts of prison life may be used in conjunction with a particular classic text to offer instructors opportunities to illustrate and explain the significance of abstract concepts, to examine issues of continuity and change in corrections theory, and to encourage critical thinking on important issues. Gresham Sykes' *The Society of Captives* and the concept of "the pains of imprisonment" provide a good opportunity to illustrate this potential for symbiosis between scholarly classics and firsthand accounts (1958). Taking the pains of imprisonment as a starting point, it is possible to show how new works may illuminate classic texts and to demonstrate how they, in turn, are given context and structure when read in conjunction with classic texts.

The Pains of Imprisonment

While many authors have written about the difficulties faced by prisoners, discussions of the pains of imprisonment often begin with consideration of Sykes' *Society of Captives* (1958). According to Sykes, the pains of imprisonment are best understood as a series of "deprivations and frustrations" that come to constitute a serious psychological assault upon the self (1958:64). Sykes linked the pains of imprisonment to deprivations of liberty, goods and services, heterosexual relations, personal autonomy, and security. For Sykes, these common "deprivations or frustrations of prison life" are at times so severe as to constitute a "serious attack on the personality" (1958:64). Sykes believed that contemporary researchers had found "only one strikingly pervasive value system" among inmates (1966:5). For Sykes, inmates develop a common culture because they confront a common set of problems as they experience incarceration. Inmate culture, for Sykes, is a collective response to the pains of imprisonment, and convict norms and roles reflect a collective effort to preserve an acceptable sense of self.

The pains of imprisonment became a key organizing concept in many of the most influential works on incarceration (Austin and Irwin 2001; Giallombardo 1966; Goffman 1961; Irwin 1970; Johnson and Toch 1982; Ward and Kassebaum 1965). Students continue to encounter the concept in these works and in many of the textbooks currently used in undergraduate courses on criminal justice, corrections, and criminology (Barlow 2000; Jacoby 1994; Martin, Mutchnick, and Austin 1990; Senna and Siegel 1995; Silverman 2001; Tewksbury 1997). There is good reason for this.

Sykes' formulation of the "pains of imprisonment" is more than a key concept in a classic text. It is a central element in a view of the prison that has attracted critical scrutiny for almost half a century. Since *Society of Captives*, corrections theory has been shaped by a debate between proponents of the "deprivation" model, who understand inmate culture as a response to the pains of imprisonment, and those who explain the social organization of prison life as a reflection of "importation" (Irwin and Cressey 1962; Simon 2000). The former view, indebted to Sykes for his discussion of the pains of imprisonment, has received substantial criticism over the years.

Subsequent research has called into question Sykes' view that the emergence of a common inmate culture could be explained as a reaction to a set of commonly experienced deprivations. Irwin and Cressey (1962), for example, argued that inmates could be grouped into not one, but three subcultures: a criminal subculture, a prison subculture, and a conventional subculture. They also argued that so-called "convict" norms were brought into the prison as an extension of previously learned criminal codes (Irwin and Cressey 1962). Irwin, in a later study of California felons, argued that the "roles, values and norms" of prisoners represent "converging subcultures . . . which emerge in other social settings" (1970:64). Heffernan, working at a women's prison in Virginia, identified three inmate social systems: "the square, the cool, and the life" (1972:41). Wheeler (1972), in summarizing the findings of his research on inmates in Scandinavian institutions, seemed to be summarizing much of the recent research in the field. For Wheeler, the data "pointed clearly to the importance of the culture outside the prison as a determinant of the life that forms within" (1972:1018).

The "deprivation" model was consistent with Goffman's (1961) account of the prison as a "total institution," isolated and insulated from changes in the larger society. As new research findings began to call into question the idea of a monolithic inmate culture formed by a common experience of deprivation, major changes in prison life began to undermine the view of the prison as a "total institution" (Farrington 1992; Simon 2000). As Farrington (1992) observes, today's prisons are hardly the isolated institutions that Goffman described in the early 1960s. New policies governing mail, education, visitation, telephone contact, television, and furloughs, many of which reflect changing judicial attitudes, are among the many links that help prisoners maintain contact with the outside world. In short, the grasp of the "total institution," which was probably never quite as strong as Goffman's work suggests, was weakened by the prisoner's rights movement, judicial activism, and changing correctional policies (Austin and Irwin 2001). While in recent years there have been a variety of efforts to reverse this trend and reduce the amenities of prison life, the pains of imprisonment are somewhat less today for many inmates than they might have been in the 1950s (Simon 2000).

The work of Irwin and Cressey (1962), Toch (1977), Wheeler (1972), Heffernan (1972), Farrington (1992) and others has undermined the primacy of the "deprivation" model of inmate culture. Even so, the concept of the pains of imprisonment continues to be regarded as an important factor shaping inmate behavior patterns (Thomas and Petersen 1977). Today, prison life is widely understood as a reflection of both external cultural influences and efforts to cope with the pains of imprisonment. As Gover, MacKenzie, and Armstrong suggest in their recent discussion of importation and deprivation, "together, the two theories offer an explanation for how institutionalized offenders adjust to correctional environments" (2000:451).

Scholars will undoubtedly continue to debate the relative importance of deprivation and importation for some time. Students who are unfamiliar with Sykes' original work on the pains of imprisonment will find themselves at a disadvantage when discussions turn to inmate culture, collective behavior, and the deprivation and importation models. In short, understanding Sykes' formulation of the pains of imprisonment makes it easier to understand a set of issues that continues to be of central importance to correctional studies almost half a century after the publication of *Society of Captives* (1958). Taking this concept as a starting point, it is possible to demonstrate some of the ways in which contemporary accounts of the prison may illuminate a classic text and to show how they, in turn, are given context and structure when read in conjunction with these works.

Firsthand Accounts

This essay uses Sykes' discussion of the pains of imprisonment as a benchmark in an examination of three recent works by Victor Hassine, Leonard Peltier, and Ted Conover. Firsthand accounts of prison constitute a remarkably rich and diverse set of resources for those who teach courses on crime and corrections. The works discussed here were chosen from the many available today because they represent three distinct perspectives commonly found within this literature. The first, Hassine's *Life Without Parole: Living in Prison Today*, is a book written from the perspective of a prisoner who has apparently come to terms with his conviction. While Hassine stops short of admitting guilt, his is a book about the process of "becoming a convict," and this is a process for which guilt or innocence is in some ways irrelevant. The second book discussed here, Peltier's *Prison Writings: My Life Is My Sun Dance*, is written by an author who is widely regarded as a political prisoner and who regards himself as an innocent man. While both Hassine and Peltier are serving life sentences for murder, their accounts of prison life represent the distinct perspectives of the convict and the political prisoner. The third work, Conover's *New Jack: Guarding Sing Sing*, views prison life from the perspective of a prison worker, a correctional officer at a maximum security institution. Certainly, there are other firsthand accounts of prison life that might be considered. Johnson and Toch's *Crime and Punishment Inside Views* (2000) and Masters' *Finding Freedom* (1997), for example, are excellent recent additions to this literature. And Behan's *Borstal Boy* (2000), while not contemporary, is now available again in a new printing. In the end, the decision to include the works of Hassine, Peltier, and Conover while leaving out other worthwhile books reflects considerations of space and the fact that each constitutes a significant contribution to the general literature on prisons. More importantly, these three books serve to make the point that firsthand accounts are a valuable teaching resource while representing something of the diversity of the genre from which they were chosen. A brief review of each of these works is followed by a discussion of some of the ways in which they may enrich our students' understanding of a central theoretical issue in corrections: the pains of imprisonment.

Life Without Parole: Living in Prison Today

Victor Hassine's *Life Without Parole* combines a thoughtful and well written prison autobiography, a series of short sketches depicting characters and incidents from prison life, and a set of Hassine's essays. The essays cover topics such as prison overcrowding, staff/inmate relations, and prison reform. Now in its second edition, *Life Without Parole* offers a foreword by John Irwin and an afterword by Richard A. Wright, which are valuable in helping students understand the book and its relationship to the academic literature on the prison.

Unlike many books written by incarcerated authors, *Life Without Parole* manages to combine observations of prison life with a level of theoretical sophistication that will please most academic readers. Hassine, we learn, is a graduate of Dickinson College in Pennsylvania, where he majored in political science and history. He had only recently finished his studies at New York Law School when he was arrested for murder.

Following his conviction in 1981, Hassine was sent to Graterford State Prison, not far from Philadelphia, where he underwent the initial classification process, began to serve his sentence, and in his own words, "became a convict." His description of his early days in Graterford and his discussion of the social situation of inmates and their captors addresses issues of identity, prisonization, penal harm, institutional violence, and the corruption of institutional authority-themes that have long been central to the academic literature on confinement.

Hassine is at his best in his discussion of the angry politics of prison life, an area that does not always receive this sort of systematic and relatively objective exploration. He succeeds in describing some of the ways in which correctional officers can inadvertently foster a convict culture that embodies values and encourages behaviors that they would not consciously choose to support. While it would be easy, as a prisoner, to explain one's experience in terms of the individual failings of depraved convicts and sadistic or uncaring guards, to create a personal mythology complete with cowardly villains, detached gods, and a cruelly used hero, Hassine refuses to settle for a simplistic account of his world. Instead, he strives to understand the historical and structural forces that work to shape his everyday experience of prison life. Rather than settle for self-serving myth, Hassine offers the reader a view of prison life that is honest, original, and thought provoking. In this respect, his work has much in common with Conover's new book.

New Jack: Guarding Sing Sing

Conover's book chronicles his experience as a correctional officer in Sing Sing, New York's maximum security prison for men at Ossining. Conover was a relatively short-term inhabitant of the world in which Hassine has spent two decades, one who chose to be there and was free to leave. Even so, perhaps because of his training in anthropology and his extensive work as an experiential journalist, his year as a correctional officer provided the foundation for a valuable account of prison life.

Conover is now well known for a series of books recounting in-depth, firsthand experiences of some of American society's more obscure subcultures. He spent a year hopping freight trains with homeless men, traveled with illegal Mexican immigrants, and once took a job driving a cab in Aspen in order to have an opportunity to observe the city's wealthy winter visitors. For this book, Conover spent a year working as a "newjack"—the inmate term for a newly minted New York State correctional officer. Upon leaving the training academy he was assigned to work in Sing Sing, where most new officers spend their first months on the job. *New Jack* tells the story of Conover's introduction to correctional work. We see a demonstrably liberal man, with a kind heart, good intentions, and a progressive political outlook overwhelmed by the violent, crowded, chaotic conditions encountered at Sing Sing. Recounting his first days supervising inmates on a crowded housing gallery, Conover explains what it is like to be a new, inexperienced officer on shifts made up of too many rookies, in housing units too short staffed to allow for good communication or adequate on-the-job training. In working in Sing Sing's "box," the Security Housing Unit, Conover learns of an inmate nicknamed "Mr. Slurpee," who uses his mouth to spray a combination of urine and feces on officers. He describes Sing Sing's PSU, the Psychiatric Satellite Unit, where because of a shortage of departmental bed space for the mentally ill, staff worked to manage inmates with antipsychotic medications so that they might be returned to the prison's general population. In doing so, Conover translates abstractions like overcrowding, staff turnover, and the deinstitutionalization of the mentally ill into real problems affecting real people in ways that can potentially alter lives forever. In recent years, legislators in many states have tended to lengthen sentences and increase prison populations while neglecting programs that promote rehabilitation and reintegration in the community (Austin and Irwin 2001). Conover's account of his year in Sing Sing helps the reader to appreciate the ways in which uninformed legislative decision-making and public indifference impact the lives of prisoners, and correctional officers. He also raises interesting questions about the eventual impact of these decisions on the larger community.

Prison Writings: My Life Is My Sun Dance

Leonard Peltier's book is an account of well over two decades of incarceration at the hands of the federal government for a crime that he possibly did not commit. The book documents the many deprivations of prison life, including the loss of safety and security in the prison environment, the loss of autonomy, and the enforced poverty of inmates. His focus on the difficulties faced by inmates trying to preserve links to family and community life in the isolation of the prison is particularly worthwhile.

Peltier is serving a life sentence for his alleged participation in the shooting of two FBI agents in June 1975 on the Pine Ridge Reservation at Oglala, South Dakota. He is regarded as a political prisoner by many, and many who have reviewed his case, including former U.S. Attorney General Ramsey Clark, contend that he is the victim of a grave injustice. Peltier and his supporters claim that, in an overzealous effort to avenge their fallen officers, the federal government convicted and imprisoned him knowing that he did not fire the gun that killed the FBI's agents.

Overall, Peltier has a good deal to say about prison life, but in the end, *Prison Writings* is far more focused on issues of social and political justice than it is on prisons. Unlike some other books describing the prison experience, this one is intensely political. A substantial part of *Prison Writings* is devoted to a very partisan discussion of the relationship between the federal government and Native Americans. Given that issues of race and class continue to be of profound significance in the American justice system, books of this sort certainly deserve a place on academic reading lists.

Teaching from Firsthand Accounts

Instructors who teach students about the pains of imprisonment face at least two challenges. First, college students typically come from relatively privileged backgrounds and rarely have firsthand experience of the kind of suffering experienced by those in jail or prison. Moreover, few students see themselves as the kind of people who will ever be incarcerated, and many students are not naturally disposed to think sympathetically about prisoners. The second challenge reflects the nature of contemporary punishment. While incidents of criminal brutality continue to occur in American prisons, formal corporal punishment is no longer the rule in modern institutions. Many of the pains of imprisonment experienced today are psychological in nature. Because such pains are largely invisible to all but those who are directly involved, it can sometimes be difficult to persuade students that even a short prison sentence represents a serious punishment. The books discussed here serve to make a persuasive case that prison continues to be a painful experience, and that the pains of imprisonment are real, substantial, and unavoidable for even the toughest, most experienced convicts.

In *Society of Captives*, Sykes describes five kinds of deprivation experienced by inmates. These include deprivations associated with: loss of liberty, goods and services, heterosexual relationships, personal autonomy, and security (1958). By considering each of these areas in turn, it is possible to explore some of the connections between Sykes' classic account of the prison and the works of Hassine, Conover, and Peltier.

Liberty

Sykes describes the prisoner's deprivation of liberty in terms of restricted opportunities for movement and social isolation. Of these two issues, he is clearly more interested in the inmate's isolation from family and friends. For Sykes:

> The mere fact that the individual's movements are restricted, however, is far less serious than the fact that imprisonment means that the inmate is cut off from family, relatives, and friends, not in the self-isolation of the hermit or the misanthrope, but in the involuntary seclusion of the outlaw (1958:65).

Sykes suggests that inmates suffer "loss of relationships" and "loneliness and boredom" as a result of their limited mobility (1958:65). More importantly, they suffer society's deliberate rejection, and they are painfully reminded of that in the many rituals and routines of institutional treatment. According to Sykes, "The prisoner is never allowed to forget that, by committing a crime, he has forgone his claim to the status of a full-fledged, trusted member of society" (1958:66).

Writing about "things missed," Victor Hassine describes his experience of lost liberty and his initial longing for "sex, love, family, and friends." After a time, Hassine comes to see privacy, quiet, and peace of mind—things unavailable to him in Graterford Prison—as even more important. Eventually, a simple trip outside becomes a major source of pleasure:

> Occasionally, when I had to make trips outside the prison for court appearances or doctor's visits, I would sit in the prison van, enraptured by the trees whizzing past. The brightness and the beautiful colors of everything around me made every trip outside an exciting experience. I know of

several men who filed lawsuits or feigned illness just to 'get some streets' (1999:19).

While Hassine writes primarily about separation from the outside world, Sykes emphasizes the fact that imprisonment involves both restriction to the prison and restriction within the prison. Peltier addresses this second issue, restrictions within the prison, in his description of Leavenworth's solitary confinement unit, a place inmates call "the shoe" or "the hole."

> I don't like being in the shoe one bit. You spend twenty-three hours a day in a small cage inside a larger cage. . . . Down in the hole, I dream. I feel myself falling, falling. Sort of like Alice down the rabbit hole, only it's a fall that never ends. There's no floor, no bottom, no stopping point. It's not space I'm falling through, or even time. It's the hole in my own self. I'm falling through the empty space where my life is supposed to be. I've been falling that way, in free fall from nowhere to nowhere, for nearly a quarter of a century now (1999:174).

Peltier's description of "the hole" provides a compelling look at what it must be like to try to sustain one's identity as a human being in almost complete isolation from others.

Sykes was aware that the loss of liberty involved the pain of separation from friends and family members outside the prison. That pain becomes particularly acute during times of family tragedy. Peltier's *Prison Writings* offers a moving account of the fate of the prisoner who is no longer permitted to take part in either the joyous or the solemn moments that mark family life. His description of prison life repeatedly returns to the themes of helplessness and separation.

> The death of a loved one is harder to take than your own. Your own death is easy by comparison. When I wasn't allowed to attend my father's funeral in 1989, I suffered pain worse than any physical pain. Pain without hope of closure, a wound eternally unhealed. He'd seen his son falsely imprisoned for fourteen years and it broke his heart (1999:17).

Peltier's discussion is consistent with that of Sykes, but his experience as a Native American inmate in an American prison brings cultural and political dimensions to the problem that Sykes neglected. Peltier understands and deals with the pains of imprisonment not as a convict, but as a Native American man wrongfully imprisoned because of his race.

> I know who and what I am. I am an Indian—an Indian who dared to stand up and defend his people. I am an innocent man who never murdered anyone nor wanted to. And, yes, I am a Sun Dancer. That, too, is my identity. If I am to suffer as a symbol of my people, then I suffer proudly (1999:14).

Peltier raises an issue here that has become increasingly important in the forty-odd years since Sykes originally described the pains of imprisonment. For those who define themselves as political prisoners, as victims of racial oppression rather than convicted criminals, for example, the psychological suffering of a prison sentence may be somewhat mitigated. In rejecting the moral authority of the dominant society, the inmate can resist the unhappy self-defining implications of confinement and continue to assert identity claims that are consistent with self-respect. Peltier's writing encourages us to address this and other issues related to minority confinement.

In *New Jack*, Conover reminds the reader that problems of restricted mobility and social isolation are problems for both correctional officers and inmates. Conover is a perceptive and articulate observer of prison life whose position as a correctional officer allowed him to see inmate suffering, as well as the corrosive effect that constant exposure to that pain has on the lives of the guards. His work offers something rarely seen in the literature on the prison: it reminds us that the pains of imprisonment are not easily limited to those we seek to punish. They must be borne by inmates and their innocent friends and family members, and also by those we pay to supervise them. Conover helps readers understand how everyone associated with the process of incarceration is ultimately diminished by it.

> A consequence of putting men in cells and controlling their movements is that they can do almost nothing for themselves. For their various needs they are dependent on one person, their gallery officer. Instead of feeling like a big tough guard, the gallery officer at the end of the day often feels like a waiter serving a hundred tables or like the mother of a nightmarishly large brood of sullen, dangerous, and demanding children (2000:234).

In his discussion of the issue of restricted liberty, Conover writes about the problems posed by "keeplocks," inmates who spend most of their time restricted to their cells as a result of violating institutional rules. Restricting inmates to their cells complicates the work of the officers assigned to manage them by making the inmates even more dependent on officers than they usually are. Keeplock status also makes it harder to control inmates who may feel that they have little left to lose. Conover describes one keeplock's response to a disciplinary citation for insubordination written after the inmate refused an order to leave a shower.

> "I don't give a fuck, CO," he explained. "I got thirty years to life, right? And I got two years' keeplock. Plus today, I got another three months. When they see this lame-ass ticket, they're gonna tell you to shove it up your ass." . . . The frustration was, he was probably right (2000:101).

Goods and Services

Inmates in American prisons are not often deprived of goods and services that most people would regard as absolute necessities, but as Sykes observes, their relative economic deprivation is experienced as a painful loss and as an assault on the inmate's sense of identity (1958:70). Goods and services that most people take for granted often form the foundation for the underground economy of the prison, with inmates willing to take substantial risks to obtain things that most people would regard as trivial. Hassine's first prison disciplinary violation occurred when he was caught with an unauthorized hamburger. It resulted in loss of a desirable prison job and a two-month cell restriction.

Sykes' sense that goods and services must be understood in terms of psychological utility as well as practical value is shared by others. Goffman reflects on the role of contraband items in his discussion of the search for "secondary adjustments" in institutional settings (1961:188). He defines secondary adjustments as:

> · · · any habitual arrangement by which a member of an organization employs unauthorized means, or obtains unauthorized ends, or both, thus getting around the organization's assumptions as to what he should do and get and hence what he should be (1961:189).

Following this, one would expect that inmate efforts to circumvent prison rules would be particularly difficult to suppress. Hassine's experience bears this out. In Graterford Prison he found a thriving underground economy, offering an unexpected array of goods and services. Laundry services were available, cooked foods and pastries could be delivered to an inmate's cell, and ice men, barbers, and cell cleaners all plied their trades within the prison. Hassine might have learned to avoid involvement in prohibited activities. Instead, he learned to be more careful about getting caught.

Peltier's experience of contraband also serves to underscore the way in which efforts to circumvent the institutionally-mandated deprivation of goods and services become central to the inmate's efforts to resist the institution's claims on his identity. Some of Peltier's first prison friendships developed over shared cigarettes in a punitive segregation unit where smoking was prohibited.

Conover approaches the issue of goods and services from the perspective of a guard rather than an inmate. Still, for the most part, his experience at Sing Sing does not contradict the analysis of Sykes or raise significant questions about the experiences of Hassine or Peltier. Initially he saw restricted access to goods and services in terms of rule enforcement and order. When he found an inmate using an unauthorized makeshift antenna to improve his radio reception, he ordered it taken down. When he caught inmates taking extra food from the kitchen, he ordered it returned.

After a time, his commitment to strict rule enforcement wavered. His experience of the chaotic world of the prison began to undermine his sense that institutional rules could and should be consistently enforced. While working an assignment on a kitchen serving line, Conover was criticized for his strict enforcement of relatively minor rules and told by one inmate that "in a few days . . . you won't give a fuck anymore." For Conover, this seems to have been a turning point in his attitude toward rule enforcement:

> He wasn't completely right, but I did realize I was wearing myself out with zeal. Other officers, though they would uniformly deny it, let the servers give away much more food than was allowed. Who really gave a damn about two extra cookies (2000:254).

Eventually, Conover made many concessions to the inmates he supervised, most of them involving inmate efforts to procure desired goods and services. He had food servers provide extra portions to the inmate porters with whom he regularly worked. He brought in contraband reading material for an inmate with whom he became friendly, and he distributed contraband cigarettes to inmates in violation of institutional rules. His account of his year as a correctional officer allows the reader a chance to understand both the psychological impact of institutionally-mandated poverty and the many pressures that mitigate against strict and consistent enforcement of institutional rules.

Conover's description of inconsistent institutional rule enforcement was, in a sense, anticipated by chapter three of *The Society of Captives*, "The Defects of Total Power" (Sykes 1958). For Sykes, prisons operate based on informally negotiated arrangements between captives and custodians. He described a system of informal rewards available to inmates who cooperate to make the correctional officer's life easier. Inmates seek to minimize the pains of imprisonment by trading cooperation for things like information, tolerance, occasional non-enforcement of rules, or favored jobs or housing assignments. By focusing our attention on issues of rule enforcement in their discussions of access to goods and services, Conover, Hassine and Peltier make it easier to understand how the pains of imprisonment may promote this kind of institutional reciprocity and play a role in shaping staff/inmate relations.

Heterosexual Relationships

Sykes describes the deprivation of heterosexual relationships as a form of figurative castration imposed upon inmates as a part of their punishment. Like other forms of deprivation, sexual deprivation has powerful implications for identity, causing Sykes to describe imprisonment as a process through which "an essential component of a man's self-conception—his status as male—is called into question" (1958:71).

Hassine, Conover, and Peltier all describe the loneliness, isolation, and violence of prison life, but it is in the works of Hassine and Conover that heterosexual deprivation is most explicitly addressed. Hassine's discussion of consensual sex between inmates offers readers insight into the thinking of at least some members of the inmate population. A search for intimacy in the prison often has tragic consequences as inmates engage in unsafe sex with multiple partners, with little awareness of the potential danger. This is described in an interview with an inmate named Toney, who although HIV positive, remained sexually active.

> It's very easy to have sex in prison. . . . Some days in prison I have twenty men a day. . . . I have allowed myself to be in a relationship where no protection was used, and it is not because I did not tell them. It is because they wanted to be a part of me and make lifelong commitments to me. . . . So once he started having unprotected sex with me, it was my spouse's way of saying 'you belong to me forever' (2000:96).

Other research on inmates is consistent with Hassine's account of this issue (Johnson and Toch 2000). That AIDS could be knowingly contracted as a kind of spiritual bond or token of commitment is a frightening comment on the institutional conditions which move men to such desperate behavior and on the lengths to which men will go to alleviate the "pains of imprisonment."

Sykes tends to describe the psychological pain associated with loss of heterosexual relations in somewhat abstract terms, and he tends to see prison sexuality largely as a response to deprivation. This is fairly clear in his description of the "argot roles" of "wolves, punks, and fags" (1958). Using the language of the era, he describes homosexual behavior as "perversion," and focuses on a struggle for power and dominance in which "wolves" prey upon "punks" and "fags." In the end he fails to communicate much of what is important in this area because he fails to consider the issue of consensual sex in anything more than a pro forma way.

Conover takes the opposite tack. Conover provides a useful supplement to Sykes' limited discussion of prison sex roles and the vulnerability of gay inmates. In doing so, he raises a number of issues that should fuel classroom debate. He describes the "punk-protector" system as "outdated or exaggerated" (2000:263). He argues that forcible rape involving inmates is less common than sex between female officers and inmates, and he rejects the view that homosexual activity in prison is a form of perversion.

Sykes and many other authors have acknowledged the increased risk of victimization faced by gay inmates. Conover does more. He introduces us to "Grandma," an aging homosexual who is denied a seat among fellow inmates in the prison dining hall. His description of "Grandma," who is publicly rejected but still sought after in private by other inmates, shows how the stigma of homosexuality colors even the most trivial moments of social interaction in prison. Conover's account of prison sex will leave many readers with doubts. His suggestion that there is more consensual sex than rape in prison, for example, may be seen as an uncritical effort to minimize his own responsibility as a correctional officer. For the most part, though, his perceptive sympathy comes in sharp contrast to the distanced "objectivity" of Sykes. To be fair, writing for 2000, Conover could take on issues that Sykes must have found more difficult in the 1950s. It is hard to imagine Sykes writing anything like Conover's description of "Baywatch," a transgender inmate he supervised at Sing Sing.

> Baywatch was slender, with plucked eyebrows and center-parted, shoulder length hair bleached a shade of light auburn. He had a boy's figure but a girl's walk, and a scared-doe look. Of all of them, he seemed the most sought after by the inmates . . . he was the "girlfriend" of a member of the Latin Kings gang, who, I was told, regarded himself as heterosexual. Baywatch was his prize. I could see them nuzzling in the yard, like a pair of junior high school lovers (2000:258).

Sykes acknowledged that the pains of imprisonment could be experienced differently by different inmates, and pointed out that while openly gay inmates might not suffer from heterosexual deprivation, they were "apt to be victimized or raped" by other prisoners (1958:71). Subsequent research confirms the view that some inmates will "see undefended homosexuals as fair game in prison" (Lockwood 1980). However, it also tends to minimize the influence of deprivation, which Bowker refers to as "the least important factor in prison rape" (1980).

While it would be a mistake to explain prison rape as a simple expression of heterosexual deprivation, Hassine's detailed discussion of prison rape is worth mentioning here because it is certain to make a vivid impression on students. Hassine's discussion will help readers to get beyond the shower room stereotypes of prison films to gain insight into an insider's perspective on consensual and non-consensual sexual activity in prison. But his description of gang rape is graphic and many will find it disturbing. On another score, Hassine also shows how a sexual liaison can form the basis for a relationship that offers power and protection for an undefended inmate. In the end, his discussion of rape and supposedly consensual sex in prison leaves the reader wondering if there is any meaningful way for authorities to distinguish between consent and coercion.

When Hassine and Conover are at their best, they begin to explore the murky world that falls in between overt coercion and honest consent. Conover is less ambitious than Hassine in his account, but even so, his sensitive discussion of the challenges faced by openly gay inmates should add considerably to the average student's understanding of these issues.

Personal Autonomy

Inmates live by a set of imposed rules governing their daily routine in minute detail. According to Sykes, inmates are infantilized by being deprived of the right to make even small and seemingly inconsequential decisions about their activities. For Sykes, deprivation of autonomy is equivalent to deprivation of one's status as an adult.

> The important point, however, is that the frustration of the prisoner's ability to make choices and the frequent refusals to provide an explanation for the regulations and commands descending from the bureaucratic staff involve a profound threat to the prisoner's self image because they reduce the prisoner to the weak, helpless, dependent status of childhood (1958:75).

Constant assaults on autonomy are the subject of many of Leonard Peltier's complaints about his treatment in the federal prison system:

> Handcuffs and leg-irons and strip searches—'spread'm Tonto'—have become my daily routine. They don't just take your freedom from you—which you'd think would be enough—but they demean and humiliate you, it seems, whenever and wherever possible (1999:143).

In "Albert Brown: Permanent Resident," an essay on the life of a longtime convict included in his book, Hassine outlines many changes that have occurred in prison life since Sykes wrote *The Society of Captives*. Court ordered prison reform has, to some extent, minimized assaults on the autonomy of prisoners and lessened the pains of imprisonment (Farrington 1992). Even so, Conover's discussion of the guard's role shows that inmates remain dependent upon correctional officers for most of the things that make prison life tolerable. For Conover, prison is a trap. In *New Jack* he shows how the officers' endless, almost ritualized efforts to limit the freedom of inmates inevitably result in a loss of their own autonomy. When Conover says, "A consequence of putting men in cells and controlling their movements is that they can do almost nothing for themselves," he is describing the limitations placed on officers who must meet the needs of those rendered helpless by prison rules. This is the other side of the coin that is "total power"—every rule that makes an inmate less competent has the potential to increase the workload of an already overworked officer. If court decisions have made the inmate's experience of prison life somewhat less restrictive today, Conover makes it clear that prisons still restrict the autonomy of everyone who comes into contact with them. This view is consistent with Sykes' 1958 account of the "defects of total power" and with more recent research on correctional officers (Lombardo 1989).

Source: From "The Pains of Imprisonment: Exploring a Classic Text with Contemporary Authors," Riley, John, *Journal of Criminal Justice Education*, Volume 13, No. 2, pp. 443–457. Copyright © 2002, by Taylor & Francis. Reprinted by permission of the publisher (Taylor & Francis Group, http://www.informaworld.com).

JONESTOWN AS A TOTAL INSTITUTION: WHY SOME PEOPLE CHOSE DEATH OVER ESCAPE FROM PEOPLES TEMPLE

by Phyllis Gardner; Mahmoud Sadri; James L. Williams

Introduction

When we look at the darker periods of history from the outside, it seems easy to tell the difference between right and wrong. That aerial snapshot of life provides certain clarity. After World War II, people were shocked and sickened at what they learned about the activities of the Nazis in desolate camps across the continent. How could things like that happen? Nearly thirty years ago,* 918 people died in Guyana, South America. Some of the dead were murdered, including U.S. Congressman Leo Ryan. The rest appear to be suicides. Some people believe that those deaths were the result of CIA and U.S. government persecution of Peoples Temple, a socialist community (R. Moore 1985). Most commentaries seem to imply an element of racism, either in the persecution or the aftermath, since the majority of the dead were African Americans (R. Moore 1985, Moore 2006, Lindt 1982, Stroud 1996). Some have concluded that the deaths were the result of cult members blindly following their paranoid leader (Mancinelli, Comparelli, Girardi, and Tatarelli 2002). Still others suggest that many people simply gave up and saw death as a release from torment, whatever its origins (Reiterman 1982, Stroud, Lindt, Layton).

Why did so many people continue their involvement with Jim Jones and Peoples Temple when they had overwhelming evidence that their faith had been misplaced (Stroud, Layton)? Newspapers are replete with accounts of groups such as Peoples Temple, the Branch Davidians and Heaven's Gate. Some people lump all of these under the heading of "cult." But Goldhammer suggests the broader term, *destructive groups.* Such groups are recognizable by the amount of control exerted by their leaders and the lack of autonomy of the membership. Stories of these groups are alarming but curious. Seemingly average people forsake what most would consider common sense, along with their instincts for survival. Some early theorists tended to believe in the sentiments expressed by the Marquess of Halifax in the late seventeenth century: "There is an accumulative cruelty in a number of men, though none in particular are ill-natured" (Goldhammer). Here a specific idea will be offered as a starting point from which to examine the attitudes of Temple members prior to their deaths. Jonestown was a complex web of obedience and conformity that became what Goffman (1961) called a *total institution.* Like Goldhammer's discussion of destructive groups and the control exerted by their leadership, Goffman's concept of the total institution offers specific steps which lead to an individual's subservience to authority in coercive circumstances.

Definitions

Obedience

Two forces are primary to the success of destructive groups, according to Goldhammer. The first is obedience. In this case, obedience is best understood by an awareness of Milgram's (1974) distinction between obedience and conformity. Obedience refers to

---

*This incident occurred on November 18, 1978, in Guyana, South America.

carrying out the will of an individual in authority. Conformity is acting as a part of a larger group – doing what others are doing. Both involve some actual or implied threat of force or punishment, but obedience is acting alone under another's authority, while conformity is acting in concert with others.

Milgram pointed out that in studying obedience, one must "take conceptions of authority and translate them into personal experience." In other words, an abstract, clinical look at obedience explains nothing. Milgram suggested that obedience is something that is deeply ingrained enough to override personal emotions such as guilt, sympathy or a belief in moral conduct. He quoted a previous author, C. P. Snow:

> *When you think of the long and gloomy history of man, you will find more hideous crimes have been committed in the name of obedience than have ever been committed in the name of rebellion. If you doubt that, read William Shirer's "Rise and Fall of the Third Reich." The German Officers' Corps were brought up in the most rigorous code of obedience . . . in the name of obedience they were a party to, and assisted in, the most wicked large scale actions in the history of the world.*

Looking at obedience to malevolent authority does not confine itself to large-scale evil. Every day people are ordered to destroy a colleague's reputation, put the competition out of business, or ostracize an individual. Those are ordinary people who are just doing their jobs. They have no particular evil ideas of their own; they just blindly do as they are told. This kind of obedience allows average people to become "agents in a terrible destructive process" (Milgram). Looking at obedience and its application in negative or destructive circumstances, it is easy to take the moral high ground. The proper thing to do would be to obey. Yet to obey becomes an evil act. Still it is the disobedience that we generally see as being wrong, not the act of obeying. So an individual might easily become confused. Milgram believed that people who are obeying an authority figure do not see themselves as in control. They are merely a tool or extension of the authority and therefore not responsible for their actions.

Conformity

The second force in destructive groups – conformity – is about group participation. Milgram referred to people acting in accordance with peers of the same status – people who had no right to impose authority or direct behavior. The term "peer pressure" becomes real in arenas other than adolescence. Solomon Asch (1951) performed experiments in which he sought to examine the nature of conformity. He showed as a result of being in the presence of complete strangers who would lie, an unknowing subject could be manipulated into reporting incorrectly in a simple matter of the length of a few straight lines. In his experiments, several confederates reported incorrectly before the subject spoke. By the time the subject was asked for an opinion about the length of the lines, he or she often reported as the others did, even though it was obvious that they were wrong. Fear and embarrassment were the apparent motivators. The confederates were total strangers to the subjects of the experiments, yet they obviously had influence. This is conformity. Milgram detailed the differences between obedience and conformity:

> Hierarchy – Obedience to authority occurs within a structure in which the actor feels that the authority figure has the right to expect compliance. Conformity

speaks to the behavior of status equals. Obedience is the link between those of different status.

Imitation – Conformity is imitation. Obedience does not have to be. The group models the behavior for the individual who is to conform. The authority figure need not model, just demand.

Explicitness – Obedience requires a specific order or demand. Conformity can be unspoken or implied. There need not be overt demands placed on an individual in order to gain conformity.

Voluntarism – Milgram stated that people will deny conformity but embrace obedience as an explanation for their behavior. People do not seem to want to admit the degree to which others influence them. It seems to be felt as vulnerability. But somehow, obeying authority is a good defense.

Total Institutions

Goffman makes a strong case for viewing some settings as what he termed "total institutions." In such cases, the requisite obedience and conformity outlined above are achieved through a much more complex and planned pattern of manipulations on the part of those in authority. In order to explore possible implications of this concept for understanding the deaths at Jonestown, it is important to understand Goffman's view:

A total institution may be defined as a place of residence and work where a large number of like-situated individuals, cut off from wider society for an appreciable period of time, together lead an enclosed, formally administered round of life.

Goffman continues with a description of what he calls the mortification of self that occurs in such settings, as residents are stripped of everything that they are accustomed to, that defines who they are, and what their standing or identity is, as individuals. The process occurs in seven steps:

Role Dispossession – Individuals are usually defined by a collection of roles, such as mother, friend, employee, and wife. In a total institution, residents lose the ability to perform the functions associated with these roles, at least in the manner in which they were accustomed.

Programming and identity-trimming – Admission processes to total institutions, such as gathering personal history, searching belongings and rules orientation are instrumental in turning individuals into "units" that follow predictable paths – a sort of standardization process.

Dispossession of name, property, and "identity kit" – Individuals might be assigned new names, first names only, or I.D. numbers. They are usually deprived of some, if not all of their personal possessions – decisions about which are not made by the individuals, themselves. Loss of personal possessions includes items such as make-up and grooming devices that assist people in maintaining a particular public image.

Imposition of degrading postures, stances, and deference patterns – Previously free citizens must now ask for permission to do basic things like go to the restroom, smoke, or watch television. In some cases, they must show deference to those in control by using "sir" or "ma'am" while not having the same deference shown to them. In extreme cases, residents must perform degrading tasks such as standing a certain way or suffering indignities such as teasing or bullying.

Contaminative exposure – This might include the disclosure of private information to others, or more literally, the exposure of self – through strip searches – and exposed or public facilities such as toilets or showers. Less obvious exposures occur when forced mingling with those who are perceived to be of lesser status violates an individual's perceived status.

Disruption of usual relation of individual actor and his acts – In general society, people can show their distaste for others as a manner and matter of self-expression. These acts serve to protect the individual in his or her own mind from the disrespect of others. In a total institution, such expressions might be prohibited, even punishable.

Restrictions on self-determination, autonomy, and freedom of action – Taken together, the previous six stages serve to strip the individual of the expression of any semblance of self-will, causing them to accept this final step.

The Mortification of Self in Peoples Temple

It is easy to picture the average American, traditional values-oriented family, fully involved and committed to their church. Move this same family to a mosquito-infested jungle with no indoor plumbing, little privacy, personal possessions or "creature comforts" but with an endless thirst for manual labor. Some would argue that not all of the people of Jonestown regretted their circumstances (A. Moore 1978, Q 042 1978, Tropp 1978, Prokes 1979). And though the logic is a bit circular, one could also argue that these individuals' lack of complaint hints that the mortification process worked better with some than with others. Transcripts of recorded meetings in the jungle indicate acquiescence – not satisfaction (Q 042). And there are some unanswered questions about the transcript of the final hours of the Peoples Temple because this tape – as were so many others recorded by Jim Jones – appears to have been edited. And if it was edited, how could that be, if everyone was dead? McGehee (2002) discusses another audiotape found that is of newscasts that were aired the day *after* the suicides (Q 875 1978). The existence of a recording after everyone was to have died suggests that perhaps some, even Jones, himself, did not die until at least a day later – leaving ample time to edit out dissenting voices from the so-called "Death Tape." Still, two people who died left written "last words" that made clear the vision that they had for their community and their belief that it was being destroyed from without – not within (A. Moore, Tropp).

Nonetheless, many survivor accounts paint a picture that includes some disgruntled followers who feared for their safety if they made their disappointment known (Stroud, Layton). Below is an overview of those privately guarded complaints, as they relate to Goffman's steps to the mortification of self.

Role Dispossession

Goffman described role dispossession in terms of the lack of freedom to schedule one's own day in such a way that fulfilling one role did not interfere with another. Some former members reported having their entire day dictated to them. In some cases, followers were unable to care for sick family members because of the demands of the work schedule. Instead, these individuals were forced to abdicate responsibility for their loved ones to the *assigned* others.

In another case, Layton told the story of a woman who toiled to develop a recipe for good tasting, nutritious jam using only the foods available at the compound. When she proudly offered one to Jones, he rebuked her publicly for wasting the valuable resources of the people on a frivolous pursuit. This woman had prided herself in being a good cook, but her efforts at continuing in this part of her identity only caused her to be shamed by the very individual with whom she sought to curry favor.

These people became drones with no other purpose than to do as they were told. There was no creative expression – that would have been viewed as selfish (Layton, Kahalas 1998).

Programming and Identity Trimming

Goffman references a process that shapes and classifies the individual into "an object that can be fed into the administrative machinery of the establishment." Upon arrival at the jungle compound, a member had all of his or her belongings searched, and they were told the basic rules of what was allowed and expected at the compound. It was here that people were assigned a place to sleep, as well as given specific jobs, such as field worker, security guard, caregiver, or cook (Stroud). Part of the human identity that is tied to roles is our belief in the value of our contribution. At Jonestown, residents were regularly reminded that they only served as tools by which greater things would be accomplished.

Dispossession of Name, Property, and "Identity Kit"

As previously mentioned, followers gave up all possessions upon entering the jungle "Utopia." One survivor (Stroud) told of the long journey to the jungle by boat, only to have to spend the next hour being searched and having his clothing taken from him. Residents were allowed a certain number of clothing items, and the rest went into a common pool for future use by those deemed to be in need. In addition, individuals who were taking medications were shocked to have their prescriptions taken from them. Make-up and extensive collections of personal hygiene items, such as hair rollers or colognes, were confiscated. But remember, these were not jungle people – they were average families who gave up their private lives to follow Jones.

Imposition of Degrading Postures, Stances, and Deference Patterns

Survivors recounted the many sleepless nights as Jones read the news – or railed at them – from loud speakers all night long. Many of these all night sessions included what Jones called "white night" drills. These were rehearsals for the mass suicide that was to eventually become real. Followers were awakened in the night by the sound of Jones' voice calling them to come. They must obey, Jones told them, because the government was out to destroy them. In their sacrificial act, they would find salvation and deny the government satisfaction for its evil plot. They did as they were told and lined up to drink Fla-Vor-Aid that was to contain poison. More than once, they did so without question.

Every day, workers sweated in the fields with little food or water, doing exactly as they were told out of fear of punishment. They grew vegetables and sugar cane, yet they rarely saw these foods on their tables, and eating even one little piece of sugarcane from the fields was considered to be stealing from the people – grounds for being sent to the "learning crew." The learning crew was a work detail that was required to do everything in double-time. They ran to their assignments and were expected to produce even more than the others (Stroud).

The Jonestown operation did not allow for any deviation from Jones' rules. Followers who complained and asked to leave were as likely as not to wind up in a secret barracks, under sedation (Stroud, Layton). The mere existence of "learning crews" and secret barracks of sedated followers makes it very clear that the structure was firmly in place to deal with any straying from the goals of the leaders. Other examples can be traced all the way back to the days before moving to the jungle compound. Survivors and apostates have told of public meetings that were held to chastise individual members for various transgressions (Stroud). These Temple members were expected to sit silently, with heads bowed, as other members of the Temple hierarchy publicly criticized them – even exposing private family matters to the entire congregation.

Contaminative Exposure

Deborah Layton's story of the woman who made jam and the public shaming she received is an example of the kind of humiliation that was commonplace within the culture of the group. Jonestown had an atmosphere of isolation from the outset (Stroud, Layton). People did not form close relationships beyond a certain point because private thoughts confided in a weak moment could end up relayed to Temple leaders. Such confessions of unhappiness or criticism were met with public humiliation or even more harsh punishment. One survivor remembers going into one particular barracks that was supposed to be part of the infirmary (Stroud). While inside, he saw a couple of members asleep in beds. The faces he saw were the faces of members that Jones had announced had chosen to leave the Temple – one of them months before. Layton corroborated this with her account of the special barracks where many outspoken or complaining members were kept sedated, using the medications taken from other members as they arrived at the compound for the first time.

Disruption of Usual Relation of Individual Actor and His Acts

While the story of Jonestown is rife with examples of this disruption or denial of one's usual recourse, the one that sticks out most vividly relates to the way parents lost the ability to discipline their own children. Further, Temple members were encouraged to tell on their peers. Layton reports that she never knew whom to trust for fear that anything she said would be repeated to church authorities. Such a consequence limited residents' ability to deal with others effectively. Imagine a situation where one individual just wants to take a break from working in the fields. The person is tired and just wants to sit for a few minutes to rest. Living in this compound was supposed to be voluntary. Therefore one's contribution, logically, should also have been voluntary. Yet failure to do exactly as prescribed was a guarantee that someone would report that individual – who would then be assigned to a "learning crew." Confronting the person who *told* would not be an option, simply because it would result in more reporting. So while one's instinct might be to confront the individual for interfering in a personal decision, to do so could have dire consequences.

Because of the atmosphere of Jonestown, people learned to keep their mouths shut, tell no one their innermost thoughts, and turn in anyone who failed to do the same because it might be a test of loyalty! Jones had the members convinced that sometimes people would tell them things that they didn't really feel in order to test their loyalty to the Temple. Failing to turn in the so-called traitor meant failing the test and putting oneself in jeopardy.

Restrictions on Self-Determination, Autonomy and Freedom of Action

Although followers were forced to work the fields, they did not all regularly enjoy the benefits. Many insist that they rarely saw the fruits and vegetables that they farmed. Some survivors reported eating mostly rice and gravy. They also reported that followers knew their own duties but often knew little about what others were doing or what was going on with Temple leadership. One member remembers working as part of the security detail and carrying a gun although he was never really sure what they were guarding because he saw no signs of the people Jones insisted were hiding in the jungle ready to strike at any moment.

There are numerous accounts of the fieldwork and the people's bewilderment at what they were doing there. They were disillusioned with the whole system, unable to see Jones' grand vision for the sweat in their eyes and the bugs on their skin. Seeman (1959) referred to people feeling a sense of meaninglessness by being unsure of what they ought to believe. Certainly some survivors reported such feelings because they knew that they were supposed to be happy to be making the sacrifices they were making, but they didn't feel grateful, and they certainly didn't see the point. This resulted in strong feelings of guilt as well as confusion. There was a feeling of disconnectedness from the real goals of the organization. Some said that they felt like prisoners in a situation that they did not understand because their activities did not seem to properly relate to the stated mission of the leaders, such as a pacifist organization having guns. In this atmosphere of fear, emotional isolation was both a defense and a consequence.

Workers had no decision-making authority, so information was pointless anyway. Every aspect of the followers' daily lives was dictated to them. In addition, they had no means of escape, so there was no incentive for those in authority to behave any differently.

Conclusion: Life and Death in a Total Institution

Goffman clearly believed that life in a total institution made people controllable. He was speaking more of institutional settings in the traditional sense of prisons and mental hospitals, but the central features are the same: the control of self through the denial of self. Whether in a prison, mental hospital, religious cult or other destructive group, the absence of personal identity and the continuous degradation led to a kind of alienation from self that must have made the idea of death seem tempting.

There were complex reasons why so many people chose to die, and for many of the dead, it seems to have had precious little to do with loyalty. Certainly, there is evidence that some followers remained loyal to Jones until the end, but that same evidence suggests that these people were probably in the minority (Layton, A. Moore, Reiterman 1998, Stroud, Tropp, Q 042). The rest were held in place by a calculated combination of factors that caused them to be more easily manipulated. This is the hallmark of the total institution. Rather than viewing Jonestown as a bizarre tragedy carried out by zealots or the mentally ill, we should focus our attention upon the salient explanations found in interpretive sociology. Each individual who joined and stayed with Peoples Temple brought his or her own reasoning, pathological or otherwise. The common element, however, is sociological not psychological in nature. To miss the sociological element is to miss the essential component of understanding its nature, causes, and outcome.

Jim Jones set up his model Utopia, and then through a variety of mechanisms he destroyed it before it ever fully came into being. It seems that Jones could not resist the temptations of control and superiority, thus he unwittingly created a total institution or at least allowed his closest followers to do so. But he lacked the formal authority to keep outsiders, such as Congressman Ryan, from invading. Coupled with his reported drug addiction and paranoia, Jones was unable to sustain his *perfect system* (Stroud, Layton). So while he espoused openness, he behaved with greed and secrecy. While he lectured on giving according to ability and need, he took while others suffered. While he enticed new followers with a sense of belonging, he rewarded them with a profound sense of isolation and meaninglessness. It was that isolation and meaninglessness that most likely led Temple members to be willing to die, not mental illness or zealotry.

There have been other tragedies like Jonestown, but they pale in comparison when one considers the number of lives involved. Still, when such a story appears in the news, people speak of the tragedy, then just shrug at the crazy things people do. So what happened at Jonestown is largely viewed as a freak action taken by an extremist group. Such actions in today's world happen not in the far away jungles, but in our cities and among our families. And the victims are not the followers, but the unsuspecting and unprepared. Perhaps in this "post-September 11th world," we need to take a more serious look at what causes people to blindly follow another – even to the point of death.

Source: Gardner, P., Sadri, M., and Williams, J. L. (2008). *Jonestown as a Total Institution: Why Some People Chose Death over Escape from Peoples Temple.* Unpublished manuscript (pp. 1–8). Reprinted by permission of Dr. Phyllis Abel Gardner, Texarkana College.

CHAPTER 5

September 11, 2001

On September 11, 2001, the mainland of the United States of America was attacked by terrorists who highjacked four passenger airliners and used them as deadly weapons of destruction. Two planes struck the World Trade Center in New York City and one airliner crashed into the Pentagon in Arlington, Virginia. Passengers on the fourth plane tried to overpower the highjackers and the aircraft crashed in a rural field in Pennsylvania. Nearly 3,000 people perished on that day. The loss of life was greater than in any previous man-made disaster in the United States.

The goal of the September 11 terrorists was not simply to kill and maim as many people as possible, but to fundamentally disrupt the predictability, security and safety that governed the lives of those living in the United States, and indeed around the world. As highlighted by Juergensmeyer (2003) in his book on religious violence, "terrorism is meant to terrify. The word comes from the Latin *terrere*, 'to cause to tremble' . . . the personal security and order that is usually a basic assumption of public life cannot in fact be taken for granted in a world where terrorist acts exist" (p. 5).

September 11 represented the arrival of institutionalized fundamentalist terrorism in the United States, and our feelings of security and self-determination were assaulted and compromised. We began to question whether we should attend a basketball game in a public arena, reside in an apartment in a high rise building, take that scheduled airline flight or whether we should open our mail during the anthrax scare. Wrested from our control were those mundane life choices and experiences that would no longer be taken for granted, but rather tempered by new considerations of safety and security. Increased vigilance has become the order of the day and most New Yorkers have been educated to pay heed to the cautionary public campaign slogan that "*if you see something, say something.*"

The terrorists operate as functionaries within an institutional network of terror that legitimizes the killing of innocents in its pursuit of "functionally rational"/operational goals. Rosenberg et al. (1964) predicted that "[g]iven the full development and diffusion of established weapons capabilities, every inhabitant of the globe will eventually find himself in this demoralized, de-legalized extreme situation" (p. 167). While the terrorists survey potential targets during the planning stages of an attack, the governmental institutions have enhanced their surveillance of the terrorists in an attempt to prevent any future attack. This governmental surveillance is necessarily extended to the entire population and is evidenced by the installation of elaborate networks of security cameras in our cities and the recent employment of both full body scanners and physical pat-downs of airline passengers. While some see these measures as troublesome but necessary components of deterrence, others view them as an unwarranted and invasive intrusion of individual rights.

Notwithstanding these measures, the reality of the terrorist threat cannot be minimized in light of the many recent aborted attacks. These include the plot to bomb the New York City subway system, the "underwear bomber's" attempt to blow up a U.S. airliner on Christmas day, 2009, the explosives laden vehicle left to detonate in Times Square, New York, on May 1, 2010, and the October 2010 discovery of concealed explosives in commercial packages shipped on cargo planes.

Given the ongoing concern with terror-related incidents, it is instructive to review several research studies that have focused on the emotional health of those affected by these events. The psychological literature is replete with studies of posttraumatic stress disorder (PTSD) after natural and man-made disasters. Several studies conducted after 9/11 have examined the degree of "emotional stress" or "distress" experienced both by residents of New York City and nationally. One notable study of slightly over 1,000 persons living in New York City found that "a total of 56.3% had at least one severe or two or more mild to moderate symptoms" three to six months after 9/11 (DeLisi et al., 2003, p. 782). The study further revealed that "[o]f those people (18.5% of the total) considered to have enough symptoms to put them at risk for PTSD, only 26.7% were receiving counseling or psychiatric treatment" (p. 782). The research team concluded that "those who could be in need of treatment may still not be adequately pursuing it" while "those with severe symptoms were far fewer than what we expected, given the magnitude and amount of personal exposure to this disastrous event" (p. 782).

Other studies have focused on the relationship between one's proximity to the World Trade Center on 9/11 and the incidence of PTSD. In an interesting psychological study of persons who were either in the World Trade Center or in proximity to it ("high exposure survivors") on 9/11, the researchers found that "highly secure adults tended to be the best adjusted following the tragedy. For example, their self reported symptom levels indicated that they had only modest PTSD symptoms at 7 months and that their PTSD symptom levels, similar to others, declined throughout the next 11 months" (Fraley et al., 2006, p. 547). While this research focused specifically on the relationship between "individual differences" in "attachment style" (i.e. indices of personality type) and adaptation to the devastation of September 11, they cite several studies indicating "that the majority of New Yorkers were able to adapt fairly well to the tragedy" (p. 546).

One study examined the impact of 9/11 on those individuals who lived within approximately eight miles from the World Trade Center; "7.5% of those living south of 110th St in Manhattan [had] symptoms related to PTSD and 9.7% [had] symptoms related to depression 1 month after the attacks" (Boscarino, Adams, and Galea, 2006, p. 607). A recent study on "spatial proximity" has concluded that "[in] the months following the attack, each 2-mile increment in distance closer to the World Trade Center site was associated with a 7% increase in anxiety-related diagnosis in the population" (DiMaggio, Galea, and Emch, 2010, p. 55). The researchers posit that these "spatial variables" will serve to "explain discrepancies in the existing literature" (p. 55) regarding the incidence of PTSD after 9/11.

Finally, it has been reported that:

> few people who were not direct victims of the attack experienced clinical levels of PTSD. However, when a less stringent definition of distress (such as the presence of stress symptoms or a lower sense of personal control) is used, reactions to September 11th were widespread and continued to persist at 6 months, though at a lower level (Thompson et al., 2006, p. 144).

It should be noted that this study focused specifically on respondents who did not live in New York during the attack (the majority of respondents were residents of California) to determine the degree to which the general public, those who were geographically distant from the place of the attack, responded.

It is interesting to juxtapose these findings, which seem to reflect a degree of fortitude in the civilian population, with Freedman's (2004) article in this chapter on the "collective resilience of first responders on 9/11." Freedman suggests that this "resilience" of the first responders in their reaction to the devastation of 9/11 was a product of their unique social and professional background. Freedman's ethnographic analysis of the rich anecdotal accounts of the first responders highlight their ability to detach their professional selves from their civilian selves wherein those individualistic dynamics that may render a person powerless in the face of disaster were repressed and overwhelmed by the primacy of their occupational responsibilities. Freedman notes that while the occupational training and cohesiveness of the first responders enabled them to respond to the disaster in a most courageous, professional and self-less manner, their subsequent "lionization" by the public complicated their self-images and impacted upon their adaptive mechanisms. This cautionary observation takes on even more significance in light of one of the research findings noted in the previously cited work on "spatial proximity" and psychopathology. The researchers found that certain "ZIP code tabulation areas experienced increased anxiety-related diagnoses in the post-attack period" (DiMaggio et al., 2010, p. 57). The most "notable" locations identified were certain areas of Staten Island, New York, home to many firemen and other first responders.

The second reading in this chapter is the personal and professional psychological insights of Dr. Judy Kuriansky (2003), a well-known radio host and author. This article is particularly informative and practical in that it identifies and elucidates, in laymen's terms, important psychological concepts that are relevant to coping with crises in general, and 9/11 in particular. Kuriansky reviews innovative models of crisis intervention and makes important suggestions toward their implementation in the enhancement of the healing process for both the professionals and their clients.

Randall Collins's (2004) article on "rituals of solidarity" after a terrorist attack suggests that the well-known sociological dictum that conflict produces solidarity is somewhat "ambiguous" and in need of clarification in regards to its application.

Specifically, Collins identifies "phases" in the evolution of group solidarity which are directly related to the unique characteristics of the actual incident. The crucial fact in solidarity is not the conflict itself but rather "the sharp rise in ritual intensity of social interaction" (p. 55) that occurs in response to the event. Collins surveyed manifestations of national solidarity such as ceremonial events and flag displays to determine whether "clusters" of ritualistic expression were influenced by variables that included geographic location, race and social class. Finally, Collins provides compelling insights and examples regarding the extent to which solidarity rituals may in fact have the opposite effect and become the catalysts for producing conflict rather than cohesiveness between various communal groups and their respective ideologies and interests.

Voices of 9/11 First Responders: Patterns of Collective Resilience

Tovia G. Freedman

Introduction

The unparalleled attacks of 9/11/01 that caused the World Trade Center buildings to collapse in an avalanche of twisted steel, black smothering smoke and debris, resulted in the deaths of thousands of people, and created a pyramid of loss that reverberated throughout the national and the world community. The psychological and physical enormity of 9/11 was impossible to comprehend. Emergency personnel, firefighters, police, and other responders rushed to the first smoking tower. From all the boroughs in the city, emergency workers poured into the tiny streets of lower Manhattan, sirens blaring, lights flashing. Simultaneously, there was a rush of office workers away from, and out of the building. As the early and first responders approached the site, the second plane hit the yet untouched tower and the realization took hold that "we were under attack." The heightened noise level of running, screaming, frightened people created a scene of chaos that would become part of an iconic historical event. The chaotic situation unfolded on what was described by firefighters as "a spectacular day, not a cloud in the sky." In this juxtaposition of catastrophe and beauty, in the words of a chaplain on the scene, "We saw two faces that day . . . the face of real evil . . . and the face of goodness."

This paper reports the results of a series of interviews undertaken in response to the events of 9/11/01 at the World Trade Center, subsequently designated, ground zero. The primary aim of the research was to increase knowledge and understanding of how emergency responders dealt with the devastating and disorienting tragedy of 9/11—the stress, risks, and terrible losses it entailed—and what contributed to their ability to engage in effective and committed action in the face of it. The chance to interview persons who were among the first to arrive on the scene and respond to it presented a unique opportunity to gather a body of data that could illuminate how they were able to function in this situation, and also that might contribute more general insights about how those who render aid in catastrophes can be of greater service in aiding victims to cope with the terror and trauma that they encounter.

Although I am familiar with the literature that has been generated by professionals who work with people involved with traumatic events, and have drawn upon it in my own clinical practice, what became immediately apparent in the 9/11 situation in which I became immersed through my research, was that the concepts around which it centers—such as "post traumatic stress," "numbing," "splitting," "dissociation" and other psychodynamic notions—were too individualistically formulated to take into account the significant social and cultural factors that affected how early responders experienced and managed 9/11. As will be seen, I quickly discovered that their social backgrounds, the occupational community to which they belonged, and the collective ways of coming to terms with disaster and death that they had learned through their professional training and socialization were crucial components in how they dealt individually and collectively with what 9/11 required of them.

Discussion

The people interviewed for this inquiry provide an "insiders" perspective on 9/11/01. What is striking about these accounts is their universal vividness and eloquence. They are infused with sense memories of sounds, sights, and smells, and with images of evocative detail. As the first plane hit the North Tower one chaplain recalled:

> It looked like a movie set. There was no time. Frozen in time. It was silence in a place that there is noise 24 h a day. But it was absolute silence, except for the clicking of the changing street lights, and through the haze you could see the colors change. It was the eeriest thing. I could not believe that I would ever see this in America.

Then, when the South Tower was hit:

> I heard a thunderous roar and looked up the street and caught a shadow. I thought it was a bird, but it turned out to be the tail of the plane sneaking behind the buildings. Then there was a thunderous roar, and a blast, and the building seemed to implode. (Fireman)

Upon emerging from life saving shelter another chaplain recounted:

> You couldn't see, you couldn't breathe . . . we started up the ramp and realized we were outside, because we found the curb. I kept looking for the garage doors, looking for the daylight. Where was the daylight? There was no daylight. The smoke started to settle. Where were the buildings?
>
> Right there people were jumping . . . A part of a torso . . . I knew that the jumpers were making a decision. They stood on the edge and made a decision. I said a prayer for them because I knew that wherever they were going had to be better than this . . . A roaring hot fire. I saw a guy fall and flip in the air and he went down on his back and his tie floated and fluttered in the air. Some kid who got up this morning, looked in the mirror, tied his tie and look where he is 2 h later. (A Deputy Fire Commissioner)

The self-analysis in which these persons on the frontlines of 9/11 engaged as they conducted their work under such extraordinary circumstances is impressive. At one and the same time they were intensely aware of what was happening externally and internally within their own thoughts and feelings. This two-layered state of consciousness, as a fireman explained, was even present when he and his comrades fled from one of the collapsing towers:

> It was a freefall. You could feel it coming. You could feel the rumble and you could hear this thunderous roar. Everybody looked, stopped in their tracks for a split second. Then everybody scattered. Everybody just ran. As I ran for safety my mind is analyzing the situation, taking in all the available cues so that I can recall every step of the way and use this to get out of the situation and help others.

Numerous emergency responders bridged and managed this duality of experience by making an intentional decision to close off some of their impressions and reactions in order to "keep going":

I took in those visions and my brain said, "You will have to deal with the tough ones later. If I focus on this now I will turn and run. . . ." If I focused on the torso I stepped across . . . I had to put that away and keep going. (A Deputy Fire Commissioner)

I was momentarily mesmerized and had to bring myself back to driving and getting to the site. (Fireman)

As soon as we heard the news and we knew cognitively there was an attack, we immediately shifted into this numb state. We were focusing on what we needed to do to accomplish the mission to survive. (Police Sergeant)

Handing out the paper cups of water on the street. . . . No uniforms, no mandate, just a kind of humanity trying to take hold, to restore the world to an emotional equilibrium. (Photographer)

As these participants in 9/11 recount, their ability to handle strong emotions in such a horror-filled emergency situation was partly the result of their professional training and experience. It entailed the learned capacity to maintain distance in order to bring objectivity to the work that had to be undertaken, while protecting their emotional selves. In effect, the firemen, police officers, and chaplains who were already dressed in distinctive garments donned extra "emotional clothing" (Fox, 1988) that protected them psychologically, and enabled them to "get the job done." In the face of the destruction and carnage with which they were confronted, a number of the first-line responders "numbed down" their feelings to a point where they described themselves as moving in an automatic, "robot"-like state:

I was numb much of the time during the long days and weeks afterward, often moving through meetings and funerals like a robot. I kept reminding myself that I had a job to do and didn't have time to indulge myself or my feelings when there was much work to be done. (Firefighter)

We understood intellectually and cognitively what we had to do as soon as we heard the news. There was no emotion. We were numb. We were focused on what we had to do to get the job done, to accomplish our mission to help others survive. (Police Officer)

I saw things that I could not register. I was focused on the ground. Things were close to me . . . a mass of body matter. You couldn't make things out. There were clothes in there . . . but there was absolutely no association with a body. This probably makes me deal with it much better. (Photographer)

Like all firefighters I have learned over the years to look directly at the most horrible things and keep them at arm's length. If you don't do that you can't get the job done. (Firefighter)

This kind of psychological state has been described in great depth in the literature on men in combat (Grinker & Spiegel, 1963; McCauley, 2003; Stouffer, 1965). The concept of "psychological numbing," and others akin to it, have subsequently been used by mental health practitioners who imply that "numbness" and "robotness" reduce an individual's lucidity and capacity to function. This does not appear to have been true of the police officers and firefighters interviewed. Quite to the contrary, these mechanisms seem to have contributed to their efficacy and to their ability to continue to work for many months at ground zero, and with its wounded and grieving victims.

As stated earlier, the ways the firefighters and policemen managed what 9/11 asked of them was not purely, or even primarily individualistic in origin. To a significant degree, they were shaped by the professional training and socialization process that the firemen and police officers had undergone, and by the culture of the occupational communities to which they belonged. Nothing was more important to their ability to deal with the catastrophe of 9/11—its associated danger, devastation, terror, loss and death—than the strong sense of group cohesion that bound firefighter to firefighter and policeman to policeman.

The distinctive social systems of these communities, their unifying common social backgrounds and shared values and beliefs, their corporate sense of identity, the brotherly unity of police partners and the extended kinship solidarity of firefighters, along with their special rituals and ceremonies were major sources of sustenance, support, endurance, and meaning.

Clinical Implications

In certain respects the clinical implications of this study are not dissimilar from those that have been reached by other studies of individuals and groups who experience traumatic events (Bloom & Reichert, 1998; Herman, 1992; North et al., 2002). In other regards, the clinical implications related to 9/11 have distinguishing characteristics that need to be taken into account. Foremost, are the particular circumstances of this traumatizing event. September 11, 2001 descended upon a psychologically and physically unprepared American consciousness. No peacetime attack of this magnitude had ever befallen the United States, and an unsuspecting population was assaulted by a seismic avalanche to mind and landscape that created a sense of disbelief and disorientation. Making sense of this terrorist act and what it meant was rendered all the more difficult by the fact that it was a narrowly focused attack experienced as an assault on a whole country and way of life. Even today, integrating the events of 9/11 is daunting for those most directly affected.

Clinicians performing disaster-related work have an obligation to help people recognize that they are most often experiencing a normal reaction to an abnormal event. The clinical work can focus on some type of experience integration in which the event or occurrence neither loses its meaning nor eclipses other life responsibilities, occurrences or emotions. Searching for the essential qualities of the experience, as one of the fire chaplains trained in Pastoral Counseling explained, "It really has to do with whether people can attach meaning to what happened—not necessarily control, but meaning. If they can make meaning of this, that is really spiritual work, not from the pulpit, but from within themselves," then perhaps they can move ahead in work and life.

When people are unable to integrate their experience and gain a sense of meaning, then clinicians are faced with a conundrum: how, when, and whether to intervene. Some of the "usual" signs of an inability to regain a sense of emotional equilibrium may include: isolation from family; alienation from others; withdrawal; emotional inaccessibility; a prevailing sense of aloneness and hopelessness; an inability to relate to "normal" feelings; and a loss of connection and purpose. An extension of these potential symptoms would be "emotional numbing," described by Bloom and Reichert (1998) as an extreme form of dissociation (APA, 1994). They suggest that this form of dissociation may go unrecognized. Because the dissociative state allows people to function on several levels simultaneously—"step across part of a torso" and continue "to get the job done"—they may appear to be coping well. However, their capacity for normal interaction could be diminished or even lost. Yet, clinicians have to be concerned about the time when the event left in a "freeze frame" state suddenly bursts forth at a vulnerable moment: When the visual reminder or whisper of the terrible act turns into a "thunderous roar," catapulting the person into the catastrophe once again, as if it is "real," he/she is no longer protected by a "numb" or dissociative state.

Clinicians hope that later in life a devastating past experience will not "sneak up" on a person, and reawaken, emotional pain in her/him. However, this is not always avoidable. Farley Mowat, a World War II veteran, underwent such an experience: "A bloody awful thing it was. So awful that through three decades I kept the deeper agonies of it wrapped in the cotton–wool of protective forgetfulness, and would have been well content to leave them buried forever . . . (in Hedges, 2002, p. 28). But, his buried feelings and experiences came alive during the subsequent war in Vietnam and affected his psychological state of mind. There is never a guarantee that any experience will stay wrapped in "cotton–wool," so it is incumbent upon mental health professionals dealing with responders to disasters to be vigilant, but not overly intrusive. Disaster mental health providers should take their primary direction from the people for whom they care. The person's observations, explanations, and interpretation of the event are critical to designing a course of psychosocial assistance and intervention. Consideration also needs to be given to the social and cultural as well as the psychological factors that have contributed to a person's use of a self-protective, "cotton–wool" type of defense and how this may delay or forestall a reaction to a traumatic event of the magnitude of 9/11, and its integration into an individual's system of meaning.

The tradition in psychological services has been to uncover all conscious and subconscious material. But re-experiencing trauma, especially when it is associated with a momentous tragic event like 9/11, needs rethinking. The images and sounds of 9/11, so enduringly entwined with individual and collective experience, need to be assessed and evaluated. Then, a period of "emotional defrosting" should be considered. This would entail providing help to move through the numb, dissociative, or stressful condition, into a state in which the experience is neither denied nor all-consuming. Ideally, this should take place in a context where the "helper" follows the lead of the "client," meeting the client where she/he is (Perlman, 1957; Smalley, 1967).

One of the major findings of the study of 9/11 first responders is that the solidarity and group cohesion that is so striking among firefighters and police officers have negative as well as positive consequences. These intra-group characteristics are significant sources of mutual support. They create a cohesiveness and an atmosphere of trust that not only contributes to firefighters and police officers' sense of individual and collective fulfillment, but also helps them to carry out their risk-fraught work as effectively and safely as possible.

However, the same group solidarity and collective sense of identity become liabilities as well. This can be seen in the impact that the "lionization" of the firefighters during and after 9/11—nationally, locally, and internationally—had upon them. The firefighters were viewed as heroes. A United States stamp, "Heroes USA," was issued showing three firemen raising the American flag at ground zero. The firemen were publicly transformed into an icon that symbolized strength and bravery. As the journalist observed, "It was great to have the image of reality of those brave men," that conveyed the message that "if you are in trouble there are people [firefighters] who will come and give their lives for you." But he, as well as many others, was chastened by the thoughts of the thousands of civilians and of the many fellow firefighters who perished on that day. Although the appreciation they received was welcomed, what they regarded as this "over-heroized" state became an additional burden to their already overloaded psychological and emotional state. The firehouses were flooded with food, cards, and people at a time when there was a need for those who survived within each firehouse to be privately together, insulated from public view. The ambivalence with which many of the surviving firefighters considered their "heroic" status was described by one firefighter this way:

> All firefighters are not heroes. They are good men who come to work and do their job. All the guys rush in. It is easy to rush in. When you get to the door there are people who become heroes and people who don't. On 9/11 regular people [civilians] became heroes. I don't think that it is good for us to be acting like everyone is a hero. If you were lucky enough to survive that day and did your job I don't think you were a hero. That's your job. . . . That is the bad part of lionization. We are all better off being human beings.

On 9/11 the subcultural norms and values of the firefighters turned out to be their "Achilles' heel." The closeness, dependence, and interdependence of the firefighters so fundamental to their work ethic and equilibrium also meant that as a result of the tremendous losses of their comrades—their "brothers"—their communal sense of identity was shaken. Having to experience their collective sense of loss on a public stage invaded their intimacy. Furthermore, the dramatically heroic image of them that emanated from the public's adulation was not congruent with how the firefighters saw themselves, and this raised the level of anxiety and self-doubt to which they became subject. Rowan Williams' (2002) conception of "prosaic heroism" comes closer to how the 9/11 firefighters and also police officers viewed their actions.

> If we are to remember that day. . . . Some people . . . practise (sic) living in the presence of death; not courting dramatic immortality through a cause, but as part of what will or may be necessary to serve the social body . . . [This is] heroism of the routine. (pp. 43–44)

Certain patterns emerged from this study that can be incorporated into professional clinical efforts to help people on the "front-lines" of responding to a catastrophe, along with those whom they assist, to deal with the deep and sustained trauma of what they have experienced individually and collectively. These patterns underlie the effectiveness and commitment with which the first responders interviewed performed their jobs, and the great fortitude and resilience they exhibited in the face of the shocking, painfully difficult circumstances that confronted them.

The most salient and significant of the patterns is the powerful and pervasive role that social and cultural factors played in what firefighters and police officers (and also chaplains and journalists) saw, heard, thought, and felt, and in how they acted and reacted at the height of the 9/11 disaster and during its aftermath. This strongly suggests how important it could be for a counselor or therapist offering them psychological aid not only to have knowledgeable understanding of their familial, ethnic, and religious backgrounds, and of the occupational communities to which they belong, but also to combine that social and cultural understanding with an individualistic approach.

There is also much of potential value to be learned from the highly developed occupational rituals—particularly those relevant to the occurrence of deaths—which both firefighters and police officers brought to the scene, the circumstances, and the consequences of 9/11. In addition to the repertoire of rituals that were already available to them, they created some new ones. One of the most striking was the way that firefighters and police officers came together at ground zero with construction workers, and sometimes with chaplains, to engage in communal acts of prayer that were often silent. This group ritual, which was described by some as "ground zero religion," took place many times during the day and throughout the night, over a period of weeks that extended into months. An indicator of how important it was to those who participated in it was poignantly expressed by a fireman who testified that it not only strengthened their comradeship with each other, but also their communion with their comrades who had died in action. "We breathed them in through the dust of their bodies and continued to feel close to them," he said. This powerfully attests to how crucial the spiritual aspects of the grief and loss experienced by those involved in a catastrophe are, how mistaken it would be to think of them purely in psychodynamic terms, and how important ritual is as a means of dealing with the existential anguish and the problems of meaning that are evoked by a disaster. Respectful awareness, understanding, and acceptance by mental health persons of this crucial dimension of the trauma experienced by individuals who have undergone a collective tragedy, and recognition of the significance of ritual in this context, even if wordlessly conveyed by therapists to the persons they are treating, can enhance the quality of rapport that is established between them, and thereby augment the healing experience.

In this connection, it was notable that at the site of ground zero and elsewhere in their 9/11 orbit, the chaplains who were interviewed and observed as part of this research often provided assistance in a non-verbal manner. Their behavior differed markedly from the "talk therapy" approach considered by many mental health providers to be a desirable, emotionally cathartic way to help a person who has undergone a calamity to "work through," and "come to terms" with it. The silent presence of the chaplains, and the consolation that they seemed to communicate were a reminder and demonstration of the therapeutic and restorative power of quietly "being there" with clients—physically and emotionally—especially in a situation like 9/11, where the problems of meaning are so overwhelming and enigmatic that no words may be adequate to express or explain them.

In conclusion, there are several caveats that emerged from these data that should be taken into consideration by social workers, as well as "helpers" involved in catastrophic events:

- Behavior and experiential accounts that would be considered "abnormal" under most circumstances are usually normal responses to abnormal circumstances and situations.
- Emotional numbing and psychological distance are useful self-adaptive tools that contribute to personal functioning and ability to perform responsibilities within

and on behalf of the occupational group. Also, high cohesion groups have their own rituals for making meaning, diminishing stress, and maintaining performance that need to be understood and supported by clinicians.

- Heroizing and lionization, created by a public and a media with favorable intentions, can be burdensome, emotionally problematic and may even contribute to disastrous sequelae.
- The enmeshment of "helpers," such as chaplains, with groups that comprise their friends, can be beneficial in terms of trust and understanding, but simultaneously create special problems for the helper who may become overburdened and even overwhelmed with responsibility toward others.

Source: With kind permission from Springer Science + Business Media: *Clinical Social Work Journal.* "Voices of 9/11 First Responders: Patterns of Collective Resilience," Volume 32, No. 4, 2004, pp. 377–378, 384–392, Freedman, Tovia G. Copyright © 2004, Springer Netherlands.

THE 9/11 TERRORIST ATTACK ON THE WORLD TRADE CENTER: A NEW YORK PSYCHOLOGIST'S PERSONAL EXPERIENCES AND PROFESSIONAL PERSPECTIVE

Judy Kuriansky

Introduction

The September 11th terrorist attack in New York City is an event that will live on in history. Its occurrence has impacted the world forever.

As a psychologist who has given mental health support at disaster sites around the country and the world, most recently at Ground Zero and the Family Assistance Center after 9/11, and who has heard many tragic stories as a radio call-in advice host for over twenty years, nothing can compare to the experiences, feelings and consequences of 9/11. In this paper, I reflect upon that event, and terrorism in general, as it impacted my personal and professional life, and explore the relevance of some fundamental, as well as newer psychological principles with regard to helping people cope with terrorism.

A Marker Event

The September 11th terrorist attack on the World Trade Center in New York is what's called in psychology a "marker" event. Like a wedding, birth of a child, or death of a loved one, a marker event is a significant experience that has a major impact on a person's life as well as potentially on history. Often a turning point, the event becomes a date against which people remember other events; for example, saying, "Before 9/11, we . . ." or "After 9/11, I no longer. . . . "

Another such marker event in recent American history is former President John F. Kennedy's assassination. An equivalent in German history is the fall of the Berlin wall.

Common qualities about these marker events are that people remember where they were when they heard the news; the people who were important at that time (who they were with or called); how they felt; and how the event has changed their life.

The 5 Questions to Ask

Given the nature of marker events, there are five helpful questions to ask people when helping them cope with the impact of such a marker event like 9/11: (1) Where were you when the 9/11 attacks happened? (2) Who were you with? (3) Whom did you call or called you? (4) How did you feel? And, (5) What impact did 9/11 have on your life?

These can be asked in various settings, whether in a therapeutic intervention, seminar, or social interaction.

The sequence of these questions helps create rapport and follows a solid psychological principle about gently guiding a person into deeper exploration of an experience. Starting with a question about location elicits factual information allowing the person an opportunity to focus on the subject in a relatively safe, unemotional left-brain way. Defining whom they were with at the time continues a factual identification. Asking whom they called or who called them begins to arouse feelings of significant others, arousing emotions and leading to the more direct question about feelings and a deeper exploration of the impact of the event on their life.

One young woman calmly described being in her office when a co-worker told her of the tragedy. Facing the question of who called her, she became emotional, describing how she ended a budding romance with a suitor because he did not call her for days after the attacks.

"Why would I want to be with someone who does care about me enough to have called me on that day?" she said. "He should have done anything to get in touch with me to see how I was."

Going through this sequence was also helpful for me.

I was in Chengdu, China on September 11th, on the eve of one of the trainings I do to teach doctors about American counseling techniques. One of the doctors came up to me and told me I better watch TV, whereupon a group escorted me to my hotel room where they translated the broadcast as we watched repeated images of the hijacked planes crash into the towers. Immediately, I tried to call my husband, my assistant and my mother, but could not get through on the phone until one of the Chinese doctors offered his cell phone that miraculously made the connection. I'll always remember those three people I worried about first and the support of those doctors who stayed by my side for hours as I watched the TV and fretted over the news. I am particularly grateful to professor Tianmin Xu, who lent me his cell phone even as he was also trying desperately to reach his daughter in New York.

After the immediate shock, I became devastated over the destruction, fearful for the future, and furious that anyone would desecrate "my city" and "my country."

As soon as I could return home, I went immediately to volunteer for the Red Cross Disaster Mental Health Services and was assigned to Ground Zero to offer mental health support for the emergency workers at the site. Later I had assignments to the Family Assistance Center, starting from the tragic day the families were offered death certificates for their lost loved ones.

Reviewing changes in life in the aftermath of the attacks can be healing. This is especially true for those directly involved or for others like myself who helped.

As requested, I committed to 12-hour shifts, suspending all else in life. I did night shifts, since I was used to working late nights on the radio and playing music in bands. Each day merged into another. Like the rescue workers, I'd go to my assignment and come home, mindlessly drop into bed and get up to start over again. Mail piled up, emails went unanswered. Nothing existed except walking the perimeter of Ground Zero, giving out water, apples, candy bars, warm socks and sweatshirts to the grateful rescue workers, firemen, police, FBI, repairmen and others working at the site; going back to the respite center (converted public schools or hotels) for food (delicious, I might add), and sharing with co-workers about the night's "walk-abouts."

Psychological Concepts in Action

Certain psychological concepts became clearly useful in assessing the impact of 9/11, and determining how best to help people.

The Importance of Contact Comfort and Transitional Objects

Contact comfort is a concept I remember learning in introductory psychology class. It refers to holding closely an object that has some comforting effect and offers nurturing. A transitional object helps the person make the adjustment from childhood to adulthood. The most common transitional object that offers contact comfort is a baby blanket. People often keep these types of items throughout life, as a symbol of comforting from childhood, and reach for them in times of stress.

Stuffed animals, particularly stuffed bears, are another good example. During my work with the Red Cross at Ground Zero and the Family Assistance Center we handed out stuffed bears to children and adults. One man hugged his bear, and told me, "This is the nicest thing someone has given me in years. I'm a grown man, but you have no idea how great this feels to hug this bear."

Of course, the best contact comfort is that which comes from another human being hugging you or a loved one holding you through the night.

Maslow's Theory of Needs

The impact of 9/11 proves the usefulness of Maslow's hierarchy of needs. Terrorism and loss (of loved ones, home, finances) sends people down to the base of the triangle, concerned over basic needs for security and safety.

But clinicians need to assess where different people are on this hierarchy, and allow them to move up and down the hierarchy. Some may be worried about survival, while others question the "meaning of life" as part of existential crises. Studies show that spirituality increases during crises, when people search for higher meaning.

Locus of Control

One of the most troublesome feelings evoked by disaster is feeling out of control.

Disaster is either "natural" (caused by the environment, as in floods, earthquakes, hurricanes, tornadoes) or man-made (as in terrorism). The latter can trigger deep emotional wounds, since human beings are the cause. Unlike in the case of natural disasters, you cannot rationalize that you have no control over the world.

Locus of control is a concept that refers to whether you believe events of life are caused by outside influences or by yourself. Rooted in social learning theory, it was applied to "alienation theory" by sociologist Melvin Seeman in 1959, who associated internal or external locus of control with alienation concepts such as powerlessness, meaninglessness, social isolation and self-estrangement.

Since introductory psychology classes, this concept has always fascinated me, as I often ponder, "Did I cause this to happen, or was this caused by events outside my control?" I have come to the conclusion that both are true: I can affect certain outcomes, but other people and unforeseen natural events also affect my life, over which I have no control. As the popular saying goes, "You can't always control what happens, but you can control how you react to it."

Therapeutic advice I offered for those feeling out of control: do something simple that you CAN control, like straightening up your closet or garage. Alabama Senator Richard Shelby even noted "the streets spilled over with trash bags" as people cleaned house, washed cars and got rid of crab grass as vicarious ways to regain control and beating the enemy. Make conscious choices, to feel empowered, even for simple things like deciding what time you will set your alarm clock for, or what you will eat for dinner.

Processing

People in crisis can function and put off processing. Yet, processing the impact of the terrorist attack on life both immediately after and in the longer term is exceptionally healing.

While terrorism can make people doubt the meaning in life, it can also do the opposite, as in my case, reaffirming purpose as a result of connecting deeply with others and forming strong bonds.

This experience is consistent with my experience for so many years working on the radio, hearing people's problems. While many people wondered how I could keep myself sane or not be drained after hearing so many problems every night for years, I actually felt energized because hope emerged from the experience of deep sharing.

The Life Stress Test

In the useful scale of life events by Holmes and Rey, various experiences in life are measured by their relative stressful impact. The scores are added to assess a person's overall amount of stress and vulnerability to breakdown. The World Trade Center attacks caused some people to score exceptionally high on such a test, putting them at risk.

Identifying their level of stress itself is helpful, giving people an explanation and acknowledgment of their situation.

Lingering Stress and Learned Helplessness

The statistics about stress after 9/11 are staggering. About 100,000 Americans either saw one of the attacks or knew someone involved. But more thousands were affected even if not close to the scene. 90 percent of Americans had at least one stress symptom, from flashbacks to insomnia, in the week after. In a recent national survey, nearly half of women and one in four men said the terrorist attacks had shaken their sense of safety and security. Some 84 percent thought future attacks were likely.

Persistent threats of terrorism can lead to learned helplessness, a well-researched psychological principle whereby constant living under stress causes frustration and giving up. Classic conditioning research on animals in cages given shocks without possibility of escape, led to the animal's passive resignation. Humans are vulnerable to a similar outcome.

The antidote to learned helplessness is reaffirmation that one can be effective in doing something to change one's circumstances, and taking small steps to do so.

Father Figures

The most common responses to the 9/11 attacks, besides depression and anxiety, were feelings of powerlessness and helplessness. Americans had felt safe, like a child in a secure family. But like a frightened child whose security was shaken, post 9/11 Americans sought the strength and reassurance of a strong authority or "father figure."

Such figures emerged. Then New York mayor Rudy Giuliani became the perfect "father figure" by displaying his ability to be strong yet also compassionate in face of hysteria and crisis (Giuliani even admitted that he becomes stronger when faced with chaos). Narrowly escaping himself from a nearby building as the towers collapsed, the mayor shared the city's grief, yet pulled together and functioned, setting an example of his advice to "get back to normal" (re-opening the Stock Exchange and Broadway theatres after only a few days, setting up a command center, all the while going to funerals of friends).

President Bush also presented a reassuring father figure. Consistent with psychological literature that victims of abuse need to feel protected and feel better if justice is done, the President responded by defying the abusers (bullies or terrorists). Public statements that "Freedom has been attacked . . . we will hunt them (the terrorists) down and punish those responsible for these cowardly acts" were well received.

Heroism of the city's uniformed officers as well as civilians further set an inspiring standard of parental protectiveness.

A New Focus on Positive Psychology

A new approach in psychology that emerged post 9/11 is a positive health-centered one, focusing on growth potential and adapting well in the face of adversity instead of focusing on dysfunction and disorders.

The now popular word describing this is "resilience."

The Practice Directorate of the American Psychological Association in collaboration with the Discovery Health TV channel launched a campaign for education, research and public service promoting the resilience of people in response to terrorism and identifying qualities that help people cope.

According to the APA executive director for professional practice, Russ Newman, "Now more than ever people seem to be examining their lives and finding new ways to cope. Resilience is a way of responding to adversity, challenges and even chronic stress, that can be learned."

Tips to achieve resilience available in a free brochure (www.helping.apa.org) include: make connections and accept support from others, avoid seeing a crisis as insurmountable, look to a better future and acknowledge how well you already deal with difficult situations, move towards your goals, keep things in perspective, and take care of yourself.

In studies before Sept 11, adults who bounced back quickly didn't bury their bad feelings after the attacks. Though only slightly less angry and sad than adults who weren't as resilient, they felt more positive feelings like gratitude and love. These positive feelings are considered to account for their ability to weather tough times caused by the terrorist attacks.

In a study by one of my colleagues at Columbia University's Teachers College, George Bonanno, a positive sense of self was crucial in adjustment to extreme adversity.

University of Michigan psychologist Christopher Peterson suggests using the word "post-traumatic growth" instead of just concentrating on "post traumatic stress."

"Throughout most of history, psychology has been concerned with identifying and remedying human ills," Peterson said. "But a positive psychology approach today puts more emphasis on strengths versus weakens, building better things in life rather than repairing the worst, and increasing fulfillment of healthy people as much as healing the distressed."

Past traumas indeed affect resilience. Those who have suffered more losses are more vulnerable. A psychologist who has studied grief, Tom Pyszcynski, uses a word-stem completion test to assess people's experiences of death. In his studies, subjects who finish the word stem "coff" with "in" spelling the word "coffin" have suffered more losses than those who complete the word with "ee" spelling a more innocuous word, "coffee."

New Models of Crisis Intervention

The most important first step in helping someone deal with disaster, experts now say, is to calm the person. "Make every effort to reassure the person and not prolong the state of terror," says psychology professor and public health associate from Johns Hopkins

University in Maryland, George Everly. "Convince them that the immediate life threat has ended."

Invoking Yogi Berra's characteristically humorous statement that "90 percent of the game is half mental," Everly advises saying, "It's over. You did OK. You can cope."

Brief Cognitive Behavior Therapy Program

Everly reported at a recent conference about a new cognitive behavior program lasting 2–5 weeks. The sessions involve relaxation training, and safely recounting the incident in a secure environment, addressing mistaken beliefs, confronting present fears, and then in-vivo desensitization by visiting the site of the disaster.

Massage and Other R and R's

Military psychologist Larry James said at the 2002 APA convention that the top request for help after the attacks on the Pentagon was for a massage. James, chief psychologist at Walter Reed Hospital in Washington D.C., noted that victims needed rest and replenishment, besides reassurance. "Before talking about [PTSD]," says James, "be sure the person is eating and sleeping well."

At the respite center in the Marriott Hotel only blocks from Ground Zero, tables were set up in a quiet area on the third floor for workers to get a massage.

In an adjacent room, there were computer stations and large TVs with soft leather reclining chairs, for comfort.

Therapy Dogs

At the Family Assistance Center, trained dogs with expert handlers roamed the floors, waiting to be petted by family members who were seeking help. Not just children, but adults, eagerly petted the animals, smiled and reported feeling happier.

Stress Inoculation

A popular concept re-emerging in response to terrorism is "stress inoculation," whereby mental health workers meet with people, often in groups, to discuss impending events that could re-trigger trauma. Such sessions took place in counseling centers around the New York area before the anniversary of the attacks, giving people a chance to share and comfort each other.

"Guerrilla Counseling"

In times of crisis, psychologists can find themselves offering counseling "on the spot," rather than always in their offices at appointed times. As a profession, we have to be prepared to do this, often pro bono, work.

People may ask questions and need help, requiring "impromptu therapeutic interactions." A variation of this model that I developed as a result of 9/11 is what I call "guerrilla counseling,"—in-person, on-the-spot advice given to people with issues related to a crisis. I found myself addressing many people's anxieties in the downtown area, especially around Ground Zero, Chinatown and Greenwich Village. Some of these sessions were videotaped by a television crew and aired on a website to show people that they are not the only one suffering with a particular problem related to 9/11. Since I am well known in the New York area, many people recognize me in the street and spontaneously asked questions. They ranged from a parent asking, "How do I tell my children about what terrorism is?" to a young Arab student asking, "How can I convince young girls to trust me enough to go out with me after what happened?" to a woman who wanted to know, "After what happened, should I break up with my boyfriend who doesn't treat me well?"

The Cell Phone Solution

Resolving to be in closer touch with loved ones was one of the silver linings of the very dark cloud of the terror attacks.

Since terrorism incidents exploded throughout the world, the fastest growing business has been that of cell phones and contact technology. Most of the couples I spoke with after 9/11 mentioned calling their loved ones more often. For example, one young man I interviewed in the Ground Zero area mentioned that he upped his cell phone usage plan so he could call his fiancé several times a day, and gifted her with a call package.

Non-techie types have had others program their phones to call loved ones at the touch of a tone.

E-mailing also became a growing means of instant communication.

A Kindler, Gentler Nation

Comparing responses to online surveys before and up to 10 months after the attacks, researchers found a sustained increase in the level of seven character strengths: gratitude, hope, kindness, leadership, love, spirituality and teamwork (www.positivepsychology.org). This pattern held regardless of gender, race, age, education and marital status. These results bode well for an index of a change in the American character.

What to Say: The Nature of Trauma Work

In the face of terrorist events in the last decade, a specialty in psychology has grown, that of dealing with trauma, post-traumatic stress, the psychology of terrorism, methods of grief counseling and techniques like "critical incident debriefing."

On most issues in this area, psychologists agree. But there are some areas of potential dispute.

One expert giving a presentation at the APA convention warned against being teary eyed as a helper. I disagreed. In some situations, with some people facing trauma, crying with them makes them feel not alone, and trust you because you are being real.

Another issue regards talking about the event.

This same expert warned against asking people questions about the event at the time, at risk of causing traumatization. "It is not necessary to talk about the grisly details," she said. "That leads to rumination. People can get better without telling the details."

In my view, this should be treated on a case-by-case basis. Experience shows me that if people want to talk, it is good clinical practice to let them do so.

This is consistent with the model of "exposure therapy" used by therapists from the Department of Psychiatry at Columbia Medical School in New York working with the New York Police Foundation. Their technique guides individuals to confront their painful memories, identify the triggers of stress, and hone in on their strengths.

The bottom line: whether revisiting the event re-traumatizes or diffuses fear depends on how and when it is done, and in what setting.

"It is safe to re-experience the traumatic event in imagination or real life if it is done properly, when the real threat is over and in a setting where there is no threat," said Professor Psychiatry at University of California San Francisco Charles Marmar. "You can prolong the trauma if a review is done before it is clear that the life threat has ended."

Interventions in the first few minutes, says trauma expert Marmar, should be aimed at soothing, calming, and reassuring the person of safety. "This does not mean telling the person to please pour out emotions," warns Marmar, as that can exaggerate feelings and reactions. Anger and panic management, he says, should precede exposure therapy.

The degree to which people talk about trauma is related to personal style. There are those (more right-brained types) who need to express emotion, and those (more left-brained types) who prefer to use defense mechanisms like denial and suppression, to keep their anxiety in check.

Every clinician knows that for some people, recounting a horrific experience can defuse the associated four major "negative" emotions: anxiety, shame, and embarrassment or fear. During the aftermath of the World Trade Attacks, I found people wanting to relate horrors (some because they trusted me, knowing me for years as a media personality in our city). One electrical worker drove me home after an overnight shift downtown at Ground Zero and immediately as I got into the truck, began to tell me about horrors he witnessed, including driving over a corpse's decapitated head.

The opposite was also true: people like to escape trauma, by talking about other aspects of life. These might be light-hearted, to distract them entirely, or heavy, addressing other problems (since trauma in one area can unleash memories of earlier past traumas).

Many patients in therapy brought up past abuses, from rape or incest to being forced to perform sexual acts on male dates.

Many people talked to me about sex, understandably since I am known as a sex counselor. Many an evening I sat in the firehouse at Ground Zero with dinner companions asking me about their sex problems, like about a wife who wasn't interested in sex after having a child, or their own disinterest because of working too hard.

Talking about sex—or sports—is a common relief from trauma. Sports talk allows the expression of aggression against a competitor or "enemy," while sex talk can offer relief from anxiety.

How do you start a conversation? On a neutral level, with a smile in your heart (even if not on your face), and usually making a statement before asking a question. On line in the cafeteria at the respite center, I might say, "We had chicken like this yesterday but this one looks more appealing than last night," and then ask, "How're you feeling today?" A good clinician can sense where to go from there and what a person needs to talk about.

The Impact on Relationships

At the 2002 annual convention of the American Psychological Association, "with almost a quarter of the 3,000 presentations related to terror and the aftermath of 9/11, psychologists uniformly agreed that in spite of stress that strains some relationships, couples generally became closer and more committed.

Responses to another online survey, replicated by my students' study at Columbia University Teachers College, revealed that up to two-thirds of women and men wanted more connection with their partners.

Asking for What You Want

Ever since the age of "assertiveness training" in the 1970's, therapists like myself have been encouraging women to ask for what they need from men. This refers to women in particular since they traditionally have a harder time than men asserting themselves. The events of September 11th were like a proverbial "kick in the pants" for many women, to finally have this message about assertion hit home. Many more women finally resolved to have courage to speak up to the men in their life about their needs, whether for love or in sex.

A Question to Assess Commitment

Classic questions have tested partner's devotion. One has been, "If you and your partner were in the Titanic and there was only one place on the lifeboat, would you go or give the spot to your spouse?" In another, women muse, "Would my husband still love me if I had breast cancer?" (an all-too-sad health problem too many women today face, and that in reality does test a relationship).

While these type questions can be threatening, they can also be fruitful. One young woman was dating a man for some time, and was upset that he was treating the relationship too casually. She asked him that question, "What would you do if I were in the towers when they went down?"

"Don't ask such a question, you weren't," he said in a stereotypically male response, focusing on the facts rather than the emotional overtones.

"What is she really asking you?" I said to him.

After much discussion, he finally admitted, "I guess she wants me to show more that I care about her."

"That's it," I said. "She wants more of a commitment."

The young man explained that he moves "far more slowly" than she does. Ultimately, however, he agreed to show her more affection that she so desired. Thus the initially disturbing question led to a discussion that the woman had longed for, yet feared bringing up (typical in so many relationships).

A Change in Sex Role Stereotypes

Men and women still fall into stereotypes, with women expressing feelings and men being less expressive. In this way, the woman offers the man vicarious emotional release and he offers her more security by being a rational "rock" in the relationship.

After September 11th, sex roles shifted. More men openly expressed emotion, giving female partners a chance to show more strength. Looking at a flyer requesting information about their missing son (as so many similar others posted on walls around Manhattan), one husband stood crying as his wife held him tight. "I am hurting inside too," she told me. "But for a change, he's the one who's showing it on the outside and I can be strong for him instead of my always being the fragile one."

September 11th gave macho men an excuse to express feelings as the whole country joined in mourning and the New York City Mayor was hailed as a perfect example of male strength and sensitivity when he publicly cried. On the day families were given death certificates of lost loved ones, a man I was counseling broke down sobbing. "Thank you for letting me cry for the first time in my life," he told me.

Finally, after so many years of my counseling women to do so, I found more women willing to give nice guys the nod and bad boys the boot. Moved by the disaster to realize they deserve to be treated well, women told me they no longer needed to continually test their desirability by winning over resistant men. More self-respecting women spell healthier relationships.

Exploring Relationships: A Valuable Classroom Assignment

As the six-month anniversary of the 9/11 terror attacks approached, a great deal of media attention again focused on the tragedy. Pundits argued whether review of scenes and feelings could re-traumatize people, and criticized the media for exploitation of the events for ratings.

From my psychological perspective, there is benefit from examining the events, given the distance of some time. As a result, I gave my summer class in "The Psychology of Intimacy" the opportunity to do projects researching the impact of the attacks on relationships, and also the assignment to ask a significant other about the impact of the events on their relationship.

The assignment: How did a conversation you had with someone about 9-11 affect the relationship you had with them?

Every student reported a positive experience from the discussion. Samples of their (abbreviated) reports included the following.

"I learned a lot about my (then) boyfriend's personality by a conversation about 9-11. We speculated about why this happened, why other tragedies happen and have happened and discussed G-d's role in them. This led to a discussion about our overall belief systems and world outlooks. I learned that he was open to hearing and thinking about my ideas and opinions, even though some of them differed from his own. He spent the whole day comforting the distraught wife of a friend who worked at Ground Zero and then aiding in the rescue and relief efforts himself. This showed me his extraordinarily giving nature. Even though he usually projects a "tough, macho" image and doesn't usually display emotion in public, he reacted to the events of 9-11 in a very appropriate and emotional way, feeling jarred, saddened and confused."

"My best friend told me that her relationship with her mother and sister changed for the better on that day, cherishing one another and realizing how fortunate they were to have a family. However, since then things have gone back to what they were before the tragedy. Bickering and petty fights are more consistent, and I've even heard her say that she hates her mom because her mother took her driving privileges away. Also, after the tragedy, she and her boyfriend became tight and spent much more time together. He even moved in with her to provide extra support, however, since then they have broken up when he assumed that she cheated on him during a vacation."

"Since the incident, my relationship with my boyfriend has become more open. We feel the need to communicate more than ever. We cherish every time we have together, especially since we are miles away. He said that he began to think about our relationship a lot and the thought of losing me; he wouldn't know what to do. He was not there and did not know anyone that was involved. However, it did help him appreciate his relationship with me because in a split second someone can be with you and then gone the next. He also gets very scared for me because I frequently fly and he prays that I always make it safely to my destination."

"My best friend of 7 years confided in me that he was glad to have a friend to share all of these feelings with. In the midst of our fears and uncertainty, we could both say I love you to one another and those three words seemed to have so much more power than they did on September 10th."

"My boyfriend's friend used to drive me crazy but after I found out he was alive when I thought he died in the tower, I ran outside and hugged him before he even got to the door. I couldn't believe that there could have been a chance that I would never see him again. He said it was weird how many people came out of the woodworks to call and see if he was ok. Now, every time I think about September 11th, 2001, I think about that feeling I had when I thought Mike was dead. And I am so grateful that he is still here to drive me crazy."

"I have since come to terms with my mother; we had constantly fought with each other. I realized that there wasn't any point in fighting with her over insignificant things. I also realized that I was lucky to even have a mother considering that so many children lost their mothers in the terrorist attack."

"My boyfriend and I are more open to new experiences and we have decided to try new activities together, experiment with different foods, and to travel to different places. We want to do as much as possible with each other while we still can. Overall, I must say that my boyfriend and I have become more loving and appreciative of each other. We have also come to accept the fact that we both have our flaws and that our relationship is not perfect."

Make Love Not War

I believe that Freud was right when he identified two major instincts: Eros (the life, love, sex drive) and Thantos (death and aggression). They're two subjects that people are most interested in talking about, and have most conflicts over. Today's television shows prove that, as viewers are treated to daily doses either of "reality" shows about relationships or shows about crime, cops, and investigations.

Sex and war are connected.

After September 11, reports surfaced about an increase in extra-marital affairs and casual sex. That meant that faced with immediate disaster, men and women were having casual even unprotected sex as in the pre-AIDS days. Thinking that the world could come to an end anyway, they were going to enjoy their last days. The media frenzy warned of "terror sex," "apocalyptic sex" and "end of the world sex."

"If I only have one day left to live," one woman told me, "I might as well have the best time of my life, whether it's buying all the clothes I like or bedding any man I want."

The urge is not new. It was presented in the classic film, recently produced on Broadway, called "The Summer of '42," where a newly widowed woman almost immediately takes a new lover upon hearing news of her loss.

I call this phenomenon "the Anne Frank Syndrome," referring to the diary of the young Jewish girl during World War II, who records her first sexual experience that happened when faced with the probability of being discovered by the enemy.

Psychologically, the connection makes sense. Confronted with death, there is a natural urge to reaffirm life by indulging in pleasurable activities like sex. In more extreme cases, overindulgence in sex, as in drugs or alcohol, represents an effort to bury painful feelings.

Tragedy can also trigger "post-traumatic sex syndrome," a phrase referring to a variation of "post traumatic stress syndrome, the recognized psychological term describing the complex of symptoms stimulated by the experience of a traumatic event that threatens life and loss, can lead to the opposite reaction – reduced libido. Symptoms like depression, anxiety, fatigue and disinterest in otherwise pleasurable activities can cause a withdrawal from sex that further increases depression in a vicious cycle.

Source: From Kuriansky, Judy. "The 9/11 Terrorist Attack on the WTC: A New York Psychologist's Personal Experience and Professional Perspective," pp. 1–7, Psychotherapie Forum, 10. Wien-New York: Springer. 2003. Copyright © 2003 by Springer-Verlag. Reprinted by permission of Springer-Verlag.

RITUALS OF SOLIDARITY AND SECURITY IN THE WAKE OF TERRORIST ATTACK

Randall Collins

Conflict produces group solidarity in four phases: (1) an initial few days of shock and idiosyncratic individual reactions to attack; (2) one to two weeks of establishing standardized displays of solidarity symbols; (3) two to three months of high solidarity plateau; and (4) gradual decline toward normalcy in six to nine months. Solidarity is not uniform but is clustered in local groups supporting each other's symbolic behavior. Actual solidarity behaviors are performed by minorities of the population, while vague verbal claims to performance are made by large majorities. Commemorative rituals intermittently revive high emotional peaks; participants become ranked according to their closeness to a center of ritual attention. Events, places, and organizations claim importance by associating themselves with national solidarity rituals and especially by surrounding themselves with pragmatically ineffective security ritual. Conflicts arise over access to centers of ritual attention; clashes occur between pragmatists deritualizing security and security zealots attempting to keep up the level of emotional intensity. The solidarity plateau is also a hysteria zone; as a center of emotional attention, it attracts ancillary attacks unrelated to the original terrorists as well as alarms and hoaxes. In particular historical circumstances, it becomes a period of atrocities.

The attack of September 11, 2001 (referred to as 9/11) gives an opportunity to study the process by which social solidarity occurs in response to external conflict. People draw together; symbols are rallied around; leaders are exalted; control becomes more centralized. This is standard sociological theory. But how long do these processes last? When are they at their height? Do they operate uniformly throughout the population, or are they clustered in pockets? How long and in what way does external conflict divert attention from internal conflict? As we shall see, ritualistic mobilization about solidarity and security generates its own processes of conflict, as persons in particular social locations struggle over control of symbols and access to the center of collective attention; and these produce ancillary conflict and sometimes violence in their own right, in a period I call the hysteria zone.

Sociological theory does not pay enough attention to the dynamics of processes over time. We tend to be stuck in a meta-theoretical dichotomy between static comparisons of how structures hang together and an actor-centered view of fluid action. But processes have shapes in time, patterns of intensity, rapid shifts, and gradual declines, which sweep people up at one moment and bring them down at another. What follows is a contribution to theorizing one important type of time process.

Solidarity and Popularity of Symbolic Leaders

The principle enunciated by Simmel [1908] (1955) and Coser (1957) is that conflict produces solidarity. The statement is vague in a number of respects. At what phase of conflict is solidarity highest? Is solidarity strongest when a group perceives itself as being attacked, or when it attacks another? On this point, as on others, the issue has been little studied. I will examine a variety of kinds of evidence.

At least on the scale of large national democracies, evidence suggests that the first moment of being attacked is a peak moment of solidarity—so are the moment of going on the offensive and the moment of celebrating victory. Prestige polls for American presidents show all three of these patterns:

- 90 percent approval rating for George W. Bush, September 21–23, 2001: 10–12 days after the 9/11 attack.
- 89 percent for George Bush, February 28–March 3, 1991: one–four days immediately following victory in the four-day battle of the Gulf War (February 23–27).
- 87 percent for Harry Truman, June 1–5, 1945: 24–28 days after Victory in Europe (V-E) Day in World War II.
- 84 percent for Franklin Roosevelt, January 8–13, 1942: one month after the Japanese attack on Pearl Harbor and the declaration of war and the same percentage two and a half weeks later, January 21–25, 1942.
- 83 percent for John F. Kennedy, April 28–May 3, 1961: 11–16 days after the disastrous U.S.-supported invasion of Cuba at the Bay of Pigs (Gallup polls, CNN/Gallup Poll; USA Today, September 24, 2001 and January 18, 2002; see also Page and Shapiro 1992).

Note some of the fine detail of these time patterns. The popularity of George W. Bush was 86 percent on September 14–15, 2001, in the immediate three-four days after the 9/11 attack; it grew still higher (to a record 90 percent) in the following 10 days. It declined again into the mid-80s through early October and then jumped again to 89 percent (nearly the all-time peak) just after the United States began its air attack on Afghanistan. U.S. victory in Afghanistan ostensibly happened by mid-December; nevertheless, Bush's popularity fell slightly during this period, to 83 percent on January 11, 2002. Similarly, George Bush's popularity remained high after the Gulf War victory for another month (from the 89 percent peak at early March 1991, declining slightly to 87 percent March 7–10; 86 percent March 14–17; 84 percent March 21–24; and 83 percent April 4–6). Roosevelt's popularity stayed at its peak for almost two months after Pearl Harbor. The solidarity aftermath of the 9/11 attack in this respect is unusually prolonged, with George W. Bush still at historically quite rarified levels of popularity four months later, declining to 75 percent in March, and toward a more normal strong presidential position (in the 60s) during summer 2002, 9–12 months later.

Periods of intense solidarity around a political figurehead hit their peak about two weeks after the dramatic onset of conflict and stay very high for another month or two; thereupon they go into a slow decline, falling back to normal levels of support for a leader within about six–nine months.

The same pattern exists in support for wars; widespread enthusiasm for wars is typical at their beginning and stays high only for short wars (Ostrom and Simon 1985; Norpoth 1987). The intense period of solidarity lasts only a few months but is replaced by normal levels of patriotic solidarity while a war goes on. It takes considerable war casualties and lack of decisive victories over a period of two to four years for a war to become widely unpopular (Keegan 1977:274–77). Soldiers often enlist at the beginning of a war in a mood of high enthusiasm (Holmes 1985:275; Scheff

1994:94–96).[1] Within a few months of combat, they withdraw from nationalist and other ideals, or at least from their overt expression, and fight mainly out of solidarity with a small local group of co-fighters (Holmes 1985:276–77).[2] Thus, even with the continuation of external conflict, the intense surge of solidarity falls back to normal political commitment at best; although an initial defeat, even a disastrous one, generates solidarity, continuation of even moderate solidarity becomes contingent on victory.

Compared to the rallying around at the outset of a war, popularity peaks from winning a war are not so prolonged; Truman's June 1945 peak is never approached again. When conflict stops, the surge of solidarity drops to levels that may be below majority support. George Bush fell from an 89 percent approval rating after the Gulf War victory to losing an election 20 months later. Winston Churchill, despite immense wartime popularity, lost an election 10 weeks after the end of the European War. And losing ventures give only a sudden jolt, like Kennedy's in April 1961. The moment of attack also gives a jolt; the beginning of air bombardment of Iraq on January 16, 1991, gave George Bush an 83 percent rating January 23–26, 7 to 10 days later. In contrast, endings of wars that become bogged down in lengthy stalemates do not give popularity for political figureheads; there are no strong popularity surges associated with the end of Korean War or with the Vietnam War.

The Simmelian principle needs to be refined; not just any conflict results in high levels of group solidarity. The key to such a pattern is the dramatic incident, the attention-focusing event: a sudden attack and response to the attack, or a dramatic celebration at the end of a conflict.[3] Solidarity is produced by social interaction within the group, not by the conflict itself as an external event. What creates the solidarity is the sharp rise in ritual intensity of social interaction, as very large numbers of persons focus their attention on the same event, are reminded constantly

---

[1]The initial mood is so powerful that it tends to attract temporarily even those who are critical politically. An instance is the behavior of Max Weber: For over a decade prior to World War I, he was highly critical of the German government for its increasing diplomatic isolation from Britain and other former allies, and from late 1915 onward he was active politically in attempting to bring a negotiated end to the war. Yet during the enthusiasm of the war outbreak in August 1914 he immediately volunteered for war service (although 50 years old at the time) and was disappointed at being given a merely administrative position on the home front. On August 28, 1914 (three and a half weeks after the beginning of the war), he wrote in response to a relative's death in battle: "For no matter what the outcome—this war is great and wonderful" (Weber 1988:521–22). By the end of 1914 Weber attempted to resign from his administrative duties, although his resignation was not accepted for another nine months. His period of war enthusiasm covered at most five months.

[2]In World War II, one of the strongest taboos among U.S. combat troops was against conventional patriotic expressions and flag-waving.

[3]The surge of presidential popularity at the end of WWII came after victory in Europe (May 7, 1945); the war with Japan went on another three months (until August 15) but without a comparable surge of presidential popularity and with notably smaller public celebrations than the spontaneous crowd gatherings that took place after V-E Day. The first celebration preempted the second one. The tail end of solidarity surges is something like an emotional refractory period, which keeps a second peak surge from happening during the time when the first surge is decaying. As we shall see, the attempted shoe-bomb attack on an airliner on December 22, 2001, occurring toward the end of the three-month solidarity plateau, did not result in renewal of high levels of solidarity ritual: the time pattern of long-term decline in collective focus was too massive a shift in emotional inertia to be disrupted.

that other people are focusing their attention by the symbolic signals they give out, and hence are swept up into a collective mood. Individual reactions to violent conflict generally are fear or paralysis (Marshall 1947; Grossman 1995); solidarity is not the aggregation of individual emotions about conflict but is an entirely different emotional process.

The onset of a period of intense solidarity often is a sharp contrast from what went before. George W. Bush's popularity, for example, varied between 52 percent and 63 percent over the seven months preceding the 9/11 attack, with a low point in early September 2001. A dramatic conflict episode raises popularity 20 to 50 percentage points, depending on how low the starting point was. New York then-mayor Rudy Giuliani was regarded with considerable hostility among a large proportion of his constituents in the two years preceding 9/11, undergoing an abrupt shift in local popularity in the week following the attack, as he became the leading figure in local activities surrounding the catastrophe and their news reports. Rallying around a leader is a symbolic gesture that swallows up rational assessment and is not based on a summary of good and bad points of the individual's record.

Popular Display of Solidarity Symbols over Time

Private individuals' display of solidarity in national conflict follows the same time pattern as solidarity around leadership symbols. As we shall see, however, private displays are confined to minorities of the population, although sometimes substantial ones; rallying around a leader appears to be the easiest and most widespread of all symbolic gestures.

My method was formulated in the immediate stir of the 9/11 atmosphere—initially by noting all indicators of solidarity display and then by settling onto counts of flags or other national symbols on buildings, cars, and personal clothing. The display of such symbols went through four phases.

The first period spanned the first two days after the attacks. For most people, there was little display of solidarity behavior except in private relationships. Individuals spread news of the attacks to one another, including some talk among strangers (as in elevators and on public transportation). The mood was largely quiet, indeed, emotionally stunned. There were few immediate outbursts of patriotic enthusiasm or of anger at an enemy.

These were days of extremely widely shared focus of attention. The major television channels broadcast all news through the fourth day, although some minor channels had gone back to entertainment shows and had resumed advertisements by the third day. Normal programming everywhere resumed the fifth day, although sports events were cancelled for the first weekend (the attacks occurred on a Tuesday). By the sixth day, newspapers scaled back coverage of the 9/11 attacks from almost total monopoly to relatively few pages and resumed normal local news; sports sections indicated that everyone was ready for resuming scheduled games. The same evening, for the first time in a week, I heard sounds of a party in the streets below my downtown Philadelphia apartment house—the usual hoots, loud drunken voices, laughter. The weekend hiatus felt right ritually for resumption of normalcy. The official ritual of national mourning, however, flags at half staff, was not ended (by presidential order) until the 12th day (the second Saturday after 9/11)—again using the weekend as a breaking point.

Social Clusterings of Solidarity Display

The display of symbols is not uniform. Conflict does not generate solidarity simply by creating a psychological current passing through everyone equally. Solidarity is orchestrated in part by rather official processes and in part by more informal and seemingly voluntary actions. Several different processes mesh over time. In the very first period, isolated individuals make idiosyncratic symbolic displays, but these generally are taken as too extreme and are met largely with embarrassment. Then official and quasi-official organizations get into the act; apartment houses put up flags and bunting very quickly in entrances and lobbies around the fifth to seventh day, as did stores. These are front-stage displays in the Goffmanian sense, a statement of what the organizational leaders believe is appropriate to be done much in the same way politicians and speakers on ceremonial occasions say what is expected. Such symbol display is not flexible; it hangs on longer than the unofficial displays, and the contrast in their rhythm after a time gives the official displays a sense of being merely formalistic, empty symbols. But at the beginning of the second period, they are important for orchestrating a sense of social consensus on the ubiquity of symbolic solidarity.

More flexible, and hence more expressive of actual emotions felt, are two further kinds of displays of national solidarity: ceremonial assemblies and popular display of symbols. Most vivid are memorial ceremonies for the victims, of which the most heavily attended and widely publicized through the media are concerts and sports events converted to national rituals. These gatherings increase the emotional significance of symbols for those who are present and to a lesser degree for those who watch them on television; they are peak experiences of solidarity. But these ceremonies mostly are concentrated in the second period (build-up) and the early part of the third period (plateau). Though very successful, they are temporary and ephemeral and can operate just as well to put closure on past events as to keep their memory alive for the future. The least orchestrated of solidarity displays, finally, are voluntary activities such as displaying flags. Despite appearances, these are not for the most part individual actions, since they are situated in local enclaves.

The display of flags is most frequent when it is part of one's recognized identity within a group. Although the symbol displays solidarity with the national group, not ostensibly with one's local ties, the local group is what sustains the display. People make their displays of solidarity with distant groups by acting together in local groups rather than as individuals.[4]

This may be corroborated with several other comparisons. As already indicated, flag displays are much lower in apartment houses than among single-family dwellings (peak frequencies on the order of 4 percent and 30–45 percent, respectively). Apartment residents may see where flags are displayed when they approach the building from outside, but they generally do not know whom the flags belong to unless they are neighbors. Where flags are displayed on apartments, they tend to clump on adjacent windows; on the same floor on opposites sides of a building (i.e., across the hall from

---

[4]We know that members of social movement demonstrations and political crowds do not come as isolated individuals but participate as little clumps of friends (McPhail 1991). A likely hypothesis, apparently as yet untested, is that members of crowds at sporting events who do the most cheering and the most extreme displays of symbolic solidarity with a team are attending as members of these little groups.

each other); or on balconies, one above the other. Moreover, over time, as the number of flags diminishes, the ones that are clumped most closely tend to stay up the longest. This pattern also is visible among single-family residences.[5] Thus, it is not only the lower level of local solidarity in apartment houses that keeps the display of national symbols down but also the higher degree of local solidarity, or at least mutual surveillance, in single-family neighborhoods that keep symbolic solidarity display up.

Patriotic display on cars has a similar pattern. Counts of flags are much higher in urban areas than on the open highway; even on the same interstate highway, the rates are much higher passing through a city than in the countryside.[6] The difference is related to the number of pick-up trucks and commercial vans, which are the most likely to carry flags.[7] This might be regarded as a class difference, with the working class and lower-middle class expressing more patriotism, but that is not the pattern found on houses, where upper-middle class neighborhoods have the highest rates of flag display. An alternative explanation is that pick-up trucks are operated by owners of small businesses, as are many commercial vans. These are the kinds of businesses that are most dependent upon a local network of personal acquaintances; thus, it is both to their commercial advantage to show their emblems of conventional solidarity (good for business) and also the display of symbols is facilitated by their group solidarity, just as it is among neighbors well known to each other.

Corroboration comes from a negative case: long-haul trucks (semi-trailers) have a much lower display of flags than any other kind of vehicle, on the order of

---

[5]Thus, the October 26 observation for San Diego: 36 of 83 houses had flags; these tended to cluster in bunches of six to eight in a row, or directly across the street from each other. December 15 observations for Philadelphia: 39 of 158 row houses, of which 20 were adjacent. The pattern was even more apparent over time as the number of flags became sparser. January 3, 2003, San Diego: 23 of 244 (9 percent) had flags, of which 19 were in adjacent clusters. Since I was making observations in the weeks around other traditional festivals, I noted also where Halloween and Thanksgiving symbols were displayed: these also tended to cluster at adjacent houses or closely in sight of each other. A combination of both types of observations comes from January 13, 2003, in Philadelphia: in 18 blocks, there were 4 flags on 340 houses; two other blocks had clusters of American flags, one consisting of 15 of 24 houses, clustered toward the middle of the block, with the flagless houses at the ends. This block also displayed nine other flags, including one German flag and one world peace flag, with the others being "personal"—flags of the kind sometimes flown in upper-middle class houses especially where there are children. The impression was of a contest of flags, between patriots and secularists; two houses (symbolic mediators?) displayed both kinds. The block also was notable in that 21 of 24 houses still had Christmas decorations up three weeks after Christmas, when decorations had disappeared almost everywhere else. A second small cluster occurred in a segment of a block where there were three American flags among five adjacent row houses, with a French flag interspersed.

[6]Five to six percent of vehicles on interstate highways in rural Delaware, Maryland, Virginia, Pennsylvania, and central California; compared to 14–15 percent on these highways in vicinity of Fresno, California, and Philadelphia; October 19–November 4, 2001. These counts exclude semi-trailers.

[7]Combining the time series presented above, pick-up trucks, commercial and official trucks, and vans (excluding semi-trailers) made up 39 percent of all urban Philadelphia vehicles observed displaying flags; 37 percent of all highway displays; 35 percent of all urban California displays; and 29 percent of all displays in rural and suburban recreation areas. These observations should be weighted for numbers of different kinds of vehicles in these settings. I counted a baseline frequency only for the urban Philadelphia observations: 22 percent of vehicles were pick-ups and commercial vehicles. The frequency clearly was not uniform in all settings; commercial vehicles were absent from recreational parking areas and were low on the open highway. Flag display on pick-ups and commercial vehicles is approximately twice as high as the frequency of such vehicles in urban Philadelphia; it seems likely that they are overrepresented by a similar order of magnitude in the other settings as well.

TABLE 5. Flags in Low-Display Neighborhoods		
October 21, 2001	2% (176)	Phila. rowhouses; WC/LMC black neighborhood
Nov. 4	2% (43)	Phila. rowhouses; LC (poverty) black neighborhood
October 21	<2% (175)	Phila. cars parked in WC/LMC black neighborhood (all stickers)
October 23	8% [203]	Phila. rowhouses (university neighborhood)

WC = working class; LMC = lower-middle class.

0.2–0.35 percent.[8] The implication is that social class is not the operative factor, since highway trucks are operated by upper-working-class individuals, or in some cases, lower-middle-class small business owners. Long-haul trucks are operating almost entirely at long distance from home and on the highway are in an anonymous environment. They lack a social community toward which they are displaying, or being recognized as displaying, their national solidarity. The apparent paradox is that solidarity with a large anonymous group is organized largely by displays within smaller more personalized groups. The national identity is sustained by the same structures as personal identities.

There are also places where symbols are not displayed. These too are part of the structuring of social clusters: either places where there is little or no informal solidarity locally so that there is indifference to national symbols, or because local clusters are in opposition to national solidarity. Table 5 shows some places where flags on houses and on cars are much lower than the middle-class residential series already presented.

Black neighborhoods show much lower display of flags, both on houses and cars; impressionistically, it appears to be much lower on stores in black neighborhoods as well (whereas in October 2001 such flags were ubiquitous on stores elsewhere). This is not to say that there was no sense of national solidarity among black Americans after 9/11. My observations include three incidents of explicit black-white solidarity focused on the disaster, all of these incidents in the first two weeks of peak solidarity after the attacks.[9] It appears that black solidarity was not as widespread, nor was it as long lasting as in the white community (see Table 5).

Another type of anomaly is illustrated by the observation of house flags for October 23, 2001, made in an area adjacent to the University of Pennsylvania and heavily populated by university faculty and students. Here the level of display (8 percent) is very low for middle-class areas at this time. Universities stood out as enclaves in opposition to the display of national symbols. This was apparent in conversations as early as the first weekend (observations at a welcoming party September 16—the fifth day—attended by about 80 persons; the 9/11 attacks were virtually absent as a topic of conversation). As noted, emblems on clothing were rare at universities, except when

[8]Observations of approximately 1,800 vehicles on interstate highways in Delaware, Maryland, Virginia, Pennsylvania, October 19–21, 2001. Similar pattern November 10–11, interstate highway in eastern Iowa.

[9]Third day: black lady, dressed in middle-class style, on the train downtown read the newspaper over my shoulder, asked about numbers killed. Eighth day: shoe-shiner discussed with me the dangers of being killed in airplanes but gave no political interpretation. Twelfth day: black taxi driver wearing American flag bandana and jacket engaged me in lengthy conversation about the attacks and said blacks and whites were on the same side now.

worn by secretaries and manual employees; flag emblems on cars were found only in employee parking lots rather than in faculty lots.[10] The main exception was among higher administrators, who tended to wear flag lapel pins, which fit with their orientation toward the outer public rather than toward the university faculty and with their playing the role of institutionally correct symbolic leader.

Yet another type of comparison suggests the importance of social connections in regulating the display of symbols. Rather than those who display no symbols at all, consider those at the opposite end of the spectrum: individuals whom we might call "superpatriots"—those who display symbols in an idiosyncratic fashion that exceeds the normal amount and kind. I have noted several of these kinds of individuals already: the vans decked with flags and banners; blaring patriotic music; the bicyclist with the flag and the "I love NY" sign who circled the downtown square in Philadelphia on the fourth and fifth days before the standard mode of display was established; or the black taxi driver on the 12th day wearing several items of flag clothing. Other instances were a homeless man with flag stickers sewn to his bags (Philadelphia, 25th day); occasional cars with two or more flags plus stickers in windows (e.g., old Cadillac with two flags and two stickers, driven by a middle-aged woman in rather elaborate dress (Baltimore suburb, October 19); a Mercedes-Benz with multiple stickers—including "Prolife"— and a personalized license plate carrying a odd slogan "GITCOWS," driven by an elderly female driver (central California, October 28)). Other people do not emulate or make gestures of solidarity with these individuals, and there are some indications that they are embarrassed by them (e.g., bystanders responded to all of the vehicles circling Rittenhouse Square September 15–16 by looking away). National solidarity quickly falls into a standard pattern of expression, and those who do not follow these patterns are given no support or encouragement. Unlike persons who display the appropriate level of symbolism, these superpatriots do not cluster but instead appear as isolated individuals, making their gestures in an unresponsive world.

Memorial rituals carried the burden of keeping up national consciousness on the conflict-generated solidarity. These included a series of memorial services for the victims collectively and then more distinctively for police officers and firefighters. Here again, the New York City attacks and the firefighters—and to a lesser degree police officers— monopolized the focus of the attention. The one-month memorial (inaccurately called "anniversary") was carried out on October 11 by a moment of silence at the WTC site of clean-up operations and by police in other cities setting off sirens simultaneously. These services were most frequent in the first two months, with well-publicized large services for the WTC dead on October 28 and on November 5 for dead firefighters. National and international political dignitaries attended the two-month commemorative in New York. Further commemoratives were held at three months and six months, although with declining public attention since these were falling into the period when solidarity indicators generally were returning to normal. The last major ceremony was held May 30, 2002, eight and a half months after the attacks, marking the ending of cleanup at the WTC site. (Notably, all the ritualism surrounding clean-up activity was at this

---

[10]A similar observation October 28 in the parking lot of a California resort hotel where a conference of environmental lawyers was taking place: <1 percent flags on cars (319); in contrast the employee parking lot had 10 percent flags (52) (all of these were on pick-up trucks).

site, not at the Pentagon.) The ceremony focused on the firefighters rather than on the mass of victims in the WTC; firefighters in their full-action outfits and helmets carried a flag-draped empty coffin, accompanied by a smaller number of uniformed police. On this occasion, newspapers carried photos of firefighters in churches wearing their helmets—a symbolic reminder of their identity and of its display to the public.

Ceremonials Promoting Revival of Hysteria

A declining sense of conflict solidarity went along with declining significance of memorial ceremonies. However, on special occasions on which great attention again was given to ceremonies, the sense of fear or even of hysteria about enemy attack revived. This was illustrated during the one-year anniversary, September 11, 2002: on this date commemorative ceremonies in New York City, Washington D.C., and the western Pennsylvania crash sites were held, as well as marches and rallies in major cities, drawing sizable crowds with a sudden (if temporary) efflorescence of patriotic symbols, especially wearing red, white, and blue colors. As is generally the case, a high degree of mass participation and attention also was associated with a rise in fear and in hysterical actions. The U.S. government put national security on a condition of "high alert," with war planes patrolling over American cities. At the same time, the government attempted to keep up an atmosphere of normalcy, advising travelers not to cancel travel plans. Nevertheless, air travel fell 30 percent from the expected level. In this condition of heightened tension, two planes were diverted by false alarms—one because two passengers changed seats after takeoff (no doubt because of availability of empty seats) and another because a man shaving was regarded as suspicious for staying in the lavatory too long. These were the same types of overreaction in a collective mood of enhanced attentiveness that characterized the security rituals at the height of solidarity immediately after 9/11.

Conflicts over Solidarity Rituals and Symbols

If rituals generate and sustain solidarity, they also promote conflict. This occurs not simply in the sense that rituals and symbols draw a group together to engage in conflict against its enemy but also in the sense that the ritual itself is a good that becomes an object of contention among those who ostensibly are members of the same side. These internecine conflicts occur chiefly during the height of symbolic mobilization, although some versions occur after the three-month plateau as solidarity is winding down.

When flags proliferated in the week after 9/11, a library director at a university in Florida ordered staff to remove "Proud to be an American" stickers in order not to offend foreign students. An insurance company in Boca Raton (in the heavily Spanish-speaking area of south Florida) prohibited workers from displaying American flags on their desks. These prohibitions were normal manifestations of so-called political correctness, self-suppression of American majoritarian symbols; however, in this early period of intense national solidarity, these actions were criticized hotly by the public and were reversed by higher authorities—the university librarian was reprimanded and was suspended for 30 days without pay (*USA Today* October 4, 2001).

A similar type of conflict is illustrated by the first month commemorative (October 11, 2001). A small group of youths in San Diego, California, put up banners with slogans such as "love" and "peace" on freeway overpasses and across prominent streets. They stated that their motive was to show solidarity with the New York City victims. These banners were removed by other persons (not by the city authorities) and were replaced by American flags. Some critics stated that the love and peace banners were antimilitary and unpatriotic. However one reads this dispute, it shows the operation of social pressure to keep symbolic display in a standard format and the dominance of feelings of moral hostility to symbols that do not take a national form.

A second type of conflict occurred over privileged access to the ritual center. At the WTC site, firefighters not only from New York City but also from elsewhere took part in the search through the ruins; after the first few days this had merely ritualistic significance, as no further victims could be found alive. After an October 28, 2001, memorial service at the site, New York City authorities attempted to convert the cleanup into a more utilitarian process, speeding up by mechanized equipment operated by professionals and reducing the number of firefighters on the site to a token 25 (the number typically had been 100–150 daily). The firefighters reacted angrily, holding mass meetings; their dispute culminated in a violent confrontation on November 2 (seven weeks after the attacks) between firefighters and police over access to the site. News photos showed firefighters wearing their helmets and active duty coats, clearly for symbolic display, since they generally did their cleanup in casual clothing. The city administrators reacted by arresting a dozen firefighters; this in turn led to further demonstrations and angry name-calling, including attacks on Mayor Giuliani, who hitherto had been a sacrosanct figure. It was a precedence struggle between symbolic leaders. The dispute went on for 10 days, finally dying down with a series of compromises, leading to dropped charges but to eventual exclusion of firefighters from the clean-up site.

The so-called Ground Zero site had become the central sacred place for the commemorative cult. It was closed to outsiders, even hidden from view for several months (again, unlike the Pentagon). It was both an object of intense curiosity by ordinary citizens, who filled the streets near the site and a place of privileged access, toured by politicians and important international guests. The firefighters thus had unique access to a sacred place; their presence there was almost totally ritualistic, since professional salvage workers could have done the job more efficiently. The firefighters as a symbolic elite were unwilling to give up their access to what must be regarded as a quasi-religious connection; they had been in the center of action and the center of the symbolic generator of public attention and solidarity. It is doubtful that they consciously regarded themselves as making a claim for status but instead felt a magnetic attraction to what they regarded as a moral calling. This magnetic, emotional impulsion toward getting in the center of attention is operative as well in the process of hysterical attacks and alarms.

A third type of conflict over symbols developed by January and February 2002, as relatives of the WTC victims began to complain publicly about their compensation. In the first flush of solidarity in late September 2001, Congress established a victim compensation fund, and a number of charities vigorously collected voluntary contributions, providing an enthusiastically welcomed opportunity for ordinary citizens to make a gesture of support. As the solidarity plateau began to recede, associations of relatives of victims began to dispute the amounts and terms of compensation; these included rules over degrees of family relationships entitled to compensation (not only spouses and children but also parents, siblings, and other relatives held themselves entitled to compensation, especially where there were no close relatives). These disputes may have involved to a degree merely monetary self-interest, and critics began to charge publicly—as the aura of sacredness around the victims' relatives had begun to dissipate—that they were merely grasping and selfish. Victims' relatives and their lawyers responded with moralistic and sometimes highly emotional statements—often in the vein that the amounts offered (typically $1.5 million) were an insult compared to the actual human worth of the person killed.

Here again, it is appropriate sociologically to view the claims as ritualistic. Relatively distant relatives put in their claims, not generally because they were unable to support themselves without the dead person (this also was the case with many spouses) but instead as a means of establishing connection. Being a relative of a WTC victim is a special status within the national catastrophe, and the denial of compensation is a denial that the connection is a legitimate one. The argument that no amount of money is an adequate measure of the value of a human life of course is a valid one; by the same token, it could be recognized that since there is no monetary equivalent, no money should be offered or taken.[11] Donors and political actors operated both with an image of the relatives as victims undergoing economic hardships and incapable of supporting themselves and with their own ritualized motive to express solidarity by making a contribution to the disaster. These idealized stances gave victims' relatives a wide symbolic field on which to make claims, depicting themselves in the light of helpless orphans while acting aggressively as militants charged up with moral outrage.

A number of organized "survivors" groups (as they came to be known) angrily denounced the government awards for requiring them to relinquish their rights to sue the airlines whose planes had crashed. Again, a tone of moralism clashed with utilitarian considerations: the airlines by this time were in serious financial straits, and some of those who lost planes in the 9/11 crashes went into bankruptcy within the following year. Lawsuits hardly would have helped the public in general and might well be described as a form of blaming the victim. A lawyer countered these charges by arguing on January 10, 2002, that the suits were motivated not by private greed but out of a desire "to know the truth, improve security, and accord accountability."

The collective utilitarian side is dubious, since security already was the subject of intense activity, and many kinds of public and political investigations were under way. What was being aimed at was the special ritualism of a court of law, which turns ordinary events into an authoritative statement of purported final interpretation of facts and of culpability. Suing the airlines follows a standard lawyers' tactic of seeking "deep pockets," the richest targets to sue; in this case, the airlines also were the most easily attackable target, since the terrorists themselves were inaccessible and since airport security companies had too low of a status to bear the brunt of such suits.

Sociologically, lawsuits calling for damages have a ritualistic component, which increases in proportion to the amount of public focus of attention on the case. The more collective solidarity around a destructive event, the more the feeling of legitimacy among those mounting a legal claim to compensation for damages. These suits are presented as if they are in the interest of the public at large (although in fact they may

---

[11]Compare Zelizer's (1994) analysis of how between 1870 and 1930, American children came to be regarded as sacred objects to be valued sentimentally rather than for their contributions as workers, yet a mark of their new social status was the high value put upon them in wrongful death suits and in a new kind of life insurance policies. In the "sentimental economy" of these institutions, the monetary value set on children increased just as their utilitarian market value decreased.

have a practical effect to the contrary, such as by bankrupting or by curtailing services to the public). Here again, the emotional mobilization of collective solidarity creates a zone of public attention, with privileged positions for those nearer the center of it. There are a number of ways of attempting to get oneself closer to the center and to improve one's position in the symbolic hierarchy. Lawsuits based on connections with victims are one form of such striving; the monetary amounts desired are always high, set at levels that are symbolic of the social importance claimed for these proceedings rather than of actual practical damages.

Source: Collins, Randall. (2004). "Rituals of Solidarity and Security in the Wake of Terrorist Attacks," *Sociological Theory*, Volume 22, No. 1, pp. 53–56, 61–64, 70–73. Copyright © 2004. Reprinted by permission of American Sociological Association and John Wiley & Sons.

CHAPTER 6

Hurricane Katrina

The first decade of the 21st century experienced numerous natural and man-made disasters of catastrophic proportion that have destroyed countless lives. These include the 9/11 terrorist attacks on the United States, Hurricane Katrina and several additional major hurricanes in the United States, the Asian tsunami of 2004, the disastrous earthquake in Haiti (2010), the flooding in Pakistan (2010) and the earthquake and tsunami in Japan (2011).

Hurricane Katrina slammed into the United States' Gulf coast on August 29, 2005. It has been described as the most devastating hurricane to hit the U.S. in the past seventy-five years. Within five to six weeks, over 1,200 people were confirmed as dead. It is estimated that over 1,800 people perished during the hurricane. The single largest percentage of the fatalities occurred in the New Orleans area. As many as 100,000 people living in New Orleans required rescue, which was not forthcoming for several days. Additionally, thousands sought refuge in the Superdome (sports arena) and Convention Center. The estimated costs for Katrina-related spending by both the federal government and private insurance companies approximated $190 billion (Horn, 2006).

The year 2010 began with the devastating earthquake on January 12 that rocked Haiti and left an estimated 230,000 people killed, 300,000 injured and 1.5 million displaced. Deborah Sontag (2010) reported six months later that "[o]nly 28,000 of the 1.5 million Haitians displaced by the earthquake have moved into new homes, and the Port-au-Prince area remains a tableau of life in the ruins" (p. A1). Noting that some officials have described the earthquake and its aftermath as the "largest urban disaster in modern history," Sontag's quotation from a young woman who is fortunate to be in a new residence speaks to the urgency of normalizing basic living conditions:

> "Even though I lost my mom in the earthquake, I feel so content, so comfortable and so lucky to have this place," Ketley Louis, 33, said, welcoming visitors into her new home on the site of the old home that collapsed on her mother (p. A1).

Unfortunately, the destructive natural disaster of the Haitian earthquake has been exacerbated by a web of man-made bureaucratic entanglements. It has been reported that, "[n]early nine months after the earthquake, more than a million Haitians still live on the streets between piles of rubble. One reason: Not a cent of the $1.15 billion the U.S. promised for rebuilding has arrived." Additionally, "[s]ome 50 other nations and organizations pledged a total of $8.75 billion for reconstruction, but just $686 million of that has reached Haiti so far—less than 15 percent of the total promised for 2010–11" (Katz and Mendoza, 2010).

On April 20, 2010, an explosion occurred on British Petroleum's *Deepwater Horizon* oil rig in the Gulf of Mexico. Eleven workers were killed and the drilling rig sank on April 22. On several occasions, the U.S. government revised its estimate of the number of barrels pouring into the Gulf, and on June 15, 2010, it estimated that number to be 60,000 barrels of oil a day (Gillis, 2010). As of July 12, 2010, it had been estimated that between 89 million and 176 million gallons of oil were released from the well into the Gulf waters, making it the largest oil spill in American history (Breen and Weber, 2010). President Obama (2010) has described the oil spill as the "worst environmental disaster America has ever faced," and preliminary estimates of cleanup and associated costs have been projected to be at least $12.5 billion.

While one can attempt to quantify the monetary losses to affected industries of the Gulf states, such as tourism and fishing, it is difficult to describe the impact of this disaster on the individuals and families whose livelihoods and traditions have been abruptly interrupted by the spill. Mireya Navarro (2010) profiles the activities of a Katrina survivor, Joycelyn Heintz, who now volunteers as a coordinator at a mental health center in Louisiana, which has opened a "satellite center" to address the needs of fishermen and their families. In the article, Navarro writes:

> Known for their self sufficiency, fishermen would be among the last to admit to mental strain, even if they are losing weight and sleep. But when a charter boat captain in Alabama, William Allen Kruse, took his own life last month, his family and friends called him another victim of the April 20 *Deepwater Horizon* rig explosion (p. A11).

The mental health center also provides much needed support services for both the wives and children of the fishermen. Heintz comments on the generational impact of the spill: "The biggest thing for them is that their children may not be able to fish . . . . We have four or five generations doing this, and now it may possibly end." Commenting on an uncertain future, she further stresses, "Katrina came and went . . . . We don't know when this is going to stop" (p. A11).

While this chapter focuses on Hurricane Katrina, many of the observations and critical comments noted in its readings apply as well to the dynamics associated with other disasters. It is particularly poignant to examine Hurricane Katrina, Haiti and other natural disasters within the sociological paradigm of extreme situations as the products of total institutions. In fact, an inverse dynamic has occurred wherein the extreme situation of the natural disaster has catalyzed an urgent need for an institutional/governmental response. In turn, the extreme situation is transformed by the confluence of bureaucratic characteristics and situational variables that impact the nature of the institutional response. Indeed several readings in this chapter explore the issues surrounding our view of Katrina as a purely natural disaster or as an event "triggered" by natural causes but significantly redefined by socioeconomic and political variables. This position is taken by Patrick Sharkey (2007), who suggests that the disastrous impact of the hurricane was differentially experienced by specific individuals and groups, that is, the elderly and the African American residents of New Orleans. Regarding the elderly victims of Katrina and other disasters, Sharkey points to a combination of their biological vulnerability and resulting "social isolation" from communal support as significant factors in explaining their high death rates. Sharkey also suggests that the disproportionate number of African American victims may very well be related to inveterate discriminatory social attitudes and policies that have situated them in neighborhoods that were more susceptible to the onslaught of the hurricane. The apparent "link" between age, race and natural forces is presented as a "geography of risk" that redefines the events of Katrina as a purely natural disaster.

In their empirical analysis of research data obtained from survivors of Hurricane Katrina, Elliott and Pais (2006) explore the intersection of race and social class as variables impacting different responses to the hurricane. In other words, are class differences or racial differences more significant in explaining behavioral responses, or is neither variable more "prominent" than the other? Notwithstanding the argument that race and class are inextricably intertwined, others have focused on the predominance of social class and the diminution of race as the essential component of understanding human relationships generally, and behavior specific to natural disasters. Others have focused on "cultural" influences that are a product of common racial identity, independent of social class. Elliott and Pais conclude that, "[b]oth 'axes of variation'—race and class—appear to have mattered in response to Hurricane Katrina" (p. 318). Additionally, they offer some interesting observations on the relationship between race, class, gender and mental health after Katrina.

Gail Garfield's (2007) reading evaluates how the media's biased presentation of the behavior of New Orleans's citizens impacted the delivery of essential humanitarian assistance to the victims of the disaster. Specifically, the article quotes extensively from the mainstream media that "detailed" the widespread looting, wanton assaults, murders and rapes that "took place" on the streets, in the Superdome and in the Convention Center. These reports portrayed New Orleans as a city torn apart at its core, where anarchy replaced human civility, morality and social order. In fact, while there was some expected looting and chaos in New Orleans the "[m]edia reports of rampant lawlessness and black criminality were largely untrue" (p. 66). The author argues that the governmental response was significantly influenced by an essentially false media accounting of the critical issues of the day. Garfield concludes that the tragedy of Katrina was in fact, "a compromised social infrastructure that was severely damaged as a result of massive flooding" (p. 67). Furthermore, the governmental response to false media information relegated the delivery of essential emergency services to a position of secondary importance in the shadow of the perceived "need" to reestablish social control.

The last reading in this chapter is the powerful oral history narrative of Kevin Owens, a forty-one-year-old African American male who took refuge with his family in the Superdome. Many of his anecdotal comments highlight the confrontational relationship between the supervisory military personnel and the black citizenry in what he describes as the "prison"-like atmosphere of the Superdome. He notes the preferential treatment given to the few white individuals, the abrupt withholding of food and water from those "imprisoned" in the stadium and the forced separation of family members during the initial stages of the evacuation. Kevin Owens's testimony is a plea for social justice for those who survived the *natural* forces of Katrina, but soon became the victims of the *social* forces of prejudice and institutionalized racism that destroyed individual self-esteem, communal relationships and aspirations for the future. Many of Owens's observations and experiences are an affirmation of the empirical analysis presented in several of this chapter's readings.

The concluding comments in this reading noted by the book's editors, Penner and Ferdinand (2009), highlight the long-term trauma experienced by survivors of Katrina, many of whom are now dispersed throughout the United States. Their focus on the breakdown of African American family and communal structures and networks as products of Katrina's destruction should be framed by another of this chapter's reading (Elliott and Pais's) that examines the relative importance of race and class in shaping "social differences" in human responses to disaster.

As an addendum to Frederick Owens's comments regarding the "criminalizing" of Katrina's victims, the following news item was reported on July 14, 2010:

> Four current and two former New Orleans police officers have been charged in connection with the killing of unarmed civilians on the Danziger Bridge in the chaotic days after Hurricane Katrina, federal law enforcement officials announced . . . . The Danziger case is the most high-profile of at least eight incidents involving New Orleans police officers that are being actively investigated by federal law enforcement officials. The case became a flashpoint, in the city and throughout the nation, a symbol of the violence, disorder and official ineptitude in the storm's wake (Robertson, 2010).

On August 6, 2011, Robertson reported on the verdict in the Danziger Bridge tragedy:

> In a verdict that brought a decisive close to a case that has haunted this city since most of it lay underwater nearly six years ago, five current and former New Orleans police officers were found guilty on all counts by a federal jury on Friday for shooting six citizens, two of whom died, and orchestrating a wide-ranging cover-up in the hours, weeks and years that followed.
>
> The defendants were convicted on 25 counts, including federal civil rights violations in connection with the two deaths, for the violence and deception that began on the Danziger Bridge in eastern New Orleans on Sept. 4, 2005, just days after Hurricane Katrina hit and the levees failed (Robertson, 2011).

RACE, CLASS, AND HURRICANE KATRINA: SOCIAL DIFFERENCES IN HUMAN RESPONSES TO DISASTER

James R. Elliott and Jeremy Pais

Introduction

The devastating and seemingly arbitrary nature of disasters such as Hurricane Katrina can reinforce the popular notion that such events are random in their social dimensions. After all, if the physical infrastructure of our communities cannot withstand such catastrophe, how can the social infrastructure that also gives them shape?

Countering this perspective is the view that natural disasters actually provide an ideal setting in which to examine core dimensions of social life. In fact, during the early days of disaster research, Merton (1969, xi) observed that, "sociological theory and research not only helps us to identify and to understand what goes on when disaster strikes but also, conversely, the investigation of these phenomena can extend sociological theories of human behavior and social organization." In this way, hurricanes and other calamities offer "strategic research sites" for sociological inquiry.

Within this scholarly vein, a growing body of research has begun to document how social identities and resources shape human responses to natural disasters (for reviews, see Drabek, 1986; Peacock et al., 1997). While diverse and relatively new, this literature, along with that emerging around issues of environmental justice, builds from the core premise that communities and regions are not homogeneous, unified systems but rather mosaics of overlapping subsystems cross-cut by social and economic inequalities. Within these subsystems, individuals and families make sense of the threats posed by environmental hazards and respond to them in ways reflective of varying social and economic resources at their disposal. The primary objective of this paper is to contribute to this line of research by examining the extent to which racial and class differences influenced human responses to Hurricane Katrina—the costliest natural disaster ever to hit the United States.

This inquiry is consistent with a core principle of contemporary social scientific research on disasters. This principle, outlined by Klinenberg (2002, 23–24) and tracing to classic observations by Mauss and Durkheim, is that extreme events such as Hurricane Katrina offer "an excessiveness which allows us better to perceive the facts than in those places where, although no less essential, they still remain small-scale and involuted" (Mauss, [1916]/1979). Our research focuses specifically on the "social facts" of racial and class differences in the Gulf South before and immediately following Hurricane Katrina.

Background

Race, Class, and Disaster

Prior research leads us to expect that although residents of the Gulf South share a common region, their responses to Hurricane Katrina varied in non-random ways reflective of racial and class divisions that have taken root and grown in the area over time (for a review see Fothergill et al., 1999). In the present paper, we treat this expectation as a matter for empirical investigation. Focusing specifically on race and class, we ask which, if either, dimension of social life most differentiated human responses to

Hurricane Katrina before and shortly after it hit the Gulf coast. Logically, the answer to this question can take one of three general forms: (1) class differences were more prominent than racial differences; (2) racial differences were more prominent than class differences; or (3) neither dimension was more prominent. We review grounds for each hypothesis below.

Hypothesis 1: Class Differences Were More Prominent than Racial Differences

For decades, social scientists have debated which is more salient for explaining observed inequalities in the US society: race or class? They have also wrestled with whether this "race versus class" framework is too simplistic for understanding the intricacies of social inequality, since race and class, while analytically distinct, constitute overlapping systems of social stratification that remain experientially entangled and causally circular. Our position is that both approaches—the analytically simple and the theoretically cautious—are useful: the first for identifying basic patterns of variation; the second for interpreting them.

From this starting point, perhaps the most influential work in the "race-class" debate is Wilson's (1978) *The Declining Significance of Race*. In this work Wilson argues that by the 1970s blacks' status in the US society had become largely a function of economic resources rather than race and racism, as in the past. This historic shift, Wilson contends, derived from a number of social and political developments (declines in white bigotry, the Civil Rights Act, affirmative action), which now allow growing numbers of blacks to pursue and attain professional, middle-class status. The catch, Wilson points out, is that as this change has occurred, it has also produced the un-intended consequence of a poor black "under-class," which has become socially and culturally isolated from mainstream society as jobs, taxes, and upwardly mobile blacks have left historically black ghettos. The plight of this new "underclass," Wilson argues, is not a contemporaneous function of racial antipathy but rather a function of concen-trated poverty that operates through a host of non-racialized mechanisms, from under-funded school districts, to ineffective job networks, to inappropriate role models.

Although Wilson's thesis has generated much debate and complex analyses, the analytical implication is straightforward. In research that Wilson calls "the best contri-bution to the race–class debate in the past two decades," Conley (1999. 7. 23) explains that. "It is not race per se that matters directly; instead, what matters are wealth levels and class positions that are associated with race in America," and "It just happens that the class structure overlays very well onto skin color, which is a lot more visible than someone's investment portfolio." To support this claim, Conley analyzed longitudinal data from the Panel Study of Income Dynamics. He found that after statistically con-trolling for class differences in family background, racial differences on a wide array of social indicators—from educational attainment to employment outcomes to wel-fare dependence—actually "disappeared," that is, they became statistically negligible, leaving class standing as the more salient, or direct, cause of observed differences and inequalities.

This "class-trumps-race" perspective also appears in recent research on hurri-cane response. For example, in their study of Hurricane Andrew, which hit the Miami area in 1992, Peacock and Girard (1997, 173) explain that, "Minorities, particularly Black households, are disproportionately located in poor-quality housing segregated into low-valued neighborhoods. This segregation creates *communities of fate* (Logan and Molotch, 1987; Stinchcombe, 1965) that can take on added salience in a disaster context." The authors go on to explain that, "Race and ethnicity are linked to housing quality—not because of ethnically based cultural variations in housing preferences . . . but because race and ethnicity are still important determinants of economic resources, such as income and credit, critical for obtaining housing." Similarly Gladwin and Peacock (1997, 66) contend that, when faced with hurricane warnings, "Ethnic minorities are less likely to evacuate than Anglos . . . probably as a result of economic conditions rather than race or ethnicity per se." In other words race "matters" but through more proximate, or direct, factors associated with class resources.

This perspective is echoed in Molotch's (2005) commentary on events immediately following Hurricane Katrina. Answering his own opening question, "Would so many white people struggling for life be ignored for so long?" Molotch writes that, "Racism explains some of what went on, but its route was indirect." Raising several possibilities, Molotch explains that, "One of the race-based explanations is that those left behind are consistently the most deprived. The legacy of slavery, exclusion, and segregation corrals those with least resources into a vulnerable space, natural, and economic."

Commenting on the same events in the wake of Hurricane Katrina, Reed (2005, 31), a political scientist, put matters more bluntly. "Granted, the images projected . . . seemed to cry out a stark statement of racial inequality. But that's partly because in the contemporary US, race is the most familiar language of inequality or injustice. It's what we see partly because it's what we're accustomed to seeing, what we look for." Reed (2005, 31) goes on to assert that,

> [C]lass—as income, wealth, and access to material resources, including a safety net of social connections—was certainly a better predictor than race of who evacuated [New Orleans] before the hurricane, who was able to survive the storm itself, who was warehoused in the Superdome or convention center or stuck without food and water on the parched overpasses, who is marooned in Houston or elsewhere, and whose interests will be factored into the reconstruction of the city, who will be able to return.

Reed and others from this perspective are not arguing that racial differences are inconsequential to human behavior and outcomes, even in times of natural disaster. Instead, they are asserting that what *look* like racial differences are more fundamentally class differences that are difficult to see without informed analysis. Supporting this perspective is the reality that thousands of working-class whites in St. Bernard Parish also suffered terribly from Hurricane Katrina. However, sparse settlement, difficult surface access, and imposition of a military no-fly zone helped to render their plight less visible to national media following the storm, thereby magnifying *apparent* racial divisions in human response to the storm and its immediate aftermath.

Hypothesis 2: Racial Differences Were More Prominent than Class Differences

Critics of the "class" perspective contend that although economic resources certainly influence individual opportunities and outcomes, racial differences persist and shape how people organize, interpret, and respond to opportunities and outcomes around them. From this perspective, emphasis falls less on material differences among individuals and more on distinctive affiliations, institutions, and world views that inform modes of thinking and knowing and doing. We might call this influence loosely "culture."

In writing about the role of culture in human response to natural disaster, Erikson (1976) explains that in addition to shaping how people think, act and feel, culture influences what people will *imagine*, and one of the persistent curiosities of human life is that the same mind that imagines a cultural form also tends to imagine (i.e., "creates") its opposite. "Thus" Erikson (1976, 82) asserts, "the idea and its counterpart become natural partners in the cultural order of things, setting up . . . an *axis of variation* that cuts through the center of a culture's space and draws attention to the diversities arrayed along it." In this way, Erikson (1976, 82) explains, "the term 'culture' refers not only to the customary ways in which a people induce conformity in behavior and outlook but the customary ways in which they organize diversity."

In US society, especially the Deep South, few "axes of variation" are as salient as racial identities, especially those contrasting white from black. Research continues to show that while white bigotry and overt discrimination may be on the decline, close friendships, neighborhoods, churches, and social clubs remain highly segregated by race (for a review at the national level, see Anderson and Massey, 2001). These divisions are important for understanding human response to natural disasters because people respond to disasters not as isolated individuals but as members of these overlapping forms of social affiliation, which interpret, affirm and support particular definitions and responses to the situation. Moreover, research shows that these social units, particularly the family, are not restricted to local life but also influence extra-local networks called upon in times of crisis. Morrow (1997, 143), for example, likens the family unit in times of disaster to "an octopus extending its tentacles outward to connect with other social units." She also explains that whether these tentacles are called "social webs" (Drabek et al., 1975), "defenses in depth" (Hill and Hansen, 1962), or "institutional and kinship embeddedness" (Bolin, 1982), they remain critical for determining human perception and response to natural disasters. They also remain racially divided and thus potentially differentiating in their operation and effects.

One example of this difference lies in how blacks and whites understand race itself. Research has long shown that blacks think and talk about race much more often than whites, in part because whites have difficulty recognizing the privilege that their skin color generally affords them in the US society (see Brown et al., 2003). Moreover, blacks of high class standing often maintain a higher level of distrust of mainstream institutions than their white or even low-income, black counterparts. Cose (1995), for example, details how black professionals, despite their class standing, are commonly frustrated and enraged by racism in contemporary America. From this perspective, it is unsurprising that Kanye West, a wealthy pop star, who also happens to be black, seized the opportunity during a televised fund raiser for Hurricane Katrina victims to proclaim to the nation that, "[President] George Bush doesn't like black people."

For our purposes, the veracity of West's claim is unimportant. What matters is the fact that even if racial hatred ceases, persistent social patterns can endure over time, affecting whom we marry, where we live, what we believe, and so forth. These patterns, in turn, bind racial subgroups across class lines, helping to forge common responses to life events, including natural disasters, in ways that differ from racial "others" in the same region. From this perspective, "communities of fate" are bound as much by racial experiences and affiliations as by common material resources. This is not to say that class differences are unimportant, but rather that in times of crisis, class differences are likely to shrink and racial differences expand as individuals define, interpret and respond to the situation before them.

Hypothesis 3: Class and Racial Differences Were Equally Prominent

A final possibility is that racial and class differences mattered equally in short-term responses to Hurricane Katrina either because neither mattered or because both mattered to more or less the same degree. The first possibility will serve as our null hypothesis. The second can be interpreted as providing weak support to the "race" perspective, since the "class" perspective asserts that economic differences are more proximate, or direct, determinants of human response than racial differences. Thus, if both factors appear to be equally influential, this would suggest that race matters *in addition* to class, not because of strong correlation between the two.

Issues of Environmental Justice

During recent years this "race–class" debate has become particularly acute in the emergent literature on environmental justice. In this literature, researchers begin with the common and well-documented observation that low-income minority communities bear a disproportionate share of environmental hazards in our society, particularly when it comes to the siting of toxic facilities (e.g., Bryant and Mohai, 1992; Bullard, 1990; Szasz, 1993). They then proceed to disagree over the primary cause of these patterns. On the "race" side of the debate, scholars who charge "environmental racism" contend that industry and government officials locate environmental hazards in low-income, minority communities because these communities lack the social, political, and economic power to resist such treatment. On the "class" side of the debate, scholars counter that low-income minority communities often emerge and solidify around environmental hazards because property values are lower and opportunities for home ownership greater than in other parts of town (e.g., Been, 1994; Been and Gupta, 1997). Under the first scenario, the key mechanism is racial discrimination in siting; under the second scenario, it is economic inequalities and market pressures that encourage "minority move-in" (Pastor et al., 2001).

In the Gulf South, researchers have documented ample evidence of both processes in the siting and development of toxic facilities (see Roberts and Toffolon-Weiss, 2001). However, as Hurricane Katrina attests, these are not the only environmental hazards in the region. In addition to polluting industries and toxic landfills, the region has long been spatially uneven with respect to elevation and flood protection, especially in and around the city of New Orleans. This unevenness, however, has never neatly conformed to racial or economic lines.

During the early 1900s, for example, the development and proliferation of new pumping stations allowed developers to drain and build new communities in New Orleans' traditional "low-land swamps" at the historic rear of the city, where significant African-American neighborhoods subsequently grew and solidified despite high vulnerability to flooding and levee failure. The same system of environmental modifications also enabled middle-class whites to expand toward the city's northern lakefront, where they used restrictive covenants to block African-Americans from the newly drained but still low-lying, and thus vulnerable, subdivisions abutting Lake Pontchartrain. Similar modifications later facilitated residential expansion into St. Bernard Parish, where working-class whites have since developed a strong and lasting attachment to land that remains largely below sea-level and compromised environmentally by the Mississippi River-Gulf Outlet (a.k.a. "Mr. Go"), a 76 mile navigational channel cut through local wetlands to permit large-hulled ships that now rarely traverse it.

These historic and geographic developments mean that exposure to the environmental hazards of hurricanes and flooding, while geographically uneven throughout the region (see Logan, 2006), are not race- or class-exclusive. Large numbers of affluent and working-class whites and blacks all lost homes, jobs and community when Hurricane Katrina hit and the levees failed.

Post-disaster Coping: Stress

When such disasters do occur, individuals understandably become stressed, and prior research suggests that this stress tends to be higher in technological disasters than in natural disasters (Erikson, 1994; Freudenberg, 1997; Norris et al., 2001). This pattern is pertinent to Hurricane Katrina because many observers now view events within the City of New Orleans as primarily a technological disaster (levee failure) and events outside the city as primarily a natural disaster (wind, rain, and storm-surge destruction). To the extent that this general distinction is meaningful, which some dispute (Alexander, 1993; Quarantelli, 1998), it would suggest that New Orleanians may experience greater post-disaster stress than residents outside the city.

To test this hypothesis, we modify our analytical approach slightly. Instead of stratifying analyses by New Orleans residence, we pool all respondents and include city residence as an explanatory variable (1 = New Orleans City resident; 0 = otherwise). Because evacuation timing, home damage and job status (non/employed) can affect stress levels as well, we also include these variables in our models as statistical controls, in addition to age, gender and parental status. We fit each model using ordinary least squares regression, which treats the dependent variable as a continuous measure ranging from low to high stress.

Results for all three indicators of stress (current, short-term, and long-term) . . . are remarkably consistent. They show that race, not class, has a strong influence on post-disaster stress associated with Hurricane Katrina, with blacks generally reporting higher stress levels than whites, all else being equal. Moreover, this racial difference increases the further into the future respondents are asked to look. For example, the average black white differential in stress is greater when respondents are asked to look five years ahead (0.20) than when they are asked to look only a few months ahead (0.15).

To place these findings in context, prior research on stress and mental health has produced inconsistent evidence of racial and ethnic differences (for a review, see Schnittker and McLeod, 2005; Vega and Rumbaut, 1991). So the findings reported here are not necessarily reflective of greater stress among racial minorities generally. Instead, they appear to be regionally and event specific. However, they also lend support to Kessler's (1979, p. 259) general assertion that, "Socially disadvantaged persons will be both more highly exposed to stressful experiences and also more highly influenced by stressful experiences than socially advantaged persons." In Kessler's study, this claim was supported by the finding that racial minorities were much more likely than whites to report "extreme distress" in times of crisis. In our analyses, it is supported by the consistency of blacks' reports of greater stress than whites following Hurricane Katrina.

In addition to these findings, results also reveal no significant difference in stress between New Orleanians and other affected respondents, all else equal. This statistically non-significant finding suggests that the technological/natural disaster distinction may be irrelevant to stress levels associated with Hurricane Katrina, at least over the short term. However, research by Picou et al. (2004) suggests that this situation could change over coming years, especially if levee failures in the city eventually lead to protracted litigation and personal time with attorneys, both of which they find contribute significantly to post-disaster stress.

In addition to these core concerns, findings for our control variables also indicate several patterns worth acknowledging: women report more stress than men following the storm, as do parents, residents with severely damaged housing, those not yet back home, and those without jobs. Results also indicate that, all else equal, residents who evacuated express more concern about the future than those who did not evacuate, perhaps raising important issues for future evacuation planning.

Conclusion

Like other disasters before it, Hurricane Katrina offers a unique laboratory in which to study the social infrastructure of its affected region. In this case, it is a region crosscut by deep and complex divisions of race and class that have hardened over time without direct, excessive interference from outsiders. As media images streamed from the region to the nation and the world following the storm, a public debate emerged over the relative importance of class and race for shaping individual, as well as institutional, responses to the disaster. In the absence of hard data, this debate came to sound much like a skit famously performed by Richard Pryor. In this skit, the comedian tells the story of his wife coming home to find him in bed with another woman. Incredulous, Pryor leaps from the mattress, denies the scene, and blurts, "Come on, baby, who're ya gonna believe, me or your own lying eyes?" As television screens filled hour after hour, day after day, with images of black Americans desperate for assistance after the storm, many viewers could not help but "see" race and racism at work. Others explained that their eyes were lying to them, and that what looked like race was in fact class in disguise. As commonly occurs in such situations, however, the vigor and volume of this debate soon dwarfed the quantity and quality of information available to assess it.

In the present study, we have sought to fill some of this empirical gap by using data from the largest, most comprehensive survey of Hurricane Katrina survivors currently available. This source cannot determine why the levees failed in New Orleans or why government officials took so long to respond, but it can begin to answer questions about how residents themselves responded to the nation's costliest natural disaster during and shortly after it occurred. Overall, results indicate that both race and class played important roles in shaping these responses and that neither can be readily reduced to the other. Thus the real issue is not either/or but where and to what degree.

With respect to race, there are two broad areas where racial differences seem to have mattered. The first involves timing of evacuation and sources of emotional support, that is, behavior more or less under the control of individuals themselves. Our findings indicate that blacks across the region were less inclined than whites to evacuate before the storm mostly because they did not believe that the hurricane would be as devastating as it eventually was. Previous experience and public assurances suggest that this personal risk assessment may not have been as irrational as it now appears. Reports indicate that had the levees been built and inspected with the integrity typically expected of the Army Corps of Engineers, they would have likely survived the storm, sparing the city from the massive flooding that eventually covered 80% of its area.

As for emotional support, our findings indicate that blacks and whites differed, at least over the short term. Specifically, blacks were more likely to report "leaning on the lord" while whites were more likely to report relying on friends and family. We have suggested that this difference might be more a matter of interpretation and world view than actual differences in network support. Another possibility is that blacks' friends and family were more likely to be adversely affected by the storm and even more widely dispersed than whites', making them more a source of concern than support. Both scenarios could easily have worked together to produce the strong racial differences observed throughout the region.

The second and more troubling set of racial difference involves something largely outside survivors' control, namely job security. Our findings indicate that black workers from New Orleans were four times more likely than white counterparts to lose their jobs after the storm, all else equal. But of course, all else is not equal. When we factor income differences and their effects into the equation, results indicate that the "average" black worker in New Orleans is actually closer to seven times more likely to have lost his or her job than the "average" white worker. This disparity will certainly have a strong effect on who is able to return to the city as it rebuilds and who is not.

This issue of return is also where class standing, specifically home ownership, exhibits its strongest and most consistent effect. We suspect that this effect cuts two ways. On the one hand, home ownership provides survivors power over when and to what extent personal return and rebuilding will occur; on the other hand, it can also create a financial weight in the form of mortgage obligations that limit resettlement options elsewhere. This interpretation is supported by the consistent effects of home ownership across the region and by aggregate analyses which indicate that less affluent homeowners are more likely to say they will return than more affluent homeowners. This pattern is also consistent with findings from Hurricane Andrew in the Miami area during 1992. In reflecting on the post-storm plight of many low-income homeowners, Morrow (1997, 168) explained that, "While they may have acquired some of the trappings associated with economic success, they may lack the 'defense in depth'—the economic security, political and social influence, and personal power of the professional classes which can be especially crucial in times of crisis."

Overall, these findings refute the apparent randomness of natural disasters as social events as well as the notion that racial differences are somehow reducible to more "fundamental" class divisions when considering human responses to such disasters. Both "axes of variation"—race and class—appear to have mattered in response to Hurricane Katrina, and while the entire region will continue to require the nation's ongoing support for years to come, results here indicate that it is low-income homeowners in particular who will need the most assistance in putting their lives and the region back together again. This will be especially true for black residents of New Orleans, who are the most likely to need new jobs as the city recovers, revives, and rebuilds. Failing this targeted assistance, mortgage foreclosures and precarious employment opportunities threaten not only working-class residents from the region but also the futures of children and grandchildren for whom they still care.

In addition to these and related assistance programs, more general efforts to improve policy and planning initiatives for future disasters may benefit from considering the following possibilities. First, with respect to evacuation, our results affirm that poor inner-city residents are often the least likely to heed formal evacuation warnings, some because they lack transportation and others because they fail to take such warnings seriously. Our findings regarding the centrality of religious faith for racial minorities, women, and the elderly coupled with the negative association of this centrality for early evacuation, suggest that emergency planning initiatives can be improved by assisting local civic and faith-based organizations in developing a coordinated, grass-roots system of hazards education and warning dissemination. The basic idea would be to buttress top-down warnings with ongoing planning and preparedness orchestrated through trusted local associations, similar to how school teachers help to educate and evacuate their own groups of students when an ominous but distant fire bell sounds and the entire school must evacuate. At a regional level, such efforts would require a great deal of organizational creativity, money, and time, but if communities are serious about disaster mitigation and saving lives, such investments seem well worth the expense, effectively reinforcing official proclamations in times of emergency with bottom-up planning and social organization.

Second, after the evacuation is over and residents begin returning to the damaged region, housing and jobs are critical to individual and community recovery, almost by definition. While such adjustments produce stress, secondary results from our analyses also indicate that the mere act of evacuation can create high levels of anxiety about the future, regardless of one's job and housing situation. In the case of New Orleans, this heightened anxiety has taken many anecdotal forms, from (even heavier) drinking and swearing to (even greater) gun purchases and racial paranoia. While it is difficult to pinpoint how or when to intervene to ameliorate such stress and its myriad manifestations, one possibility might be to rethink how military personnel are deployed and organized in post-disaster settings. Borrowing concepts and practices from community policing, one could imagine a proliferation of local substations or mobile command units that integrate themselves into respective neighborhoods over the first six to twelve months following initial search and rescue operations. Through the cultivation of sustained and highly localized relations with residents in the region, these substations could help to serve as well as protect, while simultaneously minimizing the distressful sense of living in an occupied territory, which the passing of anonymous military vehicles and the hovering of distant aircraft helped to produce after Hurricane Katrina.

Surely these will not be the last or only policy lessons proffered in the wake of the Hurricane Katrina, but one thing does appear certain: How the nation responds to this current and ongoing problem will help to define it not only as a society but as a civilization capable of communal expression of awakened conscience.

HURRICANE KATRINA: THE MAKING
OF UNWORTHY DISASTER VICTIMS

Gail Garfield

In late August 2005, Hurricane Katrina swept across the Florida, Alabama, Mississippi, and Louisiana Gulf coastline. On August 29, the eye of the storm settled over New Orleans. Water surges in excess of 10 ft high breached levee walls designed to protect this low-lying city, which sits below sea level, from the surrounding waters of Lake Pontchartrain, the Mississippi River, Lake Borgne, and the Gulf of Mexico. In the wake of Hurricane Katrina, floodwaters covered almost 80% of the "Crescent City."

Hurricane Katrina's arrival in New Orleans and her destructive nature were anticipated by government officials. Federal, state, and local government agencies had all predicted disaster scenarios for New Orleans in the event of a severe hurricane and developed emergency management plans, in an attempt to mitigate the harm a major storm would hold for city residents.[1] In fact, the Federal Emergency Management Agency (FEMA) held a simulation exercise in Baton Rouge, LA, in 2004. This exercise, called Hurricane Pam, was attended by more than 250 officials from all levels of government, and predicted a social catastrophe for New Orleans, if a major hurricane struck the city.

Alerted to Katrina's potential dangers and aware of New Orleans historical vulnerability to flooding, Mayor Ray Nagin understood that the city was "facing a storm that most of us have long feared" and recognized the potential for an "unprecedented event" (Russell 2005). However, the mayor was reluctant to issue a mandatory evacuation order because he feared legal liability. The city could face lawsuits from the business community, especially from those businesses in the tourist [trade], if there was a needless disruption to industry services due to a mandatory evacuation.[2] So, less than 24 h before Hurricane Katrina hit landfall, on August 28th, Mayor Nagin ordered the first mandatory evacuation in the history of New Orleans. But this delay as well as delays by other government officials, particularly in the aftermath of Hurricane Katrina, would prove fateful for many New Orleanians.

Prior to Hurricane Katrina's arrival, 67% of New Orleans' population of more than 450,000 was African Americans. Of the total, 28% of the city residents were living in poverty. Overwhelmingly, African Americans were among New Orleans poorest citizens. When Mayor Nagin ordered a mandatory evacuation "more than one in three black households in New Orleans (35%)—and nearly 3 in 5 poor black households

---

[1]James Carney, et al., (September 19, 2005) reported that "hundreds of regional and federal officials" had met in Baton Rouge. Louisiana to stage a hurricane simulation exercise called "Hurricane Pam," where the city of New Orleans would be covered with 10 ft of water. This simulation, sponsored by FEMA, "looked a lot like Katrina," and the report that followed "warns that transportation would be a major problem." In an article entitled, "Four Places Where the System Broke Down," (p. 41). Also, this training simulation was published in a five-part series of articles entitled "Washing Away" by McQuaid and Schleifstein for the *Times-Picayune* newspaper in New Orleans as early as June 2002. The actual plan was entitled, "Southeast Louisiana Catastrophic Hurricane Functional Plan."

[2]Carney et al. (p. 41).

(59%)—lacked a vehicle."[3] Hence, many poor black New Orleanians were unable to comply with the evacuation order. As Congressman James Clyburn (D-SC) aptly noted in a newspaper interview:

> It is one thing to receive a warning to get out and it is something else to have the ability to get out. If you do not have an automobile or some other mode of transportation, just because you are ordered to evacuate doesn't mean you have the capacity to evacuate. . . . I think that is why we see the faces on our television screens of mostly low income, black people because these are people who don't have the capacity to respond or to evacuate (Bannerman 2005).

For those who were able bodied and wanted to leave but had no private means of transportation, city buses were dispatched to twelve locations to ferry people to the designated "refuge of last resort."[4] They were taken to New Orleans Superdome. When more than 20,000 residents occupied this site, another 15,000 were allowed to ride out the storm at the Ernest M. Morial Convention Center. Both sites were ill equipped to accommodate basic shelter needs of food, water, and sanitation for the thousands who had gathered there.

Even so, they were a bit better off than the thousands of other stranded residents. For those who were the most vulnerable and should have been designated as a priority in an emergency evacuation—those who were incapacitated due to age, mental and physical disability, sickness and illness, or institutionally confined—no buses or other means of public transportation were dispatched to ferry them out of harm's way. The city's emergency evacuation strategy was aimed at those who either had cars or access to private transportation, while those who did not were stranded. No one knows for sure how many people were trapped in New Orleans on August 29 when Hurricane Katrina made landfall. However, we now know with certainty that those left in the city to face Hurricane Katrina's fury were overwhelming black and poor.

Hurricane Katrina was a natural disaster. The scope and severity of impact has made her one of the strongest storms ever recorded to sweep across the Gulf Coast region. Many lives were forever changed because of the death, damage and destruction during and following her wake. But in New Orleans, Katrina was not the major cause of the real human tragedy—the social catastrophe—visited especially upon the lives of poor black New Orleanians. For those stranded, their misery, suffering, despairs, and in to many instances death—following the breach of the levees and massive flooding—was not due solely to the working of nature. Instead, "man-made" events contributed to the indignities and deplorable conditions that many of the city's most vulnerable and needy residents would find in the immediate aftermath of Hurricane Katrina.

---

[3]Based on 2000 Census data, this assessment comes from a report by Arloc Sherman and Isaac Shapiro, (September 19, 2005) entitled "Essential Facts about the Victims of Hurricane Katrina" that was prepared for the Center on Budget and policy Priorities (p. 2).

[4]But there were no buses to ferry people out of New Orleans. In fact, as *Time* reported "a fleet of several hundred buses was left to languish in a lot that eventually flooded" (p. 41).

Those "man-made" events were deeply rooted in a body of myths that describes how people behave in the face of extreme disasters.[5] Such myths are known as "disaster mythology," and they not only influence public perceptions of what occurs during disasters, but also influence the views that shape the emergency response to disasters. The validity of established myths—such as those related to evacuation, panic, and looting behavior as well as official response that includes martial law and shelter utilization—have been disproved by noted disaster researchers in well-documented social science studies (Clarke 2002; Fischer 1998; McPhail 1991; Quarantelli and Dynes 1972; Tierney 2003).

But, as Tierney et al. (2006) point out in a recent article on Hurricane Katrina, disaster myths are not problematic simply because they are untrue. Rather, they are a problem because erroneous ideas can influence the focus and direction of the emergency response to disasters. Misguided and misleading responses informed by myths can exacerbate what occurs during disasters, thereby creating greater injury and harm as a result. Yet disaster myths persist. And in the case of New Orleans, "disaster mythology" would have a tremendous impact and hold important implications for the experiences of many poor blacks, especially those stranded in the city.

In the wake of Hurricane Katrina, a dominant disaster myth emerges. That myth, Tierney argues, characterized the behavior of stranded Hurricane Katrina victims as antisocial or deviant.[6] Furthermore, she suggests that the dominance of this myth converged with and was further bolstered by race, class, and gender stereotypes that have historically constructed lawlessness as common or typical behavior for African Americans, particularly poor black males. Following Katrina, the importance of this intersection between disaster myth and stereotypic behavior was profound: those who were stranded in New Orleans were portrayed in mass media and treated by government officials as criminals. Building upon Tierney's basic contention, I argue that by criminalizing disaster victims, their humanity and the value of their lives were rendered invisible. As such, by socially constructing Hurricane Katrina victims as criminals, the perception of unworthy disaster victims was created.

In the immediate aftermath of Hurricane Katrina, rampant black criminality was reported in news accounts. Those media portrayals, in turn, influenced the emergency response offered by government officials, whereby decisions were made largely in reaction to perceptions of widespread lawlessness. And, the emergency response—framed

---

[5]Disaster Researcher Henry Fischer has documented the effects of "disaster mythology" in shaping perceptions about how people behave and what happens during a disaster. His research focuses on such myths as: panic flight, looting, price gouging, martial law, psychological dependency, disaster shock, evacuation behavior, shelter use, and death, injury, and damage estimates. As his findings indicate, myths involving these areas of inquiry persist despite empirical evidence to the contrary. Fischer, H. (1998) Response to Disaster: Fact versus Fiction and Its Perpetuation. New York: University Press of American, Inc.

[6]Focusing on the ways media reproduced disaster myths in the aftermath of Hurricane Katrina, Tierney outlines several phases: "initial media coverage of Katrina's devastating impacts was quickly replaced by reporting that characterized disaster victims as opportunistic looters and violent criminals and that presented individual and group behavior following the Katrina disaster through the lens of civil unrest. Later, narratives shifted again and began to metaphorically represent the disaster-stricken city of New Orleans as a war zone and to draw parallels between the conditions in that city and urban insurgency in Iraq. These media frames helped guide and justify actions undertaken by military and law enforcement entities that were assigned responsibility for the post disaster emergency response. The overall effect of media coverage was to further bolster arguments that only the military is capable of effective action during disasters." Tierney et al (2006), "Metaphors Matter: Disaster Myths, Media Frames, and Their Consequences in Hurricane Katrina." *The Annals of the American Academy of Political and Social Science*, 604, p. 3.

largely within the context of "urban warfare"—was aimed at restoring law-and-order to a city that was widely perceived as being under siege from "criminal insurgents." This article focuses on the ways African Americans were portrayed in media accounts and the actions taken by government officials in response to those portrayals, as it examines how "man-made" events created the perception of unworthy disaster victims.

There are many different contextual and analytical narratives by which to examine the indignities and deplorable conditions stranded Hurricane Katrina's victims experienced, given the enormity of the human tragedy that occurred and continue to shape the lives of many poor black New Orleanians. This article, however, will focus on what happened over a one-week period: from August 29, 2006, when Hurricane Katrina made landfall in New Orleans, to September 5, 2006, when many of those left behind were finally able to leave the city. Specifically, it will examine two related social contexts that deconstructs and diminishes the value of black life: First, how the humanity of Hurricane Katrina victims was compromised through distorted media portrayals, such as "dangerous looters," "gun-toting killers," "rapists," "out-of-control crazed mob" and that of "marauding thugs." And, next, how those representations of criminality justified the [increased] use of a militaristic response that emphasized social order over humanitarian efforts in response to the needs and aspirations of black disaster victims.

Media Portrayal: The Social Construction of "Feral Fanaticism"

For most people, mass media is the primary source of public information during disasters, especially prior to, during the initial impact, and in the immediate aftermath or post-impact period. If a natural disaster can be anticipated, such as a hurricane, the media usually has time for careful reporting. Prior to the initial impact, news accounts generally focus on the more technical aspects of a storm. Media coverage often includes the location of a storm, assessment of the potential infrastructure and environmental risks, and emergency plans and preparations that are in place to mitigate human injury and harm. In the midst of a storm, media reports generally focus on the factual events that are occurring on the ground as a result of the impact. But in the aftermath of a storm, the coverage often takes on a decisively different character and tone. It is, as Henry Fischer argues, during the post-impact period that mass media plays a significant role in reproducing disaster mythology.[7] He claims that:

> The media tends to publish post-impact human interest stories which are based upon victim and local official interviews. The tendency for the media to publish unconfirmed statements made to them by their interviewees who tend to embellish their stories or pass along rumor appears to result in mythology perpetuation in the case of natural disaster news stories. Since the media tends to focus on technical aspects of pre-impact . . . it is far less likely to pass along the disaster myths commonly reported in the post-impact time period (Fischer 1998, p. 43).

[7]In his observations of media role during Hurricane Gilbert, Fischer concluded that "When myths were portrayed, those most likely to appear in any medium were myths perpetuating belief in an increase in deviance during disaster such as looting and price gouging. The behaviors most likely to be reported accurately were those dealing with the rational preparation, clean-up activities engaged in by individuals and their families, the typical disaster subculture activities such as surfing, and instances of usual altruism, e.g., search and rescue activities" (pp. 43–85).

In the aftermath of Hurricane Katrina, media accounts of rampant criminal behavior appeared to be true, plausible, and typical of the events that were occurring in New Orleans. Yet those accounts were often factually inaccurate, exaggerated, and unbalanced. In many of those accounts, disaster reporters "unwittingly passed on myths which reinforce the view that behavioral response to disaster is characterized by the breakdown of the norms of good citizenship."[8] But disaster research suggests that the opposite of this is often true (Barton 1969; Drabek 1986; Dynes 1970). That residents most often "behave proactively and prosocially to assist one another," and usually perform many critical tasks in the process of doing so, such as rescue and recovery, which leads to "greater community cohesiveness during disasters."[9]

I am not claiming that the media deliberately or intentionally misrepresented the "facts" of what occurred in the wake of Hurricane Katrina. Rather, I am suggesting, as Dennis Howitt (1998) claims that "what is read, heard and seen as news is something other than just the facts" (p. 29). I believe this is often the case, particularly when news coverage attempts to explain the situational behavior of African Americans. Whether, direct or indirect, negative racial stereotypes are often embedded within the context of news accounts of black behavior. The propensity to reproduce negative stereotypes through news reporting may not be deliberate or intentional. Yet, as Linus Abraham (2003) argues—whether intended or not—the result of visual images accompanied by the written text can create an implicit subtext, whereby racial stereotypes are revealed in the assumed and the unstated messages that are conveyed through news accounts. For instance, he notes that:

> Blackness, as race, in American culture has historically been perceived as synonymous with deviance. In many cases, blackness has become a conventional notation symbolizing abnormality. Its racist symbolic use is so ingrained that, after years of supposed egalitarian trends in the culture, this symbolic notation still appears, albeit subtly, even in arenas where such racist use of language would be most eschewed (Lester & Ross, 2003, p. 90).

Roving Gangs of Thugs: Looting

In the aftermath of Hurricane Katrina, a picture of complete anarchy in the city of New Orleans emerges from media accounts. The portrayal of "anomie, chaos, disorganization, regression to animal-like behavior, and a total collapse of social control, agencies, and personnel" was sent around the world through news coverage.[10] One of the first indicators of anarchy as portrayed by media reports was that of widespread looting. The unauthorized seizure of goods and property, even under extraordinary disaster conditions is often socially condemned, as violating the "norms of good citizenship."

---

[8]Ibid.

[9]Kathleen Tierney contends that "social cohesiveness and informal mechanism of social control increase during disasters, resulting in a lower incidence of deviant behavior than during non-disaster times" (p. 2).

[10]Rodriguez et al. (2006) note that this imagery of anarchy was particularly evident in the coverage of electronic media, and in a more restrained way in the reporting by print media. Rodriguez et al. (March 2006). "Rising to the Challenges of a Catastrophe: The Emergent and Prosocial Behavior Following Hurricane Katrina" (pp. 2–3).

Looting is generally seen as unacceptable and intolerable, regardless of the circumstances. Therefore, even if it was out of dire need, the taking of food, water, clothing, and other necessities by stranded disaster victims in the aftermath of Hurricane Katrina was often portrayed in media coverage as antisocial behavior, and viewed by many government officials as criminal behavior.

The accounts of widespread looting from both print and electronic media are [too] numerous to cite. So what follows are select representative reports taken from *Times-Picayune*, the daily newspaper of New Orleans, *The New York Times*, and *The Washington Post*.

Rampant Looting

Looting in the immediate aftermath of Hurricane Katrina was portrayed as an intergenerational affair and involved men, women, and children alike. Most accounts offered no contextual analysis as to why people were looting. Rather the coverage presented the looters as opportunistic, who were taking advantage of a disastrous situation with no regards for the private property of their fellow citizens. The taking of needed goods was not seen as a necessity under emergency circumstances, or appropriate for the situation at hand. Instead, media reports emphasized irresponsibility and frivolousness of the looters' behavior.

> From *The Times-Picayune:*
>
> The looters, who were men and women who appeared to be in their early teens to mid-40s braved a steady rain and infrequent tropical storm wind gusts to tote boxes of clothing and shoes from the store. Some had garbage bags stuffed with goods. Others lugged wardrobe-sized boxes or carried them on their heads. . . . Some looters were seen smiling and greeting each other with pleasantries as they passed. Another group was seen riding in the back of a pickup truck, honking the horn and cheering (Editorial 2005).

Not only did media accounts portray the looters as immoral "happy thieves," who had no qualms whatsoever regarding the property [of] others, they were also portrayed as dangerous thieves as well. And regardless of individual circumstances, it was the moblike behavior that was the focus of media portrayals.

> From *The Times-Picayune:*
>
> People are going in and out of businesses at Louisiana and Claiborne (avenues), taking clothes, tennis shoes and goods, Thomas (New Orleans City Council President) said. It is inconceivable to me how people can do this. . . . People are leaving the Superdome to go to Canal Street to loot, Thomas said. Some people broke into drug stores and stole the drugs off the shelves, it is looting times five. I'm telling you, it's like Sodom and Gomorrah (Anderson and Moller 2005).

> From *The New York Times:*
>
> These are not individuals looting. These are large groups of armed individuals. . . . Looting broke out as opportunistic thieves cleaned out abandoned stores for a second night. In one incident, officials said a police officer was shot and critically wounded (Treaster and Sontag 2005).

The looters were portrayed in the media as "wild animal," who possess no degree of self-control over their behavior. And the sentiments of white anger, disgust, confusion, and fear were conveyed in media analyses and commentaries.

From *The Washington Post:*

"We fear the anarchy, the feral fanaticism and, at the heart of it, the primeval bugbear of someone coming after our homes, our stores, our stuff" (Weeks 2005).

"What could be going through the minds of people who survive an almost biblical tragedy, find themselves in a hellscape of the dead and the dispossessed, and promptly decide to go looting? Obviously not much: Stealing a rack of fancy clothes when there's no place to wear them or a television when there's no electricity does not suggest a lot of deep thought" (Robinson 2005).

Katrina also brought us the faces of the detestable—the rabble who tears through the rubble, feeding off the property and misery of others: those for whom a decent society has no use. . . . Looting in the wake of Katrina was sickening. It wasn't the foraging for food, milk, diapers and toiletries that was upsetting. That part was understandable. It was the smashing of windows to steal watches, television sets, DVDs and guns that was despicable. . . . It all goes to show what happens when some people get it in their heads that they can take things that don't belong to them without getting caught. All it takes is a time and place where authority is absent. Bring on such a scene for those predators and opportunists always lurking in our midst and, bingo, you have your looters (King 2005).

Thugs Reins of Terror: Mayhem and Wanton Violence

Even though looting was a major focus of media's attention during the days following Hurricane Katrina, mayhem and wanton violence was also a significant part of the coverage as well. It included accounts of gun battles, sexual assaults, massive bloodshed, and general predatory behavior by blacks. Media accounts would characterize the social breakdown in New Orleans as analogous to a "war zone" situation. Many of the eyewitness accounts of indiscriminate violence as reported in media coverage were taken from either people in authoritative positions or from public officials. Media presumed that such individuals had accurate knowledge of the situation at hand and could be relied upon for conveying the truthfulness of what was happening. By relying on such accounts, which were based largely on rumors, the media conveyed erroneous reports that were, in turn, reproduced by other media outlets and circulated as news to the public.

Again the media reports of mayhem and wanton violence are too numerous to cite, so what follows are select representations of national and regional newspaper accounts of the indiscriminate violence that was perceived as occurring in the city:

From *The Times-Picayune:*

"There are gangs of armed men in the city moving around the city," said Ebbert, the city's homeland security chief (Mohr et al. 2005).

From *The Washington Post:*

During a briefing carried live on local radio and local and national televi sion, Sen. Mary Landrieu (D-La,) said, "We have gotten reports, but uncon-firmed, of some of our deputies and sheriffs that have either been injured or killed." . . . The New Orleans *Times-Picayune* reported that National Guard troop found 30 to 40 bodies decomposing inside a freezer in the convention center, including a girl whose throat was slashed. The Newspaper quoted a member of the Arkansas National Guard, which was deployed in the build-ing. Other news organizations then passed the information on (Pierre and Gerhart 2005).

From *The New York Times:*

Superintendent P. Edward Compass III of the New Orleans Police Department said, "armed thugs have taken control of the secondary make-shift shelter at the convention center." Superintendent Compass said that the thugs repelled eight squads of 11 officers each he had sent to secure the place and that rapes and assaults were occurring unimpeded in the neighboring streets as criminals preyed upon passers-by, including stranded tourists (Treaster and Sontag 2005).

Asked about the numerous accounts or rapes, Joseph H. Matthews, a deputy fire chief and the director of the city's Office of Emergency Preparedness, said "some were probably' true. Nothing's been confirmed, but you can't discount these reports," Mr. Matthews said (Dao and Kleinfield 2005).

From *The Seattle Times:*

In interviews with Oprah Winfrey, Compass (Superintendent of New Orleans Police Department) reported rapes of babies, and Mayor Ray Nagin spoke of hundreds of armed gang members killing and raping people inside the Dome. Other unidentified evacuees told of "children stepping over so many bodies we couldn't count." . . . The picture that emerged was one of the impoverished, overwhelmingly African-American masses of flood victims resorting to utter depravity, randomly attacking each other, as well as the police trying to protect them and the rescue workers trying to save them. The mayor told Winfrey "the crowd has descended to an almost animalistic state" (Thevenot and Russell 2005).

The media also reported accounts from disaster victims. And those reports were often based on rumors and exaggerated truths, but taken as fact as they circulate to other news outlets and to the public as news.

From the *Arizona Daily Star:*

In an interview with Greta Van Susteren on Fox News Channel, 'A Current Affair' correspondent Arthel Neville, of the famous musical family, said she "had heard that a man was beaten to death by an angry mob in the Dome after he raped and killed a 7-year-old." . . . Another Neville, blues singer

>Charmaine, 49, told a story resembling a made-for-TV movie that was broadcast as news on Baton Rouge, La., television. The distraught singer spoke of smashing through a roof with a crowbar to rescue victims, getting raped, watching alligators eat people, and walking through 'hundreds of dead bodies' before pushing two legless women in wheelchairs to dry land in the French Quarter and commandeering a bus to drive people to safety (Gillin 2005).

The different tales of "feral fanaticism" to describe what was occurring in New Orleans in the immediate aftermath of Hurricane Katrina were created and recreated through mass media accounts. Many of the reports of looting, mayhem and wanton violence that followed were based on distorted coverage: in many instances the accounts were rooted in partial and incomplete facts, embellished and exaggerated truths, or based on outright fabrications and lies.

Acknowledging that this was the case, some in the journalistic community have since begun to reassess and analyze their coverage of how disaster victims were portrayed and how their reporting contributed to the ways victims were treated. Several media outlets including the *New Orleans Times-Picayune*, *The New York Times*, *The Boston Globe*, and CNN/US have acknowledged errors and made corrections to previously erroneous reports. *The Washington Post*, for example, ran an article entitled, "In Katrina's Wake, Inaccurate Rumors Sullied Victims." This article noted that, "It's always easier to recount—and believe—the alleged inhumanity of those who are poor, less educated or of different ethnicities than of those reporting their supposed actions" (Britt 2005). Yet this on-going assessment by some media outlets, after the fact, provides little if any solace of consolation for those trapped in New Orleans, for the distortions, at the moment, had wide-ranging implications and immediate consequences for the lives of Hurricane Katrina's victims.

There is no dispute that looting occurred in New Orleans in the wake of Hurricane Katrina. However, as Tierney points out, to date:

>no solid empirical data exist regarding how widespread (or rare) looting actually was, who took part in the episodes of looting that did occur, why they were motivated to take part, whether the goods people took could have been salvaged, or how much damage and loss looting actually caused, relative to other losses the hurricane produced (Tierney et al. 2006, p. 6).

Furthermore, there is no dispute that some of the looters may have been opportunistic and taken advantage of the circumstances created in the aftermath of the storm: but for many victims, their actions were reasonable, appropriate, and needed for the life threatening situations they found themselves in.

Suggesting that this may have been the case, Benigno Aguirre, of the Disaster Research Center at the University of Delaware, noted in an interview with *The Washington Post* that the looters: "may be people taking drastic measures required by drastic times. And some, he says, are the in-an-emergency equivalent of hunters/gatherers, foraging for food, fresh water, medicine, matches, batteries, everyday essentials that are just not available. Not at home, not at shelters" (Weeks 2005).

For example, in her sworn testimony before the House Select Committee hearing on the government's response to Katrina, Denise, a 42-year-old black woman housed at the Convention Center during the storm, told the committee that:

> Many people were delirious from lack of water and food, completely dehydrated. Inside the Convention Center, conditions were horrible. The floors were black and slick with feces. Outside wasn't much better, between the heat, the humidity, the lack of water, and old and very young dying from dehydration. There were young men with guns there, who organized the crowd and got food and water for the old people and babies, because nobody had eaten in days. When buses came, it was those men who got the crowd in order. Old people in front, women and children next, men in the back (Goodman 2005a, p. 3).

Also, there is no dispute as to whether or not there was chaos in New Orleans in the immediate aftermath of Hurricane Katrina. The question, however, is whether or not that chaos was due to the looting, mayhem and wanton violence by disaster victims.

Media reports of rampant lawlessness and black criminality were largely untrue. Of the sniper attacks and gun battles, for example, the police now attribute gunshots that were heard to disaster victims who were either trapped in their homes attempting to alert rescuers of their location, or attempting to shoot their way through the attics of their home in order to reach the safety of the roof (Cooper et al. 2006, p. 6).

And, what of the atrocities—massive rapes and murders—supposedly taking place in the Superdome and Convention Center, as reported by media? There is no evidence to support the widely publicized accounts that atrocities took place. The reports of "women, children and even babies raped with abandon; people murdered for food and water: a 7-year-old raped and killed at the Convention Center," were based on rumors. Rapes may have occurred, but there was no evidence to confirm those reports. For instance, witnesses told of "the rape of two young girls in the Superdome ladies' room and the killing of one of them," but the incidents could not be confirmed (Thevenot and Russell 2005).

Yet there was confirmation that murder had taken place, and it was found that only two people had been killed—one at the Superdome (although there was dispute as to whether or not this incident was actually murder or a suicide) and one at the Convention Center. Eddie Jordan, the district attorney of Orleans Parish, said in an interview that:

> I was fully expecting that there would be many, many bodies associated with violence and also many children who would have died as a result of violence. And I expected there to be a number of killings both at the Convention Center and the Superdome. . . . And I asked the coroner and some of his employees about those allegations and the information that they had received in connection with their receipt of the bodies from New Orleans in the days immediately after the storm, and I was shocked to learn that there were only two bodies that were associated with the Convention Center and

the Superdome, and actually that was one apiece. And then there were only two other bodies associated with violence in the days immediately after the storm. So, that was a total of four, and that was clearly inconsistent with the reports that I had seen on television (Goodman 2005b, p. 2).

News reports indicated that at least 30 to 40 killings had occurred at the two sites. However, Dr. Louis Cataldie, the state Health and Human Services Department administrator overseeing the body-recovery operation, "found 10 bodies in the Dome, 4 brought in from the streets and 6 people who died onsite: 4 of natural causes, 1 of a drug overdose, and 1 of a fall from a balcony listed as an apparent suicide. . . . Of four deaths at the Convention Center, three were from natural causes and one was a homicide" (Gillin 2005).

Media portrayals of anti-social and lawless behavior influenced the perception that a complete social breakdown was occurring in New Orleans. That breakdown was widely attributed to black criminality. And, indeed, there were incidents of criminal behavior. But crime—no matter how insidious and violent it may have been—was not the cause of the social catastrophe that gripped the city, in the wake of Hurricane Katrina. It was caused by a compromised social infrastructure that was severely damaged as a result of massive flooding, and the decisions of government officials as influenced by media reports in response to this environmental disaster.

The environmental crisis created by floodwaters was made worse because of the inadequate, incompetent, and—importantly—the inappropriate response of government officials. Their response resulted in critical delays that prevented humanitarian assistance from reaching disaster victims in a timely manner. Delays occurred because officials decided that restoring social order the priority. Concomitantly, humanitarian assistance was of secondary concern, in the days following Hurricane Katrina. Those delays were critical: for delays in rescue and emergency service operations contributed to an already deteriorating environmental crisis that further jeopardized and exacerbated the life-threatening circumstances that many stranded disaster victims were in.

Source: With kind permission from Springer Science + Business Media: *Journal of African American Studies.* "Hurricane Katrina: The Making of Unworthy Disaster Victims," Volume 10, (2007), pp. 55–74, Garfield, Gail. Copyright © 2007.

SURVIVAL AND DEATH IN NEW ORLEANS: AN EMPIRICAL LOOK AT THE HUMAN IMPACT OF KATRINA

Patrick Sharkey

The death, suffering, and displacement that accompanied Hurricane Katrina generated compassion from commentators across the political spectrum. But underlying the universal understanding of Katrina as a horrible tragedy is a struggle over how to interpret the disaster. The images of New Orleans's residents stranded at the Convention Center and throughout the city left the indelible impression that the storm's impact was anything but natural. Virtually all of the faces captured by the news cameras were Black, and the visible state of desperation among the stranded victims of the storm suggested deep poverty. Based largely on these visual impressions, Katrina has come to be interpreted by some as a "metaphor" (Alba, 2005) for the inequality that pervades urban America, affecting poor, primarily Black segments of the urban populace most directly.

As has been the case with many environmental disasters, a rival interpretation of Katrina as a purely "natural" disaster has been propagated by skeptical commentators who dismiss the idea that Katrina represents anything more than a random tragedy that happened to strike a predominantly Black city (Young, 2006). The skeptics' case was strengthened by an analysis of data on the casualties of the hurricane, which appeared to show that Whites, not African Americans, seem to have been disproportionately likely to die in Hurricane Katrina (Simerman, Ott, & Melnick, 2005). The report, conducted by staff from Knight Ridder Newspapers, finds that Blacks represented only a slight majority of those who died in the storm, despite the fact that they compose a substantial majority of the population in the areas hit hardest by Katrina. The implication is that Whites may actually have been overrepresented among the victims of Katrina, which would dispel the notion that the effects of the storm were centered on the poor, Black population of New Orleans. The study compelled one columnist to write that suggestions of a link between race and the effects of Hurricane Katrina are driven by nothing more than "racial paranoia" (Young, 2006).

Though the Knight Ridder analysis is flawed in numerous ways, the reaction to it makes clear the need to move beyond mere impressions or metaphors and to document the impact of Katrina with actual evidence. Although interpretations of the storm are widespread, the evidence put forth in support of these interpretations has been sparse. An exception is the research conducted by John Logan (2006) showing that the neighborhoods experiencing flooding and structural damage in the storm were disproportionately poor and Black. The current analysis, which is based on three sources of data on Katrina's victims and those who remain missing, adds to this research in an effort to develop an interpretation of the impact of Katrina that is empirically based. I am limited in this effort by sparse data that do not allow for any analysis of the sequence of events that transpired during the storm. Still, the data used in the current analysis provide the most comprehensive description of the people and the neighborhoods that were most directly affected by Hurricane Katrina, providing the basis for a sociological interpretation of survival and death during Hurricane Katrina.

I follow a tradition of research that recasts "natural" disasters (e.g., famines, floods, or heat waves) as political, economic, and social in nature (Erikson, 1976;

Klinenberg, 2002; Sen, 1981), and I reach the same conclusion that others have reached before me: Although such disasters may be triggered by environmental sources, their impact is felt differentially by individuals and groups based on their position in the social structure. Katrina's impact was felt most acutely by elderly individuals in New Orleans and by the city's African American population. Validating the impression that the storm hit New Orleans's Black communities hardest, I find that African Americans were disproportionately likely to die in Katrina and are also disproportionately likely to remain missing. Furthermore, the neighborhoods with the highest numbers of deceased are overwhelmingly Black. These findings reflect what Briggs (2006) refers to as a "geography of risk," where the legacy of racial and economic segregation has left specific segments of urban communities isolated from institutional resources, economic opportunity, and political influence and particularly vulnerable to a disaster such as Katrina.

As I have repeated throughout the analysis, data on those who died in Katrina and those who remain missing are limited in what they reveal about the social aspects of this horrible American tragedy. Still, a rough picture emerges from these data that offers a more informed perspective on the social impacts of Katrina than the conjecture and overly simplistic analyses that have appeared in the popular press since the hurricane swept through New Orleans.

The primary conclusion to be made from these data is that the impact of the storm was felt most acutely in specific sections of the city and among specific groups within New Orleans. The elderly were clearly the most vulnerable to Katrina, as evidenced by their extraordinarily high death rates. Although a great deal of media attention has focused on the negligent actions of specific nursing homes during Katrina, the overrepresentation of the elderly among Katrina's casualties is consistent with findings from other environmental disasters. For instance, Klinenberg (2002, p. 18) found that 73% of deaths during the Chicago heat wave of 1995 occurred among the elderly. Other research on heat waves has emphasized the susceptibility of the elderly in urban areas to specific heat-related health risks (e.g., Conti et al., 2005). In effect, this research emphasizes biological explanations for the high death rates that are common among the elderly living in cities during heat waves. The current analysis demonstrates that the vulnerability of the old is not limited to heat-related crises, reinforcing the idea that the source of the elderly's vulnerability likely lies in the combination of biological as well as social factors. Klinenberg's study documents how elderly populations, especially within disadvantaged or violent urban areas, often shield themselves from the perceived dangers of the street by shutting themselves off from the social world that surrounds them. This perspective on the social isolation of the elderly, especially in violent urban areas, represents a promising interpretation of the extraordinarily high death rates found among the elderly in New Orleans.

The second unmistakable conclusion is that race was deeply implicated in the tragedy of Katrina. African Americans were disproportionately represented among both elderly and nonelderly victims, and the vast majority of those still missing are Black. These findings run counter to popular press accounts of Katrina's casualties, largely because these accounts fail to consider the age profiles of New Orleans's White and African American populations. When one takes into account the size of the elderly population of Whites and Blacks in New Orleans, it becomes clear that Whites were underrepresented among Katrina's casualties and Blacks overrepresented.

Data on the locations of recovered bodies reinforce the finding that Katrina took its largest toll on New Orleans's Black community. The group of neighborhoods with the highest death counts and highest numbers of residents who are still missing were, on average, about 80% African American. The neighborhoods hit hardest were not necessarily the poorest in New Orleans, but they were the most segregated. This conclusion confirms that Katrina's impact on African Americans is not attributable to the fact that the storm happened to strike a city with a large Black population; rather, I find that within the city of New Orleans, Black neighborhoods and Black residents were disproportionately affected by the storm.

In addition to the sparse data, the major weakness of my analysis is that it leaves unresolved the question of why Blacks were especially vulnerable to the storm. Data on Katrina's casualties can be used to suggest some hypotheses, but more research is necessary to test these hypotheses and to untangle the sources underlying Blacks' vulnerability to Katrina. The most intuitive explanation is that Blacks lived in neighborhoods that experienced the most severe flooding, leading to the high number of casualties. My results provide qualified support for this explanation. I find that neighborhoods with high death counts were much more likely to have severe flooding than neighborhoods with lower death counts and that neighborhoods with significant flooding (at least 5 feet) had higher proportions of Black residents than those with less extensive flooding. These findings are generally consistent with research on structural damage to New Orleans's neighborhoods (Logan, 2006), which shows that neighborhoods that experienced some damage had far higher proportions of Black residents than neighborhoods that did not suffer any damage. However, it is important to point out that the most severe flooding did not occur exclusively in African American neighborhoods but rather occurred in a wide variety of neighborhoods throughout the city.

A second hypothesis is that differences in income or resources among Blacks and Whites help explain the racial gap in the impact of Katrina. Relatively low income could have made it more difficult for Blacks to evacuate the city, but at a more general level, group differences in economic resources may have left Blacks in New Orleans in substandard housing within neighborhoods that were especially susceptible to flooding. Although this is a plausible hypothesis, it is well documented that group differences in socioeconomic status generally do not explain much of the gap in the residential environments of African Americans and Whites in urban America (Alba, Logan, & Stults, 2000; Massey & Mullan, 1984). Indeed, my results show that poverty was no more prevalent in neighborhoods with high death counts than in neighborhoods where no bodies were found. A more likely scenario is that racial segregation in New Orleans, arising because of a combination of historical and current discrimination (Massey & Denton, 1993; Yinger, 1995), differences in group resources, and Black/White discrepancies in preferences for "in" and "out group" neighbors (Bobo & Zubrinsky, 1996; Charles, 2001), has left African Americans in residential environments that are more disadvantaged across multiple dimensions, including their vulnerability to natural disaster.

In demonstrating the link between race and Katrina, I build on a line of research that recasts so-called natural disasters as social or economic in essence. Sen's (1981) analysis of the market failures that underlie the impact of famines is perhaps the most powerful example of how a seemingly environmental phenomenon becomes a powerful force in the lives of individuals through their position in the system of production and consumption. The current analysis extends this conceptualization to consider how individuals' and groups' position in the residential structure of the city contributes to the disproportionate vulnerability of certain groups to a tragedy such as Katrina. In this sense, I describe a "geography of risk" (Briggs, 2006) that extends beyond the constant threat of violence and other forms of disadvantage that are prevalent in America's ghettos. The social isolation that results from persistent segregation, economic disinvestment, a lack of political influence, and violence makes the residents of America's disadvantaged urban neighborhoods even more vulnerable to an environmental disaster such as Katrina.

Rather than dismiss the link between race and the impact of Katrina, it seems essential to keep exploring this link to better understand why New Orleans's Black community was so vulnerable to the storm. In doing so, we shed light on the legacy of racial and economic segregation that has structured residential New Orleans, along with so many other urban centers in America. Equally important, conceptualizing Katrina as both a social and a natural disaster reinforces the role that public policy can play before a disaster occurs. By enforcing fair housing laws, implementing policies designed to deconcentrate poverty, and creating viable, safe communities, urban policy has the potential to mitigate the vulnerability of any single population to everyday forms of disadvantage as well as to the dangers of a disaster such as Katrina.

Source: Sharkey, Patrick. (2007). "Survival and Death in New Orleans: An Empirical Look at the Human Impact of Katrina," *Journal of Black Studies,* Volume 37, pp. 482–484, 496–500. Copyright © 2007. Reprinted by permission of Sage Publications.

KEVIN OWENS—OVERCOMING KATRINA: AFRICAN AMERICAN VOICES FROM THE CRESCENT CITY AND BEYOND

D'Ann R. Penner and Keith C. Ferdinand

Raised in the Calliope Project, forty-one-year-old Kevin Owens, the only survivor of three siblings, prides himself on being a hardworking man like his father, a Vietnam veteran. Before the storm, he and his wife, Elise Ramsey, were renting a townhouse with a back yard in New Orleans East. His wife fulfilled the role of the neighborhood mom, and there was always a constant stream of guests in and out of their house. Kevin worked as a maintenance man in the B.W. Cooper Housing Development.

On December 9, 2005, Kevin, a short, muscular, extensively tattooed man with kind, expressive eyes, took off work from the University of Alabama in Birmingham to come to the Birmingham Urban League to tell his story. He was wearing work boots, blue jeans, a button-down flannel shirt, and a baseball cap. In the tightly scheduled interview blocks lined up by a conscientious Urban League staff, there wasn't nearly enough time to hear all that Kevin had to say. A follow-up interview took place in Kevin's two-bedroom apartment in Hoover, Alabama, a suburb of Birmingham.[1] Normally a quiet man, Kevin spoke on tape for a total of three hours because he felt driven to document the treatment of those he felt did not deserve to be criminalized in the wake of Katrina.

Kevin describes the experience of many working-class blacks who sought refuge in the shelter of last resort, the Superdome.[2] He arrived after he and his family abandoned an apartment in the B.W. Cooper homes, comprised of sturdy, three-story, brick buildings. After being at the Dome for a few days Kevin, a diabetic, was taken behind the guarded barricades and curtains of the main floor after he collapsed from low blood sugar. There, he observed the scenes he relates in his narrative. Within weeks of being evacuated from the Superdome to Birmingham via the Astrodome, Kevin had successfully negotiated an apartment lease in an upscale community that was initially hostile to displaced New Orleanians. He started a fulltime job on the University of Alabama's Birmingham campus where his wife's son, Carldell "Squeaky" Johnson, was a starting point guard. His reflections are recollections of black New Orleans from a man with a working-class background.

I was born in Charity Hospital in New Orleans, Louisiana in 1964. I was raised in the Calliope Housing Project. It was a rough area. My mom and them had some good values. They tried their best to move out of that area, which they did.

Right before the hurricane, I wasn't living there, but I was working there as a maintenance technician. I can just basically look at something and tell you what's wrong with it. If it's your door, your toilet, your floor, whatever. If it's broken, I can fix it or replace it.

We was living in eastern New Orleans before Hurricane Katrina came in, and we got about ten feet of water inside our home. Our house was like the typical American home. It was three bedrooms, two floors. It was really a townhouse, but it was a nice home. We had a yard with patio furniture and in the summer time, we put a little swimming pool there for the grandkids and some of the neighbor children. My wife was

---

[1]This chapter also relies on PFN, 12/12/05, 12/14/05, 12/24/05, 4/3/06, 2/10/08, and 3/13/08.

[2]On the Superdome, see also ARC, Shriff Hasan-Penner interview, Houston, TX, 10/05.

really like the neighborhood mother. She used to come out early in the morning and made sure the kids got on the school buses safe.

We knew all of our neighbors in our subdivision right off Downman and Chef. We was able, thank God, to be blessed to feed a lot of people. We felt good about that. Our home was comfortable. We was blessed to have a lot of material things, and I always looked at it like if you're in a situation to give, then you're above need. The Lord always made a way for us to be in a situation to give. We kept our house clean, and we kept company. We kept an open door.

Katrina

I stayed focused on the news days before, and we had a chance of getting out. We had transportation: a pretty reliable '99 Chevy Malibu and my stepson's truck. He had to stay because he was working for the Sewerage and Water Board, and they wouldn't let him go.

My wife just didn't believe that we was going to get hit like that. I was conscious of our levee system, but by staying focused on the news all day, I knew that we wasn't going to be missed. But I couldn't leave her. We wind up leaving our home in the East and going to her brother's house in the B.W. Cooper on the third floor. It's brick. She felt safe.

What happened was we got to her brother's home and Katrina came through. I was up through the whole thing. I was looking out the window. We watched the whole thing. They had a leak in the house that pretty much kept us woke too. The wind was pretty scary. But the building itself withstood it real good. They had some windows blown out.

When Katrina came and left, we started clapping. We was like: "We made it!" I looked out the window and I said, "Lord, look at this here. We got to roll up our sleeves and start cleaning up." A lot of the old oak trees in New Orleans is throughout the city, including the B.W. Cooper Housing. The extent of the damage was such that a lot of them just was uprooted to the point of uprooting the sidewalks, and so there was no way we was going to drive out for a while.

I had a little storm tracker radio that you wind up, and I kept winding it. I'm listening, and I'm looking at our automobile, and it was being submerged every minute that went by. I'm saying, "Something is wrong, because this water should be receding, but it's coming in faster." That's when I started cranking to find out what was wrong. I heard the man on the radio say, "If you're held up anywhere in New Orleans, you need to try your best to make it to the Superdome or the convention center, because the levees have been breached and we can't stop the water."

I turned around to them and I told them, "We need to get out of this house, because even though we're on the third floor, we're going to be trapped in the city." We was running out of food and water. Electricity had went out about 4:00 that morning.

The Superdome: "The Scariest Part of My Ordeal"

The Superdome was about half a mile away. We wasn't really trying to carry anything, because we left a lot of stuff in our house in the East, but we had a few little clothes and a few little light things like a toothbrush and your driver's license. So we had to walk through the water to about our waist. At the time, there was just a lot of stuff from the automobiles like gas, oil, and stuff like that in the water. We saw some dead bodies as we were walking, especially as we went up on the I-10 bridge. Once we walked up the

I-10 bridge, we had to walk back down at the Claiborne exit to the Superdome and go under the bridge and walk through the water again to get up in the Superdome. We left about 10:00, and we got there about 11:00 or 12:00.

We thought we was going to a shelter, but it was more of a prison. Outside the Superdome, we was searched by the military. It was like a regular little pat down. I felt like, "OK we're being searched and they might be looking for weapons or whatever." I didn't feel violated by the search. Soon as we got in there, I knew something wasn't right. We saw the water rising up by the Superdome and they wasn't trying to get us out. There wasn't no effort to try and get us out, but they constantly was bringing more people into the Superdome.

You could count the white people in the rest of the Superdome on one hand. I say 99 percent was black and poor. I know everybody else feels like we weren't in a major city in America, our country.

When we got there, I'd say about fifteen or twenty thousand people were already there that had went there earlier before the storm hit. They were stationed around on the benches and in the bleachers and sleeping in front of the restrooms and in that hall way. With every passing minute, you could see the whole situation was deteriorating. It was hard for us to find a place to lay down and get some rest, because the football field itself was wet, and they were saying, "Can't nobody sleep on the football field." There weren't any cots.

Everybody was just coming outside on the ramps, because being inside during the daytime especially was unbearable. You couldn't stay in there.

When we first got there on Monday afternoon, they was issuing the Army rationed food and water. The next day it stopped. Everything stopped. They said somebody stole the food.

I was just looking at my wife and her niece and grand-niece. My wife is a very strong woman, and she kept saying, "Baby, I'm going to just take my life. I can't take this." I was saying, "Lord, I got to get them out of here." That's what made me so mad. I didn't care if the people shot me or nothing because that was so wrong.

Every day they bringing more and more people, and we know the conditions. We're glad to see some of them because we know them. But we're trying to warn them not to come in.

When we first got to the Superdome, my wife adopted some kids that had a kid. Both of the parents were sixteen years old. And they had a kid that was physically challenged. She fell in love with them because she's that type of person. They sat next to us in the Superdome, and they was telling us that they couldn't find their family, so they clung to us.

Everybody was trying to hold each other up. If it wasn't for just everybody trying to pull together and save each other, then a lot of more of us would have died. We all we had. It was like whatever we was able to do for the elderly, we did it. Whatever we was able to do for the women, we did it, and the children. We took some clean t-shirts someone had, and tore them and made some pampers for all the babies that needed it. It was little stuff like that. People who needed medical attention, we were trying our best to get it for them. The good that we wanted to do, it was just so limited, because of the conditions, but it wasn't like everybody turned on each other, was violent or none of that toward each other. We were just praying that one day soon, we'll be out of here. We starving to death, and we hadn't touched no water in days.

I got sick, because I'm a diabetic, and I didn't eat for so long. We was going back and forward from the military to the doctors who was in there and telling them. "Look, I need something to eat. I'm going to pass out or go in a diabetic shock." So they was just sending us backward and forward for hours and hours. Finally, I passed out. That was Thursday. Some people and my wife carried me to the infirmary, which was located in the arena where the Hornets play. I had come to enough to understand what the doctor was asking my wife, "What's wrong with him?" She said, "He's a diabetic. He hasn't eaten anything." So he tested my blood sugar. My blood sugar level was like fifty or fifty-one. He said, "Take him down the hall where the people at, and get him some food and some water."

We went down this hallway in the arena, and there was this room that was being guarded, and they had cases and cases of food and cases and cases of water. So I got a case of food and a case of water. There's about six rations of food in one case. On my way out, I had asked them, "Why you all not feeding us? I thought you all said that somebody stole the food?" They said, "We giving it to the elderlies," which wasn't true, because we was with the elderly.

So on our way back with the food, the military didn't feel safe for me, so when I was about to cross back over the barricades to what's called the general population, they stopped me. They said, "Where you going with that food and water?" I said, "I'm going back over here where I've been." They said, "You going to have to stay over here with us, because you going to get mugged for food." I said, "Why is it like that? Why don't you feed them?"

We sat there all day and all night too. That's when I looked back. We was leaning against the glass, and I'm looking and they had a curtain open, and I seen all these little white children and white people sitting in a suite. They was eating good food. They wasn't eating the army rations. They had fans. The power was out, but they must have had a generator. They were with their families. I think they had one black person in there, and the rest was white.

I witnessed a black man literally try to take a little girl out of her mother's arms. That was right outside the Superdome on the ramp. Several people knew him before Katrina, and they said he was mentally ill. He should have been in a mental institution, but he was roaming the streets like that. I didn't see a little girl get raped and killed, but I was there when they took her out. She was ten. She was an African American. I witnessed the gentleman confess to doing it, and he was a white man in his late fifties. He looked raggedy. He looked like he probably had, and I'm saying probably because I don't know the man, but he probably had a mental problem before Katrina and that Superdome thing probably pushed him over. To me she's a forgotten child. But when she was reported, I wanted it to be known that it was a white man who done it regardless of his mental state, because so many black eyes had been placed on us, and, it was like I didn't want no black eyes to be placed on anyone else, but I just didn't want the world to continue to look at us like animals, because we're not. You got people that act rude and bad, but that's with every race. A lot of young girls in the Superdome was afraid, especially going to the bathroom, because there were reports of rapes. I think it was blown out of proportion. That's my feelings. But I do think some incidents is true. To be honest with you, it's probably three or four cases.

New Orleans don't have gangs. A lot of people from the same housing projects do stick together. Now if you want to classify that as a gang, then go ahead. But it wasn't much of that in the Superdome. In the Superdome, it was the people against the military. It wasn't like the people against each other. I had family in the convention center, and their stories were more violent than what I saw. They said a lot of people from different projects wound up together in the convention center, and that's when the violence probably started in there.

I think it was mostly the United States military that was patrolling everything. They carried M-16s on their shoulders and were pointing them at people. Everybody was in a military uniform, but we didn't see nobody in charge. No announcements were being made. I said, "You all need to make an announcement to let us know what you all plans are, because we don't see nobody running around in charge of you all. Who your captain is?" I thought they could tell us why we hadn't left yet. We've been in there three days. We're not eating. I didn't have my crank radio anymore, so I'm cut off from the outside world.

There was an incident in the Superdome where they were pointing their weapons at the crowd. I had asked one of the army personnel, "Sir, can I ask you questions?" He said, "yeah." I said, "What are your orders? To kill us or something?" He say, "I can't talk about it." I say, "You're pointing your gun at us, man. We're not criminals! We supposed to be in a shelter."

But you know what really got me? When I went to that bathroom for the last time and almost passed out. It broke me because I wasn't thinking about myself. I was thinking about the women, the children, the elderly who had to come to these same conditions. It was extremely dark. I done worked in some nasty jobs in my life, and that was one I wouldn't have wanted to work in. Nothing was being done about it. It was hot during that time of the year, and then in the Superdome with all them people with no kind of ventilation, no air. I say, "Now if I'm about to pass out, and I'm a man, how the women that are with us going to come use the bathroom?" I snapped. You can only take so much. This was Thursday night. So I said a lot of foul things to the military personnel, the ones over the barricades pointing guns at us.

A black man in charge said, "Why don't you settle down and let's talk?" I said, "Man, we're in a prison here. Your people point your guns at us like if we make a wrong move towards them or something, we're going to be shot. We not no prisoners, man. You need to show me one piece of paper where I committed a crime. None of us here ain't committed no crime, man. We're in here trying to save our life. If they is out there committing crimes, man, you go deal with that. We here to get away from this."

That night around 3:00, a young man on the football field, where they had at least twenty-five thousand people sleeping all over, got up and walked up to a military personnel, took his M-16 from the young military man, and shot him. They shot him four times in front of everybody. I don't know if that young man died or not, but the thing that stayed on my mind about the whole incident was he couldn't take no more. He broke. That incident to me shouldn't never of happened. It was just one big, old, desperate situation for everybody. Military personnel compounded the problem.

Leaving New Orleans

The way the military handled the evacuation was extremely bad and confusing for everybody. First they made the announcement: "Everybody back away, we're leaving from such and such gate." Obviously, everybody was with their family and making sure they got the little stuff they did carry and was able to hold on to for them days.

Everybody is sticking together and we're slowly marching to the barricade. Now you got all these thousands and thousands of people on this ramp that's going up, and you got them packed in like sardines.

When everybody gets packed in real tight, then they make another announcement: "OK we don't want nothing but women and children." That made everything worse because all families were together. So that's how me and my wife got separated for two days. If you wanted it like this, you should have said it up front. Barricades could have been put in line. "I want women and children in this line, elderly in that line, and all men in the other line." Let's keep it like that in order but everybody going to the same place, so nobody panicked about losing your family members, or being separated from them. When they caused the confusion, by everybody being packed in, now you got children, little kids, and women holding on to their husbands, their boyfriends, and their fathers. They're saying, "No! You're not going to separate us from each other because this is all I have in the world left."

Then they made a statement, "Nobody leaving. Come across this barricade, you will be shot." I'm like, "Hold up! Why would you make that statement that you going to shoot us, man? We're not criminals!" When they made that statement, a lot of us men turned around and said, "Let us make our way to the back and let our women, children, and elderly people get out."

So then they had women and their little children saying, "You know what? I don't care what you're asking. I'm not leaving my daddy." Or, "I'm not leaving my husband because we came through all this here together, we came through all that flood water together, and we staying together." If it wasn't for our women and our children not leaving us, I think we would have been murdered, to be honest with you. It was like a feeling I had, because it was like, "We going to provoke them to excite a riot." I went to telling all the men, "Look, whatever you do, don't start a riot because they already pointing guns at us for no reason and we're unarmed."

Five or six buses left already, my wife being on one of them. About an hour or so into that process, they make another statement: "This is what we want. All families, make sure you stick together." So being that I listened to the first order, now I'm separated from my wife and nieces. And it's not just me, it's a lot of us men. Now my wife's gone to Houston and if I stay back here for another day or so, Houston may stop accepting people. Where I'm going to end up at? This is already in my mind, because plans change so rapidly. They said, "Everybody in here going to the Astrodome. Don't nobody worry."

On our way to the Astrodome on Saturday evening, we had just hit Texas, the bus driver came on the intercom, and he changed the whole plan again. He said, "I have another announcement to make. This bus's destination is now San Antonio." So I jump up and I say, "Sir, I really don't care where you take this bus, but you're taking me to Houston. This is the end of the straw. You can keep rolling after Houston if you want, but drop me off and I'll walk to the Astrodome to be with my family." He say, "I can't do that."

We had to stop at a rest stop, and they had a lot of Texas law enforcement officers out there. I hurried up and jumped off the bus, and I said, "Who in charge? I need to talk to the person that's in charge." So they pointed at the gentlemen and I said, "Sir, can I please speak to you?" He said, "Yeah, what's the problem?" I said, "The problem is I've been separated from my family due to no fault of my own or Katrina, because we stuck together through it all. We got in the Superdome and because I'm trying to comply with military orders, I've been separated from my family, but they all reassured us that we was all going to be together in the Astrodome. My family's been there now for going on two days." I said, "This man here just made an announcement saying he's taking me to San Antonio. Sir, that's wrong. I don't have nobody in San Antonio, and the way I feel right now, I cannot be separated from my family no more. I don't believe none of us could." He was a nice man. He went to the bus driver and he told him, "Take this bus to the Astrodome, and if you have to, I'll escort you. But all these people's families are in the Astrodome, and that's where they should be." We had some sandwiches and water on the bus. Most of us was just breathing a sigh of relief to be out of the Superdome.

Reclaiming Existence

When we got there, the Astrodome still was taking evacuees. When I got there, it was dark. I got reunited with my family, and I went to seeing people who had been in the Superdome, paying attention to the looks on their faces. They was lost, but they was relieved because they was being fed, they was able to take a shower, and they was able to just sit back and think about where they needed to start rebuilding their lives. It was obvious to all of us that it was going to be a long time, if ever, before we was going back home. Just the shock of that was hard.

At the Astrodome, our oldest boy, Lonnie Johnson, was basically there to meet us. Our son said, "Pack your things. I'm here to take you all out of here." The children my wife adopted start crying with their little baby. But I said, "Don't worry you all. We're not leaving you." Our destination was Birmingham, by our younger son, "Squeaky."[3] At that time, he was a senior starting guard at the University of Alabama. So we called Squeaky and told him, "We adopted these children. They have a kid that's handicapped. They need help more than we do. We want to bring them with us." Fortunately, the girl's uncle recognized my wife from seeing her with the little girl one time, and he said, "Wasn't you with my niece? When you see her, please give her my number." So when they got reunited with their family, we left the Astrodome.

A Houston pastor who knew the assistant coach of the University of Alabama at Birmingham (UAB) basketball team, T.J. Cleveland, put Kevin and Elise on a bus for Birmingham.[4]

Arriving at Birmingham, we came by this lady, Miss Linda Cox, a good friend of Squeaky. Her and her two daughters, Stephanie and Sylvia, they opened their arms and their house to us. I just went to looking for a job the next day, and we was just trying to get around and put our lives together from that point on. We lost our car in New Orleans, but they was bringing us around, taking us everywhere we had to go.

We was trying to get in this apartment complex. It was upper class. It was hard for us to get in, because we black and we from New Orleans. Most everyone else is white, and they're almost all from Birmingham. At first the manager of the complex told us there wasn't nothing available. Then it was something else. I said, "What if we get a voucher from FEMA?" They said, "We don't take vouchers, we don't take Section 8." I've never been on Section 8 in my life!

---

[3]See also Erik Brady and Andy Gardiner, "Upstarting Five Takes Court," *USA Today* (3/15/06).
[4]"UAB Guard Finds Blessing in Katrina," *USA Today* (1/16/06) at usatoday.com.

In the fall of 2005, the National Fair Housing Alliance conducted sixty-five test cases to see whether African Americans were at a disadvantage compared to whites when trying to rent apartments in Florida, Alabama, Georgia, Texas, and Tennessee. They found discrimination against blacks in sixty-six percent of the cases.[5]

So I'm like, "What do I need to get in?" So he came up with 2300 dollars altogether for the deposit and first month's rent. The rent is 765 dollars every month, which we pay. We wanted to just have somewhere nice to stay where we could feel comfortable.

From there, we've just been trying to get some normalcy in our lives by me working. I'm at UAB, the same school my son goes to. They act like they're not used to work. People from Louisiana, we've been working hard our whole lives. That's how I am, because that's how my father was. He was military strict. I get bored if I'm not working.

A few churches have helped us. We found them through some friends up here from New Orleans that are searching around too, and they're carless. That sectional we bought on our own, but this table was given to us by a church. Another church gave us a Wal-Mart card when we first came. It was two hundred dollars a piece, and the Urban League gave us a gas card.

When we was allowed back in the neighborhood after Katrina, our front and back door was bust completely wide open from the water. We had a fence around the house. The whole fence had floated away somewhere. It was a wood fence but it was embedded in concrete. To look at something that was embedded in concrete completely gone, where you can't much look down the block and see it. To have about an inch-and-a-half of mud throughout your downstairs. The smell was just unbelievable. Looking at every house in your neighborhood, doors bust open: It's like the whole city was dead, I'd say from Michoud all the way to Canal Street. I don't care if you lived in a poor neighborhood, a middle-class neighborhood, or a rich neighborhood, they all was devastated. We drove around and didn't see nobody.

The whole neighborhood right now is up for grabs. Whether it is going to be rebuilt or totally demolished, we don't know. It's a fact that they're trying to keep certain people out of New Orleans. When we went back to look at our house and assess the damages, there was no construction done. This was a month and a half after Katrina. There was still no electricity, no water, and the prices of apartments that we're looking for—we'd at least need a two-bedroom—a one bedroom is over eight hundred dollars everywhere in New Orleans. We're talking about apartment complexes that ain't worth five hundred dollars a month.

Conclusion

I would love to be part of the rebuilding process. I do home improvement—my neighborhood, with some hard work, could be saved. Hopefully more and more people will come back, and then New Orleans will get its smell and its energy back. But I don't know what our politicians are doing down there. I feel like they're not for the people. They're for themselves and their friends and their families. They were corrupt before Katrina.

---

[5]Crowley, "Where Is Home?" 128.

I believe we're deliberately being kept away. The main example is that there's nowhere to stay for the people who want to go back and start to help rebuild the city. Every time I was able to get to the Internet, everywhere I looked for a two-bedroom, it's over one thousand three hundred dollars a month. Most black people who come out of New Orleans can't afford that. So people will get their little money from FEMA, and say, "I'm going to try to make my life with family here," even though we don't want to. You got to look at what you can afford.

I feel like I been robbed of everything that I love. Even if it was going to my corner store—I had my people there that I hung with. I miss being able to cook the way I want to cook. They say people from New Orleans cook from the heart. Like one time when we first got here, we drove around for five hours looking for the type of meat we need: pickled rib tips and DD smoked sausage. We went to Bessemer, which is thirty miles away. We went everywhere. I was like, "I'm tired. Forget it." So it's a culture shock.

Every day I go through my routine of working, but every day it come out of my mouth, "I want to go home." I miss seeing familiar faces and having friends call and say, "What you all doing? I'm coming over." I miss the everyday things: sitting in my back yard and just enjoying the weather, family, and friends. I miss seeing my wife putting neighborhood children on the bus in the morning. I miss seeing their faces when we barbecue and tell them to come get the hamburgers. We fed the whole neighborhood, but that was so enjoyable. Our whole neighborhood was our comfort zone. We don't have that same sense of closeness, where we at.

I'm a grown man and I'm cried out. I'm not stupid. I opened my eyes up and I seen what you was doing to me. I can ask my God to show me what's happening in front of me. I believe with all my heart the military was going to kill us. If we had been the animals that they were portraying us to be, then they would have opened fire on us. There ain't no other explanation to continuously pointing your gun at unarmed, innocent people trying to escape a flood that killed us. We were following orders.

I understand the media was portraying all the bad that was going on, like the young men shooting at the helicopters and people looting. I didn't condone that but I understood it. Before the news cameras start rolling, they weren't pulling anybody off their roofs that was begging for help. I mean the wind from the helicopter blades was literally knocking some people off, and they were drowning. That's when the shooting started, because it was like, "We going to take pictures of you all, but we not going to save you." I believe if there'd been a faster response to rescuing people, then a lot of that wouldn't have happened. I feel like my government should have and could have handled it better. I can't believe that they weren't equipped to do that given the way Americans always respond to other people's disasters that we have nothing to do with.

So many people just didn't deserve to be treated like that by our military service, the people that we trust. I've paid taxes for many years. My father did and my grandfather did. So many people you might look down on as being poor, but they was tax paying citizens. My father fought in the military. He did two tours in Vietnam, and he's disabled because of it. Everybody there wasn't no gun-toting criminals. In fact, the majority of the people there wasn't. And to be classified as something that I'm not, it's just wrong. It's like somebody decided that black people's lives in New Orleans weren't worth saving, our culture weren't worth preserving, that we just weren't worth the money, the time, and the effort. Who has the right to decide that? Katrina was an act of nature, I realize that, but it's like someone took advantage of that to get rid of what they might look at as a problem. And that was wrong because my parents always taught me you deal with everybody individually, because no two people are the same.

To me, somebody needs to be held accountable for their actions, because we go to war behind trying to save another whole country, and what's going to be done about the injustice that was done to our own people? I hope that the Lord will allow me to live to see some justice be done behind the slow response, us not getting out of there like we should have, and a lot of deaths. People died senseless. You know if a man walk up to a man on the streets and shoot him in his head, he should be dealt with. If you deliberately commit a crime against humanity, then you should be dealt with and I don't care who you is.

You might look at New Orleans people as being violent or whatever. Believe me, people from New Orleans would not be a problem to you, if you don't be a problem to them. We fun-loving people. We ain't going to rake your stuff. We are Americans, and we human beings, and we didn't deserve for our government to neglect us and look over us and let us die like that.

Katrina's Long Shadow: Death, Trauma, and Depression*

I have a ninety-four year-old lady that was like my mom, I call her Mother Baker, who was removed from her granddaughter's apartment and taken to a landfill and left for three days by the National Guard. After the storm, her son found my number, and we connected by phone. She's West Indian, so she said, "Oh my child! I've prayed so much and asked God to make you be safe, and to let me talk to you." They took her grandson and granddaughter, because she had two young kids. And they said, "We're going to have to come back for you." When they came back for her a day later, they took her to a landing field. As time went on, they brought more and more people. They were outside on the black tar road. And she said to me, "Child, it's but God that kept me on that hot, black tar three days. I had nowhere to go to the bathroom." I mean just listening to her!

—Cynthia Banks

The guards at the Birmingham Interim Shelter, all they do is laugh in your face and throw darts at your character when you turn your back. Like one night I passed by. They were talking about Hurricane Katrina people here. So I went back and I said, "Let me tell you all something. I'm here, but I own my own home. My mother done left me a home, the house my dad built. And I worked just like you worked for years. It's not like we want to be here."

—Carl Singleton, retired hopper from the Lower Ninth Ward

A lot of our old people are dying from broken hearts. One of my mama's best friends off the West Bank, Ms. Frances, never lived outside New Orleans.

---

*From "Conclusion," Penner and Ferdinand.

She went to California and she died. It ain't about no money. It's about how you killing our people by separating them from their surroundings, everything they know and love, from people who took care of them. Those people never even crossed the Mississippi River Bridge before. How you going to send somebody from New Orleans to Boston, Utah, or Alaska? We are a community of people, and we took care of each other.

—Eleanor Thornton

The men, women, and children swept out to the bayous will never be counted. Those unable to scramble up ladders to their attics drowned and were discovered, often by loved ones, weeks and months later. Many medically fragile people who obeyed the mandatory evacuation order died far removed from the petroleum-and-waste-filled floodwaters engulfing New Orleans for more than three weeks. Even a more effective rescue effort would not have prevented most of these deaths.

Between Friday morning and Sunday afternoon when the military took charge of the evacuation effort, more than sixty thousand people were evacuated from the Superdome, the convention center, the Causeway Boulevard staging area, and the Louis Armstrong International Airport.[1] In the late summer heat and humidity of New Orleans, the four-day delay in providing a reliable food and water supply to survivors had serious, long-term health repercussions. Individuals who narrowly escaped the water's mad rush by taking refuge in their attics died from dehydration, if they were not saved in time by rescuers such as Willie Pitford, Demetrius White, a volunteer in the Cajun Navy, a New Orleans firefighter, or a National Guardsman.

Public health officials and demographers have been unable to precisely detail the extent of death caused by Katrina, but it has been estimated that including those who died shortly after evacuation, 1,577 deaths could be related to the storm, thereby making it the largest natural disaster ever experienced in the United States. In the chaos during the immediate aftermath, it cannot be ruled out that some deaths went unnoticed and unaccounted for. Experts in the field of public health recognize that the exact mortality due to the aftermath of Katrina, or the so-called second wave of Katrina deaths, has not yet been fully documented. One novel attempt, spearheaded by Kevin U. Stephens, Director of the New Orleans Health Department, to document this surge in the death rate utilizes death notices from the *Times Picayune,* the New Orleans daily newspaper.[2] The study found that during the first six months of 2006, an average 1,317 deaths per 100,000 people a month were reported in comparison with an average of 924 deaths per 100,000 people a month between 2002 and 2004. The study definitively concludes that the stress of losing everything, being abandoned, and fearing for one's life caused a massive wave of strokes and heart attacks in the weeks and months after Katrina. To give just one example from the narrations, Mother Baker died shortly after she spoke to Cynthia Banks.

---

[1]*CNN Reports*, 95.

[2]Kevin U. Stephens et al., "Excess Mortality in the Aftermath of Hurricane Katrina: A Preliminary Report," *Disaster Medicine and Public Health Preparedness,* 1 (2007), 15–20. Columbia University's Earth Institute, "Accounting for Katrina's Dead," at earth.columbia.edu.

Many of those who endured the aftermath of Katrina in the city continue to fight against depression, helplessness, rage, and post traumatic stress disorder.[3] Longing for the comfort of an ordinary existence, now elusive, is the fate of tens of thousands of Americans.

The survivor's trauma is due in part to the experience of being treated like a criminal during moments of great vulnerability. This injury is partially healed when survivors recount their experiences to family and friends, who are usually of the survivor's ethnicity. Listening to detailed accounts of the indignities suffered by loved ones, however, increases the emotional burden on the listener and may also produce secondary trauma in the listener. Physicians carry with them their worries about their patients, teachers about their students, pastors about their flocks, and social workers about their clients.

Anger and despair followed in the wake of home damage caused first by the hurricane, then by the flood, and finally by the black mold that took over the houses. In some cases, individuals were prevented from returning to their homes for months. The emotional impact of this loss does not appear to have been related to the income of the narrators or the value of the houses. Before the storm, most houses in the Lower Ninth Ward were appraised at between twenty and forty thousand dollars. Even a fragile, wood-frame, shotgun-style house may reflect a lifetime's investment of resources and heart. It may also symbolically represent the ties that bind one generation to the next, and be the only tangible link to parents or grandparents no longer living. Those who tenaciously believe that they were deliberately flooded out of New Orleans carry an additional trauma beyond the loss of their possessions and home.

A home (or business) built against tremendous societal odds, in the face of segregation, institutional racism, and blacklisting, reflects a substantial emotional investment. The destruction of the heart of black middle-class New Orleans—Pontchartrain Park and New Orleans East—also meant the splintering of dreams. The floodwaters of Katrina washed away the fruits of a lifetime of sacrifice and hard work.

Another source of the emotional toll springs from the disruption of the extended network of family and friends. Black New Orleanians are now scattered throughout the United States, weakening their sense of community and interconnectedness. Social networks allowed determined African Americans to overcome the obstacles of poor education, low wages, inadequate health care, and crime to live passionate, gracious, and fulfilling lives. These support networks have been broken artificially. As survivors make decisions about where and how to rebuild, it is the loss of this community and the awareness of its collective mistreatment that deepens the mourning. Is New Orleans still home if your neighbors, cousins, and lifetime friends no longer live there?

Recent data from the *Archives of General Psychiatry* documents that the adults who experienced anxiety and stress after the attacks of September 11, 2001, were at higher

---

[3]Jose Calderon-Abbo, "The Long Road Home: Rebuilding Public Inpatient Psychiatric Services in Post-Katrina New Orleans," *Psychiatric Services*, 59, No. 3 (2008), 304–309; David Abramson, Tasha Stehling-Ariza, Richard Garfield, and Irwin Redlener, "Prevalence and Predictors of Mental Health Distress Post-Katrina: Findings from the Gulf Coast Child and Family Health Study," *Disaster Medicine and Public Health Preparedness*, 2 (2008), 77–86.

risk for heart disease, high blood pressure, and strokes. Those who developed depression were three times more likely to have heart-related illnesses one to two years later.[4] Studies from previous catastrophes, including wars, have demonstrated that with the collapse of the health infrastructure, such as New Orleans has undergone, preventable deaths continue for many years after the event.

For those of us not from New Orleans, who live eternally positioned at metaphorical crossroads, eager and ready to trade up not only jobs and partners but also cities and continents, these narratives provide detailed maps into now effaced communities with different rhythms and social values. Collectively, these histories may assist the concerned outsider, the guidance counselor, the community health worker, or the pastor to gain a better grasp on the stress and trauma still faced by survivors.

[4]E. Alison Holman et al., "Terrorism, Acute Stress, and Cardiovascular Health: A 3-Year National Study Following the September 11th Attacks," *Archives of General Psychiatry* 65 (01/08), 73–80.

CHAPTER 7

Comparative Genocide

The term "genocide" was coined by Raphael Lemkin in 1944 to describe the "Nazi policies of systematic murder, including the destruction of the European Jews." The word itself is derived from "combining geno- from the Greek word for race or tribe, with -cide, from the Latin word for killing" (United States Holocaust Memorial Museum, n.d.). In 1948 the United Nations formally designated genocide as an international crime, and adopted the following definition:

> [G]enocide means any of the following acts committed with intent to destroy, in whole or in part, a national, ethnical, racial or religious group, as such:
>
> **(a)** Killing members of the group;
> **(b)** Causing serious bodily or mental harm to members of the group;
> **(c)** Deliberately inflicting on the group conditions of life calculated to bring about its physical destruction in whole or in part;
> **(d)** Imposing measures intended to prevent births within the group;
> **(e)** Forcibly transferring children of the group to another group.
>
> (United States Holocaust Memorial Museum, n.d.).

As the comparative study of genocide has evolved, much rancor and debate have surrounded the application of the term to various historical events of mass murder. This chapter is not intended to be a presentation of "competitive" or "comparative" suffering, but rather, to familiarize the reader with major events of mass murder as extreme situations, and to highlight some of the critical issues that frame the discussion of genocidal behavior. As previously noted, Rosenberg et al. (1964) assert that "the decisive characteristic of extreme situations in sociological perspective is that they have been denormatized—morality and legality have more and more been supplanted by functional rationality as *the* operative norm of conduct . . . " (p. 167). It is precisely this abandonment of moral and legal standards that creates an institutional context wherein genocidal destruction becomes possible.

In his book on comparative genocides, Alan Rosenbaum (1996) notes that

the term Holocaust usually refers to what the Nazis called the "Final Solution to the Jewish Question," namely the deliberate, systematic extermination of all Jewish people. . . . It also encompasses the relentless persecution, enslavement, and murder of many millions more: Gypsies, Poles, Slavs, gays, the mentally ill, the handicapped, and political dissidents (p. 2).

In her classic work *The War Against the Jews*, Lucy Dawidowicz (1976) states:

> The Final Solution transcended the bounds of modern historical experience. Never before in modern history had one people made the killing of another the fulfillment of an ideology, in whose pursuit means were identical with ends. History has, to be sure, recorded terrible massacres and destruction that one people perpetrated against another, but all—however cruel and unjustifiable—were intended to achieve instrumental ends, being means to ends, not ends in themselves (p. xxiii).

Approximately 6 million Jews, or two-thirds of European Jewry, were killed during the Holocaust. The Holocaust is the quintessential genocidal event that has become the reference point for the highly charged conversation regarding genocidal atrocity.

Several readings in this chapter present a comparative analysis of the Holocaust and the Armenian Genocide. It is estimated that approximately 1.5 million Armenians were killed in the Ottoman Empire between 1915 and 1922. According to Peter Balakian (2003), "the plan to liquidate the Armenians of the Ottoman Empire was put into motion in the spring and early summer of 1915" (p. 175). Robert Melson (1996) writes that "between 1915 and the armistice in 1918, some 1 million people, out of a population of 2 million, were killed. Later a half million more Armenians perished as Turkey sought to free itself of foreign occupation and to expel minorities" (p. 160).

Referencing the Rwandan genocide, Edward Kissi (2004) notes, "Robert Melson, arguably the dean of the comparative study of genocide, has characterized the slaughter of Tutsis by extreme Hutus in Rwanda in 1994 as the 'African' version of the Holocaust" (p. 115). However, Kissi cautions that in the comparative analysis of genocide there are distinctive "fault lines," situational forces and circumstances that cannot be ignored. In the reading "Victimization, Survival and the Impunity of Forced Exile," Frank Afflitto notes that the massacres were "planned and executed with precision" (p. 83). Referencing Prunier (1995), he asserts that "[e]ven children became legitimate targets [and] [a]n estimated one million persons were killed in barely thirteen weeks, with 800,000 killed within the first five weeks" (p. 83). In his book *Eyewitness to a Genocide*, Michael Barnett (2002) outlines the grim details of the massacre: "In one hundred days, between April 6 and July 19, 1994, they murdered roughly 800,000 individuals. For the statistically inclined, that works out to 333⅓ deaths per hour, 5½ deaths per minute" (p. 1).

In the reading "Dissecting Darfur," Darren Brunk (2008) indicates that between 2003 and 2006, more than 200,000 Darfurians died while the conflict "contributed to nearly two million internally displaced people, 208,000 refugees, and 3.5 million now dependant on humanitarian assistance" (p. 27). In his book *Darfur: The Ambiguous Genocide*, Gérard Prunier (2007) states, "If we use the December 1948 definition [UN definition] it is obvious that Darfur is a genocide, but if we use the definition I proposed in my book on Rwanda it is not" (p. 156).

The highly charged and passionate genocide controversy is evident in both the academic community and between the participants involved in numerous incidents of mass murder. This chapter addresses some of the myriad factual, revisionist, socioeconomic, and geopolitical variables that influence the outcome of the dispute.

A recent case in point is Turkey's role in the Armenian massacres. In October 2009, Turkey and Armenia signed a momentous accord to "normalize" ties and create a joint commission to examine the role of the Turkish Ottoman forces in the killings. While Turkey has acknowledged the deaths of countless numbers of Armenians, it has refused to acknowledge the killing as genocide. Notwithstanding this historic accord, the United States House Foreign Affairs Committee voted by a slim margin in March 2010 to adopt a resolution stating that United States policy would formally declare the massacre of Armenians by the Ottoman forces as genocide.

> The issue puts President Barack Obama between NATO ally Turkey, which rejects calling the event genocide, and an important US-Armenian constituency and their backers in Congress ahead of a November Congressional election. . . . Turkey has said its ties with the United States would be damaged and that Ankara's efforts to normalize relations with Armenia could be endangered if the resolution is passed (Cornwell and Mohammed, 2010).

Israel Charny, author of the *Encyclopedia of Genocide*, suggests "recognizing all cases of mass murder as genocide *and* at the same time, subclassifying various cases of genocide into subgroups of similar events, so that we have a series of categories of types of genocide . . . " (as cited in Rosenbaum, 1996, p. x). With regard to the "scholarly" discussion of determining what mass murders are to be identified as genocide, he "call[s] this 'definitionalism,' or such an intense concern with establishing the boundaries of a definition that the reality of the phenomenon—in this case, human tragedy and infamy—is banished to a secondary position and no longer genuinely experienced" (p. xi).

Steven Katz (1996) begins his discussion that situates the Holocaust as unique in genocidal destruction by emphasizing that his analysis is not grounded in "comparative morality, evil or suffering." Rather, its uniqueness is "by virtue of the fact that never before has a state set out, as a matter of intentional principle and actualized policy, to annihilate physically every man, woman, and child belonging to a specific people" (p. 19). Citing Stalin's purges of academics and other leaders that began in 1929 and the subsequent Ukrainian famine of 1930–1933, Katz suggests that the ultimate goal was "the complete annihilation of Ukrainian nationalism" (p. 27). He asserts that this "is most correctly categorized as an instance of nationalist conflict and internal colonialism rather than as an example of genocide. Stalin did not intend to exterminate the entire population of Ukraine" (p. 30). He further notes that "Stalin intended that after the famine there should still be Ukrainians, though not Ukrainianism; Hitler intended that after Auschwitz there would be neither Jews nor Judaism" (p. 31).

In regard to the Armenian massacres, Katz (1996) notes that the evolution of the killings was rooted in political considerations wherein,

> the Armenians were "enemies" to the degree that they were enemies in this context, on practical and political grounds centering around long-standing policies of internal colonialism, the implications—and machinations—of national self determination, and the provocative issue of loyalty in time of war (p. 33).

In other words, the "Armenian question" was one of politics and "national iden-tity" while the "Jewish question" was one of "blood," race and biological purity. Katz asserts that the Nazis "insisted not only on the elimination of Jewish col-lective identity and communal existence, but also on the murder of every Jewish person of whatever age and gender" (p. 33). Finally, Katz considers "the possibility of Armenian Christian conversion to Islam . . . the specific character of the forced deportations . . . and the *nontotalistic* nature of the anti-Armenian crusade" (p. 34) as features characteristic of the Armenian genocide and distinguishable from the Holocaust.

Robert Melson (1996) posits that the Holocaust and the Armenian genocide are "prototypically different" in their relationship to other mass killings. He asserts that "[t]he Armenian Genocide and the Holocaust are the quintessential instances of total genocide in the twentieth century" (p. 157) and share several basic similarities. However, he argues that while the Armenian genocide was "motivated by a vari-ant of nationalist ideology [and] the victims were a territorial ethnic group . . . the Holocaust [was] motivated by ideologies of racism and anti-Semitism, an ideology of global scope" (p. 157). Melson further highlights several of the similarities and differences between the two "total" genocides and makes special note of the Nazis' extermination camp as a distinguishing characteristic of the Holocaust. He concludes that the "partial genocides" of Nigeria and Yugoslavia are more analogous to the Armenian genocide in their methods of killing and their victimization of specific ter-ritorial ethnic groups.

In his book *The Burning Tigris*, Peter Balakian (2003) details the evolutionary dynamics that precipitated the Turkish massacres of the Armenian population and concludes that "the death tolls from 1915 through 1922 range from over a million to a million and a half" (p. 180). The author references Richard Rubenstein's book *The Cunning of History* (1987), in which he describes the massacre of the Armenians by the Turks as the "first full-fledged attempt by a modern state to practice disciplined me-thodically organized genocide" (p. 180). Balakian describes the role of the "chetes—the ex-convict killer bands" (p. 182) and the gendarmes (police), in carrying out the killings and the crucial role that the railways played in facilitating the deportations and resulting massacres of the victims. The author makes numerous comparisons be-tween the Armenian genocide and the Holocaust, and emphasizes that the Armenian massacres were made possible because of their legal grounding in legislative plan-ning and authority.

Katherine Derderian (2005) emphasizes the centrality of violence against women in the Armenian genocide and the importance of such research in comparative analysis with the Holocaust and other genocidal events. Derderian describes the increased vul-nerability of women as targets of rape, sexual slavery, forced marriage and additional acts of sexual violence that took place in the absence of the Armenian men who had been separated and deported from their communities. She further suggests that sexual violence against women was used to "dehumanize" and intimidate the Armenian pop-ulation, which served to establish the "perpetrators' " control over the victim popula-tion and further the goals of the genocidal destruction. Using oral history testimonies to illuminate her analysis, Derderian also sheds light on the relationships between gender-specific violence, "reproductive continuity," assimilation, economic advantage and the enduring struggle between "stigma and survival" for those Armenian women who had married Turkish men during the genocide.

The article by Frank Afflitto (2000) briefly identifies several of the dynamics that characterized the relationship between the Hutus and Tutsis as a backdrop to the Rwandan genocide. He then notes that the *labeling* of persons as part of a group which is "deserving" of victim status, that is, "victimizable," is a salient feature in the perpetrators' rationale for their genocidal destruction of the group. The reading continues with an exploration of the victimization of a young Tutsi woman named Fleur during the Rwandan genocide. The author suggests that this case study of Fleur is in fact representative of similar experiences of victimization during the genocide. As portrayed in rich and graphic detail, the official assignment or labeling of Fleur as an ethnic Tutsi set into motion the sequential process of her tragic victimization and ultimate survival. We learn that the dynamic nature of the survivor's adaptive mode is not static but processual; it continues after the genocide and is influenced by the survivor's knowledge and internalization of whether the offenders received either appropriate justice or impunity.

The fact that the survivors' ongoing coping mechanisms are dynamic and reflect awareness of actions taken against the perpetrators after the genocide is particularly poignant. In a study of elderly survivors of the Armenian genocide, Kalayjian et al. (1996) found that the subjects' awareness of "[t]he persistent denial of the Genocide by the Turkish government evoked intense anger and rage" (p. 95). The authors cite Miller and Miller (1987) and Des Pres (1987) in their explanation of the "rage" associated with denial. According to Des Pres,

> [t]hat the world refuses to credit the central event of their fate is painful in the extreme and, for some, a cause of violent rage . . . [i]t is hardly difficult to make sense of the Armenian case in which the driving forces are historically tragedy, permanent loss and the pain of memory mocked by denial (p. 95).

Finally, the researchers cite Sullivan (1953) to note that "validation of a traumatic experience is an essential step toward resolution and closure" (p. 95).

Edward Kissi (2004) observes that while many scholars have invited comparisons between the mass murders in Rwanda, Ethiopia and Cambodia and genocidal events elsewhere, there are significant "distinctions and fault lines" that cannot be ignored. He suggests that "[w]hile genocide, as strictly defined, occurred in the course of revolution and war in Rwanda and Cambodia it did not in Ethiopia" (p. 116). Kissi and others (e.g. Harff and Gurr, 1988) make a distinction between "politicide," wherein the victims are targeted because of their "political opposition to the regime and dominant groups," and "genocide," where the victims are targeted because of their "communal characteristics i.e. ethnicity, religion or nationality" (p. 116). Kissi reviews the situational forces and various causal explanations that have been proposed to account for the mass killings in Rwanda, Cambodia and Ethiopia.

He concludes by reemphasizing the importance of clarity in identifying the role and nature of the political dimension in the etiology of mass murder. Specifically, one must examine the relationship between political groups and ideologies to their respective community and state in the analysis of mass murder and genocide.

In the final reading, Darren Brunk (2008) traces the evolutionary forces that influenced the formal organizational response to the "crisis" of violence in Darfur, and the role that the "memory" of Rwanda ultimately played in positioning Darfur in the "framework" of the genocidal debate. Brunk notes that while the conflict in Darfur between 2003 and 2006 left more than 200,000 "Darfurians" dead and 3.5 million people in need of humanitarian aid, little attention was paid to it by the United Nations, the international community or the mass media. It was not until the spring of 2004 and the approaching tenth anniversary of the Rwandan genocide that both the nature of the conflict itself and its resulting humanitarian crisis were catapulted onto the global stage.

Darfur was presented as a genocidal event viewed through the lens of the international failure in Rwanda. According to Brunk, "[i]n countless articles, the Rwandan genocide anniversary and the Darfur crisis became suffused almost into a single issue, with Darfur being presented as a contemporary recurrence of Rwanda's 'genocide' and the international community's 'failure there' " (p. 31). The "recasting" of the events in Darfur was now grounded in the diplomatic and political arena, and the United States House and Senate voted in July 2004 to "declare" Darfur a genocidal event. Notwithstanding these facts, Brunk contends that "while the invocation of Rwanda may have raised the profile of the genocide question, it is not the contention here that the situation in Darfur was in every instance perceived as genocide solely or even primarily *because* it was associated with Rwanda" (p. 37).

The debate surrounding the designation of Darfur as a genocidal event continues, and Brunk cautions that the assignment of the term to an event must flow from a precise and informed evaluation of the event itself and not from external variables (e.g. guilt) associated with previous killings. He maintains that to do so would undermine the significance of the term (genocide) itself and its "moral and legal" ramifications.

THE UNIQUENESS OF THE HOLOCAUST: THE HISTORICAL DIMENSION

Steven T. Katz

Introduction

Given the focus of this book on the issue of the uniqueness of the Holocaust, I wish to state clearly at the outset my position on this matter: The Holocaust, that is, the intentional murder of European Jewry during World War II, is historically and phenomenologically unique. No other case discussed in this book parallels it. My burden in the remainder of this chapter is to document and defend this statement.

In arguing for the uniqueness of the Holocaust, I am *not* making a *moral* claim, in other words, that the Holocaust was more evil than the other events discussed in this collection, for example, the murder of Armenians in World War I, the devastation of the Native American communities over the centuries, the decimation of Ukraine by Stalin, the treatment of the Gypsies during World War II, and the enslavement and mass death of black Africans during the enterprise of New World slavery. I know of no method or technique that would allow one to weigh up, to quantify and compare, such massive evil and suffering, and I therefore avoid altogether this sort of counterproductive argument about what one might describe as comparative suffering.

In addition, I am not suggesting that the Holocaust involved the greatest number of victims of any mass crime. It did not. Numbers of victims will not establish the uniqueness of the Holocaust—quite the contrary.

When I argue for the uniqueness of the Holocaust I intend only to claim that the Holocaust is phenomenologically unique by virtue of the fact that never before has a state set out, as a matter of intentional principle and actualized policy, to annihilate physically every man, woman, and child belonging to a specific people. A close study of the relevant comparative historical data will show that only in the case of Jewry under the Third Reich was such all-inclusive, noncompromising, unmitigated murder intended.

The Famine in Ukraine

The widespread and consequential famine in Ukraine between 1930 and 1933 also has to be accounted for in light of the current argument contra genocide. There are two main lines of scholarly interpretation as to what happened in Ukraine and why. The first of these emphasizes the nationalist dimensions of the event. Under this interpretation, both the indigenous Ukrainian population and the alien Soviet ruling class knew that Ukraine, as recently as 1918, had been independent—with its own separate historical and cultural traditions—and that it wished to be politically independent again. Accordingly, the confrontation of the late 1910s and of the 1920s and 1930s in this region is seen as having been defined by the collision of two competing claims to sovereignty: one nationalist and the other putatively internationalist, though, increasingly, the latter was merely a cover for an ever more visible Russian national chauvinism. For Stalin, the ultimate objective is seen to have been the full integration without national remainder of Ukraine into the larger, ideally homogenized, Soviet state. Anything less was dangerous, both practically—because it would interfere with Bolshevik control of the agricultural market and the essential issue of grain collection and distribution, a circumstance that often divided the local leadership—and potentially—because of the geopolitically divisive character of nationalist aspirations. In consequence, Stalin, under this nationalist reading, consciously decided on a deadly campaign—most accurately described through the political category of internal colonialism—to eradicate this recurring threat to Soviet hegemony. Beginning with the purge of Ukrainian academics and political and cultural leaders that began in April 1929 and continued into 1930, Stalin is believed to have set in motion a movement that would eventually consume literally millions of Ukrainians.

The object of the entire terror campaign was, under this exegesis, the complete annihilation of Ukrainian nationalism (a goal that was also consistent with the larger Stalinist policy of the socialization of agriculture). Much like Hitler's later strategy in, for example, Poland (and elsewhere in eastern Europe), Stalin sought to expunge local autonomy and all manifestations of cultural and political independence in order to facilitate continued domination from Moscow. Here, as in many other cases that easily come to mind (Cambodia, Nigeria, Sudan, and, most recently, Rwanda), the purpose of state-organized violence is the maintenance of political control.

Given the importance of the independent, economically autonomous peasantry in Ukraine's socioeconomic structures, Stalin's plan for the extermination of national identity required—in addition to the removal of the national intelligentsia—a crusade against this "protocapitalist" strata. As Semen O. Pidhainy has described it, Stalin had to move against Ukrainian nationalism's "social base"—the individual landholdings.[1] "Only a mass terror throughout the body of the nation—that is, the peasantry—could reduce the nation to submission."[2] As long as the *selianym* (a euphemism now for all free Ukrainian peasants) existed, nationalist (and capitalist) sentiment would remain: Both needed to be crushed.

The dominant method used to achieve this collective submission to socialism, this elimination of the base of Ukrainian national sentiment, was the forced collectivization of the agricultural sector. At the same time, and not unimportant, such a centralized agrarian policy gave the Communist Party—in the form of the All-Union Commissariat of Agriculture—control over the region's grain supply. It was the task and responsibility of this commissariat, in conjunction with the Soviet planners, to calculate, coordinate, and organize the yearly grain harvest, in other words, to set and oversee the state exactions to be levied and collected. In the event, when this direct control was expressed in an overly demanding target for grain exports from the region—ostensibly justified by the increased program of industrialization that was to be financed by the agricultural surplus—it effectively translated into a man-made famine in Ukraine in 1931 that grew worse in 1932 and 1933. For example, in 1931, the procurement quota for the region was

---

[1]Semen O. Pidhainy et al., eds., *The Black Deeds of the Kremlin: A White Book*, vol. 1 (Detroit, 1955), p. 205.

[2]Robert Conquest, *The Harvest of Sorrow: Soviet Collectivization and the Terror-Famine* (New York: Oxford University Press, 1986), p. 219. Repeated in the *U.S. Commission on the Ukraine Famine* (Washington, D.C., 1990), p. xiii: "Crushing the Ukrainian peasantry made it possible for Stalin to curtail Ukrainian national self-assertion."

set at 7 million tons out of a total of 18.3 million tons (much of which had been lost to inefficient collective harvesting). Such a level of national procurement almost certainly spelled trouble for the local community. Matters of food supply only got worse in 1932 when the procurement total was again set at 7 million tons while that year's harvest, due to drought, inefficiency, and a decline in the number of acres sown—the last partly in protest to Stalinist policy—came in at the very reduced level of 14.7 million tons. Although the local leadership, in the face of the total decline in tonnage, managed to persuade Moscow, at great cost to itself in the suspicions of disloyalty (and suspect nationalism) that such appeals raised, to reduce the quota to 6.6 million tons—itself a target never fulfilled—even this reduced sum was still far too high to make it possible to avoid massive starvation. Stalin, despite the mounting death toll, did not believe, or did not *want* to believe, the claim that the harvest was too small both to feed the Ukrainian people and to provide sufficient grain for export. Instead, already intensely suspicious of Ukrainian separatism and fearful of local disloyalty, he chose to interpret the failure to meet the inordinate quotas sent down from the center as deliberate acts of "sabotage," the peasants as no better than "wreckers" of the socialist dream. Therefore, in a deliberate act intended to punish the population of Ukraine—though justified as an act of socialist self-defense—he continued to export grain from the region, if at a lower rate: 1.73 million tons in 1932 and 1.68 million tons in 1933, compared to 5.2 million tons in 1931. This export of grain, given the greatly reduced supplies, turned an already grave situation into an occasion of mass death.

Increased pressure was now also applied against the *selianym*-class enemy, local party officials (37.3 percent of the new Ukrainian Communist Party members and candidate members were purged and 75 percent of local Soviets and members of local committees were replaced, with many of those who were replaced being arrested for failing to produce the required quota), those involved in local agricultural middle management (many of these officials were arrested in the second half of 1932 for sabotaging Bolshevik policy), and all channels of Ukrainian economic, cultural, and nutritional self-sufficiency. On December 14, 1932, the Central Committee of the All-Union Communist Party accused the leadership of the Ukrainian Communist Party "of tolerating a Ukrainian nationalist deviation in its ranks"[3] and then proceeded, on January 24, 1933, to replace it with a new ruling clique headed by Pavel Postyshev. At the same time, all available food aid to the stricken population, it is argued, was consciously denied, existing grain reserves in the region and elsewhere were not made available, and the importation of food was stopped at the border of Ukraine—all while Stalin, in an act of depravity, continued, as already noted, to export more than 3 million tons of grain in 1932 and 1933. As a result, there was massive—under this decoding, *intentional*—starvation throughout Ukraine climaxing in 1933 and 1934. Of a peasant population of upwards of 25 million, I estimate that up to 5 million persons, or 20 percent of the rural population, plus from 500,000 to 750,000 persons in the urban areas of Ukraine, died from lack of food and related medical problems in this period. In some areas, the death rate was as

---

[3]Cited from George O. Liber, *Soviet Nationality Policy* (Cambridge: Cambridge University Press, 1992), p. 166. On these political activities, interpreted from a radical Ukrainian perspective, see Hryhory Kostiuk, *Stalinist Rule in the Ukraine* (New York: Praeger, 1960), pp. 18–37; and from a less ideological perspective, see Robert S. Sullivant, *Soviet Politics in the Ukraine* (New York: Columbia University Press, 1962), pp. 195–208.

low as 10 percent, in others nearly 100 percent, depending largely upon local agricultural and ecological conditions, for example, and most importantly, the ability to find other sources of nutrition, such as fish or wildlife—in many places this also led to cannibalism and infanticide—to replace the lost grain harvests.

So goes the nationalist account of the Ukrainian famine interpreted as an intentional, man-made "genocide." Stalin purposely killed 5 million or more Ukrainians, plus hundreds of thousands of additional individuals belonging to other ethnic groups, such as the Volga Germans and Kuban Cossacks, in order both to decapitate opposition to agricultural collectivization and to eradicate Ukrainian, and other, nationalist aspirations.

Now, accepting this nationalist interpretation of Ukrainian history, at least for the sake of argument, what are we to conclude about these events constituting an instance of genocide? This is neither an irrelevant nor a trivial question given the size of the human losses involved and the evil will that is asserted to have directly caused, to have been knowingly responsible for, these losses. Moreover, I do not want to support any diminution or denial of this vast collective tragedy, the existence of which is not in doubt. However—and here I recognize that given the loss of millions of persons this conclusion will seem at first counterintuitive—even if the nationalist intentionalist thesis is correct, the results—at least 5 million deaths—do *not* constitute the technical crime of genocide, and the event, in its phenomenological specificity and totality, is not, for all of its murderous ferocity and demographic enormity, comparable to the Shoah. I would argue—assuming the correctness of this account—that the ruthless campaign against Ukrainian nationalism that destroyed a majority of the indigenous Ukrainian cultural and political elite, in addition to a significant segment of the peasant population of the region, is most correctly categorized as an instance of nationalist conflict and internal colonialism rather than as an example of genocide. Stalin did not intend to exterminate the entire population of Ukraine.

This conclusion finds immediate support from the apposite statistical indicators: Though the human carnage was enormous—approaching the number of Jewish victims during the Second World War—the portion of the Ukrainian peasant population lost was somewhere near 20 percent (plus or minus 5 percent), and the losses for the Ukrainian population as a whole were in the area of 15 percent. These demographic results resemble (if being slightly higher than) the figures for population decline in those eastern European countries overrun by the Nazis, and in both cases the numbers do not indicate that a policy of total population eradication was pursued. Had Stalin in Ukraine—and Hitler in eastern Europe—sought to pursue a genocidal war, given the destructive possibilities that lay open to him, more than 15 percent of the population would have been done away with. More people were not killed because, amid the murder that did occur, there was, odd as this may seem, restraint. There was restraint because Stalin did not want to eradicate the people of Ukraine; he wanted to exploit them. Eliminating the whole of a vanquished helot population makes no more sense than slaughtering one's slaves. However, in contrast, eliminating a conquered people's controlling elite, leaving it leaderless, anxious, and vertiginous, is a rational and functional strategy, long pursued by conquerors and adopted by Stalin, in order to achieve both enduring subordination of the subjugated and political stability in one's empire. This is not a humane imperial strategy—a regular course of action to be recommended as a form of empire maintenance—but neither is it genocide.

Ironically, this judgment is confirmed by the heartrending condition of the children, especially infants and the newborn. Throughout Ukraine, youthful cadavers lay strewn across the landscape; the entire territory had become a crude necropolis for children under the age of twelve who were unable to obtain enough nourishment to stay alive. Yet even here, in the midst of the most intense human suffering, the relevant population statistics require careful decipherment. The latest demographic data indicate that fewer than 760,000 children died,[4] largely from starvation, between 1932 and 1934. This represents, depending on one's estimation of other relevant demographic variables, between 6 percent and 33.5 percent of the age cohort and a significant percentage of the total population decline. However, recognizing the great tragedy that occurred here, even the maximum loss rate of 33.5 percent does not support a genocidal reading of this event. For, on these numbers, that is, a loss rate of between 6 and 33.5 percent, 66.5 percent of Ukrainian children, at a minimum, survived. Once the famine was past its peak in May 1933, the surviving two out of three children were not singled out for further harassment or worse. Most of those who survived the crisis of 1932–1933 survived.

This historical outcome regarding the children is not trivial. What makes the Ukrainian case non-genocidal, and what makes it different from the Holocaust, is the fact that the majority of Ukrainian children survived and, still more, that they were *permitted* to survive. Even the mountain of evidence pertaining in Stalin's evil actions produced by the proponents of the nationalist-genocide thesis—for example, James Mace and Robert Conquest—does not indicate an intent to eliminate, or any motive that would plausibly justify the extermination of, the Ukrainian biological stock. Though the number of Ukrainian children who died and, under the intentionalist reading, were murdered, was almost as high as (or higher than) the number of Jewish children who were exterminated, their deaths were the consequence of, represented, and intended something wholly different from what the murder of Jewish children at Auschwitz and Treblinka represented and intended. In the Ukrainian case, the focused object of the violence and death was national enfeeblement and political dismemberment. In the Shoah, the focused object, given its racial determinants, was physical genocide. Stalin intended that after the famine there should still be Ukrainians, though not Ukrainianism; Hitler intended that after Auschwitz there would be neither Jews nor Judaism. The loss of every child in both contexts, employing the calculus of the talmudic sages, was the loss of a world. The death of each child was an act of equal immorality. Nonetheless, there is an important, nonreductive, phenomenological difference to be drawn between mass murder (including children) and complete group extinction (including children), between a war for political and territorial domination (including children) and a war of unlimited biological annihilation (including children).

The issue, the interpretive inquiry, the dialectic of evidence and meaning regarding the Ukrainian tragedy, is still more complex. For, as noted (nonpolemically) at the

---

[4]Robert Conquest's maximum total of child deaths of 4 million—3 million as a result of the famine and 1 million due to the program of dekulakization—appears, based on currently available evidence, too high. See *Harvest of Sorrow*, p. 297. Moreover, this total includes non-Ukrainian children, for example, those of Kazakhstan, thus reducing the number and percentage of child losses in Ukraine (even on Conquest's numbers) significantly.

outset of this analysis, there are two possible explanations of the Ukrainian tragedy. The second possible, plausible, non-nationalist deconstruction of the Ukrainian tragedy argues that the famine was neither intended nor man-made—though, ultimately, it was the result of human errors connected with the program of forced collectivization. That is to say, under this alternative reading, the famine, the reality and extent of which no one denies, was not the consequence of a premeditated plan to murder large numbers of Ukrainians in support of an antinationalist political outcome in the region. Therefore, by definition, what transpired, though baleful and full of bile, was not genocide.

The case for this very different interpretation has been made by a number of scholars including, most recently, J. Arch Getty, Walter Laqueur, Mark B. Tauger, and R. W. Davies, and is supported by both Robert C. Tucker's narrative in his *Stalin in Power* and Adam Ulam's conclusion in his *Stalin: The Man and His Era*: "Stalin and his closest collaborators had not willed the famine."[5]

Now, under either interpretation of the Ukrainian tragedy, the fact is that, though something very terrible occurred in Ukraine, what happened was a very different sort of thing—structurally and as regards intention—than what transpired in the Holocaust.

The Armenian Tragedy

The Armenian tragedy was an enormous historical outrage. As I understand this event, the controlling ambition, the collective civic agenda, behind Turkish inhumanity was primarily nationalist in character and, in practice, limited in scope and purpose. The Armenian massacres were an indecent, radicalized manifestation of a most primitive jingoism activated by the exigencies of war from without and the revolutionary collapse of the Ottoman empire from within. Turkish nationalism—the extreme nationalist elites in control of the Turkish state—now under the violent cover of war, envisioned and pursued the elimination of (*not* the murder of) *all* non-Turkish elements—and most especially and specifically the eradication of the Armenian community—from the national context. The anti-Armenian crusade was, therefore, for all its lethal extravagance, a delimited political crusade. Of course, mixed in to the noxious brew that represented itself as national destiny were other obsessions: a loathing of Christians if not all non-Muslims, xenophobia, greed, jealousy, fear, desire, and the like. But, above all else, the "war against the Armenians" was a vulgar and desperate manifestation of raw nationalist politics.

As a direct and immediate consequence, anti-Armenianism is not expressed in the baroque language of metaphysical evil, nor does it require (paraphrasing Heinrich Himmler's assertion that "all Jews without exception must die") the complete annihilation of *every* Armenian man, woman, and child. It does not represent a racial collision as that term came to be understood in the ornate ontological schema of Nazism. There is no assertion of primordial reciprocity between power and being, between intrahuman aggression and metahistoric causations, between biological contingencies and noumenological principles. Rather, the elemental rationale almost universally cited by the Turks in defense of their actions is political: The Armenians were secessionists, Russian spies, fifth-columnists, and divisive nationalists who would subvert the Turkish people's revolution and destroy Turkish national and political integrity. This explanatory tack,

---

[5]Adam Uiam, *Stalin: The Man and His Era* (New York: Viking, 1973), p. 349.

this nationalist warrant, is already determinative in the prewar Turkish interpretation of, for example, the Armenian massacres at Adana in April 1909, and it reappears in full force in the explication of the events of 1915–1916. Repeated Turkish reference to the Armenian revaluation at Van in 1915 is perhaps the outstanding example of this "legitimating" mode of moral-political reasoning.

This is to argue that contrary to, for example, Helen Fein's contention that the Armenians were "enemies by definition,"[6] that is, on a priori ideological or racial grounds—thereby allowing her erroneously to equate the action against Jews and Gypsies in World War II with that against the Armenians in World War I—the Armenians were "enemies" to the degree that they were enemies in this context, on practical and political grounds centering around long-standing policies of internal colonialism, the implications—and machinations—of national self-determination, and the provocative issue of loyalty in time of war. Accordingly, the objective of Turkish action, when it came in 1915–1916, was the destruction, once and for all, of Armenian national identity. The criminality of the Armenians did not require (as I shall show in detail in a moment) the biological extinction of every Armenian man, woman, and child—especially if such individual and collective survival took place outside Turkish national boundaries and, therefore, made no claims upon Turkish sovereignty or national territory.

This is not to ignore the magnitude of the crime perpetrated against the Armenian people, the misery and death entailed by the mass deportations, the continual abuse of Armenian women, the mix of ideology, sadism, and self-interest in the massacre of Armenian men, and the theft and murder of infants and children. It is, however, to insist that these deliberate acts of despoliation and near-unlimited cruelty be deciphered aright. To decipher them aright means recognizing their particular strategic causation that (odd as this may sound, given the vast inhuman carnage that occurred) entailed limits. Being a political-national assault against a political enemy, the Young Turks could achieve their preeminent goal—the protection of the nation as they defined it—without requiring the complete physical extirpation of every person of Armenian heritage. To this degree (and here I make only this limited and very precise claim), the intentionality behind, as well as the actualized structure of, the Turkish program for the eradication of Armenian national existence was *unlike* the biocentric war that Nazism carried on against the Jews—because the "Armenian question" differed in its quintessential character from the "Jewish question." The former had been a conflicted political issue for nearly a century, had created manifold pressures and functional compromises for the Ottoman state, and now could be, once and for all, resolved by the annihilation of the organized Armenian *community* within Turkey. In contrast, the Jewish question, which had likewise been a central, exceedingly controversial, political concern in Europe since the beginning of Jewish emancipation in the eighteenth century, was categorically transformed by Hitler into an inescapable metaphysical challenge ("blood" in the Nazi universe of discourse being understood as the elementary vehicle by which ontological values become incarnate in history) that could *only* be resolved by an uncompromisingly genocidal assault. The Third Reich, therefore, insisted not only on the

---

[6]Helen Fein, *Accounting for Genocide* (New York: Free Press, 1979), p. 30.

elimination of Jewish collective identity and communal existence, but also on the murder of *every* Jewish person of whatever age and gender.

At this juncture of our argument, three seminal factors that strengthen the morphological *dis*analogy between the Armenian tragedy and the Holocaust need to be introduced. They are: (1) the possibility of Armenian Christian conversion to Islam as a way of avoiding deportation and worse; (2) the specific character of the forced deportations; and (3) the *nontotalistic* nature of the anti-Armenian crusade.

As regards the mediating role of conversion to Islam, the eyewitness accounts of the tragedy repeatedly mention this lifesaving, though communally destructive, possibility. Both "willingly" and unwillingly, large numbers of Armenians became Muslims. In particular, there appears to have been extensive, forced proselytization of Armenian women and children. It is difficult to ascertain just what role official Ittihadist ideology played in these coerced prophylactic rituals, though it is clear that the Committee of Union and Progress (CUP), devoid as it was of a racist ideology, did not oppose such re-creative, death-deflecting actions. Indeed, to the degree that Islamicization constructively reinforced the Young Turks' normative political agenda—Islam being a fundamental buttress of Turkification (whereas Christianity was the key element in Armenian self-identity)—this survivalist (flagrantly inhumane) program was consistent with CUP ambitions; and it found wide instantiation. So wide, in fact, that Johannes Lepsius again and again excoriates the Turkish government for allowing, even encouraging, this tyrannical policy, and Arnold Toynbee accusingly refers to "survival being purchased by apostatizing to Islam."[7] Likewise, the German, U.S., British, and other governments are on record as protesting this unwelcome practice.

In that neither Islam nor Turkism is predicated on inelastic, biologistic concepts, both possess absorptive capacities that create existential as well as sociopolitical possibilities unavailable in Nazism. Accordingly, the "other" is not only defined differently by the Ittihad elites than in Hitler's Reich—not genetically and without reference to metaphysical canons of ontic pollution and decadence—but the required response to the "other" allows for the remaking of the "other," primarily through the mysterious rite of conversion, so as to obviate still more complete—that is, exterminatory—forms of overcoming. We have evidence that the children in Christian orphanages were converted en masse. It was not only women and children who were forcibly converted. Lepsius, for example, records that the entire male medical staff of the German Mission Hospital in Urfa were coerced into becoming Muslim, as were Armenian army physicians at Sivas.[8] In Aleppo, the entire Armenian labor battalion was converted in February 1916, and further large-scale conversions of Armenian males occurred in March and April 1916. Lepsius also reports that "all Armenian villages in the Samsun area and in Unich has been Islamicized. No favors were granted to anyone, apart from renegades."[9] In fact, Lepsius conservatively estimates that 200,000 men, women, and children, approximately 12 to 13.5 percent of the entire Armenian community, were forcibly converted and thereby saved,[10] however

---

[7]Arnold Toynbee, "The Murderous Tyranny of the Turks" (pamphlet: New York, 1917).

[8]Johannes Lepsius, *Deutschland und Armenien, 1914–1918* (Potsdam: Tempelverlag, 1919), p. 283.

[9]Ibid., p. 160.

[10]Ibid., p. lxv.

objectionable the instrument of their salvation. In this respect, Turkish policy reproduces medieval procedures of cultural homogenization, not modern procedures of physical genocide. As such, it kept Armenians, if not Armenianism, alive.

Secondly, the Armenian deportations were not uniform events of total annihilation. Though these Armenian removals, carried out under the most brutal conditions, were regularly occasions of mass death that sealed the fate of hundreds of thousands, several hundred thousand Armenians did survive these horrific journeys. Lepsius, for example, (under)estimates the remnant at 200,000 individuals. Toynbee cites a total of 600,000 Armenian survivors up to 1916—the combined total of those who lived through the deportations and those who fled into Russian territory. He summarizes:

> In general wastage [death during the deportations] seems to fluctuate, with a wide oscillation, on either side of 50 percent; 600 out of 2,500 (24 percent) reached Aleppo from a village in the Harpout district; 60 percent arrived there out of the first convoy from the village of E. (near H.), and 46 percent out of the second; 25 percent arrived out of a convoy from the village of D. in the same neighborhood. We shall certainly be well within the mark if we estimate that at least half those condemned to massacre or deportation have actually perished.[11]

Supporting these large estimates of the number of those who were *not* killed during these forced evacuations are the figures for Armenians who found refuge in Arab countries and then, later, in western Europe and the United States. Richard Hovannisian, writing of their acceptance in the Arab world, indicates that "many of the deportees suffered a cruel fate at the hands of certain Bedouin tribes in the Syrian desert, but most were accorded sympathetic asylum by the Arab peoples, who had themselves endured four centuries of Ottoman domination. In all, the number of Armenian deportees who found refuge in Arab lands, by 1925, is estimated at well over 200,000."[12] This figure excludes the 50,000 persons who found refuge in Iran. More specifically, Hovannisian breaks these refugee figures down as follows: Syria accepted 100,000 Armenian refugees; Lebanon, 50,000; Palestine and Jordan, 10,000; Egypt, 40,000; Iraq, 25,000; and Iran, 50,000, making a total of 275,000 survivors. These numbers are supported by later governmental statistics issued by the respective Arab countries. Census data released between 1931 and 1945 by the individual Middle East states indicate that Syria had an Armenian population of 125,550 (1945); Lebanon, 72,797 (1944); Palestine, 3,802 (1931); and Egypt, 19,596 (1937). Moreover, in addition to these aggregates, we also have evidence in various national census counts of the inter-war period of sizable new Armenian communities, in France, Greece, Cyprus, Bulgaria, and the United States, with additional small populations in Czechoslovakia, Switzerland, Greece, Hungary, Austria, Yugoslavia, Italy, and

---

[11]Arnold Toynbee in Viscount Bryce, *The Treatment of the Armenians in the Ottoman Empire, 1915–1916* (London: The Knickerbocker Press [for His Majesty's Stationery Office], 1916), p. 650.

[12]Richard Hovannisian, "Ebb and Flow of the Armenian Minority in the Arab Middle East," *Middle East Journal* 1(28) (Winter 1974):20.

Canada. (The population figures for these communities overlap with Hovannisian's figures for the Arab World—though to what exact degree is uncertain.) Therefore, if we put the number of survivors of these inhumane transfers at between 300,000 and 400,000 we shall be on secure grounds—or at least grounds that are as secure as possible given all the statistical uncertainties—remembering that Hovannisian's total of 275,000 does not include any survivors in Russia, Europe, or the United States. This translates into a survival rate somewhere between 17.7 percent (300,000 out of 1.7 million, the maximum Armenian population) and 26.6 percent (400,000 out of 1.5 million, the minimum Armenian population). Then, too, beyond the mathematics alone, these substantial statistics indicate that the Turkish oppressor did not require nor demand the death of all Armenians. The Turks had all of these individuals, this entire defenseless population, within their control and could have murdered them all, despite the practical difficulties involved in murdering an entire people in a country as large as Turkey, had they so desired. Evidently, this was not necessary.

Thirdly, the enacted policy of deporting Armenians was not universally applied even within the borders of Turkey. The Armenians of Constantinople, numbering up to 200,000, and the Armenians of other large cities—for example, Smyrna, where between 6,000 and 20,000 Armenians lived, Kutahia, and, to some degree, Aleppo—were not uprooted en masse during the entire war period. Lepsius estimated (and, in his own words, perhaps "overestimated") that the number of Armenians so protected represented one-seventh to one-ninth of the total Armenian population, or some 204,700 persons (out of what he projected as an original Armenian population of 1,845,450).[13] Although recent studies[14] require that we temper Lepsius's figures and indicate that up to 30,000 Armenians were, in fact, deported from Constantinople, the need to modify all generalizations as to Turkish intentions, given the very real limitations placed upon evictions from Constantinople and elsewhere, stands.

To gain a full picture of all the relevant statistics bearing upon the question of Armenian survival, we must also add in the 300,000 or so Armenians who retreated with the Russian army back into Russian territory after the final defeat at Van in the summer of 1915 and the 4,200 who survived the famous battle at Musa Dagh and were rescued by the French in mid-September 1915. Accordingly, the comprehensive demographic picture regarding casualties and survival looks like this:

1914 Armenian Population	1,500,000–1,700,000
Converts to Islam	200,000–300,000
Survive Deportations (outside Turkey)	300,000–400,000
Survive in large Turkish Cities	170,000–220,000
Survive in Russia	250,000–300,000

[13]I will provide a fuller accounting of these statistics in my analysis of the Armenian Tragedy in vol. 2 of my *Holocaust in Historical Context*.

[14]See Vahakn N. Dadrian's important qualification regarding the Armenians of Constantinople, "Genocide as a Problem of National and International Law: The World War I Armenian Case and Its Contemporary Legal Ramifications," *Yale Journal of International Law* 14(2) (Summer 1989):262, n. 131; and again, "The Documentation of the World War I Armenian Massacres in the Proceedings of the Turkish Military Tribunal," *International Journal of Middle East Studies* 23(4) (November 1991):570, n. 26. According to Dadrian's reconstruction, based on the testimony of German Ambassador Wolff-Metternich on December 7, 1915, who gave as his source the Turkish chief of policy, 30,000 Armenians were deported from Constantinople and more deportations were feared.

Survivors of Musa Dagh	4,200–4,200
TOTAL SURVIVORS	924,200–1,224,200
TOTAL DEATHS (1915–1918, based on 1,700,000 total)	475,800–775,800

This is not the Holocaust.

Conclusion

The spatial limits imposed on this chapter prevent further comparative review and analysis. However, I believe that in all the other cases that are said to parallel the Holocaust, close study would show that they also are dissimilar insofar as they, too, would not be examples of an unlimited war that required complete annihilation—the death of every man, woman, and child—of the victim population. The Holocaust is a unique historical reality.

Source: "The Uniqueness of the Holocaust: The Historical Dimension" by Steven Katz in Alan Rosenbaum (Ed.) *Is the Holocaust Unique?* Copyright © 2008 Alan S. Rosenbaum. Reprinted by permission of Westview Press, a member of the Perseus Books Group.

PARADIGMS OF GENOCIDE: THE HOLOCAUST, THE ARMENIAN GENOCIDE, AND CONTEMPORARY MASS DESTRUCTIONS

Robert Melson

When confronted with mass death and forced deportations, the contemporary world community has often reached for the Holocaust as a paradigmatic case of genocide in order both to make sense of and to condemn current events. This article suggests that the Armenian Genocide sets a more accurate precedent than the Holocaust for current mass disasters, especially such as those in Nigeria and in the former Yugoslavia, which are the products of nationalism. Conversely, the Holocaust is a prototype for genocidal movements that transcend nationalism and are motivated by ideologies that have global scope.

In this century, the world has experienced four tidal waves of national and ethnic conflict and genocide in the wake of crashing states and empires. These waves were punctuated by the first and second world wars and by the postcolonial and post-Communist eras. During World War I and its aftermath, as the Ottoman Empire collapsed, it committed genocide against its Armenian minority. In the same period, the disintegration of the German and Austro-Hungarian empires set off *Volkisch*, nationalist and fascist movements that repressed minorities and precipitated World War II. In the context of that war, the Nazis attempted to exterminate the Jews and Gypsies and committed partial genocide against other peoples. Following World War II, as former European colonial empires, notably Great Britain and France, withdrew from their possessions, they left behind fragile regimes that lacked legitimacy. Such so-called Third World governments frequently ruled over culturally plural societies and tried to impose the hegemony of one ethnic group over the rest. In reaction, minorities rebelled and sought self-determination. This led to ethnic wars and genocide in places like Indonesia, Burundi, Sri Lanka, Nigeria, Pakistan, Ethiopia, Sudan, and Iraq. In the wake of the recent collapse of Communist regimes in the Soviet Union and Yugoslavia, we are experiencing the fourth wave of nationalist upsurge, ethnic conflicts, and genocide. Meanwhile, it should be noted, the third wave of postcolonial genocide has not yet spent its force.

The Armenian Genocide and the Holocaust are the quintessential instances of total genocide in the twentieth century. In both instances, a deliberate attempt was made by a government to destroy in part or in whole an ethnoreligious community of ancient provenance that had existed as a segment of the government's own society.[1] In both instances, genocide was perpetrated after the fall of an old regime and during the reign of a revolutionary movement that was motivated by an ideology of social, political, and cultural transformation. Also in both cases, genocides occurred in the midst of world

---

[1]On the basis of the United Nations definition, it is possible to distinguish between genocide in whole and genocide in part. In this article, a total domestic genocide is a genocide in whole directed against a group of a state's own society, while a partial genocide is a genocide in part. Total genocide implies extermination and/or massive death of such an order that a group ceases to continue as a distinct culture. Partial genocide stops at extermination and the annihilation of culture. For further discussion of these distinctions, see Robert F. Melson, *Revolution and Genocide: On the Origins of the Armenian Genocide and the Holocaust* (Chicago: University of Chicago Press, 1992), pp. 22–30.

wars. These may be said to account for some of the basic similarities between the two genocides, but there were significant differences as well.

The perpetrators of the Armenian Genocide were motivated by a variant of nationalist ideology. The victims were a territorial ethnic group that had sought autonomy, and the methods of destruction included massacre, forced deportations, and starvation. In contrast, the perpetrators of the Holocaust were motivated by ideologies of racism and antisemitism, an ideology of global scope. The victims were not a territorial group, and for the most part they had sought integration and assimilation instead of autonomy. The death camp was the characteristic method of destruction.

Though in some essential ways the Armenian Genocide and the Holocaust resemble each other, the point of this article is that contemporary instances of partial genocide such as that which occurred in Nigeria in 1966–70 and is occurring in the former Yugoslavia today have more in common with the Armenian Genocide than they do with the Holocaust. This comparison stems from the character of the victim groups, from the ideology of the perpetrators, and from the methods of destruction. As in Armenia (and unlike the Holocaust), in Nigeria and Yugoslavia the groups singled out were territorial and had sought self-determination; the ideology of the perpetrators was a variant of nationalism; and the method of destruction included forced deportation, starvation, and massacre.

The analysis in this article briefly lays out some essential similarities and differences between the Armenian Genocide and the Holocaust and then shows how the former bears more of a resemblance than the Holocaust does to contemporary partial genocides such as those that have occurred in Nigeria and Yugoslavia.

Similarities

The similarities between the course of the Armenian Genocide and the Holocaust may be briefly noted. These include the low social status and rapid ascent of the two minorities in the Ottoman Empire and imperial Germany, respectively; the revolutionary transformations of both empires and the coming to power of revolutionary vanguards like the Committee of Union and Progress (CUP) in the Ottoman Empire and the Nazis in Germany; the redefinition and recasting of the identities of the majority and minority communities (Turks and Armenians, on the one hand, and Germans and Jews, on the other); and the implementation of genocide following the revolutionary state's engagement in international war.

The Armenian Genocide

In traditional Ottoman society, Armenians, like other Christians and Jews, were defined as a *dhimmi* millet, a non-Muslim religious community of the empire. Their actual treatment by the state varied to some extent with the military fortunes of the empire, with the religious passions of its elites, and with the encroachment upon their land of Muslim refugees from the Balkans and the Caucasus and of Kurdish pastoralists.

Although by and large *dhimmis* were free to practice their religion, they were considered to be distinctively inferior to Muslims in status.[2] However, in the nineteenth

---

[2] See Roderic H. Davison, "Turkish Attitudes Concerning Christian-Muslim Equality in the Nineteenth Century," *American Historical Review*, 4:844–64 (1954).

century the Armenians challenged the traditional hierarchy of Ottoman society, as they became better educated, wealthier, and more urban. In response, despite attempts at reforms, the empire became more repressive, and Armenians, more than any other Christian minority, bore the brunt of persecution.[3]

Throughout the nineteenth century, the Ottoman sultans were caught in the vise between great power pressures on the one hand and the demand for self-determination among their minorities on the other. By the time Abdul Hamid II came to power in 1876, he had set a course of political and social repression and technological modernization. Nevertheless, he could not halt the military and political disintegration of his regime, and he was replaced in 1908 by a political revolution of the Young Turks, who had new and radical ideas of how to address the Ottoman crisis.

In the first instance, the CUP, the political organization formed by the Young Turks, attempted radically to transform the regime following liberal and democratic principles that had been embodied in the earlier constitution of 1876. They hoped for the support of the great powers for their reforms, but neither the European powers nor the minorities reduced their pressures. On the contrary, they took the opportunity of internal Ottoman disarray and revolutionary transformation to press their demands, and between 1908 and 1912 they succeeded in reducing the size of Ottoman territory by 40 percent and its population by 20 percent.[4]

Concluding that their liberal experiment had been a failure, the CUP leaders turned to pan-Turkism, a xenophobic and chauvinistic brand of nationalism that sought to create a new empire based on Islam and Turkish ethnicity. This new empire, stretching from Anatolia to western China, would exclude minorities or grant them nominal rights unless they became Turks by nationality and Muslim by religion.

This dramatic shift in ideology and identity, from Ottoman pluralism to an integral form of Turkish nationalism, had profound implications for the emergence of modem Turkey.[5] At the same time, pan-Turkism had tragic consequences for Ottoman minorities, most of all for the Armenians. From being once viewed as a constituent millet of the Ottoman regime, they suddenly were stereotyped as an alien nationality. Their situation became especially dangerous because of their territorial concentration in eastern Anatolia on the border with Russia, Turkey's traditional enemy. Thus the Armenians, at one and the same time, were accused of being in league with Russia against Turkey and of claiming Anatolia, the heartland of the projected pan-Turkic state.

This was the situation even before World War I. When war broke out, however, the Young Turks, led especially by Enver Pasha, joined the German side in an anti-Russian alliance that would allow the pan-Turkists to build their state at Russia's expense. It was in this context of revolutionary and ideological transformation and war that the fateful decision to destroy the Armenians was taken.

---

[3]See Melson, *Revolution and Genocide*, pp. 43–69.

[4]See Feroz Ahmad, *The Young Turks* (Oxford: Clarendon Press, 1969), p. 153.

[5]See Bernard Lewis, *The Emergence of Modern Turkey* (New York: Oxford University Press, 1961).

By February 1915, Armenians serving in the Ottoman army had been turned into labor battalions and either were worked to death or were killed. By April that same year, the remaining civilians had been deported from Eastern Anatolia and Cilicia, in an early form of ethnic cleansing, toward the deserts near Aleppo. The lines of Armenian deportees were set upon again and again by Turkish and Kurdish villagers who were often incited and led by specifically designated killing squads, Teshkilat-i Makhsusiye, that had been organized by members of the CUP.[6] Those who escaped massacre were very likely to perish of famine. In this manner, between 1915 and the armistice in 1918, some 1 million people, out of a population of 2 million, were killed. Later a half million more Armenians perished as Turkey sought to free itself of foreign occupation and to expel minorities. Thus, between 1915 and 1923, approximately three-quarters of the Armenian population was destroyed in the Ottoman Empire.

The Holocaust

The Holocaust had similar origins, albeit with significant variations. Jews were a traditional pariah caste in Europe that in the nineteenth century began to advance in social, economic, cultural, and political spheres. It is in this context that the antisemitic movement got its start. Initially, it was dedicated to revoke Jewish emancipation and to undermine Jewish progress. Later it spawned an ideology that identified the Jews as a biologically alien tribe that was part of a worldwide conspiracy to control the world. In imperial Germany, however, antisemitic political parties failed to make significant inroads, and on the eve of the Great War, the movement was marginalized and in retreat.[7]

Like the Young Turks, the Nazis came to power after the collapse of an old regime. The German state experienced defeat in World War I, a failed revolt from the Left, inflation, depression, and the collapse of the democratic Weimar Republic. It was this interregnum, starting with the fall of imperial Germany, that enabled the Nazis to come to power.

Led by Hitler, whose charismatic persona and ideology united them, the Nazis were a movement centered on a cult of the Führer and racialist antisemitism. Once in power, the Nazis sought to recast Germany as an "Aryan" nation from which they would eradicate Jews and banish what they called the "Jewish spirit." Between 1933 and 1945, Germans scrambled to prove to themselves and to each other that their lineage had not been "polluted" by the infusion of Jewish "blood" and that their character had not been shaped by Jewish, or even Christian, values.

Indeed, the higher one went in the Nazi hierarchy, the "purer" and more brutal one was expected to be. This attempt to recast one's identity in opposition to a mythical Jew and his weltanschauung accounts in part for the growing radicalization of Nazi policy. In order to please Hitler and the Nazi elite, various spheres of the party and state began to compete with each other over Jewish policy and over the mantle of who was most radical on the Jewish question.

---

[6]See Vahakan N. Dadrian, "Genocide as a Problem of National and International Law: The World War I Armenian Case and Its Contemporary Legal Ramifications," *Yale Journal of International Law*, 2:221–334 (Summer 1989).

[7]See Richard S. Levy, *The Downfall of the Anti-Semitic Political Parties in Imperial Germany* (New Haven, CT: Yale University Press, 1975).

The Holocaust was implemented in three overlapping stages. Between 1933 and 1939, Jews were defined, expropriated, and expelled from Germany. Between 1939 and 1941, as the Germans invaded Poland and set off World War II, Jews were concentrated in ghettos near railroad transit centers, especially in Poland and the other occupied countries of eastern Europe. Between 1941 and 1945, as Germany invaded Russia, the seat of the supposed Jewish world conspiracy, Jews were first massacred by shooting squads, and later, for the sake of efficiency and secrecy, they were deported to killing centers where they were gassed and cremated.[8]

Differences

Like their similarities, the differences between the Armenian Genocide and the Holocaust may be plotted along the same dimensions: Jews and Armenians differed in status in the two empires; Nazi racist antisemitism differed significantly from the pan-Turkist nationalism of the Young Turks; and the killing of the Armenians relied mostly on massacre and starvation rather than on death camps.

Like the Armenians in the Ottoman Empire, the Jews were an ethnoreligious community of low status in Christian Europe. Unlike the Armenians, however, who were the subject of contempt for being non-Muslims, the Jews of feudal Europe became a pariah caste stigmatized as "killers of the Son of God." Thus Jews were not only despised in most parts of Europe; they were also hated and feared in a manner that the Armenians in the Ottoman Empire were not.

In the nineteenth century, to the extent that the state became bureaucratic, society meritocratic, and the economy capitalistic, Armenians and Jews began to advance in status and wealth. Indeed, it has been suggested that Armenian and Jewish progress was viewed as illegitimate and subversive, which precipitated antagonistic reactions both in the Ottoman Empire and in Imperial Germany, respectively.[9]

Here at least two variations may be noted. Whereas Armenians were a territorial group that increasingly made known its demands for greater autonomy and self-administration within the Ottoman system, Jews were geographically dispersed, and thus, with the exception of the Zionists who sought a Jewish state in Palestine, most made no territorial demands on the larger societies in which they lived.[10] Instead, to the extent that they accepted the modern world, most Jews sought assimilation into the culture and integration into the wider society.

The reaction against Jewish progress, assimilation, and attempts at integration became a Europeanwide movement of antisemitism, a form of racism that set up unbridgeable obstacles to Jewish inclusion. According to antisemites, like Dühring, for example, not even conversion would allow Jews to become the equals of Germans or other Europeans. Already in 1881, he wrote:

---

[8]See Raul Hilberg, *The Destruction of the European Jews* (Chicago: Quadrangle, 1967; new ed., New York: Holmes & Meier, 1985).

[9]See Melson, *Revolution and Genocide*, p. 137.

[10]For discussions of the ideological crosscurrents that affected Jews in this period, see Jonathan Frankel, *Prophesy and Politics: Socialism, Nationalism, and the Russian Jews, 1862–1917* (Cambridge: Cambridge University Press, 1981); Ezra Mendelsohn, *The Jews of East Central Europe Between the World Wars* (Bloomington: Indiana University Press, 1983).

A Jewish question would still exist, even if every Jew were to turn his back on his religion and join one of our major churches. Yes, I maintain that in that case, the struggle between us and the Jews would make itself felt as ever more urgent. . . . It is precisely the baptized Jews who infiltrate furthest, unhindered in all sectors of society and political life.[11]

According to Wilhelm Marr, for example, Jews were not only an alien race; they also constituted an international conspiracy whose aim was the domination of Germany, Europe, indeed the whole world. Thus not only did antisemites found a movement that opposed Jewish progress and assimilation; they also formulated a far-reaching ideology that helped them to explain the vacillations and crises of the modern world. It was an ideology that came to rival liberalism and socialism in its mass appeal.

By way of contrast, no such ideology of anti-Armenianism developed in the Ottoman Empire. Armenians may have been popularly despised for being *dhimmis*, or *gavurs*, and later under the Young Turks they may have been feared as an alien nation supposedly making claims to Anatolia, the heartland of the newly invented Turkey. However, even pan-Turkism left the door open to conversion and assimilation of minorities, something that racism and antisemitism explicitly rejected.

Moreover, though the Young Turks may have claimed that the Armenians were in league with their international enemies, especially the Russians, their nationalism never led them to the bizarre excesses that later became Nazi antisemitism. There was no equivalent in the pan-Turkish view of Armenians to the Nazis' hysterical struggle against the "Jewish spirit," which was said to linger in Germany and Europe even after most of the Jews had been murdered. As Friedländer has noted:

It was the absolutely uncompromising aspect of the exterminatory drive against the Jews, as well as the frantic extirpation of any elements actually or supposedly linked to the Jews or to the "Jewish Spirit". . . which fundamentally distinguished the anti-Jewish actions of the Nazis from their attitude toward another group.[12]

Finally, it should be noted that the death camp, a conception of the Nazi state, was an extraordinary organization, not seen before or since. It was a factory managed by the SS but staffed at all levels by the inmates themselves. Its primary aim was to dehumanize and kill its prisoners after confiscating their property and making use of their labor. Although Jews, like Armenians, perished in massacres and by starvation, the use of the death camp as a method of extermination differentiated the Holocaust from the Armenian Genocide.

It will readily be seen that partial genocide in Nigeria and other culturally plural societies in the Third World, as well as genocide in post-Communist states like Yugoslavia, bears closer resemblance to the Armenian Genocide than to the Holocaust.

---

[11]Cited in Paul R. Mendes-Flohr and Jehuda Reinharz, *The Jews in the Modern World: A Documentary History* (New York: Oxford University Press, 1980), p. 273.

[12]See Saul Friedländer, "On the Possibility of the Holocaust: An Approach to a Historical Synthesis," in *The Holocaust as Historical Experience*, ed. Yehuda Bauer and Nathan Rotenstreich (New York: Holmes & Meier, 1981), p. 2.

Nigeria

Genocide has been committed throughout the non-Western world, in Indonesia, Burundi, Rwanda, Sudan, East Pakistan, and Iraq. In all of these instances, a shaky and hardly legitimate postcolonial state ruling over a culturally plural society attempted to establish the hegemony of a leading ethnic group over other ethnic segments of society. These attempts at domination provoked movements of resistance and self-determination, which the postcolonial state then tried to halt by force, including massacre and partial genocide.

Nigeria gained independence from Great Britain in 1960. It was organized as a federation of three states, each centering on a major ethnic group. The northern state was dominated by the Hausa-Fulani, the western by the Yoruba, and the eastern by the Ibo. The major ethnic groups jockeyed for power at the federal level, while each had its minorities that felt discriminated against at the state level of the federation.

The postindependence government, dominated by Hausa-Fulani Muslims, was resisted by southern largely non-Muslim groups, especially the Ibos. In 1966, after a failed military coup, thousands of Ibos were massacred in northern Nigeria. In 1967, a year after the massacres, the Ibos tried to secede. They called eastern Nigeria "Biafra" and fought a war of self-determination until 1970, when their secession collapsed.

During the war, over a million Biafrans starved to death as a result of the deliberate Nigerian policy of blockade and disruption of agricultural life. Thus, between 1966 and 1970, a genocide-in-part occurred in Nigeria, following the U.N. definition. It is important, however, to recall that what happened in Biafra differed from the Holocaust and the Armenian Genocide in that the policies of the Nigerian Federal Military Government (FMG) did not include extermination of the Ibos.

Yugoslavia

A definitive history of the recent and current conflict in the former Yugoslavia does not yet exist, but it is possible to render a provisional sketch. The Yugoslav disaster stems from the failure of the Communist regime to establish legitimate political institutions, a viable economy, and a compelling political culture. After Tito's death in 1980, ethnically based nationalist movements started to mobilize and to demand greater autonomy, if not yet self-determination. The process of dissolution and disintegration was drastically accelerated with the rise of Milošević, who articulated an integral form of Serbian nationalism and irredentism that called for the creation of a Yugoslavia dominated by Serbia, such as had existed after World War I. This movement frightened the other nationalities and encouraged intransigent elements.

Milošević's integral Serbian nationalism in a context of Yugoslav and Communist institutional decay and insecurity helped to sharpen ethnic enmities, to strengthen centrifugal forces throughout the federation, and to accelerate the processes of disintegration. Thus, on 27 September 1989, the Parliament of Slovenia adopted amendments to its constitution giving the republic the right to secede from Yugoslavia. Thousands of Serbs demonstrated in Novi Sad, fearing for their status in an independent Slovenia. On 3 July 1990 the Parliament of Slovenia declared that the laws of the republic took precedence over those of Yugoslavia; on 22 December 1990 Slovenia reported that 95 percent of the voters supported a plebiscite on independence; and on 25 June 1991 Slovenia declared its independence from Yugoslavia.

A similar march of events occurred in Croatia, which also declared its independence on 25 June 1991. The big difference between Slovenia and Croatia, however, was the presence of a large Serbian minority in the latter. Moreover, no sooner was independence declared in Croatia than the Tudjman regime launched an anti-Serb campaign that would have alarmed the Serbs even if nationalist elements among them had not been earlier mobilized by Milošević. Now that their kin were being threatened in Croatia, Milošević and other Serbian nationalists could call forth the terrible history of the Ustasha genocide of World War II to mobilize the Serbs against Croatian independence and in support of Serbian irredentism.

After 25 June 1991, when Slovenia and Croatia declared their independence, thereby creating Serbian minorities, especially in Croatia, the Serb radicals, using the cover of the Yugoslav army, launched an attack whose main intent was to incorporate Serbian-populated Croatian territory. To this end, Serbian forces not only initiated hostilities but set out on a path of terrorism and massacre in order to drive Croats out of areas that they desired to incorporate into greater Serbia.

This policy of terrorism and ethnic cleansing was set in motion with even greater ferocity against Bosnia when it declared its independence on 3 March 1992. Indeed, in time both Serb and Croat forces descended on Bosnia with the clear intention of carving up and destroying a state that initially had tried to stand aside from ethnic nationalism and had opted for a pluralist society. But both Serb and Croat nationalists were intent on either carving up and destroying Bosnia or making of it a rump state that would in time collapse. To this end, especially the Serbs, led by Karadzic in Bosnia, practiced massacre, ethnic cleansing, and cultural destruction against those they called the Turks. Taken together, such policies of destruction on a wide scale are called genocide.[13]

Keeping Nigeria and Yugoslavia in mind, however, it is also important to note the great fear and insecurity that possess everyone when a government is challenged and a state begins to disintegrate. This great fear, especially in culturally plural societies, leads people to seek the shelter of their families and kin and persuades various groups to band for protection and to view each other as potential enemies.

Indeed, before a culturally plural state like Nigeria or Yugoslavia disintegrates, its politics may revolve about various ethnic issues of group status and the distribution of scarce goods, but once a state crashes, for whatever reasons, ethnic groups begin to fear for their lives, as well they should. Once a political order disintegrates, who can guarantee an ethnic group that its mortal enemies will not come to power and destroy it? It is this great fear that has seized all the groups in Yugoslavia, including those Serbs who are the main perpetrators of partial genocide.

Comparisons of the Armenian Genocide with Nigeria and Yugoslavia

In both the Nigerian and Bosnian cases, we can see some parallels to the Armenian Genocide. A dominant ethnic group in a culturally plural society attempted to establish its hegemony. It was resisted by minorities that attempted some form of

---

[13]According to Helsinki Watch, genocide is taking place in Bosnia and other former areas of Yugoslavia. Although all sides have been accused of atrocities, it is the Serbian side, especially in Bosnia, that is charged with genocide. See *War Crimes in Bosnia-Hercegovina* (New York: Human Rights Watch, 1992), p. 1.

autonomy or self-determination. In reaction, the dominant group perpetrated repression and genocide. There are significant differences as well that may be even more instructive, since it is the differences that tell us how genocide varies under different conditions.

The crucial difference between a total domestic genocide, as occurred in the Armenian case, and a partial one, as occurred in Nigeria, can also be seen by comparing the two. Unlike the Armenians, once Biafra was defeated and the danger of secession passed, the Ibos were not massacred or further expelled from Nigeria. On the contrary, there was a genuine attempt to reintegrate the Ibo population into Nigeria when the war ended.

This difference may be due to two reasons. First, although the FMG was dominated by Hausa-Fulani elements, it included minorities in its leadership; indeed its commander, General Gowon, was a Christian from the north. Thus the FMG never developed an ideology of "northernization" or "Muslimization" the way the Young Turks relied on Turkification and sought to create an ethnically homogeneous Turkey. Second, the territorial issue, a crucial element in the Armenian case, was missing. The Ibos of the north were "strangers" and not "sons-of-the-soil"; thus they could not make a legitimate claim to northern territory.[14] Moreover, it is significant that the Ibos had their own area, which, except for its oil, the north did not covet. Indeed, the Biafran state was never claimed as the homeland of the Hausa-Fulani in the manner that Anatolia had been staked out by the Turks. Thus a federal solution to ethnic conflict could be implemented in Nigeria, the way it could not in the Ottoman Empire.

Once the Ibos were driven from the north back into their space, and the Biafran secession was defeated, the northern elements in the army and elsewhere succeeded in their major aims. Further massacre and starvation of the Ibos were unnecessary for ideological, territorial, or any other reasons, and the partial genocide ceased.

Two major similarities between the Armenian Genocide and the partial genocide occurring in Bosnia should be apparent. Like the Young Turks, the Serbian, and to some extent the Croat, nationalists are also dreaming of a large state that would include their peoples and exclude other ethnic and national groups. Like the Armenians, the Muslims, an ethnoreligious community making claims to land, are being massacred and driven out by Serb and Croat nationalist movements that seek to incorporate their lands and "cleanse" the area of their presence and to destroy their culture.

However, the status of Bosnia as an independent state recognized by the international community marks a significant difference between the Yugoslav case, on the one hand, and the situations of Ibos in Nigeria and of Armenians in the Ottoman Empire, on the other. Neither Armenians nor Biafrans were widely recognized as members of independent states while their destructions were in process.[15]

---

[14]See Donald L. Horowitz, *Ethnic Groups in Conflict* (Berkeley: University of California Press, 1985), for discussions of how groups validate their claims to status and power. A basic distinction lies between those who have historically dominated an area and migrants who are new arrivals. The first, the "sons-of-the-soil," make their claims on the basis of ancestral privilege; the second cannot. Thus Armenians in Anatolia could make a claim to the land, the way Ibos in the North could not.

[15]See Richard G. Hovannisian, *Armenia on the Road to Independence* (Berkeley: University of California Press, 1967); John J. Stremlau, *The International Politics of the Nigerian Civil War* (Princeton, NJ: Princeton University Press, 1977).

International Aspects

Some major similarities and differences between the Armenian Genocide and the current wave of mass murder may lie in the role of the international community. The Armenians were largely abandoned to their fate, in part because the genocide occurred in the midst of a world war. During the Cold War, both the Eastern and the Western blocs discouraged movements of self-determination, fearing superpower involvement, and the African states did the same, fearing their own disintegration along ethnic lines. This explains, in part, why the Ibos, like the Armenians, were also abandoned, except for some humanitarian relief.

In the current period, following the Cold War, the international community is giving mixed signals about how it will react to partial genocide. On the one hand, it acted forcefully to limit the Iraqi attack on the Kurds following the Persian Gulf war; on the other hand, it seemed paralyzed to act to halt the partial genocide that was being committed in Bosnia, despite the fact that on 27 and 30 May 1992 the United Nations imposed a trade embargo on Serb-controlled Yugoslavia and on 22 September 1992 it expelled that country from the United Nations. It seems that the international community intervened with force in Iraq because some member states saw their national interests threatened by Iraqi aggression. Since no such clear interests seemed to lie in Bosnia, it was abandoned like Armenia and Biafra before it.

That partial and not total genocide is occurring in Bosnia, unlike Armenia, should be very cold comfort for the world community. Seventy years after the Armenian Genocide and 48 years after the Holocaust, a European state is practicing genocide, while Europe, the United States, and the United Nations are unable or unwilling to halt the slaughter. If genocide cannot be halted in Europe, it cannot be stopped or prevented anywhere else. This then is the new world order that we are facing as we are about to enter the second millennium.

Conclusion

The Armenian Genocide, rather than the Holocaust, may serve as a closer prototype for current mass murders in the postcolonial Third World and in the contemporary post-Communist world. In Nigeria and Yugoslavia, for example, as in the Armenian case and unlike the Holocaust, minorities were territorial ethnic groups, aiming at some form of autonomy or self-determination while the perpetrators were driven by a variant of nationalism, and the methods of destruction involved massacre and starvation. In the Holocaust, the victims were not a territorial group; the ideology was a variant of a global racism and antisemitism, not nationalism; and the characteristic method of destruction was the death camp. Indeed, in the contemporary world, only the Cambodian genocide perpetrated by the Khmer Rouge bears a closer resemblance to the Holocaust than to the Armenian Genocide.[16]

On seizing power on 17 April 1975, the Khmer Rouge set about destroying various strata and segments of Cambodian society. These included the urban upper and middle classes and various ethnic communities like the Vietnamese, the Chams, and the overseas Chinese. The killing of ethnic communities was based on Cambodian racism

---

[16]See Melson, *Revolution and Genocide*, pp. 264–67.

and paranoia—the fear that if such communities were not destroyed, the indigenous Khmers would be submerged by aliens, especially the Vietnamese.

The parallel to the Nazi case becomes more apparent in the Khmer Rouge attack on the urban middle and upper classes. Here the Khmer Rouge were motivated by a global ideology—a perverted form of Marxism—in which such classes played the role of the compradore bourgeoisie that was allied to imperialism and capitalism. Unlike the Armenians of the Ottoman Empire, these classes were not a territorial group making claims to the heartland of the Khmers. Like the Jews under the Nazis, according to the Khmer Rouge, these urban classes were an ideological category that had to be killed in order to destroy imperialism and to usher in a more perfect world.

Source: Melson, Robert (1996). "Paradigms of Genocide: The Holocaust, the Armenian Genocide, and Contemporary Mass Destructions," *Annals of the American Academy of Political and Social Sciences,* Volume 548, pp. 157–168. Copyright © 1996. Reprinted by permission of Sage Publications.

GOVERNMENT-PLANNED GENOCIDE – THE BURNING TIGRIS: THE ARMENIAN GENOCIDE AND AMERICA'S RESPONSE

Peter Balakian

The relationship between World War I and Turkey's plan to exterminate the Armenians was an evolving narrative of intertwining domestic and international events. From the Adana massacres of 1909 through the Balkan Wars of 1912–13 and then to World War I, which the Ottoman Empire joined in November 1914, the Committee of Union and Progress was engaged in promoting a new Turkish nationalism, a growing and encompassing military culture at home, and a large, complex, and clandestine bureaucracy. All of these were crucial to the CUP's orchestration of the extermination of its Armenian population.

The plan to liquidate the Armenians of the Ottoman Empire was put into motion in the spring and early summer of 1915. It was well orchestrated, and in city and town, village and hamlet, and in the Armenian sections of the major cities of Asia Minor and Anatolia, Armenians were rounded up, arrested, and either shot outright or put on deportation marches. Most often the able-bodied men were arrested in groups and taken out of the town or city and shot en masse. The women, children, infirm, and elderly were given short notice that they could gather some possessions and would be deported with the other Armenians of their city or town to what they were told was the "interior." Often they were told that they would be able to return when the war was over.

The Armenian communities all over Turkey were rendered more vulnerable by the rapid elimination of the able-bodied men. Another large segment of Armenian men, in the labor battalions of the Ottoman army, was massacred from the late winter of 1915 on. The rest of the Armenian community was left increasingly helpless without those who could resist and offer protection.

A map of the Armenian genocide shows that deportations and massacre spanned the length and width of Turkey. In the west the major cities included Constantinople, Smyrna, Ankara, and Konia. Moving eastward, Yozgat, Kayseri, Sivas, Tokat, and Amasia were among the large cities of massacre and deportation. Along the Black Sea, Samsun, Ordu, Trebizond, and Rize were killing stations where Armenians were often taken out in boats and drowned. In the south, in historic Cilician Armenia, Adana, Hadjin, Zeitun, Marash, and Aintab were part of the massacre network. The traditional Armenian *vilayets* in the east—Sivas, Harput, Diyarbekir, Bitlis, Erzurum, Van—with hundreds of villages and dozens of cities, where the majority of the Armenian population of the empire lived on their historic land, were almost entirely depleted of their Armenian populations. In the southeast such towns and cities as Ras ul-Ain, Katma, Rakka, and Aleppo were both killing stations and refugee spots, where Armenians who had survived long death marches from the north lived in concentration camps, in makeshift tents, or on the desert ground, hoping to stay alive. Farther south, in the Syrian desert, more Armenians died than perhaps anywhere else. There the epicenter of death was the region of Deir el-Zor, with the surrounding towns of Marat, Busara, and Suvar, where Armenians died not only of massacre, starvation, and disease but were stuffed into caves and asphyxiated by brush fires—primitive gas chambers, as the investigative journalist Robert Fisk has noted.[1]

---

[1]Robert Fisk, "The Hidden Holocaust," Panoptic Productions, London, 1992.

The survivors were dispersed across Syria, Iraq, and Palestine in the south, and Russia and Iran to the north and east. Many survivors stayed in those areas, and many migrated in the following decades to Europe, the United States, India, China, Australia, and South America in what became a major twentieth-century diaspora.

The extermination of the Armenians proceeded from several threshold events and circumstances:

1. At the beginning of World War I, Armenian men between twenty and forty-five years old and months later men between forty-five and sixty years old were conscripted into army labor battalions (*amele taburlari*) where they were put to work in munitions and clothing factories, on roads and railway lines, or as bakers or farmers to augment the army's food supply, and often as human beasts of burden (*hamals*) carrying supplies on foot.[2]

But after Enver Pasha's humiliating defeat by the Russians at Sarikamish in December 1914–January 1915, the minister of war and his ruling elite, needing a scapegoat, blamed the Armenians, claiming that they were in sympathy with the Russians. Within a month, by February 25, 1915, all the Armenian men in the Ottoman army were officially disarmed and thrown into labor battalions. Almost immediately thereafter the army began an organized plan of massacring most of the Armenian men in the labor battalions. These killings preceded the beginning of the general deportations and massacres of the spring. Under armed guard, they were taken out into secluded areas where they were killed by gunshot or with bayonets by Turkish soldiers, often with the aid of the gendarmes and the *chetes* (organized auxiliary killing squads).[3] In this manner tens of thousands of Armenian men were disposed of. Arnold Toynbee noted that all the disarmed Armenian soldiers doing construction on the Erzurum–Erzindjan road were massacred, as were the Armenian soldiers on the Diyarbekir–Ufra and Diyarbekir–Harput roads.[4]

2. With the devastating military loss at Sarikamish, the CUP not only disarmed the Armenian soldiers but ordered all civilian Armenians who were suspected of possessing arms to surrender them to their regional and local administrators. This resulted in what James Bryce and Arnold Toynbee called a "reign of terror," unleashed by "every administrative center" in the winter and early spring of 1915.[5] It was a preliminary process: Local officials broke into Armenian homes, demanding weapons when often there were none to be found, arresting and executing innocent civilians arbitrarily. (Jay Winter suggests, too, that the landing of British, French, Australian, and New Zealand troops on Turkish soil, at Gallipoli on the Dardanelles in April 1915, propelled Turkey further into a siege mentality, which fueled the zeal for exterminating the Armenians.)[6]

---

[2]Erik Jan Zucher, "Ottoman Labor Battalions in World War I," Turkology Update Leiden Project (Leiden, Netherlands: Leiden University's Dept. of Turkish Languages and Cultures, March 2002). Christians had first been conscripted into the Ottoman army in 1909 after the implementation of new constitutional reforms, and so at the outbreak of World War I, Armenian men between the ages of twenty and forty-five were drafted into the Ottoman army. It was an army with numerous problems, among them severe ethnic discrimination. Arabs, Kurds, Armenians, Greeks, Assyrians, and others were subjected to brutal treatment. Arab soldiers, for example, were often sent to the front lines, at gunpoint, shackled in chains and escorted by Turks.
[3]Ibid.
[4]Arnold Toynbee, *Armenian Atrocities: The Murder of a Nation* (London: Hodder and Stoughton, 1915), 81–82.
[5]Bryce, *The Treatment of the Armenians in the Ottoman Empire*, 638.
[6]Jay Winter, "Under Cover of War," 4.

3. By the late winter of 1915, Dr. Behaeddin Shakir took over the leadership of the CUP's Special Organization in the eastern *vilayets*, and organized killing squads for the purpose of exterminating the Armenians.[7]

4. On April 8 the first deportation was ordered in the mountain town of Zeitun, the same place where Armenians had resisted massacre in 1895–96. It was a trial-run deportation, carried out mostly on foot, but for the first time the Turks used the railway for deportation.[8]

5. On April 17 the Armenians in Van refused what they considered to be an unrealistic demand of the *vali*, Jevdet Bey, who had terrorized the region with mass arrests and executions all winter. The *vali* demanded that the Armenian leadership deliver more than four thousand Armenian men for the Ottoman army's labor battalions. The Armenians knew full well that consenting to such a request would result in the mass murder of the men. The altercation led to Turkish attack on the city of Van and corresponding Armenian resistance during the weeks that followed. The resistance at Van became another pretext for the CUP to claim that the Armenians were disloyal during wartime.[9]

6. With the flare-up at Van, the CUP then proceeded the next week to arrest some 250 Armenian intellectuals and cultural leaders in Constantinople. This stunned the community and began the process of liquidating Armenian intellectuals and cultural leaders in every sector of the country.

7. From the spring on through the fall of 1915, the massacres and deportations, which amounted to death marches, were carried out in a deliberate and systematic way and with frenzied competence in all sectors of Turkey. Much of Cilicia was cleared of its Armenians in July and August, the eastern *vilayets* in June and July, the southeast region in August and September.

Scholars and journalists at the time estimated that between eight hundred thousand and a million Armenians died in 1915 alone.[10] Then, in the number of 1916, there was a new wave of massacres in the Mesopotamian desert (today northern Syria) in a region that included Ras ul-Ain, Rakka, and Deir el-Zor. There, about two hundred thousand Armenians who had survived the death marches were massacred. In addition tens of thousands of women were abducted into harems or Muslim families, and tens of thousands of children were taken into families and converted to Islam, and in this manner of forced conversion another segment of the Armenian population was eradicated. After the war further Armenian massacres took place in Marash in 1920 and in Smyrna in 1922. Thus the death tolls from 1915 through 1922 range from over a million to a million and a half.

The Special Organization and the Formation of the Killing Squads

When Richard Rubenstein, in *The Cunning of History*, described the Turkish extermination of the Armenians as the "first full-fledged attempt by a modern state to practice disciplined, methodically organized genocide," he was noting the skill with which the

---

[7]Vahakn Dadrian, "The Role of the Special Organisation in the Armenian Genocide during the First World War," in *Minorities in Wartime*, ed., Panikos Panayi (Oxford, England, and Providence, R.I., Berg Publishers, 1993), 64–65; Astourian, "The Armenian Genocide," 138.

[8]Bryce, *The Treatment of the Armenians*, 640.

[9]Walker, *Armenia*, 206; Ussher, *An American Physician in Turkey*, 238–43.

[10]Bryce, *The Treatment of the Armenians*, 638–43.

Turks used the bureaucracy of the state to implement mass murder, as well as its historic significance.[11] Like the Nazi Party, the Committee of Union and Progress understood the power that resided in bureaucracy.

As the inheritors of the Ottoman government, the Young Turks were the recipients of an extraordinary bureaucratic infrastructure with which the Turks had ruled a large and complex empire for centuries. The very sultan they had just deposed had expanded the size of Ottoman bureaucracy by creating the most extensive system of surveillance in the empire's history. Although Abdul Hamid's bureaucracy was riddled with corruption and manipulated by bribery, it had been essential to his rule of the empire.

What Rubenstein has noted about the Nazi final solution for the Jews was also true in the case of the Turkish plan for the Armenians. The Armenian Genocide was propelled by "a bureaucratic administration capable of governing with utter indifference [to] human needs."[12] In the end this bureaucracy was allowed to proceed without any external deterrence, and it was able to create, as the Nazis would with the Jews—a totally vulnerable, "expendable, . . . stateless people," as Rubenstein put it. A campaign of genocide, Holocaust scholar Raul Hilberg also underscores, "is a series of administrative measures which must be aimed at a definite group."[13]

The CUP's plan to exterminate the Armenians was made possible by the highest level of government planning: the harnessing of bureaucracy for the organization and implementation of the Armenian deportations; the formation and organization of killing squads; the creation and manipulation of legislation; and the use of technology and communications, such as the railway, the telegraph, and the old-fashioned but ever reliable town crier.

Like its Nazi counterpart after 1933, the CUP's Ministry of the Interior was the key to orchestrating a program of genocide. Talaat Pasha told Ambassador Morgenthau with great candor that "the Union and Progress Committee had carefully considered the matter in all its details and that the policy which was being pursued was that which they had officially adopted." Morgenthau reported, "He said that I must not get the idea that the deportations had been decided upon hastily; in reality, they were the result of prolonged and careful deliberation."[14] The Interior Ministry created another bureau called the Special Organization (SO) (*Teshkilât-i Mashusa*). The brainchild of the party's Central Committee, it was fueled by the ever-tightening relationship between the ascending military and quasi military leaders and the Committee of Union and Progress.[15]

Designed to be a clandestine operation, the Special Organization was very much in the tradition of the politics of secrecy which had defined the Young Turk movement from its origins. The Turkish political scientist Tarik Zafer Tunaya noted that the entire CUP in certain ways was "a power-wielding monopolistic clique . . . operating

[11]Richard Rubenstein, *The Cunning of History: The Holocaust and the American Future* (New York: Harper & Row Publishers, 1985), 11–12.

[12]Ibid., 34.

[13]Raul Hilberg, *The Destruction of the European Jews* (New York: Harper & Row), 1961, 43.

[14]Morgenthau, *Ambassador Morgenthau's Story*, 333.

[15]Dadrian, "The Role of the Special Organisation," 51.

behind a mysterious curtain of secrecy."[16] The surviving head of the SO later stated that it was "a secret body designed to achieve the internal and external security of the Ottoman State," and that its power was greater than that of the "official government." He confessed that the Armenian "massacres were carried out on order from the Central Committee," and that the SO was at the center of the operation.[17]

One of the SO leaders, Esref Kuscubasi, noted that the new bureau's focus was on the "non-Turkish and non-Muslim races and nationalities" in the empire because their loyalty was "suspect."[18] Throughout the war Ottoman intelligence issued propaganda to scapegoat Armenians, with statements such as: "The Armenians are in league with the enemy. They will launch an uprising . . . , kill off the Ittihadist [CUP] leaders and will succeed in opening up the Straits [Dardanelles]."[19]

While the Secret Organization included many high-ranking party officials such as Mehmed Nazim, Ziya Gökalp, and Talaat Pasha, Dr. Behaeddin Shakir seems to have been the most influential. In late fall and winter of 1914–15, he successfully lobbied for the autonomy of the SO in the eastern provinces and succeeded in placing the killing squads under the complete authority of the SO. Under his direction, in the late winter and early spring of 1915, the major phase of the Armenian extermination program was launched.[20] Colonel Düzgören Seyfi, director of the Political Department at the Ottoman General Headquarters (the Intelligence Department), worked closely with Dr. Shakir in mapping the strategy of the massacres and mobilizing the Special Organization's killing squads.[21]

The Killing Squads

The plan to exterminate the Armenians was accelerated and shaped by the rapid rise of military officers to crucial positions of power. This new military authority remained free from the restraints of the Ottoman legislature.[22] With the proclamation of the Temporary Law of Deportation of May 27, 1915, which ordered the forcible deportation of the Armenians, Ottoman officers were given the power to take charge of the

---

[16]Tarik Z. Tunaya, *Turkiyede Siyasi Pariler 1859–1952* (Political parties in Turkey) (Istanbul, 1952), 182, quoted in Dadrian, "The Role of the Special Organization," 61.

[17]Jemal Kutay, *Birinci Dunya Harbinde Teskilat-Mashusa* (The Special Organization during World War II) (Istanbul, 1962), 18, 36, 78, quoted in Dadrian, "The Role of the Special Organization"; Hafiz Mehmed, deputy at Trabzon, confessed after the war that "the massacres were carried out on order from the Central Committee of Ittihad," and the Special Organization was the center of the operation, and he admitted that "until now we remained silent about this," *Ariamard*, 13 December 1918, quoted in Dadrian, "The Role of the Special Organization," 61.

He also admitted that he had "assumed duties in missions, involving the secrets of the Armenian deportations." The Turkish historian Husamettin Erturk underscored that "the Special Organization was created by the Central Committee, for which end Enver and Talat, who in other matters were pitted against each other in a bitter struggle, joined hands. The Ittihadist Commanders of the Organization's brigands were chosen by Talat and the Central Committee; the Organization's *modus operandi* and the operational plans were determined on the basis of Enver's instructions." Mustafa Ragip Esadi, *Ittihad ve Terakki Tarihinde Esrar Perdesi* (The curtain of mystery in Ittihad's history) (Istanbul 1975), 258, quoted in ibid., 60.

[18]Kutay, *Birinci*, 18, 36, quoted in ibid., 54.

[19]Ahmed Refik Altinay, *Iki Komite, Iki Kital* (Two committees and two massacres) (Istanbul 1919), 40, quoted in ibid., 55.

[20]Dadrian, "The Role of the Special Organisation," 64–65; Astourian, "The Armenian Genocide," 138.

[21]Dadrian, "The Role of the Special Organisation," 76.

[22]Ibid., 78.

wholesale removal of the Armenian population, and the Ministry of War under Enver was authorized to administer the details.[23]

In creating an efficient killing process the Special Organization systematically recruited, organized, and deployed tens of thousands of convicted criminals for the purpose of massacring the Armenian population. In this astonishing use of the nation's criminal manpower, the military authorities were given autonomy to authorize the release of thousands of convicts from the prisons.[24] While the Ottoman government had deployed convicts in small numbers in the Balkan War of 1913, and the sultan had also emptied some prisons for the sake of killing Armenians in the 1890s, the harnessing of the criminal element of Ottoman society was brought to an entirely new threshold in 1915.

The organization of the *chetes*—the ex–convict killer bands—was similar to the Reich Security Main Office's *Einsatzgruppen*, or mobile killing units. While Raul Hilberg claims that the Reich Security Main Office conducted "for the first time in modern history . . . a massive killing operation,"[25] it appears in fact that the CUP's Special Organization was the first state bureaucracy to implement mass killing for the purpose of race extermination. Arnold Toynbee was among the first to assess the role of these killing squads when he wrote that: "Turkish 'political' *chettes* . . . made their debut on the western littoral, and in 1915, after being reinforced by convicts released for the purpose from the public prisons, they carried out the designs of the Union and Progress Government against the Armenians in every province of Anatolia except the vilayet of Aidin."[26]

The CUP's killing program also involved a hierarchy of command. At the top of this chain, Dr. Shakir played a role not unlike that of Nazi Reich Security Head, Reinhard Heydrich. The military hierarchy was essential to the operation, and accordingly the Special Organization units were mostly directed by active or reserve officers. The small detachments were commanded by lieutenants and captains, the larger ones by majors. In order to ensure that the officers would lead the killing efficiently, they were given incentives of Armenian booty and spoils. The killing squads and their leaders were motivated by both the ideology of *jihad*, with its Islamic roots, and pan-Turkism influenced by European nationalism.[27] The confession made by a Turkish gendarmerie captain named Shükrü to the Armenian priest Krikoris Balakian in Yozgat in 1916 dramatizes the role of *jihad* in the killing process. Captain Shükrü admitted to Balakian, a deportee he assumed would soon be dead, that he had been ordered to massacre all the Armenians of Yozgat because it was a "holy war." When it was over, he told the priest, he "would say a prayer and his soul would be absolved."[28]

---

[23]Dadrian, *History of the Armenian Genocide*, 221; full text of this legislation can be found in Hovannissian, *Armenia on the Road to Independence, 1918*, 55.

[24]Dadrian, "The Role of the Special Organisation," 78.

[25]Hilberg, *The Destruction of the European Jews*, 181.

[26]Arnold Toynbee, *The Western Question in Greece and Turkey* (Boston & New York: Houghton Mifflin, 1922), 280.

[27]See Bat Yéor, *The Decline of Eastern Christianity Under Islam: From Jihad to Dhimmitude*, trans., by Miriam Kochan and David Littman (London & Cranbury, N.J., Associated University Presses, 1996), 37–41; Hanioglu, *The Young Turks in Opposition*, 7–32; Dadrian, *History of the Armenian Genocide*, 1–6.

[28]Krikoris Balakian, *Hai Koghkotan* (Armenian Golgotha) (Beirut: Plenetta Printing, 1977), 227–28.

The killer bands, or *chetes*, who played such a significant role in the killing process, were estimated to be about thirty to thirty-four thousand in number.[29] While Talaat, Shakir, Enver, Gökalp, Nazim, and the others found the idea of using ex-convicts to be an effective means of carrying out genocide, there was another hidden agenda. Using ex-convicts, they believed, would enable the government to deflect responsibility. For as the death tolls rose, they could always say that "things got out of control," and it was the result of "groups of brigands."[30]

But the *chetes* were only part of a killing operation that involved military police and the provincial police, known as gendarmes. They were the ones who carried out the rigorous process of arrest and deportation city by city, town by town, village by village. Staff officers were assigned to the Ottoman army corps and became chiefs of staff in the interior, where they were put in command of their respective killing units in order to assist in "the liquidation of the Christian elements." One reserve officer put it bluntly when he said the aim of the whole process "was to destroy the Armenians and thereby to do away with the Armenian question."[31]

Acts of Legislation

In order to accelerate the extermination plan and to give it a further sense of governmental legitimacy, Talaat Pasha requested that the grand vizier, through the cabinet, pass a special law authorizing the deportations. Like the Nazis, who created "a legal solution to the Jewish problem"—as historian Lucy Dawidowcz put it—with their various anti-Jewish legislation of the 1930s, the CUP also implemented legislation to legitimize the Armenian extermination plan. The memorandum was endorsed on May 29, 1915, by the grand vizier, and the cabinet acted on it the next day, after an eager, chauvinistic wartime press had already announced this new emergency law on May 27. The members of the CUP Central Committee were always cautious about leaving traces of their genocidal plan, and so the law, called the Temporary Law of Deportation, made no overt reference to the Armenians. The commanders of armies, army corps, and divisions and commandants of local garrisons were now authorized to deport any groups of the population "on suspicion of espionage, treason, [or] military necessity."[32]

The crucial word in the law was "sensing" (*hissetmek*), which gave the authorities the power to order deportations if they had so much as a feeling or a sense that an individual or a group of people might be dangerous to the state.[33] This concept gave the legislation total license for the administrative network and the killing squads to

---

[29]Philip H. Stoddard, "The Ottoman Government and the Arabs, 1911–1918: A Preliminary Study of the Teskilat-I Mashusa," (Ph.D. diss., University of Michigan), 58, puts the number of men in the SO at thirty thousand. French historian E. Doumergue, in *L'Arménie, les massacres, set al question d'Orient* (Paris 1916), 24–25, also put the number at 30,000; Swiss historian S. Zrulinden, *Der Weltkrieg* (Zurich 1918), vol. 2, 657, puts the number at 34,000, quoted in Dadrian, "The Role of the Special Organization in the Armenian Genocide during the First World War," 59.

[30]Stoddard, The Ottoman Government and the Arabs, 49, 50.

[31]Altinay, *Iki Domite*, p. 23, quoted in Dadrian, "The Role of the Special Organization in the Armenian Genocide during the First World War," 57.

[32]Vahakn Dadrian, "Genocide as a Problem on National and International Law; the World War I Armenian Case and Its Contemporary Legal Ramifications," *Yale Journal of International Law*, 1989, vol. 14, no. 2, 266; for the English text of the law see R. Hovannisian, *Armenia on the Road to Independence* (Berkeley: University of California Press, 1967), 51.

[33]*Takvimi Vekayi*, no. 2189 (May 19/June 1, 1915), quoted in Dadrian.

round up, deport, and massacre Armenians. At the end of the war the Temporary Law of Deportation was repealed by the Ottoman parliament on the grounds that it was unconstitutional. By then it had served its purpose.

Because expropriating Armenian wealth and property was vital to the plan to destroy the Armenians, the CUP devised legal as well as purely coercive and violent means of stealing, plundering, and appropriating Armenian movable and immovable wealth. In another legislative maneuver, the Temporary Law of Expropriation and Confiscation (September 1915) was passed. This law was allegedly designed to register the properties of the deportees, safeguard them, dispose of them at public auctions, with the revenues to be held in trust until the deportees' return. It was such a transparent scheme aimed at confiscating all Armenian property and wealth that when Arthur von Gwinner, the director of the Deutsche Bank, described the new law to the German Foreign Office, he remarked with scorn that the eleven articles might be reduced to two: "1. All goods of the Armenians are confiscated. 2. The government will cash in the credits of the deportees and will repay (or will not repay) their debts."[34]

One remarkable document was discovered and translated in early 1919 by British officials in Turkey, who labeled it "The Ten Commandments." It is a blueprint of the Armenian extermination operation and appears to have been the centerpiece of a secret party meeting, which took place sometime in late December 1914 or in January 1915. The document was obtained by Comm. C. H. Heathcote Smith, the right-hand man of Adm. Somerset Calthorpe, the British high commissioner in Constantinople. Fluent in Turkish, Smith had served as British consul in Smyrna before the war, and he first learned of the "Ten Commandments" from the former British intelligence agent Percival Hadkinson, in Smyrna."[35]

The document (along with several others) came into British hands through Ahmed Essad, the wartime head of the Ottoman Ministry Department II, Intelligence. Essad had served as secretary at the conference at which the "Ten Commandments" were issued—a conference presided over by Talaat Pasha, the minister of the interior, and Drs. Nazim and Behaeddin Shakir, the masterminds of the Special Organization.

One page of a nine-page correspondence between the British High Commission in Constantinople and the Foreign Office in London in early 1919 is headed "DOCUMENTS RELATING TO COMITE UNION AND PROGRESS ORGANIZATION IN THE ARMENIAN MASSACRES." The subtitle reads: "The 10 commandments of the COMITE UNION AND PROGRES." A note following the text of the ten-point document, added by the British High Commissioner's Office in Constantinople, suggests that that office translated the document into English: "Above is a verbatim translation—dated December 1914 or January 1915."

(1) Profiting by the Arts: 3 and 4 of Comite Union and Progres, close all Armenian Societies, and arrest all who worked against Government at any time among them and send them into the provinces such as Bagdad or Mosul, and wipe them out either on the road or there.

(2) Collect arms.

---

[34]AA, Turkei 183/39, A29127 Oct. 7, 1915 report. The French text of the eleven articles is listed in Auswärtiges Amt. Turkei 183/39, A29127, and Lepsius, *Germany and Armenia*, 1914–1918, 84, quoted in Dadrian, 267.

[35]For an in-depth analysis of the document see Vahakn N. Dadrian "The Secret Young-Turk Ittihadist Conference and the Decision for the World War I Genocide of the Armenians," in *Holocaust and Genocide Studies* 7, no. 2 (Fall 1993), 173–74. The document is FO 371/4172/31307, 383–91, February 10, 1919, 388–89.

(3) Excite Moslem opinion by suitable and special means, in places as Van, Erzeroum, Adana, where as a point of fact the Armenians have already won the hatred of the Moslems, provoke organised massacres as the Russians did at Baku.

(4) Leave all executive to the people in provinces such as Erzeroum, Van, Mamuret ul Aziz, and Bitlis, and use Military disciplinary forces (i.e., Gendarmerie) ostensibly to stop massacres, while on the contrary in places as Adana, Sivas, Broussa, Ismidt and Smyrna actively help the Moslems with military force.

(5) Apply measures to exterminate all males under 50, priests and teachers, leave girls and children to be Islamized.

(6) Carry away the families of all who succeed in escaping and apply measures to cut them off from all connection with their native place.

(7) On the ground that Armenian officials may be spies, expel and drive them out absolutely from every Government department or post.

(8) Kill off in an appropriate manner all Armenians in the Army—this to be left to the military to do.

(9) All action to begin everywhere simultaneously, and thus leave no time for preparation of defensive measures.

(10) Pay attention to the strictly confidential nature of these instructions, which may not go beyond two or three persons.[36]

The Railway

Of the Nazi deportation of the Jews, Terrence Des Pres writes, "It began in the trains, in the locked box cars, eighty to a hundred people per car—crossing Europe to the camps in Poland."[37] Similarly, the century's first genocide began in part in the cattle cars of the Anatolian and the Baghdad Railway. In many cities and towns part of the Armenian population was piled into freight cars—around ninety in a car that "had a standard capacity for the military transport of 36 men or 6 horses." Crammed behind slatted bars, they were starving, in terror, and defecating on themselves. Most of the rail cars went south and east, most often to the city of Konia, where the deportees were often let out to continue on foot before they were robbed, raped, and murdered, by the killing squads. Sometimes they were shipped all the way through to Aleppo, where those who survived arrived emaciated and near death, only to confront more massacre. With the rail deportations of the Armenians, "the Ottoman government introduced into modern history," historian Hilmar Kaiser writes, "railway transport of civilian populations" as part of the plan of race "extermination."[38]

Some of the most striking evidence of the use of the railway for deporting the Armenians comes from the German eyewitness accounts of the Baghdad Railway Company. Germany's most important foreign project, the company was at the center of the kaiser's imperial designs in the Near East. It is ironic that the Turks used the

---

[36]Ibid.

[37]Terrence Des Pres, *The Survivor: An Anatomy of Life in the Death Camps* (Oxford University Press, 1975), 53.

[38]Hilmar Kaiser, "The Baghdad Railway and the Armenian Genocide 1915–1916: A Case Study in German Resistance and Complicity" in *Remembrance and Denial: The Case of the Armenian Genocide*, ed. Richard Hovanissian (Detroit: Wayne State University Press, 1998) 75.

railway in ways that the Nazis would later, and that Germans in Turkey in 1915 were on site to testify. Franz Günther, a delegate of the Deutsche Bank who headed the project's office in Constantinople and worked closely with the German embassy, reported that the Ottoman government was acting with "bestial cruelty" and noted that it was hard to justify the company's passivity in the face of what they were witnessing. When Günther sent a photograph of a deportation train to Deutsche Bank director Gwinner, Günther also noted the irony that the railway was billed as "an upholder of civilization in Turkey."[39]

The railway deportations were directed by the Ottoman government, and Talaat received reports on the numbers of deportees and their locations. On October 9 and 10, 1915, some 11,000 Armenians who had been transported from other places to Konia were sent south. Between October 13 and 16, 9,600 more followed. During the following five days 9,850 more Armenians were sent from Konia. When Ottoman military needs interrupted the rail deportations, the people were marched along the railway tracks. Still, in the month of October 1915 alone, more than 30,000 Armenians were packed into livestock cars to be sent to their deaths in the Der Zor Desert.[40]

As deportation by rail developed, detention camps sprang up alongside the tracks and stations. From Konia south to the desert, the whole stretch appeared as one long, concatenated detention camp. There was a large concentration camp by the railway station at Konia; by the end of October there were about 40,000 at Katma, a town on the deportation route north of Aleppo; the camp near Osmaniye, less than a hundred miles east of Adana, may have held as many as 70,000. In the camps the Armenians were attacked by the killing squads; women were abducted and raped; and thousands died of disease and starvation.[41]

Because of the proximity of the railway to the death camps and ultimately to the desert, the German railway engineers and employees were able to report the atrocities. At Ras-ul-Ain, a horrific refugee camp southeast of Urfa on the railway line to Mosul, two engineers reported seeing in one day three to four hundred women arriving completely naked. Hasenfratz—an employee who worked for the railway at Aleppo—reported that massacres took place beside the railway track between Tell Abiad and Ras-ul-Ain. "The bodies," he wrote, "without exception, were entirely naked and the wounds that had been inflicted showed that the victims had been killed, after having been subjected to unspeakable brutalities."[42]

As the railway and its immediate environs became a zone in which mass murder and rape were perpetually happening, the railway officials were constant witnesses to the atrocities. An engineer named Spieker reported from Ras-ul-Ain that he continually saw the arrival of remnants of the death marches; only women and children were left because all the men and boys over twelve had been killed. In his detailed reports on the systematic mass slaughter of women and children, he noted that a Turkish inspector informed him that nine out of ten Armenians had been killed on the marches. The engineer also described how Muslim railway officials and Ottoman officers raped women

---

[39]Ibid., 75, 70. See also National Archives RG 59, 867.4016/137, Dodd to Morgenthau, August 15, 1915.
[40]Ibid., 75.
[41]Ibid., 76.
[42]Ibid., 76.

and sold children and women into the slave trade. One Sergeant Nuri, the overseer of the camp at Ras-ul-Ain, actually bragged about raping children. Some of the Muslim employees of the railway left their jobs in order to take part in the killing.[43]

With nearly nine hundred skilled Armenian workers and many more Armenian laborers on the construction sites in the Taurus and Amanus Mountains and in northern Syria, the Armenian presence in the railway company was significant. Because the war made the railway even more crucial for the transportation of supplies, the Armenian employees were kept on their jobs.[44] What ensued was a poignant drama in which various Germans in respectable positions tried to intervene with their own government and the Ottoman government to save the Armenians working for the railway. Günther, the railway project director from the Deutsche Bank, who worked hard to protect the Armenian staff, "estimated that already 25 percent of the 2 million Armenians in the empire had been killed," and he was certain that the government's policy would mean the extermination of the entire Armenian population.[45] Winkler, the head railway construction engineer in Adana, who likewise tried to protect his workers, was stymied by the *vali*, who told him that nothing could be done, as the deportation orders had come directly from Talaat and Enver.[46] In the end the Armenian laborers were deported, and finally so were the Armenian staff employees of the railway. In order to cover up the massacres, the Ottoman government demanded that the railway cease its bookkeeping in German and use only Turkish. The Armenian staff was to be replaced by Muslims only.[47]

All through the summer of 1915, American consul Jesse B. Jackson in Aleppo recorded the deportation of Armenians by train. On September 29 he wrote to Ambassador Morgenthau:

> SIR: The deportation of Armenians from their homes by the Turkish Government has continued with a persistence and perfection of plan that it is impossible to conceive in those directly carrying it out, as indicated by the accompanying tables of "Movement by Railway," showing the number arriving by rail from interior stations up to and including August 31 last to be 32,751. In addition thereto it is estimated that at least 100,000 others have arrived afoot.

Of the more than thirty-two thousand deported by rail, more than nine thousand were children. In this same dispatch Jackson noted that the treatment of the deportees was "so severe" that "careful estimates place the number of survivors at only 15 per cent of those originally deported. On this basis the number of those surviving even this far being less than 150,000 up to September 21, there seems to have been about 1,000,000 persons lost up to this date."[48] Signing off to Morgenthau, he noted that he

---

[43]Ibid., 76.

[44]Ibid., 72.

[45]Ibid., 78.

[46]Ibid., 78–79.

[47]Ibid., 79, 104.

[48]Jackson to Morgenthau, U.S. State Department Record Group 59, 867.4016/219, Serial No. 382, in *United States Official Documents on the Armenian Genocide*, vol. 1, *The Lower Euphrates*, compiled and introduced by Ara Sarafian (Watertown, Mass.: Armenian Review, 1993), 94–98.

had forwarded the report in "sextuplicate, that copies thereof may be forwarded to the Governments of Great Britain, France, Russia, and Italy, respectively, if found convenient, the interests of which in this district have been entrusted to this Consulate. Copy is also being sent to the Department of State."[49]

In order to extort as much money as possible from the Armenians, the Turkish authorities often forced them to pay first-class fare before they put them into the cattle cars that would most likely take them to their deaths. On September 8, 1915, Dr. William S. Dodd wrote: "The exiles were compelled to pay the full fare and then packed forty or fifty together in box-trucks, cattle-trucks, or even open flat trucks. The Railway seems to be as conscienceless in wringing the money out of them as the Government or the Turks."[50]

Similarly, Dr. Wilfred M. Post, writing on September 3, 1915, testified to the coordination between the railway deportations and the killing squads:

> Much that I might add is as nothing, however, to what the railway employees report as going on at the end of the line, where the people leave the railway and set out on foot, only to be set upon by brigands, who rob, outrage and kill all the way from Bozanti to Adana and beyond. . . . Whether these unfortunate people are sent on towards the east or whether they remain where they are along the road, their future is very dark, and it means annihilation for the whole race.[51]

In the end between a half and two-thirds of the more than two million Armenians living on their historic homeland in the Ottoman Empire were annihilated. While the number of dead continues to be debated, as is the case with most episodes of mass killing (the U.S. Holocaust Museum, for example, places the number of Jewish dead in the Holocaust at 5.1 to 5.4 million, while other estimates go to 6 million), scholars of genocide, including the largest body of genocide scholars—the Association of Genocide Scholars of North America—conservatively assess that more than a million Armenians were killed, and probably somewhere between 1.2 and 1.3 million. Some historians put the figure at about 1.5 million, which spans the period from 1915 to 1922, when the last waves of killing took place.[52]

---

[49]Ibid., 95–96.

[50]Bryce, *The Treatment of the Armenians in the Ottoman Empire*, 423.

[51]Ibid., 423.

[52]See "Armenian Genocide Resolution Unanimously Passed by the Association of Genocide Scholars of North America, June 13, 1997," which states the genocide scholarly community's assessment that "over a million Armenians perished."

Source: Excerpts from pp. 175–176, 178–184 (top), 186 (bottom)–187, 189–193, 195–196 from *The Burning Tigris: The Armenian Genocide and America's Response* by Peter Balakian. Copyright © 2003 by Peter Balakian. Reprinted by permission of HarperCollins Publishers.

COMMON FATE, DIFFERENT EXPERIENCE: GENDER-SPECIFIC ASPECTS OF THE ARMENIAN GENOCIDE, 1915–1917

Katharine Derderian

Violence against women was a central feature of the Armenian Genocide. Even before the mass killings, sexual humiliation was used to intimidate the Armenian community. After the murder of the Armenian leadership and men of military age, Ottoman authorities and Ittihadist supporters deported surviving Armenians from Anatolia into the Syrian desert. During this ethnic cleansing, rape, kidnapping, sex slavery, and forced re-marriage became de facto instruments of genocide. Eyewitness accounts and diplomatic reports shed light on the place of gender during genocidal persecution. Although scholarship has only recently begun to explore the issue, the Armenian Genocide offers opportunities for comparative gender studies.

The recent wars in the Balkans brought sexual and gender-based violence during ethnic cleansing and genocide to the attention of the general public.[1] In the former Yugoslavia, systematic rape degraded female victims and underscored the powerlessness of the group to which they belonged. In the context of genocide, by which I mean the intentional physical and cultural extermination of a racial, ethnic, or other (even arbitrarily defined) group,[2] violence against women may be aimed at the destruction of the integrity of the group through its women, who embody its genetic and cultural continuity.[3]

Despite recent reminders of the gender-specific aspects of genocide, scholarship has only begun to address the question, generally limiting itself to the Holocaust and the war in the former Yugoslavia. Similar events such as the mass rapes in Bangladesh (1971) and Rwanda (1994) have been neglected, limiting possibilities for comparative study. Below, I argue that sexual violence and gender-specific persecution of victims were central aspects of the Armenian Genocide of 1915–17. By closely examining them I hope to contribute to the understanding of events as a whole and to suggest some features of gender violence for comparative work on the Holocaust and other genocides.

Although there is some debate about the exact number of Armenians who perished in the Genocide of 1915–17, the figure of 1.5 million people is generally

---

[1]See Kurt Jonassohn and Frank Chalk, "A Typology of Genocide and Some Implications for the Human Rights Agenda," in *Genocide and the Modern Age: Etiology and Case Studies of Mass Death*, ed. Isidor Wallimann and Michael Dobkowski (Westport, CT: Greenwood Press, 1987), pp. 3–20, esp. pp. 12–15, where the authors treat the process of real or fictive definition of the victim by a dominant group.

[2]Ruth Seifert, "Krieg und Vergewaltigung: Ansätze zu einer Analyse" in *Massenvergewaltigung: Krieg gegen die Frauen*, ed. Alexandra Stiglmayer (Freiburg: Kore, 1993), pp. 85–108.

[3]See, for example, Gisela Bock, "Equality and Difference in National Socialist Racism" in *Feminism and History*, ed. Joan Wallach Scott (Oxford: Oxford University Press, 1996), pp. 267–90; Dalia Ofer and Lenore J. Weitzman, eds., *Women in the Holocaust* (New Haven, CT: Yale University Press, 1998); Carol Rittner and John K. Roth, eds., *Different Voices: Women and the Holocaust* (New York: Paragon House, 1993); and Roger W. Smith, "Women and Genocide: Notes on an Unwritten History," *Holocaust and Genocide Studies* 8:3 (Winter 1994), pp. 315–34.

accepted as a reasonable estimate.[4] But the first killings started earlier. In 1908 the Committee for Union and Progress (CUP, *Ittihad ve Terakki Cemiyeti*, otherwise known as the Young Turks) had come to power, restoring the Ottoman constitution of 1878. Although Armenians and other minorities had supported the Young Turks, local massacres of Armenians began to occur as early as April 1909 in Adana; initial reform plans of interest to Armenians were never realized.[5] By 1913 the triumvirate of Enver Pasha (war minister), Talaat Pasha (minister of the interior), and Cemal Pasha (minister of the navy) headed both the Ottoman government and the CUP. As the CUP extended its monopoly over the government, its ideology increasingly emphasized a Turkism aimed at ethnic homogeneity within the Ottoman Empire, and a Panturanism calling for the unification of Turkic peoples from the Balkan Peninsula to Central Asia. In this context, the Armenian population of eastern Asia Minor as well as its specific efforts toward reform and autonomy came to be construed as barriers to CUP goals.

Early in 1915 measures against the Armenian population began with the disarmament of Armenian soldiers in the Ottoman military and the search for arms in private homes. On April 24, 1915, prominent Armenians in Istanbul and other cities were arrested and executed, effectively eliminating the community's intellectual and political leadership. This was followed by mass killings of men of military age and deportations of the remaining Armenians, during which the CUP and Talaat's Ministry of the Interior coordinated the activities of the regional authorities. Carried out by the "Special Organization" (*Teskilati Mahsusa*) and various other agents, the deportations disguised the Genocide as a "resettlement." Since the deportations followed the systematic elimination of the Armenian military-aged male population, they affected primarily women

---

[4]Gerayer Koutcharian, *Der Siedlungsraum der Armenier unter dem Einfluss der historisch-politischen Ereignisse seit dem Berliner Kongress 1878: Eine politisch-geographische Analyse und Dokumentation* (Berlin: D. Reimer, 1989), pp. 126–27. The exact Armenian population in the Ottoman Empire and the number of Armenian victims of the Genocide have long been the subject of debate; see Richard G. Hovannisian, *Armenia on the Road to Independence*, 1918 (Berkeley: University of California Press, 1967), pp. 34–37; and Koutcharian, *Siedlungsraum der Armenier*, pp. 80ff. The statistics from the Armenian Patriarchate in 1912 give a figure of 2.1 million Armenians in the Ottoman Empire. Of these, about 1.1 million would have resided in or near the empire's six eastern provinces (Erzurum, Van, Bitlis, Mamuret-ul-Aziz [Harput], Diyarbakir, and Sivas), representing a solid plurality in most of these areas, and perhaps a majority in Van. Turkish figures claim radically fewer Armenians in these six provinces (660,000), but rely on incomplete data (Hovannisian, *Armenia on the Road to Independence*, pp. 34–37). Official Turkish figures confirm the murder of at least 800,000 people, not counting executed wartime conscripts, women in forced marriages or sex slavery, forcibly adopted children, and those who perished in the aftermath of the deportations (Vahakn N. Dadrian, *The History of the Armenian Genocide: Ethnic Conflict from the Balkans to Anatolia to the Caucasus* [Providence, RI: Berghahn, 1995], pp. 225, 233 n. 40). Ultimately, most contemporary European observers, as well as historians of the Genocide, consider 1.5 to 2 million as the most probable population (Arthur Beylerian, *Les grandes puissances: L'Empire Ottoman et les Arméniens dans les archives françaises: Receuil de documents* [Paris: Université de Paris I, 1983], p. 509; Hovannisian, *Armenia on the Road to Independence*, p. 37; Ara Sarafian, ed., *United States Official Documents*, 5 vols. [Watertown, MA: Armenian Review, 1993], vol. 2, pp. xii, 118–19).

[5]On the history of the Young Turks and their Turkist and Turanist ideologies, see Mihran Dabag, "Katastrophe und Identität: Verfolgung und Erinnerung in der armenischen Gemeinschaft" in Hanno Loewy and Bernhard Moltmann, eds., *Erlebnis-Gedächtnis-Sinn: Authentische und konstruierte Erinnerung* (Frankfurt: Campus, 1996), pp. 177–235, esp. p. 189ff.

and children.[6] On the way to concentration camps in the Syrian desert, deportees fell victim to hunger, thirst, exhaustion, illness, and massacres perpetrated by both the gendarmes conducting the deportations and the Turkish and Kurdish civilian populations residing near their routes.

After systematic despoliation of the deportees, sexual and gender-based violence predominated,[7] including rape, sex slavery, and forced marriage (with compulsory conversion to Islam). Although women and girls might escape death through forced marriage, the ultimate result was a genocidal pattern of loss of women and children to the Armenian ethnos.

These experiences are recorded in bureaucratic documents and diplomatic correspondence of the Ottoman Empire or other countries, written accounts by eyewitnesses (usually survivors, diplomats, or missionaries of Western churches), and oral-history interviews with survivors of the Genocide.[8] The Ottoman documents have never been studied in full because of their continued inaccessibility. In addition, official communication pertaining to the deportations was often conducted so as to escape detection—oral messages, telegrams destroyed upon receipt, and "official" written orders accessible to Western observers but overridden by simultaneous oral commands to continue the deportations.[9] The Ottoman evidence is thus incomplete at best and is often contradicted by foreign sources, which consistently point to an orchestrated genocide against the Armenian community.[10]

Diplomatic documents from the United States and various European countries, as well as the eyewitness accounts of foreign observers and survivors, represent more accessible and reliable sources. Despite their Western and often Christian missionary provenance, these accounts are valuable for their contemporary perspective. Some of the most informative come from Turkey's German and Austro-Hungarian allies, who were less likely to display an anti-Turkish bias and enjoyed relatively unhindered access to the Ottoman interior.

While survivors' accounts offer greater detail and individual experience, interviews were usually conducted many years after the Genocide, which had taken place during many of the informants' childhood or youth. Interview transcripts are often difficult to obtain, as they have rarely been widely published.[11] Survivors' perspectives

---

[6]See for example Johannes Lepsius, *Rapport secret sur les massacres d'Arménie* (Beirut: Edition Hamaskaïne, 1968), pp. 44–49, or *New York Times* reports confirming that the majority of deportees were women and children (see Richard D. Kloian, *The Armenian Genocide: News Accounts from the American Press, 1915–1922* [Richmond, CA: ACC Books, 1985], pp. 20, 142, 148).

[7]Vahakn N. Dadrian, "The Armenian Genocide in Official Turkish Sources: Collected Essays," *Journal of Political and Military Sociology* 22:1 (1994), p. 121 n. 63.

[8]Rouben Adalian, "The Armenian Genocide" in *Genocide in the Twentieth Century: Critical Essays and Eyewitness Accounts*, ed. Samuel Totten, William S. Parsons, and Israel W. Chamy (New York: Garland, 1995), pp. 49–96.

[9]Taner Akçam, *Armenien und der Völkermord: Die Istanbuler Prozesse und die türkische Nationalbewegung* (Hamburg: Hamburger Edition, 1996), pp. 61–70.

[10]Sarafian, *United States Official Documents*, vol. 1, pp. xv–xxii. While Turkish historiography continues to insist that the deportations were simply a resettlement, documents released from the Ottoman archives to date give no evidence of the arrival or resettlement of any deportees.

[11]See Donald E. Miller and Lorna Touryan Miller, "Women and Children of the Armenian Genocide" in *The Armenian Genocide: History, Politics, Ethics*, ed. Richard G. Hovannisian (New York: St. Martin's, 1992), p. 213, for a comprehensive list of institutional and individual oral history projects in the United States, representing an estimated 1,696 audio and 934 video interviews.

may be colored by years of repeated narration as well as by their American socialization, both through contact with American relief organizations and during their adult lives in the United States. Ideally, one would contrast the views of Armenian-American survivors with those of Armenians who resettled in European or Near Eastern countries, but the latter published few accounts. Because of the limitations of the available materials, my discussion often juxtaposes the contemporary accounts of foreign eyewitnesses with later oral history interviews.[12]

The Role of Gender in the Armenian Genocide

Various hallmarks of genocide illustrate a definite link between genocidal and gender ideologies. These include the character of genocide as an act of physical and cultural aggression and as an attack on the social and biological reproduction of the victims, including the prevention of births or the assimilation of children. In addition, the institutionalized marginalization of the victim group before genocide strongly suggests analogies with the institutionalized differentiation between the genders.[13]

Gender-specific practices marked every stage of the Armenian Genocide. Sexual insults, intimidation, and violence reinforced the everyday marginalization of the Armenian community in the Ottoman Empire and may have constituted a violent precedent to the 1915–17 Genocide.[14] Gender ideology influenced the perpetration of the Genocide, beginning with the separation and massacre of the men, which left Armenian women and children defenseless. Rape, kidnapping, sex slavery, and forced conversion to Islam furthered the genocidal program, in which women and girls represented a productive and reproductive force targeted for forced labor and biological assimilation.[15] Because the treatment of Armenian women varied, they were able to devise strategies of evasion and survival, often related to traditional female

[12]Scholars of women's history argue for negotiating between larger patterns of social history and the experiences of individual women to provide an integrated account of historical events or movements. See Kathryn Anderson and Dana C. Jack, "Learning to Listen: Interview Techniques and Analyses" in *Women's Words: The Feminist Practice of Oral History*, ed. Sherna Berger Gluck and Daphne Patai (New York: Routledge, 1991), pp. 11–26; and Ann D. Gordon, Mari Jo Buhle, and Nancy Schrom Dye, "The Problem of Women's History" in *Liberating Women's History: Theoretical and Critical Essays*, ed. Bernice A. Carroll (Urbana: University of Illinois Press, 1976), pp. 75–92.

[13]Raphael Lemkin, *Axis Rule in Occupied Europe: Laws of Occupation, Analysis of Government, Proposals for Redress* (Washington, DC: Carnegie Endowment for International Peace, 1944), p. 79; Helen Fein, "Genocide: A Sociological Perspective," *Current Sociology* 38:1 (1990), p. 24; Vahakn N. Dadrian, "The Comparative Aspects of the Armenian and Jewish Cases of Genocide: A Socio-Historical Perspective" in *Is the Holocaust Unique? Perspectives on Comparative Genocide*, ed. Alan S. Rosenbaum (Boulder, CO: Westview, 1996), pp. 111–13; Leo Kuper, *Genocide: Its Political Use in the Twentieth Century* (New Haven, CT: Yale University Press, 1982), pp. 41–42, 86ff; and Yves Temon, *Der verbrecherische Staat: Völkermord im 20. Jahrhundert* (Hamburg: Hamburger Edition, 1996), p. 140.

[14]Vahakn N. Dadrian, "The Circumstances Surrounding the 1909 Adana Holocaust," *Armenian Review* 41:4 (1988), pp. 8–12.

[15]Vahakn N. Dadrian, "The Naim-Andonian Documents on the World War I Destruction of Ottoman Armenians—The Anatomy of a Genocide," *International Journal of Middle East Studies* 18:3 (1986), pp. 311–60, esp. pp. 314–18; idem, "The Secret Young-Turk Ittihadist Conference and the Decision for the World War I Genocide of the Armenians," *Holocaust and Genocide Studies* 7:2 (Fall 1993), pp. 174–75; Mabel Evelyn Elliott, *Beginning Again at Ararat* (New York: Fleming H. Revell, 1924), pp. 26–29, 104, 185; Henry Morgenthau, *Ambassador Morgenthau's Story* (Garden City, NY: Doubleday, Page, 1918), pp. 291, 321.

activities or to their subordinate status as women and as members of a minority group.[16]

Ironically, the early Ittihad regime, strongly secular, had made significant improvements in the situation of women.[17] The era saw progress in girls' education, reforms in family law, and the emergence of various women's organizations,[18] including the Society for the Advancement of Women (*Teali-i Nisvan Cemiyeti*), which was founded by the Turkish feminist and Ittihad figure Halidé Edib and maintained close connections with the Ittihad Party.[19] The Ittihad movement supported progress for women

---

[16]Armenian women are reported to have feigned labor pains to avoid contact with perpetrators, camouflaged themselves as Americans or other foreigners, and even undertaken active resistance activities. See Elliott, *Beginning Again at Ararat*, pp. 254–55, 259–61; Zabel Essayan, "Chronique: Le rôle de la femme arménienne pendant la guerre," *Revue des Études Arméniennes* 2:1 (1922), passim; Stanley E. Kerr, *The Lions of Marash: Personal Experiences with American Near East Relief, 1919–1922* (Albany: State University of New York Press, 1973), pp. 165–66, 249.

[17]The family in Asia Minor was patriarchal; see James Creagh, *Armenians, Koords, and Turks* (London: S. Tinsley, 1880), p. 116; Lucy M. J. Garnett, *The Women of Turkey and Their Folk-Lore*, 2 vols. (London: David Nutt, 1890), vol. 1, pp. 202–7; Béatrice Kasbarian-Bricout, *La société arménienne au XIXe siècle* (Paris: Pensée universelle, 1981), pp. 58–59, 61–62; Raymond H. Kévorkian and Paul B. Paboudjian, *Les Arméniens dans l'Empire Ottoman à la veille du génocide* (Paris: Éditions d'art et d'histoire, 1992), pp. 61–62; Donald E. Miller and Lorna Touryan Miller, *Survivors: An Oral History of the Armenian Genocide* (Berkeley: University of California Press, 1993), pp. 55–60. While Armenian men moved in the public sphere, Armenian women oversaw the household, including preparation of meals and the preservation of food for winter, cleaning and laundry, textile production, and child rearing; see Creagh, *Armenians, Koords, and Turks*, p. 92; Garnett, *Women of Turkey*, vol. 1, pp. 202, 215, 232–33; Susie Hoogasian Villa and Mary Kilbourne Matossian, *Armenian Village Life before 1914* (Detroit: Wayne State University Press, 1982), pp. 48–58, 110–15, 120–24; Kasbarian-Bricout, *Société arménienne*, pp. 40–43; Hratch A. Tarbassian, *Erzurum (Garin): Its Armenian History and Traditions* (New York: Garin Compatriotic Union of the United States, 1975), pp. 121, 129–31. Note traditional Armenian proverbs on the separate spheres in Arshag Tchobanian, *La Femme Arménienne: Conférence faite à Paris le 18. Janvier 1917* (Paris: Librarie Bernard Grasset, 1918), pp. 72–77. Some women acquired additional skills such as weaving, tailoring, teaching, nursing, and midwifery, many of which became essential for survival in the period following the Genocide.

As of the nineteenth century, most Armenian women, even in rural areas, had some schooling because of European and American missionary work as well as the more liberal Armenian attitudes toward women than in the general Ottoman population; see Fanny Davis, *The Ottoman Lady: A Social History from 1718 to 1918* (Westport, CT: Greenwood, 1986), pp. 49–52, 61, 87–89; Garnett, *Women of Turkey*, vol. 1, pp. 217–21; Hoogasian, pp. 71–72, Miller and Miller, *Survivors*, p. 122. Of forty-eight female informants in the Miller interviews, thirty-five mention some formal schooling, nine received no schooling (four of these because of the deportations), and four give no clear information about their education.

In the countryside, Armenian women's freedom of movement was limited by the dangers of traveling in public; unmarried Christian women were often abducted, while their kidnappers went unpunished. Motivated by the desire to avoid payment of the bride price and to assimilate Christians, this practice persisted until the 1970s and 1980s without Turkish governmental interference. See *Evangelischer Pressedienst* (EPD), " 'Christliche Minderheiten aus der Türkei': Ein Bericht eines Ausschusses von Kirchen" (Frankfurt am Main: EPD, November 12, 1979); Norwegian Helsinki Committee, "Report: From a Journey to Turkey, April 3–14, 1981" (Oslo: EPD, 1981); Churches Committee of Migrant Workers in Europe (CCMWE), Working Party on Christian Minorities in Turkey, "Kurze Darstellung über christliche Minderheiten der Türkei," *Pogrom* 86 (April 1982), pp. 50–54; *Die Lage der christlichen Minderheiten in der Türkei seit dem Staatsstreich im September 1980 (Bericht vom Juni 1982)* (Frankfurt am Main: EPD, 1984).

In the Ottoman Empire Muslim women's freedom of movement was often more limited than that of Armenian women, and they might be veiled or be fully secluded from the public and even from male family members beyond the age of puberty. Muslim women's experience also differed radically from that of Christian women because of polygamy. Muslim society persistently limited girls' education well into the era of the Young Turks.

[18]Including the expansion of girls' education in 1911 and the opening of the university in Istanbul to women from 1914 to 1916; see Davis, *Ottoman Lady*, pp. 50–55, 94–95.

[19]Deniz Kandiyoti, "End of Empire: Islam, Nationalism, and Women in Turkey" in *Women, Islam, and the State*, ed. Deniz Kandiyoti (Philadelphia: Temple University Press, 1991), pp. 22–47, esp. p. 29.

and a departure from gender differentiation in the interest of national unity, as can be seen in Edib's writings.[20] Other Ittihad supporters espoused similar views, including Ziya Gökalp, who based his nationalistic ideals on a hypothetical Pan-Turkic past that featured a tradition of gender equality. This unifying ideological link between the Turkish women's movement and the Ittihad Party proved advantageous to the progress of both.

The gender-neutral nationalism espoused by Ittihad ideologues reverberated in gender-neutral orders for (though not implementation of) the Genocide. Interior Minister Talaat's telegrams called for universal deportations without attention to gender: "It has been previously communicated that the government, by orders of the *Cemiyet* [CUP], has decided to exterminate entirely all the Armenians living in Turkey . . . without regard for women, children, and the infirm."[21] These telegrams explicitly condemn the practice of forced intermarriage with Armenian women, which would have saved the latter from deportation, as did Talaat's communication of 29 September 1915: "We have heard that certain people and officials have married Armenian women. I strictly forbid this and enjoin the dispatch of women of this kind into the desert, after they have been separated from their husbands."[22]

Despite Talaat's and other official orders for implementation without regard to gender, the Genocide's local implementation continued to include forced assimilation, coinciding with traditional ideas of gender and nationality. Most important among the latter were that men are the bearers of ethnicity but that women and children are susceptible to assimilation. In specific instances local authorities ignored orders only to be subsequently overruled. The German missionary Johannes Lepsius observed this:

> The *vali* [provincial governor] allowed the sick, families without men, and single women to stay in Erzurum. This humane procedure, for which I also interceded, was suddenly brought to an end by some influence from the Committee [CUP]. . . . The papers already distributed to the women and the sick still remaining in the town were taken away again and they were driven onto the road—to a certain death.[23]

Still, if women's experiences vary, this should not be understood to lessen the gravity of the Genocide but rather to allow us to examine women's divergent experiences in their full complexity, ranging from assimilation and physical violence to escape and even rescue in Ottoman homes.

---

[20]Halidé Edib, *Memoirs of Halidé Edib* (New York: Century, 1926), p. 258; *Das neue Turan: Ein türkisches Frauenschicksal* (Weimar: Verlag Gustav Keipenheuer, 1916), pp. 7, 25, 38; and *Turkey Faces West* (New Haven, CT: Yale University Press, 1930), pp. 5–6, 46, 129–32.

[21]Telegram to the prefecture of Aleppo, September 15, 1915; cited in Aram Andonian, *Documents officiels concernant les massacres arméniens* (Paris: H. Turabian, 1920), p. 145. For insight into the 1980s debate about the authenticity of the Naim-Andonian documents, which concluded with a general scholarly consensus on their authenticity, see Dadrian, "Naim-Andonian Documents," pp. 311–60.

[22]Tessa Hofmann, ed., *Der Völkermord an den Armeniern vor Gericht: Der Prozess Talaat Pascha* (Göttingen: Die Gesellschaft, 1980 <1985>), pp. 133–36.

[23]Johannes Lepsius, *Dentschland und Armenien, 1914–1918: Sammlung diplomatischer Aktenstücke* (Potsdam: Der Tempelverlag, 1919), p. 113 (hereafter: *DA*); cf. also Andonian, *Documents officiels*, p. 51; and Sarafian, *United States Official Documents*, vol. 2, p. 26.

After, and even during, the Genocide, the Armenian community acknowledged the specificity of the experiences of Armenian women. The problem of Armenian women in forced marriages remained general knowledge long afterwards. The conference "La Femme Arménienne" in Paris on January 18, 1917, and Zabel Essayan's 1922 essay "Chronique: Le rôle de la femme arménienne pendant la guerre" were contemporary attempts to approach women's experience as representative of the overall Genocide and as a specific extraordinary development in which they were thrust out of their traditional roles in the household.[24] Over the following decades, however, research rarely concentrated on the divergent experiences of male and female victims,[25] or when it did, only in individual, thematic studies. Eliz Sanasarian studies the roles of women as victims and perpetrators of genocide. Basing their work on oral history interviews, Donald E. Miller and Lorna Touryan Miller establish valuable experiential motifs and psychological categories for the effects of the Genocide on survivors. In particular, their thematization of survival strategies and ethical decision-making contribute to understanding the psychological significance of the Genocide for women. Further scholarly examination of gender-specific experience in the Genocide would aid in the understanding of the Genocide as a whole and provide a crucial basis for comparative work with other genocides.[26]

During the initial stages of the Armenian Genocide, sexual intimidation created an environment of rumor and alarm, recalling memories of the sexual insults and attacks that had preceded earlier massacres in Adana (1909) and elsewhere.[27] Incidents sometimes provoked Armenian communities, whose reaction then served as the pretext for

---

[24]Essayan, "Rôle de la femme arménienne," pp. 121–38, esp. p. 124; Tchobanian, *Femme arménienne*; Edib, *Tukey Faces West*, pp. 5–6, 46, 129–32.

[25]For example, Dadrian, *History of the Armenian Genocide*, pp. 400–01: "It is evident that in genocide victim differences, whether among members of a single victim group or among several victim groups, are of little significance. The differences simply collapse into an abyss of irrelevance as they are leveled by the mechanisms and claws of a mammoth engine of destruction."

[26]Miller and Miller, "Women and Children," pp. 152–72, esp. p. 161, for a discussion of survivors' "tragic moral choices"; and idem, "The Experience of Women and Children," in *Survivors*, chap. 5; Eliz Sanasarian, "Gender Distinction in the Genocidal Process: A Preliminary Study of the Armenian Case," *Holocaust and Genocide Studies* 4:4 (Winter 1989), pp. 449–61, esp. pp. 453–55. Drawing on oral history interviews with fourteen female survivors, Sanasarian observes how Turkish, Arab, and Kurdish women were involved in the purchase and forced labor of Armenian women in their own households, as well as complicit in arranging forced marriages and even directly involved in genocidal violence. Sanasarian also recognizes the role of Ottoman women as rescuers, concluding, "No ethnic group or gender stands out as rescuers. Women acquired all possible roles traditionally ascribed to men; they were perpetrators and collaborators. . . . The 14 case histories . . . seem to [corroborate] Israel Charny's thesis that 'all "normal" people are capable of being genociders, accomplices or bystanders' " (p. 459). Cf. Roger Smith ("Genocide and Women," pp. 328–29), who argues that while female perpetrators' roles have often been determined by their gender (e.g., torturers of men, kidnappers of children, subordinate actors dealing with female victims), their role converges with men's in terms of moral assent to the genocidal project and—with an increasing level of bureaucratic and technical involvement in genocide in the modern era—a greater potential for direct and sustained participation in genocide. On theoretical issues see Susan Brownmiller, *Against Our Will: Men, Women, and Rape* (New York: Simon and Schuster, 1975), pp. 33–38, 56, 124, 376; and Lee Ellis, *Theories of Rape: Inquiries into the Causes of Sexual Aggression* (New York: Hemisphere, 1989), pp. 55–60.

[27]As Dadrian notes, accusations against alleged Armenian rapists, gang rapes of Armenian girls, and sexual insults and threats to an Armenian couple figured in the onset of the Adana massacre of 1909: "What is so unusual about this particular act of Turkish provocation and the disastrous Armenian response to it is its erotic-sexual angle" ("Adana Holocaust," pp. 11–12).

massacre. Repeated verbal and physical assaults went unpunished, with the authorities' indifference emboldening the attackers to further outrages.[28] Eyewitnesses did not fail to note the targeting of Armenian women, as in Van:

> Things continued in . . . suspense until the 20th of April [1915], when some Turkish soldiers tried to seize some village women on their way to the city. The women fled. Two Armenians came up and asked the Turks what they were doing. The Turkish soldiers fired on the Armenians and killed them. This served as a signal. The booming of cannons and rattle of rifles began from every side, and it was realized that the Armenian quarter was besieged.[29]

Contemporary observers also noted the severe treatment of women whose relatives were suspected of resistance. For example, in Malatya a girl whose brother was allegedly aiding the Russians received a particularly harsh prison sentence.[30] In particular, physical abuse and rape of female relatives was also used to intimidate the Armenian leadership and dampen its will to resist. An Armenian eyewitness from Sassun reported that "Early in July [1915] . . . the leading Armenians of the town [Sassun] and the headmen of the villages were subjected to revolting tortures. . . . The female relatives of the victims who came to the rescue were outraged in public before the very eyes of their mutilated husbands and brothers."[31] A survivor from the town of Marash recalled a comparable instance: "[My mother-in-law's] husband [an Armenian priest] was in hiding and when they came to see where he was, she would not tell them; [when] she said that you have killed him, they tortured her. When the husband finds out that they had tortured his wife, he gives himself up and is put in prison."[32]

Attackers often targeted wives of leading figures in the Armenian community, priests, political activists, the heads of resistance groups, and the like. Persecution of the Armenian leadership and their families affirmed both the vulnerability of the community and the impunity of those who attacked it, while reducing the community's

[28]See Dadrian, "Comparative Aspects," p. 114; and *History of the Armenian Genocide*, pp. 386–87.

[29]Letter dated Van, June 7, 1915, from Mr. Y. K. Rushdouni, published in the *Manchester Guardian*, August 2, 1915 (Viscount Bryce, *The Treatment of the Armenians in the Ottoman Empire, 1915–1916* [Beirut: G. Donigian & Sons, 1972], p. 49). Cf. Bryce, *Treatment*, pp. 63, 483 (Zeitun); Lepsius, *DA*, pp. 256–57 (Aleppo); Lepsius, *Der Todesgang des armenischen Volkes: Bericht über das Schicksal des armenischen Volkes in der Türkei während des Weltkrieges* (Potsdam: Tempelverlag, 1919; hereafter: *TAV*), p. 43 (Erzurum), p. 204 (Zeitun); and Morgenthau, *Ambassador Morgenthau's Story*, p. 298 (Van).

[30]Tessa Hofmann and Méliné Pehlivanian, *"Der schlimmsten Orte einer. . . . "*: *Malatia, 1915–1918*, p. 273; this is an originally unpublished manuscript now published as "Malatia 1915: Carrefour des convois de déportés d'après le journal du missionaire allemand Hans Bauernfeind" in Raymond H. Kévorkian, *L'extermination des déportés arméniens ottomans dans les camps de concentration de Syrie-Mésopotamie (1915–1916): La deuxième phase du génocide* (Paris: Revue d'histoire arménienne contemporaine, 1998), vol. 2, pp. 247–69.

[31]Interview with Roupen of Sassun by Mr. A. S. Safrastian, Tiflis (Tbilisi), November 6, 1915, quoted in Bryce, *Treatment of the Armenians*, p. 85, cf. pp. 434, 480 (Zeitun); Lepsius, *DA*, p. 40; Lepsius, *TAV*, p. 126 (Adapazari); and Morgenthau, *Ambassador Morgenthau's Story*, p. 305.

[32]Lousaper Derghevondian, female native of Marash, in unpublished Miller interviews. Similar accounts come from Bogzliyan; Mezre, a town near Harput (Elazığ); Siverek; and Urfa.

ability to defend itself when the deportations were getting underway. The authorities separated Armenian men from their families by conscription into the army, by decree within individual towns prior to the deportation, and by recurring massacres during the deportations themselves. Since men were the traditional heads of their families, their separation reduced the community's ability to resist. Usually the men were killed immediately upon removal, the women having been assured that they would be reunited after evacuation. At least initially, this strategy prevented women's resistance and delayed their assumption of familial leadership.[33] In the absence of male protection and organized female resistance, women became defenseless targets for sexual violence or massacre.

As the deportations were starting, massacres took place, often targeting those who resisted or who had previously been politically active.[34] Gendarmes and *çetes* (irregular armed bands, often specially organized from released prisoners) massacred deportees in the caravans, particularly those who attempted escape or straggled. Victims were sometimes thrown from cliffs or into rivers. As the deportees arrived at the concentration camps in Syria, renewed large-scale massacres occurred. Deportees who did not fall victim to massacre died of hunger, thirst, illness, and exposure.[35]

Rape

Violence directed at female deportees included rape, sexual torture, kidnapping, sexual slavery, and forced marriage. While gender violence is typically mentioned in accounts of the Genocide as a way to emphasize the suffering of the victims, documentary evidence remains understandably scarce, survivor interviews scarcer still.

---

[33]On the normalization of genocidal processes as central to their implementation, see Dabag, "Katastrophe und Identität," p. 185. The victims are convinced by rhetoric camouflaging genocidal intent (e.g., husbands will be reunited with wives, Armenians will return to their homes after the "deportation"), and the perpetrators are convinced of the normalcy of violence against minorities and are thus reinforced in their role.

[34]On the targeting of resisters or the politically active, see three informants from the unpublished Miller interviews; cf. Bryce, *Treatment of the Armenians*, p. 434; Lepsius, *TAV*, p. 89. On massacres within the caravan: eleven accounts from the unpublished Miller interviews; cf. Bryce, *Treatment of the Armenians*, pp. 238, 266, 353–54, 365–66, 553; Faiz El-Ghassein, *Martyred Armenia* (New York: G. H. Doran, 1918), pp. 8, 28; Kloian, *Armenian Genocide*, p. 291; Lepsius, *TAV*, pp. 25, 45–47, 52, 118, 138; Sarafian, *United States Official Documents*, vol. 1, p. 107. On the large-scale massacres in the Syrian desert, four informants from the unpublished Miller interviews; Miller and Miller, *Survivors*; cf. Sarafian, *United States Official Documents*, vol. 1, p. 148–49.

[35]On hunger, see Bryce, *Treatment of the Armenians*, pp. 262, 269, 274–75, 337–38, 473, 552, 564, 567; Pailadzo Captanian (ed. Meliné Pehlivanian), *1915: Der Völkermord an den Armeniern: Eine Zeugin berichtet* (Leipzig: Gustav Kiepenheuer, 1993), p. 49; Kloian, *Armenian Genocide*, pp. 28–29, 61, 106, 142; Lepsius, *DA*, p. 107; Lepsius, *TAV*, pp. 9–10, 26, 151; Sarafian, *United States Official Documents*, vol. 1, pp. 18–19, 31, 130–34; vol. 2, pp. 94, 99. On thirst, see Bryce, *Treatment of the Armenians*, pp. 266, 274–75, 473, 543, 561, 567; Captanian, *1915*, p. 75; El-Ghassein, *Martyred Armenia*, p. 7; Kloian, *Armenian Genocide*, p. 36; Lepsius, *TAV*, p. 152; Sarafian, *United States Official Documents*, vol. 1, pp. 107–8. On exposure, see Bryce, *Treatment of the Armenians*, pp. 266, 277, 323, 543; Kloian, *Armenian Genocide*, p. 61; Lepsius, *DA*, p. 107; Sarafian, *United States Official Documents*, vol. 1, pp. 129, 145–46; vol. 2, p. 121. On physical abuse, see Sarafian, *United States Official Documents*, vol. 1, pp. 31, 49, 129; vol. 2, p. 120. On the forced marches, see Bryce, *Treatment of the Armenians*, pp. 295, 403; Kloian, *Armenian Genocide*, pp. 28–29; Sarafian, *United States Official Documents*, vol. 1, p. 129; vol. 2, p. 121. On disease (typhus in particular), see Bryce, *Treatment of the Armenians*, pp. 260, 262, 337, 429, 431–34, 473, 564, 567; Captanian, *1915*, pp. 48–49; Kloian, *Armenian Genocide*, p. 28; Lepsius, *TAV*, p. 26; Sarafian, *United States Official Documents*, vol. 1, pp. 18–19, 95, 131–32, 146, 165; vol. 2, pp. 94, 123–24.

Contemporary observers often cited their discomfort openly discussing sexual violence, and some accounts explicitly expunge passages recounting it, or else summarize it only superficially.[36]

Despite such limitations, the evidence points to relatively consistent patterns. One survivor from Balıkesir recounted her family's experience as follows:

> My brother [was sent] to the front lines. That's the last we heard of him. . . .
> They took my dad away. . . . Then the turn came for young women and girls.
> At midnight they would come and take some of them away. This was before
> the deportations. Once they took a girl away, forget it, you'll never know her
> whereabouts. I know this because they took one of my girlfriends too. . . .
> You know the Turks did a lot of things but you cannot even talk about
> them. They did everything—if they liked them they made them wives, if
> not they would do all of their bad acts and then kill them. But of course you
> never really know what happened to them—all you know is that they have
> disappeared.[37]

As this survivor noted, the onset of sexual violence preceded mass deportations but followed the elimination of the men. In her account, the assault on women generally took two forms: forced marriage or sex slavery, often entailing physical survival; or rape followed by murder or return to the caravan, essentially consigning the women to death.

Deportation convoys fell victim to nightly raids during which men from neighboring communities and convoy guards alike abducted women, raped them, and then either killed them or returned them to the caravans. "Every night when we would try to sleep under the stars," one male deportee testified, "the gendarmes would come among the people and snatch young girls and women and after doing all sorts of bad things to them, they would return them bloody or dead to their mothers. Those things I can never forget."[38] An American missionary witnessed much the same:

> All tell the same story and bear the same scars: their men were all killed
> on the first day's march from their cities, after which the women and girls
> were . . . robbed of their money, bedding, [and] clothing [,] and beaten,

---

[36]See Beylerian, *Grandes puissances*, p. 208; Bryce, *Treatment of the Armenians*, p. 506; and Captanian, *1915*, p. 45. One particularly good example is the English translation of El-Ghassein's account of the Genocide. In a section entitled "The Violation of Women before or after Death," the main text is abridged and the following footnote appears: "I refrain from particulars. The gendarmes and Kurds are stated to have been the perpetrators of these acts. — Translator" (El-Ghassein, *Martyred Armenia*, p. 30). Another section, "Price of Armenian Women," is curtailed with the note "An unimportant anecdote omitted. — Translator" (p. 34); "The Mutesarrif and the Armenian Girl" is likewise edited, with the comment "Unfit for reproduction. — Translator." The sections "A Caravan of Women" (p. 35) and "Chastity of Armenian Women" (p. 36) are likewise summarized or edited out, leaving only titles to suggest what the author originally discussed.

[37]Satenig Marashlian, female native of Balıkesir, unpublished Miller interviews; cf. Sarafian, *United States Official Documents*, vol. 1, p. 130.

[38]Hovsep Janjikian, male native of Arapkir; similar accounts by informants from Kessab, Sebaste (Sivas), and Hadjin in the unpublished Miller interviews.

criminally abused, and abducted along the way. Their guards . . . allowed the baser element in every village through which they passed to abduct the girls and women and abuse them. We not only were told these things but the same things occurred right here in our own city before our very eyes and openly on the streets. . . . There must be not less than five hundred abducted now in the homes of the Muslims of this city and as many more have been sexually abused and turned out on the streets again.[39]

The available accounts point to other recurring aspects of mass sexual violence during the Genocide: gang rapes or rapes involving more than one individual as perpetrator or enabler, rape in public areas, the coincidence of robbery and rape, and most notably the tolerance and even the agency of government gendarmes in rape.[40]

From the gendarmes and their immediate supervisors all the way up to higher government officials, authorities at all levels were complicit in, direct perpetrators of, or beneficiaries of sexual violence. In September 1915, the *New York Times* reported that Armenian girls were "taken over" or sold by Ottoman officials: "One hundred [Armenian] girls who were attending a mission school . . . were divided into groups, and those that were the best looking in the opinion of the Turkish officers were taken over by those officers. Those considered not quite so good-looking were given over to the soldiers, while those still less attractive were put up for sale to the highest bidders."[41] The German missionary Johannes Lepsius also cites "verifiable cases" in which "attractive Armenian girls were kidnapped by Turkish civil servants in [Merzifon]. A Muslim reported that a gendarme offered to sell him two girls. . . . All Armenians were deported from Gemerek, but they did not reach Sivas. The men and boys were killed [while the] women and children were distributed among the Turkish officials and civil servants."[42] Other observers note the distribution of Armenian women among Turkish officials and the population, as well as police encouragement of sexual outrages, including forced prostitution.[43]

Rape and physical abuse served to dehumanize the Armenian population, something necessary for the successful prosecution of any genocide. For the

---

[39]Letter from Rev. L. M. Leslie, American missionary and American consular agent (Urfa), to Jesse B. Jackson, Esquire, American consul, Aleppo, August 6, 1915 (cited in Sarafian, *United States Official Documents*, vol. 1, pp. 49–50); cf. Hofmann, *Völkermord an den Armeniern*, p. 8; Ephraim K. Jernazian, *Judgment unto Truth: Witnessing the Armenian Genocide* (New Brunswick, NJ: Transaction, 1990), pp. 68, 88; Sarafian, *United States Official Documents*, vol. 1, p. 107.

[40]Cf. in particular Captanian, *1915*, pp. 42ff., 50–52; Kloian, *Armenian Genocide*, p. 36 (Zeitun); Sarafian, *United States Official Documents*, vol. 1, p. 31; vol. 2, p. 135.

[41]"Armenian Women Put Up At Auction," *New York Times*, September 29, 1915 (cited in Kloian, *Armenian Genocide*, p. 47). Cf. Bryce, *Treatment of the Armenians*, p. 20; Kloian, *Armenian Genocide*, pp. 54, 90, 297, 337; Sarafian, *United States Official Documents*, vol. 1, pp. 6–7, 15, 26, 36; vol. 2, pp. 27, 38–39; and account of Takouhi Levonian, female native of Kighi, by Erzurum, unpublished Miller interviews.

[42]Lepsius, *TAV*, pp. 61–62.

[43]On the distribution of women among officials and population see Bryce, *Treatment of the Armenians*, pp. 225, 238, 347–48, 475; Sarafian, *United States Official Documents*, vol. 1, pp. 7, 26, 31, 36, 49; vol. 2, p. 27. On police violence, see Bryce, *Treatment of the Armenians*, pp. 426, 475. On forced prostitution, see Bryce, *Treatment of the Armenians*, p. 91; Hofmann and Pehlivanian, "Malatia 1915," pp. 318–19.

perpetrators, the inferior status of the Armenians remained closely linked with rape, as emerges from the following story related by a male survivor from Ailanji, a village by Yozgat:

> One day my *agha* [master] took me with him. . . . We saw from far off that some people were fighting or rolling on the ground and there was a soldier in the road. My *agha* asked the soldier what was going on. He replied that the Turk had a *gavur* [infidel]. Obviously he was raping her. *Agha* called him and her over. She was bleeding, beaten up, in bad shape. He asked the man what this was all about. The Turk replied that she was only a *gavur*.[44]

The dehumanization of the Armenians was furthered by the fact that so many of the rapes were perpetrated in public, indeed in many instances in front of family members.[45] Survivors confirm that rape or the threat of rape thus functioned as a means of intimidation throughout the Genocide. A female survivor from Kighi by Erzurum relates: "It used to be said that if we harmed the gendarmes, then others would come and harm our women. We were not the ones who were afraid, only the men in our group were. They used to say that if they did something to a Turkish gendarme, they would only be hurting their own women."[46]

Rape also constituted a threat hanging over the heads of those women who escaped the deportations or entrusted themselves to rescuers. Five informants in the Miller interviews speak of rapes that occurred outside the context of the deportations. Two of them refer to sexual attacks on groups of women traveling unaccompanied, while two others report rape or attempted rape of women or girls entrusting themselves to Turkish "protectors." One other informant implies that a gendarme raped an escaped woman in his charge while returning her to the deportations.

Beyond sexual abuse, female deportees were particularly vulnerable to other forms of physical violence. According to some, these included horrible medical "experiments."[47] The theft of clothing also represented an assault on women's bodily integrity and decreased victims' chances of survival during the hardships of the deportations. In

---

[44]Albert Ailanjian, male native of Ailanji (village by Yozgat), unpublished Miller interviews.

[45]Sarafian, *United States Official Documents*, vol. 1, pp. 49–50; cf. Bryce, *Treatment of the Armenians*, p. 24; El-Ghassein, *Martyred Armenia*, pp. 34–35; Martin Niepage, *The Horrors of Aleppo, Seen by a German Witness* (London: T. Fisher Unwin, 1975 <1917>), p. 12. For the full account see German original, *Ein Wort an die berufenen Vertreter des deutschen Volkes: Eindrücke eines deutschen Oberlehrers aus der Türkei* (Potsdam: "Der Reichsbote" GmbH, 1916), p. 7.

[46]Baydzar Idris, female native of Kighi, by Erzurum, unpublished Miller interviews. Cf. Kerr, *Lions of Marash*, p. 25, who reports men killed for protesting against rapes, and Seifert, "Krieg und Vergewaltigung," pp. 5, 9, on rape or the threat of rape aimed at dampening resistance by highlighting the helplessness of the men and the corresponding defenselessness of "their" women.

[47]Vahakn N. Dadrian, "The Role of Turkish Physicians in the World War I Genocide of Ottoman Armenians," *Holocaust and Genocide Studies* 1:2 (Fall 1986), pp. 169–92. Both men and women were said to have been subject to massacres and medical experiments performed under the leadership of doctors; especially noteworthy were mutilations of the eyes of girls and of infants (pp. 181–82; Elliott, *Beginning Again at Ararat*, pp. 25–26). Some contemporaries claimed that doctors were also involved in the selection of children and girls for placement as slaves or concubines (Bryce, *Treatment of the Armenians*, p. 262).

particular, the nakedness of female deportees contributed to their dehumanization in the eyes of the general population; as one foreign observer recounted: "Farther on, all the survivors . . . were entirely stripped of their clothing. . . . They were brought into Aleppo the last few miles in third-class railway carriages, herded together like so many animals. When the doors of the carriages were opened, they were jeered at by the populace for their nakedness."[48]

There have been various scholarly efforts to explain the function of rape and sexual violence in group conflicts. Most agree that rape, in both individual and collective contexts, is not a sexual act but an exercise of the perpetrator's power over the victim. Scholars have argued that rape may demonstrate perpetrators' control over a subordinate group by violating the personal integrity of its women, or may create solidarity through complicity among male perpetrators.[49] Sexual violence is also understood to dehumanize the victims, thereby facilitating the implementation of genocide.

Sexual intimidation and abuse were used to dampen Armenian resistance, thus expressing and bolstering Ottoman power. Early in the Genocide sexual attacks on women destroyed men's roles as protectors of their families, and, by targeting female relatives of the Armenian leadership in particular, minimized potential resistance. Throughout the Genocide most rapes were perpetrated, or at least enabled, by groups. While we lack explicit evidence that these rapes created solidarity among male perpetrators (as scholars of rape theorize), the complicity among various levels of the Ottoman hierarchy does suggest a concerted dehumanization of the victims.

Prevention of Reproduction, Forced Marriage, Assimilation

Pregnant women and young mothers occupied a distinctive position in the eyes of the Ittihadists and other perpetrators. While many Armenian women and children were assimilated into Ottoman households, pregnant women, infants, and small children were often targets of violence as the embodiment of biological continuity. A typical eyewitness reported "Turkish soldiers us[ing] cudgels upon women in advanced pregnancy."[50] Eight informants in the Miller interviews also saw or heard of pregnant women whose bellies were slit open or stabbed. One informant mentions that pregnant women in Zeitun were separated from the Armenian population before the deportations, presumably to be massacred.

Pregnant women also succumbed to the exhaustion and physical abuse suffered during the deportations, if they were not compelled to deliver their babies outdoors and under extreme conditions. There is extensive evidence for female deportees undergoing childbirth during the deportations only to be forced to continue with the convoy

---

[48]Bryce, *Treatment of the Armenians*, p. 543, cf. pp. 20, 266 (reproduced in Sarafian, *United States Official Documents*, vol. 1, p. 108); Captanian, *1915*, pp. 123–24; Niepage, *Horrors of Aleppo*, p. 13; Sarafian, *United States Official Documents*, vol. 1, p. 145.

[49]Brownmiller, pp. 33–38, 56, 124, 376; Lee Ellis, *Theories of Rape: Inquiries into the Causes of Sexual Aggression* (New York: John Benjamins, 1989), pp. 55–60.

[50]Niepage, *Horrors of Aleppo*, p. 8, cf. p. 13.

shortly afterwards.[51] Mortality was high among infants, and some new mothers ended up giving away, abandoning, or neglecting newborns.[52]

Both foreign observers and survivors note that children, particularly younger females, were assimilated into Muslim households or assigned to Turkish orphanages.[53] Girls were often kidnapped from caravans, often with the involvement or express consent of gendarmes and government officials.[54] In Van, Trabzon, Urfa, and other cities, children were killed en masse in coordinated actions. In some cases, abandoned children or those in orphanages were killed.[55] Two survivors interviewed by the Millers report the massacre of children in Armenian communities that resisted deportation. One informant mentions a separate deportation of children from Aleppo to Deir-el-Zor, while another recalls a group of children from his convoy being thrown into a well.[56] Such actions represent an important facet of gender violence—the perpetrators' attack on reproduction in the Armenian community.

Written and oral accounts refer to sex slavery and forced marriages as phenomena that paralleled outright physical violence. Although "marriages" were discouraged by the central government, regional differences in the implementation of orders permitted the kidnapping of some women and girls from the deportation columns, while others were given the choice of converting to Islam, marrying Muslim men, and thus escaping deportation. Whether as wife, concubine, or laborer, the assimilation of female deportees into Ottoman households coincided with the Genocide's goals by furthering the assimilation of survivors and thus eradicating the Armenian community.

---

[51]Bryce, *Treatment of the Armenians*, pp. 27, 472–73, 534–35; Captanian, *1915*, pp. 30, 72; Kloian, *Armenian Genocide*, pp. 9, 54, 143; Lepsius, *DA*, p. 53; Lepsius, *TAV*, p. 8, 142; Sarafian, *United States Official Documents*, vol. 1, pp. 26, 36. Two informants from the Miller interviews mention childbirths during the deportations; in both cases, the infant died shortly after birth.

[52]Of the survivors interviewed by the Millers, two report seeing abandoned infants, one reports the abandonment of a newborn sibling, and two recall infant siblings dying of hunger.

While one informant mentions her mother getting a respite from the deportation because of childbirth, such cases appear to have been exceptional. On mortality among infants and new mothers, see Bryce, *Treatment of the Armenians*, p. 27; Captanian, *1915*, pp. 79–80; El-Ghassein, *Martyred Armenia*, p. 13; Kloian, *Armenian Genocide*, pp. 29, 54; Sarafian, *United States Official Documents*, vol. 1, pp. 26, 36, 83; vol. 2, p. 124. On the abandonment or neglect of infants see A. S. Baronigian, *Armenien und die Türkei: Erzählungen und Erlebnisse aus Armeniens jüngster Martyriumsgeschichte* (Post Kötzschenbroda in Sachsen: Armenisches Hilfskommittee e.V., n.d. [ca. late 1910s–mid-1920s]), p. 519; Bryce, *Treatment of the Armenians*, pp. 472–73; El-Ghassein, *Martyred Armenia*, pp. 7–8; Kloian, *Armenian Genocide*, p. 36; Lepsius, *TAV*, p. 142; Sanasarian, "Gender Distinction in the Genocidal Process," p. 451.

[53]Baronigian, *Armenien und die Türkei*, pp. 18–20; Beylerian, *Grandes puissances*, p. 131; Bryce, *Treatment of the Armenians*, pp. 12, 14, 92, 295–96, 323, 363, 477, 488, 506; Lepsius, *DA*, p. 184; Sarafian, *United States Official Documents*, vol. 1, pp. 14–15, 21, vol. 2, pp. 38, 48, 53, 94.

[54]Adalian, "Armenian Genocide," p. 86; Bryce, *Treatment of the Armenians*, pp. 334, 338; Captanian, *1915*, pp. 109–10, 119; Kloian, *Armenian Genocide*, p. 297.

[55]Beylerian, *Grandes puissances*, p. 469; Bryce, *Treatment of the Armenians*, pp. 86, 243, 260, 316, 359; Leslie A. Davis (ed. Susan Blair), *The Slaughterhouse Province: An American Diplomat's Report on the Armenian Genocide, 1915–1917* (New Rochelle, NY: Aristide D. Karatzas, 1988), p. 169; Jernazian, *Judgment unto Truth*, p. 88; Kloian, *Armenian Genocide*, pp. 291, 299; Lepsius, *DA*, p. 209; Sarafian, *United States Official Documents*, vol. 2, p. 38.

[56]For the massacre of children in resisting communities, see two informants (Kighi by Erzurum, Urfa); for children's deportation, see one informant (Osmaniye); for separation and murder of children, see informant Arapkir in unpublished Miller interviews.

Forced intermarriage and the resulting assimilation of women and girls were rooted in the traditional perception of men as the sole bearers of ethnicity. This perception was particularly apparent in the refusal of men's conversions to Islam, the refusal of female converts with male children, and ongoing ambivalence about intermarriage with Armenian women as inconsistent with the larger genocidal program. One contemporary reported that "At Harpug [Elazığ], they would not accept the conversion of the men; in the case of the women, they made their conversion conditional in each instance upon the presence of a Muslim willing to take the convert in marriage."[57] Similarly, a foreign observer told the American Committee for Armenian and Syrian Relief that "a company of young Armenian brides [Armenian: *hars*, young married woman] with their little boys, all of whom had become Mohammedans, were sent away. The order had come privately, not to the Governor but to the police, that women who had boys, no matter if they were babies in arms, should be deported with their children."[58] A telegram of Talaat Pasha dated December 17, 1915, likewise recognizes the inconsistency of local conversions and assimilation with the overall genocidal program: "To the Prefecture of Aleppo. . . . Advise the Armenians who have requested to embrace Islam in the intention of avoiding the general deportation (toward the desert) that they are not at all able to become Muslims except after arriving at their place of exile.[59] While Armenian men and boys were effectively excluded from local assimilation, women and girls were viewed as potentially salvageable. This perspective was reinforced by the general identification of the children of forced intermarriages as Turkish.

A Western missionary relates the following about an Armenian woman who ultimately left behind her Turkish rescuer and, consequently, their children:

> When she heard of the Armistice she took off all the jewels and clothes her husband had given her . . . and she said to him, "I am leaving you. I will never see you again." . . . I said to her, "You love your husband. . . . [W]hy do you not go back to him?" She looked at me with astonishment in her miserable eyes and said, "But he is a Turk." He was a Turk, her baby was a Turk, and she was Armenian. She felt that her love for them was a sin. . . . Many Armenian girls, of course, did remain in Turkish households. Of the thousands who disappeared into the seclusion of the high-walled gardens, only a few hundreds came out.[60]

---

[57]Bryce, *Treatment of the Armenians*, p. 14. For similar incidents, cf. Beylerian, *Grandes puissances*, pp. 153, 289; Bryce, *Treatment of the Armenians*, pp. 5, 12, 14, 247, 296, 313, 352, 363, 384; Captanian, *1915*, pp. 38–39; Elliott, *Beginning Again at Ararat*, p. 33; Kloian, *Armenian Genocide*, pp. 5, 31, 77; Lepsius, *TAV*, pp. 253–57; Niepage, *Horrors of Aleppo*, p. 14; Sarafian, *United States Official Documents*, vol. 1, p. 48; vol. 2, pp. 53, 93–94, 133.

[58]Bryce, *Treatment of the Armenians*, p. 353. For similar incidents, cf. Captanian, *1915*, p. 134; El-Ghassein, *Martyred Armenia*, p. 39; and Morgenthau, *Ambassador Morgenthau's Story*, p. 291, where it is noted that younger boys whose identity could still be influenced would be assimilated into Turkish families, while girls would be taken as wives or concubines.

[59]Talaat Pasha, telegram, December 17, 1915 (cited in Andonian, *Documents officiels*, p. 148). On Talaat's telegrams bearing specific references to integration and elimination of Armenian children, see Dadrian, "Naim-Andonian Documents," p. 315.

[60]Elliott, *Beginning Again at Ararat*, pp. 28–29. See also Baronigian, *Armenien und die Türkei*, p. 142. The Armistice of Mudros of October 30, 1918 implicitly required the release of forcibly kept Armenian women: "All Allied prisoners of war and Armenian interned persons and prisoners are to be collected in Constantinople and handed over unconditionally to the Allies." See Hovannisian, *Armenia on the Road to Independence*, pp. 238–40.

Fourteen informants in the Miller interviews mention forced marriages known from personal experience. During one a female survivor, requesting that the tape recorder be turned off, recounted the following details from her life (as reported by the interviewer):

> In Boğazlıyan when she spoke of living separately from her mother, it was because she was forced to marry (at the age of fifteen) a much older Turkish man. He saved her family and several others and seemed to have been very kind to her. . . . She feels very ashamed of this part of her life. But she told me that later in Adana to save her honor her brother and mother made her marry an Armenian man, who was married before with children and turned out to be "crass and uncivilized." . . . They moved to the United States, but eventually got divorced. She said that everywhere she went Armenians always pointed their finger at her, saying how could she not live with that [Armenian] man.[61]

While the survivors tell of women's lack of agency in forced marriages or marriages where they took refuge from the deportations, shame and stigma attached to their survival. Their experiences demonstrate another way marriages may have saved the physical lives of female deportees, but nonetheless sundered them from their people.

Self-Enrichment and Forced Labor

The forced intermarriage of Armenian women was also a means to material gain for those involved. By assimilating an Armenian woman into his household, a man could save the traditional dowry paid to a Muslim girl's parents, while gaining rights both to the deportees' children and to her family's property. In the words of an Armenian observer from Van, "by the permission of the Government, the Armenian households—that is, the women and children and property—were divided among the Turks. In order to secure their property, the Turks betrothed themselves to Armenian girls and women, with the intention of marrying them."[62] In other ways too, the trade in Armenian women that attended the deportations offered opportunities for self-enrichment. Surrounding communities and the Ottoman authorities alike stood to benefit from the despoliation of the victims, from the sale of women as workers or as wives, and from Armenian women's slave labor.

Many sources report the plundering of the deportees. In the absence of men the women and girls became defenseless targets for robbery not only by the communities through which the caravans passed, but by the very gendarmes assigned to convoy them. Molestation and plunder intertwined when men "searched" the bodies of women for hidden money or valuables. One victim later recounted how "they took us to the top of a tall hill and the same *effendi* and the other gendarmes searched us all over in a

---

[61]Anonymous female native of Kayseri; see similar accounts from female natives of Besni, Eskişehir, and Sivrihisar, unpublished Miller interviews.

[62]Bryce, *Treatment of the Armenians*, p. 63.

shameful manner; they took everything made of silk and everything else of value in our clothes and bedding.[63]

Gendarmes supplemented their pay by selling Armenian women to surrounding communities. Deportees were sold at auction as sex slaves, marketed in Damascus naked so that bidders might better judge their worth: "Soldiers were pushing in front of them 300 or 400 naked Armenian girls and women. These were put up for auction and the whole lot disposed of, some for two, three, and four francs. Only Mohammedans were allowed to buy. The salesman kept on exclaiming: 'Rejoice oh ye faithful in the shame of the Christians.'"[64] In Turkish, Kurdish, and Arab households, Armenian women and girls ended up as servants, farmhands, and maids, remaining totally vulnerable because of their absolute dependence.[65] Of the survivors interviewed by the Millers, at least two worked as servants and one as a nanny. Another survivor related her brother's account of witnessing female deportees being forcibly prostituted or traded at an inn.[66]

Aftermath

Contemporary observers viewed the assimilation of women and children into Muslim households as an intentional policy aimed at disintegrating the Armenian community simultaneously with the physical annihilation of men and boys. As a report in the *New York Times* put it, "The object of the conversion of children reported from some districts and the very general sale of women and girls appear [sic] to be political. Foreigners believe Talaat has countenanced these crimes with the object of breaking up the strong social structure of the Armenian community in Turkey."[67] Even after the Mudros Armistice of October 1918 required the release of all forcibly married women, those who left their Turkish homes faced the prospect of having to support themselves and their children in the hostile environment and broken economy of a defeated country. At the time, the American Committee for Armenian and Syrian Relief reported on the situation of Armenian women as follows: "After the signing of the armistice, many of the Turks, believing that by so doing they could escape punishment, turned the women—many of them with babies—into the streets. Cable dispatches to the Committee have reported that numbers of these women were wandering about the country, crazed

---

[63]Bryce, *Treatment of the Armenians*, pp. 271–72; cf. Captanian, *1915*, pp. 35–36, 77, 83; Kloian, *Armenian Genocide*, p. 289; Lepsius, *TAV*, p. 146; Sarafian, *United States Official Documents*, vol. 1, pp. 105–08. Cf. also Ofer and Weitzman, *Women in the Holocaust*, pp. 333, 336 on sexualized body searches in the Holocaust, and Brownmiller, *Against Our Will*, pp. 89–90, 108–9 on a similar usage of rape as a method of "strip-searching" or "interrogation" in the Vietnam War.

[64]Beylerian, *Grandes puissances*, p. 206; cf. Bryce, *Treatment of the Armenians*, p. 23 (Vezirköprü by Merzifon); Captanian, *1915*, p. 124; El-Ghassein, *Martyred Armenia*, pp. 33–34 (Deir-el-Zor); Jernazian, *Judgment unto Truth*, p. 68; Lepsius, *TAV*, p. 61. Other researchers' survivor interviews point to the prevalence of trade in Armenian women as servants or slaves who were thus subject to physical and sexual abuse; see Sanasarian, "Gender Distinction in the Genocidal Process," pp. 453–54.

[65]On Armenian women as servants or slaves, see Bryce, *Treatment of the Armenians*, pp. 23, 262, 410; Captanian, *1915*, pp. 98–105, 109–10, 124; Hofmann and Pehlivanian, "Malatia 1915," p. 317; Sarafian, *United States Official Documents*, vol. 1, p. 145; on Armenian women in agricultural work, see Adalian, "Armenian Genocide," p. 94; Bryce, *Treatment of the Armenians*, p. 261; on Armenian women as nannies, see Captanian, *1915*, pp. 98–105.

[66]Arousiag Aivazian, female native of Kayseri, unpublished Miller interviews.

[67]"Criticizes Mr. Morgenthau," *New York Times*, October 8, 1915 (cited in Kloian, *Armenian Genocide*, p. 63).

by starvation and exposure. As fast as possible they are being gathered up by . . . relief workers and placed in homes established for their care."[68] Despite the presence of missionary and relief groups such as Near East Relief, harsh conditions persisted for Armenian survivors long after war's end. Deciding among the options of orphanage life, emigration, or resettlement in Turkey posed daunting questions.[69]

In fact, relief organizations had made concerted efforts to gather women and girls from Muslim households as early as 1916, offering "ransom" to Muslim families and Ottoman officials who had helped distribute the women among the populace and who could offer information about their location.[70] But even after the armistice, when both Armenians and foreign residents were gathering the scattered women and children into orphanages, trying to undo the assimilation of young women and children was occasionally punished by the authorities. One survivor recalled that "a lot of those people who went around gathering Armenians were imprisoned and some killed."[71] As late as July 1919 reports estimated about 50,000 Armenian women and girls were still being "held captive."[72]

While many Armenian women and children were rescued during this period, some were now pregnant by their Muslim "husbands," others had been traumatized by physical abuse, and yet others still had been infected with sexually transmitted diseases.[73] Adding insult to injury, a large number were stigmatized because of their experience. This latter rift convinced many such women to remain with their Turkish households. Perhaps they were right: women returning to, and even accepted by, the Armenian community nonetheless continued to encounter tension in their relationship with it. "Listen to me," one Armenian witness confided,

> those girls who were mature and had married Turkish men, it was so sad—I can hardly talk about it. I had girl friends who had married Turks [and] used to say, "I want my *effendi*." They wanted their husbands—they had a comfortable life. In the same way that they took me to the [American orphanage in Konya], they took those girls to the orphanage as well. They were girls from good homes [i.e., before the Genocide]. Some wanted their [Turkish] husbands, others did not. Those who did were young and simple. I had one friend whose fiancé they killed and took her [for a Turkish man]. . . . [Later] she was engaged [to an Armenian man] and some people objected that the man should not marry this girl. So he did not, but later another man married her.[74]

---

[68]"Armenian Girls Tell of Massacres," *New York Times*, June 1, 1919 (cited in Kloian, *Armenian Genocide*, p. 297).

[69]See Miller and Miller, "Orphanage Life and Family Reunions" in *Survivors*, pp. 118–36.

[70]"The Turkish officers for so much money will give information as to where these young women may be found. Further payments will cause them to be brought to some appointed place, and then it is a matter of how much money will be paid for their release" ("Ransoms Armenian Girls," *New York Times*, February 13, 1916 [cited in Kloian, *Armenian Genocide*, p. 140]).

[71]Mayreni Shahinian, female native of Urumdigin by Yozgat, unpublished Miller interviews.

[72]"Tells of Armenia's Woes," *New York Times*, July 20, 1919 (cited in Kloian, *Armenian Genocide*, p. 333).

[73]Major Stephen Trowbridge, "Stories of Liberated Armenians," *Missionary Review of the World*, July 1919 (cited in Kloian, *Armenian Genocide*, pp. 302–5); Sanasarian, "Gender Distinction in the Genocidal Process," p. 455.

[74]Yeghisapet Manjikian, female native of Afyon Karahisar, unpublished Miller interviews.

A male survivor from Urfa also recalls the dilemma of Armenian women married into Ottoman households during the genocide, as they were caught between social stigma and the need to survive:

> Now there are many Armenian women among the Turks. They were taken in and remained with them and bore their children. They are all Turkicized [sic] now—gone from our blood. The children don't know their identity, only their mothers do. . . . After the deportations they gathered up a lot of the . . . women and children. Many of them objected and did not want to leave because they had nowhere to go and no one to go to. Many of them would have left if they had had parents living. But here they were with children and a home, after all, and did not want to leave. . . . There are many such cases. . . . Everyone used to look down and find it shameful when an Armenian married a Turk.[75]

Another male survivor, from Sivas, also confirms that stigma prevented the return and reintegration of Armenian women into their community:

> My brother . . . and a few others . . . came to Adana and wanted to go to the village to get their wives. I told them not to because I had already gone to the court three times. . . . [The former wives] all came dressed like Turks with veils on their heads. [Their new husbands] told [the Armenian men] that anything can happen during wartime. . . .[The Armenian women] would not leave—one of them said that if they returned, people would say that they have been Turks' wives and would all mock them. [The Armenian husbands] all gave up, returned to Adana, and remarried; and all of them returned to the U.S.[76]

In any case, the fact that even many Armenians considered the children of the forced marriages "Turkish" made the reintegration of Armenian women into their community all the more problematic. A female survivor from Aleppo recounts the following story:

> When we were living in the Turkish village. . . . We knew an Armenian woman who was married to a Turk. She used to come to us and help with our house cleaning. We guess[ed] that she was Armenian, and talked to her. She gave us her father's name. We wrote letters and advertised in the U.S., and, sure enough, we found her father. He wrote to her, saying: you are my daughter and I will take you back, but not your children who also belong to a Turk. She had a boy and a girl. She herself had gotten married very young, only twelve or so. Obviously she was taken during the deportation. She kept crying and crying, not knowing what to do. Finally she decided to leave and went to Beirut; once in Beirut, she could not take it without her children but was too afraid to return. . . . She was miserable.[77]

---

[75]Kevork Voskeritchian, male native of Urfa, unpublished Miller interviews.

[76]Hagop Elmassian, male native of Sebaste (Sivas), unpublished Miller interviews.

[77]Azniv Yousoufian, female native of Aleppo, unpublished Miller interviews.

Conclusion

Although there are basic differences between the motives and perpetration of the Armenian Genocide, the Holocaust, and other genocidal episodes,[78] some aspects of the former shed light on the situation of women during genocide in general.

(1) Insults and intimidation of women as an antecedent

Sexual intimidation can function as an antecedent of genocide by dehumanizing the victims, making them a ready target for attacks that could be conducted with impunity. In Turkey, where attacks did provoke responses on the part of the Armenian community, these were used as a rationale for further violence. Genocidal actors singled out women married or related to leaders and resistance figures as a means of paralyzing the community.

(2) The targeting of men and the isolation of women

The separation of victims by gender and the elimination of most of the male population left women vulnerable to sexual abuse, exploitation, and forced assimilation. The men were targeted for killings in their double capacity as heads of household and bearers of Armenian ethnicity. In their absence, female deportees were viewed as susceptible to assimilation. Once incorporated into a Muslim household, they and their children were no longer seen as representatives of the Armenian people.

(3) Attacks on reproduction of the victim group

Genocides involve concerted intervention in the reproductive cycles of women in conjunction with the perpetrators' genocidal program. Impregnation by the perpetrator group, attacks on pregnant women, and the abduction and assimilation of existing children are some of the methods employed by genocidal actors. As the Armenian Genocide was aimed at not only the physical but also the cultural elimination of the Armenian community, means such as these were widely considered consistent with the CUP's genocidal plans, if only in particular localities.

(4) Exploitation and sexual slavery

Genocidal actors derived economic, social, and other benefits from the use of women's bodies. In the absence of male family members and traditional coping mechanisms, women became vulnerable to sexual abuse and victimization as a slave labor force. While the absorption of Armenian women into Ottoman households as workers, wives, or (essentially) sex slaves may represent an exception to the CUP's genocidal program, they also highlight the economic and other benefits motivating perpetrators.

---

[78]On similarities and differences between the Armenian Genocide and the Holocaust, see Dadrian, "Comparative Aspects," passim; Dadrian, *History of the Armenian Genocide*, pp. 395–99; Florence Mazian, *Why Genocide? The Armenian and Jewish Experiences in Perspective* (Ames: Iowa State University Press, 1990), esp. pp. 243ff. Ternon (*Verbrecherische Staat.* pp. 153–55) makes a significant point on the difference between Armenian and Jewish women's experience of sexual violence: while the Armenian Genocide allowed for local variations (e.g., forced assimilation, survival of orphans), the racial-biological uniformity aimed at by the Nazi regime led to a more global annihilation with fewer variations. While the CUP was motivated by racist ideology, this ideology was not widespread among local perpetrators, whose actions often varied from the general plan, as we have seen; by contrast, the Nazi perpetrators selected victims according to physical constitution for forced labor or death—gender violence was less prominent because sexual contact with Jewish men or women represented "Rassenschande" ("racial shame")—a punishable crime.

(5) Rape

In genocide, rape marks the subordinate status of the victimized community as the latter succumbs to widespread violence. In addition, rape often functions as a means of social control to stifle resistance and to stigmatize victims. Rapes perpetrated against women isolate them from their own community, creating a crisis in its communal life. Rape took many forms in the Armenian Genocide: forced marriage, sex slavery, individual and gang rapes perpetrated or enabled by Ottoman authorities. This abuse left its mark on the Armenian community; rape victims continued to suffer stigmatization after their experience, while many women remained in forced marriages in Turkey for years following the deportations, or sometimes for the rest of their lives.

* * *

The Armenian Genocide exhibits the impact and significance of gender violence in a way that could be fruitful for comparative studies. Gender-based violence attends the overall implementation of genocide. It can create a long-lasting rift between abused female survivors and their community. Where it is a product of genocidal intent, sexual and gender-based violence contribute to the destruction of the victims' culture parallel to the attempt at physical elimination of the community in whole or in part. This violence should be understood as a distinct and important element of genocide.

Source: From Derderian, Katharine. (2005). "Common Fate, Different Experience: Gender-Specific Aspects of the Armenian Genocide, 1915–1917," *Holocaust and Genocide Studies*, Volume 19, No. 1, pp. 1–25. Copyright © 2005. Reprinted by permission of Oxford University Press.

VICTIMIZATION, SURVIVAL AND THE IMPUNITY OF FORCED EXILE: A CASE STUDY FROM THE RWANDAN GENOCIDE

Frank M. Afflitto

Introduction

The basis of any empirical enterprise is the collection of observed data which can be subjected to theoretical speculation. To begin building a criminological understanding of genocide, then, scholars need a foundation of observations suitable as objects for study within the epistemological framework of criminology. This paper contributes to that process by presenting a case study of a survivor of the Rwandan genocide, focusing on experiences during the genocide and the post-victimization perspectives of the respondent. The interview data reported here are interpreted in terms of the respondent's sense of justice and how formal sanctions, or their absence, affect the quality of experience of victims in the aftermath of the crime.

The revelatory, holistic case study (Yin, 1984) found in this article relates the experiences of a young Tutsi woman during the Rwandan genocide of the period April to July of 1994. This case study is relevant in that it is far from unique. It is because it is representative of many similar cases of victimization in the Rwandan genocide that it is of value and is revelatory as a case study.

Another reason case studies such as the present one are of empirical worth is that the information provided by the research subject deals with issues beyond victimization. These contextual data include post-victimization perceptions of justice and other perspectives beyond the cross-sectional experience of direct genocidal victimization. This current case study of one Rwandan genocide victim and survivor provides the reader with not only the circumstances surrounding victimization, but a context in which her current reactions can be examined. These reactions center on her perceptions of the socio-legal aftermath of the genocide in her country and her continued persecution as a Tutsi woman.

A third and salient point of relevance of the case study method is the position of the professional researcher in the research process. This article is being written from a place of partiality (Benedetti, 1984). While the research has been conducted with the standard perpetual focus on the enhancement of scientific objectivity and empirical validity, I would be misrepresenting myself as a criminologist were I not to state that I am partial in exposing the reader to data detailing a process of genocide.

The production of such a research article is part of a process of "writing against terror" (Sluka, 2000). This methodological genre has been a developing professional trend in political anthropology and ethnography over the past decade. "Writing up genocide," then, is a methodological act that is also, inseparably, an "ethical stance" (Afflitto, 1998b) in my view. Not only are ethics exercised in guarding the respondent's identity and hometown, but the presentation of the data themselves is one small piece in the fight against genocide. Anthropologist Nancy Scheper-Hughes (1992) has eloquently addressed the responsibility of exercising morality in one's ethnographic fieldwork in her book on poverty and violence in northeast Brazil. Other powerful recent work on fieldwork techniques (Lee, 1995) and on researching the violence in and around Northern Irish Catholic ghettos (Sluka, 1989, 2000) has also addressed this methodological orientation.

Criminologists, in general, face similar dilemmas of partiality and objectivity as part of more common research topics. After all, who among us does not study subject matter that is somehow repulsive and unacceptable, such as child sexual molestation, police corruption, domestic violence, or savings and loan fraud? Our field is replete with scholars researching phenomena which they somehow seek to overcome, affect or modify. I feel no shame, therefore, in letting the reader know that this criminologist writes from a place of condemnation of genocide and state violence, in Rwanda and elsewhere. It is my hope that the data in this article provide the reader a name and a face for the word "genocide" and motivate criminologists and victimologists to include genocide in their research agendas.

Methodology

The case study is based on a number of contacts between the author and the research subject over an eighteen-month period. The author first witnessed the informant speak in public on two separate occasions during a six-month period, from October 1998 into April 1999. In October 1998, the research subject spoke at the First International Genocide Conference in Sacramento, California, hosted by the Ethnic Studies Department of the California State University at Sacramento. The subject was then invited to speak in April 1999 at The University of Memphis as part of several academic projects commemorating the fifth anniversary of the Rwandan genocide.[1] It was during that visit in April, when the then twenty-year old informant addressed several University of Memphis Department of Criminology and Criminal Justice classes and a group of faculty, that a full-length recorded interview was conducted with her for purposes of this case study.

Information about the young woman's genocide experiences was relayed to the author in fora other than the public speaking engagements and the formal interview. A personal relationship developed between the author and research respondent via telephone and cyberspace. She subsequently spoke on the Fox 13 evening news in Memphis during her April 1999 visit and she was interviewed more extensively while visiting Memphis several months later for a five-hour video documentary on genocide due to be released late in the year 2000 (Media Entertainment, Inc., 2000). The author was also present for and participated in those media events, having facilitated them.

The data for this article were gathered from all of the above-named sources. Information was principally garnered from the private, semi-structured interview, which lasted approximately 60 minutes. The interview schedule was adapted from two questionnaires previously utilized by the author in research with state terrorism survivors in Guatemala in 1990 and 1992. Further questions were tailored to elicit clarifying elements based on the author's previous exposures to the research subject's stated

---

[1]The informant was brought to Memphis through the auspices of a grant (5–36256) by the American Bar Association for research on genocide awarded to The University of Memphis's Department of Criminology and Criminal Justice.

memories. In this way, general questions directed towards victims of state repression were used to gather data that could be solicited from any survivor, while specific details of the Rwandan experience were collected from the individual research subject as she reflected on her own genocide experiences.

Definition

While many definitions of genocide exist, two main points are necessary in order to place the reported experiences of the research subject in the proper context. The first of these is that genocide entails the real or attempted annihilation of a group, "in whole or in part" (United Nations, 1948). While the main polemic in the definition of genocide has tended to center on what *kinds* of groups the attempted annihilation refers to, it is not necessary to enter into this debate for the purposes of this article.

Essential for understanding the case of Rwanda, however, is one caveat to the definition process which is brought into the literature by philosopher Thomas W. Simon (1996). Simon refers to the fact that genocide is not limited to the simple killing of people in a particular group for the purposes of elimination. For Simon the violence is perpetrated on the victims because the perpetrators negatively identify, and sometimes assign, the group identity of those victimized or "victimizable." This notion of negative group identity and assignment is essential to understanding the motives for genocide should one seek to establish work towards prevention and amelioration of the phenomenon.

Comments on the Available Literature in English on the Rwandan Genocide

Much of the published literature on the Rwandan genocide has dealt with collective case studies providing bits and pieces of detail on victimization (African Rights, 1995, 1998a). Some of the books in question give a general historical background to the violence, portraying the victimization of various sectors of the Rwandan population (Keane, 1995). None of these above-mentioned sources, however, addresses the consequences for victims in any theoretical context. Many recent works are more global analyses of victim or survivor experiences with experiential testimonies interspersed throughout a body of journalistic commentary (Gourevitch, 1998; Vanderwerff, 1996).

The present article will briefly address the history of Rwanda, the global historical circumstances surrounding the 1994 genocide, and some of the causes or social conditions present in the genocide. More detailed historical information can be found in several major works in English (Destexhe, 1995; Eller, 1999; Prunier, 1995). Several noted academicians have also called for studying Burundi alongside any study of Rwanda (LeMarchand, 1996; Melady, 1974; Melson, 1999). The interested reader or serious student should heed such a call.

The Origins of Intergroup Conflict in Rwanda

Group assignment to a bipolar ethnic category in Rwanda and Burundi is complicated at best and even shares some random elements. Most of the authors writing in English who have addressed this in their journalistic and scholarly works agree that there were many class or socioeconomic dimensions to ethnicity formation in Rwanda and Burundi (Eller, 1999; Gourevitch, 1998; LeMarchand, 1996; Prunier, 1995). As a more random, yet deeply defining element, the Belgian identity card system with bipolar "ethnic" categories implemented in the second quarter of the twentieth century was and had been the main catalyst in individual ethnic formation among Rwandans (Feil, 1998; Gourevitch, 1998). Their German colonial predecessors propagated an ideology of racialist division based largely on aesthetics and cattle-owning (Destexhe, 1995) and were an influence on the European view of Rwanda for the Belgians who received the nation as one of the spoils of World War 1.

There are four dominant trends related to the explaining of who is a Tutsi and who is a Hutu in Rwanda. The first explanation for Tutsi/Hutu differentiation is a political thesis. This was effectively used by Hutu nationalists to point out the perceived dangers of Tutsi domination. The political thesis states that the Tutsi served Belgian colonialism. Tutsis were supposedly a more educated class of people who had constituted the pre-Belgian monarchy in Rwanda (*Mwami*). The aristocratic Tutsis had then worked at the side of the colonizers to further enslave or rule over the Hutu, or Bahutu ("servant"), peoples with a double yoke of oppression; one of these being domination by Europeans and the other by indigenous Tutsis (Prunier, 1995).

The second explanation for Hutu-Tutsi differentiation is a class thesis. This class thesis states that the Hutu were the people who worked the land in more or less hunter-gatherer and subsistence-based agricultural communities. The Tutsis were those who were cattle herders and, more importantly, livestock owners, favored in wealth succession, (i.e., livestock inheritance) by the Europeans through the *ubuhake* system (Destexhe, 1995). The ownership and grazing of livestock necessitates more land than most subsistence or local market crop farming does. The non-governmental organization African Rights (1995) even states that the terms themselves may have been simply distinguishing signifiers for cultivator ("Hutu") and cattle herder ("Tutsi"). Therefore, the Tutsis, as cattle herders, were also the Rwandan equivalent of large landowners, according to this class thesis. It this class division, argue adherents to this thesis, that is essential to understanding the differentiation between Tutsi and Hutu.

The third thesis has been called the "Hamitic myth" (LeMarchand, 1996). The Hamitic thesis states that the Tutsis really are persons of a different ethnicity, or race, with different body types and complexions. The Hutu are considered to be of sub-Saharan racial/ethnic stock, with shorter, wider bodies, flatter, wide noses and darker complexions than the Tutsi. The Tutsi are alleged to be descendants of northeast African immigrants who emigrated down the Nile and into the area south of Lake Victoria. Their taller, slighter features and lighter complexions are evidence of their different "racial stock" according to adherents of the Hamitic theory (Melady, 1974; Prunier, 1995).

The fourth thesis is an instrumental thesis. While the proponents of the instrumental thesis may admit to the influence of perceived class divisions and aristocratic divisions on Rwandan society, they are not proponents of the Hamitic thesis. The instrumental thesis emphasizes the widespread presence of "mixed marriages," the social mobility from "Hutu" to "Tutsi" upon acquiring cattle, the fact that both groups speak exactly the same language, and the unreliable dependence on eugenic-related notions of nineteenth century Europe (where do tall Hutus or short, squat Tutsis fit into the racialist categories?) in order to dismiss the validity or the political, class and Hamitic theses (Destexhe, 1995). It is exactly the racial categorizations of the Germans, and later the Belgians, that constructed the indelible nature of "ethnic" or "tribal" identification for Rwandans (Prunier, 1995). According to this instrumental theory, this closed ethnic caste system is not of Rwandan making.

Hutu extremists have used the first three theses to varying degrees while seeking to justify the destruction of the Tutsis. Supposed rejection of class domination, aristocracy, pro-colonialism, and domination by those of foreign origin had predominated as Hutu supremacist themes and rallying cries in their propaganda outlets. When the military conflicts began in the Democratic Republic of the Congo in 1998, these three themes were also fundamental components of the anti-Tutsi campaigns of the new regime's allies in the eastern part of the country. There, the Banyarwanda, or Banyamulenge peoples, considered to be of Tutsi origins, suffered violence and calls for extinction just as they had in episodes of conflict throughout neighboring Rwanda's post-independence history (Mwangachuchu, 1999). This possible extermination campaign, along with the persistence of cross-border raids of Hutu extremists into western Rwanda, prompted the Rwandan and Ugandan governments to become militarily involved in the Congolese conflict.

There is some truth to the assumption that Tutsis, at least in the eastern Congo, are on the more comfortable end of any continuum of class divisions in the country, if not the region. The Congolese Tutsis are often the teachers, shopkeepers and public functionaries of the highly underdeveloped eastern zones of the former Zaire (Anonymous, 1998). Much like the Jews during the Holocaust, the Tutsi are available to serve as scapegoats, as class enemies of the poor and working "majority" peoples of Rwanda and the Democratic Republic of the Congo. If only the Tutsi will disappear, the Hutu extremist logic contends, then the Hutus will be able to live in peace and prosper.

The Rise of Hutu Supremacist Ideology

Rwanda gained formal independence from Belgium in 1962. The party that ruled Rwanda's political and military spheres after independence was the National Republican Movement for Development (or MRND, its French acronym). The *Interahamwe* ("those who work together") (Prunier, 1995) were their clubs and their militias. A more openly extremist party which was also Hutu-dominated and played a leading role in the atmosphere leading up to the genocide by shunning any negotiations with the Tutsi-dominated rebel Rwandan Patriotic Front was the CRD or Coalition for the Defense of the Republic (Destexhe, 1995). The CRD had its own clubs and militias, known as the *Impuzamugambi* or "those who have only one aim" (Destexhe, 1995). At the time of the genocide, Rwanda was approximately 85% Hutu, 14% Tutsi and 1% Twa, or pygmy, out of a national population of around eight million (Feil, 1998).

It is important to observe that not all Hutu nationalism was necessarily extremist. As a reaction to class and political rule discrepancies of the past, Hutu nationalism could be bent on majority rule without necessarily calling for majority dictatorship or genocide. It is evident, however, that the extremists controlled the military. Habyarimana, in fact, rose from his position as head of the military in 1973 to take state power until his death in April 1994.

Hutu supremacist-inspired massacres against mostly male Tutsis occurred in 1959, the early 1960's, the early 1970's, and throughout the early 1990's after the commencement of war between the Rwandan Patriotic Front and the government forces. Such widespread, episodic violence became a justification for many Tutsi and non-supremacist Hutus to form and fight in the Rwandan Patriotic Front, in order to unite the divided groups as Rwandans and take the reins of political and military power from the Hutu supremacists.

The genocide of 1994 went way beyond selective massacres, however cruel those may have been. It was planned and executed with precision (African Rights, 1995). Even children became legitimate targets. An estimated one million persons were killed in barely thirteen weeks, with 800,000 killed within the first five weeks (Prunier, 1995). The *Interahamwe* boasted they could kill one hundred Tutsis in twenty minutes and they proceeded to do just that. Machetes were stockpiled for several months before the April occurrences. Purportedly imported from China en masse, some were hidden in plastic containers at the bottoms of bogs and marshes, while others were buried underground in impermeable plastic. Upon the assassination of President Habyarimana, the military and the *Interahamwe* set up roadblocks throughout Kigali after unearthing the machetes, and the killing began. The killing did not end until July with the fall of the Rwandan armed forces at Gisenyi (Destexhe, 1995). The Ugandans upriver from northern Rwanda spent weeks pulling the 60,000-plus corpses out of the river (Prunier, 1995) on their way "back to Ethiopia." Within these larger events our case study unfolded.

A Young Woman of Sixteen

Fleur grew up in what she describes as a middle-class family. Her family had passports and would go to other African countries for their yearly vacations. In fact, one of her uncles worked in the Rwandan diplomatic corps in West Africa. Her father was a small business owner working in the print industry. Her family lived in the urbanized seat of a prefecture relatively close to Rwanda's capital, Kigali. Both of her parents had migrated from other parts of Rwanda to live in the prefectural seat.

Fleur's family lived quite well by Rwandan standards. The circumstances of her social status were understandably quite comfortable if one considers that 90% of Rwanda's population lives in rural areas outside of the cities, and is engaged in agricultural activities on small plots (Feil, 1998; Panafrican News Agency, 1999), with coffee being the main market crop (Prunier, 1995).

Additionally, having money for international travel, even to neighboring states, was a luxury most Rwandans could never hope to afford. Even her cultural preferences belied her social standing. For example, Fleur's favorite television show was "Melrose Place," which she would watch each week in French.

The Victimization of Fleur's Family in Ethno-Historical Context

Fleur found out in elementary school that she was a Tutsi. While the regime was Hutu, and lauded Hutu "togetherness" (Prunier, 1995) as an alternative to Tutsi "domination" (Eller, 1999), Fleur's parents never told her "what she was." At age six or seven, as my informant recalls, she was asked to fill in her ethnicity on a form at school and found that she could not. She went home to ask her father. He fell silent. After a hushed adult discussion between her parents, it was explained to Fleur that she and her family were Tutsis. This identification had made no difference in her life up until this point. She returned to school with the news and her life changed forever.

This is where Simon's (1996) previous point about the perpetrator's imposition of a negative identity on the victim is important. For Fleur, the matter of being a Tutsi or a Hutu was essentially meaningless until the school system decided to implement restrictive ethnic policies in order to keep Tutsi quotas down and Tutsis out of education. The group membership to which she was supposedly intrinsically tied was no less than imposed upon her by the Hutu supremacist-dominated education system of the time, which was itself an artifact of Belgian colonialism. From that day on, Fleur was no longer Rwandan, but a Tutsi.

Criminologist Margaret Vandiver has poignantly addressed the ludicrousness of the group assignment of persons to be victimized in the context of the genocidal events in Bosnia in the 1990's. What Serb nationalism ended up labeling as a Muslim, according to the author was, in many instances, the antithesis of the individual's own identification of self. Blonde, blue-eyed, beer-drinking, pork-eating Bosnians became Muslims overnight, according to the spelling of their last names or other such perpetrator-imposed criteria (Afflitto and Vandiver, 2000). Such was Fleur's case in Rwanda.

The school requirement for establishing my informant's "ethnic identity" marked her formative years. Her social identity at school was changed from that of a good friend, student and playmate to that of a "snake." Fleur became a snake, as Tutsis were snakes and Fleur was a Tutsi. Snakes are considered sly and sneaky in Rwandan culture, coming up upon one without one's being aware and, therefore, of intrinsic danger. Consequently, Fleur was no longer judged on personal attributes by her teachers or fellow students, but by the identity assigned to her by the state.

Being a snake was not the only negative characteristic attributed to the Tutsis by the dominant Hutu ideology, which in many ways flaunted a discourse of supremacy while simultaneously portraying the anti-Tutsi fight as a fight against subjugation. The Tutsis have been portrayed as "cockroaches" (*Inyenzi*) when alluding to former RPF guerrillas[2] (Prunier, 1995), as "foreigners" from Ugandan exile (Destexhe, 1995; Prunier, 1995), as "southerners" in Rwanda (Keane, 1995), class (Eller, 1999; Feil, 1998) and/or racial oppressors (LeMarchand, 1996) or "accomplices/traitors" (*Ibyitso*) (Keane, 1995; Prunier, 1995). The traitor label alluded to supposed Tutsi participation in the RPF, which was, in fact, a mostly Tutsi army at the time.

It is this last idea, setting up all Tutsi as a "fifth column" (Keane, 1995) of the RPF, that the genocidal regime used as its political logic in calling for death to the Tutsis. Being fifth columnists[3] made all Tutsi eligible for the death sentence as foreign invaders with lethal potential and designs. During the genocide, as well, Hutus who had married Tutsis, who befriended or protected Tutsis, who voiced opposition to the Hutu supremacy ideology or who would not participate in the killings were also identified as "*Ibyitso*" (Prunier, 1995). There is also evidence that some perpetrators killed fellow perpetrators who they did not find zealous enough in the matter of killing (Prunier, 1995).

A Young Woman's Victimization

When the killing began in April 1994, Fleur and her immediate family went into hiding. Her father, having faced tortures and arbitrary detention during previous epochs of MRND regime round-ups of Tutsis, left home to hide in the bush. Fleur's family believed that, as before, the Hutu Power regime would spare women and children in its murderous rampages, so she, her mother and eleven-year old brother stayed at their home while hiding. According to some sources, there may even have been a certain

---

[2]Now the RPA, or Rwandan Patriotic Army.

[3]For a discussion of this ethnic/political linkage in the making of genocide in Guatemala, see Afflitto and Vandiver (2000).

amount of truth to that perception in those early days (African Rights, 1995; African Rights, 1998a).

The respondent described to me how the three family members were in hiding in a back bedroom, having heard that a certain Hutu gentleman was looking for her Tutsi father. Fleur and her mother knew quite well that there were reports of widespread killings and that many of her relatives had already been killed in other regions. For example, Fleur's older brother had called from Kigali when the killings intensified there in the first weeks of genocide. After being shot in the chest, he called his mother to tell her what had happened to him and to the rest of the family. While his mother listened over the phone, he succumbed to his wounds and died. By the end of the 1994 genocide, my informant lost her parents, her older brother, her paternal grandmother, three aunts, two uncles and a multitude of cousins, many of whom were children at the time of their murders.

She also lost her older sister, who was a medical student at the National University. She was killed in Butare, the major southern city near the border with Burundi, where she studied. Most of the University's faculty, students and medical staff were killed during the genocide (Prunier, 1995). While most people killed were actually Hutu (Prunier, 1995), the National University is portrayed in more than one text as a focused killing ground (African Rights, 1995; Prunier, 1995), resembling a genocide of the intelligentsia and the professional class. At the time of the attack on the house where her mother and brother were in hiding with her, however, Fleur did not know of this event. A surviving best friend of her older sister was able to tell her subsequently that her sister had died, though Fleur does not know how nor does she know exactly when. Given the fact that Fleur's sister's roommate was tortured by the University fraternity *"Interahamwe"*[4] and left without eyes or ears, Fleur has been left to imagine in strands of painful thought the conditions under which her sister expired.

On the day Fleur lost her mother, their bedroom sanctuary provided no refuge. Five men in army uniforms armed with AK-47's burst through the door when she and her mother did not answer the pounding and yelling. They went through the house searching for them until the three of them were found and brought into the living room. My informant described the men as *"Interahamwe,"* though they came in army camouflage uniforms with helmets similarly colored in the black, grey and pink camouflage pattern of the former Rwandan National Army (FAR).

My informant makes a clear distinction between the military personnel of what she calls "Habyarimana's army"[5] and the *Interahamwe* militias. Her conceptual distinction centers on both the level of organizational formality as paid agents of the state versus being state-sponsored paramilitaries, as well as on the violence-perpetration model to which each group subscribed when killing. Regarding this second facet, Fleur told me that the "Habyarimana army come [sic] to shoot you and you die," whereas the *Interahamwe*" always torture you before you die." "People prefer to be killed by the army," she further stated.

---

[4]Literally "those who work together" (Prunier, 1995). These were the rank-and-file killing groups, organized by the MRND politicians and the FAR (former Rwandan army). They acted much like death squads and paramilitaries.

[5]The Rwandan National Army, or FAR.

Her conceptual distinction may be difficult to understand, but becomes clearer during a later interview. While Fleur related to me how the army was an organized and professional force who came in military uniform and always killed people via gunshot wounds, she perceived the group that came to her house as *Interahamwe*, even though they were dressed in full military gear. Her attribution of the death squad that arrived at her home as *Interahamwe* stems from the fact that the man who was looking for her father was a Hutu who worked with him. This man, she stated, was the man who had sent the group to her house. He was also the leader of the group. Due to the fact that this group was not a detail of professional soldiers, but was comprised of men who worked in civilian capacities in her city, she has concluded that they were *Interahamwe*.

These five men came in asking for her father. They went straight to the rear bedroom as if they knew where the three people were hiding. After she and her family responded that they did not know his whereabouts, the men herded Fleur's mother, brother and herself into the living room, then her mother was shoved against the wall. Two gunshots from an AK-47 occurred nearly simultaneously into the head of her mother, resulting in the vertical propulsion and horizontal dispersion of blood-soaked brain matter over the room's occupants. Upon seeing her mother's head explode, Fleur remembers "screaming." The *Interahamwe* death squad had not necessarily come to find Fleur's father. They had come to kill, she said. They had come to kill Tutsis. They had come to commit genocide.

Fleur's eleven-year old brother was attacked with one rifle-butt blow to the head. He dropped to the floor. She imagined him dead, as the blow to his head had been "really strong." Screaming all the while, Fleur fought to survive. Two men attacked her head as well. Rifle-butt blows from one and machete strokes from the other pursued Fleur's life. She described crouching on the floor like a turtle, all balled up, with her hands and forearms protecting her head. The machete scars on her skullcap and forearms map out the will to live which she so ardently exhibits today. She succumbed to unconsciousness and was left for dead.

Why did a man who worked with her father and was a "friend of the family" lead a squad of men to eliminate her family? He was a "really good man," she stated, before speculating on his reasoning for desiring to terminate their collective existence. He was my "father's best friend," she said. "He just changed," Fleur told me, " . . . maybe because of the radio[6] . . . of this whole propaganda thing. I was surprised when I first heard it [that he had organized a militia group to seek out the family]. I denied it . . . [I believed] that it was not true."

Unknown to my informant, her father was still alive at this time, still hiding in the bush. Upon hearing the news that his family had been victimized, Mr N. came out of hiding. He began the walk home, to be with his loved ones, even in death. He wanted to give them a Christian burial. He never made it home. Hungry, weary and certainly fearful, Mr N. was set upon by a Hutu supremacist militia as he walked back to his house. Hog-tied and brutalized, Fleur's father died of the multiple blows perpetrated by clenched hands clutching bloodied stones.

---

[6]The RTLM station, or Radio Télévision Libre des Milles Collines, which provided continuous Hutu supremacist broadcasts and genocidal indoctrination.

The example of her father's love continues to move Fleur. Mr N. made an incredible sacrifice in the face of obvious lethal dangers. He was a wanted Tutsi in a town where everyone knew him. He had been arrested previously and tortured. These memories are prominent in Fleur's recollections and conversations. She believes that the spirit of this noble man lives on in the souls of good people who are alive now.

Survival

Survival to my informant is unbounded by individual considerations and approached by her in an ethnic, regional and even global context (see African Rights, 1998a; United States Committee for Refugees, 1998). "I am proud to have survived this 'kind of thing' and to still be here," states Fleur. There is a sense of triumph emanating from her words and posture. She ardently believes that the genocide was supported by France and China and ignored by much of the rest of the world. It is in the face of world indifference that she talks of the elation of survival. She even minimizes her injuries by saying that, due to the covering of her head with her arms, her "head didn't get hurt too bad."

What did it take for this young woman to survive, besides the foresight and fortitude of covering her head with her hands and forearms? Ironically, while the Hutus brought death to the woman who brought her life, she owes her present life to a Hutu man who she has never been able to thank.[7] A "friend of ours came home, a Hutu", upon seeing what had happened at the N. household. While they were both still unconscious, he took Fleur and her brother to the hospital.

Fleur awoke in a hospital. Fleur's eleven-year old brother would be in a coma for almost four weeks, but he lived. Her hospitalization was anything but pleasant. At the hospital, Fleur began to learn that survival was ongoing and continually unfolded in a process (Walter, 1969) of genocide; it was not to be an either/or phenomenon. The painful memories of her brain-spattered living room, the brother who she assumed was dead and the family members she already knew about losing the weeks before were her surreal bed partners in an overcrowded, medicine-sparse and hostile hospital environment ruled and continuously invaded by Hutu Power militias.

"You are N.'s daughter, correct? You are N.'s daughter! You are Tutsi!" they screamed at her as she recuperated in her hospital ward, the sounds of gunfire and mob violence accompanying her painful memories as she lay relatively immobile. "No," she said forcefully, fearfully. "I am so-and-so." She denied her relationship to a man who gave his life at the thought of her having lost her own. She denied her ethnic identification, or at least that which her identity card told her to have. She learned that survival was plagued with pain. My informant now knew that with survival came guilt, denial, deceit, and even shame. The role of survivor guilt in the known repertoire of posttraumatic sequelae has been well-documented in U.S. and European psychiatric and psychological literature.

To Fleur, however, survival also meant hope, and the importance of winning the fight to live and breathe another day as a human being and as a Tutsi. The odds were stacked against this. Fleur was determined not to be another fatality of the Hutu supremacists' genocide. Who else would carry on the N. name?

Survival also meant winning at the daily gamble of living while others around her perished. For nearly two months, while recuperating in the local hospital, my informant

---

[7]Prunier addresses this phenomenon in his book The Rwanda Crisis (1995).

was witness to the sounds of mob violence and gun-fire, screams, pleas for mercy and haunting death throes of fellow Rwandans. At least once in her hospital stay, she was taken out of the hospital with a group of persons and accused of being Tutsi. As the drunken mob fired shots at her feet and those of the other members of the group of accused Tutsis, once again her guardian angel stepped in. "These people are Hutu," someone shouted, and she was saved once again while facing death.

One of the most horrific moments she related about her hospitalization centered on the impalement of a woman outside her hospital ward window. A sharpened stake was jabbed into the victim's vagina. Fully conscious and shrieking in torment, she was raised up on the stake so that the weight of her body pressed down, forcing it through her cervix, into her uterus and beyond.

The more she squirmed and yelled the farther down she sank and the closer to her horrible death she came. "There is not a day that goes by that I don't think about all this," my informant has stated more than once. To Fleur, survival has now become a responsibility. It is a delicate balance to be navigated and achieved. Painful memories invade the psyche at the same time that the pride of knowing she has lived to tell about her ordeal fills her countenance with an unsurpassable glow.

Impunity and Forced Exile: A Symbiotic Relationship Precluding Justice

Justice has remained an elusive ideal for Fleur. This was as true for her estimations of justice nationally in Rwanda as it was for her desires for justice in her individual situation. While no action will ever bring her family back, certain actions may help dignify their memory. The militia organizer who led the group that killed her mother was arrested some time after Fleur and her brother were freed from the hospital, when the opposition Rwandan Patriotic Front liberated the country from the Rwandan armed forces (FAR) in July 1994, thus ending the genocide. While he remained incarcerated for more than four years, he was released sometime late 1998 or early 1999. All charges were dropped against him and he was allowed to go free. Fleur attributes this to the connections he had in the judicial system.

The fact that the Rwandan judicial system has had some fairly stiff witness requirements has been cited as an impediment to the successful resolution of cases by surviving victims of the genocide still living in Rwanda (African Rights, 1998b). Fleur's case is no different. Upon his release from incarceration, the man who led the attack on her and her family publicly threatened the lives of Fleur and her brother, vowing never to rest until sure of their demise by his own hands. The respondent also worries about the one remaining cousin she has living in the area, because the génocidaire knows her family and Fleur continually expresses worry about what he might do to that cousin.

Impunity can be defined as the "freedom from legal sanction or accountability" (McSherry and Molina, 1992) for the perpetration of illegal acts. Lack of prosecution and weak judiciaries have been identified as major mechanisms of impunity (Afflitto, 1998a; McSherry and Molina, 1992).

The violence itself and the continuing threat of violence, are, in and of themselves, also major impediments on the road to justice. The initial violence during the genocide eliminated many persons from a potential pool of witnesses who could have been available to testify. The ongoing nature of the violence, however, especially the invasions by Hutu extremists of Rwandan territory (African Rights, 1998b), and the calculated assassinations of witnesses reported in all major texts are all factors in the present situation of impunity in which my respondent finds herself. Fleur is unable to return to Rwanda, in her mind, as long as her father's "best friend" lives, as he has sworn that he will never be happy until both she and her brother lie "dead at his feet."

Conclusion

Despite the ongoing conditions of impunity and exile which present painful and strenuous challenges in Fleur's young life, she has worked at finding direction in her adult life and in creating a future for herself. She is a successful student in an engineering program in the United States and works to support herself and to put herself through school. She keeps in regular contact with her brother in Canada, as well as with many Rwandans living in the U.S. through telephone and the internet. Even the small African community at the modest state university she attends is a source of support and encouragement for her.

The case study method is important to the criminological study of genocide. It is essential to refrain from relying solely on a positivist approach and a numerical summary of human losses when studying the phenomenon. Rather than seeing the genocide victim-survivor solely as a person coping with loss(es), it is imperative to remind ourselves that how we are embedded in empathetic communities and how we are attacked by multiple traumatizing processes, such as impunity, are factors that one cannot ignore in evaluating and explaining anyone's survival. Survival itself must be taken as an active, conscious strategy and not simply as a mere static fact or the continuation of life. Survival is something much more profound than a heart continuing to beat.

Source: With kind permission from Springer Science + Business Media: *Crime, Law and Social Change.* "The Armenian Massacres in Ottoman Turkey," Volume 34, 2000, Frank Afflitto, copyright © 2000 by Kluwer Academic Publishers.

Rwanda, Ethiopia and Cambodia: Links, Faultlines and Complexities in a Comparative Study of Genocide

Edward Kissi

Introduction

About two million people of diverse ethnic backgrounds dead in Ethiopia from 1974 to 1991. Between two and three million mainly Khmer ethnic groups killed by the Khmer Rouge in Cambodia from 1975 to 1979. Approximately 800,000 Tutsi and politically moderate Hutu killed in Rwanda between April 6 and July 15, 1994.

These are the visible epitaphs in the public memory of mass murder in Ethiopia, Cambodia and Rwanda in the last three decades of the twentieth century. But the death toll alone, as important as it is, does not offer us a better perspective of the complex processes behind the numbers. It often creates in the public mind a hierarchy of mass murder based on mortality statistics. Writers and scholars who have looked beyond the scale of murder in their analysis of what happened in Rwanda, Ethiopia and Cambodia have often not resisted the temptation of drawing comparisons between them and other historical cases of genocide. Dawit Wolde Giorgis, a defected member of Ethiopia's revolutionary regime, and journalist Robert Kaplan see a mirror image of Cambodia in Ethiopia of the early 1970s. As Dawit argues, "like Pol Pot, Mengistu . . . massacred thousands . . . , and brought death, suffering, and displacement to millions (Dawit, 1989, p. 57). Robert Kaplan has described Ethiopia under Mengistu as the "African killing field." Evoking this powerful imagery of Cambodia under Pol Pot, Kaplan contended that the "manner in which Ethiopians died" resembled "the slaughter of millions of Cambodians by the Khmer Rouge" (Kaplan, 1988, p. 32). Robert Melson, arguably the dean of the comparative study of genocide, has characterized the slaughter of Tutsis by extreme Hutus in Rwanda in 1994 as "the African version of the Holocaust" (Melson, 2003, p. 337). But comparisons of mass murder in the developing world that seek common characteristics or links with genocide in other parts of the world should also discover instructive distinctions and faultlines produced by specific histories and circumstances.

This article is inspired by calls from scholars who study genocide for the integration of mass murder in Africa and Asia into the study of genocide (Fein, 1993, p. 796; Gellately and Kiernan, 2003, p. 9). It puts the Rwanda genocide in the context of mass murder in Ethiopia and Cambodia and analyzes their notable similarities and differences. It also focuses on lessons to the extent that the three cases offer any about the roles that history, ideology, revolution, states and culture play in the genocidal process. The paper observes that while ideology and revolution created conditions for the destruction of groups in Rwanda, Ethiopia and Cambodia, the scope, pace and success of murder depended on the degree of control and influence that the perpetrators exercised in their respective society. While genocide, as strictly defined, occurred in the course of revolution and war in Rwanda and Cambodia, it did not in Ethiopia. Mass killing in Ethiopia was a case of political mass murder or what Barbara Harff and Ted Robert Gurr have called *politicide* (Harff and Gurr, 1988, p. 360).

Harff and Gurr distinguish between "genocide" and "politicide" (political mass murder) on the basis of the "characteristics" by which perpetrators define and target their victims. In the opinion of Harff and Gurr, victims of *genocide* are defined by their "communal characteristics, i.e., ethnicity, religion, or nationality." However, in *politicide*, the members of the target group are defined by their "political opposition to the regime and dominant groups" of their society (p. 360). But in the most recent "expansion" of this concept of genocide and politicide, Harff (2003, p. 58) has acknowledged that genocide or politicide is more than "an act of the state." As she now notes, "nonstate actors can and do attempt to destroy rival ethnic and political groups." Thus Harff's revised concept of genocide and politicide sees both crimes as "the promotion, execution, and, or implied consent of sustained policies by governing elites or their agents—or, in the case of civil war, either of the contending authorities—that are intended to destroy, in whole or part, a communal, political or politicized ethnic group" (p. 58).

The relevance of Harff's revised concept of politicide for analysis of what happened in Ethiopia cannot be overstated. In Ethiopia, politicide was more than an act of state. It was also a crime of armed political groups or insurgents against one another and against state officials and their sympathizers who constituted a collectivity.

Perpetrators of Genocide: States, Insurgents and Extremists

Cambodia, Rwanda and Ethiopia demonstrate the complex nature of genocide and political mass murder in developing societies in transition. The three cases also highlight the ambiguous role of the state in the process of mass murder. In Cambodia, the role of the state in the destruction of groups can be clearly established despite questions about the degree of control the Khmer Rouge exercised over that process. Politicide in Ethiopia was the result of 17 years (1974–1991) of uncompromising struggle for state power between a beleaguered state and its well-armed opponents. Eventually, the opponents succeeded in destroying the state and assuming power. In Rwanda, genocide was perpetrated not by a strong state, but rather a weakened one. At the dawn of the 1994 genocide, a militarized Hutu society was struggling to keep intact a state losing its grip on power. Therefore, the Rwandan genocide was the clearest case of a collaboration between a weakening state and organized sections of society in the destruction of groups whose existence, in the 1990s, symbolized the passing of an era—the era of Hutu monopoly on power.

Debates on national reconciliation in Rwanda's second republic (1973–1994) had taken place in a volatile atmosphere of war with the Rwandan Patriotic Front (RPF), an insurgent army formed in 1989 by Tutsi refugees in Uganda. RPF military successes, between 1990 and 1993, had exposed the weakness of the Rwandan state and its armed forces. They had also split the Hutu of Rwanda into two political camps: moderates willing to share power with the now stronger RPF and extremists eager to defend Hutu power to the point of exterminating every Tutsi (Mamdani, 2001, pp. 190, 203).

The declining ability of the state to preserve Hutu power after October 1990 intensified Hutu consciousness of a changing status quo. Under these circumstances, the anger and anxiety of the most extreme among the Hutu middle class grew to a level where it needed only a trigger to erupt into a large-scale slaughter of the Tutsi and the politically moderate Hutu. That happened on April 6, 1994 when Habyarimana's plane was shot down—possibly by extremists within his government—on its return flight from national reconciliation talks with the RPF in Arusha, Tanzania. Under the changing political circumstances, a genocide against Tutsi and moderate Hutu, following the death of Habyarimana, could not be organized by the state alone. A successful genocide came to depend on the mobilization of large numbers of Hutu society. As Mamdani (2001, pp. 185–193) accurately states, although some state functionaries took part in the planning of the genocide, the physical killing of the Tutsi and moderate Hutu was done by ordinary people and armed militia.

The chief organizers of the 1994 genocide were the interim government under Jean Kambanda: the army, Hutu intellectuals, armed militia and sections of Rwanda's clergy. Scholars who have studied the genocide in Rwanda point to the influential role of the *Akazu*, a group formed in the late 1980s by senior officers of the Rwandan army, civilian advocates of Hutu power from northwestern Rwanda and relatives of Habyarimana's wife (Des Forges, 1999, p. 44; Scherrer, 2002, p. 105). This "informal structure of the Rwandan state," as Scherrer describes it, organized its own paramilitary organ, *the Interahamwe* (Scherrer, 2002, p. 105). From April 12 to July 15, 1994, the Interahamwe and Akazu encouraged and participated in the killing of a broad category of Tutsis: women, children and the elderly (IPEP/OAU, 2000, p. 117; Scherrer, 2002, p. 111). But as Alison Des Forges (1999, pp. 4–5, 261), Mahmood Mamdani (2001, pp. 184, 204, 217–218) and Christian Scherrer (2002, p. 111) remind us, the perpetrators of genocide in Rwanda were a broad range of people: clergymen; unemployed youth; teachers; peasants and ordinary people displaced by RPF attacks. Included in this diverse group of perpetrators were Hutu refugees from Burundi who had entered Rwanda to avenge the assassination of the Hutu president of that country in a failed Tutsi-led abortive coup in Burundi in October 1993.

It was this motley group of perpetrators that committed, in Rwanda, all but the last of the five actions constituting genocide under the UN Genocide Convention of 1948: (1) "killing members of the group"; (2) "causing serious bodily or mental harm to members of the group"; (3) "deliberately inflicting on the group conditions of life calculated to bring about its physical destruction in whole or in part"; (4) "imposing measures intended to prevent births within the group"; and (5) "forcibly transferring children of the group to another group" (Chalk and Jonassohn, 1990, p. 44). What happened in Rwanda, in 1994, is an example of mass murder that meets the terms of the Genocide Convention which defines genocide as "acts committed with intent to destroy, in whole or in part, a national, ethnical, racial or religious group, as such." As Frank Chalk (1998, pp. 10–11) argues, the Akazu's target groups of women, children and the elderly demonstrate its intent to prevent the biological reproduction of the Tutsi as a group, destroy the seeds of its future generations and erase the repository of Tutsi memory and cultural identity.

From the perspective of motivations behind the killing, and the degree of involvement of the society in it, the genocide in Rwanda was unique compared to the genocide in Cambodia and the political mass murder in Ethiopia. Genocide in Rwanda was a form of retribution exacted on Tutsi living in Rwanda for the actions of Tutsi exiles who had invaded the country. That sets it apart from what happened in Ethiopia. The Dergue did not kill or harass ethnic Somalis in Ethiopia when Somalia invaded Ethiopia in June 1977 (Kissi, 1997). But like the RPF invasions of Rwanda, the Somali invasion of Ethiopia increased nationalism and patriotism in the country. Ethiopia successfully repelled the Somali invasion. Rwanda could not defeat the RPF. And nationalists in Ethiopia did not rally to save the beleaguered Ethiopian state, even in its victory over external forces, as Hutu nationalists did in Rwanda, even in the defeat of the Rwandan state by the RPF.

Genocide in Cambodia and politicide in Ethiopia, on the other hand, were motivated by the desire of the state, without the aid of broad segments of society, to implement an ideology: ethnic purity in Cambodia and national unity in Ethiopia. In the pursuit of its revolution, the Khmer Rouge targeted large numbers of Chinese, Vietnamese, and Cham ethnic groups as well as Muslims and Buddhist religious groups. By expelling and also killing the entire Vietnamese ethnic population of Cambodia, killing and forcibly relocating about 50% of the Chinese who lived mainly in urban areas, and by killing and imposing deadly conditions of life on nearly 36% of the Cham people, the Cambodian state demonstrated its intent to transform the ethnic composition of Cambodian society (Kiernan, 1997, pp. 340–341). In 1975, the Khmer Rouge made public its ideology of ethnic purity. It outlawed the existence of all ethnic groups and made the Khmer language the only language to be spoken in revolutionary Cambodia (Becker, 1986, p. 253; Kiernan, 1997, pp. 353, 358). Here, the Khmer Rouge was motivated by ideology and not by retribution.

The greatest majority of the people who died in the hands of the Khmer Rouge were members of the Khmer ethnic group—a common element that links genocide in Cambodia and Rwanda with political mass murder in Ethiopia. But this commonality reveals as much as it disguises. Hutu supremacists in Rwanda killed in reaction to a situation in which control of power was fast slipping away from them. They did not intend, as the Khmer Rouge did, to create a nation of only one dominant ethnic group and language. Involvement of broader sections of society in Khmer Rouge murders was also limited. Certainly, there were peasants and teenage cadres in Cambodia who killed Khmers the Pol Pot regime labeled as "new people" (Jackson, 1989, p. 115; Kiernan, 1996, pp. 175–176). "New people" in revolutionary Cambodia included Khmers from urban areas, intellectuals, merchants and rich farmers who did not live in Khmer Rouge areas of control during the civil war. By virtue of their geographical location during the civil war, the Khmer Rouge suspected their political loyalties and considered them as ideologically impure. "New people" bore the brunt of Khmer Rouge atrocities. However, there was no Cambodian or Ethiopian equivalent of the successful mobilization of thousands of ordinary people by the Rwandan state and extreme sections of society to kill specific communal groups in Rwanda—the Tutsi and their Hutu sympathizers. Whereas the Khmer Rouge destroyed religion and churches, and the Dergue both persecuted and patronized the Church, the perpetrators of genocide in Rwanda used the Hutu clergy to sanction the genocide.

What took place in Ethiopia also demonstrates that with greater access to weapons and ideas in modern societies, the state no longer has the monopoly over coercion and violence. The Dergue sought political power to create a society in which no ethnic group would be targeted for extermination or forced to join one single nationality (author's taped interview, 1999b). For their part, the Dergue's armed opponents—the educated elites who had cooperated with the soldiers to hasten the downfall of the Haile Selassie regime—envisioned an Ethiopia in which all ethnic groups exercised the right to self-determination including the freedom to secede from the country. They also killed in defense of secessionism as an ideology.

Genocide in Rwanda and Cambodia and politicide in Ethiopia also took forms that diverged from what the UN Genocide Convention calls "acts committed with intent" to destroy groups. In Rwanda, some advocates of Hutu power killed Tutsi and moderate Hutu for the purpose of robbing them of property (Jefremovas, 1997, p. 99). Similarly, in Cambodia knowledge of foreign languages and possession of wrist-watches and eyeglasses, for instance, could make one a target irrespective of religion or ethnicity (Criddle and Mam, 1987, pp. 50, 149, 161). Elizabeth Becker dismisses the "eyeglasses fables" as exaggerated expressions of pervasive state control in Cambodia under the Khmer Rouge (Becker, 1998, p. 162). In Ethiopia, rich people and individuals married to beautiful women were easy targets of armed mobs (author's taped interview, 1995a,b).

Thus, all three cases of mass murder exhibit characteristics that lack the requisite intent to completely or partially exterminate particular groups of people. It is these often murky intentions and arbitrary actions of perpetrators that make Mamdani's caution significant. As he advises, "if we are to understand the context of . . . mass killing, we need to move away from an assumption of genocide as a conspiracy from above" to examine how "perceptions" and "circumstances" alter intent and motivations of perpetrators (Mamdani, 2001, p. 195). Here, Mamdani shifts the focus of the study of genocide from state actions to the shifting motivations of groups in society. Like Lemarchand (2002, p. 500), Mamdani emphasizes context and circumstance over intent and ideology in examining genocide and political mass murder.

Scope of Genocide and Politicide: Role of Opposition

Scholars who have studied the genocide in Cambodia have debated the contexts and circumstances under which it occurred. Michael Vickery (1983, pp. 101, 112) has questioned the extent to which state policy sanctioning genocide differed from the "caprice of individual cadres" and how local conditions affected both. For David Chandler (1999, pp. 115, 161), the blurred relationship between intent and unintended consequences of human actions or state-sanctioned killing and the excesses and misperceptions of ordinary people in society undermine the case of genocide against the Khmer Rouge. Like Vickery and Chandler, Serge Thion (1983, p. 28) does not see the Khmer Rouge government as having wielded the extent of state power and control required for killing about three million people.

Perpetual surveillance such as separation of families, relocation of people and closely-supervised communal eating which the Khmer Rouge exercised over Cambodian society constitutes substantial control and enormous state power. A survivor of the Khmer Rouge revolution put it succinctly: "nobody liked the Khmer Rouge but they did not know where to turn" (Kiernan, 1996, p. 193). Kiernan is, therefore, correct in arguing that the Cambodian state's "top–down domination" and unprecedented power allowed it to conduct a broader scope of genocide in Cambodia from April 1975 to January 1979 (Kiernan, 1996, pp. 26–27).

What happened in Cambodia, Rwanda and Ethiopia also reinforce Vahakn Dadrian's contention that genocide is more likely to occur in societies in which great disparities in power exist between powerful perpetrators and relatively powerless victims (Dadrian, 1998, p. 1). In all three societies, power relations determined the scope, pace and success of killing. Between June and November 1978, the Khmer Rouge encountered armed opposition from Cham Muslims. In a series of rebellions in Krauchmar district, in the Eastern Zone of Cambodia, following Khmer Rouge attempts to seize

Cham religious texts, the Cham "slaughtered half a dozen of [Khmer Rouge soldiers] with swords and knives" (Kiernan, 1996, pp. 262–267). Here, the Cham resisted systematic attempts by the Khmer Rouge to impose on them conditions of life aimed at undermining their faith and livelihood as a group. Opposition from the relatively powerless Cham did not significantly affect Khmer Rouge determination to eliminate the Cham as an ethnic and religious group in the new and purified society. With its preponderant military strength, the Khmer Rouge responded by massacring the entire populations of several Cham villages (Kiernan, 1997, pp. 341–342). Similar force was exerted by the Akazu and the perpetrators of genocide in Rwanda in 1994. Many Tutsi victims fought for their lives. Nonetheless, with overwhelming power in the numbers of Hutu in Rwandan society willing to kill Tutsis, the perpetrators of genocide in Rwanda overcame individual and less organized Tutsi and Hutu opposition (Des Forges, 1999, pp. 216–221).

The situation was different in Ethiopia. Those who did not like the Dergue or share its national unity ideology could more easily turn to the numerous anti-Dergue groups to express their dissent. The Dergue's armed opponents included the Eritrean Peoples Liberation Front (EPLF), Ethiopian Peoples Revolutionary Party (EPRP), the Tigrayan Peoples Liberation Front (TPLF), the Oromo Peoples Liberation Front (OLF), the Ethiopian Democratic Union (EDU), the Afar Liberation Front (ALF) and the Western Somalia Liberation Front (WSLF). Each group had a substantial, independent and organized military machinery and controlled particular regions of Ethiopia (Amnesty International, 1987, p. 4; Kiflu, 1998, pp. 30–36, 70–75, 259). Ultimately, it was the TPLF's and EPRP's objective of overthrowing the state, and the EPLF's, OLF's and WSLF's opposition to the national unity ideology of the Dergue, that brought these insurgent groups and the military regime into a protracted and violent power struggle.

In January 1977, the power struggle between the Dergue and the EPRP, in particular, descended into violence. The EPRP, a multi-ethnic political group with Amhara leadership, orchestrated what it called "The White Terror"—a rural and urban campaign of assassination of members and supporters of the Dergue. That provoked the Dergue's infamous "Red Terror" counter-campaign of assassination of EPRP members and supporters. Between February 1977 and March 1979, the Dergue issued "hundreds of orders" and "directives" to state agents and revolutionary cadres to kill EPRP leaders and members. Civilians suspected of having links with or sympathies for the EPRP were also targeted (Dawit, 1989, p. 22; Ethiopian News Agency, 1998, p. v). Both the White and Red Terror campaigns claimed between 15,000 and 20,000 lives (*Abyot*; 1976, p. 72; author's taped interview, 1999a). Here, the Dergue aimed its terror mainly against organized armed groups bent on destroying it. Certainly, Ethiopia's "political groups" opposed to the Dergue consisted of people from particular ethnic groups who had political and ideological beliefs different from the Dergue's. It is, therefore, not impossible to argue that in the atmosphere of war, the Dergue could have converted real ethnic groups into political enemies to be destroyed. But very little evidence exists to suggest that the Dergue intended to eliminate every Amhara because of the Amhara leaders of the EPRP or every Oromo in Ethiopia because it was at war with the OLF. Thus, unlike Cambodia and Rwanda, state-organized killing in Ethiopia was not based on ethnic identity, but rather membership in armed groups that actively opposed the state.

The Ethiopian case highlights a fact often overlooked in the study of political mass killing. The death toll cannot be attributed to the Dergue alone. Members and supporters of the armed groups opposed to the Dergue settled their own internecine scores by eliminating one another (Medhane, 1995, p. 9). As Medhane Tadesse argues, the relationship between the EPRP and the TPLF, for instance, was characterized by "killing and counter-killing" (Medhane, 1995, pp. 8–9). Kiflu Tadesse confirms that "[h]undreds of EPRP members and followers were lost [sic] in the hands of the EPLF" (Kiflu, 1998, p. 259). Hence, it was the struggle for state power between the Dergue and its equally powerful armed opponents to implement competing nationalist ideologies that intensified war and facilitated politicide in Ethiopia.

Culture and Genocide

Some scholars attribute genocide and political mass murder to the culture of the societies in which they take place. In Cambodia, Ethiopia and Rwanda, perpetrators of mass murder either included or attempted to include the family members of individuals they killed or people who had blood ties with the victims. Between 1977 and 1978, the Khmer Rouge ordered the killing of high-ranking cadres such as Siet Chhae, Regiment Staff Member, Ruos Mau, Northwest Zone Party Chief of Staff, Sua Va Sy, Party Secretary of the Commercial Branch, and Mau Khem Nuon, Deputy Chief of Staff of S-21 Security Office and Sien An, the Cambodian Ambassador to Hanoi. As Chandler (1999, p. 131) argues, these individuals were killed "along with their relatives" and close friends.

The Dergue attempted this method of organized murder. After eliminating many members of the EPRP and weakening it as a political force, the Mengistu regime turned its attention to the ethnopolitical groups: the OLF, TPLF and EPLF. It imprisoned and tortured "hundreds of people belonging to the Oromo ethnic group" on grounds of being Oromo, and therefore likely to have sympathies for the OLF (Ethiopian News Agency, 1998, p. 19). The Dergue made similar arbitrary connections between the EPLF and TPLF and Tigrinya-speaking people from the secessionist province, of Eritrea and the insurgent province of Tigray. By persecuting ethnopolitical opposition groups and innocent Ethiopians with whom they shared language, the Dergue attempted to transform its destruction of political groups into genocide of people on the basis of their biological affinity with the regime's armed opponents (Ethiopian News Agency, 1998, p. 19). Hutu supremacists in Rwanda acted in a similar manner in 1994 as they had done in previous years. They linked the Tutsi living in Rwanda to the RPF and regarded them as accomplices in RPF invasions by virtue of their biological relationship. But the Ethiopian state failed where Hutu extremists succeeded.

Some scholars have offered cultural explanations for the enormous scale of popular participation in the genocide in Rwanda, the successful broadening of the scope of killing beyond target groups to family members in Cambodia and the unsuccessful attempt of the Dergue to turn political mass murder into genocide against ethnic groups. Gerard Prunier, Christian Scherrer and Bill Berkeley have attributed the participation of large numbers of ordinary Hutu in the killing of the Tutsi in Rwanda to the "notorious culture of obedience" to authority in Rwandan society shaped by "submissiveness" and "illiteracy" (Berkeley, 2002, p. 70; Prunier, 1995, pp. 141–142; Scherrer, 2002, p. 114).

Similarly, anthropologist Alexander Hinton has attributed Khmer Rouge destruction of the entire families of its targets to a "culture of disproportionate revenge" in Cambodian society (Hinton, 1997, pp. 1–4). That culture, Hinton argues, seeks revenge in total destruction and obliges people who kill to eliminate the family of the deceased to break the inevitable cycle of revenge. In the same vein, Ethiopian historian Merid Wolde Aregay sees the influence of culture in the Dergue's political killings. But unlike Prunier and Hinton, Merid regards culture as having prevented rather than encouraged genocide. Merid argues that, historically, Ethiopians have tolerated murder of political and ideological opponents. But extermination of people on the grounds of their ethnicity or the extension of political mass murder to the destruction of families of political opponents is a cultural threshold that Ethiopians have never crossed in their multi-ethnic society (author's taped interview, 1999c). Thus, Ethiopian culture, according to Merid, limited the Dergue's killings to armed political opponents.

Cultural explanations of mass murder have their limitations. They seek to explain human conduct to some natural predispositions of people, abnormal or moral behavior peculiar to particular groups of people and societies. Very often, these cultural explanations overlook the historical contexts of killing and the clearly political choices perpetrators make. Prunier's conformist mentality thesis or an illiterate mass argument overlooks evidence of disobedience and resistance to genocide in Rwanda and participation of educated middle class Hutu in the genocide. In fact the obedience thesis revives the discredited colonial myth of the Hutu as obedient and docile. From a historical perspective, the genocide in Rwanda was a product of self-interest and perception more than a national habit of obedience and submission. The political self-interest of Hutu participants in the genocide was rooted in their perception that an RPF rule would constitute a return to Tutsi power and, therefore, a reversal of the gains of the 1959 revolution (Mamdani, 2001, pp. 191, 202–203).

Pent-up anger was also an important historical force in genocide in Rwanda and Cambodia. RPF invasions had displaced many and the insurgents' depredations built a force of anger that did not need cultural prodding to generate its own genocidal sentiment against the Tutsi inside Rwanda. Similarly, pent-up anger and perception explain the atrocities committed by ordinary Khmer Rouge cadres against officials of the Lon Nol regime and urban people. Many peasants in rural Cambodia perceived those officials and urban people as responsible for the displacements and refugee situations created by the US bombardment of the Cambodian countryside from 1969 to 1973 (Chandler, 1999, pp. 96–97; Kiernan, 1996, pp. 19–25).

There was more to the Dergue's failure to convince many Ethiopians to follow it down a genocidal path than national culture suggests. Throughout its 17 years of rule (September 1974–May 1991), Ethiopia's revolutionary military government—unlike the Akazu and the Khmer Rouge—never succeeded in imposing its authority on the society. Organized opposition limited the Dergue's scope of target groups to those who threatened its tenuous grip on power. Since the Dergue did not have monopoly over the instruments of violence, as the Akazu and the Khmer Rouge did, consolidating power inevitably required building popular support in Ethiopia's multi-ethnic society. That was a political decision rather than a cultural choice. What happened in Rwanda, Ethiopia and Cambodia has both empirical and theoretical lessons for the study of genocide.

Conclusion

The lethal combination of revolution and genocide was evident in Rwanda from 1957 to 1962 and in Cambodia from 1975 to 1979. The Hutu Revolution of 1959 excluded the Tutsi of Rwanda from power and marked them for deportations and annihilation. Similarly, the Khmer Rouge revolution of 1975 excluded non-Khmer ethnic groups and Khmers the Pol Pot regime considered impure from membership in the "new society." But Ethiopia demonstrates that not every revolution embodies the idea of excluding particular ethnic groups from membership of society or leads to genocide through radical transformation of the ethnic fabric of society. The Ethiopian revolution preserved rather than destroyed the pre-existing ethnic composition of Ethiopia.

Cambodia, Rwanda and Ethiopia were societies undergoing rapid change that also experienced mass murder. While the Khmer Rouge annihilated its target groups as part of changing its society, the Interahamwe and the Dergue killed as part of resisting change. The Khmer Rouge wanted to return Cambodia to an imagined glorious past. But Hutu extremists and Ethiopian nationalists within the Dergue wanted to maintain a status quo under threat: Hutu power in Rwanda and national unity and military rule in Ethiopia. Thus genocide and politicide do not necessarily occur in the context of change. They can be products of resistance to change.

It is also important to note the different bases on which the perpetrators of mass murder in the three societies defined the groups they destroyed. In Cambodia, the victims of genocide were defined on the bases of their ethnic and religious identity within Khmer Rouge determination of who was pure enough to be part of the utopian society it envisioned. Ethiopia's beleaguered revolutionary regime defined its targets from the prism of their armed opposition to the state or threat to the power of the Dergue. The Dergue's victims of politicide were members of domestic insurgent groups that threatened the Dergue's power. The interim government of Rwanda and Hutu nationalists defined those they killed on the basis of their ethnic affiliation with an external insurgent group that threatened Hutu monopoly on power. In Rwanda, the victims of genocide were not members of the RPF.

The three cases compared here suggest that states are not the definitive perpetrators of mass murder. State machinery was used extensively to commit genocide in Cambodia because the Khmer Rouge exercised tremendous power over a subdued society. But in Ethiopia and Rwanda, non-state actors played key roles in the killing. The Dergue's political opponents were not defenseless rivals in the struggle for state power. Non-state armed opposition groups in Ethiopia also settled their differences by murder. The success of genocide in Rwanda came to depend on the collaboration of a weakened state and organized groups in society with diverse intentions. Power, more than ideology, motivated the motley group of killers in Rwanda in 1994. The underlying lesson here is that like states, non-state groups (insurgents and organized nationalists), under certain circumstances, have the potential of creating the conditions of genocide and politicide or committing the crime themselves.

Social structures and domestic opposition are just as important in the process of mass murder as revolution, war, ideology and state power. With their ideologies of the domination of one ethnic group, the mono-ethnic Khmer Rouge and advocates of Hutu Power had no scruples about destroying other ethnic groups. But because of the strong opposition it faced from many armed opponents, it was impossible for the Dergue, a multi-ethnic military junta, to physically destroy particular ethnic groups in its multi-ethnic society. Hence, it would be an exaggeration to speak of organized and systematic extermination of ethnic groups in Ethiopia comparable to that of Pol Pot's Cambodia or post-Habyarimana Rwanda.

If the study of genocide aims at creating a peaceful and tolerant world, then integration of developments in Rwanda, Cambodia and Ethiopia into the study of mass murder should have one key impact. It should encourage a clearer definition of the concept of "political groups." Organized murder of defenseless "political groups" who pursue their objectives through non-violent means should be distinguished from the killing of "political activists" or insurgent groups who are well-armed and aim at seizing state power through war and violence. Such distinction should also emphasize that unless the killing of "political groups" and " political activists" includes or leads to the total or partial destruction of the ethnic communities to which members of the political groups belong—as it did not in Ethiopia—then such killing ought not be called genocide.

Source: Kissi, Edward. (2004). "Rwanda, Ethiopia and Cambodia: Links, Faultlines and Complexities in a Comparative Study of Genocide," *Journal of Genocide Research*, Volume 6, No. 1, pp. 115–116, 122–131.

DISSECTING DARFUR: ANATOMY OF A GENOCIDE DEBATE

Darren Brunk

Introduction

The Rwandan genocide of 1994 is remembered throughout the international commu-nity today not only for what extremist Hutus did in their attempted programme of ethnic annihilation, but, just as importantly, for what the international community is perceived *not* to have done. The international community did not reinforce the exist-ing UNAMIR mission in the first weeks of the genocide. Instead, the United Nations Security Council chose to draw down its modest force to near irrelevance after the death of ten Belgian troops. The great Western powers present on the Security Council – Britain, France and the United States – did not call the violence in Rwanda by what is widely accepted today as the conflict's proper name, genocide, until weeks after its scope and organized nature were already well understood. Ultimately, those interna-tional agents seen to possess the ability to stop the genocide at the time did not act, and as a result are recurrently condemned today for having failed a significant test of global moral leadership to name and prevent genocide perpetrated against the world's most vulnerable populations.

Former US President Bill Clinton clearly expressed the dual nature of the inter-national community's failure when he admitted on the tarmac of Kigali airport in 1998 that:

> The international community . . . must bear its share of responsibility for this tragedy. We did not act quickly enough after the killing began. . . . We did not immediately call these crimes by their rightful name: genocide.[1]

It is this second category of perceived international failures with which this article is principally concerned. Specifically, it seeks to investigate how the force of guilt in-scribed by the narrative of international failure has influenced the debate among some of the principal political actors throughout the international community towards the contemporary crisis in Darfur, Sudan.

As the article will contend, the memory of the Rwandan genocide, once invoked, became an important frame through which many actors perceived and engaged with the emerging Darfur crisis. Darfur entered public consciousness in a number of key per-ception and policy forums – in the UN system, in US legislative and executive branches of government, among international humanitarian NGOs, and in mass media outlets – through 2003 and early 2004. Shaped in part by the occasion of the tenth anniversary of the Rwandan genocide, the Darfur crisis was informed by the resurgent memory of the international community's failure to end the 1994 Rwandan conflict, and, more specifi-cally, to call it by its proper name – genocide.

---

[1]Bill Clinton quoted in Michael Barnett, *Eyewitness to a Genocide: The United Nations and Rwanda* (London: Cornell University Press, 2002), p. 155.

Few events in the twentieth century have shaken the conscience of human-kind like the 1994 Rwanda genocide. In the span of 100 days an estimated 800,000 Tutsis and moderate Hutus were killed by the extremist interim Hutu government and its youth militias. Though a small UN mission was present on the ground, the international community was variously unwilling or unable to stem the violence. Today, the memory of this tragic episode is dominated by two central meanings – genocide and international failure. On 19 March 2004, these meanings were given new relevance when the UN Humanitarian Coordinator for Sudan, Mukesh Kapila, declared that 'the only difference between Rwanda and Darfur now is the numbers involved'.[2] Although a chasm of context separated these two unique regions of Africa, the comparison first publicly expressed by Kapila has found widespread resonance with policy-makers and concerned observers throughout the international community.

Darfur entered international concern as a reincarnation of the Rwandan past, rather than as an independent and novel event. This article is centrally concerned with this surprising prevalence of the Rwandan memory and its component meanings in the debate around Darfur, particularly during the first two years of international attention to the conflict (2003–4). Within this context, it asks the central question: *to what extent have the memory and meanings of the Rwandan genocide influenced the international community's perceptions of and policy towards the Darfur crisis?* The aims in answering this question are to determine both the influence of Rwanda's memory upon our understanding of Darfur, and whether the memory of Rwanda has caused us to *misrepresent* the violence occurring there.

By examining key UN Security Council deliberations and US Congressional debates, as well as media and NGO reporting, the article will examine how Darfur entered public consciousness in a number of key perception and policy forums through 2003 and early 2004. The first section will provide a historical examination of the Darfur conflict, and of its emergence within the international consciousness. The second section will examine the prevalence of the Rwandan genocide in Darfur deliberations, and provide some possible explanations for this recurrent association. A third section will critically reflect upon the memory and meanings of Rwanda, how these memories and meanings have influenced the framing of Darfur, and, finally, the potential legitimacy of resultant policy responses formed within this frame.

This article is, at heart, a plea for caution. Frequently the lessons of the past are presumed to be the surest guides for policy action in the present. Yet the past can sometimes shroud our understanding of the present with false meanings. In this respect, the past may influence our perception of the present, though this perception may be different from the reality. Darfur is not Rwanda. And yet, through the analogical lens of the Rwandan genocide, Darfur has been perceived through meanings and memories which are not its own. By summoning the memory of Rwanda, international actors also invoked the meanings within it – most notably, the twin spectres of genocide and international failure. These perceptions influenced the terms of policy debate at

---

[2]Mukesh Kapila, quoted in Eric Reeves, 'Catastrophe in Darfur', *Review of African Political Economy*, 31 (99), 2005, pp. 160–1 at p. 161.

important policy junctures within the international community, with tangible policy effects. For this reason, it is important to understand where and how the memory of the Rwandan past has impacted upon the reality of the Darfur present, with both positive and negative effects.

Darfur – from Humanitarian to Human Rights Crisis

Darfur's most recent round of violence is typically traced back to February 2003, when a new militant political movement drawn from among the marginalized Fur, Zaghawa and Masalit populations of Darfur initiated a violent campaign against government targets in the west of the country. Since its initial success, the government of Sudan has sought a military solution to counter the insurgency. The government's strategy has borrowed from its experiences and military structures developed in the 1980s in its long war of attrition against the southern self-determination movement, the Sudanese People's Liberation Army/Movement (SPLA/M).[3] Most notably, the government has employed proxy militias – trained, armed, funded and mobilized by political leaders in Khartoum – to raid the Fur, Masalit and Zaghawa civilian bases of support for the rebel insurgency.

Prior to the current expression of violence, the chief actors and their grievances developed over many years and even decades of identity formation and modern nation-state building.[4] With the formation of an organized armed resistance in 2003, however, the dynamics of conflict in Darfur have escalated to previously unmatched proportions. An estimated 9000 were killed during a previous round of intra-Darfurian violence between 1985–8.[5] By comparison, in the first three years of the current conflict (2003–6), the number of Darfurians believed to have died is widely agreed to have surpassed 200,000, while contributing to nearly two million internally displaced people, 208,000 refugees, and 3.5 million now dependent on humanitarian assistance.[6]

---

[3]For a detailed account of Sudan's north–south civil war, see Douglas Johnson, *The Root Causes of Sudan's Civil Wars* (Oxford: James Curry, 2003).

[4]For a more detailed account of the history behind the Darfur conflict, and the formation of the predominant identities and grievances at issue therein, see Julie Flint and Alex de Waal, *Darfur: A Short History of a Long War* (London: Zed Books, 2005). Gérard Prunier, *Darfur: The Ambiguous Genocide* (London: Hurst, 2005). Alex de Waal, 'Who Are the Darfurians? Arab and African Identities, Violence and External Engagement', *African Affairs*, 104, 2005, pp. 181–205.

[5]Prunier, *Darfur: The Ambiguous Genocide*, p. 65.

[6]As of March 2007, four years into the violence, estimates on the numbers killed in the Darfur violence vary wildly. Numbers proposed by the government of Sudan set the death toll at around 7000. A UK parliamentary committee placed the total at 300,000, while the Coalition for International Justice (CIJ) estimated closer to 400,000. In the September 2006 edition of the journal *Science*, John Hagan and Alberto Palloni compare the different estimates of crude mortality rates (CMR) calculated by a range of organizations – including the US State Department, the British government, the World Health Organization and Médecins sans Frontières – and make a critical study of the methodologies by which these estimates were derived. The authors argue, based on the most conservative interpretation of these contrasting estimates and methodologies, that 'although we cannot overcome the limitations in the basic information, on the basis of the surveys available, we conclude that the death toll in Darfur is conservatively estimated to be in the hundreds of thousands rather than tens of thousands of people'. See Active Learning Network for Accountability and Performance in Humanitarian Action (ALNAP) Report, *Review of Humanitarian Action in 2004*, available at: www.odi.org. ukALNAP/RHA2004/contents.html (accessed 16 May 2006), p. 78; John Hagan and Alberto Palloni, 'Death in Darfur', *Science*, 313, 15 September 2006, pp. 1578–9; Human Rights Watch Report, 'Darfur: Humanitarian Aid Under Siege', May 2006, available at: http://hrw.org/backgrounder/africa/sudan0506/3.htm#_ Toc134524595 (accessed 29 June 2006).

Moreover, in contrast to previous decades when violence was largely conducted between Darfurians, the government has taken a much more assertive and active role on the side of the 'Arab' militias – the Janjawiid. Government aircraft supported Janjawiid raids through 2003 and early 2004, using Antonov bomber aircraft, fighter jets and combat helicopters to bomb 'non-Arab' target villages ahead of ground assaults by mounted Janjawiid.[7] Additionally, government troops have at times directly participated alongside the militias in coordinated air and ground attacks.[8] The raids have caused incredible suffering and disruption for the civilian population in Darfur. Many have been killed, raped, kidnapped, mutilated, assaulted, abused and dispossessed of property.[9]

The government initiated its military solution to the Darfur crisis in mid-2003. At the end of the year, the scale and effect of the violence prompted Jan Egeland, the United Nations' Under-Secretary for Humanitarian Affairs, to assert that Darfur was possibly 'the worst [crisis] in the world today'.[10] Later the same month another UN officer, Tom Vraalsen, clarified the nature of the crisis when he described Darfur as 'nothing less than the "organized" destruction of sedentary African agriculturalists – the Fur, the Masalit and the Zaghawa'.[11] By December 2003, the crisis in Darfur had already been raging for nearly a year since the first coordinated attacks by local rebels and the destructive reprisals by government and militia forces.

And yet, for much of 2003, the international response to Darfur was muted, at best. In the United Nations, the Office of the High Commission for Human Rights (OHCHR) in Sudan first reported an 'ostensible effort by the Sudan government to purge Darfur of African tribes' in March 2003, while in September the UN launched a 'Greater Darfur Initiative' funding drive for $23 million.[12] Yet the effects of these announcements were weak, producing few tangible reactions from the international community, even from within the UN system itself. Though the UN had a country team in place in Khartoum through most of the year, 'the minutes of its meetings . . . were found to "reflect a general lack of urgency until December 2003"',[13] while the UNHCR's 'Greater Darfur Initiative' failed to raise a single cent by the end of the year.[14] Moreover, at the highest levels of UN policy formation, Darfur was a non-issue for the first 13 months of the rebellion and the Sudanese government's counter-insurgency campaign. Although

---

[7]Human Rights Watch (HRW), 'Darfur in Flames: Atrocities in Western Sudan' (Human Rights Watch, April 2004), 16(5)A, p. 16.

[8]HRW, 'Darfur in Flames', p. 16.

[9]United Nations, 'Report of the United Nations High Commissioner for Human Rights and Follow-Up to the World Conference on Human Rights: Situation of Human Rights in the Darfur Region of the Sudan', E/CN.4/2005/3, 7 May 2004, p. 12. HRW, 'Darfur Destroyed: Ethnic Cleansing by Government and Militia Forces in Western Sudan', (Human Rights Watch, May 2004), 16(6) A, pp. 7–39.

[10]Samuel Totten and Eric Markusen, 'Research Note: The US Government Darfur Genocide Investigation', *Journal of Genocide Research*, 7(2), 2005, pp. 279–90, at p. 280.

[11]Totten and Markusen, 'Research Note', p. 280.

[12]ALNAP, *Review of Humanitarian Action in 2004*, p. 79.

[13]ALNAP, *Review of Humanitarian Action in 2004*, p. 79.

[14]Prunier, *Darfur: The Ambiguous Genocide*, p. 112.

concern was mounting among UN staff on the ground, Darfur would not appear on the UN Security Council agenda until March 2004.[15]

In NGO circles, Darfur was generally slow to appear as an agenda priority. Part of the blame for this lack of attention may be attributable to the government of Sudan's restrictive access policies for foreign journalists and NGO workers to the conflict region. Early investigative efforts by the few international NGOs aware of the crisis were frequently thwarted by the Sudanese government's travel and visa restrictions.[16] Other prominent organizations failed to investigate the crisis until much later. The International Crisis Group, for example, did not report on the region until June 2003, while Human Rights Watch did not produce its first press release until March 2004.[17] Some groups did, however, endeavour to report on the crisis through research and re- sources outside the region. Amnesty International, to its credit, issued its first press release relating to Darfur in February 2003, warning the international community that the newly emerging tensions in Darfur must not 'be allowed to escalate into all-out war'.[18] With limited interstate and NGO attention to this inaccessible crisis, howev- er, the media were equally absent in their coverage. A cursory LexisNexis survey of 19 British national newspapers between 1 January 2003 and 31 March 2004 identified 19 articles mentioning 'Darfur', though not a single instance of 'Darfur' appeared in an article headline during this period.[19]

Moreover, what little direct engagement there was within the international com- munity to address the crisis during the first year was largely concerned with secur- ing *humanitarian* outcomes. One extensive report from London's Foreign Policy Centre examined policy responses to the crisis from the UK and US governments, as well as the EU and the UN, through the autumn of 2003 and spring of 2004.[20] The report con- cluded that most in the international community were concerned with addressing only

---

[15]John Borton and John Eriksson, *Lessons from Rwanda – Lessons for Today: Assessment of the Impact and Influence of the Joint Evaluation of Emergency Assistance to Rwanda*, April 2005, available at: www.um.dk/en/menu/ DevelopmentPolicy/Evaluations/ReportsByYear/2004/Lessons+from+Rwanda+-+Lessons+for+Today.htm (accessed 7 June 2006), p. 102.

[16]ALNAP, *Review of Humanitarian Action in 2004*, p. 80.

[17]Borton and Eriksson, *Lessons from Rwanda*, p. 103.

[18]Amnesty International Press Release, 'Sudan: Urgent Call for Commission of Inquiry in Darfur as Situation Deteriorates', 21 February 2003, available at: http://web.amnesty.org/library/Index/ ENGAFR540042003?open&of=ENG-SDN (accessed 1 July 2006). For additional Amnesty coverage from 2003 and 2004, see Amnesty Press Releases: 'Sudan: Crisis in Darfur – Urgent Need for International Commission of Inquiry and Monitoring', 28 April 2003; 'Sudan: Looming Crisis in Darfur', 1 July 2003; 'Sudan: Immediate Steps to Protect Civilians and Internally Displaced Persons in Darfur', 29 August 2003; 'Sudan: Humanitarian Crisis in Darfur Caused by Sudan Government's Failures', 27 November 2003, all available at: http://web. amnesty.org/library/Index/ENGAFR541012003?open&of=ENG-SDN (accessed 2 July 2006).

[19]LexisNexis Search, 1 January 2003 to 31 March 2004, available at: http://web.lexis-nexis.com/professional (accessed 2 July 2006). For the purposes of this LexisNexis search, the UK's 'national' newspapers included 19 titles.

[20]Greg Austin and Ben Koppelman, 'Darfur and Genocide: Mechanisms for Rapid Response, an End to Impunity' (London: The Foreign Policy Centre, July 2004). The Foreign Policy Centre's findings have been reinforced by further assessments of the international response. See, for example, International Crisis Group, *Darfur Rising: Sudan's New Crisis*, 25 March 2004, available at: www.crisisgroup.org/home/index. cfm?l=1&id=2550 (accessed 4 April 2004), p. 27. Alex Bellamy and Paul Williams, 'The Responsibility to Protect and the Crisis in Darfur', *Security Dialogue*, 36(1), 2005, pp. 27–47, at p. 32.

the humanitarian dimensions of the conflict; their attention was directed towards the easing of the effects of the violence rather than confronting the root causes.[21] In the ten-year retrospective by the Danish development agency (Danida) on the lessons of Rwanda, the authors similarly criticized the international community's singularly humanitarian focus during the first formative months of the Darfur crisis. Recalling its own Joint Evaluation of the international response to Rwanda ten years earlier, and reiterating the concerns raised by UN officials in Darfur at the time, the report warned that 'humanitarian action cannot substitute for political action', as had become the prevailing policy trend in Darfur.[22]

After March 2004, however, the weak international response underwent a sudden transformation. Consider, for example, that through March only two articles citing Darfur appeared in any of the United Kingdom's national newspapers.[23] Through the month of April, by contrast, Darfur featured in 27 articles nationwide.[24] Furthermore, in contrast to the 19 articles mentioning Darfur over the preceding fifteen months, a LexisNexis search of the UK's national newspapers over the following 15 months, from April 2004 to the end of June 2005, recorded 334 articles including 'Darfur' in the headline alone.[25] Similarly, across the Atlantic the *New York Times* produced five articles and opinion columns mentioning Darfur between 20 March and 31 March 2004, though none earlier in the month.[26] The number of articles published in April rose to 12.[27] Similar trends in reporting appear consistently through a number of prominent Western press outlets, including the *Washington Post*, *Le Monde*, and CNN.[28]

In NGO and intergovernmental agency reports, strikingly similar conclusions began to emerge about the form and degree of violence occurring on the ground. The International Crisis Group produced its first extensive investigation of the conflict in March 2004, in a report entitled *Darfur Rising: Sudan's New Crisis*.[29] Far from depicting a purely humanitarian disaster, the report carefully traced the complex political roots

---

[21]Austin and Koppelman, 'Darfur and Genocide', p. 32.

[22]Borton and Eriksson, *Lessons from Rwanda*, p. 102.

[23]LexisNexis Search, 1 March 2004 to 31 March 2004, available at: http://web.lexis-nexis.com/professional (2 July 2006).

[24]LexisNexis Search, 1 April 2004 to 30 April 2004, available at: http://web.lexis-nexis.com/professional (accessed 2 July 2006).

[25]LexisNexis Search, 1 April 2004 to 30 June 2005, available at: http://web.lexis-nexis.com/professional (accessed 11 July 2006).

[26]New York Times Archive Search, 20 March 2004 to 31 March 2004, available at: http://query.nytimes.com/search/query?frow=0&n=10&srcht=a&query=Darfur&srchst=nyt&hdlquery=&bylquery=&daterange=period&mon1=03&day1=01&year1=2004&mon2=03&day2=31&year2=2004&submit.x=29&submit.y=13 (accessed 10 July 2006).

[27]New York Times Archive Search, 1 April 2004 to 30 April 2004, available at: http://query.nytimes.com/search/query?frow=0&n=10&srcht=a&query=Darfur&srchst=nyt&hdlquery=&bylquery=&daterange=period&mon1=03&day1=01&year1=2004&mon2=03&day2=31&year2=2004&submit.x=29&submit.y=13 (accessed 10 July 2006).

[28]In the *Washington Post*, articles mentioning Darfur in March and April respectively rose from 5 in March to 11 in April. In *Le Monde*, not a single article was recorded dealing with the conflict through March, though 12 articles appeared in April. The first web article headline relating to Darfur appeared on the CNN website on 7 April 2004. See http://search.cnn.com/pages/search.jsp?currentPage=21&query=Darfur&sortby=Date (accessed 10 July 2006).

[29]ICG Report, *Darfur Rising*.

of the conflict, arguing that 'Darfur . . . has more to do with the structural imbalances of governance and economic development that characterise the relations of the centre with peripheral regions than with the north/south divide.'[30] On 2 April, Human Rights Watch followed with its first in-depth report on the crisis.[31] The report emphasized the critical need to address the root causes of the conflict as an essential precursor to any positive humanitarian outcome.[32]

The United Nations also began to take greater note and engagement with the violent foundations of the crisis. In April, a United Nations High Commission for Human Rights team led by the acting High Commissioner Bertrand Ramcharan left for Darfur to investigate 'reports of massive and criminal violations of human rights'.[33] Summarizing the character of the violence, the resultant report concluded that:

> It is clear that there is a reign of terror in Darfur. While the Government appears to employ different tactics to counter the rebellion, the mission encountered a consistency of allegations that government and militia forces carried out indiscriminate attacks against civilians; rape and other serious forms of sexual violence; destruction of property and pillage; forced displacements; disappearances; and persecution and discrimination.[34]

Following this growing global concern, the Security Council convened its first informal deliberations on Darfur in the last week of March.[35] On 7 May, Ramcharan briefed the Council, highlighting the government-initiated human rights abuses compiled in his report.[36] Subsequently, on 11 June, the Council adopted its first resolution relating to Darfur. Though reiterating its primary concern for the successful resolution of the north–south conflict, Resolution 1547 also called on the primary north/south parties to lend their influence 'to bring an immediate halt to the fighting in the Darfur region'.[37]

Increasingly, Darfur was claiming space on the global agenda as a violent political crisis, rather than a purely humanitarian one. How do we explain this sudden shift in attention? In part we may explain Darfur's rising visibility in terms of increasing access to the crisis zone afforded to the international community after February 2004, when the government of Sudan eased access to the country for humanitarian organizations, their staff, and other foreign professionals – including journalists and some NGO workers.[38] After February, greater analysis and experience of the crisis were possible,

---

[30]ICG Report, *Darfur Rising*, p. 1.

[31]HRW, *Darfur in Flames*.

[32]HRW, *Darfur in Flames*, p. 2.

[33]United Nations, Report E/CN.4/2005/3.

[34]United Nations, Report E/CN.4/2005/3.

[35]Borton and Eriksson, *Lessons from Rwanda*, p. 102.

[36]Cheryl Igiri and Princeton Lyman, Council on Foreign Relations, *Giving Meaning to 'Never Again': Seeking an Effective Response to the Crisis in Darfur and Beyond*, CSR 5, September 2004, p. 7.

[37]United Nations, Document S/RES/1547, 11 June 2004.

[38]According to the ALNAP review, the government of Sudan adopted an 'accordion' strategy to impede humanitarian access. 'Although authorities eased strictures in February 2004 and again in May 2004 in response to international pressure, by then valuable time had been lost. Approaching humanitarian space as something of an accordion, the authorities restricted access again in early 2005 and then relaxed restrictions again in April 2005. ' See ALNAP, *Review of Humanitarian Action in 2004*, p. 81.

alongside increased international activity on the ground. Through first-hand reports, Darfur further penetrated the public consciousness, and into policy debate. Greater access to the region may explain Darfur's increased visibility, but what about its changing character within international perception?

This second shift began to assume a new form through the spring of 2004. The first signs of a change, however, were clearly expressed on 19 March 2004. The occasion for the expression of this change in perception was the critical statement given by Mukesh Kapila. In front of the world's media, Kapila framed the conflict in terms that would resonate and be reproduced throughout the international community when he stated:

> I was present in Rwanda at the time of the genocide, and I've seen many other situations around the world and I am totally shocked at what is going on in Darfur. . . . The only difference between Rwanda and Darfur now is the numbers involved.[39]

Kapila's appeal to the memory of the Rwanda genocide was a significant derivation from the preceding humanitarian representational trend. Kapila cast the crisis in terms of genocide – a representation which spoke to the underlying violent roots of the crisis rather than its surface humanitarian effects. Moreover, eschewing quiet diplomatic entreaties to the Sudanese government, his remarks were also a very public admonition of the violent government-driven campaign. Moreover, the timing for his comments was propitious, with the tenth anniversary of the Rwandan genocide less than a month away. Following Kapila's comments, Rwanda figured frequently in the rising media, NGO, state and intergovernmental attention to the conflict. It is during this anniversary period in which analogical framings of the conflict in terms of 'genocide' – and the Rwandan genocide in particular – become apparent.

Rwanda and Darfur – A Memory and Its Meanings

Through the spring and summer of 2004, reports on Rwanda, often in tandem with Kapila's statement in particular, were frequently reprinted around the world, featuring, among other major media outlets, on the BBC, in the *New York Times*, Associated Press, the UK's *Guardian and Daily Telegraph*, and Canada's national English-language daily, the *Globe and Mail*.[40] In countless articles, the Rwandan genocide anniversary and the Darfur crisis became suffused almost into a single issue, with Darfur being presented as a contemporary recurrence of Rwanda's 'genocide' and the international community's 'failure' there. On 7 April, in a release on the genocide anniversary, Agence France Presse reported that 'UN Secretary General Kofi Annan said that the international community must be ready to take decisive action against Sudan . . . if Khartoum

---

[39]Austin and Koppelman, 'Darfur and Genocide', p. 36.

[40]'Mass Rape Atrocity in West Darfur', BBC, 19 March 2004, available at: http://news.bbc.co.uk/1/hi/world/africa/3549325.stm (11 July 2006). 'World Briefing – Africa: Sudan: "Greatest Humanitarian Crisis"', *New York Times*, 20 March 2004. 'UN Official Says Fighting in Western Sudan Creating World's Worst Humanitarian Crisis', Associated Press, available at: http://pqasb.pqarchiver.com/ap/results.html?st=advanced&qryTxt=Darfur&sortby=REVERSE_CHRON&datetype=6&frommonth=03&fromday=01&fromyear=2004&tomonth=04&today=30&toyear=2004&By=&Title= (accessed 11 July 2006). LexisNexis Search, 18 March to 10 April 2004, available at: http://web.lexis-nexis.com/professional (accessed 10 July 2006). 'The Next Rwanda?: Sudan's Neglected Nightmare', *Globe and Mail*, 5 June 2004.

denies aid workers access to the strife-torn Darfur region.'[41] On 22 April, a CNN investigation of genocide claims in Darfur chastised the international community for its failure to act. Couched in the context of Rwanda, the article argued that 'The world is not dealing with [Darfur]. . . . And in the light of these commemorations and talk about Rwanda, it comes as increasingly double standards again by the international community.'[42] On 3 June, Emma Bonino wrote in *Le Figaro* that 'the ghost of Rwanda and the current powerlessness of the international community should give us all pause to reflect', in the face of the international community's failure and indifference over Darfur.[43] Similar accounts were reported by the BBC and the UN's own in-house press agency, IRIN.[44] Beginning in late March and continuing through the summer of 2004 (and beyond), 'Rwanda', 'international failure' and 'genocide' were raised together as mutually constitutive and mutually evocative historical memories and meanings. Prior to April 2004 and the Rwandan genocide anniversary commemorations, however, these framing images were entirely absent from the paucity of awareness and coverage provided by the international community.

International human rights NGOs were also quick to use the powerful Rwanda imagery to their advantage, particularly in publicity campaigns conducted through press releases, newspaper columns and even in conjunction with major television network investigations. In an article in the *Boston Globe* on 20 May, former US National Security Advisor Anthony Lake and the ICG's John Prendergast claimed that 'Sudan is Rwanda in slow motion'.[45] Drawing on the memory of international failure to act in Rwanda, the authors inferred the same potential meaning for Darfur in the international community when they warned that 'if we do not act now, in 2014 we will have to face another 10-year anniversary of shame'.[46] On 28 April, Human Rights Watch (HRW) produced a column, also reprinted in the *Los Angeles Times*, lamenting the poor press coverage of Darfur. Drawing on the failure of the international press to cover both Rwanda and a new emerging genocide in Darfur, the article argued that 'the international media don't send reporters to cover genocides, it seems. They cover genocide anniversaries'.[47] Merging once more Rwanda's twin meanings of 'failure' and 'genocide' in a *New York Sun* article that same month, HRW's Minky Worden concluded, 'thanks to the UN Commission on Human Rights and its member countries' willingness to look the other way in Sudan, "never again" is looking like "once again" in Africa'.[48] The

---

[41]'Main Ceremony Begins to Mark 10th Anniversary of Rwanda Genocide', Agence France Presse, 7 April 2004, available at: www.afp.fr/english/home (accessed 7 April 2004).

[42]'Probe into Sudan Genocide Claims', CNN, 22 April 2004, available at: http://www.cnn.com/2004/WORLD/africa/04/22/sudan.genocide/index.html (accessed 11 July 2006).

[43]Emma Bonino, 'Soudan: Une Insupportable Indifférence', *Le Figaro*, 3 June 2004.

[44]Paul Welsh, 'Darfur: A Repeat of Rwanda?', BBC, 23 August 2004, available at: http://news.bbc.co.uk/1/hi/world/africa/3591924.stm (accessed 3 November 2004). 'Sudan: US Considering whether Darfur Displacements, Killings Constitute Genocide', IRIN, 17 June 2004.

[45]'Stopping Sudan's Slow-Motion Genocide', *Boston Globe*, 20 May 2004.

[46]'Stopping Sudan's Slow-Motion Genocide', *Boston Globe*. See also Prendergast's column with Samantha Power: 'Break Through to Darfur', 2 June 2004.

[47]Carroll Bogert, 'Another Africa Calamity – Will Media Slumber On?', *Los Angeles Times*, 28 April 2004.

[48]Minky Worden, 'Sudan's Silent Scream', *New York Sun*, 28 April 2004.

memory of failure in Rwanda blended seamlessly with the anticipation of genocide in Darfur in many additional reports, releases and columns.[49]

Human rights NGOs were not the only concerned groups to adopt Rwanda's evocative imagery and meanings to guide their understanding of and fears for Darfur. State policy-makers and intergovernmental statesmen and women were equally captivated by the seeming similarities between the two cases. UN Secretary-General Kofi Annan used the occasion of the Rwandan genocide anniversary to launch his own personal appeal to the international community for action on Darfur. Speaking before the Commission on Human Rights Annan appealed to his global audience not to forget the lessons of Rwanda. 'In this connection', he argued, 'let me say here and now that I share the grave concern expressed last week . . . at the scale of reported human rights abuses and at the humanitarian crisis unfolding in Darfur, Sudan.'[50] He continued:

> Mr Chairman, such reports leave me with a deep sense of foreboding. Whatever terms it uses to describe the situation, the international community cannot stand idle. . . . Let us, Mr Chairman, be serious about preventing genocide. Only so can we honour the victims whom we remember today. Only so can we save those who might be victims tomorrow.[51]

Roméo Dallaire, the former UN force commander in Rwanda during the genocide, reiterated these parallels in a *New York Times* column later in the year. Cautioning the international community against a repeat of its failure to intervene in Rwanda he made the following appeal:

> In April, on the tenth anniversary of the start of his country's genocide, President Paul Kagame told his people and the world that if any country ever suffered genocide, Rwanda would willingly come to its aid. He chastised the international community for its callous response to the killing spree of 1994. . . . And sure enough, Rwanda sent a small contingent to Darfur. President Kagame kept his word. Having called what is happening in Darfur genocide and having vowed to stop it, it is time for the West to keep its word as well.[52]

Media stories and public discussions on Darfur became an occasion to vent recriminations for failing to act in genocides past, and expressed the fear of failure in genocide present. Yet, this fear was also frequently an appeal for action – a purging of the guilt felt personally by those directly involved in Rwanda, and the generation informed by its meanings for the international community. Rwanda, put simply, was everywhere, and its meaning was ubiquitous.

[49]See, for example, Amnesty International press release, 'Sudan: UN Commission Statement on Darfur – Bland Words in Response to a Deepening Human Rights Crisis', 23 April 2004, available at: http://web.amnesty.org/library/Index/ENGIOR410292004?open&of=ENG-SDN (accessed 11 July 2006).

[50]'Secretary-General Observes International Day of Reflection on 1994 Rwanda Genocide', United Nations, 7 April 2004, available at: www2.unog.ch/news2/documents/newsen/sg04003e.htm (accessed 16 May 2006).

[51]'Secretary-General Observes International Day of Reflection'.

[52]Roméo Dallaire, 'Looking at Darfur, Seeing Rwanda', *New York Times*, 4 October 2004.

Policy-makers were not immune to these memories and meanings within the United States government. Indeed, some of the most vocal in their Rwandan memories were members of the US Congress. Following the first two months of heightened public attention to Darfur's perceived 'genocide', the crisis quickly rose up the Congressional agenda. Moreover, after the US government's perceived failure to respond adequately in Rwanda, the language of 'genocide' and Rwanda in relation to Darfur left many members of Congress with a deep sense of foreboding. Fearing another genocide failure on their watch, numerous members of Congress – Republican and Democrat – became actively involved in bringing Congressional influence to bear on the US government's policy response. Speaking before the House on 4 May 2004, Republican Senator Frank R. Wolf challenged Congress to take up the issue of Darfur and to pressure the executive into a more active policy response. According to Senator Wolf:

> if we fail to act, in another ten years Darfur will be today's Rwanda and some Member of Congress will be standing here on the floor asking those in the body at that time to remember the genocide that took place in Darfur. Is that what this world wants?[53]

Wolf's plea to Congress once more drew on the evocative imagery of Rwanda. From this invocation he also inferred Rwanda's composite meanings – the guilt of failure and the spectre of genocide.

Rwanda's meaning and influence became a recurrent theme throughout Congressional debate on Darfur. On 29 April, speaking on a proposed joint resolution to declare the Darfur crisis 'genocide', Senator Edward Kennedy (D-MA) reflected:

> It has been ten years since the Rwanda genocide. A decade ago . . . the international community was silent. We did not stop the deaths of 800,000 Tutsis and politically moderate Hutu, in spite of our commitment that genocide must never again darken the annals of human history. . . . Sadly, we may now be repeating the same mistake in Sudan.[54]

Speaking on the same resolution several days later, Jon Corzine (D-NJ) declared:

> UN Secretary Kofi Annan has compared the genocide in Rwanda ten years ago to events that are now unfolding. . . . So I hope by speaking out today and as we go forward that this Darfur situation will not fall off the radar screen. This is a real risk of genocide evolving.[55]

The Darfur debate reached fever pitch in both houses through June and July, as Congress debated in earnest whether to declare Darfur 'genocide' under a Concurrent

---

[53]Frank Wolf, 'Stop Genocide in Sudan', United States House of Representatives, 4 May 2004, available at: http://thomas.loc.gov/ (accessed 14 May 2006).

[54]Edward Kennedy, 'On Sudan', United States Senate, 29 April 2004, available at: http://thomas.loc.gov/cgi-bin/query/C?r108:./temp/~r108VZPSOC (accessed 14 May 2006).

[55]Jon Stevens Corzine, 'Sudan Darfur Crisis', United States Senate, 6 May 2004, available at: http://thomas.loc.gov/cgi-bin/query/C?r108:./temp/~r108th6Z5h (accessed 14 May 2006).

Congressional resolution (H. Con. Res. 467, S. Con. Res. 133).[56] The same message of Rwandan memories and meanings was echoed in statements and speeches from both sides of the House and Senate as the debate wore on. Speakers repeated variations of the same conflation of meanings inferred by Rwanda then permeating debate throughout the international community – failure and genocide.[57] Finally, on 22 July, after two months spent in debate around the harsh memories and meanings of Rwanda, both houses declared Darfur to constitute genocide – the House by a unanimous vote of 422 to 0, the Senate by a voice vote.[58] In an emphatic conflation of Darfur and its perceived predecessor ten years previously, chairman of the House Subcommittee on Africa, Ed Royce (R-CA), declared after the vote, 'I fully support this resolution's determination that genocide is occurring in Sudan, as it played out in Rwanda ten years ago!'[59]

For Royce, and indeed for many in Congress who spoke in the debate, the resolution was not just a statement about genocide in Darfur. Rather, strikingly consistent within the Congressional debate is the retrospective regret for failure to invoke the term genocide around Rwanda. Following this regret is the recurrent expression of fear of repeating the same failure in Darfur. Taken together, the fear of failure and the memory of past regret over Rwanda provide one of the key arguments motivating Congress's genocide resolution on Darfur.

Following pressure from this joint Congressional resolution, and at the urging of former International Criminal Tribunal for Rwanda (ICTR) prosecutor Pierre-Richard Prosper, the State Department organized its own mission to the region. The investigation drew on experts recruited by the Coalition for International Justice (CIJ), who conducted over a thousand interviews with Darfurian refugees in Chad. Drawing on the mission's findings, Secretary of State Colin Powell was sufficiently compelled to announce before the Senate Foreign Relations Committee on 9 September that 'genocide has been committed in Darfur and . . . the Government of Sudan and the Jingaweit bear responsibility – and that genocide may still be occurring'.[60] Pressed into action by Congressional concern, the administration soon adopted its own determination of genocide in Darfur. Though the memory of Rwanda was never directly invoked in the administration's assessment, its influence on Congress was critical to building the necessary political will for the administration to ask, and answer, the genocide question in Darfur.

---

[56]US Congress HCON 467 IH, 24 June 2004, 'Declaring Genocide in Darfur, Sudan', adopted by United States House of Representatives, available at: www.genocidewatch.org/SudanUSHouseResolutionofGenocide-22July2004.htm (accessed 14 May 2006).

[57]See, for example, speeches from Thomas Harkin, 'Executive Session', United States Senate, 6 May 2004, available at: http://thomas.loc.gov/cgi-bin/query/F?r108:132:./temp/~r108MPOiEk:e144737: (accessed 14 May 2006).

[58]Charles Corey, 'US Congress Terms Situation in Darfur "Genocide" ', US Department of State, 22 July 2004, available at: http://usinfo.state.gov/is/Archive/2004/Jul/26–233176.html (accessed 12 July 2006).

[59]Quoted in Corey, 'US Congress Terms Situation in Darfur "Genocide" '.

[60]Colin Powell, 'The Crisis in Darfur', US Department of State, 9 September 2004, available at: www.state.gov/secretary/rm/36042pf.htm (accessed 15 September 2004).

Determining Genocide – Dealing with Darfur, Seeing Rwanda

What conclusions might be drawn from the international community's perception of and engagement with Darfur? The genocide debate was inaugurated by the Rwandan genocide anniversary; it had no independent existence prior to this 'trigger' event. Moreover, the genocide debate was repeatedly raised in connection to this powerful memory. In this respect, the genocide debate appears to have been invoked through and initially triggered by the Rwandan analogy, along with the spectre of international failure.

For Alex Bellamy and Paul Williams, however, the invocation of 'genocide' precedes and explains the emergence of Rwanda within the Darfur debate. According to the authors, as the perception of Darfur shifted from humanitarian crisis to security concern, 'inevitably, the use of the word "genocide" invited comparisons with the slaughter in Rwanda during 1994 and highlighted the need to avoid a repeat of international society's feeble response there'.[61] Bellamy and Williams' explanation presumes that the 'genocide' issue arose prior to the invocation of Rwanda. However, this sequence of events confuses the order of precedence. The Rwandan analogy played an integral part in transforming the Darfur debate from humanitarian crisis into an extreme human rights and security concern. This claim is true for all of our primary areas of investigation – whether at the UN, in the NGO community, through the media, or within the US policy-making machine. Given this prevalence within debate over Darfur, how much influence has the Rwandan analogical perception had upon policy in these different arenas?

Rwanda, as we have observed, was frequently invoked in conjunction with its core meanings – the international failure to act and the prospect of genocide. These meanings, and their associated regrets and fears invoked by elite policy-makers and attributed to Darfur in public debate, raised the spectre of genocide and failure. Through this analogical prism, some policy actions bearing superficial similarities to policy processes that occurred in the Rwandan case may have stoked these fears. Through the spring and summer of 2004, as we have variously observed, both Rwanda 1994 and Darfur 2004 seemed to share an emphasis on securing a peace agreement, slow international awareness and attention to the conflict, and lengthy Security Council debate with few material enforcement mechanisms.[62] These perceived similarities reinforced public and policy-maker fears that the conflict unfolding in Darfur might also share other similarities with Rwanda.

Even the way in which the term 'genocide' itself was used – or not used – became part of the pattern of foreboding similarities between the two events. 'This is similar to the situation that had existed over Rwanda', wrote Linda Melvern in an *International Relations* article in March 2006, 'when in July 1994, faced with overwhelming proof of genocide, the Council thought of one action: to create a committee of experts to "evaluate the evidence"'.[63] According to Hugo Slim's review of the initial international

[61]Bellamy and Williams, 'The Responsibility to Protect and the Crisis in Darfur', p. 31.

[62]See, for example, Hugo Slim, 'Dithering Over Darfur? A Preliminary Review of the International Response', *International Affairs*, 80(5), 2004, pp. 811–28. Council on Foreign Relations, *Giving Meaning to 'Never Again'*, p. iii. Linda Melvern, 'Rwanda and Darfur: The Media and the Security Council', *International Relations*, 20(1), 2006, pp. 93–104.

[63]Melvern, 'Rwanda and Darfur', p. 102.

response to Darfur in this respect, 'another common feature between the two conflicts has been the reluctance in the international community to use the "G-word," genocide. . . . as it was in Rwanda'.[64] As Salih Booker and Ann-Louise Colgan of Africa Action argued in *The Nation* in the spring of 2004, for example, 'we should have learned from Rwanda that to stop genocide, Washington must first say the word'.[65] Resistance to the term 'genocide' was one powerfully symbolic expression of international failure to act in Rwanda. As such, the pressure to deploy the term in reference to Darfur became an equally powerful symbolic expression of action within the international community.

For Melvern and others, the international community's failure to use the term 'genocide' in Rwanda was a deliberate omission. Consequently, for these same critics, resistance to the term in Darfur was seen through the symbolic meaning of the term in relation to the Rwandan genocide. After the failure to use the term during the Rwanda crisis, the absence of its use around Darfur became in its own right a frightening similarity of omission. This omission was viewed as a denial of a presumed 'genocidal' reality. After Rwanda, these commentators seemed to imply, the refusal to use the term 'genocide' echoed the perceived conspiracy of genocide denial that had occurred during the Rwanda genocide, and thus was in fact evidence of the presence of genocide in Darfur.

Far from an act of bad faith, however, it was the memory of Rwanda that seems to have compelled the international community to consider the genocide question to the extent that it has. It was the spectre of similarities to the past, and its associated fear of repeating past failures, which in many instances accompanied the key policy debate: 'Is Darfur genocide?' In this respect, numerous and serious efforts have been made to determine whether Darfur fits this extreme category of violence on its own terms. Based on several interpretations of criteria laid out in the 1948 Genocide Convention, Darfur has repeatedly and in different state and non-governmental forums been determined a potential, if not actual, genocide. In July 2004, the Foreign Policy Centre in London determined that 'there was one side perpetrating a genocide and their actions were in stark contrast to the low-intensity military operations of the other side, the SLA'.[66] The US Department of State determination of genocide was made after an extensive field investigation of the violence conducted by the Coalition for International Justice (CIJ) over the summer of 2004.[67] Drawing on evidence compiled through extensive interviews with Darfurian refugees in Chad, the mission then determined that the violence in Darfur was in violation of the Genocide Convention. Claus Kress has also provided a methodical legal analysis of genocide claims in the *Journal of International Criminal Justice*.[68] Physicians for Human Rights (PHR) declared in June 2004 that a 'genocidal process is unfolding in Darfur, Sudan'.[69] This statement was adopted after a careful

---

[64]Slim, 'Dithering Over Darfur?', p. 811.

[65]Quoted in Scott Straus, 'Darfur and the Genocide Debate', *Foreign Affairs*, 84(1), 2005, p. 123.

[66]Austin and Koppelman, 'Darfur and Genocide', p. 27.

[67]Totten and Markusen, 'Research Note', p. 286.

[68]Claus Kress, 'The Darfur Report and Genocidal Intent', *Journal of International Criminal Justice*, 3, 2005, pp. 562–78.

[69]Physicians for Human Rights (PHR), 'PHR Calls for Intervention to Save Lives in Sudan: Field Team Compiles Indicators of Genocide', 23 June 2004, available at: http://www.phrusa.org/research/sudan/pdf/sudan_genocide_report.pdf (accessed 4 June 2006), p. 1.

dissection of Darfur's violence against a series of six indicators of genocide, 'all of which indicate organized intent to effect group annihilation'.[70]

These claims have been made with careful attention to the context-specific details of the Darfurian case, its history, actors, and methods of violence as they might be interpreted within the legal boundaries of the 1948 Genocide Convention. Even within this context, however, many groups have in the end not been convinced of the appropriateness of the genocide label. Notably, the September 2004 Report of the International Commission of Inquiry on Darfur to the UN Secretary-General, in addition to reports from the African Union, Human Rights Watch and Amnesty International, have all examined Darfur's genocide credentials, and elected to shy away from the term.[71] As the International Commission of Inquiry reasoned in its negative determination:

> the crucial element of genocidal intent appears to be missing, at least as far as the central Government authorities are concerned. Generally speaking the policy of attacking, killing and forcibly displacing members of some tribes does not evince a specific intent to annihilate, in whole or in part, a group distinguished on racial, ethnic, national or religious grounds.[72]

As such, the debate around whether Darfur constitutes genocide may have been aroused by meanings and fears generated by the Rwandan analogy, but within this debate, arguments for and against the determination of genocide have largely been conducted according to the unique characteristics of the Darfur case. The effect or output of the Rwanda analogy was felt most keenly in eliciting this policy debate.

What do these observations mean? In terms of its influence as an analogy, Rwanda shaped perception insofar as it helped raise the spectre of genocide in Darfur. Though it raised the genocide question in relation to Darfur, Rwanda's identity was not always uncritically transferred onto the Darfur crisis. Darfur was not seen to be genocide because of its association to Rwanda. Rather, the determination of genocide in Darfur was conducted in many quarters according to criteria independent of the memory of Rwanda. Thus, Rwanda's primary influence was in framing Darfur within the genocide debate. Furthermore, the urgency of this debate was fuelled by one consistent set of recurrent meanings Rwanda held for many policy-makers, academics, humanitarian advocates and journalists: namely, regret over the failure to name and stop the Rwandan genocide, coupled with the fear of recurrent failure today. However, the terms upon which this determination was being made were in large part determined by the specific features and characteristics unique to the Darfur case. While the invocation of Rwanda may have raised the profile of the genocide question, it is not the contention here that the situation in Darfur was in every instance perceived as genocide solely or even primarily *because* it was associated with Rwanda. The invocation of Rwanda facilitated a discussion of genocide in Darfur, and even fed moral pressure to represent Darfur as

---

[70]PHR, 'PHR Calls for Intervention', p. 4.

[71]United Nations, 'Report of the International Commission of Inquiry on Darfur to the United Nations Secretary-General', 18 September 2004, available at: www.ohchr.org/english/darfur.htm (accessed 17 May 2006). Council on Foreign Relations, *Giving Meaning to 'Never Again'*, p. 18.

[72]United Nations, 'Report of the International Commission of Inquiry on Darfur'.

genocide. This invocation did not, however, always determine that the genocide label would be applied.

To summarize therefore, the emergence of the Rwanda analogy does appear to co-incide and converge with several critical shifts in the international community's treatment of Darfur. Most notably, the memory of Rwanda arose alongside the changing terms of debate, and rising attention to Darfur's violent roots, rather than its humanitarian effects. The tenth anniversary of the Rwandan genocide merged public awareness around Rwanda and Darfur into a single narrative stream of 'failure' and 'genocide'. Framed within the memories and meanings of Rwanda, Darfur was perceived in the international community less as a humanitarian crisis and increasingly as a prospective genocide. The genocide debate among global media, NGOs and UN and US policy-makers was conducted through the memory of and seeming similarities to the international community's failure in Rwanda. As the 2004 Council on Foreign Relations review clearly summarizes, 'the anniversary recall[ed] the horrific way in which some 800,000 Rwandans lost their lives and serv[ed] as an unforgettable reminder of the international community's failure to prevent that genocide', a memory made all too clear in the recriminatory statements from the US Congress, the UN Secretary-General and media and NGO reports.[73] 'This failure', the Council concludes, 'pervades the current consciousness as the tenor rises over how to react to credible reports of ethnic cleansing in Sudan'.[74]

The genocide debate in relation to Darfur, though useful insofar as it drew attention to government involvement, was fuelled by a powerful sense of failure deeply ensconced within the memory and experience of the Rwandan genocide. However, the failure to call the situation in Rwanda genocide was a failure for a particular time and place. Rwanda invokes the memory of failure. This failure was expressed at the time in a powerful and particular way – namely the reluctance to utter the term 'genocide', with all the uncertain legal and moral responsibilities raised with the term.[75] Subsequently, the subject of Rwanda, when raised around Darfur today, invokes these meanings of failure, compelling those touched by that sense of failure to act. And yet, from out of the very particular way international failure was expressed around the Rwanda crisis, this memory also encourages that action to assume a very particular form: namely, to confront and apply the term 'genocide'.

Conclusion

This article opened with the premise that the Rwandan genocide was a prominent historical referent and framing mechanism for the Darfur crisis. The tenth anniversary of the 1994 Rwandan genocide replayed the message of 'never again' before an attentive

---

[73]Council on Foreign Relations, *Giving Meaning to 'Never Again'*, p. 1.

[74]Council on Foreign Relations, *Giving Meaning to 'Never Again'*, p. 1.

[75]In his review of the Atrocities Documentation Project, Gregory Stanton examines the reasons why many, particularly in the United States, have resisted application of the term 'genocide' to the conflict in Darfur. His examination provides a brief review of how the State Department in particular sustained its resistance to the term during the Rwandan genocide, and the extensive arguments developed by the Atrocities Documentation Project to counter the enduring scepticism of those who would use legal arguments to 'deny' the existence of genocide in Darfur. See Gregory Stanton, 'Proving Genocide in Darfur: The Atrocities Documentation Project and Resistance to its Findings', Genocide Watch, available at: www.genocidewatch.org/about genocide/stantonprovinggenindarfur.htm (accessed 22 March 2007).

international audience. Through the spring and summer of 2004, Darfur emerged as a prominent cause for international concern out of this reflective context. The Rwandan genocide anniversary was used by many international observers to frame, and give new impetus to, action in a previously marginalized conflict. The commitment of 'never again' which many in the international community so readily reasserted after the Rwandan genocide was put to the test against a crisis framed in terms of yet another 'Rwanda' perceived to be unfolding in Darfur, Sudan.

Clearly, the memory and meanings of Rwanda are tightly woven into the current Darfur debate. In the face of the horrible suffering experienced by so many directly affected by the war in Darfur, why should these abstract questions matter? They matter because this narrative-weaving may have an effect on the resultant policy fabric, with very direct effects on the lives of Darfurians. By perceiving Darfur through the twin fears of failure and genocide, diplomats, bureaucrats, journalists, activists and citizens have manufactured a policy discussion that is shaped in part by the woven strands of the Rwandan genocide. This discussion favours or enables some policy options, to the omission of others. Insofar as the memory of Rwanda may have played into our perception and treatment of Darfur we must firstly be wary of this influence, and secondly question whether it is likely to help or hinder a successful and effective policy response. In this respect, the emergence of the Rwandan anniversary and the language of genocide invoked by it changed the visibility of Darfur within the international community, with both positive and negative effects.

On the positive side, by framing the Darfur crisis within the Rwandan genocide anniversary, Darfur was represented less as a marginal humanitarian crisis and more as a prominent human rights disaster. The genocide debate within this Rwandan anniversary context broadened the scope of attention to the Sudanese government's active role in the region. Consequently, policy debate around Darfur has focused on both the civil war and the targeted killing dynamics of the violence. This, it is important to note, is in stark *contrast* to the Rwanda experience, in which the international community's policy discussion through the month of April was directed exclusively at ending the civil war violence, to the tragic neglect of the concurrent genocide. At the time, in April 1994, policy debate on the UN Security Council centered on securing a ceasefire between the civil war combatants, the likely result of which would have freed Rwandan government resources to expedite the genocide. In the Darfur conflict today, the debate has progressed rather differently. The Security Council has raised the possibility of sanctions against Sudan, though at the time of writing it has failed to build a consensus on their application.[76] It has initiated criminal investigations of the conflict's chief architects and human rights abusers, and has agreed to bring their cases before the International Criminal Court.[77] It has invoked travel and financial sanctions on specific individual actors.[78] While the cumulative effects of these policies have as yet failed to bring a conclusive end to the conflict, the current perception of the crisis is far more attuned to the government's involvement – an element which will be a critical consideration in any ultimately successful peaceful resolution.

---

[76]United Nations, Document S/RES/1564 (2004), 18 September 2004.

[77]United Nations, Document S/RES/1593 (2005), 31 March 2005.

[78]United Nations, Document S/RES/1591 (2005), 29 March 2005. United Nations, Document S/RES/1672 (2006), 25 April 2006.

While some useful policy lessons may well have been drawn from the Rwandan experience, the spectre of international failure raised out of the Rwandan analogy also misdirected attention in the international community in significant ways: the Rwandan genocide anniversary provided a context for debate in which both the Darfur conflict, and even the Rwandan genocide itself, were sorely misrepresented. First, international failure in relation to the Rwandan genocide was interpreted as a failure of omission rather than commission. As such, the memory turned attention away from the policy mistakes made during the Rwandan genocide and towards the imperative to act, without offering any concrete guidance as to the form such action should take, short of redressing the omission of Rwanda to call the genocide by its proper name. This debate, once invoked, has done little to help build international consensus and common action in relation to the crisis. As we have seen, the genocide debate in Darfur has been a divisive one. To the degree that some multilateral action has been built towards addressing the genocide, this has occurred without consensus around the genocide question as such.

Secondly, pressure within the international community to adopt the genocide label risks fundamentally undermining the effectiveness of the term. Indeed, the US Congress and the Bush administration were quick to adopt this determination, largely on the guilty inspiration of their failure to invoke the term during the Rwandan genocide. This determination has not, however, drastically altered America's policy approach towards Darfur. The US government continues to address the crisis through multilateral forums such as the UN Security Council in which the genocide question remains a contested claim, both among council member states and within the institutional bodies of the UN itself. In this respect, the invocation of the term has not necessarily elicited a novel international consensus, nor encouraged a significantly more robust policy response. Rather, where there has been policy consensus amongst member states on the UN Security Council, it has occurred entirely without agreement on the genocide term, and its presumed rallying force for collective action. Far from a central part of this consensus, as we have observed, the genocide question is a point of contention within the international community.

At the same time, we must be cautious about how we interpret opposition to the genocide label. Resistance is not necessarily indicative of a deliberate denial of an otherwise obvious genocide reality. Scepticism has been expressed in many different quarters and by a number of individuals and institutions across the international community, grounded in genuine engagement with and interpretation of the Genocide Convention. Consequently, resistance within the international community to the term genocide should not be interpreted as a conspiracy of silence. This is not to deny the wilful resistance and obstruction to the term at the time of the Rwandan genocide. If there is resistance to the term, it may well be because the Darfur crisis did not, through the spring and summer of 2004 when the genocide question first appeared and was most hotly debated, constitute genocide.

The invocation of Rwanda as a meaningful policy referent through the spring and summer of 2004 helped raise the profile of the Darfur crisis within the international agenda. However, debate around Rwanda and its component meanings has also at times distracted international attention from meaningful policy debate, and the formation of a common agenda for action towards what is, undoubtedly, an intolerable humanitarian disaster demanding immediate international collective action. Certainly, we must hold on to the lessons of the past. In this vein, the international community is right to critically reflect upon what could have been done, and indeed what was not done, to end the Rwandan genocide. However, these same failures, and their perceived remedies, do not translate with predictable and formulaic application into the policy choices and challenges we face in Darfur today.

Genocide is a powerful term, infused with moral and legal gravitas that, once invoked, can be used to compel those who use it to action. Consequently, caution should be exercised over invoking the term in particular cases, lest we undermine its force and influence. It is out of respect for this term that this debate is so important – it is to ensure that we are invoking it not only in the right place, but for the right reasons. The failure to name Rwanda's conflict 'genocide' was specific to a time and a place in history. If Darfur is to assume this label, it must not be to redress the tragic memories and failures of an immutable past. This is the danger presented by the memory and meanings of Rwanda for Darfur today.

Source: Darren Brunk, "Dissecting Darfur: Anatomy of a Genocide Debate," *International Relations*, Volume 22, pp. 25–40. Copyright © 2008. Reprinted by permission of Sage.

REFERENCES

Introduction

1. Bettelheim, B. (1980). *Surviving and Other Essays.* New York: Vintage.
2. Goffman, E. (1961). *Asylums: Essays on the Social Situation of Mental Patients and Other Inmates.* New York: Anchor Books, Doubleday.
3. Marcus, P. (1999). *Autonomy in the Extreme Situation: Bruno Bettelheim, the Nazi Concentration Camps and Mass Society.* Connecticut: Praeger.
4. Rosenberg, B., Gerver, I. and Howton, F. W. (1964). *Mass Society in Crisis: Social Problems and Social Pathology.* New York: Macmillan.
5. Wallace, S. (1971). *Total Institutions.* United States of America: Transaction.

Chapter One

1. Bettelheim, B. (1980). *Surviving and Other Essays.* New York: Vintage.
2. Davies, C. (1989). Goffman's Concept of the Total Institution: Criticisms and Revisions. *Journal of Human Studies.* 12, 77–95.
3. Des Pres, T. (1976). *The Survivor: An Anatomy of Life in the Death Camps.* New York: Oxford University Press.
4. Giddens, A. (1991). *Modernity and Self Identity: Self and Society in the Late Modern Age.* California: Stanford University Press.
5. Goffman, E. (1961). *Asylums.* New York: Anchor Books, Doubleday.
6. Krell, R. (1997). *Medical and Psychological Effects of Concentration Camps on Holocaust Survivors.* New Brunswick, NJ: Transaction.
7. Langer, L. (1982). *Versions of Survival.* Albany: State University of New York Press.
8. Marcus, P. (1999). *Autonomy in the Extreme Situation: Bruno Bettelheim, the Nazi Concentration Camps and Mass Society.* Connecticut: Praeger.
9. McEwen, C. A. (1980). Continuities in the Study of Total and Nontotal Institutions. *Annual Review of Sociology.* 6, 143–185.

10. Miller, J. A. and Miller, R. (October 1987). Jeremy Bentham's Panoptic Device. *M.I.T. Press.* 41, 3–29.
11. O'Farrell, C. (2005). *Michel Foucault.* London: Sage.
12. Pytell, T. (2007). Extreme Experience, Psychological Insight, and Holocaust Perception: Reflections on Bettelheim and Frankl. *Psychoanalytic Psychology.* 24(4), 641–657.
13. Rosenberg, B., Gerver, I. and Howton, F. W. (1964). *Mass Society in Crisis: Social Problems and Social Pathology.* New York: Macmillan.
14. ____. (1971). *Mass Society in Crisis: Social Problems and Social Pathology.* (2nd ed.). New York: Macmillan.
15. Volpato, C. and Contarello, A. (1999). Towards a Social Psychology of Extreme Situations: Primo Levy's *If This Is a Man* and Social Identity Theory. *European Journal of Social Psychology.* 29, 239–258.

Chapter Two

1. Adler, H. G. (1958). Ideas Toward a Sociology of the Concentration Camp. *American Journal of Sociology.* 63(5), 513–522.
2. Andrews, W. L. and Gates, H. Jr. (2000). *Slave Narratives.* New York: The Library of America.
3. Blassingame, J. (1972). *The Slave Community: Plantation Life in the Antebellum South.* New York: Oxford University Press.
4. Davis, D. B. (2006). *Inhuman Bondage: The Rise and Fall of Slavery in the New World.* New York: Oxford University Press.
5. Elkins, S. (1959). *Slavery: A Problem in American Institutional and Intellectual Life.* New York: Grosset and Dunlap.
6. Encyclopaedia Britannica Online, s. v. Frederick Douglass. http://www.britannica.com/EBchecked/topic/170246/Frederick-Douglass. Accessed on November 6, 2011.

7. Kolchin, P. (1993). *American Slavery: 1619–1877*. New York: Hill and Wang.

8. Lester, J. (1968). *To Be A Slave*. New York: Scholastic.

9. Stampp, K. (1963). *The Peculiar Institution: Slavery in the Antebellum South*. New York: Knopf.

10. Tadman, M. (1996). *Speculators and Slaves: Masters, Traders, and Slaves in the Old South*. Madison: University of Wisconsin Press.

Chapter Three

1. Bettelheim, B. (1943). Individual and Mass Behavior in Extreme Situations. *Journal of Abnormal and Social Psychology*. 38(4), 417–452.

2. Bettelheim, B. (1980). *Surviving and Other Essays*. New York: Vintage.

3. Dawidowicz, L. (1976). *The War Against the Jews 1933–1945*. New York: Bantam Books.

4. Des Pres, T. (1976). *The Survivor: An Anatomy of Life in Death Camps*. New York: Oxford University Press.

5. Elkins, S. (1959). *Slavery: A Problem in American Institutional and Intellectual Life*. New York. Grosset and Dunlap.

6. Frankl, V. (1959/1985). *Man's Search for Meaning*. New York: Washington Square Press, Pocket Books.

7. Goldenberg, M. (1996). Lessons from Gentle Heroism: Women's Holocaust Narratives. *Annals of the American Academy of Political and Social Science*. 548, 78–93.

8. Levi, P. (1958/1996). *Survival in Auschwitz*. New York: Simon and Schuster.

9. Sofsky, W. (1997). *The Order of Terror: The Concentration Camp*. Translated by Templer, W. New Jersey: Princeton University Press.

10. United States Holocaust Memorial Museum. Concentration Camps, 1933–1939. *Holocaust Encyclopedia*. http://www.ushmm.org/wlc/en/article.php?ModuleId=10005263. Accessed on July 27, 2010.

11. Yad Vashem. The World of the Camps; Labor and Concentration Camps. http://www1.yadvashem.org/yv/en/holocaust/about/06/camps.asp. Accessed on July 21, 2010.

12. Yad Vashem. Concentration Camps. http://www1.yadvashem.org/odot_pdf/Microsoft%20Word%20-%205925.pdf. Accessed on July 27, 2010.

13. Yad Vashem. Muselmann. http://www1.yadvashem.org/odot_pdf/Microsoft%20Word%20-%206474.pdf. Accessed on July 27, 2010.

14. Yad Vashem. The Implementation of the Final Solution; Auschwitz-Birkenau Extermination Camp. http://www1.yadvashem.org/yv/en/holocaust/about/05/auschwitz_birkenau.asp. Accessed on July 27, 2010.

15. Yad Vashem. The Implementation of the Final Solution; The Death Camps. http://www1.yadvashem.org/yv/en/holocaust/about/05/death_camps.asp. Accessed on July 27, 2010.

Chapter Four

1. Arcaro, T. (1984, February). Self-identity of Female Prisoners: The Moral Career of the Inmate. *Humanity and Society*. 8, 73–89.

2. Arnold, R. (1994). Black Women in Prison: The Price of Resistance. In M. B. Zinn and B. T. Dill (Eds.), *Women of Color in U.S. Society* (pp. 171–184). Philadelphia: Temple University Press.

3. Asch, S. (1951). The Effects of Group Pressure upon the Modification and Distortions of Judgment. In H. Guetzkow (Ed.), *Groups, Leadership and Men.* (pp. 117–190) Pittsburgh: Carnegie Press.

4. Austin, J. and Irwin, J. (2001). *It's About Time: America's Imprisonment Binge*. (3rd ed.). Belmont, CA: Wadsworth.

5. Barlow, H. D. (2000). *Criminal Justice in America*. Upper Saddle River, NJ: Prentice Hall.

6. Bartollas, C., Miller, S. J. and Dinitz, S. (1976a). *Juvenile Victimization: The Institutional Paradox*. New York: Halsted Press. (a Sage Publications book).

7. ____. (1976b). The White Victim in a Black Institution. In M. Riedel and P. A. Vales (Eds.), *Treating the Offender: Problems and Issues.* (pp. 97–108) New York: Praeger.

8. Behan, B. (2000). *Borstal Boy.* Boston: Godine.

9. Belknap, J. (1996). *The Invisible Woman: Gender, Crime, and Justice.* Belmont, CA: Wadsworth.

10. Bentham, J. (1843). *Works,* ed. Bowring, IV.

11. ____. (1791). *Panopticon.* London: T. Payne.

12. Bettelheim, B. (1960). *The Informed Heart.* Glencoe, IL: Free Press.

13. ____. (1975). *A Home for the Heart.* New York: Bantam Books.

14. Bowker, L. H. (1980). *Prison Victimization.* New York: Elsevier.

15. Carlen, P. (1983). *Women's Imprisonment: A Study in Social Control.* London: Routledge/Kegan Paul.

16. Chesney-Lind, M. and Pollock, J. (1995). Women's Prisons: Equality with a Vengeance. In A. Merlo and J. Pollock (Eds.), *Women, Law, and Social Control* (pp. 157–175). Boston: Allyn and Bacon.

17. Clark, J. (1995, September). The Impact of the Prison Environment on Mothers. *Prison Journal.* 75(3), 306–329.

18. Conover, T. (2000). *New Jack: Guarding Sing Sing.* New York: Random House.

19. Daragahi, B. and Katz, B. L., Iran Says Woman Won't be Stoned to Death. http://articles.latimes.com/2010/jul/09/world/la-fg-iran-stoning -20100710. Accessed on July 9, 2010.

20. Davis, A. J. (1968). Sexual Assaults in the Philadelphia Prison System and Sheriff's Vans. *Trans-Action.* 6, 8–12.

21. Dostoyevski, F. (2006). Ballads. In F. R. Shapiro, (Ed.), *The Yale Book of Quotations* (p. 210). New Haven, CT: Yale University Press.

22. Durkheim, E. (1938). *The Rules of Sociological Method.* The Free Press.

23. Erikson, K. T. (1962). Social Problems. *Spring.* 9(4), 307–314. University of California Press.

24. Faith, K. (1993). *Unruly Women: The Politics of Confinement and Resistance.* Vancouver, Canada: Press Gang.

25. Farrington, K. (1992). The Modern Prison as Total Institution? Public Perception versus Objective Reality. *Crime and Delinquency.* (38), 6–26.

26. Fisher, S. (1961). Social Organization in a Correctional Residence. *Pacific Sociological Review.* 4, 87–93.

27. Fletcher, B., Shaver, L. and Moon, D. (Eds.) (1993). *Women Prisoners: A Forgotten Population.* Westport, CT: Praeger.

28. Fogel, C. (1993). Hard Time: The Stressful Nature of Incarceration for Women. *Issues in Mental Health Nursing.* 14, 367–377.

29. Foucault, M. (1979). *Discipline and Punish: The Birth of the Prison.* New York: Vintage.

30. Gardner, P., Sadri, M., and Williams, J. L. (2008). *Jonestown as a Total Institution: Why Some People Chose Death over Escape from Peoples Temple.* Unpublished manuscript (pp. 1–8).

31. Giallombardo, R. (1966a). Social Roles in a Prison for Women. *Social Problems.* 13(3), 268–287.

32. ____. (1966b). *Society of Women: A Study of a Women's Prison.* New York: John Wiley and Sons.

33. Girshick, L. (1997). *No Safe Haven: Stories of Women in Prison.* Boston: Northeastern University Press.

34. Goffman, E. (1961). *Asylums: Essays on the Social Situation of Mental Patients and Other Inmates.* Garden City, NY: Anchor Books.

35. Goffman, E. (1961). *Asylums.* New York: Anchor Books, Doubleday.

36. Goldhammer, J. (1996). *Under the Influence: The Destructive Effects of Group Dynamics.* New York: Prometheus Books.

37. Gover, A., MacKenzie, D. L. and Armstrong, G. S. (2000). Importation and Deprivation Explanations of Juveniles' Adjustment to Correctional Facilities. *International Journal of Offender Therapy and Comparative Criminology.* 44, 450–467.

38. Hassine, V. (1999). *Life without Parole: Living in Prison Today.* (2nd ed.). Los Angeles: Roxbury.

39. Heffernan, E. (1972). *Making It in Prison: The Square, The Cool, and The Life.* New York: Wiley.

40. Henriques, Z. (1996). Imprisoned Mothers and Their Children: Separation-Reunion Syndrome. *Women and Criminal Justice.* 8(1), 77–95.

41. Irwin, J. (1970). *The Felon.* Englewood Cliffs, NJ: Prentice Hall.

42. Irwin, J. and Cressey, D. (1962). Thieves, Convicts, and the Inmate Culture. *Social Problems.* (10), 142–155.

43. Jacobs, J. E. (1994). *Classics of Criminology.* Prospect Heights, IL: Waveland Press.

44. Johnson, R. and Toch, H. (1982). *The Pains of Imprisonment.* Beverly Hills, CA: Sage.

45. Johnson, R. and Toch, H. (2000). *Crime and Punishment: Inside Views.* Los Angeles: Roxbury.

46. Kahalas, L. (1998). *Snake Dance: Unravelling the Mysteries of Jonestown.* New York: Red Robin Press.

47. Langer, S. (1980). The Rahway State Prison Lifers' Group: A Critical Analysis. PhD Dissertation. New York: City University of New York.

48. Larson, J. and Nelson, J. (1984). Women, Friendship, and Adaptation to Prison. *Journal of Criminal Justice.* 12, 601–615.

49. Layton, D. (1998). *Seductive Poison: A Jonestown Survivor's Story of Life and Death in the Peoples Temple.* New York: Anchor Books.

50. Lindt, G. (1981). Journeys to Jonestown: Accounts and Interpretations of the Rise and Demise of the Peoples Temple. *Union Seminary Quarterly Review.* 37(1 & 2) Fall/Winter 1981–1982, 159–174.

51. Lockwood, D. (1980). *Prison Sexual Violence.* New York: Elsevier.

52. Loisel, G. (1912), *Histoire des menageries*, II. Paris.

53. Lombardo, L. X. (1989). *Guards Imprisoned: Correctional Officers at Work.* (2nd ed.). Cincinnati, OH: Anderson.

54. Lord, E. (1995, June). A Prison Superintendent's Perspective on Women in Prison. *Prison Journal.* 75(2), 257–269.

55. MacKenzie, D., Robinson, J. and Campbell, C. (1989, June). Long-Term Incarceration of Female Offenders: Prison Adjustment and Coping. *Criminal Justice and Behavior,* 16(2), 223–238.

56. MacKinnon, C. (1987). *Feminism Unmodified: Discourses on Life and Law.* Cambridge: Harvard University Press.

57. Mahan, S. (1984). Imposition of Despair: An Ethnography of Women in Prison. *Justice Quarterly.* 1, 357–384.

58. Mancinelli, I., Comparelli, A., Girardi, P. and Tatarelli, R. (2002). Mass Suicide: Historical and Psychodynamic Considerations. *Suicide & Life-Threatening Behavior.* 32(1), 91–100.

59. Martin, R., Mutchnick, R. J. and Austin, W. T. (1990). *Criminological Thought: Pioneers Past and Present.* New York: Macmillan.

60. Masters, J. J. (1997). *Finding Freedom: Writings from Death Row.* Junction City, CA: Padma.

61. McGehee, F. (2002). November 19 tape adds perplexing postscript: A commentary by Fielding McGehee, *The Jonestone Report.* 4.

62. Milgram, S. (2004 [1974]). *Obedience and Authority: An Experimental View.* New York: Harper Collins.

63. Miller, J. A. and Miller, R. (October 1987). Jeremy Bentham's Panoptic Device. *M.I.T. Press.* 41, 3–29.

64. Moore, A. (1978) "Last Words." http://jonestown.sdsu.edu/AboutJonestown/PrimarySources/annie.htm.

65. Moore, R. (1985). *A Sympathetic History of Jonestown: The Moore Family Involvement in Peoples Temple.* Lewiston/Queenston: The Edwin Mellen Press.

66. Moore, R. (2006). http://jonestown.sdsu.edu/, Rebecca Moore, site manager; F. McGehee, archivist.

67. Moyer, I. (1984, March). Deceptions and Realities of Life in Women's Prisons. *Prison Journal.* 64, 45–56.

68. Nordland, R. (2010). In Bold Display, Taliban Order Stoning Deaths. http://www.nytimes.com/2010/08/17/world/asia/17stoning.html. Accessed on August 16, 2010.

69. Peltier, L. (1999). *Prison Writings: My Life is My Sun Dance.* New York: St. Martin's Press.

70. Prokes, M. (1979). Statement at his suicide/press conference. http://jonestown.sdsu.edu/AboutJonestown/PrimarySources/Prokes_statement.htm.

71. Propper, A. (1982, May). Make-believe Families and Homosexuality among Imprisoned Girls. *Criminology*. 20(1), 127–138.

72. Q 042 transcript (also known as "The Death Tape")

73. Q 875 summary.

74. Reiterman, T. (1998). Remembering Jonestown: Twenty Years after the Mass Deaths in Guyana. [A reporter tells how time has not diminished the horror.] *Los Angeles Times*. 11, 14–98.

75. Reiterman, T. and Jacobs, J. (1982). *Raven: The Untold Story of the Rev. Jim Jones and His People*. New York: E.P. Dutton.

76. Riley, J. (2002). The Pains of Imprisonment: Exploring a Classic Text with Contemporary Authors. *Journal of Criminal Justice Education*. 13(2), 444–456.

77. Seeman, M. (1959). On the Meaning of Alienation. *American Sociological Review*. 24, 783–791.

78. Senna, J. J. and Siegel, L. J. (1995). *Essentials of Criminal Justice*. New York: West.

79. Siegel, L. J. (2009). *Criminology* (10th ed.). Belmont, CA: Thomson Wadsworth.

80. Silverman, I. J. (2001). *Corrections: A Comprehensive View*. (2nd ed.). Belmont, CA: Wadsworth.

81. Simon, J. (2000). The 'Society of Captives' in the Era of Hyper-Incarceration. *Theoretical Criminology*. 4, 285–308.

82. Stroud, R. (1996). Unpublished personal interview.

83. Sultan, F., Long, G., Kiefer, S., Schrum, D., Selby, J. and Calhoun, L. (1984). The Female Offender's Adjustment to Prison Life: A Comparison of Psychodidactic and Traditional Supportive Approaches to Treatment. *Journal of Offender Counseling, Services, and Rehabilitation*. 9, 49–56.

84. Sykes, G. (1966). *The Society of Captives*. New York: Atheneum.

85. Sykes, G. M. (1958). *The Society of Captives: A Study of A Maximum Security Prison*. Princeton: Princeton University Press.

86. Sykes, G. M. and Messinger, S. L. (1960). The Inmate Social System. In R. A. Cloward (Ed.), *Theoretical Studies in the Social Organization of the Prison* (pp. 5–19). New York: Social Science Research Council.

87. Tewksbury, R. A. (1997). *Introduction to Corrections*. New York: Glencoe.

88. Thomas, C. W. and Petersen, D. W. (1977). *Prison Organization and Inmate Subcultures*. Indianapolis, IN: Bobbs-Merrill.

89. Toch, H. (1977). *Living in Prison: The Ecology of Survival*. New York: The Free Press.

90. Tropp, R. (1978). "Last Words." http://jonestown.sdsu.edu/AboutJonestown/PrimarySources/tropp.htm. Accessed by Langer on November 17, 2011.

91. Turnbo, C. (1993). Differences That Make a Difference: Managing a Women's Correctional Institution. In American Correctional Association, *Female Offenders: Meeting Needs of a Neglected Population* (pp. 12–16). Laurel, MD: American Correctional Association.

92. Ward, D. and Kassebaum, G. (1964). Homosexuality: A Mode of Adaptation in a Prison for Women. *Social Problems*. 12(2), 159–177.

93. Ward, D. A. and Kassebaum, G. G. (1965). *Women's Prison: Sex and Social Structure*. Chicago: Aldine.

94. Wheeler, S. (1972). Socialization in Correctional Institutions. In D. A. Goslin (Ed.), *Handbook of Socialization Theory and Research* (pp. 1005–1023). Chicago: Rand McNally.

Chapter Five

1. American Psychiatric Association, (1994). *Diagnostic and Statistical Manual of Mental Disorders*. (4th ed.). Washington, DC: American Psychiatric Press.

2. Bloom, S. L. and Reichert, M. (1998). *Bearing Witness: Violence and Collective Responsibility*. New York: The Haworth Maltreatment and Trauma Press.

3. Boscarino, J. A., Adams, R. E. and Galea, S. (2006). Alcohol Use in New York after the Terrorist Attacks: A Study of the Effects of Psychological Trauma on Drinking Behavior. *Addictive Behaviors*. 31, 606–621.

4. Collins, R. (2004). Rituals of Solidarity and Security in the Wake of Terrorist Attacks. *Sociological Theory*. 22(1), 53–87.

5. Coser, L. (1957). *The Social Functions of Conflict*. New York: Free Press.

6. DeLisi, L. E., Maurizio, A., Yost, M., Papparozzi, C. F., Fulchino, C., Katz, C. L., Altesman, J., Biel, M., Lee, J. and Stevens, P. (2003). A Survey of New Yorkers After the Sept. 11, 2001, Terrorist Attacks. *The American Journal of Psychiatry*. 160(4), 780–782.

7. DiMaggio, C., Galea, S. and Emch, M. (2010). Spatial Proximity and the Risk of Psychopathology After a Terrorist Attack. *Psychiatry Research*. 176, 55–61.

8. Fox, R. C. (1988). The Human Condition of Health Professionals. In R. C. Fox (Ed.), *Essays in Medical Sociology: Journeys into the Field* (2nd enlarged ed., pp. 572–587, especially p. 586). New Brunswick, NJ/ Oxford: Transaction Books.

9. Fraley, R. C., Fazzari, D. A., Bonanno, G. A. and Dekel, S. (2006). Attachment and Psychological Adaptation in High Exposure Survivors of the September 11th Attack on the World Trade Center. *Personality and Social Psychology Bulletin*. 32, 538–551.

10. Freedman, T. G. (2004). Voices of 9/11 First Responders: Patterns of Collective Resilience. *Clinical Social Work Journal*. 32(4), 377–393.

11. Grinker, R. R. and Spiegel, J. (1963). *Men under Stress*. New York: McGraw Hill.

12. Grossman, D. (1995). *On Killing: The Psychological Cost of Learning to Kill in War and Society*. Boston: Little, Brown.

13. Hedges, C. (2002). *War is a Force that Gives Us Meaning*. New York: Anchor Books.

14. Henry, V. E. (2004). *Death Work: Police, Trauma, and the Psychology of Survival*. New York: Oxford University Press.

15. Herman, J. L. (1992). *Trauma and Recovery*. New York: Basic Books.

16. Holmes, R. (1985). *Acts of War. The Behavior of Men in Battle*. New York: Free Press.

17. Juergensmeyer, M. (2003). *Terror in the Mind of God: The Global Rise of Religious Violence*. (3rd ed.). Los Angeles: University of California Press.

18. Keegan, J. (1977). *The Face of Battle*. New York: Random House.

19. Kuriansky, J. (2003). The 9/11 Terrorist Attack on the WTC: A New York Psychologist's Personal Experience and Professional Perspective. *Psychotherapie Forum*. 10, 1–11.

20. Marshall, S. L. A. (1947). *Men against Fire: The Problem of Battle Command*. Norman: University of Oklahoma Press.

21. McCauley, C. (2003). *Men in Combat*. www.psych.upenn.edu/sacsec/online/bib-agg.htm

22. McPhail, C. (1991). *The Myth of the Madding Crowd*. New York: Aldine de Gruyter.

23. Norpoth, H. (1987). Guns and Butter and Government Popularity in Britain. *American Political Science Review*. 81, 949–970.

24. North, C. S., Tivis, L., McMillen, J. C., Pferfferbaum, B., Cox, J., Spitznagel, E. L., Bunch, K., Schorr, J., and Smith, E. M. (2002). Coping, Functioning, and Adjustment of Rescue Workers after the Oklahoma City Bombing. *Journal of Traumatic Stress*. 15, 171–175.

25. Ostrom, C. W., Jr. and Simon, D. M. (1985). Promise and Performance: A Dynamic Model of Presidential Popularity. *American Political Science Review*. 79, 334–358.

26. Page, B. I. and Shapiro, R. Y. (1992). *The Rational Public: Fifty Years of Trends in Americans' Policy Preferences*. Chicago, IL: University of Chicago Press.

27. Perlman, H. H. (1957). *Social Casework: A Problem-Solving Process*. Chicago: University of Chicago Press.

28. Rosenberg, B., Gerver, I. and Howton, F. W. (1964). *Mass Society in Crisis: Social Problems and Social Pathology*. New York: Macmillan.

29. Scheff, T. J. (1994). *Bloody Revenge: Emotions, Nationalism, and War*. Boulder, CO: Westview Press.

30. Simmel, G. (1955[1908]). *Conflict and the Web of Group Affiliations*. New York: Free Press.

31. Smalley, R. E. (1967). *Theory for Social Work Practice*. New York: Columbia University Press.

32. Smith, D. (1972, 1999). *Report from Engine Co. 82*. New York: Warner Books.

33. _____. (2002). *Report from Ground Zero*. New York: Viking.

34. Stouffer, S. A. (1965, c1949). *The American Soldier*. New York: John Wiley & Sons.

35. The Staff of The New York Times. (2002). Portraits: 9/11/01: The collected portraits of grief from the *New York Times*. New York: The New York Times.

36. Thompson, S., Schlehofer, M., Bovin, M., Dougan, B., Montes, D. and Trifskin, S. (2006). Dispositions, Control Strategies, and Distress in the General Public After the 2001 Terrorist Attack. *Anxiety, Stress and Coping*. 19(2), 143–159.

37. Von Essen, T. (2002). *Strong of Heart: Life and Death in the Fire Department of New York*. New York: Regan Books.

38. Weber, M. (1988). *Max Weber: A Biography*. New Brunswick, NJ: Transaction Books.

39. Williams, R. (2002). *Writing in the Dust: After September 11*. Grand Rapids. Michigan/Cambridge: William B. Eerdmans Pub. Co.

40. Zelizer, V. (1994). *Pricing the Priceless Child: The Changing Social Value of Children*. Princeton, NJ: Princeton University Press.

Chapter Six

1. Abraham, L. (2003). Media Stereotypes of African Americans. In P. M. Lester and S. D. Ross (Eds.), *Images That Injure: Pictorial Stereotypes in the Media* (2nd ed., pp. 87–92). Westport, CT: Praeger.

2. Alba, R. D. (2005). New Orleans and Katrina: A Powerful New Metaphor for the Impacts of Systemic Inequality and Racism. *CUSS News: Newsletter of the Community and Urban Sociology Section*. http://www.commurb.org/Newsletters/CUSSNewsletter%20FallWinter%202005.pdf. Accessed on May 1, 2006

3. Alba, R. D., Logan, J. R. and Stults, B. J. (2000). The Changing Neighborhood Contexts of the Immigrant Metropolis. *Social Forces*. 79, 587–621.

4. Alexander, D. (1993). *Natural Disasters*. London: Chapman and Hall.

5. Anderson, E. and Massey, D. S. (Eds.) (2001). *Problem of the Century: Racial Stratification in the United States*. New York: Russell Sage Foundation.

6. Anderson, E. and Moller, J. (2005, August 30). Looting Difficult to Control. *New Orleans Times-Picayune*. http://www.nola.com/t-p/archives.ssf?/mtlogs/nola_tporleans/archives/2005_08_30.html. Accessed on July 22, 2006.

7. Bannerman, L. (2005, September 3). The Big Uneasy: Katrina Exposes Race Divide that Splits America. *The Herald (Glasgow), Newsquest Media Group*. http://www.lexisnexis.com/universe/document?_m=d903e838cc6e65. Accessed on June 23, 2006.

8. Barton, A. H. (1969). *Communities in Disaster: A Sociological Analysis of Collective Stress Situations*. Garden City, New York: Doubleday.

9. Baum, D. (2006, January 9). Deluged. *The New Yorker*. http://www.levity.com/mavericks/bau-int. Accessed on July 22, 2006.

10. Been, V. (1994). Locally Undesirable Land Uses in Minority Neighborhoods: Disproportionate Siting or Market Dynamics? *Yale Law Journal*. 103, 1383–1422.

11. Been, V. and Gupta F. (1997). Coming to the Nuisance or Going to the Barrios? A Longitudinal Analysis of Environmental Justice Claims. *Ecology Law Quarterly*. 24, 1–56.

12. Bobo, L. D. and Zubrinsky, C. L. (1996). Attitudes on Residential Integration: Perceived Status Differences, Mere In-Group Preference, or Racial Prejudice? *Social Forces*. 74, 883–909.

13. Bolin, R. C. (1982). *Long-Term Family Recovery from Disaster*. Boulder, CO: University of Colorado.

14. Breen, T. and Weber, H. R. (July 12, 2010). BP Affixes New Cap on Gulf

Oil Well; Tests Ahead. *Associated Press,* http://www.boston.com/business/articles/2010/07/12/bps_new_oil_cap_headed_for_well_then_testing/. Accessed on October 4, 2011.

15. Briggs, X. (2006). After Katrina: Rebuilding Lives and Places. *City & Community.* 5(2), 119–128.

16. Britt, D. (2005, September 30). In Katrina's wake, inaccurate rumors sullied victims. *The Washington Post.* http://www.washingtonpost.com. Accessed on June 23, 2006.

17. Brown, M. K., Carnoy, M., Currie, E., Duster, T., Oppenheimer, D. B., Shultz, M. M. and Wellman, D. (2003). *White-Washing Race: The Myth of a Color-Blind Society.* Berkeley: University of California.

18. Bryant, B. and Mohai, P. (Eds.). (1992). *Race and the Incidence of Environmental Hazard: A Time for Discourse.* Boulder, CO: Westview Press.

19. Bullard, R. D. (1990). Dumping in Dixie: Race, Class and Environmental Quality. Boulder, CO: Westview Press.

20. Charles, C. Z. (2001). Processes of Residential Segregation. In A. O'Connor, C. Tilly and L. Bobo (Eds.), *Urban Inequality: Evidence from Four Cities* (pp. 217–271). New York: Russell Sage Foundation.

21. Clarke, L. (2002). Panic: Myth or reality? *Contexts.* 1(3), 21–26.

22. Conley, D. (1999). *Being Black, Living in the Red: Race, Wealth, and Social Policy in America.* Berkeley: University of California.

23. Conti, S., Meli, P., Minelli, G., Solimini, R., Toccaceli, V., Vichi, M., Beltrano, C. and Perini, L. (2005). Epidemiologic Study of Mortality during the Summer 2003 Heat Wave in Italy. *Environmental Research.* 98, 390–399.

24. Cooper, A., Myers, C., Tuchman, G., Mattingly, D., Meserve, J., Kaye, R., *et al.* (2006, June 10). *Encore presentation: CNN Presents: The Devastation of Hurricane Katrina.* New York: Cable News Network CNN. http://www.lexis-nexis.com/universe/document?_m=a10cb5c131e5251. Accessed on June 19, 2006.

25. Cose, E. (1995). *The Rage of a Privileged Class: Why are Middle-Class Blacks Angry? Why Should America Care?* New York: HarperCollins.

26. Dao, J. and Kleinfield, N. R. (2005, September 3). More troops and aid reach New Orleans; Bush visits area chaotic exodus continues. *The New York Times.* http://www.nytimes.com. Accessed on June 22, 2006.

27. Drabek, T. E. (1986). *Human System Responses to Disaster: An Inventory of Sociological Findings.* New York: Springer-Verlag.

28. Drabek, T. E., Key, W. H., Erikson, P. E. and Crowe, J. L. (1975). The Impact of Disaster on Kin and Relationships. *Journal of Marriage and the Family.* 10, 481–494.

29. Dynes, R. R. (1970). *Organized Behavior in Disaster.* Lexington, MA: Heath Lexington Books.

30. Editorial (2005, October 5). Civilian-led response is best. *The Denver Post.* http://www.denverpost.com. Accessed on June 23, 2006.

31. Elliott, J. R. and Pais, J. (2006). Race, Class and Hurricane Katrina: Social Differences in Human Response to Disaster. *Social Science Research.* 35(2), 295–321.

32. Erikson, K. (1976). *Everything in Its Path: Destruction of Community in the Buffalo Creek Flood.* New York: Simon and Schuster.

33. Erikson, K. (1994). *A New Species of Trouble: Explorations in Disasters, Trauma and Community.* New York: Norton.

34. Fischer, H. W. (1998). *Response to Disaster Fact versus Fiction and Its Perpetuation: The Sociology of Disaster.* (2nd ed.). New York: University Press of America.

35. Fothergill, A., Maestas, E. G. M. and Darlington, J. D. (1999). Race, Ethnicity and Disasters in the United States: A Review of the Literature. *Disasters.* 23(2), 156–173.

36. Freudenberg, W. R. (1997). Contamination, Corrosion and the Social Order: An Overview. *Current Sociology.* 45(3), 19–39.

37. Garfield, G. (2007). Hurricane Katrina: The Making of Unworthy Disaster

Victims. *Journal of African American Studies*. 10, 55–74.

38. Gillin, B. (2005, September 28). Katrina Unleashed Flood of Rumors. *Arizona Daily Star*. http://www.dailystar.com. Accessed on July 23, 2006.

39. Gillis, J. (June 15, 2010). Estimates of Oil Flow Jump Higher. *The New York Times*, http://www.nytimes.com/2010/06/16/us/16spill.html?scp=1&sq=US%20government%20revised%20estimates%20for%20BP%20oil%20spill%20&st=cse. Accessed on October 4, 2011.

40. Gladwin, H. and Peacock, W. G. (1997). Warning and Evacuation: A Night for Hard Houses. In W. G. Peacock, B. H. Morrow and H. Gladwin (Eds.), *Hurricane Andrew: Ethnicity, Gender and the Sociology of Disasters* (pp. 52–74). New York: Routledge.

41. Goodman, A. (2005a, September 16). The Militarization of New Orleans: Jeremy Scahill Reports from Louisiana. *Democracy Now!* http://www.democracynow.org/article.pl?sid=05/09/16/122225. Accessed on July 12, 2006.

42. _____. (2005b, September 16). Trapped in New Orleans: Emergency medical worker describes how police prevented evacuation. *Democracy Now!* http://www.democracynow.org/article.pl?sid=05/09/16/1223207. Accessed on July 12, 2005.

43. Horn, G. M. (2006). The Katrina Disaster. In *The World Almanac and Book of Facts*. (pp. 5–6).

44. Howitt, D. (1998). *Crime, the Media, and the Law*. New York: Wiley.

45. Katz, J. M. and Mendoza M. (2010). Haiti Still Waiting for Pledged U.S. Aid, http://www.huffingtonpost.com/2010/09/29/haiti-still-waiting-for-p_n_743002.html. Accessed on September 29, 2010.

46. Kessler, R. C. (1979). A Strategy for Studying Differential Vulnerability to the Psychological Consequences of Stress. *Journal of Health and Social Behavior*. 20, 100–108.

47. King, C. (2005, September 3). A time for action, not outrage. *The Washington Post*. http://www.washingtonpost.com. Accessed on June 22, 2006.

48. Klinenberg, E. (2002). *Heat Wave: A Social Autopsy of Disaster in Chicago*. Chicago: University of Chicago.

49. Lester, P. M. and Ross, S. D. (2003). *Images That Injure: Pictorial Stereotypes in the Media*. (2nd ed., revised). Santa Barbara, CA: ABC-CLIO, Inc.

50. Logan, J. R. (2006). The Impact of Katrina: Race and Class in Storm-Damaged Neighborhoods. Unpublished manuscript. Spatial Structures in the Social Sciences Initiative, Brown University.

51. Logan, J. R. and Molotch, H. L. (1987). *Urban Fortunes: The Political Economy of Place*. Berkeley: University of California.

52. Massey, D. and Denton, N. (1993). *American Apartheid: Segregation and the Making of an Underclass*. Cambridge, MA: Harvard University Press.

53. Massey, D. and Mullan, B. P. (1984). Processes of Hispanic and Black Spatial Assimilation. *American Journal of Sociology*. 89, 836–874.

54. Mauss, M. ([1916]/1979). *Sociology and Psychology: Essays*. Translated by Brewster, B. Boston: Routledge.

55. McPhail, C. (1991). *The Myth of the Maddening Crowd*. New York: Aldine de Gruyter.

56. Merton, R. (1969). Foreword. In A. H. Barton (Ed.), *Communities in Disaster: A Sociological Analysis of Collective Stress Situations*. (pp. 7–37). Garden City, NY: Doubleday.

57. Mohr, H., Foster, M., Breed, A. G., Nossiters, A. and Reeves, J. (2005, August 31). Blanco says evacuation buses on the way to N.O. *New Orleans Times-Picayune*. http://www.nola.com/t-p/archive.ssf?/mtlogs/nola_tporleans/archives/2005_08_31.html. Accessed on July 22, 2006.

58. Molotch, H. L. (2005). *Death on the Roof: Race and Bureaucratic Failure. Electronic Essay from Understanding Katrina: Perspectives from the Social Sciences*. New York: Social Science Research Council, http://understanding-katrina.ssrc.org/Molotch/ (pp. 141–170). New York: Routledge.

59. Morrow, B. H. (1997). Stretching the Bonds: The Families of Andrew. In W. G. Peacock, B. H. Morrow and H. Gladwin (Eds.), *Hurricane Andrew: Ethnicity, Gender and the Sociology of Disasters* (pp. 141–170). New York: Routledge.

60. Navarro, M. (July 12, 2010). With Help After Storm, A Chance To Give Back. *The New York Times.* P. A11.

61. Norris, F., Byrne, C. C., Diaz, E. and Kaniasty, K. (2001). *The Range, Magnitude, and Duration of Effects of Natural and Human-Caused Disasters: A Review of the Empirical Literature.* National Center for PTSD, http://www.ncptsd.org/facts/disasters/fsrange.html

62. Obama, B. H. (2010). Oval Office Address—Remarks by the President to the Nation on the BP Oil Spill. http://www.whitehouse.gov/the-press-office/remarks-president-nation-bp-oil-spill. Accessed on June 15, 2010.

63. Pastor M., Jr., Sadd, J. and Hipp, J. (2001). Which Came First? Toxic Facilities, Minority Move-in, and Environmental Justice. *Journal of Urban Affairs.* 23(1), 1–21.

64. Peacock, W. G. and Girard, C. (1997). Ethnic and Racial Inequalities in Hurricane Damage and Insurance Settlements. In W. G. Peacock, B. H. Morrow and H. Gladwin (Eds.), *Hurricane Andrew: Ethnicity, Gender and the Sociology of Disasters* (pp. 171–190). New York: Routledge.

65. Peacock, W. G., Morrow B. H. and Gladwin, H. (1997). *Hurricane Andrew: Ethnicity, Gender and the Sociology of Disasters.* New York: Routledge.

66. Penner, D. R. and Ferdinand, K. C. (2009). *Overcoming Katrina: African American Voices from the Crescent City and Beyond.* New York: Palgrave Macmillan.

67. Picou, J. S., Marshall, B. and Gill, D. A. (2004). Disaster, Litigation and the Corrosive Community. *Social Forces.* 82(4), 1493–1522.

68. Pierre, R. E. and Gerhart, A. (2005, October 5). News of pandemonium may have slowed aid: Unsubstantiated reports of violence were confirmed by some officials, spread by news media. *The Washington Post.* http://www.washingtonpost.com. Accessed on July 23, 2006.

69. Quarantelli, E. L. (1998). *What is Disaster? Perspectives on the Question.* New York: Routledge.

70. Quarantelli, E. L. and Dynes, R. R. (1972). *Images of Disaster Behavior: Myths and Consequences.* Newark, DE: Disaster Research Center, University of Delaware.

71. Reed A. L., Jr., (2005). The Real Divide. *The Progressive.* 69(11), 31.

72. Roberts, J. T. and Toffolon-Weiss, M. M. (2001). *Chronicles from the Environmental Justice Frontline.* New York: Cambridge University Press.

73. Robertson, C. (July 13, 2010). Police Are Charged in Post-Katrina Shootings. *The New York Times.* P. A1.

74. Robertson, C. (August 6, 2011). Officers Guilty of Shooting Six in New Orleans. *The New York Times.* P. A1.

75. Robinson, E. (2005, September 2). Where the good times haven't rolled. Editorial. The Washington Post. http://www.washintonpost.com. Accessed on June 22, 2006.

76. Russell, G. (2005, August 28). Nagin orders first-ever mandatory evacuation of New Orleans. *New Orleans Times-Picayune.* http://www.nola.com/t-p/archive,ssf?/mtlogs/nola_tporleans/archives/2005_08_28.html. Accessed on September 23, 2006.

77. Schnittker, J. and McLeod, J. (2005). The Social Psychology of Health Disparities. *Annual Review of Sociology.* 31, 75–103.

78. Sen, A. (1981). *Poverty and Famines: An Essay on Entitlement and Deprivation.* Oxford, UK: Clarendon.

79. Sharkey, P. (2007). Survival and Death in New Orleans: An Empirical Look at the Human Impact of Katrina. *Journal of Black Studies.* 37, 482–501.

80. Simerman, J., Ott, D. and Melnick, T. (2005, December 29). Assumptions about

Katrina victims may be incorrect, data reveal. *Knight Ridder Newspapers.*

81. Sontag, D. (July 11, 2010). In Haiti, the Displaced Are Left Clinging to the Edge. *The New York Times.* P. A1.

82. Stinchcombe, A. L. (1965). Social Structure and Organizations. In J. March (Ed.), *The Handbook of Organizations* (pp. 142–193). New York: Rand McNally.

83. Szasz, A. (1993). *Ecopopulism: Toxic Waste and the Movement for Environmental Justice.* Minneapolis: University of Minnesota Press.

84. Thevenot, B. and Russell, G. (2005, September 26). Reports of anarchy at superdome overstated. *The Seattle Times.* http://www.seattletimes.com. Accessed on July 22, 2006.

85. Tierney, K. J. (2003). Disaster Beliefs and Institutional Interests: Recycling Disaster Myths in the Aftermath of 9-11. In L. Clarke (Ed.), *Research in Social Problems and Public Policy, Terrorism and Disaster: New Threats, New Ideas* (Vol. 11, pp. 33–51). New York: Elsevier.

86. Tierney, K. J., Bevc, C. and Kuligowski, E. (2006). Metaphors Matter: Disaster Myths, Media Frames, and Their Consequences in Hurricane Katrina. *The Annals of the American Academy of Political and Social Science.* 604(57). http://www.lexis-nexis.com/universe/document?_m=8a9a2c0a279f4bc. Accessed on June 20, 2006.

87. Treaster, J. and Sontag, D. (2005, September 2). Despair and lawlessness grip New Orleans as thousands remain stranded in squalor. *The New York Times.*

88. Vega, W. A. and Rumbaut, R. (1991). Ethnic Minorities and Mental Health. *Annual Review of Sociology.* 17, 351–383.

89. Weeks, L. (2005, September 1). Carried away; Looting has it Roots in the Chaos of Catastrophe. *The Washington Post.* http://www.washingtonpost.com. Accessed on June 22, 2006.

90. Wilson, W. J., 1978. *The Declining Significance of Race: Blacks and Changing American Institutions.* Chicago: University of Chicago.

91. Yinger, J. (1995). *Closed Doors, Opportunities Lost: The Continuing Costs of Housing Discrimination.* New York: Russell Sage.

92. Young, C. (2006, January 16). Katrina's racial paranoia. *The Boston Globe.* p. A13.

Chapter Seven

1. Afflitto, F. (2000). Victimization, Survival and the Impunity of Forced Exile: A Case Study from Rwandan Genocide. *Crime, Law and Social Change.* 32, 77–97.

2. Afflitto, F. M. (1998a). Experience and Evaluation: Social Perceptions of Justice in Guatemala's 'Popular' Movement, 1990–1992, Unpublished doctoral dissertation, University of California, Irvine.

3. _____. (1998b). Methodological Demands of Qualitative Research under Regimes of State-Sponsored Terrorism. *Political and Legal Anthropology Review.* 21(2), 96–108.

4. Afflitto, F. M. and Vandiver, M. (2000). The Political Determinants of Ethnic Genocide. In A. Kimenyi and O. L. Scott (Eds.), *Anatomy of Genocide* (pp. 7–24). Lewiston, NY: E. Mellen Press.

5. African Rights. (1995). *Rwanda: Death, Despair and Defiance* (Revised 1995 ed.). London: African Rights.

6. _____. (1998a). *Resisting Genocide: Bisesero, April–June, 1994.* London: African Rights.

7. _____. (1998b). *Rwanda: The Insurgency in the Northwest.* London: African Rights.

8. Anonymous (1998). *Interview with the Author.* Sacramento, CA.

9. Balakian, P. (2003). *The Burning Tigris: The Armenian Genocide and America's Response.* New York: HarperCollins.

10. Barnett, M. (2002). *Eyewitness to a Genocide.* Ithaca: Cornell University Press.

11. Benedetti, M. (1984). *Cotidianas [Daily Occurrences].* 6th ed. Mexico City: Siglo.

12. Brunk, D. (2008). Dissecting Darfur: Anatomy of a Genocide Debate. *International Relations.* 22 (1) 25–44.

13. Charny, I. (2000). *Encyclopedia of Genocide.* Santa Barbara, California: ABC-CLIO.

14. Cornwell, S. and Mohammed, A. (March 4, 2010). U.S. Armenia Genocide Vote Looms, Angering Turkey. *Reuters.* http://www.reuters.com/article/2010/03/04/us-turkey-usa-idUSTRE6233L320100304

15. Dawidowicz, L. (1976). *The War Against the Jews 1933–1945.* New York: Bantam Books.

16. Derderian, K. (2005). Common Fate, Different Experience: Gender Specific Aspects of the Armenian Genocide 1915–1917. *Holocaust and Genocide Studies.* 19(1), 1–25.

17. Des Pres, T. (1987). Introduction: Remembering Armenia. In R. G. Hovannisian (Ed.), *The Armenian Genocide in Perspective* (pp. 9–17). New Brunswick, NJ: Transaction, Inc.

18. Destexhe, A. (1995). *Rwanda and Genocide.* New York: New York University Press.

19. Eller, J. D. (1999). Rwanda and Burundi: When Two Tribes Go to War? In J. D. Eller (Ed.), *From Culture to Ethnicity to Conflict: An Anthropological Perspective on International Ethnic Conflict.* (pp. 195–241) Ann Arbor: University of Michigan Press.

20. Feil, S. R. (1998). *Preventing Genocide: How the Early Use of Force Might Have Succeeded in Rwanda.* New York: Carnegie Corporation.

21. Gourevitch, P. (1998). *We Wish to Inform You That Tomorrow We Will Be Killed with Our Families: Stories from Rwanda.* New York: Farrar, Straus and Giroux.

22. Harff, B. and Gurr, T. R. (1988). Toward Empirical Theory of Genocides and Politicides: Identification and Measurement of Cases Since 1945. *International Studies Quarterly.* 32, 359–371.

23. Kalayjian, A. S., Shahinian, S. P., Gergerian, E. L. and Saraydarian, L. (1996). Coping with Ottoman Turkish Genocide: An Exploration of the Experience of Armenian Survivors. *Journal of Traumatic Stress.* 9(1), 87–95.

24. Katz, S. (1996). The Uniqueness of the Holocaust: The Historical Dimension. In A. S. Rosenbaum (Ed.), *Is The Holocaust Unique? Perspectives on Comparative Genocide.* (pp. 19–38) Boulder, CO: Westview Press.

25. Keane, F. (1995). *Season of Blood.* London: Viking.

26. Kissi, E. (2004). Rwanda, Ethiopia and Cambodia: Links, Fault-lines and Complexities in a Comparative Study of Genocide. *Journal of Genocide Research.* 6(1), 115–133.

27. Melson, R. (1996). Paradigms of Genocide: The Holocaust, the Armenian Genocide and Contemporary Mass Destructions. *Annals of the American Academy of Political Sciences.* 548, 156–168.

28. Lee, R. (1995). *Dangerous Fieldwork.* Thousand Oaks, CA: Sage.

29. Lemarchand, R. (1996). *Burundi: Ethnic Conflict and Genocide.* 1st paperback ed. Cambridge: Woodrow Wilson Press and Cambridge University Press.

30. McSherry, J. P. and Molina Mejía, R. (1992). Confronting the Question of Justice in Guatemala. *Social Justice: A Journal of Crime, Conflict and World Order.* 19(3), 1–28.

31. Media Entertainment. (2000). *The Genocide Factor,* Film. New York: Media Entertainment.

32. Melady, T. P. (1974). *Burundi: The Tragic Years.* Maryknoll, NY: Orbis Books.

33. Melson, R. (1998). Interview with the author (West Lafayette, IN).

34. Miller, D. E. and Miller, L. T. (1987). An Oral History Perspective on Responses to the Armenian Genocide. In R. G. Hovannisian (Ed.), *The Armenian Genocide in Perspective* (pp. 187–204). New Brunswick, NJ: Transaction, Inc.

35. Mwangachuchu, B. (1999). Interview with the author (Sacramento, CA).

36. Panafrican News Agency. (1999, October 11). *Rwandan Population on the Rise,* Available FTP: Hostname: africannews.org Directory: PANA/news/19991011 File: feat21.html

37. Prunier, G. (1995). *The Rwanda Crisis: History of a Genocide.* New York: Columbia University Press.

38. Prunier, G. (2007). *Darfur: The Ambiguous Genocide*. Ithaca: Cornell University Press.

39. Rosenbaum, A. S. (1996). *Is The Holocaust Unique? Perspectives on Comparative Genocide*. Boulder, CO: Westview Press.

40. Rosenberg, B., Gerver, I. and Howton, F. W. (1964). *Mass Society in Crisis: Social Problems and Social Pathology*. New York: Macmillan.

41. Rubenstein, R. (1987). *The Cunning of History*. New York: Harper Perennial.

42. Scheper-Hughes, N. (1992). *Death without Weeping: The Violence of Everyday Life in Brazil*. Berkeley: University of California Press.

43. Simon, T. W. (1996). Defining Genocide. *Wisconsin International Law Journal*. 15(1), 243–256.

44. Sluka, J. A. (1989). *Hearts and Minds, Fish and Water: Support for the IRA and INLA in a Northern Irish Ghetto*. Berkeley: University of California Press.

45. _____. (2000). Introduction: State Terror and Anthropology. In J. A. Sluka (Ed.), *Death Squad: The Anthropology of State Terror*. (pp. 1–45) Pittsburgh: University of Pennsylvania Press.

46. United Nations, (1948, December 9). *Convention for the Prevention and Punishment of the Crime of Genocide* Article I, 78 U.N.T.S. 229.

47. United States Committee for Refugees. (1998). *Genocide Widows: A World Apart. Informational Flyer*.

48. United States Holocaust Memorial Museum. What Is Genocide? *Holocaust Encyclopedia*. http://www.ushmm.org/wlc/en/article.php?ModuleId=10007043. Accessed on July 27, 2010.

49. Vanderwerff, C. (1996). *Kill Thy Neighbor*. Boise: Pacific Press.

50. Walter, E. V. (1969). *Terror and Resistance: A Study of Political Violence with Case Studies of Some Primitive African Communities*. New York: Oxford University Press.

51. Yin, R. K. (1984). *Case Study Research: Design and Methods*. Thousand Oaks, CA: Sage.